The Gypsum Construction

Construction

HANDBOOK

Sixth Edition

RSMeans

WILEY

John Wiley & Sons, Inc.

Copyright © 2009 by USG Corporation, 555 West Adams Street, Chicago, IL 60661. All rights reserved.

Published by John Wiley & Sons, Inc., Hoboken, New Jersey

Published simultaneously in Canada

Managing Editor: Mary Greene. Editorial Supervisor: Andrea Sillah. Editor: Barbara Balboni. Editorial Assistant: Jessica deMartin. Production Manager: Michael Kokernak. Composition: Sheryl Rose. Cover design: Jessica deMartin. Technical Artist: Steven Kalter.

Library of Congress Cataloging-in-Publication Data:

ISBN: 978-0-87629-258-7

Printed in the United States of America

10 9 8 7 6 5 4

Contents

1   Drywall & Veneer Plaster Products   1

Describes complete line of construction products, including SHEETROCK brand gypsum panels and IMPERIAL brand gypsum base for drywall and veneer plaster construction, sheathing and ceilings. Also, beads, trims, framing, insulation, fasteners, adhesives, joint compounds, coatings, tapes, plaster finishes and textures.

2   Framing   69

Framing practices and procedures for wood and steel framing. Includes details for resilient channel installation, chase walls, furred ceilings and walls, and door and window openings.

3   Cladding   101

Detailed instructions for installing drywall and veneer bases in single and multiple layer configurations. Also covers predecorated panels, water resistant panels, sheathing, insulation, fixtures and specialty materials. Provides information on fastener requirements and special constructions such as curved surfaces, arches, soffits, etc.

4   Backerboard Installation   145

Durock brand cement board products and installation procedures, including proper attachment, taping and finishing. Encompasses moisture and climatic considerations, proper framing, fasteners, and finishing options in baths, kitchens, floors and specialty uses.

5   Finishing Drywall Systems   161

Complete guide to proper joint treatment and surface preparation for drywall construction. Includes installation of corner beads, trim and control joints; hand and mechanical finishing with setting-type and drying-type compounds; addresses special environmental and lighting situations. Covers textures, resurfacing and redecorating.

6   Finishing Veneer Plaster Systems   209

In-depth instructions for selecting, preparing and installing veneer plaster systems appearance and abuse-resistance options. Encompasses one-coat and two-coat veneer plaster systems and specialty finishes.

7   Conventional Plaster Products   231

Describes full line of conventional plasters, laths and accessories for successful completion of plaster systems. Helps evaluate specific situations and end-use requirements to match plaster products to needs. Includes gypsum and plaster laths, beads and trims, clips and screws, framing components and specialty plasters.

8   Conventional Plaster Applications   251

Comprehensive guide to plaster systems, including framing installation, base and lath application, accessories and control joints, plaster mixing and application and finishing options.

9

Acoustical Ceiling Design & Application   287

Complete information on selection and installation of acoustical ceiling systems, including design considerations. Also contains information on standards, building codes, sound control, lighting and light reflectance, fire safety, seismic considerations and HVAC.

10

System Design Considerations   317

Outlines methods for matching systems to specific performance criteria. Covers fire and sound criteria, wood and steel partitions and sound control systems. Specialty systems include area separation walls, cavity shaft walls, fireproofing, curtain wall/fire containment systems, thermal insulation, air water and vapor control.

11

Planning, Execution & Inspection   347

Selection of materials, regulatory requirements, handling, job conditions, movement in structures, product quality and inspection.

12 Problems, Remedies & Preventive Measures 369

Trouble shooting for drywall, veneer plaster, conventional plaster and cement board problems. Cites problems and how to handle them.

13 Safety Considerations & Material Handling 403

Provides health and safety considerations relative to drywall and plaster applications.

14 Tools & Equipment 417

Defines tools and how to use them. Includes framing tools, board and lath tools, mixing equipment, finishing tools, hand and spray texturing equipment, machines, hoses, guns, nozzles, etc.

15   Building Sciences   441

A review of building science principles that relate to design, selection and installation of building materials, with emphasis on gypsum panel products. Includes building movement, fire resistance, heat transfer, sound transmission and vapor control.

16   Sustainability   467

An overview of sustainability as it applies to building design and construction materials, including USG efforts.

17   USG: America's Building Industry Leader   481

A review of USG Corporation, it's industry products, history and core values. Also includes useful online resources.

Appendix

Agencies, ratings, testing procedures, comparisons, standards, conversions, rating designations, company literature, plant locations.

Welcome to the Sixth Edition of *The Gypsum Construction Handbook.* This edition is the successor to a long line of earlier versions stretching back for more than a hundred years. Since it was first published in 1905, the *Handbook* has been a trusted reference and an invaluable toolbox companion. We believe this latest edition will faithfully maintain and build on that century-long tradition of excellence.

The people of USG are honored to provide the *Handbook* in light of the book's heritage and relevance to the building industry. This sixth edition, like its predecessors, represents a true collaborative effort on the part of our company, our people and our partners. It pools the collective experience, best knowledge and practices, and hands-on expertise of hundreds of USG employees. And it draws from USG's long history of innovative research and product development, cutting-edge production technologies and the delivery of high-performance solutions, decade after decade.

The *Handbook* symbolizes USG's total commitment to its customers and its industry. Our dedication to unexcelled service, state-of-art products, dynamic leadership and the development of lasting relationships motivates us to *go the distance* in everything we do—with no short-cuts and no tolerance for less than our best effort. We want the professionals who use our products to be confident that USG will deliver high-performance, cost-effective building solutions every time.

At USG, we are proud of our products and the dedication and innovation inherent in our manufacturing processes. We will continue to focus our company and people on the development of new materials, broader applications and improved construction technologies. That is our pledge to our customers and our industry, because, at USG, we have always been committed to "Building a Better Way."

Sincerely,

William C. Foote
Chairman and Chief Executive Officer, USG

Trademarks

The following trademarks used in this edition are owned by United States Gypsum Company or an affiliated company: ACOUSTIBOND, ACRI-ADD, A/P LITE, AQUA-TOUGH, ASPEN, ASTRO, AX, BEADEX, BABY BULL, BILLO, BRIO, CADRE, CELEBRATION, CENTRICITEE, CHAMPION, CLEAN ROOM, *CLIMA-PLUS*, COMPÄSSO, COVER COAT, CURVATURA, DIAMOND, DONN, DUR-A-BEAD, DURABOND, DUROCK, DX, DXL, DXLA, DXW, EASY SAND, ECLIPSE, "F" FISSURED, FIBEROCK, FINELINE, FIRECODE, FRESCO, FROST, GEOMETRIX, GLACIER, GRIDWARE, HALYCON, HYDROCAL, IMPERIAL, LEVELROCK, LIBRETTO, MARS, MICRO BEAD, MILLENIA, MOLD TOUGH, OLYMPIA MICRO, ORIENTAL, PANZ, PARALINE, PEBBLED, PLUS 3, PREMIER HI-LITE, PREMIER NUBBY, QUADRA, RADAR, RED TOP, ROCK FACE, ROCKLATH, SANDRIFT, SECUROCK, SHEETROCK, SMOKE SEAL, STRUCTO-BASE, STRUCTOCORE, STRUCTO-GAUGE, STRUCTO-LITE, SUMMIT, TEXOLITE, TOPO, TOUCHSTONE, TUFF-HIDE, TUF-TEX, ULTRACODE, USG, WIREWORKS, ZXA, ZXLA.

BONCRETE, GRAND PRIZE, IVORY, MORTASEAL AND SNOWDRIFT are trademarks of Graymont Dolime Inc. BUILDEX, CLIMASEAL, CONDRIVE, and TAPCON are trademarks of Illinois Tool Works Inc. YVEK and HOMEWRAP are trademarks of E. I. du Pont de Nemours and Company. MASTERSPEC is a trademark of American Institute of Architects. MASTERFORMAT is a trademark of The Construction Specifications Institute, Inc. SWEET'S is a trademark of McGraw-Hill Companies, Inc. COLORTREND and AMBIANCE are trademarks of Creanova, Inc. LEXAN is a trademark of Sabic Innovative Plastics. WELD-CRETE is a trademark of Larsen Products Corporation. BAZOOKA is a trademark of Ames Taping Tools Systems Company.

Editorial Committee

The Editorial Board for the sixth edition of *The Gypsum Construction Handbook* consisted of:

USG
Scott Feste, Jake Gress, Bob Grupe, Rik Master, Linda McGovern, Brad Nemeth, Kurt Peterson, Tom Sheppard and Jean Wilcox

Reed Business Information
Julian Francis, Mary Greene and John Shea

Residential Design
Jaime Manzo

Thorne Associates
Dan Degnan

Additional editorial contributors to this edition were Chris Baker, Chris Borovka, Sam Copell, Scott Crandall, Bobbi Gruca, Grant Guenther, Jeff Hartin, Jeff Johnston, Ted Kellam, John Koch, Chris Lawson, Kevin Moyer, John Koch, Don Schaefer, Andrew Seidel, Paul Shipp, Chris Skelton, Rich Willett, and Robert Williams of USG, Steve Kalter of Kalter Design, as well as David Morton, an independent consultant.

Using *The Gypsum Construction Handbook*

For over a century, *The Gypsum Construction Handbook* has been a trusted, reliable resource for architects, engineers, builders, dealers, distributors and contractors. *The Handbook* was first introduced as *The Red Book for Builders and Plasterers.* Over the course of 100 years and more, it has been the building industry's most relied-on reference for gypsum products and systems and has grown and evolved with each new edition to meet the industry's changing needs.

The book is a comprehensive guide to the selection and use of gypsum drywall, veneer plaster, tile backers, ceilings and conventional plaster building materials. It provides information on current products and systems and describes correct, time- and cost-saving installation methods designed to simplify and speed construction.

The book has served as a standard text for training and apprenticeship classes, a guide for building inspectors and code officials, and a source of detailed product information and installation procedures for building professionals worldwide.

For architects and engineers: technical information on gypsum product construction standards, including available system descriptions, fire- and sound-rated construction, limitations and installation procedures.

For contractors, builders and dealers: full data on all aspects of gypsum products and accessories, tools and equipment, and applications, including information needed to estimate and plan projects.

For apprenticeship training schools: illustrated, easy-to-understand directions for applying gypsum products—from framing to finish.

For journeymen: a comprehensive index of contents and clear, concise, illustrated instructions and techniques for applying gypsum products at every stage of the construction process.

For building inspectors and code officials: an excellent source of fire, sound and physical test data and proper construction techniques for gypsum products to ensure compliance with performance criteria.

The Handbook contains the latest information about proper gypsum drywall, plaster and cement board construction available at the time of its writing. The text describes framing installation, drywall and veneer plaster construction, joint treatment and plaster finishing, interior cement board construction, and conventional plaster application and the tools required for each job. *The Handbook* also covers special engineered systems, product application factors, problems and solutions, and various repair and remodeling techniques.

Readers may use the table of contents or fully cross-referenced index to find desired information on drywall, veneer or conventional plaster, or tile backers construction. The book also includes a comprehensive glossary of terms with definitions of terms used throughout the text.

New in This Edition

The new Sixth Edition covers the latest USG products, including abuse-resistant gypsum panels and sustainable materials, as well as three new chapters:

- Chapter 15: "Building Sciences," with expanded information on building movement, fire resistance, heat transfer, sound transmission and vapor control.

- Chapter 16: "Sustainability," a review of sustainable building approaches and USG's products and manufacturing processes that comply with green construction standards.

- Chapter 17: "USG: America's Building Industry Leader," information on USG Corporation, its categories of products and their applications, and useful customer tools, including the latest online resources.

Chapter 14, "Tools & Equipment," now includes the latest on SHEETROCK brand tools.

Drywall & Veneer Plaster Products

Since their introduction over 90 years ago, SHEETROCK® brand gypsum panels from USG have led the drywall industry and have become the standard for quality interior walls and ceilings. With the addition of veneer plaster bases and finishes, USG has the nation's largest-selling, broadest line of gypsum products with the highest quality and the best performance.

The gypsum products described in this chapter conform to product standards recommended by USG, as well as applicable ASTM, government and commercial standards. These materials meet the essential requirements of economy, sound isolation, workability, strength, fire resistance and ease of decoration that are characteristic of quality construction.

USG continues to be at the forefront of technological advances in the industry. In recent years, the company's research and development staff has produced a series of materials that offer exceptional strength and durability. Those materials now are commercially available as abuse-resistant products and systems. These systems were initially developed for government buildings, commercial construction, schools, prisons and other structures where walls and ceilings are subject to considerable traffic and abusive wear and tear. They will also provide longer lasting quality in typical commercial and residential construction. You will find information on abuse-resistant products and systems throughout this text.

USG sales and technical representatives are available to consult with tradespeople, contractors, architects, dealers and code officials on gypsum products and systems and their application to individual job problems and conditions. For more in-depth information, visit the USG websites (**usg.com** and **usgdesignstudio.com**).

Gypsum Panel Products

SHEETROCK is the preferred and most widely used brand of gypsum panels. It is available in more specialized forms than any other gypsum panel line. When used with USG's other high-quality components, SHEETROCK brand gypsum panels provide high-performance walls and ceilings.

A SHEETROCK™ brand panel is composed of a noncombustible gypsum core encased in a strong, smooth-finish paper on the face side and a natural-finish paper on the back side. The face paper is folded around the long edges to reinforce and protect the core, and the ends are square-cut and finished smooth. The long edges of the panels are available in a choice of designs (including tapered), allowing joints to be reinforced and concealed with a USG joint treatment system.

Advantages

Interior walls and ceilings built with SHEETROCK panels have a durable surface suitable for most types of decorative treatment and for redecoration throughout the life of the building.

1

Dry Construction Factory-produced panels do not contribute moisture during construction. The joint finishing system contributes very little.

Fire Protection The gypsum core will not support combustion or transmit temperatures greatly in excess of 212°F until completely calcined. Fire-resistance ratings of up to 4 hours for partitions, 3 hours for floor-ceilings and 4 hours for column and beam assemblies are available with specific assemblies. (See Chapter 10, "System Design Considerations," for specific ratings and related assemblies.)

Sound Control SHEETROCK gypsum panels are a vital component in sound-resistive partition and floor-ceiling systems. (See Chapter 10 and the Appendix for specific rating data.)

Low In-Place Cost The easily cut gypsum panels install quickly, simplifying fixture attachment and installation of electrical and mechanical services.

Dimensional Stability Expansion or contraction under normal temperature and humidity changes is small and normally will not result in warping or buckling. With joints properly reinforced, SHEETROCK panels are exceptionally resistant to cracking. (See the Appendix for thermal and hygrometric coefficients of expansion.)

Availability Over 40 USG manufacturing plants produce gypsum board and related products described herein throughout North America. Special warehouse facilities, in addition to these plants, increase total distribution and service efficiency to major markets and rural areas from coast to coast. All standard gypsum board products are readily available on short notice. Many products are available from USG subsidiary plants in Mexico and Canada.

Gypsum Panel Limitations

1. Exposure to excessive or continuous moisture and extreme temperatures should be avoided. Not recommended for use in solar or other heating systems when board will be in direct contact with surfaces exceeding 125°F.

2. Adequate protection must be provided against wetting when panels are used as a base for ceramic or other wall tile (see foil-back panel limitation, page 6). DUROCK® brand cement board, FIBEROCK® brand AQUA-TOUGH™ interior panels, or FIBEROCK AQUA-TOUGH tile backerboard are recommended for partitions in moisture-prone areas.

3. Maximum spacing of framing members: 1/2" and 5/8" gypsum panels are designed for use on framing centers up to 24"; 3/8" panels are designed for use on framing centers up to 16". In both walls and ceilings, when 1/2" or 5/8" gypsum panels are applied across framing on 24" centers and joints are reinforced, blocking is not required. 1/4" SHEETROCK panels are not recommended for single-layer applications on open framing.

4. Application of panels is not recommended over 3/4" wood furring applied across framing, since the flexibility of the furring under impact of the hammer tends to loosen nails already driven. Furring should be 2 x 2 minimum (may be 1 x 3 if panels are to be screw-attached).

5. Application of gypsum panels is not recommended over an insulating blanket that has first been installed continuously across the face of the framing members. Blankets should be recessed and flanges attached to the sides of studs or joists.

6. To prevent objectionable sag in new gypsum panel ceilings, the weight of overlaid unsupported insulation should not exceed: 1.3 psf for 1/2"-thick panels with frame spacing 24" o.c.; 2.4 psf for 1/2" panels on 16" o.c. framing (or 1/2" SHEETROCK brand interior gypsum ceiling board, sag-resistant on 24" o.c. framing); 2.2 psf for 5/8" panels on 24" o.c. framing. 3/8"-thick panels must not be overlaid with unsupported insulation. A vapor retarder should be installed in all exterior ceilings, and the plenum or attic space should be properly vented.

During periods of cold or damp weather, where a polyethylene or equivalent vapor retarder is installed on ceilings behind the gypsum board, it is important to install the ceiling insulation before or immediately after installing the ceiling board. Failure to follow this procedure may result in moisture condensation on the back side of the gypsum board, causing the board to sag.

Water-based textures, interior finishing materials and high ambient humidity conditions can produce sag in gypsum ceiling panels, if adequate vapor and moisture control is not provided. The following precautions must be observed to minimize sagging of ceiling panels:

a) Where vapor retarder is required in cold weather conditions, care must be taken to avoid moisture condensation. The temperature of the gypsum ceiling panels and vapor retarder must remain above the interior air dew point temperature during and after the installation of panels and finishing materials.

b) The interior space must be adequately ventilated and air circulation must be provided to remove water vapor from the structure.

Most sag problems are caused by the condensation of water within the gypsum panel. The placement of vapor retarders, insulation levels and ventilation requirements will vary by location and climate and should be reviewed by a qualified engineer if in question.

7. Certain recommendations regarding surface preparation and painting products and systems must be adhered to for satisfactory performance and intended results.

8. Precaution should be taken against using gypsum panels as a base for highly water-vapor-resistant coverings when the wall already contains a vapor retarder, as this will create a double vapor retarder. Moreover, do not create a vapor retarder by such wall coverings on the interior side of exterior walls of air-conditioned buildings in hot-humid climates where conditions dictate a vapor retarder be located near the exterior side of the wall. Such conditions require assessment by a qualified mechanical engineer.

Products Available

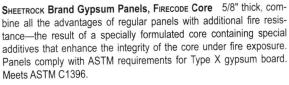

SHEETROCK **Brand Gypsum Panels, Regular** These 48"-wide panels have long edges tapered on the face side to form a shallow recess (nominal 0.050" deep) to accommodate joint reinforcement. Made in three thicknesses for specific purposes:

- 1/2", recommended for single-layer application typical new construction and remodeling. The thickness provides resistance to fire exposure, sound transmission and sagging.
- 3/8", lightweight, applied principally in repair and remodel work over existing surfaces.
- 1/4", lightweight, low-cost, utility gypsum panel, used as a base layer for improving sound control in multi-layer partitions and in covering old wall and ceiling surfaces. Also used for forming curved surfaces. Meets ASTM C1396.

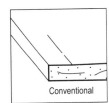

Conventional

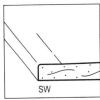

SW

Types of Tapered Edges

SHEETROCK **Brand 54" Gypsum Panels** Same as 1/2" regular core SHEETROCK brand gypsum panels, but 6" wider. The added width reduces cutting, waste, joint finishing and labor costs for walls that are 8'-6" or 9' tall.

SHEETROCK **Brand Gypsum Panels, SW** Feature an exclusive tapered rounded edge design to help minimize ridging, beading and other joint imperfections. This edge produces a much stronger joint than a regular tapered edge when finished with joint treatment. Except for the rounded edge, panels are tapered like, and otherwise identical to, regular tapered-edge gypsum panels. Made in 5/8" and 1/2" thicknesses. Panels are available in regular or FIRECODE® Core (Type X and Type C) formulations. Meets ASTM C1396.

SHEETROCK **Brand Gypsum Panels, FIRECODE Core** 5/8" thick, combine all the advantages of regular panels with additional fire resistance—the result of a specially formulated core containing special additives that enhance the integrity of the core under fire exposure. Panels comply with ASTM requirements for Type X gypsum board. Meets ASTM C1396.

SHEETROCK **Brand Gypsum Panels, FIRECODE C Core** Available in 1/2" and 5/8" thicknesses. Improved formulation exceeds ASTM requirements for Type X gypsum board. Based on tests at Underwriters Laboratories Inc. (UL) and other nationally recognized testing agencies, certain partition, floor-ceiling and column fire-protective assemblies using these special products provide 1-hr. to 4-hr. fire-resistance ratings.

In order to attain fire-resistance ratings, the construction of all such assemblies must be consistent with the assembly tested. (See Chapter 10 for assemblies.) Meets ASTM C1396.

SHEETROCK **Brand 1/4" Flexible Gypsum Panels** Designed specifically for curved partitions, these panels are more flexible than standard panels of the same thickness, making them ideal for use anywhere a tight radius is required for curved walls, arches and stairways. (See curved surface section, Chapter 3, "Cladding.") They make construction of curved surfaces easy and fast. Double-layer installation improves surface smoothness and fire protection. Meet ASTM C1396.

SHEETROCK **Brand Gypsum Panels, ULTRACODE® Core** 3/4" thick, UL tested to provide a 2-hr. fire rating with single-layer construction and a 4-hr. fire rating with double-layer construction in certain specified systems (steel studs only). Because fewer layers are needed to meet fire ratings, ULTRACODE Core panel systems reduce labor and material costs.

Gypsum Panels, Foil-Back

SHEETROCK brand gypsum panels, foil-back are made by laminating special kraft-backed aluminum foil to the back surface of regular, SW, FIRECODE or FIRECODE C panels. Where required in cold climates, this panel forms an effective vapor retarder for walls and ceilings when applied with foil surface next to framing on interior side of exterior wall in single-layer application or as the base layer in multi-layer systems. Foil-backed gypsum panels provide a water-vapor retarder to help prevent interior moisture from entering wall and ceiling spaces. In tests per ASTM E96 (desiccant method), 1/2" foil-back panels showed a vapor permeability of 0.06 perms. The permeance of the total exterior wall system is dependent on the closure of leaks with sealants at periphery and all penetrations such as outlet boxes.

These panels are designed for use with furred masonry or wood or steel framing. Thickness: 5/8", 1/2" and 3/8". Sizes, edges and finish are the same as for base panels.

Foil-Back Panel Limitations

1. Not recommended as a base for ceramic or other tile.

2. Not to be used in air-conditioned buildings in climates having sustained high outside temperature and humidity, such as the Southern Atlantic and Gulf Coast areas. Under these conditions, a qualified mechanical engineer should determine vapor retarder location.

Foil-back panels applied to steel framing over the interior of exterior walls provide an effective vapor retarder.

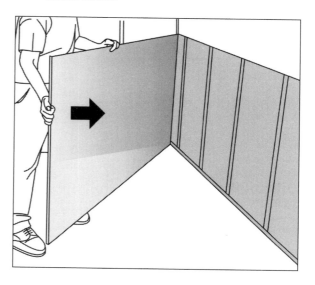

Gypsum Panels, Moisture & Mold Resistant

SHEETROCK Brand MOLD TOUGH® Gypsum Panels Have a noncombustible, moisture- and mold-resistant gypsum core encased in moisture- and mold-resistant, 100-percent-recycled green face and brown back paper. The 5/8" FIRECODE and 1/2" FIRECODE C Core panels are UL classified for fire resistance (Type X).

Although all SHEETROCK brand MOLD TOUGH gypsum panels have improved moisture and mold resistance over standard gypsum panels by treating the core and surface, independent lab tests conducted at the time of manufacture on only 5/8" SHEETROCK brand FIRECODE MOLD TOUGH gypsum panels, 1/2" SHEETROCK brand MOLD TOUGH FIRECODE C Core gypsum panels (Type X) and SHEETROCK ULTRACODE gypsum panels per ASTM D3273, "Standard Test Method for Resistance to Growth of Mold on the Surface of Interior Coatings in an Environmental Chamber," the panel score was 10.

This ASTM lab test may not guaranty the mold performance of building materials in actual use. Given unsuitable project conditions may be present at any time during construction, any building material can be overwhelmed by mold. To manage the growth of mold, the best and most cost-effective strategy is to protect building products from water exposure during storage and installation and after completion of the building. This can be accomplished by using good design and construction practices.

SHEETROCK Brand Gypsum Panels, MOLD TOUGH, Regular 1/2" thickness for single-layer application in residential construction.

SHEETROCK Brand Gypsum Panels, MOLD TOUGH, FIRECODE Core 5/8" thickness with a Type X core to provide fire resistance for required ratings.

SHEETROCK Brand Gypsum Panels, MOLD TOUGH, FIRECODE C Core 1/2" and 5/8" thicknesses with a special core to provide improved fire resistance for required ratings.

SHEETROCK Gypsum Panels MOLD TOUGH 3/4" ULTRACODE Core The 3/4" ULTRACODE Core panel is UL classified as to fire resistance. One layer of 3/4" ULTRACODE Core panels may be substituted for two layers of 5/8" FIRECODE Core panels in many UL Listed assemblies. Refer to the *UL Fire Resistance Directory* for details.

MOLD TOUGH Panel Limitations

1. Not suitable for sustained temperatures exceeding 125°F (52°C).

2. Should not be exposed to excessive, repetitive or continuous moisture before, during or after installation. Eliminate sources of moisture immediately.

3. Not suitable for use as a substrate for tile in wet areas such as tubs and showers, gang showers and other areas subject to direct water exposure. DUROCK brand cement board is recommended for these uses. (See DUROCK applications, Chapter 4, "Backerboard Installation.")

4. Non-load-bearing.

FIBEROCK® Brand AQUA-TOUGH™ Interior Panels Offer finishing flexibility and superior mold and moisture resistance in a single panel. Manufactured using USG's unique gypsum-fiber technology, these durable panels provide moisture and mold resistance superior to conventional drywall, but can be installed and finished using basic drywall techniques. Uniform composition, without face paper, is based on a uniquely engineered gypsum/cellulose-fiber combination that won't weaken if the surface is penetrated by moisture. Panels comply with ASTM C1278.

FIBEROCK Brand AQUA-TOUGH Tile Backerboard Unique fiber-reinforced gypsum product that represents a new era in substrate performance for wet or dry areas. This durable panel offers superior performance and tile bond because of its integral water-resistant core. Unlike traditional water-resistant gypsum board, FIBEROCK tile backerboard derives both strength and water resistance from its uniquely engineered gypsum/cellulose-fiber combination, With no paper to delaminate, FIBEROCK tile backerboard maintains its integrity even when wet.

FIBEROCK Panel Limitations

Panels are not intended for use in areas subject to constant moisture, such as interior swimming pools, gang showers, steam showers and saunas (DUROCK brand cement board is recommended for these uses. See Chapter 4 for further information.)

Exterior Gypsum Ceiling Board

SHEETROCK Brand Exterior Gypsum Ceiling Board Weather-resistant board designed for use on the soffit side of eaves, canopies and carports and other commercial and residential exterior applications with indirect exposure to the weather. Noncombustible core is simply scored and snapped for quick application. Panels can be painted and provide good sag resistance.

Installed conventionally in wood- and metal-framed soffits. Batten strips or mouldings can be used over butt joints or joints can be treated. Backing strips are required for small vent openings. Natural finish. Available in 1/2" thickness with regular core and in 5/8" thickness with fire-rated Type X and Type C cores—both with eased edges. Board complies with ASTM C1396.

SECUROCK Glass-Mat Sheathing Also can be used for exterior ceiling applications where extra weather protection is desired. A direct-applied synthetic-type stucco system applied in accordance with the manufacturer's recommendations is recommended as a final finish.

FIBEROCK Brand AQUA-TOUGH Interior Panels Suitable for use in exterior soffit and ceiling applications not directly exposed to the weather, such as open porches, walkways, soffits and similar applications that are horizontal or inclined downward away from the building. Manufactured using USG's unique gypsum-fiber technology, these durable panels provide moisture and mold resistance superior to conventional paper-faced products. Panels comply with ASTM C1278.

Sag-Resistant Ceiling Panels

SHEETROCK Brand Interior Ceiling Panels, Sag-Resistant Significantly lighter in weight than 5/8" gypsum panels and provide greater sag resistance. These panels also support sprayed textures and overlaid insulation better than 5/8" gypsum panels. Panels are 1/2" thick and are available in 8' or 12' lengths, 4' wide. Meet ASTM C1396.

Abuse-Resistant Panel Products

SHEETROCK **Brand Abuse-Resistant Gypsum Panels** Offer greater indentation and through-penetration resistance than standard gypsum panels. Available in 5/8" FIRECODE Core.

Abuse-resistant panels are made with strong face paper and a heavy-duty backing sheet, which improve the integrity of the board. As a result, the panels are able to withstand impact better than standard gypsum board and are less likely to allow penetrations or show indentations. Meets ASTM C1396.

FIBEROCK **Brand Abuse-Resistant Panels** Engineered to provide increased resistance to abrasion, indentation and penetration for interior walls and ceilings in demanding construction applications. These gypsum fiber panels are designed to outperform paper-faced gypsum board. Strong, solid and durable, they resist denting, breaking and puncturing—even in high-traffic areas. They also are manufactured with 95% recycled content. They have exceptional surface-burning characteristics (ASTM E84, Flame Spread 5, Smoke Developed 0) and fire resistance (ASTM E119). 5/8" FIBEROCK abuse-resistant panels may be used in lieu of Type X gypsum panels in over 50 fire rated wall assemblies as listed in the *UL Fire Resistance Directory* under "Type FRX."

Specifications—Gypsum Panel Products

	Thickness		Length	Approx. wt.	
	in.	mm	ft.[1]	lb./SF	kg/m²
SHEETROCK Brand Regular Panels[2]	1/4	6.4	8 and 10	1.2	5.9
	3/8	9.5	8, 9, 10, 12, 14	1.4	6.8
	1/2	12.7	8, 9, 10, 12, 14	1.7	8.3
FIRECODE Core Panels[2]	5/8	15.9	8, 9, 10,12, 14	2.2	10.7
FIRECODE C Core Panels[2]	1/2	12.7	8, 9, 10, 12, 14	1.9	9.3
	5/8	15.9	8, 9, 10, 12, 14	2.5	12.2
ULTRACODE Core Panels	3/4	19.0	8, 9, 10, 12	2.8	13.7
MOLD TOUGH Panels	1/2	12.7	8, 10, 12	1.8	8.8
MOLD TOUGH FIRECODE Core Panels	5/8	15.9	8, 10, 12	2.2	10.7
MOLD TOUGH FIRECODE C Core Panels	1/2	12.7	10	1.9	9.3
FIBEROCK Brand AQUA-TOUGH Interior Panels/FIBEROCK Brand Tile-Backerboard	1/2	12.7	5, 8, 9,10	2.2	10.7
	5/8	15.9	5, 8, 9, 10	2.7	13.2
Exterior Ceiling Board Regular Board	1/2	12.7	8, 12	1.9	9.3
FIRECODE Board	5/8	15.9	8, 12	2.4	11.7
Interior Ceiling Panels Sag Resistant	1/2	12.7	8, 12	1.6	7.8
1/4" Flexible Panels	1/4	6.4	8 and 10	1.2	5.9
54" Panels	1/2	12.7	8, 9, 10, 12, 14	1.7	8.3
Abuse Resistant Panels	5/8	15.9	8, 9, 10,12, 14	2.7	13.2
FIBEROCK Brand Abuse Resistant Panels	1/2	12.7	8, 9, 10, 12	2.2	10.7
	5/8	15.9	8, 9, 10, 12	2.7	13.2

FIBEROCK Brand AQUA-TOUGH Interior Panels Have all the benefits of FIBEROCK abuse-resistant panels with the added benefit of mold and moisture resistance. Available in 1/2" and 5/8" FIRECODE Core.

FIBEROCK Brand VHI Abuse-Resistant Panels Very high impact (VHI) panels have all the benefits of the FIBEROCK abuse-resistant panels, but are also glass-fiber-mesh reinforced to provide penetration resistance and rigidity for a single-layer gypsum panel. Available in 1/2" and 5/8" FIRECODE Core.

Veneer Plaster Gypsum Base Products

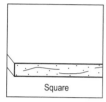

Square

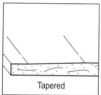

Tapered

Types of Edges

Gypsum bases finished with veneer plasters are recommended for interior walls and ceilings in all types of construction. For these interiors, a veneer of specially formulated gypsum plaster is applied in one coat (1/16" to 3/32" thick) or two coats (approximately 1/8" thick) over the base. The resulting smooth or textured monolithic surfaces are preferred for hard-wear locations where durability and resistance to abrasion are required.

IMPERIAL® gypsum bases are 48"-wide gypsum board panels that are rigid and fire-resistant. A gypsum core is faced with specially treated, multi-layered paper (blue) designed to provide a maximum bond to veneer plaster finishes. The paper's absorbent outer layers quickly and uniformly draw moisture from the veneer plaster finish for proper application and finishing. The moisture-resistant inner layers keep the core dry and rigid to resist sagging. The face paper is folded around the long edges. Ends are square-cut and finished smooth.

Gypsum Base Advantages

Gypsum bases, in conjunction with selected veneer plaster finishes, provide the lasting quality of plaster walls and ceilings at a lower cost and with less weight and residual moisture than conventional plaster.

Rapid Installation Walls and ceilings can be completed quickly—in 3 to 4 days, from bare framing through decorated interiors.

Fire Resistance Ratings of up to 4 hours for partitions, 3 hours for floor-ceilings and 4 hours for column fire protection assemblies have been obtained.

Sound Control Gypsum base partitions faced with veneer plaster finishes on both sides have high resistance to sound transmission. (Resilient attachment of base and use of insulation further improve sound isolation.)

Durability Hard, high-strength surfaces provide excellent abrasion resistance, resulting in minimum maintenance, even in high-traffic areas.

Easily Decorated Smooth-surfaced interiors readily accept paints, texture, fabric and wallpaper. Veneer plaster finishes also may be textured. If completely dry, finishes can be painted with breather-type paints the day following application. For additional information, reference PM15, Gypsum Plaster Finishes.

**Gypsum Base
Limitations**

1. Maximum frame and fastener spacing is dependent on thickness and type of base used.

2. Recommended for use with IMPERIAL veneer basecoat, IMPERIAL veneer finish, DIAMOND® veneer basecoat and DIAMOND veneer finish. Do not apply gauged lime-putty finishes or Portland cement plaster directly to base; bond failure is likely.

3. Not recommended for use in areas exposed to moisture for extended periods or as a base for adhesive application of ceramic tile in wet areas (DUROCK brand interior cement board and FIBEROCK AQUA-TOUGH tile backerboard are recommended for this use).

4. Gypsum base that has faded from the original light blue color due to exposure to sunlight should be treated with either USG plaster bonder or a solution of USG accelerator—alum catalyst before DIAMOND veneer finish or any veneer plaster finish containing lime is applied. When using USG plaster bonder, a two-coat veneer system (basecoat and finish coat) is required for adequate smoothness. IMPERIAL veneer basecoat and veneer finish and DIAMOND veneer basecoat plasters do not contain lime and are not susceptible to bond failure over faded base.

5. Joints and internal angles must be treated with SHEETROCK joint tape and setting-type joint compound (DURABOND®) or lightweight setting-type joint compound (EASY SAND™) when building temperature-humidity conditions fall in the "rapid-drying" area of the graph when metal framing is specified or when 24" o.c. wood-frame spacing and a single-layer gypsum base veneer system is specified (5/8" base with one-coat veneer finish and 1/2" or 5/8" base with two-coat veneer finish). Single-layer 1/2" base is not recommended with 24" o.c. spacing and one-coat veneer plaster.

**Plaster Drying
Conditions**

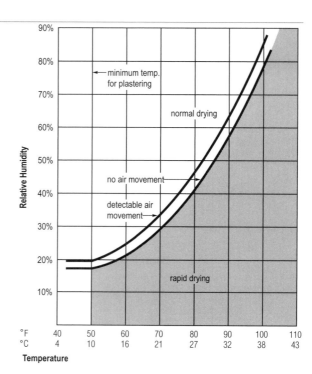

**Products
Available**

IMPERIAL **Gypsum Base** A special gypsum board that has been specifically engineered for use with IMPERIAL veneer finish and DIAMOND veneer finish or IMPERIAL and DIAMOND veneer basecoat plasters. It provides the strength and absorption characteristics necessary for top-quality veneer plaster finishing performance. Large sheets minimize the number of joints and speed installation. The high-density, fire-resistant gypsum core has a superior controlled-absorption paper lightly tinted blue on the face side and a strong liner paper on the back side. Available in two thicknesses with square or tapered edges: 1/2" for single-layer application in new light construction; 5/8" recommended for the finest high-strength veneer plaster finish construction. The greater thickness provides increased resistance to fire exposure and sound transmission and allows 24" o.c. spacing of wood framing. IMPERIAL gypsum base may be used with DIAMOND veneer finish to embed cables for radiant heat ceilings. Meets ASTM C588.

IMPERIAL **Gypsum Base**, FIRECODE **and** FIRECODE **C Core** IMPERIAL gypsum base, FIRECODE Core in 5/8" thickness and FIRECODE C Core in 1/2" and 5/8" thicknesses combine all the advantages of regular IMPERIAL gypsum base with additional resistance to fire exposure—the result of specially formulated mineral cores. UL-classified for fire resistance. Meets ASTM C588.

IMPERIAL **Gypsum Base, Ultracode Core** In 3/4" thickness, has a fire-resistant core that permits fire ratings to be achieved with fewer layers of panels. Meets ASTM C588.

Other Veneer Plaster Base Products

DUROCK **Brand Cement Board** A glass-fiber-mesh reinforced aggregated Portland cement panel that provides a high-strength substrate for improved abuse resistance. Requires the use of USG plaster bonder, which is only suitable for two-coat plaster application. Available 1/2" thick (5/8" available under minimum order conditions) in 4' x 8' and 4' x 10' dimensions.

FIBEROCK **Brand Abuse-Resistant Panels and** FIBEROCK **Brand VHI Abuse-Resistant Panels** Deliver greater impact and puncture resistance than any other gypsum panel. Made with a unique gypsum/cellulose fiber core, the panels impede penetrations by sharp objects, including sharp blows from small objects, and exhibit more rigidity than standard gypsum panels. They also provide greater flexural strength and screw withdrawal properties than other gypsum panels. Requires the use of USG plaster bonder, which is only suitable for two-coat plaster application. VHI panels are glass-fiber-mesh reinforced to provide extraordinary penetration resistance and rigidity for a single-layer gypsum panel. Available in 1/2" and 5/8" thicknesses. They have exceptional surface-burning characteristics (ASTM E84, Flame Spread 5, Smoke Developed 0) and fire resistance (ASTM E119). 5/8" FIBEROCK brand abuse-resistant panels may be used in lieu of Type X gypsum panels in over 50 fire rated wall assemblies as listed in the *UL Fire Resistance Directory* under "Type FRX."

Specifications—Gypsum Bases

	Thickness		Length	Approx. wt	
Product	in.	mm	ft.[1]	lb./SF	kg/m²
IMPERIAL Gypsum Base[2]					
Regular	1/2	12.7	8, 9, 10, 12, 14	1.8	8.8
Regular	5/8	15.9	8, 9, 10, 12, 14	2.3	11.2
FIRECODE	5/8	15.9	8, 9, 10, 12, 14	2.3	11.2
FIRECODE C	1/2	12.7	8, 9, 10, 12, 14	2.0	9.8
FIRECODE C	5/8	15.9	8, 9, 10, 12, 14	2.5	12.2
ULTRACODE	3/4	19.0	8, 9, 10, 12, 14	3.0	14.6
Abuse-Resistant FIRECODE	5/8	12.7	8, 9, 10, 12, 14	2.0	9.8
Abuse-Resistant FIRECODE C	5/8	15.9	8, 9, 10, 12, 14	2.5	12.2
DUROCK Brand Cement Board	1/2	12.7	8, 9, 10, 12, 14	3.0	14.6
FIBEROCK Brand Abuse Resistant Panels	1/2	12.7	8, 9, 10	2.2	10.9
FIBEROCK Brand VHI Abuse Resistant Panels	5/8	15.9	8, 9, 10	2.7	13.4

(1) Metric lengths: 8 ft. = 2440 mm; 9 ft. = 2745 mm; 10 ft. = 3050 mm; 12 ft. = 3660 mm; 14 ft. = 4270 mm.
(2) Also available in Foil-Back Base.

Gypsum Liner & Sheathing Products

Double Beveled

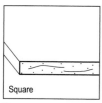

Square

Types of Edges

SHEETROCK Brand Gypsum Liner Panels Have a 1" thick, special fire-resistant gypsum core that is encased in multi-layered, moisture-resistant green paper. Panels are used in USG cavity shaft walls, area separation walls, select floor assemblies and infill panel systems for exterior curtain walls. Panels have beveled edges for easy insertion between the supporting flanges of steel C-H studs, E-studs or H-studs. Meets ASTM C1396.

SHEETROCK Brand Gypsum Liner Panels, MOLD TOUGH Have a non-combustible, moisture- and mold-resistant gypsum core that is encased in moisture- and mold-resistant, 100-percent-recycled blue face and back papers. The panels are UL-classified as to fire resistance (Type SLX) and feature double beveled edges for easy installation. May be substituted for SHEETROCK gypsum liner panels in all SHEETROCK shaft-wall and area-separation-wall systems.

Note: These SHEETROCK gypsum liner panels have been comprehensively tested for fire resistance, structural performance and sound control *only* when used with SHEETROCK shaft wall and area separation wall framing components. All SHEETROCK shaft-wall and area-separation-wall system components must be used together to ensure superior system performance and safety. Substitutions of any components are not recommended and are not endorsed by the United States Gypsum Company.

SHEETROCK Brand Gypsum Sheathing A fire-resistant gypsum board, with a water-resistant gypsum core encased in specially treated water-repellent paper on both sides and long edges. Its weather resistance, water repellency, fire resistance and low applied cost make it suitable for use in exterior wall construction of garden apartments and light commercial buildings as well as in homes. Also used in steel stud curtain wall construction.

SHEETROCK brand gypsum sheathing is suitable for a wide range of exterior finishes such as, but not limited to, masonry veneer, wood, vinyl and aluminum siding, wood shingles and stucco. Exterior finish attachment is limited to mechanical fastening through sheathing into the framing.

Available in 1/2" and 5/8" thick in two economical types: 4' wide, 8' and 9' long with square edges for vertical application. Meets ASTM C1396.

FIBEROCK Brand AQUA-TOUGH Sheathing Manufactured using USG's unique patented technology, FIBEROCK sheathing offers exceptional strength, durability and superior water resistance. Unlike other gypsum sheathings, FIBEROCK sheathing derives both strength and water resistance from its uniform core formulation. FIBEROCK sheathing is strong and water resistant all the way through its cross section and won't lose its strength when cut. FIBEROCK sheathing is warranted for 10 years against manufacturing defects and for 12 months of weather exposure.

Meets ASTM C1278 standards and meets or exceeds the physical property requirements of ASTM C1177, ASTM C1396 and ASTM C931. Available 1/2" and 5/8" thick.

Sheathing Limitations

1. Sheathing may be stored outside for up to one month, but must be stored off the ground and must have a protective covering.

2. Maximum stud spacing is 24" o.c.

3. When applied to a structure, sheathing must not be left exposed to the elements for more than one month unless the procedure as outlined in limitation 5 (below) is followed.

4. Exterior finish systems applied over gypsum paper-faced sheathing must be applied with mechanical fasteners through the sheathing into the wall framing. Alternate methods of application are not endorsed, and their performance and that of the substrate are solely the responsibility of the specifier. Direct application of paint, texture finishes and coatings over gypsum sheathing is not recommended.

5. For paper-faced sheathing in-place exposure up to six months, all gaps resulting from cuts, corners, joints and machine end cuts of the sheathing should be filled with exterior caulk at time of erection, or wrapped with a suitable water barrier.

6. For curtain wall construction, cover the sheathing with No. 15 asphalt felt or other suitable water barrier within 30 days of sheathing installation. Felt should be applied horizontally with 2" overlap and immediately anchored with metal lath, masonry ties or corrosion-resistant screws or staples. (See SA923 Technical Folder for additional curtain wall details.)

7. Paper-faced sheathing is not recommended for exterior ceilings and soffits, unless covered with metal lath and exterior Portland cement stucco.

8. System should be designed to allow free movement of water out of the system where the sheathing is installed to allow it to dry.

9. Specific requirements regarding framing spacing, fastener spacing and fastener specifics to provide required lateral wind-load resistance are the responsibility of the design professional.

10. For FIBEROCK AQUA-TOUGH sheathing, no weather-resistant barrier is required for exposure warranty. Where system air- and water-penetration resistance are required while the building is being enclosed, joints between FIBEROCK sheathing can be treated with a sealant such as Dow Corning 795 silicone sealant (or equivalent), or Bituthene 3000 tape (or equivalent).

SECUROCK Glass-Mat Sheathing

SECUROCK glass mat sheathing has a treated gypsum core combined with a fiberglass mat face and back, and offers superior strength. It is a non-combustible, moisture- and mold-resistant panel designed for use under exterior claddings where conventional gypsum sheathing products have traditionally been used, such as brick veneer, properly detailed Exterior Insulation Finish Systems (EIFS), clapboard siding, panel siding, shingle siding, shake siding and conventional stucco. The panels offer quick score-and-snap cutting with no sawing or special tools, and rapid screw or nail attachment. Available in 1/2" regular and 5/8" fire-rated thicknesses, 48"-wide square edges and 8', 9' and 10' lengths.

SECUROCK™
Glass Mat
Sheathing

1. Must not be used as a nail base for exterior cladding.

2. Specific requirements regarding framing spacing, fastener spacing and fastener specifics to provide required lateral wind-load resistance are the responsibility of the design professional.

3. Offers improved resistance to weather, but is not intended for constant exposure to water.

4. Not recommended for lamination to masonry surfaces. (Use furring strips or framing.)

5. Maximum stud spacing is 24" o.c.

6. Not a finished surface.

7. Not intended for tile applications.

8. Does not meet CHPS formaldehyde interior requirements.

Specifications—Liner and Sheathing Products

| | Thickness | | Width | | | Length | Approx.wt. | |
Product	in.	mm	in.	mm	Edges	ft.	lb./SF	kg/m²
SHEETROCK Brand Liner Panels	1	25.4	24	610	Bevel	up to 16	4.1	20.0
SHEETROCK Brand Sheathing	1/2	12.7	24	610	"V"T&G	8	2.0	9.8
	1/2	12.7	48	1219	Square	8, 9	2.0	9.8
SHEETROCK Brand FIRECODE Sheathing	5/8	15.9	48	1219	Square	8, 9	2.4	11.7
SECUROCK Glass Mat Sheathing	1/2	12.7	48	1219	Square	8, 9, 10	2.0	9.8
SECUROCK Glass Mat FIRECODE Sheathing	5/8	15.9	48	1219	Square	8, 9, 10	2.7	13.2
FIBEROCK Brand Sheathing	1/2	12.7	32, 48	815,1219	Square	8	2.2	10.7
	5/8	15.9	32, 48	815,1219	Square	8	3.0	14.6

Roof Board

SECUROCK® **Brand Roof Board** is a fiber-reinforced gypsum panel developed specifically to meet the demands of low-slope commercial roofing assemblies. It provides high wind uplift performance, fire resistance and resistance to moisture intrusion. The roof board protects, separates and supports the membrane and insulation, preventing early roof failures due to traffic, hail, snow loads or high winds. The smooth top surface provides an exceptional bonding surface for fully adhered or self adhering membrane applications. SECUROCK roof board meets ASTM C1278 and is made from 95% recycled content. For additional information, please visit **usg.com**.

Floor Underlayment Products

1

FIBEROCK Brand AQUA-TOUGH Underlayment   Engineered to meet water-, mold- and indentation-resistance needs under ceramic tile, resilient flooring, carpeting, hardwood flooring and laminate flooring in residential and light-commercial construction. This all-purpose underlayment is manufactured from a specially engineered combination of gypsum and cellulose fibers, and has a uniform, moisture- and mold-resistant composition. It is an environmentally friendly alternative to wood-based underlayments because it is made from 95 percent recycled material. Residential and light-commercial performance rating based on Robinson Floor Test (ASTM C627), conducted by TCNA. Meets ASTM C1278 standards.

DUROCK Brand Underlayment   Glass fiber-mesh reinforced aggregated Portland cement panel for floors and countertops. Its nominal 5/16" thickness helps eliminate transition trim when abutting carpet or wood flooring, and it helps minimize level variations with other finish materials. Its 4' x 4' size is easy to handle and helps cut down on waste. It may be applied directly over old substrate on countertops to save time. Regular 1/2" DUROCK brand cement board may also be used for underlayment applications.

LEVELROCK® Brand Floor Underlayments   are poured cementitious floor systems available in compressive strengths ranging from 2,500–8,000 psi. They require no shot blasting and include the first "green" underlayments in the industry made from recaptured gypsum, a byproduct of flue gas desulfurization. LEVELROCK floor systems provide fire resistance, sound control and durability for a variety of applications. All LEVELROCK floor underlayments are expertly installed by authorized applicators who receive and maintain certification following comprehensive onsite and field training from United States Gypsum Company. For additional information, please visit **usg.com**.

Suspended Ceiling Products

Suspended ceilings offer the advantages of variable ceiling height and expanded plenum usage that are not always available with conventional ceiling construction. USG offers several products for suspended ceiling construction that provide superior performance in the areas of fire resistance and sound attenuation. See Chapter 9, "Acoustical Ceiling Design & Application," for information on acoustical ceilings.

SHEETROCK Brand Lay-in Ceiling Tile

SHEETROCK lay-in ceiling tile, with CLIMAPLUS™ performance, is designed for use in standard ceiling suspension systems for exceptional economy, ease of installation and accessibility to the plenum.

Panels also qualify for UL design fire-rated assemblies to 1-1/2 hours (UL design G222) and 2 hours (UL design G259) when used with fire-rated steel suspension systems such as DONN® DXL™, DXLA™ or ZXLA™ grid systems. SHEETROCK Lay-In Ceiling Tile, with CLIMAPLUS performance, are made of 1/2" FIRECODE C Core gypsum board in both 2' x 2' or 2' x 4' sizes. Both sizes are available with either laminated white vinyl facing or natural paper facing.

All CLIMAPLUS performance products carry a warranty to withstand conditions up to 104°F and 90% relative humidity without visible sag when used with DONN brand suspension systems. The panels are guaranteed for 10 years against visible sag, or 30 years when used with DONN suspension systems.

Vinyl facing is embossed in a stipple pattern for a soft, lightly textured look. It is 2 mil. thick for toughness and durability, and can withstand repeated washings with no sign of abrasion. Natural paper facing can be left plain for utilitarian applications or can be painted to match room color scheme.

SHEETROCK lay-in ceiling tiles, with CLIMAPLUS performance, are safe, sanitary and washable. They meet USDA requirements for kitchens, restaurants and other food-service areas, and are suitable for hospitals, laboratories, nursing homes and other health care facilities. These tiles attain interior finish classification Type III, Form A, Class 3; Class A (NFPA 101). Panels with white vinyl facing achieve light reflectance LR1. Panels also can be used in applications such as covered entryways and parking garages.

CLEAN ROOM™ CLIMAPLUS Vinyl Panels

CLEAN ROOM CLIMAPLUS Class 100 and Class 10M–100M panels have embossed vinyl laminated aluminum facing and meet federal standard 209E, "Clean Room and Work Station Requirements, Controlled Environment."

Advantages

Easy Installation Conventional installation tiles install quickly and easily in standard exposed grid.

Easy Maintenance Embossed vinyl facing is washable to keep surface bright and light-reflecting.

Outdoor Applications Excellent in protected areas when used with compatible suspension system (such as DONN) Environmental ZXLA grid, which features 25-gauge, hot-dipped galvanized steel with corrosion-resistant aluminum face. 4' hanger spacing achieves intermediate-duty rating vs. 3' spacing for aluminum grids.

Sound Attenuation Tiles provide STC range of 45–49.

Performance Tiles qualify for fire-rated assemblies. Surface-burning characteristics: Flame Spread 25, Smoke Developed 50. Class A rated on all products (ASTM E84 test procedure). Thermal performance up to R-0.45. Weight 2.00 lb./SF

Specifications—SHEETROCK Brand Lay-In Ceiling Tile

	Size	Edge	Regular			FIRECODE		
			Item No.	NRC Range	CAC Range	Item No.	NRC Range	CAC Min
Stipple Pattern SHEETROCK Brand Lay-In Ceiling Tile	2'x2'x1/2"	Square	N/A	—	—	3260	N/A	35
	2'x4'x1/2"	Square	N/A	—	—	3270	N/A	40
Unfinished Paper Facing SHEETROCK Brand Lay-In Ceiling Tile	2'x4'x1/2"	Square	N/A	—	—	3450	N/A	40
CLEAN ROOM CLIMAPLUS Vinyl Panels	2'x4'x1/2"	Square	N/A	—	—	3200	N/A	40

USG Drywall Suspension System

The USG drywall suspension system provides a fast and economical method of installing gypsum panel ceilings while supplying support for lighting and air handling accessories. The system is designed for direct screw attachment of gypsum panels to produce either flat or curved surfaces. Single panels may be up to 5/8" thick. Double-layer panel applications may be up to 1-1/4" combined thickness.

1

Vault Drywall Ceilings

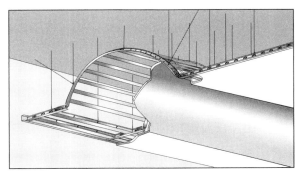

Flat Drywall Ceilings

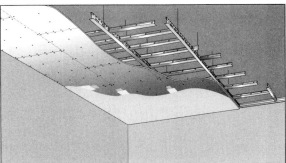

The USG drywall suspension system is made of hot-dipped galvanized steel. Main tees are 1-1/2" high x 144" long with a rectangular top bulb and 15/16" or 1-1/2" wide flange. The system offers the option of using 1-7/16" wide-faced furring cross channels or 1-1/2" wide furring cross tees for gypsum panel attachment. The face of both cross channels and cross tees is knurled to improve fastening of drywall screws. Also available are tees with 15/16" exposed flange to be used with lay-in light fixtures.

Direct-hung drywall suspension system is used in UL designs with fire ratings of 1, 1-1/2, 2 and 3 hours. The most current list of UL designs is available at **usgdesignstudio.com**, where you can search floor/ceiling and roof/ceiling assemblies by fire rating, type of structural framing, IIC and STC. Downloadable REVIT™ and CAD files are available on this site. You can also consult the *UL Fire Resistance Directory* and revisions for further information and construction details.

Advantages

Labor Saving Factory-controlled module spacing and snap-lock connection of cross channels and cross tees with main tees cuts installation time.

Cost Saving Components are low in cost compared with conventional construction to achieve the same result.

Strength Strong metal components are designed with interlocking tabs and splicing mechanisms to resist twisting of assembly.

Sound Control A vital component in sound-resistive floor-ceiling systems. Visit **usgdesignstudio.com** for details.

Accommodates Light Fixtures Accepts NEMA type G and type F light fixtures.

System Components

Main Tee Conforms to ASTM C635 Heavy-Duty Main Tee Classification. Designed to support gypsum board ceiling with maximum deflection of 1/360 of the span. Double-web design, 1-1/2" high x 144" long, rectangular top bulb, 15/16" wide or 1-1/2" wide flange, integral reversible end splice. Furring cross channel holes 4" from ends, spaced 8" o.c., hanger wire holes 4" o.c.

Wall-to-Wall Main Tee Conforms to ASTM C635 Heavy-Duty Main Tee Classification. Designed to support gypsum board ceiling with maximum deflection of L/240 of each span, per ASTM C645. 1-1/2" high x 6', 8', 10', 12' and 14' lengths, double-web design, rotary stitched and knurled.

DGCL Cross Channel Hat-shaped formed section, 1-7/16" wide x 7/8" high knurled screw surface, integral end locks stamped at each end. For fire-rated assemblies.

DGLW Cross Tee 1-1/2" high, roll-formed into double-web design with rectangular bulb, 1-1/2" knurled face and a steel cap, high-tensile-steel, double-locking and self-indexing end clenched to web. For fire-rated assemblies.

DGL Cross Tee 1-1/2" high, roll-formed into double-web design with rectangular top bulb, 15/16" exposed flange, high-tensile-steel, double-locking and self-indexing end clenched to web.

Channel Moulding U-shape, 1" flange x 1-9/16"

Angle Moulding L-shape, 1-1/2" flange x 1"

Hanger Wire Galvanized carbon steel, soft temper, pre-stretched, yield stress load at least five times design load, but not less than 12-gauge wire.

USG Drywall Suspension System— Curved Surfaces

The USG drywall suspension system is uniquely engineered to take advantage of curved metal framing components and flexible gypsum panels to produce arched and/or wavy ceiling surfaces. Framing components are formed tees available in a wide range of radii from 31" to over 240". The system is designed for direct screw attachment of gypsum panels, IMPERIAL gypsum base or metal lath when using conventional plaster systems.

The system easily accommodates transferring from straight to curved members and from concave to convex directions. Tees can be field-cut to specific arc or chord lengths. Main tees are 144" long before bending. Spans from single sections vary. Main tees and cross tees or channels both have knurled surfaces to aid screw attachment of gypsum panels.

The system is completed with attachment of SHEETROCK gypsum panels. Joints are taped and finished with a SHEETROCK joint treatment system. Fire-rated constructions are achievable with multiple layers of the gypsum panels. Additional details, photographs, system estimators and assembly animations are available at **usgdesignstudio.com**.

Advantages

Labor Saving Components are factory-prepared for easy installation of the main-tee and cross-tee assembly.

Accuracy Uniform arched components ensure accurate fit of attached components, including gypsum panels.

Aesthetic Appearance Dynamic arched or wavy surface is aesthetically pleasing.

Curved System Components

Curved Main Tees Conform to ASTM C635 Heavy-Duty Main Tee Classification. 1-1/2" high, galvanized cold-rolled-steel tee with 15/16" flange comes with various radius curvatures in either concave or convex direction. Tee length before bending is 144". Tee web is punched 4" from the end and thereafter at 8" intervals to accept cross channels. Web also is punched at 3' intervals with holes to accept hanger wire.

Cross Channel Hat-shaped, galvanized-steel channel has 1-7/16"-wide knurled screw surface for convenient attachment of gypsum panels.

Hanger Wire Galvanized carbon steel, soft temper, prestretched, yield stress load at least five times design load, but not less than 12-gauge wire.

USG Drywall Suspension System—Fascia Applications

A special feature of the USG drywall suspension system is the array of fascia trim designed to finish edges that do not abut walls, soffits or adjacent ceilings. The trim strips, called COMPÀSSO™, are available either flat or curved (convex or concave) to meet design requirements. The trim system is designed for parallel, perpendicular or angled attachment to suspension system tees. Curved fascia applications are also available.

Advantages

Labor Saving Components are factory prepared for easy installation.

Cost Saving Trim is low in cost compared with conventional construction to achieve the same result.

Aesthetic Appearance Flat or curved fascia trim is aesthetically pleasing.

**Compässo™
Fascia Trim
Components**

Compässo Trim Available flat or in a variety of radii to match design requirements. Widths available up to 8".

Compässo Drywall Clip Provides ready attachment of Compässo trim to main or cross tees, either parallel or perpendicular to the tee direction. Clip edges fit snugly inside trim edges; screw-attach to tees.

Bead & Trim Accessories

USG offers a wide variety of bead and trim products that are utilized in finishing drywall corners.

**Paper-Faced
Metal Bead and
Trim**

Sheetrock and Beadex® Brand Paper-Faced Metal Bead and Trim Offer the most cost-effective, problem-free, high-quality corners. Fast, easy installation reduces labor costs while superior product performance eliminates costly job callbacks, saving money and ensuring customer satisfaction. Tape-on profiles do not require nailing, so installation and corner alignment is easier, and there are no nails to pop when wood framing shrinks. USG's formulated paper tape ensures excellent adhesion to joint compounds, textures and paints for a strong, clean finish.

Tape-on paper-faced metal corner bead and trim also provide superior resistance to edge cracking. In fact, USG offers a lifetime warranty against edge cracking using recommended application techniques (refer to USG Lifetime Warranty J1302 for details).

Sheetrock and Beadex Brand Paper-Faced Metal Outside Corner, Tape On Bead (B1W, B1XW EL, Micro Bead™, B1 Super Wide) For 90° outside corners. Suitable for use on any thickness of wallboard.

Sheetrock and Beadex Brand Paper-Faced Metal Inside Corner, Tape On Trim (B2) Designed to form a true inner 90° corner. For use with any thickness of wallboard.

Sheetrock and Beadex Brand Paper-Faced Metal Offset Outside Corner, Tape On Bead (B1 OS) For 135° corners. Offset bead is designed to give a true offset corner with a smaller bead height for less compound fill. Can be used with any thickness of wallboard.

Sheetrock and Beadex Brand Paper-Faced Metal Offset Inside Corner, Tape On Bead (B2 OS) Designed to provide a true offset angle on inside corners greater than 90°. Use on any thickness of wallboard.

Sheetrock and Beadex Brand Paper-Faced Metal 3/4" Bullnose Outside Corner, Tape On Bead (SLOC) Designed to create a rounded 3/4" radius, 90° corner angle. For use with 1/2" or 5/8" gypsum panels.

SHEETROCK and BEADEX Brand Paper-Faced Metal Inner Cove, Tape On Trim (SLIC) Creates a rounded 3/4" radius, 90° inside corner. For use with 1/2" or 5/8" gypsum panels.

SHEETROCK and BEADEX Brand Paper-Faced Metal Bullnose Offset Outside Corner, Tape On Bead (SLOC OS) Forms a rounded 135° offset outside corner. Ideal for bay-window offsets and similar applications.

SHEETROCK and BEADEX Brand Paper-Faced Metal Offset Inner Cove, Tape On Trim (SLIC OS) Forms a smooth cove for 135° inside corners.

SHEETROCK and BEADEX Brand Paper-Faced Metal 1-1/2" Bullnose Outside Corner, Tape On Bead (Danish) Broader and gentler corner than 3/4" radius bullnose. Use with 1/2"- or 5/8"-thick wallboard.

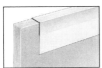

SHEETROCK and BEADEX Brand Paper-Faced Metal "L" Shaped Tape On Trim (B4 Series) For use where wallboard abuts suspended ceilings, beams, plaster, masonry and concrete walls, as well as untrimmed door and window jambs.

SHEETROCK and BEADEX Brand Paper-Faced Metal Outside Corner (MICRO BEAD) Reduced bead height results in less joint compound consumption. Extra-wide flanges for maximum corner coverage.

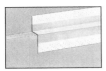

SHEETROCK and BEADEX Brand Paper-Faced Metal Reveal, Tape On Trim (B4 NB) Modified tape-on "L" trim solves problems with reveals on soffits, wall offsets, ceilings, light boxes and other interior architectural features. B4 reveal features a paper flange on both trim legs, eliminating the need to caulk the edge of reveal details and providing a cleaner, straighter line.

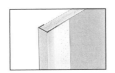

SHEETROCK and BEADEX Brand Paper-Faced Metal "J" Shaped Tape on Trim (B9) Used to finish rough drywall panel ends. Ideal for use at window and door openings and casements.

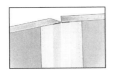

SHEETROCK and BEADEX Brand Flexible Metal Corner Reinforcing Tape Flexible reinforcing tape that ensures straight, sharp corners on any angle. Provides durable corner protection on cathedral and drop ceilings, arches and around bay windows. Tape is 2-1/16" wide and has 1/16" gap between two 1/2" wide galvanized steel strips. When folded, tape forms a strong corner bead. Applied with standard joint compound feathered at the edges for a smooth wall surface. Also used to join drywall partition to plastered wall in remodeling and for repairing chipped and cracked corners. Available in convenient 100' rolls in dispenser box.

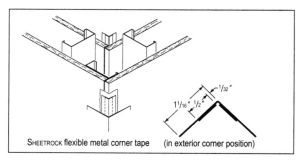

SHEETROCK flexible metal corner tape   (in exterior corner position)

Metal Beads

Metal corner beads permit traditional fastening to studs and construction of true, concealed external angles with gypsum base and panels.

DUR-A-BEAD® Corner Bead Specially galvanized steel reinforcement for protecting external corners in drywall construction. It is screwed or nailed to framing through the panels and concealed with USG joint compounds as a smooth, finished corner. Flanges also may be attached with a clinch-on tool. Available in 1-1/4" x 1-1/4" flange width (No. 103).

Expanded Flange Corner Bead No. 800 A galvanized steel external corner reinforcement with 1-1/4"-wide fine-mesh expanded flanges, tapered along outer edges to enhance concealment. It is easily nailed or stapled and provides superior bond to panels and base with joint compound and veneer plaster finishes through approximately 90 keys per linear foot. It also provides proper 1/16" grounds for one-coat veneer finishes.

Expanded Flange Corner Bead No. 900 Used with two-coat veneer plaster systems, it provides 3/32" grounds and its 1-1/4" fine-mesh flanges can be either stapled or nailed. Provides reinforcement equivalent to No. 800.

DUR-A-BEAD Corner Bead

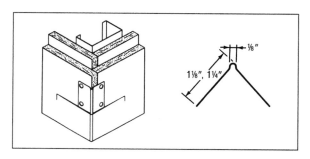

1

Expanded Flange Corner Bead, Nos. 800 and 900

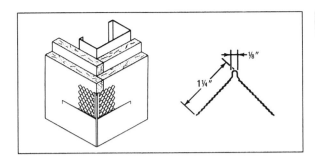

Metal Trim

Metal trim provides protection and neat finished edges to gypsum panels and bases at window and door jambs, at internal angles and at intersections where panels abut other materials. Easily installed by nailing or screwing through the proper leg of trim. Made in following types and sizes:

L-Trim & J-Trim Galvanized steel casing for gypsum panels, includes No. 200-A J-shaped channel in 1/2" and 5/8" sizes and No. 200-B L-shaped angle edge trim without back flange (to simplify application), in 1/2" and 5/8" sizes. Both require finishing with USG joint compounds.

No. 200-A Metal J-Trim

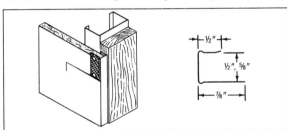

No. 200-B Metal L-Trim

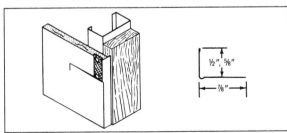

No. 701-A Metal Trim
No. 801-A Metal Trim

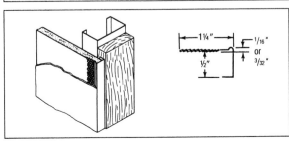

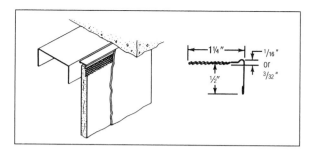

Expanded Flange L-Trim & J-Trim, No. 700 series All-metal trim provides neat edge protection for two-coat veneer plaster finishes at cased openings and ceiling or wall intersections. Fine-mesh expanded flanges strengthen veneer bond and eliminate shadowing. No. 701-A J-shaped channel-type and No. 701-B L-shaped angle edge trim provide 3/32" grounds. Sizes for 1/2"- and 5/8"-thick gypsum base.

Expanded Flange L-Trim & J-Trim, No. 800 series All-metal trim companion to 700 series, but with 1/16" grounds for one-coat veneer plaster finishes or finishing with joint compound in drywall applications. Fine-mesh 1-1/4" expanded flanges strengthen veneer bond, eliminate shadowing, provide a superior key and are easily nailed or stapled. No. 801-A J-shaped channel-type and No. 801-B L-shaped angle-edge trim come in sizes for 1/2"- and 5/8"-thick panels and bases.

Framing Components

USG pioneered the development of steel framing components for gypsum construction. They offer the advantages of light weight, low material cost, quick erection and high strength and versatility in meeting job requirements.

Today, steel studs and runners are available from a number of manufacturers. It is important to note that while manufacturers produce the same gauge of material, the steel properties and thicknesses can vary from manufacturer to manufacturer. To ensure the best system performance, manufacturer specifications should be checked against the design and minimum thicknesses provided by USG. Failure to do so could result in excessive deflection or overstressed or even buckled steel studs.

USG does not sell common steel framing, but does sell framing components for its proprietary systems and accessory products for high-performance systems. All components are noncombustible, made from corrosion-resistant steel.

It is important that light-gauge steel components such as steel studs and runners, furring channels and resilient channels be adequately protected against rusting in the warehouse and on the job site. In marine areas, particularly sea coasts, and especially such areas as the Caribbean, Florida and the Gulf Coast where salt-air conditions exist with high humidity, components that offer increased protection against corrosion should be used.

Steel Studs and Runners Steel studs and runners are channel-type, roll-formed from corrosion-resistant steel and designed for quick screw attachment of facing materials. They are strong, non-load-bearing components of interior partitions, ceilings and column fireproofing and also framing for exterior curtain wall systems. Heavier thickness members are used in load-bearing construction. Limited chaseways for electrical and plumbing services are provided by punchouts in the stud web. Matching runners for each stud size align and secure studs to floors and ceilings, which also function as headers.

25-ga. (18-mil) Studs and Runners Efficient, low-cost 25-ga. members for framing non-load-bearing interior assemblies. Studs come in widths to match wood framing dimensions and are available in lengths up to 20'. Runners come in matching stud widths—10' lengths. Not recommended for high-density board applications, such as for DUROCK cement board, FIBEROCK abuse-resistant panels or SHEETROCK abuse-resistant panels.

22-ga. (27-mil) Studs and Runners Heavier gauge, stronger studs in widths of 2-1/2", 3-5/8", 4" and 6". Runners come in widths to match studs. Not recommended for high-density board applications, such as for DUROCK brand cement board, FIBEROCK brand abuse-resistant panels or SHEETROCK abuse-resistant panels.

20-ga. (33-mil) Studs and Runners Heavier 20-ga. members used in framing interior assemblies requiring greater-strength studs and as reinforcement for door frames. Also used in curtain wall assemblies. Studs available in 2-1/2", 3-5/8", 4" and 6" widths, and cut-to-order lengths up to 28'. Runners come in stud widths, 10' lengths.

Studs and runners should be hot-dip galvanized.

Load-Bearing Studs and Runners Used for framing load-bearing interior and exterior walls and non-load-bearing curtain walls. These studs have stiffened flanges and are available in several sizes.

Typical Steel Thickness—Steel Studs and Runners[2]

Minimum Thickness[1] (mils)	Design Thickness (in)	Reference Only Gauge No.
18	0.0188	25
27	0.0283	22
30	0.0312	20 - Drywall
33	0.0346	20 - Structural
43	0.0451	18
54	0.0566	16
68	0.0713	14
97	0.1017	12

(1) Minimum Thickness represents 95% of the design thickness and is the minimum acceptable thickness delivered to the job site based on Section A3.4 of the 1996 AISI Specification. (2) Data is from Steel Stud Manufacturers Assocation (SSMA) catalog.

There is a serious misconception within the construction industry regarding the substitution of one manufacturer's studs for those of another manufacturer. The assumption is that all studs of a given size and steel thickness are interchangeable. It is possible that the substitution can safely be made, but the decision should not be made until the structural properties of the studs involved are compared. Most reliable manufacturers publish structural property tables in their technical literature. USG includes recommended minimum thickness data in all architectural technical literature covering steel-framed systems.

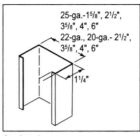

Steel stud
(25, 22, 20-ga.)

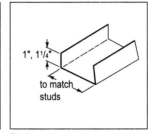

Steel runner
(25, 22, 20, 18, 16, 14-ga.)

Cavity Shaft Wall & Area Separation Fire-Wall/Party-Walls

These steel components are lightweight, versatile non-load-bearing members of economical fire- and sound-barrier systems: (1) Area separation walls between units in multi-family wood-frame buildings; (2) Shaft walls around elevator and mechanical shafts, return air ducts, stairwells and smoke shafts in multi-story buildings. Components are formed from corrosion-resistant steel: C-H Stud base metal meets structural performance standards in ASTM A446, Grade A. Components should be hot-dipped galvanized.

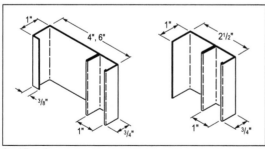

Steel E-studs

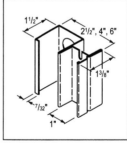

Steel C-H stud

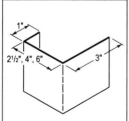

Steel jamb strut (20 ga.)

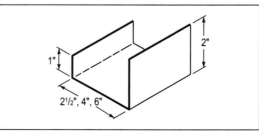

Steel J-runner

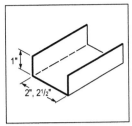

Steel C-runner

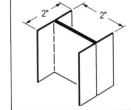

Steel H-stud (two piece)

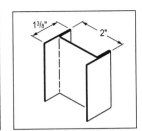

Steel H-stud (one piece)

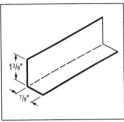

Breakaway clip

Metal angle runner

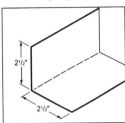

Corner angle

Thickness—Area Separation, Shaft Wall and Furring Components[1]

Component Designation	Design[2]		Minimum		
	in.	mm	in.	mm	Gauge[3]
CR, CH, ES25	0.0188	0.48	0.0179	0.45	25
JR24	0.0239	0.61	0.0227	0.58	24
Metal Angles	0.0239	0.61	0.0227	0.58	24
CH22	0.0310	0.79	0.0294	0.75	22
ES, JR, JS, CH20	0.0359	0.91	0.0341	0.87	20

(1) Uncoated steel thickness; meets ASTM A568. Studs and runners meet ASTM C645. Base metal meets ASTM A446 standards for structural performance. Min. yield strength 33 ksi, except C-H stud 40 ksi. Coatings are hot-dip galvanized per ASTM A525; aluminized per ASTM A463, or aluminum-zinc per ASTM A792. (2) Conforms to AISI Specification for the Design of Cold Formed Steel Structural Members, 1986 edition. (3) For information only; refer to limiting height tables and structural properties for design data.

Cavity Wall Components 2-1/2", 4" and 6" wide and designed for use with 1" thick SHEETROCK brand gypsum liner panels. USG steel C-H studs 2-1/2", 4" and 6" are non-load-bearing sections installed between abutting liner panels. They have 1" holes spaced 12" to 16" from each end for easy installation of horizontal pipe and conduit. USG steel E-studs are 2-1/2", 4" or 6" wide, used singly to cap panels at intersections with exterior walls or back-to-back as studs in unusually high partitions. USG steel J-runners, made with unequal legs, are used at floor and ceiling in shaft walls. USG steel C-runners are used singly at terminals, top and bottom of wall and back-to-back between vertical liner panels at intermediate floors in area separation walls. USG steel jamb struts (20-gauge), 2-1/2", 4" and 6" wide, are used in jamb framing for fire-rated elevator doors.

Solid Wall Components 2" wide and used with two thicknesses of 1" gypsum liner panels: USG steel H-studs fit over and engage edges of adjacent liner panels. USG steel C-runners are used in area separation walls as floor and top runners and back-to-back between liner panels at intermediate floors. Also used singly to cap area separation walls.

USG Aluminum Breakaway Clip A 2"-wide angle clip made of 0.63"-thick aluminum. Used to attach area separation walls to intermediate floor and roof framing. Clips are designed to melt and break away when exposed to fire. 2-1/2" x 2"; approximately 60 lb./1,000 pcs.

Specifications—Area Separation Wall & Shaft Wall Components

Component Designation[1]	Section Depth		Length		Approx. Weight	
	in.	mm	ft.	mm	lb./1000 ft.	kg/100 m
C-H Studs						
212CH25	2-1/2	63.5	8 to 24	2440 to 7315	519	77.2
212CH22	2-1/2	63.5	8 to 24	2440 to 7315	861	126.5
212CH20	2-1/2	63.5	8 to 24	2440 to 7315	1000	148.8
400CH25	4	101.6	8 to 24	2440 to 7315	612	91.1
400CH20	4	101.6	8 to 24	2440 to 7315	1245	185.3
600CH20	6	152.4	8 to 24	2440 to 7315	1366	203.3
E-Studs						
212ES25	2-1/2	63.5	8 to 28	2440 to 8530	358	53.3
212ES20	2-1/2	63.5	8 to 28	2440 to 8530	729	108.5
400ES25	4	101.6	8 to 28	2440 to 8530	472	70.2
400ES20	4	101.6	8 to 28	2440 to 8530	970	144.3
600ES25	6	152.4	8 to 28	2440 to 8530	689	102.5
600ES20	6	152.4	8 to 28	2440 to 8530	1285	191.2
J-Runners						
212JR24	2-1/2	63.5	10	3050	535	79.6
212JR20	2-1/2	63.5	10	3050	736	109.5
400JR24	4	101.6	10	3050	680	101.2
400JR20	4	101.6	10	3050	937	139.4
600JR24	6	152.4	10	3050	860	128.0
600JR20	6	152.4	10	3050	1191	177.2
C-Runners						
200CR25	2	50.8	10	3050	270	40.1
Metal Angles						
2-1/2" x 2-1/2"	2-1/2	63.5	10	3050	425	63.2
1-3/8" x 7/8"	1-3/8	34.9	10	3050	190	28.3
Jamb Strut						
212JS20	2-1/2	63.5	8 to 12	2440 to 3660	826	122.9
400JS20	4	101.6	8 to 12	2440 to 3660	1026	152.7
600JS20	6	152.4	8 to 12	2440 to 3660	1256	186.9

(1) All components shipped unbundled, additional charge for bundling.

Framing & Furring Accessories

Metal Angles Made of 24-ga. galvanized steel in two standard sizes. The 1-3/8" x 7/8" size is used to secure 1" core board or liner panels at floor and ceiling in laminated gypsum drywall partitions. Length: 10'; 1-3/8" x 7/8": approximate weight 190 lb./1000, 2-1/2" x 2-1/2": approximate weight 425 lb./1000. (Angles in other sizes and gauges available on request. See page 32 for illustration.)

Cold-Rolled Channels   Made of 16-ga. steel. Used in furred walls and suspended ceilings. Available either galvanized or black asphaltum painted. Sizes 3/4" with 1/2" flange, 1-1/2" and 2" with 17/32" flange; lengths 16' and 20'; 3/4": approximate weight 300 lb./1,000', 1-1/2": approximate weight 500 lb./1,000', 2": approximate weight 590 lb./1,000'. (See page 32.)

Resilient Channel   Made of 25-ga. corrosion-resistant steel. One of the most effective, lowest-cost methods of reducing sound transmission through wood- and steel-frame partitions and ceilings. Used for resilient attachment of SHEETROCK brand gypsum panels and IMPERIAL brand gypsum bases. Prepunched holes 4" o.c. in the flange facilitate screw attachment to framing; facing materials are screw-attached to channels. Length: 12'; 1/2" x 2-1/2": approximate weight 200 lb./1,000'. (See page 32.)

Limitations: Not for use beneath highly flexible floor joists; should be attached to ceilings with 1-1/4" type W or type S screws only—nails must not be used; see Chapter 2, "Framing Requirements."

Z-Furring Channels   Made of minimum 24-ga. corrosion-resistant steel used to mechanically attach mineral wool FS-15 insulating blankets, polystyrene insulation (or other rigid insulation) and gypsum panels or base to interior side of monolithic concrete and masonry walls. Length: 8'-6"; sizes 1", 1-1/2", 2" and 3"; approximate weight (lb./1,000'): 224 (1"), 269 (1-1/2"), 313 (2") and 400 (3"). (See page 32.)

Metal Furring Channels   Roll-formed, hat-shaped sections made of 20- and 25-ga. corrosion-resistant steel. Designed for screw attachment of gypsum panels and gypsum base in wall and ceiling furring. Size 7/8" x 2-9/16"; length 12'; approximate wt.: 25-ga.: 276 lb/1,000', 20-ga.: 515/1,000'. (See page 33.)

Furring Channel Clips   Made of galvanized wire and used in attaching metal furring channels to 1-1/2" cold-rolled channel ceiling grillwork. For use with single-layer gypsum panels or base. Clips are installed on alternate sides of 1-1/2" channels; where clips cannot be alternated, wire-tying is recommended. Size 1-1/2" x 2-3/4"; approximate weight 38 lb./1,000 pcs. (See page 33.)

Adjustable Wall Furring Brackets   Used for attaching 3/4" cold-rolled channels and metal furring channels to interior side of exterior masonry walls. Made of 20-ga. galvanized steel with corrugated edges, brackets spaced not more than 32" o.c. horizontally and 48" o.c. vertically are attached to masonry and wire-tied to horizontal channel stiffeners in braced furring systems. Permits adjustment from 1/4" to 2-1/4" plus depth of channel. Approximate weight 56 lb./1,000 pcs. (See page 33.)

Hanger and Tie Wire   Galvanized soft annealed wire available in three sizes: (1) 8-ga. wire, used for hangers in suspended ceiling grill work, available in 50-lb. coils (approx. 730'); (2) 12-ga. wire for the USG drywall suspension system; (3) 18-ga. wire, used for wire-tying channels in wall furring and ceiling construction, available in 50-lb. coils (approximately 8,310') and 25-lb. hanks (48" straight lengths— 4,148' total). (See page 33.)

Metal angles

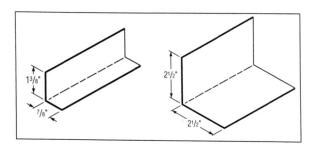

Cold-rolled channel

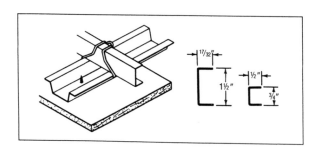

Resilient channel

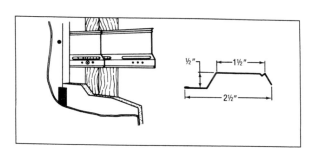

Z-furring channel

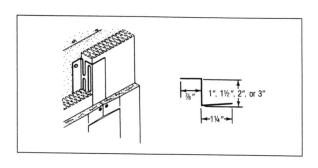

Metal furring channel

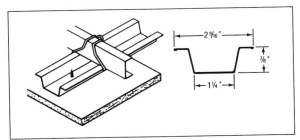

Furring channel clip

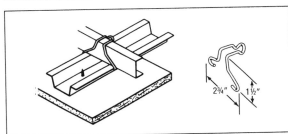

Hanger and tie wire

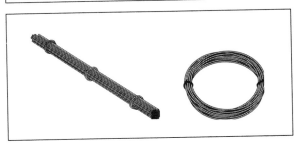

Adjustable wall furring bracket

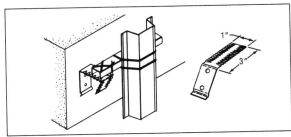

Sound Control & Insulation Products

Adequate sound control and energy conservation are among the most important requirements in today's buildings. The public has become sufficiently aware of these factors to demand effective measures to control unwanted sound and heat transfer in both commercial and residential construction. With its advanced research, USG has been a leader in developing new systems and products for efficient, low-cost sound control and thermal insulation for new construction and remodeling.

Products Available

Sheetrock **Brand Acoustical Sealant** A highly elastic, water-based-caulking compound for sealing sound leaks around partition perimeters, cutouts and electrical boxes. May be easily applied in beads or worked with a knife over flat areas. Provides excellent adherence to most surfaces. Highly resilient, permanently flexible, shrink- and stain-resistant and has a long life expectancy. Accepted for use in 1- to 3-hour fire-rated assemblies with no adverse effect on assembly fire performance. Complies with ASTM C919. Not to be used in contact with PVC or plastic pipe.

Coverage—Sheetrock **Brand Acoustical Sealant**

| Product | Bead size | | |
	in.	mm	Approx. coverage
Sheetrock Brand Acoustical Sealant	1/4	6.4	392 ft./gal
	3/8	9.5	174 ft./gal.
	1/2	12.7	98 ft./gal.

Sheetrock Brand Acoustical Sealant at partition perimeters seals leaks to help deliver tested sound attenuation.

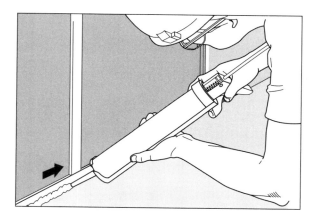

Firestop Products

USG Fire/Smoke Containment Products

Through-penetration openings—where metallic pipes and conduit pass through floors and walls—can also be passage points for fire and smoke to spread through the building.

USG Fire/Smoke-Stop System restores the floor or wall as a fire barrier by preventing smoke and fire from passing through such openings.

Firecode **Compound** Mortar-type material applied wet over the forming material (where applicable). It then sets or dries to form a tough, curable seal. Available in either a powder or ready-mixed form.

Firecode Compound is UL-Classified and low in cost. It has been tested in a variety of penetration conditions.

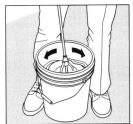

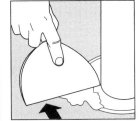

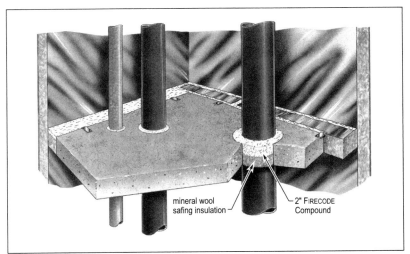

mineral wool
safing insulation

2" FIRECODE
Compound

*Mineral Wool Through-
Penetration Fire/Smoke-
Stop System*

FIRECODE **Compound**   Non-toxic compound developed for use with safing insulation to provide wall and floor through-penetration fire-stop systems that combine exceptional economy and performance. Rated noncombustible as defined by NFPA Standard 220 when tested in accordance with ASTM E136. Surface-burning characteristics: flame spread 0, smoke developed 0, when tested in accordance with ASTM E84. Effectively seals openings around pipe and cable poke-through openings. Comes ready-mixed in 3-qt. or 4.5-gal. pails, or in 15-lb. bags to mix easily with water at the job site. More economical to use than tube products, especially in large-scale jobs. See Chapter 10 for floor and wall penetrations. Tested in accordance with ASTM E814, UL 1479, CAN-S115 and UL 2079.

Coverage—FIRECODE Compound

Dry Powder Compound	Approx. Water Additions (pts.)	Approx. Applied Firestop (cu. in.)*	Premixed Compound (qts.)	Approx. Applied Firestop (cu. in.)
1	0.5	33.6	1.0	57.8
5	2.5	172.5	4.0 (1 gal.)	231.0
7.5	3.8	257.6	18.0 (4.5 gal.)	1039.5
10	5.0	344.9	—	—
15	7.5	517.4	—	—

*Based on approximately 7.5 pints water per 15 lb. bag for wall penetrations. For floor penetrations, approximately 8.3 pints water per 15 lb. bag is recommended and yields approximately 537 cu. in. of applied firestop.

FIRECODE **Firestop Sealant Acrylic** is a single component, water-based, acrylic sealant for use in wall and floor through-penetrations and head-of-wall construction joint applications.

FIRECODE **Firestop Sealant Acrylic Spray** is a sprayable single component, water based acrylic sealant for use in head-of-wall construction joint applications.

FIRECODE **Firestop Sealant Intumescent** expands to fill voids caused from combustible material burned or melted in a fire, for example plastic pipe. For wall and floor through penetrations.

Fasteners

Gypsum Board Screws

Although USG does not produce fasteners, there are many manufactures that offer a complete line of special self-drilling, self-tapping steel screws, including types with a double-lead thread design that produces up to 30% faster penetration, less screw stripping and greater holding power and pull-through resistance than conventional fasteners.

Screws should be corrosion-resistant and (except Hex Washer Head type) have a Phillips-head recess for rapid installation with a special bit and power-driven screw gun. The bugle head spins the face paper into the cavity under the screw head for greater holding power and helps prevent damage to the gypsum core and face paper. Defects associated with improper nail dimpling are eliminated. Other head types are designed specifically for attaching metal to metal and installing wood and metal trim. Screws should meet ASTM C1002 (type S and type W) and ASTM C954 (type S-12).

Type S screws have specially designed drill point and threads that minimize stripping, provide maximum holding power and pull-through resistance in steel studs and runners. Type S screws are designed for use with steel up to .04" thick; type S-12 screws for steel from .04" to .07" thick. (See table on page 38.) The special threads on type G and type W screws offer superior holding power in attachment to gypsum boards and wood framing, respectively. Tapcon anchors provide fast, safe attachment of steel components to poured concrete and concrete block surfaces. Special 1-15/16" type S-12 bugle head pilot point screws are designed for attachment of plywood to steel joists and studs.

The superior pull-through resistance of type W screws has virtually eliminated loose panel attachment and nail pops in wood-frame construction. Tests have shown the type W screw to have 350% greater pullout strength than GWB-54 nails. Fewer screws than nails are generally required, and the speed of installation using electric screw guns compares favorably with nailing.

The secret to superior screw attachment is shown by comparative diagrams. Bugle-head (left) screw depresses face paper of gypsum panel without tearing; threads cut into and deform wood to hold tightly. Longer drywall nail (right) grips with friction, loosens hold as wood shrinks, which may pop nailhead above surface to create callback situation.

Selector Guide for Screws

Fastening Application	Fastener used	Fig[2]
Gypsum panels to steel framing[1]		
1/2″ single-layer panels to steel studs, runners, channels	1″ TYPE S bugle head	1
5/8″ single-layer panels to steel studs, runners, channels	1″ TYPE S bugle head 1-1/8″ TYPE S bugle head	1 1
3/4″ single-layer panels to steel studs, runners, channels	1-1/4″ TYPE S bugle head	1
1″ coreboard to metal angle runners in solid partitions	1-5/8″ TYPE S bugle head	1
1/2″ double-layer panels to steel studs, runners, channels	1-5/8″ TYPE S bugle head	1
5/8″ double-layer panels to steel studs, runners, channels	1-5/8″ TYPE S bugle head	2
3/4″ double-layer panels to steel studs, runners, channels	2-1/4″ TYPE S bugle head	2
1/2″ panels through coreboard to metal angle runners in solid partitions	1-7/8″ TYPE S bugle head	2
5/8″ panels through coreboard to metal angle runners in solid partitions	2-1/4″ TYPE S bugle head 3″ TYPE S bugle head	2 2
1″ double-layer coreboard to steel studs, runners	2-5/8″ TYPE S bugle head	2
Wood to steel framing		
Wood trim over single-layer panels to steel studs, runners	1″ TYPE S or S-12 trim head 1-5/8″ TYPE S or S-12 trim head	5 5
Wood trim over double-layer panels to steel studs, runners	2-1/4″ TYPE S or S-12 trim head	5
Steel cabinets, brackets through single-layer panels to steel studs	1-1/4″ TYPE S oval head	6
Wood cabinets through single-layer panels to steel studs	1-5/8″ TYPE S oval head	6
Wood cabinets through double-layer panels to steel studs	2-1/4″, 2-7/8″, 3-3/4″, TYPE S oval head	6
Steel studs to door frames, runners		
Steel studs to runners 25 & 22-ga.	3/8″ TYPE S pan head	9
Steel studs to runners		
Steel studs to door frame jamb anchors 20-ga.	3/8″ TYPE S-12 pan head 5/8″ TYPE S-12 low-profile head	10 11
Other metal-to-metal attachment (12-ga. max.)		
Steel studs to door frame jamb anchor clips (heavier shank assures entry in clips of hard steel)	1/2″ TYPE S-12 pan head 5/8″ TYPE S-12 low-profile head	10 11
Metal-to-metal connections up to double thickness of 12-ga. steel	3/4″ S-4 hex washer head Anticorrosive-coated	12
Gypsum panels to 12-ga. (max.) steel framing		
1/2″ and 5/8″ panels and gypsum sheathing to steel studs and runners; specify anticorrosive-coated screws for exterior curtain wall applications	1″ TYPE S-12 bugle head	3
Self-Furring Metal Lath and brick wall ties through gypsum sheathing to steel studs and runners; specify anticorrosive-coated screws for exterior curtain wall applications	1-1/4″ TYPE S-12 bugle head 1-1/4″ TYPE S-12 pancake head	4 13
1/2″ and 5/8″ double-layer gypsum panels to steel studs and runners	1-5/8″ TYPE S-12 bugle head	4

Selector Guide for Screws continued

Fastening Application	Fastener used	Fig[2]
Gypsum panels to 12-ga. (max.) steel framing		
Multi-layer gypsum panels and other materials to steel studs and runners	1-7/8", 2, 2-3/8", 2-5/8", 3" Type S-12 bugle head	4
Cement board to steel framing		
Durock Brand Cement Board or Exterior Cement Board direct to steel studs, runners	1-1/4", 1-5/8" Durock Brand Steel Screws	17
Rigid foam insulation to steel framing		
Rigid foam insulation panels to steel studs and runners; Type R for 20-25-ga. steel	1-1/2", 2, 2-1/2", 3" Type S-12 or R wafer head	15
Aluminum trim to steel framing		
Trim and door hinges to steel studs and runners (screw matches hardware and trim)	7/8" Type S-18 oval head anticorrosive-coated	7
Batten strips to steel studs in demountable partitions	1-1/8" Type S bugle head	1
Aluminum trim to steel framing in demountable and Utrawall partitions	1/4" Type S bugle head anticorrosive-coated	1
Gypsum panels to wood framing		
3/8", 1/2" and 5/8" single-layer panels to wood studs, joists	1-1/4" Type W bugle head	8
Cement board to wood framing		
Durock Brand Cement Board or Exterior Cement Board to wood framing	1-1/4",1-5/8", 2-1/4" Durock Brand Wood Screws, with anticorrosive coating	18
Resilient channels to wood framing		
Screw attachment required for both ceilings and partitions	1-1/4" Type W bugle head	8
	1-1/4" Type S bugle head	1
For fire-rated construction	1-1/4" Type S bugle head	1
Gypsum panels to gypsum panels		
Multi-layer adhesively laminated gypsum-to-gypsum partitions (not recommended for double-layer 3/8" panels)	1-1/2" Type G bugle head	8
Plywood to steel joists		
3/8" to 3/4" plywood to steel joists (penetrates double thickness 14-ga.)	1-5/16" Type S-12 bugle head, pilot point	16
Steel to poured concrete or block		
Attachment of steel framing components to poured concrete and concrete block surfaces	3/16" x 1-3/4" acorn slotted HWH Tapcon Anchor	14

Notes: (1) Includes 25, 22 and 20-ga. steel studs and runners; metal angles; metal furring channels; resilient channels. If channel resiliency makes screw penetration difficult, use screws 1/8" longer than shown to attach panels to resilient channels. For other gauges of studs and runners, always use Type S-12 screws. For steel applications not shown, select a screw length which is at least 3/8" longer than total thickness of materials to be fastened. Use anticorrosive-coated screws for exterior applications. (2) Figures refer to screw illustrations on page 40.

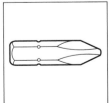

No. 1 Bit for trim and pancake heads

No. 2 Bit for bugle pan, water, low-profile & oval heads

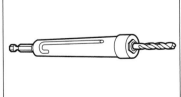

Condrive Tool/Bit for HWH Tapcon Anchors Note: Hex-head bit not illustrated

Basic Types of Screws—Numbers refer to desciptions on pages 38–39.

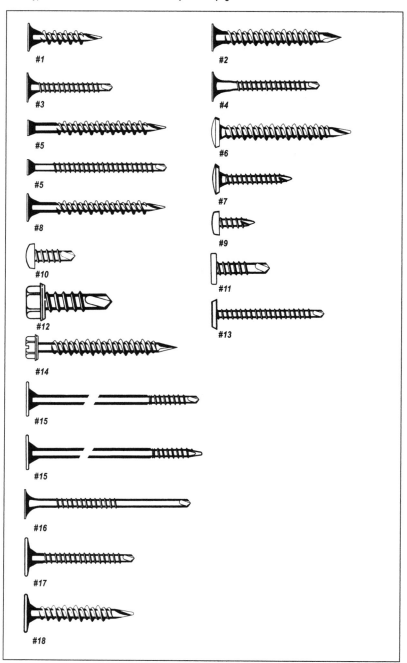

Specifications—Screws

Description	Length in.	mm	Type	Head
Base Screws	1	25.4	Type S	bugle
	1-1/8	28.6	Type S	bugle
	1-1/4	31.8	Type S	bugle
	1-5/8	41.3	Type S	bugle
	1-7/8	47.6	Type S	bugle
	2-1/4	57.2	Type S	bugle
	2-5/8	66.7	Type S	bugle
	3	76.2	Type S	bugle
Specialty Screws	3/8	9.5	Type S	pan
	3/8	9.5	Type S-12	pan
	1/2	12.7	Type S-12	pan
	1/2	12.7	Type S-12	pancake
	1/2	12.7	Type S-16	pan[1]
	5/8	15.9	Type S-12	low-profile
	3/4	19.1	Type S-4	hex washer[1]
	7/8	22.2	Type S-18	oval[1]
	1	25.4	Type S	trim
	1	25.4	Type S-12	trim
	1	25.4	Type S-12	bugle
	1-1/4	31.8	Type S-12	bugle
	1-1/4	31.8	Type S	bugle[1]
	1-1/4	31.8	Type W	bugle
	1-1/4	31.8	Type S-12	pancake
	1-1/4	31.8	Type S	oval
	1-1/2	38.1	Type G	bugle
	1-1/2	38.1	Type R	wafer
	1-1/2	38.1	Type S-12	wafer
	1-5/8	41.3	Type S	oval
	1-5/8	41.3	Type S	trim
	1-5/8	41.3	Type S-12	bugle
	1-5/8	41.3	Type S-12	trim
	1-7/8	47.6	Type S-12	bugle
	1-15/16	49.2	Type S-12	bugle, pilot pt.
	2	50.8	Type S-12	bugle
	2	50.8	Type R	wafer
	2	50.8	Type S-12	wafer
	2-1/4	57.2	Type S	trim
	2-1/4	57.2	Type S	oval
	2-1/4	57.2	Type S-12	trim
	2-3/8	60.3	Type S-12	bugle
	2-1/2	63.5	Type R	wafer
	2-1/2	63.5	Type S-12	wafer
	2-5/8	66.7	Type S-12	bugle
	2-7/8	73.0	Type S	oval
	3	76.2	Type S-12	bugle
	3	76.2	Type R	wafer
	3	76.2	Type S-12	wafer
	3-3/4	95.3	Type S	oval
Tapcon Screw	1-3/4	44.5	conc.	hex

(1) Anticorrosive-coated

Screw Applications

Application	Screw Size and Length (no. x Inches)
1" (25.4 mm) Bugle Head Type S Attaches 1/2" or 5/8" single-layer gypsum panels and bases to steel framing.	6 x 1
1-1/8" (28.6 mm) Bugle Head Type S Attaches 5/8" gypsum panels and bases to resilient channels or other steel framing, also batten strips for demountable partitions.	6 x 1-1/8
1-1/4" (31.8 mm) Bugle Head Type S Attaches 1" coreboard to steel runners. Attaches 1/2", 5/8" and 3/4" gypsum panels and bases to wood studs.	6 x 1-1/4
1-5/8" (41.3 mm) Bugle Head Type S Attaches double-layer gypsum panels to steel framing.	6 x 1-5/8
2" (50.8 mm) Bugle Head Type S 2-1/4" (57.2 mm) Bugle Head 2-1/2" (63.5 mm) Bugle Head 3" (76.2 mm) Bugle Head Attaches multiple layers of gypsum panels and other compatible materials to steel framing.	6 x 2 6 x 2-1/4 7 x 2-1/2 8 x 3
1-1/4" (31.8 mm) Bugle Head (Type W) Attaches 1/2" or 5/8" single-layer gypsum panels, bases, or resilient channels to wood framing.	6 x 1-1/4
7/16" (11.1 mm) Pan Head Attaches 25-ga. steel studs to runners.	6 x 7/16 7 x 7/16
1-1/2" (38.1 mm) Bugle Head-Laminating Temporary attachment of gypsum to gypsum.	10 x 1-1/2
1-5/8" (41.3 mm) Trim Head 2-1/4" (57.2 mm) Trim Head Attaches wood trim to 20 to 25-ga. steel framing.	6 x 1-5/8 6 x 2-1/4

Double Thread Screw Applications

Application	Screw Size and Length (no. x Inches)
Bugle Head Attaches gypsum board to 20 to 25-ga. steel framing	6 x 1 6 x 1-1/8 6 x 1-1/4 6 x 1-5/8 6 x 2 6 x 2-1/4 7 x 2-1/2 8 x 3

Drill Tip Screw Applications

Application	Screw Size and Length (no. x Inches)
Bugle Head Attaches single-layer gypsum board to steel framing up to 14-ga.	6 x 1 6 x 1-1/8 6 x 1-1/4
Bugle-Head Attaches multi-layer gypsum board to steel framing up to 14-ga.	6 x 1-5/8 6 x 1-7/8 8 x 2-1/8 8 x 2-5/8 8 x 3
Pan Head Attaches stud to runner up to 14-ga.	7 x 7/16 8 x 5/8
Hex Washer Head Attaches steel to steel up to 14-ga.	8 x 1/2 8 x 5/8 8 x 3/4 8 x 1
Modified Truss Head Attaches metal lath to steel framing up to 14-ga.	8 x 1/2 8 x 3/4 8 x 1 8 x 1-1/4

Gypsum Board Nails

The design of nails has vastly improved since the relationship of wood shrinkage to nail popping was identified. Nails have been developed to concentrate maximum holding power over the shortest possible length—notably the annular ring type nail, which has about 20% greater holding power than a smooth-shank nail of the same length and shank diameter. However, under lengthy, extreme drying conditions, such as a cold, dry winter or in arid climates, resultant wood shrinkage may cause fastener pops even with the shorter annular ring nail.

As with screws, specification of the proper nail for each application is extremely important, particularly for fire-rated construction where nails of the specified length and diameter only will provide proper perfor-

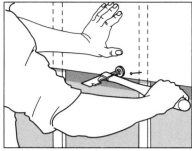

*Hand pressure is applied
to panel as nail is driven.*

mance. When wood-frame gypsum panel systems are subjected to fire, nails on surface attain temperatures that tend to char the wood, thereby reducing their holding power. Nails used in gypsum construction should comply with performance standards of ASTM C514. Nails are not available from USG.

Selector Guide for Gypsum Board Nails[1]

Fastener description[2]	Fastener length		Total thickness of surfacing materials[3]									Approx Usage	
	in.	mm	in. 1/4	3/8	1/2	5/8	3/4	7/8	1	1-1/4	1-3/8	lb/1,000 ft²	kg/100m²
			mm 6.4	9.5	12.7	15.9	19.1	22.2	25.4	31.8	34.9		
Annular Ring Drywall Nail 12-1/2 ga. (2.50 mm) 1/4" (6.35 mm) diam. head. Med. diamond point	1-1/4	31.8	X	X	X							4.50	2.20
	1-3/8	34.9				X						5.00	2.44
	1-1/2	38.1					X					5.25	2.56
	1-5/8	41.3						X				5.75	2.81
Same as above except 19/64" (7.54 mm) diam. head	1-1/4	31.8	X	X	X							4.50	2.20
	1-3/8	34.9				X						5.00	2.44
	1-1/2	38.1					X					5.25	2.56
	1-5/8	41.3						X				5.75	2.81
	1-3/4	44.5							X			6.00	2.93
	2	50.8								X		7.00	3.42
12-1/2 ga. (2.50 mm) 19/64" (7.54 mm) diam. head	1-1/4	31.8	X	X	X							4.50	2.20
	1-3/8	34.9				X						5.00	2.44
	1-1/2	38.1					X					5.25	2.56
	1-5/8	41.3						X				5.75	2.81
Same as above except 1/4" (6.35 mm) diam. head													
14 ga. (2.03 mm)	1-3/8 (4d)	34.9				X						3.50	1.71
13-1/2 ga. (2.18 mm)	1-5/8 (5d)	41.3					X					4.50	2.20
13 ga. (2.32 mm)	1-7/8 (6d)	47.6							X			5.75	2.81
13-1/2 ga. (2.18 mm)	2-1/8 (7d)	54.0									X	7.50	3.66

(1) For wood framing 16″ o.c., nails 8″ o.c. for walls, 7″ o.c. for ceilings. (2) All nails treated to prevent rust with joint compounds or veneer plaster finishes. Fire-rated assemblies generally require greater nail penetration; therefore, for fire-rated assemblies, use exact nail length and diameter specified for rated assembly (see Fire Test Report). (3) In laminated double-layer construction, base layer is attached in same manner as single layer.

Adhesives

SHEETROCK Brand Lightweight Setting-Type (EASY SAND) Joint Compound

SHEETROCK Brand Ready-Mixed All Purpose Joint Compound

Drywall adhesives make an important contribution to gypsum panel attachment when high quality room interiors are desired. Their use greatly reduces the nail or screw fastening otherwise required, thus saving labor on spotting and sanding, as well as minimizing nail pops and other fastener imperfections.

USG offers reliable, field-tested adhesives designed for professional use. Each is formulated to produce strong attachment, freedom from fastener imperfections and high-quality results. Recommended for laminating gypsum panels in multi-layer fire-rated or non-rated partitions and ceilings. All provide tight bond when dry yet permit adjustment of panels after contact.

SHEETROCK Brand Setting-Type (DURABOND) or Lightweight Setting-Type (Easy Sand) Joint Compounds Dry, powder products to be mixed with water, used for laminating gypsum panels in multi-layer fire-rated or non-rated partitions and ceilings. Spreader-applied, these compounds require temporary fastening in application. They provide tight bond when dry, yet permit panel adjustment after contact. Meet ASTM C475.

SHEETROCK Brand Ready-Mixed Joint Compound Taping or All Purpose Compounds Formulated to a creamy, smooth consistency for fast spreader application. Used for laminating gypsum panels in multi-layer fire-rated or non-rated partitions and ceilings. These offer ready-to-use convenience and eliminate extensive mixing and waste. Provide good bond and strength when dry. Use above grade; keep from freezing. Meet ASTM C475.

Commercial Adhesives Available in drywall stud and construction types meeting ASTM C557; used in non-fire-rated gypsum construction. These adhesives bridge minor irregularities in the base or framing, making it easier to form true joints and level surfaces. The use of adhesive adds strength to an assembly, reduces fasteners required, and helps eliminate loose panels and nail pops.

Coverage—Laminating Adhesives

| Product[1] | Type of laminating | Approx. coverage[2] | |
| | | Lam. blade notch spacing | |
		2" o.c.	1-1/2" o.c.
SHEETROCK Brand Ready-Mixed Joint	sheet	340	465
Compounds—Taping or All Purpose	strip	170	230
SHEETROCK Brand Lightweight All Purpose	sheet	23.0	31.7
Ready-Mixed Joint Compound (PLUS 3)	strip	11.5	15.5
SHEETROCK Brand Setting-Type	sheet	184	246
Joint Compounds (DURABOND)	strip	93	123
SHEETROCK Brand Lightweight Setting-Type	sheet	134	179
Joint Compounds (EASY SAND)	strip	68	90

(1) See Joint Compound Specifications for standard package sizes. (2) Coverage in lb./1000 SF of packaged product, not including water, necessary to achieve working consistency. Exception: PLUS 3 is gal./1000 SF.

Joint Compounds

Today's complete USG Sʜᴇᴇᴛʀᴏᴄᴋ brand joint compound line includes both ready-mixed and powder products in drying and setting (hardening) types. In addition to conventional joint finishing and fastener spotting, some of these products are designed for repairing cracks, patching, spackling, back-blocking, texturing and for laminating gypsum panels in double-layer systems. Products comply with ASTM C475.

Advantages

Low Cost High-quality products reduce preparation time, save application labor and prevent expensive callbacks.

Versatility Job-tested compounds are available in specialized types to meet finishing requirements.

Safety Safe to handle and use; meet OSHA and Consumer Product Safety Standards.

Use of USG joint compounds brings the important added advantage of dealing with one manufacturer who is responsible for all components of the finished walls and ceilings—formulated in our laboratories, and manufactured in our plants for maximum system performance.

General Limitations

1. USG joint compounds are not compatible with and should not be inter-mixed with any other compounds.

2. For interior use only except for the use of Sʜᴇᴇᴛʀᴏᴄᴋ brand setting-type (Dᴜʀᴀʙᴏɴᴅ) and Sʜᴇᴇᴛʀᴏᴄᴋ lightweight setting-type (Eᴀsʏ Sᴀɴᴅ) joint compounds with Sʜᴇᴇᴛʀᴏᴄᴋ exterior gypsum ceiling board.

3. Not recommended for laminating except Sʜᴇᴇᴛʀᴏᴄᴋ brand setting-type (Dᴜʀᴀʙᴏɴᴅ) and Sʜᴇᴇᴛʀᴏᴄᴋ brand lightweight setting-type (Eᴀsʏ Sᴀɴᴅ) compounds and Sʜᴇᴇᴛʀᴏᴄᴋ brand ready-mixed compounds—all purpose and taping.

4. Protect bagged and cartoned products against wetting; protect ready-mixed products from freezing and extreme heat.

5. Each compound coat must be dry before the next is applied (except Sʜᴇᴇᴛʀᴏᴄᴋ brand setting-type [Dᴜʀᴀʙᴏɴᴅ] and Sʜᴇᴇᴛʀᴏᴄᴋ brand lightweight setting-type [Eᴀsʏ Sᴀɴᴅ] compounds); and completed joint treatment must be thoroughly dry before decorating.

6. Use only Sʜᴇᴇᴛʀᴏᴄᴋ brand setting-type (Dᴜʀᴀʙᴏɴᴅ) 90 for treating joints of Fɪʙᴇʀᴏᴄᴋ panels to be covered with ceramic or plastic tile.

7. With regard to the following products: Sʜᴇᴇᴛʀᴏᴄᴋ brand lightweight all-purpose joint compound (Pʟᴜs 3®), Sʜᴇᴇᴛʀᴏᴄᴋ brand topping joint compound ready-mixed and Sʜᴇᴇᴛʀᴏᴄᴋ lightweight all-purpose joint compound (A/P Lɪᴛᴇ™). If smoothing by dry sanding, use nothing coarser than 150-grit sandpaper or 220-grit abrasive mesh cloth.

8. For painting and decorating, follow manufacturer's directions for materials used. All surfaces must be thoroughly dry, dust-

free and not glossy before decorating. SHEETROCK brand First Coat should be applied and allowed to dry before decorating.

9. Gypsum panel surface should be skim coated with joint regular weight all-purpose compound or COVER COAT® or spray applied TUFF-HIDE™ to equalize suction before painting in areas where gypsum panel walls and ceilings will be subjected to severe artificial or natural side lighting and be decorated with a gloss paint (eggshell, semi-gloss or gloss).

10. If dry sanding is used to smooth the joint compound, avoid roughening the gypsum panel face paper.

11. Do not use topping compound for taping or as first coat over bead.

12. Not recommended for texturing by spray application.

13. Children can fall into joint compound bucket and drown. Keep children away from bucket if even a small amount of liquid is inside. Do not reuse bucket.

SHEETROCK Brand Ready-Mixed Drying-Type Joint Compounds

SHEETROCK ready-mixed joint compounds are drying-type products that are vastly superior to ordinary ready-mixed compounds and are preferred for consistently high-quality work. These formulations are specially premixed to a creamy, smooth consistency essentially free of crater-causing air bubbles. They offer excellent slip and bond and easy workability. Available for hand or machine-tool applications.

Six specialized products:

Ready Mixed Taping

Ready Mixed Topping

Ready Mixed All Purpose

PLUS 3

Midweight

Plus 3 with Dust Control

SHEETROCK **Brand Taping Joint Compound Ready-Mixed** High-performance product for embedding paper tape. Also used as a first fill coat over metal bead, trim and fasteners in some areas. Check suitability of the formula with your local sales office. Also used for laminating.

SHEETROCK **Brand Topping Joint Compound Ready-Mixed** Low-shrinkage, easily applied and sanded product recommended for second and third coats over SHEETROCK taping and all-purpose joint compounds. Also used for simple hand-applied texturing in some geographic areas. Check suitability of the formula with your local sales office. Not suitable for embedding tape or as first coat over metal corners, trim and fasteners, or for skim coating.

SHEETROCK **Brand All-Purpose Joint Compound Ready-Mixed** Used for embedding, finishing, skim coating, simple hand-applied texturing and for laminating. Combines single-package convenience with good taping and topping characteristics. Recommended for finishing SHEETROCK gypsum panels, SW Edge, joints over prefill of SHEETROCK setting-type (DURABOND) or lightweight setting-type (EASY SAND) compound; also for repairing cracks in interior plaster and masonry not subject to moisture.

SHEETROCK **Brand Lightweight All-Purpose Joint Compound Ready-Mixed (PLUS 3®)** Offers all the benefits of an all-purpose compound, plus three exclusive advantages: up to 35% less weight, less shrinkage and exceptional ease of sanding. Usually needs only two coats over metal. Eliminates need for separate taping and topping compounds—sands with ease of topping compound, bonds like taping compound. Not recommended for skim coating.

SHEETROCK **Brand Lightweight All-Purpose Joint Compound Ready-Mixed (PLUS 3 with Dust Control)** Offers the additional advantage of drastic reduction of airborne dust. The dust particles bind together, falling directly to the floor, concentrating along the walls for faster clean up.

SHEETROCK **Brand All-Purpose Joint Compound Ready-Mixed (Mid-weight)** Ready-mixed compound that weighs 15% less than conventional-weight compounds, offers excellent tape-embedding properties and easy workability and sandability. Works well for both taping and topping applications. Lower shrinkage means that only two coats typically are required over metal bead, trim and fasteners.

SHEETROCK Brand Powder Joint Compounds

SHEETROCK brand powder joint compounds are top-quality, non-asbestos, drying-type products providing easy mixing, smooth application and ample working time. Designed for embedding tape, for fill coats and finishing over drywall joints, corner bead, trim and fasteners. Included in product line:

SHEETROCK **Brand Taping Joint Compound** Designed for embedding tape and for first fill coat on metal corner beads, drywall trims and fasteners; also used for patching plaster cracks. Offers excellent bond and resistance to cracking.

Sheetrock **Brand Topping Joint Compound** A smooth-sanding material for second and third coats over taping or all-purpose compound. Produces excellent feathering and superior finishing results.

Sheetrock **Brand All-Purpose Joint Compound** Incorporates good taping and topping characteristics in a single product, for use where finest results of the specialized compounds are not necessary. Also has good hand-applied texturing properties.

Sheetrock **Brand Lightweight All-Purpose Joint Compound (A/P Lite)** All-purpose compound weighs 20% less than conventional compounds; offers lower shrinkage, better crack resistance and easier mixing, application and sanding.

Sheetrock **Brand Powder Setting-Type Joint Compounds**

These setting-type powder products were developed to provide faster finishing of drywall interiors, even under slow drying conditions. Rapid chemical hardening and low shrinkage permit same-day finishing and usually next-day decoration. Features exceptional bond; virtually unaffected by humidity extremes. Ideal for laminating double-layer systems, particularly fire-rated assemblies, and for adhering gypsum panels to above-grade concrete surfaces. May be used for surface texturing and for filling, smoothing and finishing interior above-grade concrete. Also used to treat joints in exterior gypsum ceiling board; as prefill material for Sheetrock brand gypsum panels, SW Edge; treating fastener heads in areas to receive ceramic or plastic tile; and (except for Sheetrock brand lightweight setting-type joint compound) to embed tape and fill beads in veneer plaster finish systems when rapid drying conditions exist.

Sheetrock **Brand Lightweight Setting-Type Joint Compound (Easy Sand)** Weighs 25% less than conventional setting-type compounds for easier handling, faster application and improved productivity on the job. Provides sanding ease similar to a ready-mixed, all-purpose joint compound. Offers varied setting times of 8 to 12 minutes (Easy Sand 5), 20 to 30 minutes (Easy Sand 20), 30 to 80 minutes (Easy Sand 45), 85 to 130 minutes (Easy Sand 90) and 180 to 240 minutes (Easy Sand 210).

Sheetrock **Brand Setting-Type Joint Compound (Durabond)** Provides the strongest joint bond of all setting-type compounds. Available in a number of setting times to meet varying job requirements: 20 to 30 minutes (Durabond 20), 30 to 80 minutes, (Durabond 45), 85 to 130 minutes (Durabond 90) and 180 to 240 minutes (Durabond 210).

Easy Sand   *Durabond*

Joint Compounds for Manufactured Housing

USG has formulated special joint compounds for manufactured housing. These are setting-type compounds designed for the industry's controlled manufacturing environment, and the strength characteristics required for over-the-road transit of factory-built homes. For information about these products, recommended applications and instructions for their use, contact your local USG sales office.

Joint Compound Selection

Choosing the right joint compound for a specific job requires an understanding of a number of factors: job conditions, shop practices, applicators' preferences, types of available joint systems, characteristics of products considered and recommended product combinations.

Joint compound products are usually named according to function, such as taping, topping and all-purpose. Taping typically performs as the highest shrinking, strongest bonding, hardest sanding of the three compounds, and is used for embedding tape. Topping usually is the lowest shrinking and easiest applying and sanding of the compounds for use in second and third coats; may occasionally be designed for simple hand-applied texturing. Taping and topping are usually designed as companion products to give the highest quality finish. All-purpose is generally a compromise of taping and topping and may be used as a simple hand-applied texturing material. Lightweight all-purpose joint compound is also an all-purpose compound, but is lighter, shrinks less and sands easier.

Types of Joint Compounds

Two-Compound Systems   Formulated for superior performance in each joint finishing step. Separate taping compounds develop the greatest bond strength and crack resistance. Separate topping compounds have the best sanding characteristics, lower shrinkage and smoothest finishing.

All-Purpose Compounds   Good performance in all joint finishing steps; do not have the outstanding bond strength, workability and sandability of separate taping and topping compounds. However, all-purpose compounds minimize inventories, avoid job site mix-ups and are especially good for scattered jobs.

Ready-Mixed Compounds   Open-and-use convenience; save time and mistakes in mixing, leading to minimum waste. Require minimal water supply at the job. Ready-mixed compounds have the best working qualities of all compounds—excellent performance plus factory-controlled batch consistency.

These compounds do require heated storage. Should they freeze, they can be slowly thawed at room temperature, mixed to an even viscosity and used without damaging effect. However, repeated freeze/thaw cycles cause remixing to become more difficult.

1

Powder Compounds Have the special advantage of being storable (dry) at any temperature. If they are stored in a cold warehouse, however, they should be moved to a warm mixing room the day before they are to be mixed. Best results require strict adherence to proportioning of powder and water.

Specifications—SHEETROCK **Brand Joint Compounds**

Product	Container size	Approx. coverage
SHEETROCK Brand Ready-Mixed Joint Compound—Taping, Topping, All Purpose	12-lb. (5.4 kg), 42-lb. (19 kg) or 61.7-lb. (28 kg) pail; 48-lb. (21.8 kg), 50-lb. (22.7 kg) or 61.7-lb. (28 kg) carton	138 lb./1,000 SF (67.4 kg/100 m²)
SHEETROCK Brand Lightweight All Purpose Joint Compound, Ready-Mixed (PLUS 3)	1 gal, (3.8L) or 4.5 gal. (17L) pail; 4.5 gal. (17L) or 3.5-gal. (13L) carton	9.4 gal./1,000 SF (38.3L/100 m²)
Plus 3 with Dust Control	1 gal. pail; 3.5 gal. pail, 3.5 gal. carton Patch Repair pan	9.4 gal./1,000 SF (38.3L/100 m²)
SHEETROCK Brand All Purpose Joint Compound, Ready-Mixed (Midweight)	4.5 gal. (17L) pail; 4.5 gal. (17L) or 3.5-gal. (13L) carton	9.4 gal./1,000 SF (38.3L/100 m²)
SHEETROCK Brand Powder Joint Compound-Taping, Topping, All Purpose	25-lb. (11.3 kg) bag	83 lb./1,000 SF (40.5 kg/100 m²)
SHEETROCK Brand Lightweight All Purpose joint Compound (AP LITE)	20-lb. (9 kg) bag	67 lb./1,000 SF (32.7 kg/100 m²)
SHEETROCK Brand Setting-Type Joint Compound (DURABOND) 20, 45, 90, 210, 300	25-lb. (11.3 kg) bag	72 lb./1,000 SF (35.2 kg/100 m²)
SHEETROCK Brand Lightweight Setting-Type Joint Compound (EASY SAND) 20, 45, 90, 210, 300	18-lb. (8.1 kg) bag	52 lb./1,000 SF (25.3 kg/100 m²)

Concrete Finishing Compounds

COVER COAT Compound

Cover Coat Compound Formulated for filling and smoothing monolithic concrete ceilings, walls and columns located above grade—no extra bonding agent needed. Supplied in ready-mixed form (sand can be added), easily applied with drywall tools in two or more coats. Dries to a fine white surface usually making further decoration unnecessary. Not washable unpainted. Also can be used for embedding tape, for first coat over metal bead and trim and for skim coating over gypsum panels.

SHEETROCK **Brand Setting-Type (**DURABOND**) and Lightweight Setting-Type (**EASY SAND**) Joint Compounds** These setting-type compounds are ideally suited to fill offsets and voids left in concrete. They produce a hard finish in various shades of white. Overpainting may be required.

Where deep fills are required, SHEETROCK brand setting-type (DURABOND) and SHEETROCK brand lightweight setting-type (EASY SAND) compounds are especially recommended for the first coat, then followed by COVER COAT compound. This practice minimizes check cracking.

Reinforcing Tapes

From the originator of modern joint finishing, USG reinforcing tapes add strength and crack resistance for smooth concealment at flat joints and inside corners. Two products—both quickly and easily applied—are available for specialized uses: paper tape for treatment with joint compounds and glass-fiber tape for veneer plaster finishes.

SHEETROCK **Brand Joint Tape** Special strong, cross-fibered paper tape for use with USG joint compounds in reinforcing joints and corners in gypsum drywall and veneer plaster finish interiors. Exceptional wet and dry strength; resists stretching, wrinkling and other distortions; lies flat and resists tearing under tools. The wafer-thin tape is lightly sanded for increased bond and lies flat for easy concealment on next coat. Precision-processed with positive center creasing, which simplifies application in corners; uniform winding provides accurate, trouble-free attachment to angles and to flat joints.

SHEETROCK brand joint tape is designed for both embedding by hand (below) and application with mechanical taping tool (right). Joint is covered with thin layer of compound before taping.

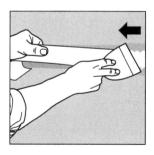
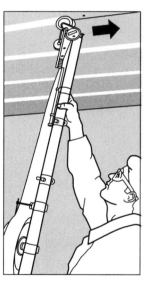

Preferred for its consistent high performance in gypsum drywall finishing, SHEETROCK brand joint tape with SHEETROCK setting-type (DURABOND) joint compound is also used with veneer plaster finish systems. The regular SHEETROCK brand joint tape is 1-31/32" wide in 75', 250' and 500' rolls. SHEETROCK brand joint tape-heavy provides added strength and crack-resistance in drywall joint treatment; it is 2-1/16" wide in 250' and 500' rolls. Approximate coverage: 370 LF tape per 1,000 SF panel.

A joint treatment system (reinforcing tape and joint compound) must provide joints as strong as the gypsum board itself. Otherwise, normal structural movement in a wall or ceiling assembly can result in the development of cracks over the finished joint.

1

Repeated joint strength tests conducted at the USG Research Center have shown that joints taped and finished with conventional fiberglass leno-weave mesh tape and conventional joint compounds are more prone to cracking than joints finished with paper tape and conventional joint compounds. This is because fiberglass mesh tapes tend to stretch under load, even after being covered with joint compounds.

Permanent repair of these cracks is difficult. Accordingly, USG does not recommend using conventional fiberglass leno-weave mesh tape with conventional ready-mixed, powder or chemically setting compounds for general drywall joint finishing.

SHEETROCK **Brand Fiberglass Drywall Tape** Made with a unique cross-fiber construction to provide greater drywall joint strength than conventional fiberglass leno-weave mesh tapes. This self-adhesive tape goes on quickly, eliminating the bedding coat. Smooth, finished joints are accomplished in two coats by using SHEETROCK setting-type joint compound (DURABOND or EASY SAND) for at least the first application. The setting-type joint compound also provides the added bond to provide desired joint strength. Second SHEETROCK brand joint compound application can be either setting-type or drying-type (ready-mixed or powder). This tape is also ideal for patching small holes and cracks.

IMPERIAL **Brand Tape** Strong, glass-fiber tape used in wood-frame construction to conceal and reinforce joints and interior angles of IMPERIAL gypsum base prior to veneer plaster finishing with IMPERIAL veneer basecoat, IMPERIAL veneer finish, DIAMOND veneer basecoat and DIAMOND veneer finish. High-tensile strength glass fibers are woven into an open mesh, coated with binder and slit to roll width.

The open weave of IMPERIAL brand tape (100 meshes per sq. in.) provides excellent reinforcing and keying of plaster to resist cracking. The glass fibers lay flat and minimize stretching for wrinkle-free attachment without springback or distortion. Spirally woven (leno) long strands and a binder coating reduce edge raveling and fraying and keep loose threads from defacing finished surfaces. Tape flexes readily to permit fast application to flat joints and corners. Available in two types:

Type P with pressure-sensitive adhesive backing. Selected for quick, self-stick hand application; saves installation time and fastener cost.

Type S with plain back, fastened with staples. Lower in cost than Type P.

Availability: Type S in 300' rolls, 2-1/2" wide; Type P in 300' rolls, 2" and 2-1/2" wide; 12 rolls per ctn. Approximate coverage: 370 LF tape per 1,000 SF gypsum base.

Both types of glass-fiber IMPERIAL *Brand Tape are quickly applied—Type S with 3/8" staples at staggered 24 intervals (left), self-stick Type P by light hand pressure and bonding with finishing knife or trowel (right). Use of Type P Tape cuts taping time up to 50%, simplifies embedding and saves cost of staples.*

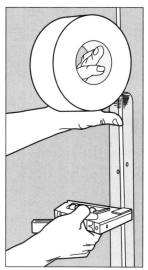

Veneer Plaster Finishes

Veneer plaster finishes offer the opportunity to trim days from interior finishing schedules and provide strong, highly abrasion-resistant surfaces. These products are designed for one- or two-coat work over gypsum bases or directly to concrete block or properly prepared monolithic concrete. Formulated for hand application (IMPERIAL veneer finish and DIAMOND veneer finish), they provide a thin, lightweight veneer that sets rapidly.

Conventional plaster is the best system to attain a uniform, monolithic, blemish-free, smooth surface with excellent wear resistance. By contrast, veneer plaster systems utilize large-size gypsum panels to improve speed of installation, while providing more monolithic, harder, abuse-resistant surfaces than are achievable with drywall. Plaster thickness is reduced from the standard 1/2" associated with conventional plaster to a mere 1/16" to 1/8" using high-strength gypsum in the product formulations. While RED TOP® Keenes cement-lime-sand provides the most universal texture finish in two-coat application, IMPERIAL veneer finish and DIAMOND veneer finish provide better surface hardness, abrasion resistance and wearability. Ready for final finish in as little as 24 hours if completely dry. (See "Comparing Plaster Systems" in Appendix.)

Advantages

Rugged, Abuse-Resistant Surfaces High-strength IMPERIAL veneer-finishes provide hard, durable interiors that require minimal maintenance.

Quicker Completion/Faster Occupancy Veneer plaster finishes apply rapidly, set fast, dry quickly to save days in finishing interior walls and ceilings. DIAMOND veneer finish can be decorated in 24 hours (if completely dry) with breather-type paint or left undecorated if desired.

When abraded 1000 cycles by 25-lb. weighted wire brush in laboratory test, IMPERIAL brand veneer plaster finish showed virtually no penetration— proof of outstanding abrasion resistance.

Competitive Costs   Veneer plaster finishes are easily applied and cover more area per ton than conventional plasters. Joints and interior angles are preset with the same veneer plaster finish that goes on the walls and ceilings.

Easily Decorated   Veneer plasters are readily finished in smooth-trowel, float or texture surfaces. The hard, smooth surface is decorated easily and economically with paint, fabric, wallpaper or texture.

Versatile   A wide choice of assemblies is available to meet design requirements: fire- and sound-rated systems for wood or steel framing, hard and abuse-resistant surfaces for high-traffic areas and electrically heated ceilings.

Products Available

IMPERIAL Brand Basecoat Plaster

IMPERIAL **Veneer Basecoat** For use as a basecoat in two-coat veneer application finished with proper lime or gypsum finishes. Can be applied to either IMPERIAL gypsum base, directly to concrete block, or over USG plaster bonder on monolithic concrete. Formulated as the basecoat for high-strength IMPERIAL finish veneer, gauged lime putty, DIAMOND veneer finish, STRUCTO-GAUGE® lime smooth trowel, or Keenes lime sand float finishes. Available in hand formulation. Complies with ASTM C587. Available in 50-lb. bags.

IMPERIAL **Veneer Finish**   For single-coat application composed of scratch coat and immediate doubling back directly over special IMPERIAL gypsum base, glass-fiber tape or SHEETROCK brand joint tape or SHEETROCK brand setting-type joint compound (DURABOND or EASY SAND). Also used over IMPERIAL veneer basecoat in a two-coat system. Available for hand application—provides a smooth-trowel or float or spray-texture finish ready for decoration. Complies with ASTM C587. Available in 50-lb. bags.

Coverage—IMPERIAL Brand Basecoat and Finishes

	SF/ton		m²/ton (metric)[1]	
Product	Gypsum base	Masonry	Gypsum base	Masonry
IMPERIAL Brand Basecoat	3250-4250	2700-3600	335-435	275-370
IMPERIAL Brand (1-coat) Finish	3500-4000	not recommended	360-410	not recommended
IMPERIAL Brand (2-coat) Finish	3200-3600	3200-3600	330-370	330-370

(1) Coverage rounded to nearest 5m² per metric ton.

DIAMOND Brand Veneer Basecoat Plaster

DIAMOND **Veneer Basecoat**   Provides quality walls and ceilings for residential construction where superior strength of IMPERIAL veneer basecoat is not essential. Offers superior workability and ease and speed of application. Formulated to receive a variety of finishes. Apply to IMPERIAL gypsum base, concrete block or monolithic concrete. Complies with ASTM C587. Available in 50 lb.bags.

Coverage—Diamond Brand Basecoat

Product	SF/ton		m²/ton (metric)[1]	
	Gypsum base	Masonry	Gypsum base	Masonry
Diamond Brand Basecoat	4000-5000	3500-4500	410-510	360-460

Diamond Brand Interior Finish Plaster

Diamond Veneer Finish A white finish formulated for hand application directly to Imperial gypsum base or over USG Plaster Bonder on monolithic concrete. Also suitable in a two-coat system over Imperial veneer or Diamond veneer basecoats or a sanded gypsum basecoat. Applied to a nomimal 1/16" thickness, this finish is unaggregated for a smooth or skip-trowel finish; may be job-aggregated with up to an equal part by weight of clean, fine silica sand for Spanish, swirl, float or other textures. Not recommended for use over Portland cement basecoat or masonry surfaces. Complies with ASTM C587. Available in 50-lb. bags.

Diamond veneer finish should be applied only to Imperial gypsum base having blue face paper. Faded base must be treated with USG accelerator—alum catalyst or USG plaster bonder before finish is applied to prevent possible bond failure. See page 223 for specific application instructions.

Diamond veneer finish is also suitable for use with electric cable ceilings. Allows higher operating temperatures than with other products, provides more heat transmission and greater resistance to heat deterioration. Finish is job-sanded and hand-applied 3/16" thick to cover cable. A finish coat of the same material is applied 1/16" to 3/32" thick to bring the total plaster thickness to 1/4". Applied over Imperial gypsum base attached to wood joists, to metal furring channel or suspended metal grillage, or over USG plaster bonder directly to monolithic concrete ceilings (5/16" fill coat plus finish coat for 3/8" total thickness.) For additional information, see PM16, Application of Diamond Interior Finish in Electric Heat Cable Systems.

Coverage—Diamond Veneer Finish

Conventional walls and ceilings

Surface applied to	Neat		Sand float finish sanded 1:2[1] (Sand:DIF)[1]		Heavy texture finish sanded 1:1[1] (Sand:DIF)[1]	
	SF/ton	m²/ton[2]	SF/ton	m²/ton[2]	SF/ton	m²/ton
Imperial Gypsum Base	6000	610	4660	475	3500	355
Imperial or Diamond Veneer Basecoat	5500	560	4330	440	3250	330
Sanded Red Top Basecoat	5000	510	4000	410	3000	305
Monolithic concrete[3][4]	5500	560	4330	440	3250	330
Veneer basecoat over monolithic concrete[3]	5500	560	4330	440	3250	330

Electric cable heat ceilings

Surface applied to	fill coat[5] sanded 1:1[1]		1/16" finish coat sanded 1:4[1]		1/16" finish coat sanded 1:1[1]	
	SF/ton	m2/ton[2]	SF/ton	m2/ton[2]	SF/ton	m2/ton[2]
Imperial Gypsum Base	2300	235	5000	510	3250	330
Monolithic concrete[3]	900	84	5500	560	4500	418

(1) Coverage based on one ton of aggregated mixture (combined weight of sand and Diamond Brand Interior Finish Plaster). (2) Coverage rounded to nearest km² per metric ton. (3) USG Plaster Bonder required. (4) Must be job sanded, minimum 1/2:1, sand to plaster. (5) Fill coat over gypsum base is 3/16" thick—over monolithic concrete is 5/16".

Primers

SHEETROCK Brand First Coat—Read-Mixed

SHEETROCK Brand First Coat—Ready-Mixed Decorating problems such as "joint banding" or "photographing" are usually caused by differences between the porosities and surface textures of the gypsum board face paper or concrete on one hand, and the finished joint compound on the other. SHEETROCK brand First Coat is a flat latex basecoat paint-type product specially formulated to provide a superior prime coat over interior gypsum board, wood and concrete surfaces.

In contrast to a sealer, SHEETROCK brand First Coat does not form a film that seals the substrate surface. Instead, it minimizes porosity differences by providing a base that equalizes the absorption rates of the drywall face paper and the finished joint compound when painted. SHEETROCK brand First Coat also provides the proper type and amount of pigments and fillers, lacking from conventional primers and sealers, that minimize surface texture variations between the gypsum board face paper and the finished joint compound.

SHEETROCK brand First Coat is designed for fast, low-cost application. It can be applied with a brush, roller or airless or conventional sprayer. It dries in less than 30 minutes under 72°F/50% R.H. conditions. White finish is ready for decoration in an hour. Not intended as a final coating—it should be overpainted when dry. The product comes ready-mixed in 5-gal. and 1-gal. pails.

SHEETROCK Brand Wallcovering Primer— Ready-Mixed

SHEETROCK Brand Wallcovering Primer—Ready-Mixed Ideal basecoat product for wallcoverings. Also, the required primer for joint-treated areas of walls and ceilings to receive the USG Decorative Interior Finish System; in these applications the primer is then covered with USG plaster bonder—clear. For wallpaper applications, SHEETROCK brand wallcovering primer prevents wallcovering adhesive from soaking into porous wall surfaces and improves adhesion and slip. Also, permits later removal of wallpaper. May be used on cured new or old plaster, stripped wallpaper, masonry and gypsum panels. Not recommended over lime-gauging or lime-containing plaster finishes. Available in 5-gal. and 1-gal. containers.

Interior Texture Finishes

Texture finishes from USG offer a wide variety of possible texture patterns to provide distinctive interior styling. They are fast and easy to apply and quick drying, so save labor time to preserve job profits. They hide minor surface blemishes, which reduces the amount of surface preparation needed. All products are non-asbestos containing.

Powder Texture Products

SHEETROCK Brand Ceiling Spray Texture (QT)—(Fine) (Medium) (Coarse) Powder product with polystyrene aggregate, available in three finishes. It creates a simulated acoustical ceiling finish but with no acoustical correction. Requires only addition of water and short soaking period at job site. Produces excellent bonding qualities for application to gypsum panels, concrete, plaster or wood. High wet and dry hide masks minor surface defects. Dries to a white finish, which is usually left unpainted but may be overpainted if desired. Not recommended for use where constant humid conditions exist.

Examples of high-style textures produced by SHEETROCK Brand Ceiling Spray Texture (QT): (1) Fine Finish for light effect; (2) Medium Finish for striking texture; (3) Coarse Finish for unusual decorating effect.

1

2

3

Surface designs available with SHEETROCK Brand Wall and Ceiling Spray Texture include Spatter Finish (left) and Spatter/Knockdown Finish (right).

SHEETROCK **Brand Wall and Ceiling Spray Texture** Available in aggregated and unaggregated forms for texture variety on most interior wall surfaces. This product produces light spatter, and light "orange peel" texture with spray application. It dries to a soft-tone white surface with good concealment that should be overpainted on walls, but can be left unpainted on ceilings if adequate amount has been applied to provide sufficient hiding properties. However, it is not washable if left unpainted.

SHEETROCK **Brand Wall and Ceiling Texture (TUF-TEX®)** Unaggregated texture coating that produces a variety of patterns from bold spatter/knockdown to light orange peel. May be by spray-applied and/or hand tooled with a broad knife, brush or roller, depending on pattern desired. Dries to a hard, white finish and helps conceal minor substrate defects. Not intended as a final coating—should be overpainted when dry. If left unpainted, it is not washable.

1

Distinctive medium stipple texture is achieved with SHEETROCK Brand Wall and Ceiling Texture (TUF-TEX).

Variety of effects obtained with SHEETROCK Brand Wall and Ceiling Texture— Multi-Purpose include (clockwise from left) bold shadowing with roller application, medium-light finish applied by spray and lightly stippled surface applied with small brush or roller-stippler.

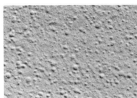

SHEETROCK Brand Wall and Ceiling Texture—Multi-Purpose An economical, unaggregated powder product that is mixed with water to create desired texturing consistency. Excellent for producing fine to medium texture patterns (such as fine orange peel and crow's foot stipple finishes) on drywall or other interior surfaces. The textured effect is obtained by brush, roller or spray application and helps conceal minor surface defects. It dries to a soft-tone white finish that should be overpainted on walls, but can be left unpainted on ceilings when adequate amount of material is applied. It is not washable if left unpainted.

SHEETROCK Brand Wall and Ceiling Spray Texture Sand Finish Texture 12 Spray-applied powder product that yields a fine sand finish on walls and ceilings. Combines easy mixing, fast drying, excellent coverage and good concealment. Ideal base for wall paints. May be left unpainted on ceilings, but unpainted it is not washable.

Close-up view shows typical sand-effect finish obtained with aggregated SHEETROCK Brand Wall and Ceiling Spray Texture—Sand Finish Texture 12. In application, fan technique is used on walls, cross-spray on ceilings (left).

Simple roller-applied texture is obtained with vinyl-base SHEETROCK Brand Powder, Joint Compounds. Same products can be used for joint finishing and texturing on job (right).

SHEETROCK **Brand Powder Joint Compound (All-Purpose)** Easy-mixing, smooth-working product that can be used to produce attractive light to medium textures. It is applied with a brush, roller or trowel. Color is white but may vary in degree of whiteness. Surfaces should be painted. It is not washable if left unpainted.

SHEETROCK Brand Ceiling Spray Texture (QT)—(Fine) (Medium) (Coarse)

SHEETROCK Brand Wall and Ceiling Spray Texture—(Unaggregated) (Aggregated)

SHEETROCK Brand Wall and Ceiling Texture (TUF-TEX)

SHEETROCK Brand Wall and Ceiling Texture—Multi-Purpose

SHEETROCK Brand Wall and Ceiling Spray Texture Sand Finish Texture 12

Sound-Absorbing Plaster Finish

USG Acoustical Plaster Finish

USG Acoustical Plaster Finish An attractive spray plaster texture for application to gypsum basecoats, interior monolithic concrete, metal decks and gypsum panel ceilings. Chemically setting-type product gives a sound-absorbing, sound-rated decorative finish to gypsum panels, concrete and non-veneer-type plaster ceilings and other non-contact surfaces. Produces a natural-white, evenly textured finish. Requires no application of a bonding agent except over metal decking. Reduces surface preparation time and costs. For use on new or renovation construction. Surface-burning characteristics: flame spread 10, smoke developed 25 per ASTM E1042-85. Sound rated: NRC 0.55 for concrete and conventional plaster at 1/2" finish thickness; NRC 0.75 for concrete and conventional plaster at 1" finish thickness, NRC 0.50 for gypsum panels at 1/2" finish thickness. Use on noncontact surfaces only. For additional information, see P720, USG Acoustical Plaster finish Data Submittal Sheet.

USG acoustical plaster Finish absorbs sound and gives dramatic appeal to ceilings and other non-contact surfaces (left).

Extra-thick finish applied in one coat provides eye appeal and decorative charm (right).

Ready-Mixed Texture Products

SHEETROCK **Brand Wall and Ceiling Texture**   Offers unique super thickness with just one coat, plus the fast start of ready-mixed material. Massive thickness in just one pass eliminates doubling back. This white, latex-type finish develops a tough, durable surface with stubborn resistance to fissure cracks. Apply with trowel, roller, brush or spray, depending on pattern desired. Bonds well with excellent hide over many surfaces—gypsum panels, concrete, primed plaster, interior masonry and non-staining wood surfaces. Painting not required on non-contact surfaces. Overpaint if desired. Not washable unpainted.

SHEETROCK **Brand Wall and Ceiling Spray Texture**   A ready-mixed vinyl formulation for texturing interior, above-grade surfaces. Ideal where moderate to bold texture patterns are desired. Designed for spray application over gypsum panel, concrete and most other interior wall and ceiling surfaces. Formulated to create unique texture patterns such as spatter, spatter/knockdown and orange peel designs. Dries to a white surface, but should be overpainted when dry. Not washable unpainted.

SHEETROCK **Brand Wall and Ceiling Texture Paint (Sand Finish Texture 1)** White; produces a sand finish on walls and ceilings. Sanded effect is obtained by brush, roller or spray application. Durable finish; may be left unpainted.

SHEETROCK **Brand Wall and Ceiling Texture Paint (Ripple Finish Texture 2)** Produces an orange peel to moderate ripple texture patterns on ceilings and sidewalls; textured effect obtained by roller or spray, depending on the desired texture finish; may be left unpainted.

SHEETROCK Brand Wall and Ceiling Texture

SHEETROCK Brand Wall and Ceiling Spray Texture

SHEETROCK Brand Wall and Ceiling Texture Paint (Sand Finish Texture 1)

SHEETROCK Brand Wall and Ceiling Texture Paint (TEXOLITE® Sanded Paste Stipple)   White; produces a sand finish on ceilings and side-walls. Texture effect is obtained by roller application that can be left as-is or brushed to create a sanded-swirl texture finish. Durable finish; may be left unpainted.

SHEETROCK Brand Ready-Mixed Joint Compounds (Topping or All-Purpose) Virtually ready to use, these products will produce textures ranging from light to medium depending upon method of application. Color is white, but may vary. Surfaces should be painted. Applied with brush, roller or trowel. Not recommended for spray application or for texturing in all areas. Not washable unpainted. Check local sales office for suitability of formulation for texturing in your area.

SHEETROCK Brand Wall and Ceiling Texture Paint (Ripple Finish Texture 2)

SHEETROCK Brand Wall and Ceiling Texture Paint (TEXOLITE Sanded Paste Stipple)

SHEETROCK Brand Ready-Mixed Topping Joint Compound

SHEETROCK Brand Ready-Mixed All Purpose Joint Compound

SHEETROCK Brand Textures

	Product	SHEETROCK Brand Ceiling Spray Texture (QT) (Fine)	SHEETROCK Brand Ceiling Spray Texture (QT) (Medium)	SHEETROCK Brand Ceiling Spray Texture (QT) (Coarse)	SHEETROCK Brand Wall and Ceiling Spray Texture (Aggregated)
Surfaces	prime coat required	yes	yes	yes	yes
	ceilings	yes	yes	yes	yes
	walls	no	no	no	yes
Properties	type of aggregate	polystyrene	polystyrene	polystyrene	perlite
	aggregate size	fine	medium	course	fine-med.
	ability to hide sub-strate imperfections	good	excellent	excellent	very good
	water dilution gal./lb.[4]	varies**	varies**	varies**	4-5/50, 3-4/40
Application	solution time	very good	very good	very good	good
	machine	yes	yes	yes	yes
	hand	no	no	no	yes
Spray Equipment	pole gun	yes	yes	yes	no
	7E2 type texture gun	yes	yes	yes	yes
	18D type texture gun	no	no	no	yes
	hopper gun	yes	yes	yes	yes
	aggregate fallout (bounce)	min. to. mod.	min. to. mod.	min. to. mod.	min.
	abrasiveness on equipment	min.	min.	min.	mod.
Features	drying time	slow-med.	slow-med.	slow-med.	very fast
	bond of dry aggregate	mod.	mod.	mod.	good
	dried whiteness	excellent	excellent	excellent	good
	crack resistance	good	good	good	good
	coverage SF/lb. -spray[1]	up to 8	up to 8	up to 8	up to 40
	coverage SF/lb. -hand[1]	N/A	N/A	N/A	N/A

N/A—not applicable   * no primer required under painted walls.   ** Varies—see Chapter 5, "Finishing Drywall Systems." Also see footnotes.

(1) **Coverage,** as considered here, is intended to provide a relative comparison between products when mixed and applied according to directions—not to provide a figure for job estimating. Coverage can vary widely depending on factors such as condition of substrate, amount of dilution, spray techniques and procedures, thickness and uniformity of coating and market preferences in texture appearance.

(2) **Joint Compounds** are designed for treating joints, fasteners, metal bead and trim. However, these products have been used in many markets for hand-applied textures and because of this trade practice, are included as texturing materials.

(3) SHEETROCK Ready-Mixed Topping Joint Compound is not recommended for texturing in all areas. Check local sales office for suitability of joint compound in your area.

(4) Water dilution properties shown here are only approximate. Check product container for actual dilution requirements.

Texture/Compound Selector

Product	SHEETROCK Brand Wall and Ceiling Spray Texture (Unaggregated)	SHEETROCK Brand Wall & Ceiling Spray Texture (TUF-TEX)	SHEETROCK Brand Wall and Ceiling Texture Multi-Purpose	SHEETROCK Brand Wall and Ceiling Spray Texture Sand Finish Texture 12
Surfaces prime coat required	yes	yes	yes	yes
ceilings	yes	yes	yes	yes
walls	yes	yes	yes	yes
Properties type of aggregate	N/A	N/A	N/A	perlite
aggregate size	N/A	N/A	N/A	fine
ability to hide sub-strate imperfections	good	good	good	good
water dilution gal./lb.[4]	4-5/50, 3-4/40	4-4.8/40	2-3/25, 3-4/40	2-1/2–3-1/4/25
Application solution time	good	good	good	good
machine	yes	yes	yes	yes
hand	yes	yes	yes	no
Spray Equipment pole gun	no	no	no	no
7E2 type texture gun	yes	yes	yes	no
18D type texture gun	yes	yes	yes	yes
hopper gun	yes	yes	yes	yes
aggregate fallout (bounce)	N/A	N/A	N/A	min.
abrasiveness on equipment	min.	min.	min.	mod.
Features drying time	fast	fast	fast	fast
bond of dry aggregate	N/A	N/A	N/A	excellent
dried whiteness	good	good	good	very good
crack resistance	good	good	good	good
coverage SF/lb. -spray[1]	up to 40	up to 40	up to 20	20-35
coverage SF/lb. -hand[1]	N/A	10-20	10-15	N/A

N/A—not applicable   * no primer required under painted walls.   ** Varies—see Chapter 5. Also see footnotes.

(1) **Coverage,** as considered here, is intended to provide a relative comparison between products when mixed and applied according to directions—not to provide a figure for job estimating. Coverage can vary widely depending on factors such as condition of substrate, amount of dilution, spray techniques and procedures, thickness and uniformity of coating and market preferences in texture appearance.

(2) **Joint Compounds** are designed for treating joints, fasteners, metal bead and trim. However, these products have been used in many markets for hand-applied textures and because of this trade practice, are included as texturing materials.

(3) SHEETROCK Ready-Mixed Topping Joint Compound is not recommended for texturing in all areas. Check local sales office for suitability of joint compound in your area.

(4) Water dilution properties shown here are only approximate. Check product container for actual dilution requirements.

Texture/Compound Selector

Texture Finishes

Product		USG Acoustical Plaster Finish	USG Ready-Mixed Texture Compound	SHEETROCK Brand Powder All-Purpose[2]
Surfaces	prime coat required	yes	yes*	yes
	ceilings	yes	yes	yes
	walls	no	yes	no
Properties	type of aggregate	polystyrene	N/A	N/A
	aggregate size	fine-medium	N/A	N/A
	ability to hide substrate imperfections	excellent	very good	very good
	water dilution gal./lb.[4]	3.5/30	1/2-2 / 50	2-1/4–2-3/4 / 25
Application	solution time	good	N/A	good
	machine	yes	yes	no
	hand	no	yes	yes
Spray Equipment	pole gun	yes	no	no
	7E2 type texture gun	yes	yes	no
	18D type texture gun	no	yes	no
	hopper gun	no	yes	no
	aggregate fallout (bounce)	min. to. mod.	N/A	N/A
	abrasiveness on equipment	min.	min.	min.
Features	drying time	slow	slow-med.	slow-med.
	bond of dry aggregate	very good	N/A	N/A
	dried whiteness	good	fair	good
	crack resistance	excellent	good	good
	coverage SF/lb. -spray[1]	1-1/2 – 3	7-8	N/A
	coverage SF/lb. -hand[1]	N/A	4-6	4-7

N/A—not applicable   * no primer required under painted walls.   ** Varies—see Chapter 5. Also see footnotes.

(1) **Coverage,** as considered here, is intended to provide a relative comparison between products when mixed and applied according to directions—not to provide a figure for job estimating. Coverage can vary widely depending on factors such as condition of substrate, amount of dilution, spray techniques and procedures, thickness and uniformity of coating and market preferences in texture appearance.

(2) **Joint Compounds** are designed for treating joints, fasteners, metal bead and trim. However, these products have been used in many markets for hand-applied textures and because of this trade practice, are included as texturing materials.

(3) SHEETROCK Ready-Mixed Topping Joint Compound is not recommended for texturing in all areas. Check local sales office for suitability of joint compound in your area.

(4) Water dilution properties shown here are only approximate. Check product container for actual dilution requirements.

Texture/Compound Selector

Texture Finishes

Product		SHEETROCK Brand Ready-Mixed Topping[3] or All-Purpose[2]	SHEETROCK Brand Lightweight All Purpose Joint Compound (PLUS 3)[2]
Surfaces	prime coat required	yes*	yes*
	ceilings	yes	yes
	walls	yes/no[3]	no
Properties	type of aggregate	N/A	N/A
	aggregate size	N/A	N/A
	ability to hide substrate imperfections	very good	very good
	water dilution gal./lb.[4]	1–1-1/2 / 62	1–1-1/2 / 40
Application	solution time	N/A	N/A
	machine	no	no
	hand	yes	yes
Spray Equipment	pole gun	no	no
	7E2 type texture gun	no	no
	18D type texture gun	no	no
	hopper gun	no	no
	aggregate fallout (bounce)	N/A	N/A
	abrasiveness on equipment	min.	min.
Features	drying time	slow-med.	slow-med.
	bond of dry aggregate	N/A	N/A
	dried whiteness	good	fair
	crack resistance	good	good
	coverage SF/lb. -spray[1]	N/A	N/A
	coverage SF/lb. -hand[1]	6-11	9-17

N/A—not applicable   * no primer required under painted walls.   ** Varies—see Chapter 5. Also see footnotes.

(1) **Coverage,** as considered here, is intended to provide a relative comparison between products when mixed and applied according to directions—not to provide a figure for job estimating. Coverage can vary widely depending on factors such as condition of substrate, amount of dilution, spray techniques and procedures, thickness and uniformity of coating and market preferences in texture appearance.

(2) **Joint Compounds** are designed for treating joints, fasteners, metal bead and trim. However, these products have been used in many markets for hand-applied textures and because of this trade practice, are included as texturing materials.

(3) SHEETROCK Ready-Mixed Topping Joint Compound is not recommended for texturing in all areas. Check local sales office for suitability of joint compound in your area.

(4) Water dilution properties shown here are only approximate. Check product container for actual dilution requirements.

Interior Patch & Repair Products

Finished interior walls are subject to abuse and damage from time to time. USG has developed a line of repair products to deal with a variety of holes, cracks, dents and abrasions. Many of these products may be found in retail hardware and home center stores.

SHEETROCK **Brand Spackling Powder** Easy-to-mix hole-filling compound.

SHEETROCK Brand Spackling Powder

SHEETROCK **Brand Plaster of Paris** Fast-setting plaster excellent for first fill of large holes. Expands upon setting. Not sandable.

SHEETROCK Brand Plaster of Paris

SHEETROCK **Brand Floor Patch/Leveler** High-compressive-strength compound for leveling concrete floors or patching holes in concrete. Expands upon setting.

SHEETROCK Brand Floor Patch/Leveler

SHEETROCK Brand Patching Plaster Fiber-reinforced plaster for patching larger holes in plaster or drywall walls. Expands upon setting. Not sandable.

SHEETROCK Brand Patching Plaster

SHEETROCK Brand Patching Compound, EASY SAND 5 Easy-to-mix, low-expansion compound for quick fills and rapid finishing of cracks and holes. Working time of 5–10 minutes.

SHEETROCK Brand Patching Compound

SHEETROCK Brand Drywall Repair Clips Metal clips that provide for ready attachment of a drywall patch to an existing wall. Use with replacement drywall to repair larger holes.

SHEETROCK Brand Drywall Repair Clips

Framing

General Requirements

The choice and installation of framing materials and methods depends on a number of factors. In the case of wood framing, these include the species, size and grade of lumber. For steel framing, factors include the cross-sectional shape of the framing member, as well as the size, thickness and grade of steel. Equally important are the wall height, stud spacing and maximum span of the surfacing material. Steel stud size is usually derived from limiting heights tables, which are based on the capacity of the steel and the allowable deflection of finish surfaces. The limiting heights tables included in *The Gypsum Construction Handbook* are from the Steel Stud Manufacturers Association, SSMA, *Product Technical Information Manual*. Current SSMA information on steel stud properties and limiting heights can be found on their website **ssma.com**. USG presents these limiting heights as a reference, but is not responsible for resulting wall performance.

Tip
For framing safety instructions, see Chapter 13, "Safety Considerations & Material Handling."

Loads Framing members must be selected according to their ability to support the loads to which they will be subjected. These include live loads (contributed by the occupancy and elements such as wind, snow and earthquake) and dead loads (weight of the structure itself). Minimum lateral load for interior partitions is 5 psf; for exterior walls 15 psf to 45 psf—or greater depending on building height and geographic location. Design loads are determined based on model building codes with jurisdiction in the local area.

Deflection Even though an assembly is structurally capable of withstanding a given load, its use may be restricted if the amount of deflection that would occur when the lateral load is applied exceeds that which the surfacing materials can sustain without damage. The deflection criteria used in a design are dictated by the surfacing material and desired stiffness of the assembly.

For drywall assemblies it is desirable to limit deflection to L/240 (L = length of the span in inches) and to never exceed L/120 (L/180 in some codes). The preferred limit for veneer assemblies is L/360 and should not exceed L/240. Using L/240 as an example, and where the length of a span (distance between framing members) is 10', deflection is determined as follows:

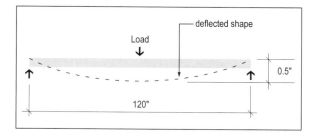

$$D = \text{Deflection Limit} = \frac{L}{240}$$

$$L = 10' \text{ or } 120"$$

$$D = \frac{120}{240}$$

$$D = 0.5"$$

Bending Stress Framing members also must withstand any unit force exerted that will break or buckle the stud, based on the individual stud strength/capacity.

End Reaction Shear This factor is determined by the amount of force applied to the stud that will bend or shear the runner or buckle the web of the stud.

Frame Spacing A factor in load-carrying capability and deflection, it also is a limiting factor for the finishing materials. Every finishing or surfacing material is subject to a span limitation—the maximum distance between framing members that a material can span without undue sagging. For that reason, "maximum frame spacing" tables for the various board products are included in this chapter. However, where frame spacing exceeds maximum limits, furring members can be installed to provide necessary sag-resistance support for the surfacing material.

Insulation and Services Chase walls provide vertical shafts where greater core widths are needed for pipe runs and other service installations. These walls consist of a double row of studs with gypsum panel or metal cross-braces between rows. Plumbing, HVAC and electrical piping, vents and wiring within the framing cavities must be flush with or inside the plane of the framing. Fasteners used to assemble the framing must be driven reasonably flush with the surfaces.

In wood frame construction, the flanges of batt-type insulation must be attached to the sides of frame members, not to their faces. Any obstruction on the face of frame members that will prevent firm contact between the gypsum board and framing can result in loose or damaged board and fastener imperfections.

Wood Framing

Wood framing must meet the following minimum requirements for proper performance of all gypsum drywall and plaster base assemblies:

1. Framework should meet the minimum requirements of applicable building codes.

2. Framing members should be straight, true and of uniform dimension. Studs and joists must be in true alignment; bridging, fire stops, pipes, etc., must not protrude beyond framing.

3. All framing lumber should be the correct grade for the intended use, and 2" x 4" nominal size or larger should bear the grade mark of a recognized inspection agency.

4. All framing lumber should have a moisture content of 19% or less at the time of gypsum board application.

Failure to observe these minimum framing requirements, which are applicable to screw, nail and adhesive attachment, will substantially increase the possibility of fastener failure and surface distortion due to warping or dimensional changes. This is particularly true if the framing lumber used has greater than normal tendencies to warp or shrink after erection.

The moisture content of wood framing should be allowed to adjust as closely as possible to the level it will reach in service before gypsum drywall or plaster base application begins. After the building is enclosed, delay board application as long as possible (consistent with schedule requirements) to allow the moisture content adjustment to take place.

Framing should be designed to accommodate shrinkage in wide dimensional lumber such as is used for floor joists or headers. Gypsum wallboard and veneer plaster surfaces can buckle or crack if firmly anchored across the flat grain of these wide wood members as shrinkage occurs. When building tall, uninterrupted walls, such as are a part of cathedral ceiling designs or in two-story stairwells, regular or modified balloon framing can minimize the problem.

Framing Corrections If joists are out of alignment, 2" x 6" leveling plates may be attached perpendicular to and across the tops of ceiling joists. Toenailing into joists pulls framing into true horizontal alignment and ensures a smooth, level ceiling surface. Bowed or warped studs in non-load-bearing partitions may be straightened by sawing the hollow sides at the middle of the bow and driving a wedge into the saw kerf until the stud is in line. Reinforcement of the stud is accomplished by securely nailing 1" x 4" wood strips or "scabs" on each side of the cut.

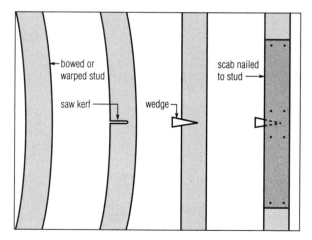

Framing Member Spacing

To ensure adequate support for gypsum panels and the integrity of walls and ceilings, attention must be paid to the distance between framing members. Spacing requirements will depend on a number of variables, including the location of the paneled surface (ceiling or wall), the thickness of the gypsum panels, the number of panel layers on each side of the completed wall, and the orientation of the panels to the framing members. For a fire-rated assembly, the frame spacing may also be limited based on the test design. For thicker gypsum panels or double-layer applications, the distance between framing members can be increased. For wood framing installed in the conventional manner, with lumber meeting requirements outlined above, maximum frame spacing is as shown in the tables on the following pages.

2

Maximum Frame Spacing—Drywall Construction

Direct Application

Panel thickness[1]	Location	Application method[2]	Max. frame spacing o.c.	
Single-Layer Application			in.	mm
3/8″ (9.5 mm)	ceilings[3]	perpendicular[4]	16	406
	sidewalls	perpendicular	16	406
		parallel	16	406
1/2″ (12.7 mm)	ceilings	perpendicular	24[5][6]	610
		parallel[4]	16	406
	sidewalls	parallel or perpendicular	24	610
		parallel[4]	16	406
5/8″ (15.9 mm)	ceilings[6]	perpendicular	24	610
	sidewalls	parallel or perpendicular	24	610
Double-Layer Application				
3/8″ (9.5 mm)	ceilings[7]	perpendicular	16	406
	sidewalls	perpendicular or parallel	24[8]	610
1/2″ & 5/8″ (12.7 & 15.9 mm)	ceilings	perpendicular or parallel	24[8]	610
	sidewalls	perpendicular	24[8]	610

(1) 5/8″ thickness is recommended for the finest single-layer construction, providing increased resistance to fire and transmission of sound; 1/2″ for single-layer application in new residential construction and remodeling; and 3/8″ for repair and remodeling over existing surfaces. (2) Long edge position relative to framing. (3) Not recommended below unheated spaces. (4) Not recommended if water-based texturing material is to be applied. (5) Max. spacing 16″ if water-based texturing material is to be applied. (6) If 1/2″ SHEETROCK brand Sag-Resistant Ceiling Board is used, max. spacing is 24″ o.c. for perpendicular or parallel application with water based texture, and the weight of unsupported insulation not exceeding 2.2 psf. (7) Adhesive must be used to laminate 3/8″ board for double-layer ceilings. (8) Max spacing 16″ o.c. if fire rating required.

Maximum Frame Spacing—Veneer Plaster Construction
Direct Application

Gypsum base thickness	Construction	Location	Application method[1]	Max. frame spacing o.c. in.	mm
1/2" (12.7 mm)	one layer, 1-coat finish	ceilings	perpendicular	16	406
		sidewalls	perpendicular or parallel	16	406
	one layer, 2-coat finish	ceilings	perpendicular	16 or 24[2]	406 or 610[2]
		sidewalls	perpendicular or parallel	16 or 24[2]	406 or 610[2]
	two layer, 1 & 2-coat finish	ceilings	perpendicular	24	610
		sidewalls	perpendicular or parallel	24	610
5/8" (15.9 mm)	one layer, 1-coat finish	ceilings	perpendicular	16 or 24[2]	406 or 610[2]
		sidewalls	perpendicular or parallel	16 or 24[2]	406 or 610[2]
	one layer, 2-coat finish	ceilings	perpendicular	24[2]	610[2]
		sidewalls	perpendicular or parallel	24[2]	610[2]
	two layer, 1 & 2-coat finish	ceilings	perpendicular	24	610
		sidewalls	perpendicular or parallel	24	610

(1) Perpendicular preferred on all applications for maximum strength. Where fire rating is involved, application must be identical to that in assembly tested. Parallel application not recommended for ceilings. (2) 24" o.c. frame spacing with either one or two-coat veneer application requires Sheetrock Brand Joint Tape Reinforcement and Sheetrock Brand Setting-Type (Durabond or Easy Sand) Joint Compound.

Sagging To prevent objectionable sag in new gypsum panel ceilings, the weight of overlaid unsupported insulation should not exceed 1.3 psf for 1/2" thick panels with frame spacing 24" o.c.; 2.2 psf for 1/2" panels with frame spacing 16" o.c. (or 1/2" Sheetrock interior gypsum ceiling panels, sag-resistant, with framing 24" o.c.) and 5/8" panels 24" o.c. Panels 3/8" thick must not be overlaid with unsupported insulation. A separate vapor retarder should be installed where required in roofed ceilings, and the plenum or attic space vented with a minimum 1 SF of free vent area per 150 SF of horizontal space, or per local code.

See "Ceiling Sag Precautions" on page 345 for more information on the application of water-based textures and interior finishing materials.

Resilient Application On ceiling assemblies of both drywall and veneer plaster, install resilient channels perpendicular to framing and spaced 24" o.c. for joists 16" o.c. Channels should be spaced 16" o.c. for joists 24" o.c. For sidewalls, install channels at 24" o.c. maximum. See single-layer sections in tables on the preceding pages for limitations for specific board thicknesses. Fasten channels to framing with screws only.

Note: As an alternate to resilient channel for ceiling construction, drywall suspension, described below, may be used in conjunction with wood framing to achieve fire and acoustic separation design requirements. Specific assembly designs, searchable by minimum fire separation, STC and IIC are available at **usgdesignstudio.com**. Assemblies are available in downloadable PDF, CAD and REVIT files.

Spray-Textured Ceilings Where water-based texturing materials or any slow-drying surface treatments are used over single-layer panels, maximum frame spacing is 16" o.c. for 1/2" panels applied perpendicular to framing. Parallel application is not recommended, nor is use of 3/8" thick panels. For best results use Sʜᴇᴇᴛʀᴏᴄᴋ brand interior ceiling board, sag-resistant, with maximum spacing 24" o.c. Note: Airless spraying of latex paint in one heavy application (10 to 14 mil) may also cause ceilings to sag between framing members. See "Ceiling Sag Precautions" in Chapter 10, "System Design Considerations."

Water-based texturing materials applied to ceilings should be completely dry before insulation and vapor retarder are installed. Under most conditions, drying takes several days.

Partition Layout

Properly position partitions according to layout. Snap caulk lines at ceiling and floor. Be certain that partitions will be plumb. Where partitions occur parallel to and between joists, ladder blocking must be installed between ceiling joists. Double joists are recommended beneath partitions.

Steel Framing

Steel stud framing for non-load-bearing interior partitions is secured to floors and ceilings with runners fastened to the supporting structure.

Runner Installation

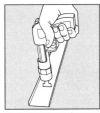

Fastening channel runners

Fastening angles

Securely attach runners to:

1. **Concrete and masonry** using stub nails, power-driven fasteners.

2. **Foam-backed metal (max. 14-ga.) concrete inserts** using 3/8" type S-12 pan head screws.

3. **Suspended ceilings** using expandable hollow wall anchors, toggle bolts, screws or other suitable fasteners

4. **Wood framing** using 1-1/4" type S oval head screws or 8d nails

To all substrates, secure runners with fasteners located 2" from each end and spaced a maximum of 24" o.c. (Tall walls require that fasteners be spaced closer together. Contact the steel stud manufacturer for more detailed information.) Attach runner ends at door frames with two anchors when three-piece frames are used. (One-piece frames should be supplied with welded-in-place floor anchor plates, pre-punched for two anchors into structure.)

At partition corners, extend one runner to the end of the corner and butt the other runner to it. Runners should not be mitered.

Interior Framing Limiting Heights

Stud Depth (in.)	Stud Spacing (in.)	Design Limit (psf)	Allowable Deflection	(18 mil) 25 Gauge 0.01799 min. (0.455 mm min.)		(33 mil) 20 Gauge 0.03299 min. (0.836 mm min.)	
				ft.-in.	(mm)	ft.-in.	(mm)
1-5/8 (162S125-18/33)	24	5	L/120	9-9	(2970)	11-0	(3350)
1-5/8 (162S125-18/33)	24	5	L/240	7-11	(2410)	8-9	(2670)
1-5/8 (162S125-18/33)	24	5	L/360	7-1	(2160)	7-8	(2030)
1-5/8 (162S125-18/33)	16	5	L/120	10-7	(3230)	12-1	(3680)
1-5/8 (162S125-18/33)	16	5	L/240	8-4	(2540)	9-8	(2950)
1-5/8 (162S125-18/33)	16	5	L/360	8-2	(2490)	8-5	(2570)
2-1/2 (250S125-18/33)	24	5	L/120	11-10	(3610)	14-10	(4520)
2-1/2 (250S125-18/33)	24	5	L/240	10-7	(3230)	11-7	(3530)
2-1/2 (250S125-18/33)	24	5	L/360	9-3	(2820)	10-0	(3050)
2-1/2 (250S125-18/33)	16	5	L/120	13-3	(4040)	16-5	(5000)
2-1/2 (250S125-18/33)	16	5	L/240	11-3	(3430)	12-10	(3910)
2-1/2 (250S125-18/33)	16	5	L/360	9-10	(3000)	11-2	(3400)
3-5/8 (362S125-18/33)	24	5	L/120	13-9	(4190)	18-6	(5640)
3-5/8 (362S125-18/33)	24	5	L/240	13-5	(4090)	14-9	(4500)
3-5/8 (362S125-18/33)	24	5	L/360	11-7	(3530)	12-9	(3890)
3-5/8 (362S125-18/33)	16	5	L/120	15-4	(4670)	20-8	(6300)
3-5/8 (362S125-18/33)	16	5	L/240	14-4	(4370)	16-5	(5000)
3-5/8 (362S125-18/33)	16	5	L/360	12-4	(3760)	14-3	(4340)
4 (400S125-18/33)	24	5	L/120	15-1	(4600)	20-9	(6330)
4 (400S125-18/33)	24	5	L/240	14-2	(4320)	16-5	(5000)
4 (400S125-18/33)	24	5	L/360	12-4	(3760)	14-3	(4340)
4 (400S125-18/33)	16	5	L/120	17-2	(5230)	23-1	(7040)
4 (400S125-18/33)	16	5	L/240	15-4	(4670)	18-4	(5590)
4 (400S125-18/33)	16	5	L/360	13-4	(4060)	15-11	(4850)
6 (600S125-18/33)	24	5	L/120	16-9	(5110)	27-2	(8280)
6 (600S125-18/33)	24	5	L/240	16-9	(5110)	21-7	(6580)
6 (600S125-18/33)	24	5	L/360	16-9	(5110)	18-10	(5740)
6 (600S125-18/33)	16	5	L/120	19-9	(6020)	30-10	(9400)
6 (600S125-18/33)	16	5	L/240	19-9	(6020)	24-6	(7470)
6 (600S125-18/33)	16	5	L/360	17-11	(5770)	21-4	(6500)

Notes: The number following the stud depth is new industry-wide product identification, created by the Steel Stud Manufacturers Association; the number identifies the member depth, style, flange width and material thickness in mils.

This limiting heights data is from ASTM C754. USG presents this information only as a reference, and will not be responsible for the performance of walls based on this table. Consult current information from ASTM C754 and SSMA (Steel Stud Manufacturers Association ssma.com), and the stud manufacturers for limiting heights characteristics of their particular products.

Limiting heights apply to walls constructed with minimum 1/2" (12.7 mm) thickness of gypsum board and with a minimum of one full-height layer on both sides of the stud framing.

Limiting heights are based on tests conducted with gypsum board attached with screws spaced 12" (305 mm) o.c. to framing members.

Stud Installation

Insert floor-to-ceiling steel studs between runners, twisting them into position. Position studs vertically, with the open sides facing in same direction, engaging floor and ceiling runners and spaced 16" or 24" o.c. maximum, as required. Proper alignment will provide for proper bracing, utility runs and prevention of stepped or uneven joint surfaces. The recommended practice for most installations is to anchor to the runner track only those studs adjacent to door and borrowed light frames. This would also be applicable to partition intersections and corners. In cases where a significant slab live load deflection must be accommodated, anchoring these studs may restrict slab movement and cause partition cracking. In such cases, stud anchoring may need to be omitted. A design professional can identify these instances and address them on a case-specific basis.

2

Steel studs are positioned in floor and ceiling runners.

Place studs in direct contact with all door frame jambs, abutting partitions, partition corners and existing construction elements. Spot grouting of door frames with a suitable joint compound is always suggested and is required where heavy or oversize doors are used. Contact door frame manufacturers for specific requirements and recommendations.

Where a stud directly abuts an exterior wall, and there is a possibility of condensation or water penetration through the wall, place a No. 15 asphalt felt strip between the stud and the wall surface.

Place a section of runner horizontally with a web-flange bent at each end over metal doors and borrowed light frames. Secure the runner to the strut-studs with two screws in each bent web. For vertical joints over the door frame header, install a cut-to-length stud extending to the ceiling runner. (See "Framing—Door & Window Openings" section later in this chapter.)

Contact the steel stud manufacturer for their specific recommendations when stud splicing is required.

Resilient Channel Framing—Steel Framing

Stud System Installation Attach steel runners to structural elements at the floor and ceiling with suitable fasteners located 2" from each end and spaced 24" o.c. Position studs vertically, with the open sides facing in same direction, engaging floor and ceiling runners, and spaced 24" o.c. For non-fire-rated resilient channel systems, anchor the studs to the floor and ceiling runners on the resilient side of the partition. Fasten the runner to the stud flange with 3/8" type S pan head screw.

Resilient Channel Installation Position resilient channel at right angles to steel studs, spaced 24" o.c., and attach it to stud flanges with 3/8" type S pan head screws driven through holes in channel mounting flange. Install channels with the mounting flange down, except at the floor, to accommodate attachment. A strip of gypsum panel is sometimes used at the base of a partition in lieu of the first inverted resilient channel. Locate channels 2" from the floor and within 6" of the ceiling. Splice channel by nesting directly over the stud and screw-attach it through both flanges. Reinforce it with screws located at both ends of the splice.

Chase Wall Framing

Align two parallel rows of floor and ceiling runners according to partition layout. Spacing between outside flanges of each pair of runners must not exceed 24". Follow instructions above for attaching runners.

Position steel studs vertically in runners, with flanges in the same direction, and with studs on opposite sides of the chase directly across from each other. Except in fire-rated walls, anchor all studs to floor and ceiling runner flanges with 3/8" or 1/2" type S pan head screws.

For cross-bracing, cut gypsum board to be placed between rows of studs. It should be 12" high and the width required for the chase wall. Space braces 48" o.c. vertically and attach them to the stud web with screws spaced 8" o.c. maximum per brace.

Steel studs can also be used for bracing. Use 2-1/2" minimum steel studs. Anchor the web at each end of the metal brace to the stud web with two 3/8" pan head screws. When chase wall studs are not opposite one another, install steel stud cross-braces 24" o.c. horizontally, and securely anchor each end to a continuous horizontal 2-1/2" runner, screw-attached to chase wall studs within the cavity.

Methods of cross bracing

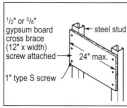

Gypsum brace

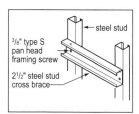

Steel stud brace

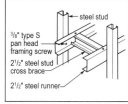

Steel stud & runner brace

Drywall & Plaster Ceiling Suspension Systems

Suspended drywall and plaster ceilings can be framed with conventional framing materials or drywall suspension systems. Conventionally framed suspended ceilings typically include the use of carrying channel and furring or "hat" channel suspended by 8- or 9-gauge hanger wire. Drywall suspension systems are a time saving alternative to traditional framing. These grid systems are comprised of a selection of main and cross tees that can be used for a variety of suspended ceiling applications. These systems include labor saving accessories that reduce hanger wire and speed design details such as control joints, light fixtures and utility framing.

USG Drywall Suspension System

The USG drywall suspension system includes a selection of main tees, cross tees and accessories designed for framing suspended ceilings and soffits. The system includes solutions for flat ceilings, corridors and small rooms, and curved ceilings. The system can be used with gypsum panels or plaster and in interior and exterior applications.

2

Flat Ceilings

Main tees shall be spaced a maximum of 72" on center and supported with hanger wires spaced a maximum 48" on center. Cross tees, if required, are spaced in accordance with manufacturer's recommendations. For fire-resistive assemblies, the hanger wire, main tees and cross tees shall be spaced in accordance with the assembly design. Searchable fire resistive assemblies with downloadable PDF, CAD or REVIT files are available on **usgdesignstudio.com** or refer to the UL directory.

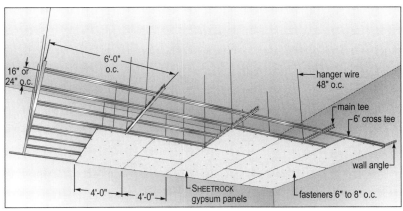

Flat ceilings

Small Rooms and Corridors

Wall-to-wall main tees are spaced 16" or 24". Wall-to-wall main tees can span up to 8' unsupported with a single layer of 1/2" gypsum panels and up to 7'-6" with a single layer of 5/8" gypsum panels. With center support or support at 1/3 points, wall-to-wall main tees can be used to span rooms or corridors up to 24'. Refer to the system catalog AC3152 for load tables.

Curved Ceilings

Space valley and vault main tees a maximum 48". Space hanger wires a maximum 48" for vault main tees, and a maximum 24" for valley main tees. Space cross tees per manufacturers' recommendations. Additional hanger wires may be necessary to stabilize any curved ceiling during and after drywall attachment.

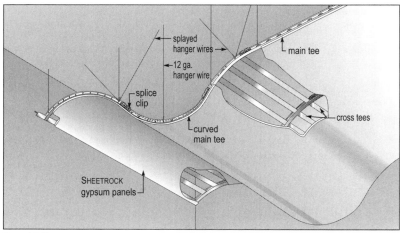

Curved Ceilings

**Transitions:
Changes in
Elevation
in Soffit
and Fascia**

When constructing stepped soffits, it may be necessary to brace the drywall suspension system and/or install additional hanger wires to ensure stability and structural performance during and after drywall attachment. The maximum vertical soffit height is 48". (Maximum un-supported drywall area shall not exceed 48" x 24".) Intermediate cross tees are not necessary unless bulkhead dimensions exceed 24".

Cross tee spacing in a horizontal soffit plane should not exceed 24". Intermediate cross tees may be necessary to maintain visually acceptable drywall planes and corners.

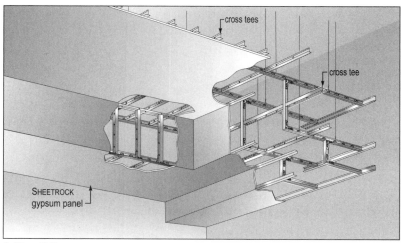

Soffits on Ceilings

General Hanger Wire Notes   Hanger wires are required within 12" on both sides of a pivoted splice clip. At least 1 hanger wire is required within 12" of a transition clip.

Limitations   Do not support wires from mechanical and/or electrical equipment above the ceiling.

Accessories   Install accessories as applicable to meet project requirements. System accessories are outlined in the system catalog AC3152.

Gypsum Panel Installation   Apply gypsum panels first to the ceiling and then to walls. Position all ends and edges of gypsum panels at framing members. Extend the ceiling board to the corners and make firm contact with the wall angle, channel or top plate. To minimize end joints, use panels of maximum practical lengths. Fit ends and edges closely, but don't force them together.

Cut ends and edges and scribe or make cut-outs within the field of panels in a workmanlike manner. Cut and score gypsum board to size using a knife and straight edge.

Attach gypsum panels to the suspension system's main runners, cross tees and cross channels with conventional gypsum panel fasteners (No. 6 type S HiLo bugle head, self-drilling, self-tapping steel screws) spaced 8" o.c. at the periphery of gypsum panels and located 3/8" in from panel edges and spaced 12" o.c. in the field. To keep the surface flat, drive fasteners in the field of panels first, working toward ends and edges. Hold panels in firm contact with the framing while driving fasteners slightly below the surface of gypsum panels in a uniform dimple—without breaking the face paper.

Install trim at all internal and external angles formed by the intersection of panel surfaces or other dissimilar materials. Apply corner bead to all vertical or horizontal external corners in accordance with manufacturer's directions.

Traditionally Framed Suspended Ceilings

Furring Channels   Space metal furring channels 24" o.c. at right angles to bar joists or other structural members. As an alternate, 1-5/8" steel studs may be used as furring. Saddle-tie furring channels to bar joists with triple-strand 18-ga. tie wire at each intersection. Provide 1" clearance between furring ends and abutting walls and partitions. At splices, nest furring channels with at least an 8" overlap and securely wire-tie each end with triple-strand 18-ga. tie wire. Frame around openings such as light troffers with additional furring channels and wire-tie them to bar joists.

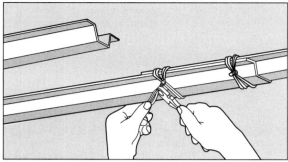

Wire Tieing Hat Channel

Maximum allowable spacing for metal furring channels is 24" o.c. for 1/2" and 5/8" thick gypsum panels or plaster base. See frame spacing tables below for limiting spans.

For bar joist spacing up to 60", steel studs may be used as furring channels. Wire-tie studs to the supporting framing as shown in the following diagram. Position 1-5/8" studs with open side up; position larger studs with opening to side. See table below for stud spacing and limiting spans.

Limiting Span[1]—Metal Furring Members[2]

Type furring member	Member spacing (in. o.c.)	Single layer panels (2.5 psf max.)		Double layer panels (5.0 psf max.)	
		1-span	3-span	1-span	3-span
DWC-25-ga.	16	5'9"	7'1"	4'7"	5'8"
	24	5'0"	6'2"	4'0"	4'11"
DWC-20-ga.	16	6'11"	8'6"	5'5"	6'9"
	24	6'0"	7'5"	4'9"	5'11"
1-5/8" stud, 25-ga.	16	7'2"	8'10"	5'8"	7'0"
	24	6'3"	7'9"	5'0"	6'2"

(1) For beams, joists, purling, sub-purling; not including 1-1/2" cold rolled channel support spaced 4'0" max. Check Manufacturer's literature to verify that the selected furring member is appropriate for the indicated span. (2) Limiting spans for 1/2" and 5/8" thick panels, max. L/240 deflection and uniform load shown. Evaluate concentrated loads such as light fixtures and exhaust fans separately.

Metal furring channel

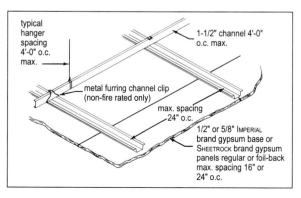

typical hanger spacing 4'-0" o.c. max.

1-1/2" channel 4'-0" o.c. max.

metal furring channel clip (non-fire rated only)

max. spacing 24" o.c.

1/2" or 5/8" IMPERIAL brand gypsum base or SHEETROCK brand gypsum panels regular or foil-back max. spacing 16" or 24" o.c.

Steel stud furring

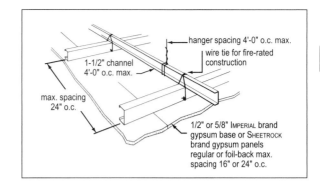

Control joint

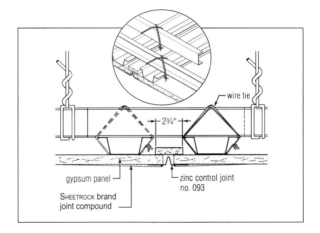

Suspended Ceiling Grillage

Space 8-ga. hanger wires 48" o.c. along carrying channels and within 6" of ends of carrying-channel runs. In concrete, anchor hangers by erection attachment to reinforcing steel, by loops embedded at least 2" or using approved inserts. For steel construction, wrap the hanger around or through beams or joists. Do not attach components to air ducts.

Install 1-1/2" carrying channels 48" o.c. (spaced as tested for fire-rated construction) and within 6" of walls. Position channels for proper ceiling height, level and secure with hanger wire saddle-tied along channels. Provide 1" clearance between runners and abutting walls and partitions. At channel splices, interlock flanges, overlaps ends 12" and secure each end with double-strand 18-ga. tie wire.

Erect metal furring channels at right angles to 1-1/2" carrying channels. Space furring member within 6" of walls. Provide 1" clearance between furring ends and abutting walls and partitions. Attach furring channels to 1-1/2" channels with wire ties or furring channel clips installed on alternate sides of the carrying channel. Saddle-tie furring to channels with double-strand 18-ga. tie wire when clips cannot be alternated. At splices, nest furring channels with at least an 8" overlap and securely wire-tie each end with double-strand 18-ga. tie wire.

Where required, in fire-rated assemblies, install double furring channels to support gypsum panel ends, and back-block with gypsum board strip. When staggered end joints are not required, control joints may be used.

At light troughs or any openings that interrupt the carrying or furring channels, install additional cross-reinforcing to restore the lateral stability of the grillage.

Steel Stud Framing System

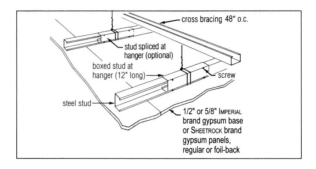

Lighting Fixture

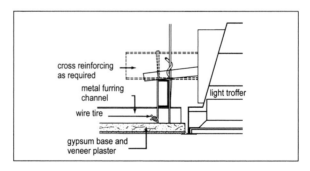

Single span   *Double span*   *Triple span*

Limiting Span—Steel Stud Ceiling System[1]

Stud Style		Stud Spacing (in.)	Single Span (ft.-in.) (uniform load-psf)				Double and Triple Span (ft.-in.) (uniform load-psf)			
			5	10	15	20	5	10	15	20
2-1/2″	25-ga.	12	10′11″	8′8″	7′7″	6′9″	13′6″	10′2″	8′2″	6′11″
		16	9′11″	7′11″	6′10″	5′4″	12′4″	8′8″	6′11″	5′9″
		24	8′8″	6′9″	4′9″	—	10′2″	6′11″	5′9″	4′4″
3-5/8″[2]	25-ga.	12	14′7″	11′7″	9′8″	7′3″	17′5″	11′2″	8′4″	6′8″
		16	13′3″	10′6″	7′3″	5′5″	14′8″	9′2″	6′8″	5′3″
		24	11′7″	7′3″	4′9″	—	11′2″	6′8″	4′9″	—
4″[2]	25-ga.	12	15′9″	12′6″	10′4″	9′0″	17′6″	11′0″	8′0″	6′3″
		16	14′4″	11′0″	9′0″	7′6″	14′7″	8′9″	6′3″	4′10″
		24	12′6″	9′0″	6′8″	5′0″	11′0″	6′3″	4′4″	—
2-1/2″	20-ga.	12	13′2″	10′5″	9′1″	8′3″	16′4″	12′11″	11′4″	10′0″
		16	11′11″	9′6″	8′3″	7′6″	14′10″	11′9″	10′0″	8′9″
		24	10′5″	8′3″	7′3″	6′4″	12′11″	10′1″	8′2″	7′1″
3-5/8″	20-ga.	12	17′6″	13′11″	12′2″	11′0″	21′9″	17′3″	15′0″	13′3″
		16	15′11″	12′8″	11′0″	10′0″	19′9″	15′8″	13′3″	11′6″
		24	13′11″	11′0″	9′8″	8′4″	17′8″	13′3″	10′10″	9′4″
4″	20-ga.	12	19′0″	15′0″	13′2″	11′11″	23′6″	18′8″	16′3″	14′3″
		16	17′3″	13′8″	11′11″	10′10″	21′4″	16′11″	14′3″	12′4″
		24	15′0″	11′11″	10′4″	9′0″	18′8″	14′3″	11′7″	9′9″
6″	20-ga.	12	26′3″	10′10″	18′2″	16′6″	32′6″	25′9″	20′3″	16′10″
		16	23′10″	18′11″	16′6″	14′9″	29′6″	21′10″	16′10″	13′10″
		24	10′10″	16′6″	13′11″	12′0″	25′9″	16′10″	13′10″	10′2″

(1) Based on L/240 allowable deflection. Bracing of top flanges is required and must not exceed 48″ o.c. Check manufacturer's literature to verify that the selected framing member is appropriate for the indicated span. (2) Stud end stiffening required. Additional hangers are necessary when span area exceeds 16 ft.²

Light Fixture Protection When required in fire-rated construction, protection should be installed over recessed lighting fixtures in a direct suspension grid. Cut pieces of 1/2" or 5/8" SHEETROCK brand gypsum panels or IMPERIAL brand gypsum base with FIRECODE C core to form a five-sided enclosure, trapezoidal in cross-section (see detail). Fabricate the box larger than the fixture to provide at least 1/2" clearance, and in accordance with the fire test report.

Light fixture fire protection

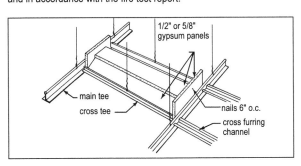

1/2" or 5/8" gypsum panels

main tee

cross tee

nails 6" o.c.

cross furring channel

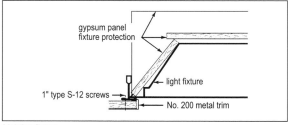

Lighting fixture

Ceilings Note

Spacing of drywall grid is designed to support only the dead load. Heavy concentrated loads should be independently supported. Lighting fixtures or troffers, air vents and other equipment should be separately supported from the structure; gypsum panels will not support these items.

To prevent objectionable sag in new gypsum panel ceilings, the weight of overlaid unsupported insulation should not exceed 1.3 psf for 1/2" thick gypsum panels with spacing of 24" o.c., and 2.2 psf for 1/2" thick gypsum panels 16" o.c. framing. Where SHEETROCK brand interior gypsum ceiling panels, sag-resistant, are used, framing should be spaced 24" o.c. for 1/2" or 5/8" panels. Note that 3/8" thick gypsum panels must not be overlaid with unsupported insulation. Install a vapor retarder in exterior ceilings, and properly vent plenum or attic spaces.

During periods of cold or damp weather when a polyethylene vapor retarder is installed on ceilings behind the gypsum panels, it is important to install the ceiling insulation before or immediately after installing the gypsum panels. Failure to follow this procedure may result in moisture condensation in the back of the gypsum panels, causing them to sag.

Spray-Textured Ceilings

Where water-based texturing materials or any slow-drying surface treatments are used over single-layer panels, maximum frame spacing is 16" o.c. for 1/2" panels applied perpendicular to framing.

Expansion Joints

Provide a separation in the suspension system at expansion joints as shown on the drawings and carry the joint through the gypsum panels. Expansion joints are installed between two main tees to separate the suspension system and allow for movement in large ceiling areas.

Control Joints

Provide control joint No. 093, which has a 3/32" ground for drywall and veneer plaster. Ceiling areas should not exceed 50' (2,500 SF) with perimeter relief, and 30' (900 SF) without perimeter.

Wall Furring

Exterior walls are readily furred using steel or wood furring to which 1/2" regular or foil-back gypsum panels are screw-attached. Use of foil-back board can provide an effective, low-cost vapor retarder in appropriate climates. In these systems, different framing methods may be used to provide for a vapor retarder, thermal insulation, and chase space for pipes, conduits and ducts. Vinyl wall coverings are not recommended in furred walls containing foil-back gypsum panels or plaster base. A qualified mechanical engineer should determine the need for, and location of a vapor retarder.

Metal furring channels are fastened directly to the inside of exterior walls or monolithic concrete and to virtually any type of masonry—brick, concrete block or tile. This economical system provides an excellent vapor retarder and a durable, easily decorated interior surface. Foil-back gypsum panels or plaster base should be screw-attached to channels and appropriate sealants applied at the periphery and penetrations.

Use Z-furring channels with insulating blankets or rigid plastic foam insulation on the inside face of exterior walls. Apply insulation panels progressively as the Z-furring channels are attached to the wall. Gypsum panels are screw-attached to channel flanges to provide an interior surface isolated to a great degree from the brick, concrete or concrete masonry wall. In new construction and remodeling, this system provides insulation properties with a self-furring solid backup for gypsum board installation.

Steel studs erected vertically between floor and ceiling runners serve as free-standing furring for foil-back gypsum panels screw-attached to one side of studs. This free-standing system with 1-5/8" studs provides maximum clear chase space and minimizes possibilities for photographing or shadowing (accumulated dust) to occur. When heights greater than 12'-0" are required, secure the stud framing to the exterior wall with adjustable wall furring brackets at mid-height, in addition to the normal attachment of studs at their head and base. Other furring providing greater height may be constructed with wider and heavier steel studs.

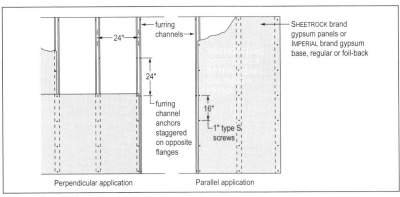

Wall elevation—furring

Temperature differentials on the interior surface of exterior walls may result in collection of dust on the colder areas of the surface. Consequently, shadowing may occur at fastener or furring channel locations where surface temperatures are the lowest. U.S. Gypsum cannot be held responsible for surface discoloration of this nature. Where temperature, humidity and soiling conditions are expected to cause objectionable blemishes, use free-standing furring with insulation against the exterior wall.

Furring Channel Erection— Direct Attachment

Attach metal furring channels to masonry or concrete surfaces, either vertically (preferred) or horizontally (for spacing, see frame spacing tables). For channels positioned horizontally, attach a furring channel not more than 4" from both the floor line and the ceiling line. Secure channels with fasteners placed on alternate channel flanges and spaced 24" o.c. Use a 2" cut nail in mortar joints of brick, clay tile or concrete block, or in the field of lightweight aggregate block; use a 5/8" concrete stub nail or other power-driven fasteners in monolithic concrete.

Channels may be furred using adjustable wall furring brackets and 3/4" cold-rolled channels to provide additional space for pipes, conduits or ducts.

At window locations, attach furring channels horizontally over the substrate returns to support gypsum board at corners (see detail).

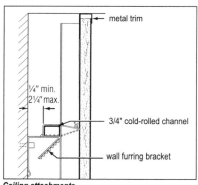

Ceiling attachments — metal trim, 1/4" min. 2 1/4" max., 3/4" cold-rolled channel, wall furring bracket

Suspended ceiling — dustproof membrane, metal furring channel

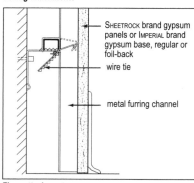

Floor attachments — SHEETROCK brand gypsum panels or IMPERIAL brand gypsum base, regular or foil-back, wire tie, metal furring channel

Direct furring — SHEETROCK brand gypsum panels or IMPERIAL brand gypsum base, regular or foil-back, asphalt strip

Free-Standing Furring

Free-standing furring consists of 1-5/8" steel studs in 1-5/8" steel runners. To erect, plumb and align runners at the desired distance from the exterior wall. Fasten runners to floor and ceiling with suitable anchors. Snap studs into place in runners. (See framing spacing tables for required stud spacing.)

If greater height is required than can be attained with 1-5/8" studs, wider or heavier gauge studs can be used. However, if space is critical, heights greater than 12'-0" can be attained with 1-5/8" studs by bracing them to the exterior wall at mid-height or at more frequent intervals. For bracing, install adjustable furring brackets or sheet metal "L" pieces to the exterior wall and attach it to the stud webs with 3/8" pan head type S screws.

Z-Furring Channel Erection

Erect insulation vertically and hold it in place with Z-furring channels spaced 24" o.c. Except at exterior corners, attach narrow flanges of furring channels to the wall with concrete stub nails or power-driven fasteners spaced 24" o.c. At exterior corners, attach a wide flange of furring channel to the wall with a short flange extending beyond the corner. On the adjacent wall surface, screw-attach a short flange of furring channel to the web of the attached channel. Start from this furring channel with a standard-width insulation panel and continue installing Z-furring and insulation progressively along the wall. At interior corners, space the second channel no more than 12" from the corner and cut the insulation to fit. Hold mineral wool insulation in place until the gypsum panels are installed with 10" long staple, field-fabricated from 18-ga. tie wire and inserted through a slot in the channel. Apply wood or other appropriate blocking around window and door openings and as required for attachment and support of fixtures and furnishings.

Apply gypsum drywall or plaster base panels parallel to channels with vertical joints occurring over channels. Attach gypsum panels with 1" type S screws spaced 16" o.c. in the field and at edges, and with 1-1/4" type S screws spaced 12" o.c. at exterior corners.

Metal window—jamb

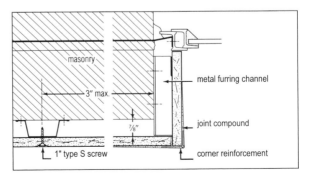

masonry

3″ max.

metal furring channel

⁷⁄₈″

joint compound

1" type S screw

corner reinforcement

Z-furring application details

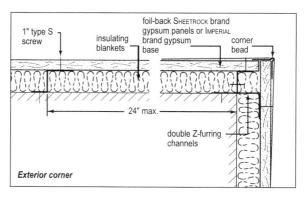

1" type S screw

insulating blankets

foil-back SHEETROCK brand gypsum panels or IMPERIAL brand gypsum base

corner bead

24" max.

double Z-furring channels

Exterior corner

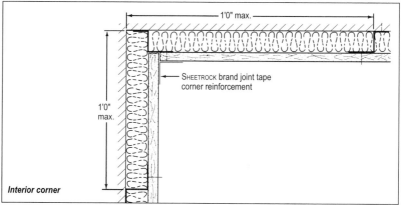

1'0" max.

1'0" max.

SHEETROCK brand joint tape corner reinforcement

Interior corner

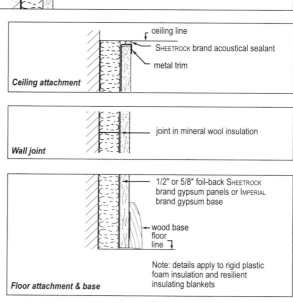

ceiling line

SHEETROCK brand acoustical sealant

metal trim

Ceiling attachment

joint in mineral wool insulation

Wall joint

1/2" or 5/8" foil-back SHEETROCK brand gypsum panels or IMPERIAL brand gypsum base

wood base floor line

Note: details apply to rigid plastic foam insulation and resilient insulating blankets

Floor attachment & base

Z-furring application details

Design of Z-furring channels helps prevent wicking of moisture to inside surfaces.

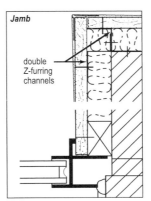

Jamb

double Z-furring channels

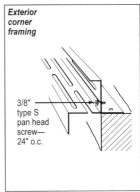

Exterior corner framing

3/8" type S pan head screw— 24" o.c.

2

For gypsum base, space screws 12" o.c. in the field and at edges. For double-layer application, apply the first layer parallel to channels, facing it either perpendicular or parallel to channels, with vertical joints offset at least one channel. Attach the first layer with screws 24" o.c. and attach the face layer with 1-5/8" screws 16" o.c.

Wood Furring Erection

Wood furring strips over wood framing must be 2" x 2" (nom.) minimum size or nail-on application. Strips may be 1" x 3" (nom.) if gypsum board is to be screw-attached.

When panels are to be applied parallel to furring strips securely attached to masonry walls, use strips 2" x 3" or 1" x 3" (nom.) minimum size. Where the long edges of the board are to be applied across the furring, use strips 2" x 2" or 1" x 2" (nom.) minimum size. Space furring strips as specified by frame spacing tables. For board application, select a screw length that will not penetrate through the furring.

Where there is a possibility of water penetration through the walls, install a layer of asphalt felt between the furring strips and the wall surface.

Note: Nail application of gypsum board over 1" (nom.) thickness wood furring applied across framing members is not recommended since the relative flexibility of undersize furring prevents proper fastening and tends to loosen nails already driven.

Resilient Framing—Wood Frame

Resilient attachment of gypsum board with resilient channels provides low-cost, highly efficient, sound-rated drywall and veneer partitions and floor-ceiling assemblies. The steel channels float the panels away from the studs and joists and provide a spring action that isolates the gypsum board from the framing. This spring action also tends to level the panel surface when it is installed over uneven framing. Additional features include excellent fire-resistance (from the total assembly) and simple, fast installation for overall economy. For fire- and sound-resistant assemblies, refer to *USG Fire-Rated Assemblies Catalog, SA100.*

Resilient Channels Partitions

Attach resilient channels flange down and at right angles (perpendicular) to wood studs. Position the bottom channel with the attachment flange up for ease of attachment. Use 1-1/4" type W screws driven through the flanges. Nails are not recommended. Fasten channels to studs at each intersection with the slotted hole directly over a framing member.

Locate channels 2" maximum above the floor, within 6" of the ceiling and at no more than 24" intervals. (For some veneer assemblies, the maximum channel spacing is 16" o.c. Refer to frame spacing tables earlier in this chapter.) Extend channels into all corners and attach to corner framing. Splice channels directly over studs by nesting (not butting) the channels and driving the fastener through both flanges into the support.

Where cabinets are to be installed, attach resilient channels to studs directly behind cabinet hanger brackets. When the distance between hangers exceeds 24" o.c., install additional channels at midpoint between hangers.

For cabinet installation with resilient framing, refer to the section "Fixture Installation" in Chapter 3, "Cladding."

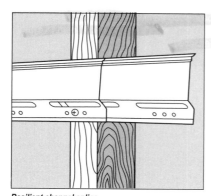

Resilient channel splice

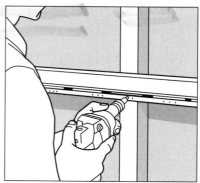

Channel attachment to stud

Resilient Channels Ceilings

Attach resilient channels at right angles to wood joists. Drive 1-1/4" type W or 1-1/4" type S screws through the channel attachment flange for single-layer construction. Fasten channels to joists at each intersection. Do not use nails to attach channels to joists in either single- or double-layer assemblies. For the channels to function acoustically, they should be held away from adjacent walls a minimum of one inch. Mineral wool SAFB is required for sound control.

A 2-hr. floor/ceiling system with STC ratings as high as 60 is achievable with a ceiling of double-layer 5/8" SHEETROCK brand gypsum panels, FIRECODE C Core, attached to resilient channels mounted across joists and 3" mineral wool SAFB in the cavity. The same fire rating applies to the system using IMPERIAL FIRECODE or FIRECODE C gypsum base and any USG veneer plaster finish. When attaching drywall to a resilient channel, avoid contact between the screw and the framing member.

For a two hour fire-rated, double-layer assembly, apply resilient channels over the base layer. Attach channels with 1-7/8" type S screws driven through channel flange and base layer into the wood joist (see UL Des L511—not recommended when sound control is a major consideration).

Framing—Partition Corners

Framing for partition corners must ensure firm fastening of the gypsum panels to vertical studs—and allow enough room from the inside corner to perform this task. Studs should be attached to runners a minimum of 2", but not more than 6" from where the runners intersect. While the panel edges will extend slightly beyond these corner studs, the edge of the second-applied panel will overlap the plane of the first enough to ensure proper taping of the inside corner. Outside corners of partition intersections require firm attachment of panels to perpendicular edges of the outside corner stud.

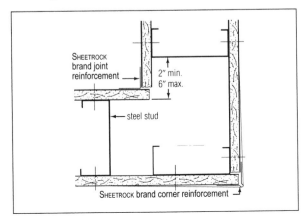

Framing—Door & Window Openings

Rough framing for most door and window openings is the same for gypsum panels and gypsum base veneer systems.

Wood Framing

Install additional infill cripple studs above the header and 1/2" from bearing studs where control joints are required. Do not anchor the cripple stud to the bearing stud, header or plate.

In long runs, treat window openings in the same manner as shown for doors.

Steel Framing

For doors up to 2'-8" wide and weighing 100 lbs. or less, and borrowed light openings use 25 ga. Steel studs and runners to frame the opening. The recommended practice for most installations is to position floor-to-ceiling height jamb strut studs vertically, adjacent to frames, and anchor them securely to the top and bottom runners with screws. However, in cases where significant slab live-load deflection must be accommodated in the vicinity of the door, anchoring of these studs may need to be omitted to accommodate the slab movement. Contact a design professional to determine whether slab deflection is an issue and address each installation case-by-case. Where heavy or oversize doors are used, install additional jamb strut-studs at door openings. Fabricate sill and header sections from steel runners and install over less-than-ceiling-height door frames and above and below borrowed light frames. Fabricate header sections from a piece of runner, cut-to-length (approximately 6" longer than the rough opening). Slit flanges and bend the web to allow flanges to overlap adjacent vertical strut-studs. Securely attach to jamb-studs with screws. For frames with jamb anchor clips, fasten clips to jamb strut-studs with two 3/8" type S pan head screws. Install cripple studs in the center above the door opening and above and below borrowed light openings spaced 24" o.c. maximum.

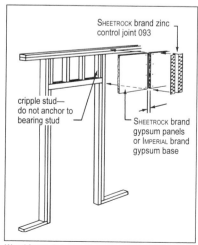

SHEETROCK brand zinc control joint 093

cripple stud—
do not anchor to
bearing stud

SHEETROCK brand
gypsum panels
or IMPERIAL brand
gypsum base

Wood frame door opening

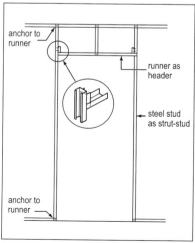

anchor to
runner

runner as
header

steel stud
as strut-stud

anchor to
runner

Door frame with steel runner as header

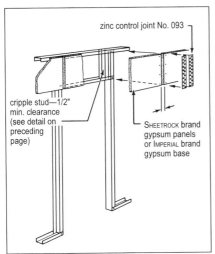

Steel stud door opening

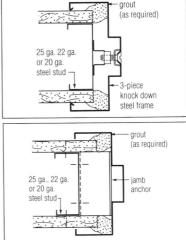

Jamb standard door

Where control joints in header panels are required, install cripple studs 1/2" away from strut-studs. Do not attach the cripple studs to the runners or jamb strut-studs.

Note: Three-piece frames are recommended for drywall and veneer plaster construction since these frames are installed after drywall or plaster base is in place. One-piece frames, which must be installed before the gypsum panels, are more difficult to use because the panels must be inserted under the frame returns as they are installed.

Framing for Heavy and Oversize Doors

For doors that are wider or heavier than shown above the framing must be reinforced. For solid-core doors and hollow-core doors 2'-8" to 4'-0" wide (200 lb. maximum), rough framing should be 20-ga. steel studs and runners. For heavy doors up to 4'-0" wide (300 lb. maximum), two 20-ga. studs should be used to form the jambs struts. For doors over 4'-0" wide, double doors and extra-heavy doors (over 300 lb.), framing should be specially designed to meet load conditions. Rough framing for all doors in fire-rated partitions should be 20-ga. studs and runners.

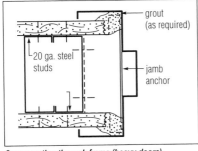

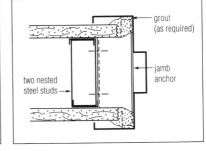

Cross-section through frame (heavy doors)

For added door frame restraint, grouting of the frame is often required for solid-core doors and doors over 2'-8" wide. Apply Sheetrock brand setting-type joint compound (Durabond or Easy Sand) or Red Top gypsum plaster (job-aggregated) just before inserting board into frame. This spot of material is installed only at the door jamb anchor clip. Do not terminate the gypsum panel against the trim return. The use of grout in a door frame is a suggestion by USG, but not universally required by all door frame manufacturers.

Several ANSI door frame standards and door frame industry technical notes call for not grouting the frame in any drywall wall applications due to a concern for possible corrosion within their frame. USG recommends contacting the door frame manufacturer for their particular requirements and tested installation practices.

Door Frame Installation

The following general recommendations apply to one-piece and three-piece door frames and are basic considerations for satisfactory performance.

Rough framing and rough frame reinforcement for these frames should be installed as previously described.

Frame for standard door

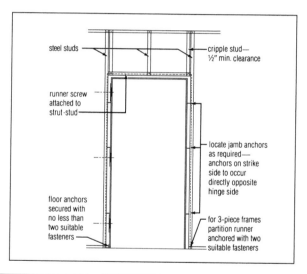

Jamb anchors (furnished with frame)

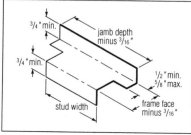

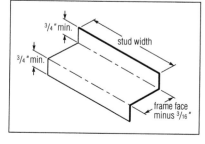

2

Installation One-piece metal door (and borrowed light) frames used with gypsum panel and gypsum base partitions must be constructed and installed properly to prevent twisting or movement. Basic considerations for satisfactory performance are:

1. Frames must be securely anchored. If frames are free to twist upon impact, or trim returns are free to vibrate, movement of the frame will tend to pinch gypsum board face paper and crush the core, resulting in unsightly cracks in the finish, in addition to loose frames.

2. The partition must fit securely in the frame so that the wall and frame work as a unit. Impact stresses on the frame will then be dissipated over the entire partition surface, and local damage minimized.

3. Select frame sizes that have a throat opening between trim returns that properly fits the overall thickness of the partition. The face-layer panels should be enclosed by the trim and not butted against the trim return. This throat opening measurement is critical, as too large a tolerance between panels and trim return will cause a door frame to twist and vibrate against the panels. Too small a tolerance will prevent the panels from fully entering the frame opening and, as a result, the door frame will not be held securely by the partition.

4. One-piece metal door (and borrowed light) frames should be formed from 18-ga. steel minimum, shop-primed. Floor anchor plates for door frames should be 16-ga. steel minimum, designed with two anchor holes to prevent rotation, and shop-welded to frame rabbets to dampen door impact vibrations. Floor anchorage is achieved by two power-driven anchors or equivalent per plate. Jamb anchors should be formed of 18-ga. steel minimum, fit tightly in jambs and screw-attached to the stud. At least three anchor clips per jamb are recommended. Position the clips along the jamb at approximately the hinge points.

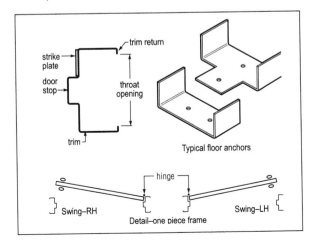

strike plate — trim return — throat opening — door stop — trim

Typical floor anchors

hinge — Swing–RH — Swing–LH

Detail–one piece frame

5. Spot-grouting of one-piece door jambs will increase the rigidity of the frame and improve resistance to frame rotation caused by the weight of the door. To spot-grout, apply SHEETROCK brand setting-type joint compound (DURABOND), mixed in accordance with bag instructions. Apply to each jamb anchor, filling the inside face of the jamb at each point. Immediately insert the gypsum panels into the jamb and attach to framing. Do not terminate the gypsum board against the trim.

An alternative to spot-grouting is full grouting of the jambs, flush with the jamb anchors, and prior to installation of framing. RED TOP gypsum plaster (job-aggregated) or STRUCTO-LITE® gypsum plaster (mill-mixed) is recommended for this purpose. Check with the door frame manufacturer for their recommendation on grouting for the particular door frame and door being used.

To improve the acoustical performance seal around door frames by applying a continuous bead of SHEETROCK brand acoustical sealant to the return of the jamb at the intersection with the gypsum board. Tool the bead of sealant smooth and allow it to dry before finishing the door jamb.

6. Door closers and bumpers are required on all doors where door weight (including attached hardware) exceeds 50 lbs., or where door width exceeds 36". These doors require grouting.

7. When installing a three-piece knock-down door frame, secure runner ends with two floor anchors and allow space in the rough framing for the adjustment shoes in the frame.

8. When ordering metal door frames, the factors to be considered include: Gauge of frame; width and height of door; swing direction of door; type and thickness of door; stud size, and overall thickness of partition.

Metal Window Framing

In climates where extremes in summer or winter temperatures may result in condensation on metal frames, gypsum board (drywall and veneer) should be isolated from direct contact with the frame.

Metal trim (No. 200-B, No. 801-A and B and No. 400 for drywall assemblies No. 801-A and B for veneer plaster assemblies) placed between the gypsum board and window frame provides protection against moisture damage.

Waterproof insulating tape, 1/4" thick and 1/2" wide, or a waterproof acrylic caulk is required to separate metal sash from metal trim and will provide some measure of insulation between the two different metals. Direct contact of an aluminum frame with steel trim, in the presence of condensation moisture, may cause electrolytic deterioration of the aluminum frame.

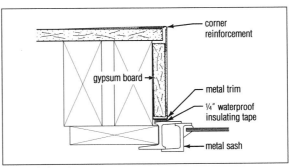

Detail—window trim

Cladding

General Planning Procedures

In most instances, job planning requirements and application techniques are the same for gypsum board—whether it is gypsum panels or gypsum bases. The term "gypsum board" is used throughout this chapter wherever the recommendations apply to both types of products. Where the requirements differ, the products are treated separately.

Various organizations provide information about recommended standards or tolerances for installation of drywall systems. See the Appendix for more information.

For instructions on the safe use of gypsum panels, gypsum base and other products, see Chapter 13, "Safety Considerations & Material Handling."

Planning the Job

Advance planning by the wall and ceiling contractor can mean savings in time and material cost and a better appearance of the finished work. Planning also helps ensure that the materials are properly matched to the intended purpose of the walls.

A number of gypsum board products and systems have been developed that either speed the construction process or improve the abuse resistance and performance of the finished wall. Wider gypsum board, for example, reduces the number of joints that need to be taped on walls between 8' and 9' tall. And the use of gypsum boards with heavy-duty face paper and backing sheets (Sheetrock brand abuse-resistant panels) or fiber-reinforced gypsum panels (Fiberock abuse-resistant panels, Fiberock Interior Aqua-Tough panels, or Fiberock abuse-resistant VHI panels) improve the overall impact and abuse resistance- of the finished wall system. In addition, panels have been developed to reduce ceiling sag (Sheetrock brand interior gypsum ceiling board, sag-resistant). Performance factors should be revisited in the planning stage to make sure that the cladding products selected are the best suited to meet the project's performance requirements.

Note that installation of Fiberock brand products sometimes varies from the procedures used to install conventional drywall panels and gypsum base. See **usg.com** for the most current literature on Fiberock panels.

Proper planning not only achieves the most effective use of materials and elimination of unnecessary joints, but also makes it possible to place necessary joints in the least conspicuous locations. One gypsum board should span the entire length or width of the wall or ceiling, if possible. By using the longest practical board lengths obtainable, end joints are kept to a minimum. Where they do occur, they should be staggered.

In double-layer construction, end joints in the face layer must be offset at least 10" from parallel joints in the base layer. Layout of the base layer should be planned to accommodate this offset while still providing optimum joint-finishing conditions and efficient use of materials in the face layer.

Fire-rated designs stipulate framing, fastener spacing, use of adhesive, joint details, etc. These stipulations must be factored into the planning. See Chapter 10, "System Design Considerations," for details.

Estimating Materials

Gypsum Board Professional estimators have developed various methods for determining square footage of walls and ceilings required to complete different types of jobs. Basically, these methods stem from the simple principle of "scaling a plan" and determining the length, width and ceiling height of each room on the plan. (Frequently, door and window openings are "figured solid" with no openings considered. Exceptions may be floor-to-ceiling board required for openings.) From these dimensions, the estimator determines the square footage of each room. The totals for each room are added to determine total square footage for that part of the project. From these figures the number of gypsum boards needed may be determined. (Refer to Chapter 1, "Drywall & Veneer Plaster Products," for available lengths of each type of panel.)

Screws For single-layer wall application to 16" o.c. framing, approx. 1,000 type W screws are required for wood, or type S or S-12 for steel per 1,000 SF of gypsum board; approximately 850 for 24" o.c. framing. See the Appendix for complete information on estimating screws.

Fastener usage for other assemblies varies with the construction and spacing. Refer to specific system descriptions for fastener requirements.

Nails Usage for nails is shown in the Selector Guide for Gypsum Board Nails, page 44.

Acoustical Sealant The approximate linear feet (LF) of bead realized per gallon of Sheetrock brand acoustical sealant is: 392 LF for 1/4" bead, 174 LF for 3/8" bead, and 98 LF for 1/2" bead.

Adhesive The following table shows the amount of adhesive needed per 1,000 SF of laminated board surface.

Coverage—Adhesives for Lamination

Product	Application	Approx. quantity			
		lb./1000 ft.²		kg/100 m²	
		Lam. blade 1/4″ notch spacing			
		2″	1-1/2″	50 mm	38 mm
SHEETROCK Brand Ready-Mixed Joint Compound	Strip lam.	170	230	83	112
	Sheet lam.	340	465	166	227
SHEETROCK Brand Setting Type (DURABOND) Joint Compound	Strip lam.	93	123	45	60
	Sheet lam.	184	246	90	120
SHEETROCK Brand Lightweight Setting Type (EASY SAND)	Strip lam.	68	90	33	44
	Sheet lam.	134	179	66	87
		gal./1000 ft.²		L/100 m²	
		2″ 1-1/2″		50 mm	34 mm
SHEETROCK Brand Lightweight All Purpose Ready-Mixed (PLUS 3)	Strip lam.	11.5	15.5	45.6	63
	Sheet lam.	23.0	31.7	93.5	129

Joint Treatment–Gypsum Panels Approximate quantities required for finishing 1,000 SF of gypsum panels: 370 LF of SHEETROCK brand joint tape; 83 lbs. of conventional drying-type powders, 67 lbs. of lightweight drying-type powder (A/P LITE), 72 lbs. of conventional setting type powders, 52 lbs. of lightweight setting-type powder (EASY SAND); 138 lbs. of SHEETROCK brand all-purpose ready-mixed or 9.4 gallons of SHEETROCK lightweight all-purpose ready-mixed compound (PLUS 3).

Joint Treatment–Veneer Plaster Gypsum Base For regular application, approx. 370 LF of either type "P" or "S" IMPERIAL brand tape is required per 1,000 SF of base surface.

For application over metal framing, approximately 370 LF of SHEETROCK brand joint tape and 72 lbs. of SHEETROCK brand setting type (DURABOND) joint compound are required per 1,000 SF of surface. This application also is needed to meet certain spacing requirements, and when building temperature/humidity conditions fall within the rapid drying area of the graph on page 211.

Handling and Storage

When drywall and veneer construction moved into high-rise buildings, it brought with it the new challenge of moving large gypsum boards from ground level to the point of use in the stories above. Inefficient materials handling at the job site can add cost and reduce profit. Correct handling procedures can result in substantial time and money savings.

Gypsum boards, like millwork, must be handled with care to avoid damage. Gypsum products, including joint compound, should be ordered for delivery several days in advance of installation, but should not be stored on the job for a long period of time, as boards are susceptible to damage, and joint compounds and veneer finishes are subject to aging.

Boards should be placed inside, under cover, and stacked flat on a clean floor in the centers of the largest rooms. Where heavy loads are involved, it may be preferable to make smaller stacks of panels and distribute them around the perimeter of the room.

Gypsum boards intended for use on ceilings should be placed on the top of the pile for removal first. Avoid stacking long lengths atop short lengths.

All successful veneer plaster finish jobs require adequate equipment: power mixers, mortar boards, scaffolding and tools. Ample scaffolding should be provided. Rather than ship all veneer plaster finish to the job at one time, fresh material should be sent to the job every few days as needed. Plaster stored for long periods is subject to damage, variable moisture conditions and aging that probably will produce variations in setting time and create performance problems.

Store veneer plaster products inside, in a dry location and away from heavy-traffic areas. Stack bags on planks or platforms away from damp floors and walls. Protect metal corner beads, casing beads and trim from being bent or damaged. All materials used on the job should remain in their packages until used.

Tip
See Chapter 13, "Safety Considerations & Material Handling," for more on the safe use of gypsum panels and base.

Environmental Conditions

In cold weather (outdoor temperature less than 55°F), controlled heat in the range of 55°F to 70°F must be provided, starting 24 hours before, and then during and after the entire gypsum board joint finishing process, day and night, until the permanent heating system is in operation, or the building is occupied. A minimum temperature of 50°F should be maintained during gypsum board application.

Methods for Applying Drywall & Veneer Bases

3

Gypsum panels and bases may be applied in one or two layers directly to wood framing members, steel studs or channels, or interior masonry walls. Use of stilts can make application easier. See Chapter 13 for safety precautions.

Single Layer vs. Double Layer

Single-Layer Application This basic construction is used to surface interior walls and ceilings where economy, fast erection and fire resistance are required. This method is equally suitable for remodeling, altering and resurfacing cracked and defaced areas.

Double-Layer Application With this method, a face layer of gypsum board is applied over a base layer that is directly attached to framing members. This construction can offer greater strength and higher resistance to fire and to sound transmission than single-layer applications. Double-layer construction, when adhesively laminated, is especially resistant to cracking and provides one of the finest, strongest walls available. Also, these adhesively laminated constructions are highly resistant to sag and joint deformation. In double-layer application, always apply all base-layer board in each room before beginning face-layer application.

Nailing technique for single-layer application

Attachment Methods

Gypsum boards are attached to framing by several methods, depending on the type of framing and the desired results.

Single Nailing Conventional attachment for wood framing.

Double Nailing Minimizes defects due to loose board. See page 112 for more on double nailing.

Screw Attachment Screws are excellent insurance against fastener pops caused by loosely attached board. Screws are recommended for wood frame attachment, and required for attachment to steel framing and resilient channels. When mounting to resilient channels, take care not to locate screws where they will also penetrate studs, thereby "shorting out" or negating the resiliency.

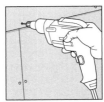

Screw attachment along vertical edges of face-layer board in double-layer application

Adhesive Attachment A continuous bead of drywall stud adhesive applied to wood framing, along with supplemental nail or screw attachment, improves bond strength and greatly reduces the number of face nails or screws needed.

Adhesive Lamination (Double Layer) Produces the highest quality surfaces. Adhesive attachment of face layer to base layer in double-layer construction, and of single-layer board to interior masonry walls, usually requires only supplemental mechanical fastening until the adhesive attains full bond. This method reduces the number of nails or screws required, saves finishing labor and minimizes fastener pops and joint ridging. A SHEETROCK brand setting-type (DURABOND) or light-weight setting-type (EASY SAND) joint compound or SHEETROCK brand ready-mixed joint compound—taping or all-purpose–is required for adhesive lamination with fire-rated assemblies.

Perpendicular vs. Parallel Application

Gypsum board may be applied perpendicular (long edges of board at right angles to the framing members) or parallel (long edges parallel to framing). Fire-rated partitions may require parallel application. (See Chapter 10 for specific information on fire-rated systems.)

Perpendicular application is generally preferred because it offers the following advantages:

1. Reduces the lineal footage of joints to be treated by up to 25%.
2. Strongest dimension of board runs across framing members.
3. Bridges irregularities in alignment and spacing of frame members.
4. Better bracing strength—each board ties more frame members together than does parallel application.
5. Horizontal joints on wall are at a convenient height for finishing.

For wall application, if ceiling height is 8'-1" or less, perpendicular application of standard 4' wide panels results in fewer joints, easier handling and less cutting. If ceiling height is greater than 8'-1", or wall is 4' or less wide, parallel application is more practical.

Walls ranging in height from 8'-1" to 9'-1" can be clad with perpendicular 54" wide panels to eliminate the addition of more joints. (See SHEETROCK brand gypsum panels—54" in Chapter 1.)

For ceiling application, use whichever method—parallel or perpendicular—results in fewer joints, or is required by frame spacing limitations.

For double-layer ceiling application, apply base-layer boards perpendicular to frame members; apply the face layer parallel to framing with joints offset. On walls, apply the base layer parallel with long edges centered on framing; apply face layer perpendicular.

Starting at ceiling line, horizontal board is screw-attached (left). Parallel application (right) is used in special situations.

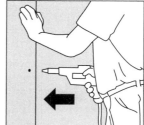

Gypsum Drywall & Plaster Base Application

General Recommendations

When applying gypsum panels to wood and steel framing:

1. Apply ceiling boards first.
2. Cut boards so that they slip easily into place.
3. Butt all joints loosely. Never force panels into position.
4. Whenever possible, place tapered or wrapped edges next to one another.
5. Wherever possible, apply boards perpendicular to framing and in lengths that will span ceilings and walls without creating end (butt) joints. If butt joints do occur, stagger and locate them as far from the center of walls and ceilings as possible.
6. Support all ends and edges of gypsum board on framing, except long edges at right angles to framing and where end joints are to be floated between frame members and back-blocked. Back-blocking is covered later in this chapter on pages 117–118.
7. When fastening, apply hand pressure on the panel next to the fastener being driven to ensure the panel is in tight contact with the framing member.
8. If metal or plastic trim is to be installed around edges, doors, or windows, determine whether the trim is to be installed before the panels. Refer to Chapter 1 for a description of products.
9. Do not anchor panel surfaces across the flat grain of wide dimensional lumber such as floor joists and headers. Float panels over these members or provide a control joint to compensate for wood shrinkage.
10. To ensure level surfaces at joints, plan to apply boards so that the leading edge of each board is attached to the open or unsupported edge of a steel stud flange. All studs must be placed so that their flanges point in the same direction. Board application should advance in the direction opposite to the flange direction. When this simple procedure is followed, attachment of each board holds the stud flange at the joint in a rigid position for attachment of the following board.

If the leading edge of the gypsum board is attached to the web edge of a flange, the open edge of the flange can deflect under the pressure of attachment of the next gypsum board. Friction between the tightly abutted board edges can cause them to bind, preventing return of the second board to the surface plane of the first. A stepped or uneven joint surface results.

This recommended application procedure is absolutely essential for good results in steel-framed veneer and drywall assemblies. (See the drawings on the following page for correct methods.)

Measurements All measurements must be accurate. Make two measurements as a check. This procedure will usually warn of partitions

Correct application

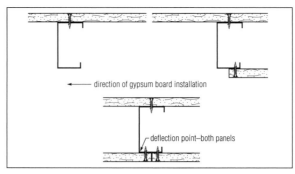

Incorrect application

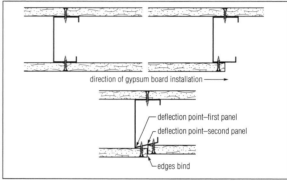

Cut edges of board are smoothed with a rasp, coarse sandpaper or piece of metal lath stapled around wood block (top). Measurements for cutouts are carefully made with flexible rule (bottom).

or door openings that are out of plumb or out of square. Framing corrections can then be made before the board is hung. A 12' to 25' steel power tape is recommended. Tools for measuring and cutting are shown in Chapter 14, "Tools & Equipment."

Cutting Make straight-line cuts across the full width or length of the board by scoring the face paper, snapping the board core and then cutting the back paper. The tool most often used to score and cut gypsum board is a utility knife with replaceable blades. Regardless of the type of knife used, its blade should be kept sharp so that the paper can be scored without being torn or rolled up into the gypsum core. For FIBEROCK panels, multiple scores may be required on the panel surface and into the core; it is not necessary to cut the panel back unless it is a very high impact (VHI) panel.

Note that installation of FIBEROCK products sometimes varies from the procedures used to install conventional drywall panels and gypsum base. See **usg.com** for the most current literature on FIBEROCK panels.

For cuts across the board width, a straightedge is recommended. An aluminum 4' drywall T-square, ruled on both edges, facilitates clean, straight cuts. For cuts along the long length of the board, use a steel tape with an adjustable edge guide and a tip that accepts the utility knife blade. With this tape, the edge guide is set for the desired width and placed against the board edge. The knife blade is then inserted

3

Left to right, gypsum board is cut by scoring with utility knife against drywall T-square, then snapping toward back (top), cutting back paper with same knife and separating sections (bottom)—quick method to obtain clean edges and precise fit.

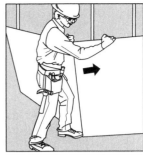
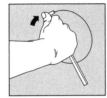

Adjustable cutting tool makes quick work of circular holes, as cutter wheel on calibrated shaft rotates from center pin (top). Edges are trimmed with hook-bill knife (bottom). Stiff drywall saw and other tools are used to make odd-shaped cuts.

into the slotted tape tip, and by moving both hands together, the tool is drawn down the full length of the board to make a smooth and accurate cut. (See manufacturer instructions for proper use and any safety precautions.)

Cut and fit the board neatly around pipes, electrical outlet boxes, medicine cabinets, etc. Holes for electrical outlet boxes can be made with a special outlet box cutting tool. For circular holes, use an adjustable circular cutting tool or drywall router. Keyhole saws and similar cutting tools can be used for any type of cut-out. After cutting the hole, remove any loose face paper at the cut. Refer to Chapter 14, "Tools & Equipment," for examples of appropriate tools.

Screw Application

Screws are applied with an electric screw gun, equipped with an adjustable screw-depth control head and a Phillips bit. The use of screws provides for positive mechanical attachment of gypsum board to either wood or steel framing.

Adjust Screw Gun   Set the adjustment to the proper screw depth. For gypsum panels (drywall), the screw head must be driven slightly below the face of the panel (maximum 1/32"), but not deep enough to break the paper. For gypsum bases (veneer plaster), the screw head is set flush with the base surface. To adjust the depth, rotate the control head to provide proper screw depth. Then secure the control head to maintain the setting.

Secure control head to maintain adjustment.

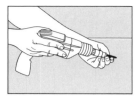

Phillips-head tip holds drywall screw for driving.

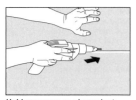

Hold screwgun as shown (not by pistol grip) to avoid stress on wrist.

Place Screw A Phillips head tip holds the drywall screw for driving (above, center). The bit tip does not rotate until pressure is applied to the gypsum board.

Start Screw Straight A firm hand grip on the electric screw gun is important for a straight line of entry. To avoid stress on the wrist, hold the gun as shown (above), not by the pistol grip. The screw must enter perpendicular to the board face for proper performance. Drive screws at least 3/8" from the ends or edges of the board.

Operate the electric screw gun continuously during screw application. When the screw head is driven solidly against the board, the screw gun head will automatically stop turning as the positive clutch disengages.

The electric screw gun technique is relatively simple. An installer can gain proficiency in use of the tool in a few hours. For a description of screws, see Chapter 1; for screw spacing, see the fastener spacing table on the next page.

Staple Application

Staples are recommended only for attaching base layer boards to wood framing in double-layer assemblies. Staples should be 16-ga., flattened galvanized wire with 7/16" wide crown, divergent points and leg lengths to provide a minimum of 5/8" penetration into supports. Drive staples with the crown perpendicular to gypsum board edges except where edges fall on supports. Drive staples so the crown bears tightly against the board, but does not cut the paper.

Single-Nailing Application

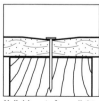

Nail driven to form slight dimple in drywall panel.

1. Begin nailing from the abutting edge of the board and proceed toward opposite ends or edges. Do not nail the perimeter before nailing the field of the board. Ceiling application may cause the board to deflect or sag in the center and prevent firm fastening.

2. Position nails on adjacent ends or edges opposite each other.

3. Drive nails at least 3/8" from ends or edges of gypsum board.

4. Apply hand pressure on the board adjacent to the nail being driven to ensure that the board is in tight contact with the framing member.

5. Drive nails with the shank perpendicular to the board face.

6. Use a drywall hammer with a crowned head for gypsum panels.

7a. For gypsum panels (drywall), seat nails so their heads are in a shallow, uniform dimple formed by the last hammer blow.

Do not break the paper or crush the core at the nail head or around the dimple's circumference by over-driving. Never use a nail set. The depth of the dimple should not exceed 1/32" for gypsum panels.

7b. For gypsum bases (veneer plaster), nail heads should be driven flush with the board surface without dimpling.

3

Maximum Fastener Spacing—Constructions Using Drywall, Gypsum Base and Similar Products[1]

				Maximum Fastener Spacing			
				Drywall Assemblies		Veneer Plaster Assemblies	
				SHEETROCK Brand Gypsum Panels or FIBEROCK Brand Abuse-Resistant Panels		IMPERIAL Brand Gypsum Base or FIBEROCK Brand Abuse-Resistant Panels	
Framing	Type const.	Type Fastener	Location	in	mm	in	mm
wood	single layer[2]—mechanically attached	nails	ceilings	7	178	7	178
			sidewalls	8	203	8	203
		screws	ceilings	12	305	12	305
			sidewalls	16[3]	406	12	305
		screws—with resilient channels	ceilings	12	305	12	305
			sidewalls	12	305	12	305
	single layer—adhesively attached	nails/ screws	ceilings (perpendicular)	16" or 406 mm o.c. at ends, edges—1 field fastener per frame member at mid-width of board		same as for gypsum panels	
			ceilings (parallel)	16" or 406 mm o.c. along each edge and 24" or 610 mm o.c. along intermediate framing		same as for gypsum panels	
			walls (perpendicular)	16" or 406 mm o.c. at ends, edges—1 field fastener per frame member at mid-width of board		same as for gypsum panels	
	base layer of double layer—both layers mechanically attached	nails	ceilings	24	610	24	610
			sidewalls	24	610	24	610
		screws	ceilings	24	610	24	610
			sidewalls	24	610	24	610
		staples	ceilings	16	406	16	406
			sidewalls	16	406	16	406
	face layer of double layer—both layers mechanically attached	nails	ceilings	7	178	7	178
			sidewalls	8	203	8	203
		screws	ceilings	12	305	12	305
			sidewalls	16	406	12	305
	base layer of double layer—face layer adhesively attached	nails	ceilings	7	178	7	178
			sidewalls	8	203	8	203
		screws	ceilings	12	305	12	305
			sidewalls	16	406	12	305
		staples	ceilings	7	178	7	178
			sidewalls	7	178	7	178
	face layer of double layer—face layer adhesively attached	nails/screws	ceilings	16" or 406 mm o.c. at ends, edges—1 field fastener per frame member at mid-width of board		same as for gypsum panels	
			sidewalls	fasten top and[4] bottom as required		same as for[4] gypsum panels	

Maximum Fastener Spacing—Constructions Using Drywall, Gypsum Base and Similar Products[1]

Framing	Type const.	Type Fastener	Location	Maximum Fastener Spacing				
				Drywall Assemblies			Veneer Plaster Assemblies	
				SHEETROCK Brand Gypsum Panels or FIBEROCK Brand Abuse-Resistant Panels			IMPERIAL Brand Gypsum Base or FIBEROCK Brand Abuse-Resistant Panels	
				in	mm		in	mm
steel	single layer	screws	ceilings	12	305		12	305
			sidewalls	16[3]	406		12	305
	base layer of double layer— both layers mechanically attached	screws	ceilings	16	406		16	406
			sidewalls	24	610		24	610
	face layer of double layer— both layers mechanically attached	screws	ceilings	12	305		12	305
			sidewalls	16	406		12	305
	base layer of double layer— face layer adhesively attached	screws	ceilings	12[4]	305[5]		12[5]	305[5]
			sidewalls	16[4]	406[5]		12[5]	305[5]
	face layer of double layer— face layer adhesively attached	screws	ceilings	16" or 406 mm o.c. at ends and edges— 1 field fastener per frame member at mid-width of board			same as for gypsum panels	
			sidewalls	fasten top and[4] bottom as required			same as for[4] gypsum panels	

(1) Fastener spacings based on wood framing 16″ o.c., steel framing 24″ o.c. Spacings are not for fire-rated assemblies; see test listing for fastener spacing for specific fire-rated assemblies. (2) See page 115 for fastener spacing using adhesive. (3) Water-resistant board spacing is 12″ o.c. (4) When board has been pre-bowed. For flat boards, use temporary nails or Type G screws called for in sheet or strip lamination section. (5) Spacing is 8″ (203mm) o.c. at joint edges.

Double-Nailing Application (Walls and Ceilings)

In the double-nailing method for attaching gypsum board to wood framing, space the first nails 12" o.c. along the supports in the field of the board and around the perimeter spaced 7" o.c. for ceilings and 8" o.c. for walls. Drive the second nails about 2" from the first in the board field and make sure the first nails are properly seated.

This method helps prevent loose panels and resultant nail pops that may occur when boards are not applied correctly and drawn tightly to the framing. Double-nailing will not reduce the incidence or severity of nail pops due to wood shrinkage.

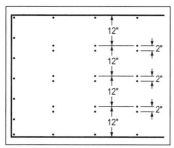

Double-nailing in field of board

Adhesive Application

A continuous bead of drywall stud or construction adhesive is applied to the face of wood framing. Adhesives should meet ASTM C557 standards. Gypsum boards are applied and attached with only a minimum number of supplementary fasteners, compared to conventional fastening methods. (See table on preceding page for fastener spacing requirements.)

The framing member spacing is the same as that used for conventional attachment.

Advantages of attachment with adhesives:

1. Reduces the number of fasteners used (up to 75%).
2. Is stronger than conventional nail application—up to 100% more tensile strength, up to 50% more shear strength.
3. Is unaffected by moisture or by high or low temperatures.
4. Results in fewer loose panels due to improper fastening.
5. Bridges minor framing irregularities.
6. Will not stain or bleed through most finishes.

Adhesives are readily available in 29-oz. cartridges and applied with hand or powered-guns.

General Directions

The following recommendations will help explain the proper use of adhesives and the conditions that may affect the quality of the finished job.

1. Select the proper adhesive for specific job requirements. Read container directions carefully.
2. Make sure that all substrates are clean, sound and free from oil, dirt or contamination.
3. Exercise care regarding open flames when using flammable solvent adhesives in poorly ventilated areas.
4. Prevent freezing of adhesives.
5. Apply adhesives at temperatures between 50°F and 100°F except as directed by the manufacturer. Extremely high temperatures may cause solvent-base products to evaporate rapidly, shortening the time containers can be open and damaging bond characteristics.
6. Close containers whenever adhesive is not in use. Evaporation of vehicle can affect adhesive's wetting, bonding and application properties.
7. Do not exceed open time specified by manufacturer. Failure to follow instructions may cause poor bonding.
8. Follow manufacturer's recommendation on proper amounts of adhesive to apply. Too small or too large a bead will lead to performance problems or waste.
9. Apply adhesive with manufacturer-recommended tools.

Cartridge Preparation

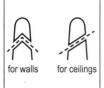

for walls   for ceilings

Nozzle cuts

Cut the cartridge tip in two different ways: for walls, make a chevron or "V" cut in order to produce a round, uniform bead. The cut edge of the nozzle rides along the stud easily. For ceilings, use a single, angled slash across the nozzle. This enables the adhesive to be wiped on the ceiling joist to minimize dripping.

With a 3/8" bead, approx. 3 to 5 gallons of adhesive will prepare framing for 1,000 SF of gypsum board. See adhesive manufacturer information for specific product coverage.

Proper nozzle opening and gun position (see illustrations) are required to obtain the right size and shape of bead for satisfactory results. Initial height of the bead over framing should be 3/8" and of sufficient volume to provide 1/16" adhesive thickness over the entire support when compressed.

Apply adhesive in a continuous 3/8" bead in the center of the attachment face (below) and to within 6" of ends of all framing members. Where two gypsum boards meet on a framing member, apply two continuous 3/8" beads to framing members at extreme edges of face, to ensure adequate contact with the paper on the back of the board. Do not apply adhesive to members such as bridging, diagonal bracing, etc., into which no supplemental fasteners will be driven. Adhesive is not required at inside corners, top and bottom plates or bracing and is not ordinarily used in closets.

Place gypsum boards shortly after adhesive bead is applied and fasten immediately, using proper screws or nails. After board has been fastened hand press along each stud or joist to ensure good contact at all points.

Where fasteners at vertical joints are objectionable (such as with pre-decorated panels), boards may be pre-bowed and adhesively attached with fasteners at the top and bottom only.

Pre-bow boards by stacking them face up with their ends resting on nominal 2" x 4" lumber or other blocks, and with center of the boards resting on floor. Allow boards to remain overnight or until they have a 2" permanent bow. (Under very humid conditions, board may be too flexible to assume the stiff bow needed to provide adequate pressure against framing.)

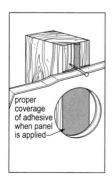

proper coverage of adhesive when panel is applied

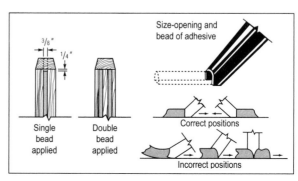

Size-opening and bead of adhesive

$3/8"$ $1/4"$

Single bead applied   Double bead applied

Correct positions

Incorrect positions

To ensure a good bond, no more adhesive should be applied than can be covered in 15 minutes. If adhesive is left exposed to the air for longer periods, the volatile materials will evaporate, causing surface hardness or skimming that prevents a full bond. Remove excess adhesive from board and other finished surfaces and tools with a solvent-base cleaner before the adhesive dries. Follow the solvent manufacturer's safety procedures.

Allow adhesive to dry at least 48 hours before treating drywall joints or applying veneer finishes.

Fastener Spacing Using Adhesive

Ceilings–Long Board Edges Across Framing Fasten board at each framing intersection and 16" o.c. at each end. Install one temporary field fastener per framing member at mid-width of the board.

Ceilings–Long Board Edges Parallel to Framing Space fasteners 16" o.c. along the board edges and at each framing intersection on the ends. Space fasteners 24" o.c. on intermediate supports.

Walls–Long Board Edges Across Framing Application Same as Ceilings, above, except that no field fasteners are required.

Walls–Long Board Edges Parallel to Framing Same as Ceilings, above, except that no fasteners are required on intermediate supports. Where fasteners at the vertical joints are objectionable, pre-bow the gypsum board and apply fasteners 16" o.c. only at the top and bottom of the board.

Note: If using vinyl foam tape as a temporary supplementary fastener, follow manufacturer's directions for additional fasteners required.

Gypsum Board Ceiling Installation

The size and weight of standard gypsum boards make them somewhat cumbersome for ceiling installation, even with two people doing the work. Installation typically is easier if the installers wear stilts or erect temporary platforms from which they can easily drive initial fasteners. Marking the panel face for anticipated joist locations may also be helpful.

Use of aids such as panel lifters or T-jacks is recommended for safety, ease of adjustment and more secure panel attachment. Panel lifters are essentially scissor jacks that lift panels into position and enable accurate alignment with ceiling joists. Panel lifters can also hold the panels firmly in place so that the gypsum board can be secured directly to the framing. T-jacks are simply bars on adjustable poles. They do a good job of holding the panels in place once they are in position, but do not facilitate alignment in the same manner as panel lifters. (See Chapter 13 and equipment manufacturer instructions for safety precautions.)

Wood Frame Single-Layer Application

This basic construction provides economical, quickly completed walls and ceilings with wood framing and wall furring. All types of gypsum boards may be used in this assembly. Measuring and cutting, perpendicular or parallel application, framing requirements and fastening are covered earlier in this chapter. For complete information on fire- and sound-resistant assemblies, refer to USG publication, Fire-Resistant Assemblies, SA100.

Installation

Wood Studs and Joists Apply gypsum boards so that ends and edges overlap with framing members, except when joints are at right angles to the framing members (as in perpendicular application) or when the end joints are to be back-blocked. (See the following section.)

To minimize end joints, use boards of maximum practical lengths. End joints should be staggered. Arrange joints on opposite sides of a partition so they occur on different studs.

Apply gypsum boards first to the ceiling, and then to the walls. If foil-back gypsum boards are used, apply the foil side against the framing. Fit the ends and edges closely, but do not force boards into place. Cut boards accurately to fit around pipes and fixtures.

Usually two mechanics are required to install long-length board on ceilings. Fasten boards with screws or nails starting from abutting edges and working toward the opposite ends and edges. While fasteners are being driven, the boards must be held in firm contact with the framing or joists. When single fasteners are used, attach boards to framing with screws or nails spaced as shown in the Fastener Spacing Table on pages 111–112. Drive fasteners at least 3/8" from the edges and ends of the board.

Fasteners are placed at least 3/8" from edges and ends.

Apply gypsum boards to the sidewalls after ceilings are erected. Where long panel edges are across studs (perpendicular application), apply top wall board first, butted against the ceiling. When long edges are parallel to studs (parallel application), span the sidewall from ceiling to floor with a single length of board. For situations where the ceiling height is greater than 8'-1" but less than 9'-1", SHEETROCK brand gypsum panels—54" provide the added board width needed to avoid additional joint finishing. Use parallel application where ceiling height is over 9'-1" or where this method reduces waste and joint treatment.

On sidewalls, space screws 16" o.c. max. for gypsum panels, 12" o.c. maximum for gypsum base. Space nails 8" o.c. (If wall is fire-rated, follow specific design specifications.)

Wherever possible, use board of sufficient length to span wall areas. If joints occur near an opening, apply boards so vertical joints are centered, if possible, over the opening. Keep vertical joints at least 8" away from external corners of windows, doors or similar openings except at interior or exterior angles within the room or when control joints are used.

After installation, exert hand pressure against wall and ceiling surfaces to detect loose fasteners. If any are found, drive them tight. Where nails or screws have punctured the paper, hold the board tight against the framing and install another fastener properly, about 1-1/2" from the screw or nailhead that punctured the paper. Remove faulty fasteners. When nailing boards to the second side of a partition, check the opposite side for nails loosened by pounding and drive them tight again.

With platform framing and sidewall expanses exceeding one floor in height, fur the gypsum boards over floor joists using resilient channels. (See detail.)

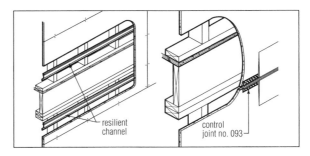

resilient channel

control joint no. 093

As an alternate, install a horizontal control joint between gypsum boards at the junction of the bottom of top plates and the first-floor studs. (See detail.) Do not fasten gypsum boards to the side face of joists or headers.

Acoustical Sealant Application

To prevent flanking and loss of the sound-control characteristics of sound-rated partitions, SHEETROCK brand acoustical sealant must be used at all wood and steel floor runners (detailed below) to seal the bottom edge of the gypsum board and at wall angles where dissimilar materials meet. Caulking is required at possible leaks in all sound-rated systems to achieve sound reduction comparable to that obtained in the laboratory.

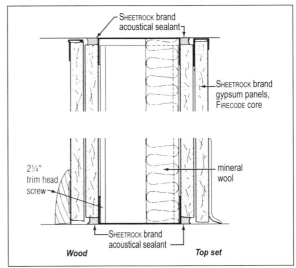

SHEETROCK brand acoustical sealant

SHEETROCK brand gypsum panels, FIRECODE core

2¼″ trim head screw

mineral wool

SHEETROCK brand acoustical sealant

Wood   *Top set*

Back-Blocking Application

Back-Blocking is a system designed to minimize an inherent joint deformation, called "ridging," in single-layer gypsum board construction. Ridging sometimes occurs under a combination of adverse job and weather conditions. The Back-Blocking System, developed by USG, enables floating of end joints between studs or joists and makes it easier to form a good surface over a twisted stud or joist. The system has been widely used for years and produces outstanding results.

Back-Blocking consists of laminating cut-to-size pieces of gypsum board to the back surface of boards directly behind joints to provide resistance to ridging. To install the system, follow these steps:

1. Cut backing blocks 8" wide and long enough to fit loosely between framing.

2. Install separate gypsum strips along sides of studs, set back enough to accommodate the block thickness and keep the face of blocks flush with or slightly behind stud faces.

3. Spread the surface of the blocks with SHEETROCK brand setting-type (DURABOND) or lightweight setting-type (EASY SAND) joint compound or SHEETROCK brand ready-mixed joint compound—taping or all-purpose. Apply the compound in beads 1/2" high, 3/8" wide at the base, spaced 1-1/2" o.c.

4. Apply gypsum boards horizontally with long edges at right angles to joists. Place backing blocks along full length of edge and ends of board.

5. Immediately after all blocks are in place, erect the next board, butting ends loosely.

6. After fastening the abutting board, install a block and bracing as shown in the cross-section illustration. This method forms a taper that remains after bracing strips are removed.

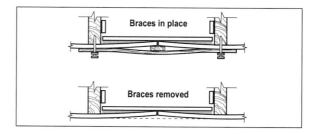

Braces in place

Braces removed

Double-Layer Adhesive Lamination

In adhesive application, face-layer gypsum boards are job-laminated to a base layer of gypsum board or interior masonry partitions.

In multi-layer adhesive systems, the base layer must be attached with the same fastener, fastener spacing, and framing spacing as for a single-layer assembly of the same thickness as the base layer.

In fire-rated assemblies, permanent fasteners and the type of board used must be the same as in the particular tested assembly. (See specific design for complete description.)

In applying the base layer, the long edges can be either parallel or perpendicular to the framing. Plan the layout of the face layer so that all joints are offset a minimum of 10" from parallel base-layer joints. It is preferable to apply the face layer perpendicular to the base layer. At inside vertical angles, only the overlapping base layer should be attached to the framing to provide a floating corner. Omit all face-layer fasteners within 8" of vertical angles.

Application—Laminating Adhesive

Apply laminating adhesive in strips to the center and along both edges of the face layer board. Apply strips with a notched metal spreader that has four 1/4" x 1/4" minimum notches spaced a maximum of 2" o.c. Position the face layer against the base layer and fasten at the top and bottom (vertical application) as required. For laminated ceilings, space fasteners 16" o.c. along edges and ends, with one permanent field fastener per framing member installed at mid-width of the board. Press board into place with firm pressure to ensure bond; re-impact within 24 hrs. if necessary.

3

Application—Joint Compound (Used as Laminating Adhesive)

All SHEETROCK brand setting-type (DURABOND) and lightweight setting-type (EASY SAND) joint compounds and ready-mixed joint compounds—all-purpose and taping may be used for two methods of lamination: sheet lamination and strip lamination.

When using SHEETROCK setting-type compounds, supplemental or temporary fasteners or supports are required until the compound has hardened (minimum of three hours, depending on which type of compound is used). Because the compound is a heavy consistency, it provides a leveling action not obtainable with thinner-bodied adhesives. When using SHEETROCK ready-mixed joint compounds for laminating, temporary nailing or permanent type G screws are needed until the compound is dry (usually overnight). In cold weather, provide heat to keep compound from freezing until adhesive is dry.

Corner detail

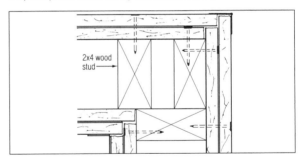

2x4 wood stud→

Mixing—SHEETROCK Brand Setting-Type Compounds

1. Mix in a clean plastic container.
2. Use only clean, potable water.
3. Mix according to bag directions, making sure compound is uniformly damp.
4. Do not contaminate with previously mixed SHEETROCK setting-type joint compound (DURABOND), lightweight setting-type (EASY SAND) joint compound, other compounds or dirty water, as this will affect the setting time.
5. Mix only as much compound as can be used within the time period indicated on the bag—usually one hour for SHEETROCK setting-type (DURABOND) or lightweight setting-type (EASY SAND) 90 and two hours for 210, for example.
6. The addition of extra water (retempering) will not prevent set or increase working time with SHEETROCK setting-type joint compounds.

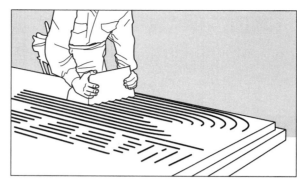

In sheet lamination (right), notched spreader is used to spread compound over entire back surface of face-layer board. In strip lamination of vertical sidewall boards (above), adhesive can be applied to either base surface or face panel. Mechanical tool used is Ames Lamination Spreader.

Mixing—
SHEETROCK
Brand
Ready-Mixed
Compounds

Use the compound at package consistency for best leveling action. If a thinner adhesive is desired, add cool water in half-pint increments to avoid over-thinning. Remix lightly with a potato masher-type mixer and test-apply after each water addition. If compound becomes too thin, add thicker compound from another container and remix.

See Chapter 13, "Safety Considerations & Material Handling," for more information on the safe use of joint compounds.

On all laminated ceilings, the face layer must be permanently attached with fasteners spaced 16" o.c. maximum at the ends and edges, plus one field fastener in each frame member at mid-width of the board. Nails must penetrate wood framing a minimum of 3/4". Screws must penetrate steel framing a minimum of 3/8".

On walls, permanently attach the top and bottom of the face layer with fasteners driven 24" o.c. maximum (except pre-bowed boards). Provide temporary support fasteners, or type G screws 24" o.c. maximum in the field of the board.

1. **Temporary Nailing** Use double-headed scaffold nails driven through wood or gypsum board scraps so that the nail penetrates framing a minimum of 3/4".

2. **Type G Screws** Permanently attach the face layer with screws driven into the base layer to avoid contact with the framing. Apply compound just prior to face board erection to prevent wetting the base layer, as this would reduce the screws' holding power. Press the face layer firmly against the base layer when driving the screws. Compound should be thin enough to spread as the screw is driven. Type G screws should not be used with base-layer boards less than 1/2" thick.

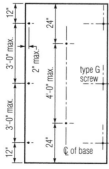

Strip Lamination (vertical face layer, sidewalls only) This method is often preferred because it requires less compound and improves sound attenuation. Apply strips (4 beads, each 3/8" wide by 1/2" high spaced 1-1/2" o.c.) 24" o.c. max. Place permanent fasteners 24" o.c. max. at each end of the face layer. Drive type G screws as shown in diagram.

**Application—
Liquid Contact
Adhesive**

Apply liquid contact adhesive according to manufacturer's directions. Use a short nap paint roller to cover both contact surfaces. Let adhesive air-dry to the touch. Apply boards as soon as possible after drying occurs. On walls, fasten 16" o.c. at top and bottom (vertical application) as required. In ceiling lamination, apply permanent supplementary fasteners at each corner of the board, and along the edges spaced a maximum of 48" o.c. Press the board into place with firm pressure to ensure bond.

Resilient Board Application

**Gypsum
Board—
Sidewalls**

Apply gypsum boards perpendicular to framing with the long dimension of boards parallel to resilient channels. (Make sure that resilient channels are oriented with the attachment flange down, except for baseboard channel which should be oriented with the attachment flange up for easier board attachment.) To avoid compromising sound insulation, lift panels off the floor and ensure there is a 1/8" relief around the perimeter to be filled later with SHEETROCK brand acoustical sealant. Attach boards with 1" type S screws spaced 12" o.c. along channels. Center horizontal abutting edges of boards over screw flange of channel, and screw-attach. Take particular care that these screws do not penetrate the resilient channels and enter studs since this "grounding" will nullify the resilient properties of the channels. For vertical applications, butt joints should be centered over the resilient channels. Where a fire rating is required, the board must be applied with the long dimension vertical.

For two-layer application of gypsum board, apply the base layer vertically and attach to resilient channels with 1" type S screws spaced 24" o.c. Apply the face layer with the long dimension at right angles to the long edges of the base layer. Fasten with type S screws of sufficient length to penetrate channels 3/8" min, spaced 16" o.c.

**Gypsum
Board—
Ceilings**

Single Layer Apply boards of maximum practical length with the long dimension at right angles to resilient channels, and with end joints staggered. To avoid compromising sound insulation, make sure there is a 1/8" relief around the perimeter to be filled later with SHEETROCK acoustical sealant. End joints may occur over resilient channels or midway between channels with joints floated and back-blocked with sections of resilient channels. Fit ends and edges closely, but not forced together. Fasten boards to channels with 1" type S screws spaced 12" o.c. in field of boards and along abutting ends. Cut boards neatly and provide support around cut-outs and openings.

Two-Plane Assembly Provides two layers of gypsum panels for a specific fire-endurance rating, with a resilient channel between layers. The base layer of gypsum board is applied with long edges across joists and end joints staggered. Attach resilient channels perpendicular to framing with 1-7/8" type S screws through the base layer. Face layer of gypsum boards is applied in the same manner as for a single layer, but at right angles to the base layer. Fasten boards to resilient channels with 1" type S screws. (See specific fire-rated assembly design for board type, fastener requirements and fastener spacing.)

Double-Layer Assembly Provides two layers of gypsum panels with a resilient channel between panels and framing. Resilient channel is applied 16" o.c. perpendicular to joists. Base layer of 5/8" gypsum boards is attached to resilient channel with 1" type S screws. Face layer is attached at right angles to the base layer. For added sound control and fire protection, install 3" mineral wool SAFB in cavity. (See specific fire-rated assembly design for board type, fastener requirements and fastener spacing.)

Steel Frame Single-Layer Partition Application

This noncombustible assembly has won wide acceptance because of its sound attenuation, low cost, speed of erection and light weight—only 4 to 6 lbs./SF. Partitions are ideal for space division within units. Ceilings, both suspended and furred, conceal overhead structural and mechanical elements and provide a surface ready for either final decoration or adhesively applied acoustical tile.

Gypsum Board Erection

With long edges of panels applied parallel to steel framing, worker places screws at 16" o.c. intervals for drywall, 12" o.c. for gypsum base.

Apply gypsum boards with the long dimension parallel or perpendicular to framing. (See Frame Spacing Tables on page 74 for limitations.) Use maximum practical lengths to minimize end joints. Position boards so all abutting ends and edges (except edges with perpendicular application) will be located in center of stud flanges. Plan the direction of board installation so that the lead edge or end of the board is attached to the open end of the stud flange first. Make sure joints are neatly fitted and staggered on opposite sides of the partition so they occur on different studs. Cut boards to fit neatly around all outlets and switch boxes.

For single-layer application, fasten boards to supports with 1" type S screws spaced according to Fastener Spacing Table. Stagger screws on abutting edges or ends.

For fire-rated construction, apply gypsum boards and fasten as specified in the fire-tested assembly. (See specific design.)

Steel Frame Double-Layer Partition Application

Double-layer construction using steel studs offers some of the best performances in both fire- and sound resistance—up to 2-hour fire ratings and 55 STC sound rating. These economical, lightweight partitions are adaptable as party walls or corridor walls in virtually every type of new construction.

In these assemblies a face layer of gypsum board is job-laminated to the base layer or screw-attached through the base-layer gypsum board to steel studs. The installation of steel studs and runners is the same as for single-layer application.

Base-Layer Erection

Apply gypsum board with the long dimension parallel to studs. Position the board so that abutting edges will be located in the center of stud flanges. Make sure joints are neatly fitted and staggered on opposite sides of the partition so they occur on different studs. For double-layer screw attachment (both layers screw-attached), fasten panels to studs with type S screws spaced 24" o.c. Use 1" screws for 1/2" and 5/8" thick board. For double-layer adhesively laminated construction, fasten board with 1" screws spaced 8" o.c. at joint edges and 12" o.c.

in the field for panels and gypsum base. For fire-rated construction, fasten the board as specified in the fire-tested design being erected. (See specific design.)

Face-Layer Erection

Apply gypsum board with the long dimension parallel to studs. Position the board so abutting edges will be located in the center of stud flanges. Stagger joints from those in the base layer and on opposite sides of partition. For double-layer screw attachment (both layers screw-attached), fasten the face layer to studs with type S screws spaced 16" o.c. for gypsum panels and 12" o.c. for gypsum base. Use 1-5/8" screws for 1/2" and 5/8" -thick board. (As a rule of thumb, screws should be a minimum of 3/8" longer than the total thickness of the material to be attached to steel studs.) For double-layer laminated construction, attach the face layer using adhesive lamination described earlier in this chapter. For fire-rated construction, fasten gypsum boards with screws as specified in the fire-tested design. (See specific design.)

Steel Frame—Multi-Layer Application

Multi-layer construction, using steel studs, 1-1/2" or greater mineral wool SAFB insulation and 1/2" or 5/8" SHEETROCK gypsum panels, FIRECODE C Core, SHEETROCK brand abuse-resistant gypsum panels, SHEETROCK gypsum panels, ULTRACODE Core or 1/2" IMPERIAL brand gypsum base, FIRECODE C Core. This application offers 3- and 4-hour fire ratings and up to 65 STC sound rating. These superior assemblies are low cost, much lighter weight and thinner than concrete block partitions offering equivalent performance.

3-Layer Application

Apply gypsum panels vertically with the long dimension parallel to studs (except face layer may be applied horizontally across studs). Position base so abutting edges are located in the center of stud flanges. Stagger joints from those in adjacent layers and on opposite sides of the partition.

Fasten the first layer to studs with 1" type S screws spaced 48" o.c. Fasten the second layer to studs with 1-5/8" type S screws spaced 48" o.c. Fasten the face layer to studs with 2-1/4" type S screws spaced 12" o.c. Horizontally applied face layer requires 1" type G screws in the base between studs and 1-1/2" from horizontal joints.

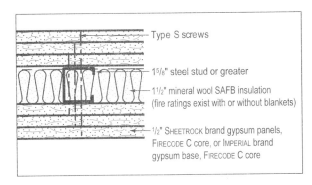

Type S screws

1⁵/₈" steel stud or greater

1¹/₂" mineral wool SAFB insulation (fire ratings exist with or without blankets)

¹/₂" SHEETROCK brand gypsum panels, FIRECODE C core, or IMPERIAL brand gypsum base, FIRECODE C core

4-Layer Application

Apply gypsum boards vertically with the long dimension parallel to studs (except face layer may be applied horizontally across studs). Position base so abutting edges are located in center of stud flanges. Stagger joints from those in adjacent layers and on opposite sides of the partition.

Fasten first layer to studs with 1" type S screws spaced 48" o.c. Fasten second layer to studs with 1-5/8" type S screws spaced 48" o.c. Fasten third layer to studs with 2-1/4" type S screws spaced 12" o.c. Fasten fourth layer to studs with 2-5/8" screws spaced 12" o.c. Horizontally applied face layer requires 1-1/2" type G screws in base between studs and 1" from horizontal joints.

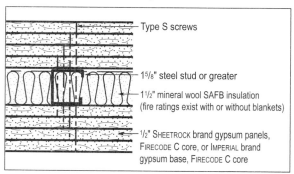

Type S screws

1⁵/₈" steel stud or greater

1¹/₂" mineral wool SAFB insulation (fire ratings exist with or without blankets)

¹/₂" SHEETROCK brand gypsum panels, FIRECODE C core, or IMPERIAL brand gypsum base, FIRECODE C core

Furred Framing Board Application

Apply gypsum board of maximum practical length with the long dimension at right angles to the furring channel. Center end joints over channel web; fit joints neatly and accurately; stagger end joints from those in adjacent rows of board. Fasten boards to furring channels with type S screws spaced according to Fastener Spacing Table. Use 1" screw length for 1/2" or 5/8" thick boards.

Masonry Single-Layer Direct Application

Gypsum boards adhesively applied directly to interior, above-grade monolithic concrete or unit masonry are laminated using a SHEETROCK brand setting-type (DURABOND) or lightweight setting-type (EASY SAND) joint compound or ready-mixed joint compound (all-purpose or taping) or an appropriate subfloor plywood construction adhesive. Use the metal furring channels or Z-furring channels system to apply gypsum board to the interior of exterior and below-grade wall surfaces. If cavity walls have been erected inside of exterior walls and have a continuous (1" min.) clear air space, and the masonry wall surface is well damp-proofed, the wall surfaces may be considered as interior.

Note: Gypsum panels should not be installed where they will be in continuous contact with moisture.

Preparation

Mortar joints on the surface of unit masonry to which gypsum boards are to be bonded should be cut flush with the masonry to provide a level surface. The wall surface should be plumb and true. Grind off rough or protruding areas before starting lamination. Fill pockets or holes greater than 4" in diameter and 1/8" deep with grout, mortar, or SHEETROCK brand setting-type (DURABOND) or lightweight setting-type (EASY SAND) joint compound. Allow to dry before laminating.

Remove all form oils, grease and other release agents from the masonry surface and make sure it is dry and free of dust, loose particles and efflorescence. If masonry has been coated or painted, test by attaching a small section of board to the surface. If it pulls from the surface after a sufficient adhesive bonding time, the surface coating must be removed or a furring system used.

If wood base is used, attach a wood nailer to the wall with mechanical fasteners before laminating gypsum boards. The nailer should be equal to the board thickness and at least 1-1/2" high (or 3/4" less than the wood base height).

Board Installation with Adhesive

Cut face boards to allow continuous clearance (1/8" to 1/4") at the floor. Apply SHEETROCK brand setting-type (DURABOND) or lightweight setting-type (EASY SAND) joint compound, ready-mixed joint compound–all-purpose or taping at center and near each board edge in strips consisting of 4 beads, 3/8" wide by 1/2" high and spaced 1-1/2" to 2" o.c. Position boards vertically over the wall surface, press into place and provide temporary support until the adhesive has hardened.

Trim & Finishing

Upon mounting the board, walls and ceilings are ready for trims and corner beads in preparation for finishing. Information regarding correct application of beads and trims is covered in Chapter 5, "Finishing Drywall Systems."

Gypsum Sheathing Application

The benefits of weather- and fire-resistance plus low applied cost make SHEETROCK brand gypsum sheathing suitable for application under many exterior surfaces—masonry veneer; wood; exterior finish systems; aluminum; steel and vinyl siding; wood and mineral shingles; and stucco. It is ideal for use in exterior steel- or wood-framed construction on single-family housing, apartments, motels and light commercial buildings. In commercial work with exterior plaster, SHEETROCK brand gypsum sheathing provides flatter walls, more uniform plaster thickness, reduced "shadowing" over steel studs and improved racking resistance in panelized construction.

Paper-faced gypsum sheathing is not intended for use where the subsequent building materials (such as expanded polystyrene foam insulation) are to be adhesively applied with no mechanical fasteners. SECUROCK™ Glass Mat Sheathing or FIBEROCK AQUA-TOUGH sheathing should be used for such applications. Paper-faced sheathing should be covered with a continuous water barrier over its face. Refer to page 15 for other limitations.

Installation   SHEETROCK **Brand Gypsum Sheathing or** SECUROCK **Glass Mat Sheathing** Apply 4' x 8' or 9' (1/2" or 5/8") square-edge SHEETROCK gypsum sheathing or SECUROCK Glass-Mat sheathing vertically with face side out. For SECUROCK sheathing, the face side is labeled "USG SECUROCK." Fasteners should be 1-1/2" or 1-3/4" hot-dipped galvanized roofing nails, or 1-1/4" or 1-5/8" wood or steel type fasteners with corrosion resistance of more than 800 hours, per ASTM B117. Space fasteners 8" o.c. on framing members. For ½" thick sheathing, use 1-1/2" nails or 1-1/4" screws, for 5/8", use 1-3/4" nails or 1-5/8" screws. Sheathing may also be installed horizontally. Refer to Technical Folder SA700 for full details on exterior sheathing application.

FIBEROCK AQUA-TOUGH **Sheathing** Apply FIBEROCK AQUA-TOUGH sheathing with the logo side toward the exterior. Fit ends and edges closely, but not forced together. Use 11-gauge hot-dipped galvanized roofing nails, 7/16" diameter head, or corrosion-resistant exterior screws for fastening. Minimum fastener penetration into wood framing is 3/4" and into steel framing is 3/8". Screws with low-profile heads should be used where screwheads protrude beyond the plane of framing. Unless otherwise specifically required, FIBEROCK AQUA-TOUGH sheathing may be applied either perpendicular or parallel to wood or steel framing spaced a maximum of 24" o.c. Maximum spacing for vertical surfaces (walls) is 8" o.c. for nails, and 12" o.c. for screws.

The sheathing products above are not designed to perform as shear or racking braces. Install diagonal corner braces, or equal, at all external corners as required by applicable code.

For shear values for FIBEROCK AQUA-TOUGH sheathing and SECUROCK Glass-Mat sheathing, see your local USG representative.

Interior Gypsum Ceiling Panel Application

1/2" SHEETROCK brand interior gypsum ceiling panels, sag-resistant, are specially formulated to support water-based spray texture paints and overlaid insulation with the same sag resistance as regular 5/8" gypsum board. These panels can be substituted for regular 1/2" board in other applications, such as on sidewalls, reducing waste and lowering in-place cost. The panels are ideal for new construction or renovation over wood or steel framing.

Handling Store and handle these panels in the same manner as other gypsum board. Stack boards flat and store them under cover.

Installation Apply these panels to ceilings before applying gypsum boards to walls. Joists must be spaced 24" o.c. or less. Board may be cut by scoring and snapping in the same manner as other gypsum board.

These ceiling panels are designed for parallel or perpendicular application to framing components spaced up to 24" o.c. with a maximum 2.2 lbs./SF insulation loading and wet texturing for ceiling application. For single-layer wood-framed ceilings, nails are spaced 7" o.c.; 1-1/4" type W screws are placed 12" o.c. Adhesive/nail-on fastening improves bond strength and reduces face nailing. Finish with a USG joint treatment system.

In new construction or renovation applications, steel furring channels can be used (resilient channels or metal furring channels spaced a maximum of 24" o.c., fastened to bottom of joists).

Caution: Careful attention should be paid to framing construction and alignment. Problems will "telegraph" through the board if the framing is not true. Excessively long drying times may also cause ceiling finish problems, such as joint banding and staining. Ensure proper ventilation to remove excess moisture during and after finishing. Supplemental heat or dehumidification may be required.

Surface Preparation Before texturing, apply a high-quality, undiluted latex or alkyd primer/sealer. Follow manufacturer's directions for application. See page 74 for ceiling frame spacing and supported insulation limitations.

Exterior Ceiling Board Application

SHEETROCK brand exterior gypsum ceiling board embodies a specially treated gypsum core encased in chemically treated paper. The result is an ideal surface material for sheltered exterior ceiling areas such as covered walkways and malls, large canopies, open porches, breezeways, carports and exterior soffits.

Weather- and fire-resistant, 1/2" or 5/8" thick exterior ceiling board may be applied directly to wood framing or to cross-furring of wood or metal furring channels attached to main supports.

Special Conditions

Where frame spacing exceeds 16" o.c. for 1/2" board or 24" o.c. for 5/8" board, furring is required to provide support for gypsum board.

Wood Framing Requirements 1 x 3 wood furring may be used for screw application where support member spacing is 24" o.c. maximum. Furring of 2" nominal thickness should be used for nailing board or where framing spacing is from 24" to 48" maximum o.c.

Steel Framing Requirements Installation of grillage should be the same as for "Steel Frame Single-Layer Application" previously described in this chapter on page 122.

Ventilation Where the area above the ceiling board opens to an attic space above habitable rooms, the space should be vented to the outside in accordance with local building codes. Where the ceiling board is applied directly to rafters or to roof-ceiling joists (as in flat roof construction) that extend beyond habitable rooms, vents are required at each end of each rafter or joist space. Vents should be screened and be a minimum of 2" wide x full length between rafters (or joists). Vents should be attached through the board to minimum 1 x 2 backing strips installed prior to board application. Vent openings should be framed and located within 6" of the eave's outer edge.

Soffit ventilation

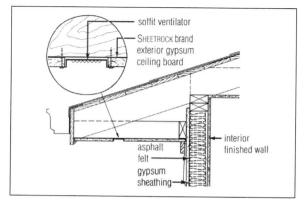

soffit ventilator
SHEETROCK brand
exterior gypsum
ceiling board

asphalt
felt
gypsum
sheathing

interior
finished wall

*Exterior ceiling board
application showing wall
intersection (top) and
control joint*

Weather Protection At the perimeter and at vertical penetrations, the exposed core of panels must be covered with No. 401 metal trim or securely fastened moldings.

In areas subject to freezing temperatures and other severe weather conditions, shingled roofs should be installed in accordance with industry-accepted roofing practices.

Fascia boards should extend at least 1/4" below the ceiling board or adjacent trim mouldings, whichever is lower, to provide a drip edge.

Intersections Where ceiling board expanse exceeds 4', a space of at least 1/4" should be provided between its edge and the adjacent walls, beams, columns and fascia. This space may be screened or covered with moulding, but must not be caulked.

Control Joints SHEETROCK exterior gypsum ceiling board, like other building materials, is subject to structural movement, expansion and contraction due to changes in temperature and humidity.

Install a control joint no. 093 or a control joint consisting of two pieces of No. 401 metal trim back-to-back in ceiling board where expansion or control joints occur in the exterior wall or roof.

Long, narrow areas should have control joints spaced no more than 30' apart. Wings of "L", "U" and "T"-shaped areas should be separated with control joints. Also, intersections of dissimilar materials should be separated with control joints. These joints usually are placed so that they intersect light fixtures, vents, etc. to relieve stress concentrations. The canopy must be designed to resist uplift.

Fixtures Provide backing or blocking for electrical boxes, vents and heavy fixtures. Cut board neatly and accurately to fit within 1/4" of fixtures and vents. Cover openings with trim.

**Steel frame canopy
(commercial)**

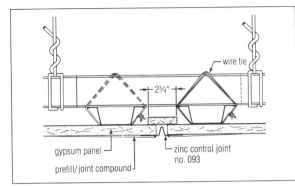

Steel frame furred canopy

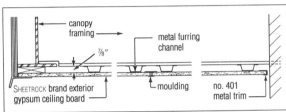

Installation

Apply exterior ceiling board with the long dimension across supports. For 1/2" board, the maximum support spacing is 16" o.c.; for 5/8" board, 24" o.c. maximum. Position end joints under supports. Use maximum practical lengths to minimize end joints. Allow 1/16" to 1/8" space between butted ends of board. Fasten board to supports with screws spaced 12" o.c. or nails spaced 8" o.c.

Hotel entrance canopy; faced with SHEETROCK brand exterior ceiling board.

For steel framing, use 1" type S corrosion-resistant screws (type S-12 for 20-ga. and thicker steel). For wood framing, use 1-1/4" type W screws or 1-1/2" galvanized box nails or 1-1/2" aluminum nails. Treat fasteners and joints using a SHEETROCK brand setting-type (DURABOND) or lightweight setting-type (EASY SAND) joint compound. If desired, panel joints may be concealed with batten strips or by installing panels with ends inserted into aluminum H-mouldings (by others). After joint compound has dried, apply one coat of oil-based primer-sealer and one coat exterior oil or latex paint (or other balanced finishing system recommended by the paint manufacturer) to all exposed surfaces.

Gypsum Board Suspended Ceilings

Gypsum board applications for suspended ceilings provide excellent fire protection and appearance with exceptional economy. Applications include SHEETROCK ceiling lay-in tiles in standard DONN suspension grid or surface-mounted SHEETROCK brand gypsum panels on USG drywall suspension system.

Lay-In Tiles   SHEETROCK brand ceiling lay-in tiles have a FIRECODE C Core and square-cut edges. They are available in 2' x 2' or 2' x 4' sizes and either natural paper facing or a laminated white vinyl facing with a stipple pattern. Tiles may be installed in DONN brand DX, DXL or DXLA suspension systems for most interior applications or ZXA, ZXLA or AX suspension systems for exterior applications or high humidity areas. (See USG ceilings catalogs for complete information.)

Install tiles beginning at one corner of the room and work one row at a time. Tilt the tile up through the opening and lower it to rest squarely on all four tees. Snap firmly in place. Where partial tiles are required, use a straight edge and cut face of tiles with a utility knife, snap at the score and cut through the backing. Trim rough edges as necessary to fit.

Surface-Mounted Panels   SHEETROCK brand gypsum panels provide a monolithic ceiling when mounted to USG Drywall Suspension System. The system offers 1, 1-1/2, 2 and 3-hr. fire ratings when constructed with SHEETROCK brand gypsum panels, FIRECODE C or Type X formulations (consult UL Fire Resistance Directory).

Beginning at one corner of the room, mount panels parallel to main tees with butt ends meeting in the center of the cross channels. Hold panels firmly in place against channels and secure them with 1-1/4" type S screws. Complete the assembly in the same manner as conventional gypsum board ceiling construction. Finish with a USG joint treatment system and caulk perimeter with SHEETROCK brand acoustical sealant.

Mineral Wool Blanket Application

Many USG drywall and veneer partitions have been developed to meet the demand for increased privacy between units in residential and commercial construction. Designed for wood stud, steel stud or laminated gypsum board construction, these assemblies offer highly efficient sound-control properties, yet are more economical than other partitions that offer equal sound isolation. These improved sound-isolation properties and ratings are obtained by using mineral wool sound attenuation fire blankets and decoupling the partition faces. Decoupling is achieved with resilient application or with double rows of studs on separate plates. General application procedures for these products follow. See Chapter 1 for product descriptions.

Installation

Install blankets to completely fill the stud cavity from bottom to top, and with the vapor retarder oriented according to job specifications. If necessary to tightly fill height, cut stock-length blankets with a serrated knife for insertion in the void. Tightly butt ends and sides of blankets within a cavity. Cut small pieces of mineral wool blankets for narrow stud spaces next to door openings or at partition intersections. Fit blankets carefully behind electrical outlets, bracing, fixture attachments, medicine cabinets, etc.

In ceilings, insulation should be carefully fitted around recessed lighting fixtures. Covering fixtures with insulation causes heat to build up, which could possibly result in a fire.

Creased Mineral Wool Sound Insulation Systems

Creased mineral wool assemblies are non-load bearing, steel-framed, 1-hr. fire-rated systems that offer high sound ratings (50-55 STC) plus the lower in-place cost of lightweight single-layer gypsum board. The systems consist of 5/8" SHEETROCK brand gypsum panels, FIRECODE C Core; 3- 5/8" steel studs spaced 24" o.c. and set in runners; and mineral wool sound attenuation fire blankets, 25" wide.

Since the blanket is 1" wider than the cavity, it is installed with a slit that is field-cut down the center and partially through the blanket. This allows the blanket to flex or bow in the center, easing the pressure against the studs and transferring it to the face panel, thereby dampening sound vibrations more effectively. Gypsum panels may be screw-attached directly or resiliently to the steel framing.

Creased mineral wool application—mineral wool SAFB 1 wider than stud cavity is field cut with utility, carpet or hook-blade knife. Crease will press against gypsum panel to dampen sound vibrations.

Perimeter Isolation

Perimeter relief should be provided for gypsum construction surfaces where (a) a partition or furring abuts a structural element (except a floor) or dissimilar wall or ceiling; (b) a ceiling or soffit abuts a structural element, dissimilar partition or other vertical penetration; (c) a ceiling, partition or furring run exceeds 30' in either direction; (d) expansion or control joints occur throughout the building itself.

In addition, less-than-ceiling-height frames should have control joints extending to the ceiling from both corners. Ceiling-height door frames may be used as control joints. Treat window openings in the same manner as doors.

Isolation is important to reduce potential cracking in partitions; ceilings; and wall, column, and beam furring. It reduces the likelihood of sound flanking in rated construction. Generally, methods for isolating surfaces are detailed and specified according to the job. The typical intersection application described below may be adapted as required.

Gypsum Board Edge Treatment Where boards intersect dissimilar materials or structural elements, appropriate trim should be applied to the face-layer perimeter, and SHEETROCK brand acoustical sealant applied to close the gap. P-1 vinyl trim may be used without sealant or joint treatment.

Partition-Structural Ceiling Attach the steel runner to the structural ceiling to position the partition. Cut the steel stud 3/8" min., 1/2" maximum less than the floor-to-ceiling height. Attach the gypsum board to the stud at least 2-1/2" down from the ceiling. Allow 3/8" minimum clearance atop gypsum boards; finish as required. Special detailing may also be required to meet fire ratings. Check UL listings for specifications.

Partition-Radiant Heat Ceiling Allow at least 1/8" clear space between radiant-heated ceilings and walls or partition framing. Finish ceiling angle with P-2 vinyl trim or wood moulding fastened to wall members only.

Partition-Exterior Wall or Column Attach the steel stud to the exterior wall or column to position the partition. Attach the gypsum board only to the second steel stud erected vertically at a maximum of 6" from the wall. Allow at least 3/8" clearance between the partition panel and the wall. Caulk as required with SHEETROCK brand acoustical sealant.

Perimeter relief at columns reduces possibility of cracking.

Exterior Wall Allow a 1/4" minimum clearance between acoustical trim and the intersecting exterior wall or column. Apply SHEETROCK brand acoustical sealant as required.

Ceiling-Exterior Wall On suspended or furred ceilings, locate supports for gypsum board within 6" of abutting surfaces, but do not allow the main runner or furring channels to be let into or come into contact with abutting masonry walls.

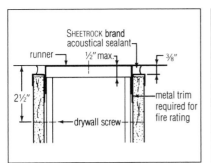

Partition-structural ceiling

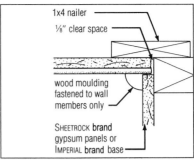

Partition-radiant heat ceiling

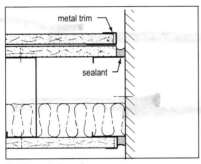

Partition-exterior wall

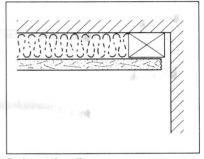

Furring-exterior wall

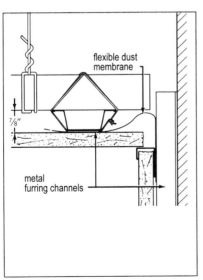

Ceiling-exterior wall

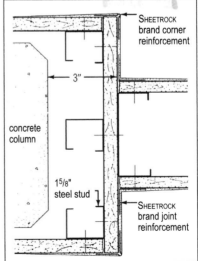

Partition-column

Partition-Column Fur gypsum board away from concrete columns using vertical steel studs. Attach the stud in the intersecting partition to the stud within the free-standing furring.

Floating Interior Angle Application

The floating interior angle method of applying gypsum board effectively reduces angle cracking and nail pops resulting from stresses at intersections of walls and ceilings. Fasteners are eliminated on at least one surface at all interior angles, both where walls and ceilings meet and where sidewalls intersect. Follow standard framing practices for corner fastening. Conventional framing and ordinary wood back-up or blocking must be provided where needed at vertical and horizontal interior angles. Apply gypsum board to ceilings first.

Ceilings

Use conventional single nail or screw application. Apply the first nails or screws approximately 7" from the wall and at each joist. Use conventional fastening in the remainder of the ceiling area.

Sidewalls

Apply gypsum board on walls so that its uppermost edge (or end) is in firm contact with and provides support to the perimeter of the board already installed on the ceiling. Apply the first nails or screws approximately 8" below the ceiling at each stud. At vertical angles omit corner fasteners for the first board applied at the angle. This panel edge will be overlapped and held in place by the edge of the abutting board. Nail or screw-attach the overlapping board in the conventional manner. Use conventional fastening for the remainder of the sidewall area.

Double Nailing

When double nailing is used with a floating interior angle, follow the above spacing on the first nail from the intersecting point and use double nailing in the rest of the area. Provide conventional framing and ordinary wood back-up or blocking at vertical internal angles.

Detail—floating interior angle

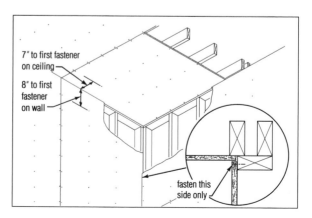

7" to first fastener on ceiling

8" to first fastener on wall

fasten this side only

Fixture Installation

Electrical Fixtures

After electrical services have been roughed in, and before gypsum board is installed, cut the necessary openings in the base and face layers of the board to accept switches, outlet and fixture boxes, etc. Cut out openings with a keyhole saw or with specially designed cutting tools, which produce more precise openings. (See Chapter 14.)

Sealant Where the partition is used as a sound barrier, do not install boxes back-to back or in the same stud cavity. Apply SHEETROCK brand acoustical sealant around all boxes to seal the cut-out. See acoustical sealant application earlier in this chapter. Electrical boxes with a drywall ring or device cover (for use as a stop in caulking) are recommended.

Fixture Attachment

Gypsum board partitions can provide suitable anchorage for most types of fixtures normally found in residential and commercial construction. However, it is important to have an understanding of requirements for attachment of each fixture type. In this way, sound-control characteristics will be retained, and attachment will be within the allowable load-carrying capacity of the assembly—ensuring satisfactory job performance.

In wood-frame construction, fixtures are usually attached directly to the framing or to blocking or supports attached to the framing. Blocking or supports should be provided for plumbing fixtures, towel racks, grab bars and similar items. Fixture supports used with DUROCK brand cement board are shown in Chapter 4, "Backerboard Installation." Single- or double-layer gypsum boards are not designed to support loads imposed by these items without additional support to carry the main part of the load.

Only lightweight fixtures should be attached to resilient wall surfaces constructed with resilient channel unless special framing is provided. (See "Cabinet Attachment Method," following.) Refrain from attaching fixtures to party walls where they may provide a direct flow path for sound. Gypsum boards used in the ceiling are not designed to support light fixtures or troffers, air vents or other equipment. Separate supports must be provided.

Fixture Attachment Types

Loading capacities of various fasteners and fixture attachments used with gypsum board partitions appear in the load table on page 493. Fasteners and methods follow.

No. 8 Sheet Metal Screw Driven into 25-ga. min. sheet metal plate or strip, laminated between the face board and the base board in laminated gypsum partitions. Also may be driven through gypsum board into a steel stud. Ideal for planned light fixture attachment.

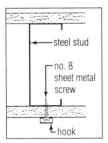

Continuous Horizontal Bracing   Back-up for fixture attachment is provided with notched runner attached to steel studs with two 3/8" type S pan head screws.

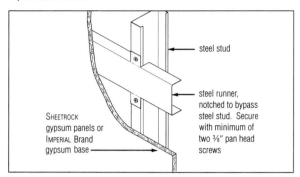

SHEETROCK gypsum panels or IMPERIAL Brand gypsum base

steel stud

steel runner, notched to bypass steel stud. Secure with minimum of two ⅜" pan head screws

Bolt and Nested Channels   Bolt welded to nested 1-1/2" channels for use in mounting hanger brackets for heavy fixtures. Suitable for use in laminated gypsum partitions, provided that fixture attachments do not contact opposite coreboard.

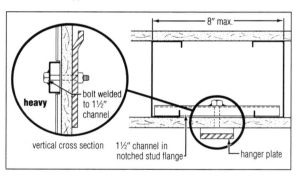

8" max.

heavy

bolt welded to 1½" channel

vertical cross section   1½" channel in notched stud flange

hanger plate

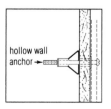

hollow wall anchor

Hollow Wall Anchors   1/4" hollow wall anchors installed in gypsum boards only. One advantage of this fastener is that the threaded section remains in the wall when the screw is removed. Also, widespread spider support formed by the expanded anchor spreads the load against the wall material, increasing the load capacity.

Anchor Inserts   Inserted into drilled holes, these anchors spread when a fastener is inserted, gripping the inside of the hole. Good for fastening small objects.

Screw Anchors   Also inserted into a drilled hole, these anchors have broad screw planes for more positive attachment to the gypsum board. The screw attachment improves pull-out resistance capacity.

toggle bolt

wood block

Toggle Bolt   1/4" toggle bolt installed in gypsum board only. One disadvantage of toggle bolts is that when they are removed, the wing fastener on the back will fall down into the hollow wall. Another disadvantage is that a large hole is required to allow wings to pass through wall facings.

Bolt and 1-1/2" Channel Bolt welded to single 1-1/2" channel and inserted in notches cut in steel stud for use in mounting hanger brackets for heavy fixtures.

Fixture Attachment Load Data—Drywall and Veneer Plaster Construction

fastener type	size in.	mm	base[1]	allowable withdrawal resistance lb.	N[2]	allowable shear resistance lb.	N[2]
Toggle Bolt or	1/8	3.18	1/2" gypsum board	20	89	40	178
Hollow Wall Anchor	3/16	4.76		30	133	50	222
	1/4	6.35		40	178	60	267
	1/8	3.18	1/2" gypsum board and	70	311	100	445
	3/16	4.76	25-ga. steel stud	80	356	125	556
	1/4	6.35		155	689	175	778
No. 8 sheet metal screw			1/2" gypsum board and 25-ga. steel stud or	50	222	80	356
Type S bugle head screw			25-ga. steel insert	60	267	100	445
Type S-12 bugle head screw			1/2" gypsum board and 20-ga. steel stud or 20-ga. steel insert	85	378	135	600
3/8" Type S pan head screw			25-ga. steel to 25-ga. steel	70	311	120	534
Two bolts welded to steel insert	3/16	4.76	1/2" gypsum board, plate and steel stud	175	778	200	890
	1/4	6.35	1/2" gypsum board, plate and steel stud	200	890	250	1112
Bolt welded to 1-1/2" chan.	1/4	6.35	(see drawing)	200	890	250	1112

(1) Comparable information is available for Fiberock Brand Panels. See the most current literature on Fiberock Brand Panels for data.
(2) Newton.

Cabinet Attachment Method Detailed below, allows the following items to be mounted without reducing the sound rating: kitchen, bathroom and other cabinets and fixtures (except lavatories and wall-mounted toilets) of moderate weight, and "Hollywood" style headboards on party walls using resilient channel. Recommended only for residential and light commercial wood-frame construction. Suitable for loads including cabinet weight of 67.5 lbs. for studs spaced 16" o.c. and 40 lbs. for studs 24" o.c. Loads are a maximum per linear foot of resilient channel installed for cabinet attachment. Mounting cabinets back-to-back on a partition should be avoided since this practice creates a flanking path that increases sound transmission.

In this system, 5/8" gypsum board is installed with the long dimension parallel to the channels and fastened with 1" type S screws spaced 12" o.c. along the channels. Cabinets are attached to channels with 2-1/4" type S screws spaced 12" o.c. and located between studs. Screws must be driven between studs. Screws that penetrate the stud cause a significant loss in the partition's sound rating.

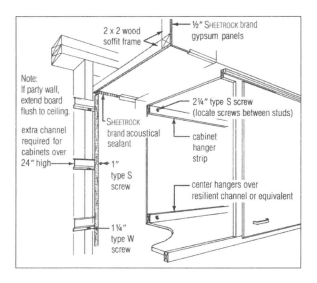

2 x 2 wood soffit frame

½″ SHEETROCK brand gypsum panels

Note:
If party wall, extend board flush to ceiling.

extra channel required for cabinets over 24″ high

SHEETROCK brand acoustical sealant

1″ type S screw

1¼″ type W screw

2¼″ type S screw (locate screws between studs)

cabinet hanger strip

center hangers over resilient channel or equivalent

Curved Surfaces

Versatile SHEETROCK brand gypsum panels and IMPERIAL brand gypsum base can be formed to almost any cylindrically curved surface. Boards can be applied either dry or wet depending on the radius of curvature desired and the thickness and flexibility of the board. To prevent flat areas between framing, shorter bend radii require closer than normal stud and furring spacing.

SHEETROCK brand 1/4″ flexible gypsum panels are specifically designed for this purpose. These 1/4″ panels are more flexible than standard gypsum panels of the same thickness and adapt quickly to the curved framing for walls, archways and circular stairways. Multiple layers may be applied.

Boards are horizontally or vertically applied, gently bent around the framing, and securely fastened to achieve the desired radius. When boards are applied dry, the minimum radius of curvature meets many applications. (See table below for dry gypsum boards.) By thoroughly moistening the face or back paper prior to application, and replacing in the stack for at least one hour, the board may be bent to still shorter radii. (See table for wetted gypsum board.) When the board dries thoroughly, it will regain its original hardness.

Curved stairwell, faced with drywall, forms attractive design element in a shopping mall (right). Radius of curved gypsum board, joints treated, is shown in construction view (below).

3

Minimum Bending Radii of Dry Gypsum Board[1]

Board Thickness		Board Applied With Long Dimension Perpendicular to Framing		Board Applied with Long Dimension Parallel to Framing	
in.	mm	ft.	m	ft.	m
1/4	6.4	3	0.9	5	1.8
3/8	9.5	6	1.8	9	2.7
1/2	12.7	12	3.7	—	—
5/8	15.9	18	5.5	—	—

(1) Comparable information is available for FIBEROCK Brand Panels. See the most current literature on FIBEROCK Brand Panels for data.

Minimum Radii of SHEETROCK Brand 1/4″ Flexible Gypsum Panels

Application	Condition	Lengthwise Bend Radii in.	mm	Max. Stud Spacing in.	mm	Widthwise Bend Radii in.	mm	Max. Stud Spacing in.	mm
Inside (concave)	Dry*	32	813	9	229	45	1143	9	229
Outside (convex)	Dry*	34	864	9	229	20	508	6	152

*@75°F/50% relative humidity.

Minimum Bending Radii of Wetted Gypsum Board[1]

Board Panel Thickness	Radius	Inside Length of Arc[2]	Outside Length of Arc[2]	No. of Studs on Arc Including at Tangents[3]	Approx. Stud Spacing c. to c.[4]	Max. Stud Spacing c. to c.[4]	Oz. of Water Required per One Side—oz[5]
1/4"	2'0"	3.14'	44.0"	9	5.50"	6"	30
1/4"	2'6"	3.93'	53.4"	10	5.93"	6"	30
3/8"	3'0"	4.71'	62.8"	9	7.85"	8"	35
3/8"	3'6"	5.50'	72.2"	11	7.22"	8"	35
1/2"	4'0"	6.28'	81.6"	8	11.70"	12"	45
1/2"	4'6"	7.07'	91.1"	9	11.40"	12"	45

(1) For gypsum board applied horizontally to a 4" thick partition (2) Arc length = $\frac{3.14 \cdot R}{2}$ (for a 90° arc).

(3) No. studs = outside arc length/maximum spacing +1 (rounded up to next whole number). (4) Stud spacing = outside arc length/no. of studs -1 (measured along outside of runner). (5) Wet only the side of board that will be in tension. Water required per board side is based on 4' x 8' sheet.

Installation

Framing Cut one leg and web of the top and bottom steel runners at 2" intervals for the length of the arc. Allow 12" of uncut steel runners at each end of the arc. Bend the runners to a uniform curve of the desired radius (90° max. arc). To support the cut leg of the runner, clinch a 1" x 25-ga. steel strip to the inside of the leg. Select the runner size to match the steel studs; for wood studs, use a 3-1/2" steel runner. Attach steel runners to structural elements at the floor and ceiling with suitable fasteners as previously described.

Position studs vertically, with open side facing in the same direction and engaging floor and ceiling runners. Begin and end each arc with a stud and space intermediate studs equally as measured on the outside of the arc. Secure steel studs to runners with 3/8" type S pan head screws; secure wood studs with suitable fasteners. On tangents, place studs 6" o.c., leaving the last stud free-standing. Follow directions previously described for erecting balance of studs.

Panel Preparation Select the length and cut the board to allow one unbroken panel to cover the curved surface, and 12" tangents at each end. The outside panel must be longer than inside panels to compensate for additional radius contributed by the studs. Cut-outs for electrical boxes are not recommended in curved surfaces unless they can be made after boards are installed and thoroughly dry.

When wet board is required, evenly spray water on the surface (which will be in tension when the board is hung). Apply water with a conventional garden sprayer using the quantity shown in the table. Carefully stack boards with wet surfaces facing each other and cover the stack with a plastic sheet (polyethylene). Allow boards to set at least one hour before installation.

Panel Application Apply panels horizontally with the wrapped edge perpendicular to the studs. On the convex side of the partition, begin installation at one end of the curved surface and fasten the panel to the studs as it is wrapped around the curve. On the concave side of the partition, start fastening the panel to the stud at the center of the curve and work outward to the ends of the panel. For single-layer panels, space screws 12" o.c. Use 1" type S screws for steel studs and 1-1/4" type W screws for wood studs.

For double-layer application, apply the base layer horizontally and fasten it to the stud with screws spaced 16" o.c. Center face layer panels over joints in the base layer and secure them to studs with screws spaced 12" o.c. Use 1" type S screws for the base layer and 1-5/8" type S screws for the face layer. Allow panels to dry completely (approximately 24 hours under good drying conditions) before applying joint treatment.

3

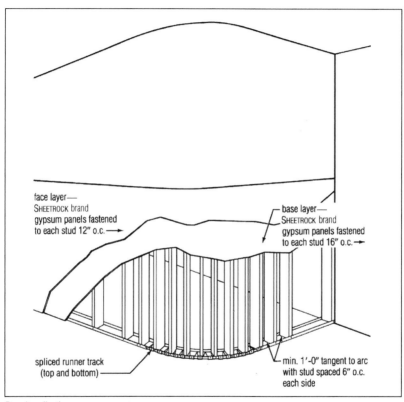

face layer—
SHEETROCK brand
gypsum panels fastened
to each stud 12″ o.c. →

base layer—
SHEETROCK brand
gypsum panels fastened
to each stud 16″ o.c. →

spliced runner track
(top and bottom)

min. 1′-0″ tangent to arc
with stud spaced 6″ o.c.
each side

Board application

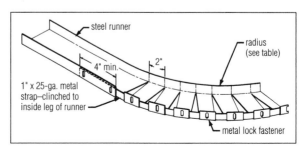

steel runner

radius
(see table)

4" min.

2"

1" x 25-ga. metal
strap—clinched to
inside leg of runner

metal lock fastener

Runner installation

Arches

Arches of any radii are easily faced with gypsum panels or base and are finished with a USG joint system or veneer plaster finish. Score or cut through the back paper of panels at 1" intervals to make them flexible. The board should previously have been cut to the desired width and length of the arch.

After the board has been applied to the arch framing with nails or screws, apply tape reinforcement (SHEETROCK brand joint tape for drywall panels or IMPERIAL brand type P or S for plaster base). Crease the tape along the center. Make scissor cuts half-way across the tape and 3/4" apart to make the tape flexible. Apply the uncut half to the curved surface, and fold the cut half of the tape onto the wall surface. Finish as appropriate for drywall or veneer plaster construction.

Soffits

Gypsum board soffits provide a lightweight, fast, economical way to fill over cabinets or lockers and housing for overhead ducts, pipes or conduits. Soffits are made with wood framing or steel stud and runner supports, faced with screw-attached gypsum board. Braced soffits up to 24" deep are constructed without supplementary vertical studs. Select components for the soffit size desired from the table on the next page. Unbraced soffits without horizontal studs are suitable for soffits up to 24" x 24". To retain fire protection, finish partitions and ceilings with gypsum board before installing soffits.

Installation

Braced Soffit Attach steel runners to the ceiling and sidewall as illustrated on page 143, placing fasteners close to the outside flange of the runner. On stud walls, space fasteners to engage the stud. Fasten vertical gypsum face board to the web of the face corner runner and flange of the ceiling runner with type S screws spaced 12" o.c. Place screws in the face corner runner at least 1" from the edge of the board. Insert steel studs between the face corner runner and sidewall runner and attach alternate studs to runners with screws. Attach the bottom face board to studs and runners with type S screws spaced 12" o.c. Attach corner bead and finish. Where sound control is important, attach resilient channel to the framing before attaching gypsum board.

Unbraced Soffit Attach steel studs and runners to the ceiling and sidewall, placing fasteners to engage wall and ceiling framing. Cut gypsum board to the soffit depth and attach a soffit-length stud with type S screws spaced 12" o.c. Attach this preassembled unit to the ceiling stud flange with screws spaced 12" o.c. Attach the bottom panel with type S screws spaced 12" o.c. Attach corner bead and finish.

Braced Soffit Design Maximum Dimensions[1]

Gypsum Board Thickness[2]		Steel Stud Size		Maximum Vertical[3]		Max. Horizontal for Max. Vertical Shown	
in.	mm	in.	mm	in.	mm	in.	mm
1/2	12.7	1-5/8	41.3	60	1525	48	1220
1/2	12.7	2-1/2, 3-5/8	63.5, 92.1	72	1830	36	915
5/8	15.9	1-5/8	41.3	60	1525	30	760
5/8	15.9	2-1/2, 3-5/8	63.5, 92.1	72	1830	18	455

(1) The construction is not designed to support loads other than its own dead weight. (2) Double-layer applications and 3/8″ board are not recommended for this construction. (3) Widths shown are based on construction having no supplemental vertical studs.

3

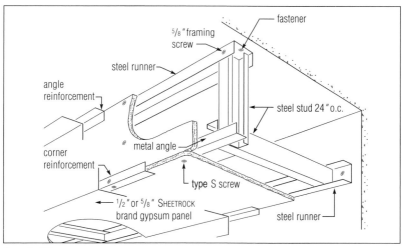

Braced soffit

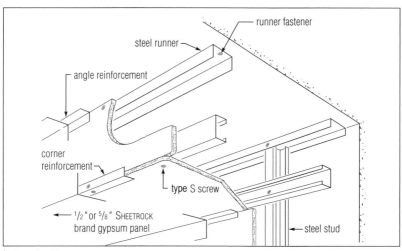

Unbraced soffit

Backerboard
Installation

4

Cement Board Products

Durock® brand cement board offers architects, builders and contractors a strong, water-durable base for ceramic and stone tile in tub and shower areas. It is also an abuse- and fire-resistant substrate for tile (quarry tile, lugged tile, thin stone tile, thin brick, glass and ceramic mosaics) in floor and wall applications. Cement board is applied over load-bearing or non-load-bearing wood or steel framing to produce high-performance systems.

Durock cement board is formed in a continuous process and consists of an aggregated Portland cement core, reinforced with polymer-coated glass-fiber mesh embedded in both surfaces and wrapped around the edges. This composition makes the product noncombustible and dimensionally stable.

Durock cement board products can also be used in exterior applications, such as fences, mobile-home skirting, agricultural buildings, exterior chimneys and garage wainscoting. See Chapter 6, "Finishing Veneer Plaster Systems," for veneer plaster applications over Durock cement board.

Various organizations provide information about recommended standards or tolerances for installation of cement board systems. See the Appendix for information for more on standards and tolerances.

For instructions on the safe use of cement board and related products, see Chapter 13, "Safety Considerations & Material Handling."

Cement Board Sizes[1] and Packaging

Thickness	Width	Lengths	Shipping Units[2]
1/2"	32"	5'	50
1/2"	3'	4', 5', 6'	50
1/2"	4'	8'	30
5/8"	4'	8'	24
5/16"	3'	5'	40
5/16"	4'	4'	40

(1) Other lengths may be available. Contact your USG Representative.
(2) Stretch wrapped and shipped in packaging units as shown.

Durock Brand Cement Board is sized and formulated for use in interior areas that may be subject to water or high moisture/humidity conditions, such as bathtub or shower enclosures, gang showers, bathroom floors, bath and kitchen countertops and steam rooms. The aggregated Portland cement core resists water penetration and will not deteriorate when wet.

Durock cement board is a superior substrate for ceramic, slate and quarry tile on all interior surfaces. Panels are manufactured in three widths for minimum cutting and easy handling and installation. Use larger panel sizes for bigger projects such as commercial kitchens and gang showers. Smaller panels are designed to fit typical tub and shower enclosures.

This product exceeds the ANSI standards for cementitious backer units (CBU). See ANSI A118.9 for test methods and specifications for CBU; and ANSI A118.9 for interior installation of CBU. The ASTM designation for DUROCK cement board is C1325. All DUROCK cement board products meet ASTM Standard E136 for noncombustibility.

DUROCK Brand Cement Board Limitations

1. Steel framing must be 20-ga. or heavier.

2. Systems using DUROCK cement board are designed for positive or negative uniform loads of up to 30 psf with studs spaced maximum 16" o.c. (See publication SA700 for design recommendations on systems requiring uniform loads up to 40 psf.)

3. Maximum stud spacing: 16" o.c. (24" o.c. for cavity shaft wall assembly, requires intermediate adhesive bead); maximum allowable deflection, L/360. Maximum fastener spacing: 8" o.c. for wood and steel framing on floors and walls; 6" o.c. for ceiling applications.

4. Maximum dead load for ceiling system is 7.5 psf, including cement board.

5. Drywall screws and drywall nails should not be used, as they do not provide adequate holding capacity.

6. Not recommended for vinyl flooring.

7. 5/16" thickness should not be used for walls or ceilings.

8. Drywall joint compounds must not be used directly over cement board unless it is properly sealed; see page 158.

DUROCK Brand Cement Board features.

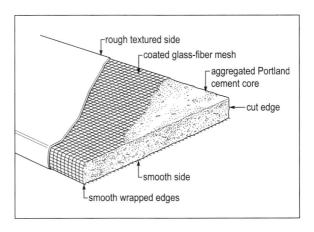

rough textured side

coated glass-fiber mesh

aggregated Portland cement core

cut edge

smooth side

smooth wrapped edges

Durock Brand Cement Board

Typical Physical Properties

Property	Test Method	1/2"	5/16"
Flexural strength—psi	ASTM C947	750	1250
Indentation strength—psi 1" dia. disc @ 0.02" indent.	ASTM D2394	>1250	>1250
Uniform load—psf studs 16" o.c.	—	30 max,	—
Water absorption -% by wt. 24 hrs.	ASTM C473-84	15	15
Nail pull resistance—lb. 0.4" head diameter (wet or dry)	ASTM C473-84	90	—
Weight-psf	ASTM C473-84	<3	<2.3
Freeze/thaw resistance—Procedure B number of cycles with no deterioration	ASTM C666-84	100	100
Non Combustibility	ASTM E136	Pass	Pass
Surface burning characteristics—flame/smoke	ASTM E84	0/0	0/0
Thermal "R"/k value	ASTM C177	0.37/1.35	—
Standard method for evaluating ceramic floor tile installation systems	ASTM C627	Lt. Commercial	Lt. Commercial
Min. bending radius—ft.	—	6	—

Fiber-Reinforced Gypsum Panels

FIBEROCK tile backerboard and underlayment are manufactured from a specially engineered combination of gypsum and cellulose fibers and have a uniform water- and mold-resistant composition. They are also environmentally friendly with a certified recycled content of 95%.

FIBEROCK panels can be used on floors under ceramic tile, carpeting, hardwood, resilient and laminate flooring and on walls under ceramic tile or paint finishes. FIBEROCK underlayment has been tested by the Tile Council of North America and is recognized for residential and light commercial use. FIBEROCK tile backerboard is also recognized for use by both the Tile Council of North America and the *International Residential Code* as a backerboard for both wet and dry areas of the home including tub and shower surrounds. The 1/4" and 3/8" underlayment panels are ideal for floors, with 1/2" and 5/8" tile backerboard recommended for walls. FIBEROCK underlayment and tile backerboard meet ASTM Standard C1278. For the most current installation recommendations on all types of finishes, including resilient flooring, please refer to **usg.com**.

Sizes[1] and Packaging

Thickness	Width	Lengths	Shipping Units
1/4"	3'	5'	60
1/4"	4'	4'	60
3/8"	3'	5'	60
3/8"	4'	4'	60
3/8"	4'	8'	40
1/2"	3'	5'	50
1/2"	4'	5'	50
1/2"	4'	8'	30
5/8"	3'	5'	40

[1]Other lengths available. Contact your USG Representative.

Limitations

1. Maximum stud and fastener spacing:

Wall Panel	Frame Spacing	Nails	Screws
1/2"	16" o.c.	8" o.c.	12" o.c.
5/8"	16" o.c.	8" o.c.	12" o.c.

2. Maximum deflection L/360 for ceramic tile and L/720 for natural stone.

3. For marble and stone applications, consult current TCNA and MIA guidelines for recommendations.

4. Do not use in areas subject to prolonged exposure to standing water—for instance, in gang showers, saunas, steam showers or hot-tub decks.

5. Fiberock tile backerboard must be tiled or painted, not used as a finish surface.

6. Panels should not be exposed to sustained temperatures above 125°F (51.6°C).

7. For fire-resistant or abuse-resistant construction over steel framing, a minimum of 20 gauge steel framing is required.

8. For interior use only.

9. Do not install directly over concrete subfloors.

10. Do not install over heavily cushioned, thick-foam-backed vinyl flooring.

11. Do not install using drywall screws or drywall nails.

12. For ceramic tile flooring applications, underlayment must be bonded using mortar or adhesive, and mechanically fastened to subfloor.

4

FIBEROCK Tile Backerboard
Typical Physical Properties

Performance Attributes	Test Method	1/2"	5/8"
Compressive Strength	ASTM D2394	500 psi	500 psi
Shear-Bond Strength	7 Day Cure ANSI A108	> 50 psi	> 50 psi
Flexural Strength	ASTM C473	120 (minimum) lbf	161 (minimum) lbf
Nail-Head Pull-Through Resistance	ASTM C473	120 (minimum) lbf	145 (minimum) lbf
Water Absorption	ASTM C473	5%	5%
Surface Water Absorption (Cobb)	ASTM C473	1.6 grams	1.6 grams
Linear Variation with Moisture Change	ASTM D1037	0.03%	0.03 %
Coefficient of Thermal Expansion	ASTM E831	9.0×10-6 in./in./°F	9.0×10-6 in./in./°F
Mold Resistance	ASTM D3273	10	10
Flame Spread	ASTM E84	0	0
Smoke Development	ASTM E84	5	5
Thermal "R" Value	ASTM C518	0.3 hr.ft.2 °F/Btu	

DUROCK Brand Accessory Products

DUROCK Brand Wood (above) and Steel Screws (below)

DUROCK **Brand Wood and Steel Screws** are made with a special corrosion-resistant coating that is superior to cadmium plating or zinc. Wafer head design with countersinking ribs allows flush seating while preventing strip-outs. Increased bearing surface provides greater pull-through resistance. (Drywall screws do not provide adequate pull-through resistance and must not be used.). For 14- to 20-ga. steel framing, use 1-1/4" and 1-5/8" DUROCK steel screws. For wood framing, use 1-1/4", 1-5/8" or 2-1/4" DUROCK wood screws. Packaging: 1-1/4" screws, 5,000 pieces per carton, or twenty 150-pc. boxes; 1-5/8" screws, 4,000 pieces per carton; 2-1/4" screws, 2,000 pieces per carton. Ensure minimum thread penetration of 3/4" into steel framing and 1/2" into wood framing.

Hot-Dipped Galvanized Roofing Nails

Durock *Brand Alkali-Resistant Tape*

Nails 1-1/2" hot-dipped galvanized roofing nails may be used for Durock cement board, Durock underlayment, Fiberock tile backerboard and Fiberock underlayment attachment to wood framing.

Staples 1/4" crown or larger chisel point staples may be used only for Fiberock underlayment attachment to wood framing.

Durock Brand Tile Backer Tape is a specially designed, alkali-resistant tape. Tape is 2"-wide, polymer-coated, open glass-fiber mesh. Packaging: 2" (nom.) x 75' rolls; 24 rolls per carton.

Adhesives, Mortars and Grout Use only adhesive products compatible with alkaline or Portland-cement-based substrates. Multi-purpose adhesive for subfloor attachment to framing must meet ASTM C557-73; ceramic tile adhesive must be Type I meeting ANSI A136.1; dry-set mortar mixed with acrylic latex additive must meet ANSI A118.1; latex Portland cement mortar must meet ANSI A118.4; and grout must meet ANSI A118.6.

Job Preparation & Design Considerations

Estimating

Material requirements for underlayment and backerboard applications are estimated in much the same manner as gypsum drywall. There are, however, some important differences:

Measure surface area "solid," ignoring cut-outs for doors and windows. For wall or ceiling applications, use 1/2" or 5/8" panels as necessary to match adjacent gypsum panel thickness. 5/8" Durock cement board may be substituted for 1/2" Durock cement board to meet surface dimension requirements without diluting the fire-rated performance of fire-rated assemblies that call for 1/2" Durock board.

It is permissible to substitute 5/8" Fiberock panels for 5/8" Sheetrock Firecode Core gypsum panels or 1/2" Sheetrock Firecode C Core gypsum panels without compromising the fire rating.

A water barrier, not a vapor retarder, may be required behind tile backerboard in many applications as dictated by local building codes. The water barrier must be Grade D building paper, No. 15 asphalt felt or equivalent. Ensure that the total square footage of water barrier exceeds the total square footage of cement board to take into account material overlaps required to prevent moisture penetration.

To estimate quantities of mortars, grouts and adhesives, consult packaging and coverage information for those products.

Environmental Conditions

All materials should be delivered and stored in their original unopened packages in an enclosed shelter that provides protection from damage and exposure to the elements. Even though the stability and durability of Durock cement board is unaffected by the elements, moisture and temperature variations may have an effect on the bonding effectiveness of basecoats and adhesives.

Various humidity and temperature conditions may require a vapor retarder. A qualified engineer should be consulted to determine the proper location of the retarder to prevent moisture condensation within the wall.

Control Joints

Certain types of interior wall surface construction should be isolated with surface control joints (also called expansion joints) or other means where: (a) a wall abuts a structural element or dissimilar wall or ceiling; (b) construction changes within the plane of the wall; (c) tile and thin brick surfaces exceed 16' in either direction. Surface control joint width should comply with architectural specifications. Location and design of building control joints must be detailed by a professional architect. Steel framing at building control joints that extend through the wall (with top and bottom runner tracks broken) should have 1-1/2" cold-rolled channel alignment stabilizers spaced a maximum of 5'-0" o.c. vertically. Channels should be placed through holes in the stud web of the first two adjacent studs on both sides of the joint and securely attached to the first adjacent stud on either side of the joint. (See Moisture-Resistant Assemblies publication SA934 for further information.)

Panels should be separated at all surface and building control joints. Where vertical and horizontal joints intersect, the vertical joint should be continuous, and the horizontal joint should abut it. Splices, terminals and intersections should be caulked with a sealant that complies with architectural specifications and sealant manufacturer recommendations. Do not apply tile or finishes over caulked, sealed expansion joints.

High-Moisture Areas

Pool Enclosures DUROCK cement board systems may be used for the walls and ceilings around indoor swimming pools. Adequate consideration should be given to ventilation to protect against deterioration of metal hangers and framing members in areas of high moisture and chlorine content.

Steam Rooms and Saunas Where temperatures exceed 120°F for extended periods, use DUROCK cement boards with dry-set or latex-fortified Portland cement mortar; do not use organic adhesive.

Leaching and Efflorescence

Latex leaching and efflorescence are natural phenomena that occur with the use of latex-modified mortars and grouts, through no fault in the products. Follow current manufacturer guidelines and recommendations to help prevent these problems.

Applications

Framing

For wall applications, frame spacing for DUROCK cement board and FIBEROCK tile backerboard attachment must not exceed 16" o.c. (24" o.c. for cavity shaft wall assembly). Studs of freestanding furred walls must be secured to an exterior wall with furring brackets, or laterally braced with horizontal studs or runners spaced 4' o.c. max. Laterally brace all steel-framed walls before applying joint treatment. If necessary for tub or shower surround applications, fur out studs to allow fixtures and components to be flush with the ceramic tile face. Install appropriate blocking or headers to support tub and other plumbing fixtures and to receive soap dishes, grab bars, towel racks and other accessories and hardware.

Ceiling framing must be capable of supporting the total ceiling dead load, including insulation, ceramic tile, bonding materials and tile-backer board, with deflection not exceeding L/360.

For floor applications, maximum joist spacing is 24" with a minimum subfloor thickness of 23/32". The subfloor should be designed for a defection limit of L/360 for ceramic tile and L/720 for natural stone. The subfloor should be APA Span-Rated Plywood or OSB with an Exposure 1 classification or better with tongue and groove or back-blocked at the unsupported edges. Apply 3/8" bead of multi-purpose adhesive to the center of the top flange of the joists. Place plywood panels with the long dimension across or parallel to wood or steel joists spaced maximum 16" o.c. Fasten plywood to steel joists with 1-15/16" pilot point type S-12 screws spaced 16" o.c. Fasten plywood to wood joists with suitable nails or screws spaced 12" o.c. or as required by code.

For countertops, install minimum 3/4" exterior grade plywood base across wood cabinet supports spaced 16" o.c. Position the ends and edges over the supports.

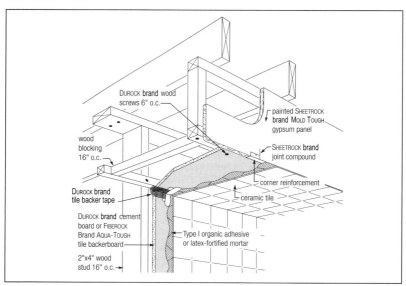

Wood soffit framing

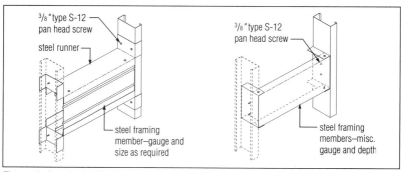

Fixture attachment—steel framing

Fixture Attachment

Framing and bracing must be capable of supporting the partition elements and fixture additions within L/360 allowable deflection limit.

Install bracing and blocking flush with the face of the framing to keep the stud faces smooth and free of protrusions.

Heavy gauge metal straps mounted on the studs are not recommended as supports because the metal thickness and/or screwheads used to attach them cause bowing in the board and interfere with the flat, smooth application of the tile backerboard and ceramic tile. When heavy anchor plates must be used, fur out the studs with a metal strap or wood shim to provide an even base for the tile backerboard.

Panel Fabrication

___

Tip

See Chapter 13, "Safety Considerations & Material Handling," for safety considerations.

DUROCK panels, FIBEROCK panels and gypsum panels are similar in terms of cutting and shaping. For DUROCK cement board, a utility knife or cement board cutting tool is used to cut through the top side glass-fiber mesh scrim of the board. The board is then snapped in the same manner used for gypsum board and the back side glass-fiber mesh scrim is then cut. Cut-outs for penetrations must be made on both sides of the board, and then tapped out with a hammer. To ensure that the cuts occur at the right locations on both sides, it is often useful to drive nails through the board at key locations, such as the center or corners of required penetration locations. A wood rasp is useful for shaping cut-outs and board edges. For safety, wear eye protection and gloves while cutting or shaping.

For FIBEROCK tile backerboard and underlayment, panels may be cut by scoring and snapping with a utility knife and straight edge, working from the face side. With score-and-snap method, score panel once or twice and snap upwards. Where necessary, use a rasp to smooth the cut edges. Holes for pipes, fixtures, and other small openings can be cut with a utility knife, saw or a drywall router equipped with a purpose-made bit. Always wear an OSHA-approved dust mask and eye protection when cutting FIBEROCK panels with a power tool.

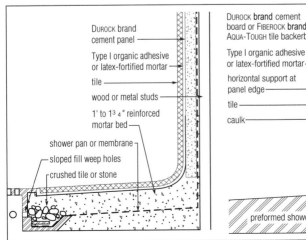
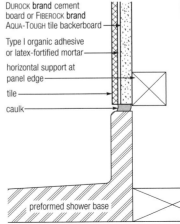

Tub and shower—single layer board

Panel Application

For Ceramic Tile Floors For both Durock brand cement board and Fiberock underlayment, laminate panels to the subfloor using Type I ceramic tile adhesive, latex-fortified mortar, or thin-set mortar mixed with acrylic latex additive. Apply thin-set mortar to subfloor with a 1/4" square-notched trowel and mastic with a 5/32" V-notched trowel. Durock cement board is rough on one side, and smooth on the other. Typically, the smooth side is used for mastic applications of tile and the rough side for mortar applications, (although mastic and mortar can be used on either side). Place Durock cement board with joints staggered from subfloor joints. Fit the ends and edges closely, but not forced together. Fasten the cement board to the subfloor with 1-1/4" Durock wood screws or 1-1/2" galvanized roofing nails spaced 8" o.c. in both directions, with perimeter fasteners at least 3/8" and less than 5/8" from the ends and edges.

For Fiberock underlayment, lay cut edges against the wall; only factory edges should be joined. Begin laying panels at one corner. Panels should be placed with logo facing up. Maintain 1/4" space between panels and perimeter walls. Stagger joints a minimum of 16" o.c. so that four panel corners never meet, and offset end and edge joints of panels a minimum of 12"–16" from subfloor panel joints. Butt panel edges and ends lightly together. A maximum 1/32" gap is allowed. Fasten panels to subfloor with staples, screws or nails, spaced 8" o.c., with perimeter fasteners 1/2" from ends and edges.

Floors, wood or steel joists

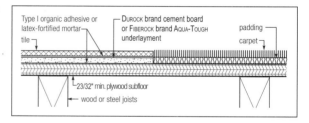

Type I organic adhesive or latex-fortified mortar
tile
Durock brand cement board or Fiberock brand Aqua-Tough underlayment
padding
carpet
23/32" min. plywood subfloor
wood or steel joists

Note: For bonding cement board to plywood subfloor, use Type I organic adhesive or latex-fortified mortar that is suitable for this kind of application. For application of various types of tiles to cement board on floors or countertops, contact the tile manufacturer for the appropriate type of tile-setting mortar.

Tile/Carpet underlayment

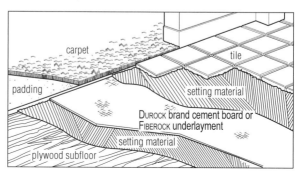

carpet
tile
padding
setting material
Durock brand cement board or Fiberock underlayment
setting material
plywood subfloor

For Walls After the tub, shower pan, or receptor is installed, place temporary 1/4" spacer strips around the lip of the fixture. Installation of a water barrier over the studs and overlapping the vertical flange of the fixture is highly recommended.

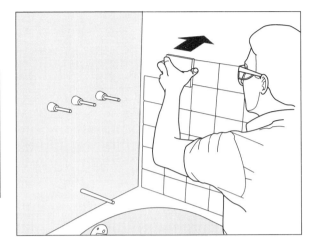

tile

DUROCK brand steel or wood screw 8" o.c.

Type I organic adhesive or latex-fortified mortar

DUROCK brand tile backer tape

setting material

DUROCK brand cement board or FIBEROCK Brand AQUA-TOUGH tile backerboard

vapor permeable water membrane (if required)

wood or steel studs 16" o.c. max.

Walls, interior—wood or steel studs

4

DUROCK cement board has both a rough and a smooth surface. Typically, the smooth side is used for mastic applications of tile and the rough side for mortar applications (mastic and mortar can be applied to either side). FIBEROCK panels should be hung with logo side facing out.

Cut the DUROCK or FIBEROCK panels to required sizes and make any necessary cut-outs. Fit the ends and edges closely, but do not force them together. Install board abutting top of spacer strip. Stagger end joints in successive courses. Fasten panels to wood studs spaced a maximum of 16" o.c., and bottom plates with 1-1/4" DUROCK wood screws or 1-1/2" galvanized roofing nails spaced 8" o.c. Fasten cement boards to steel studs spaced maximum 16" o.c. and bottom runners only with 1-1/4" DUROCK steel screws spaced 8" o.c. with perimeter fasteners at least 3/8" and less than 5/8" from ends and edges. Do not fasten to, or within 1" of, top runner. For FIBEROCK tile backerboard, screw spacing can be increased to 12" o.c.

In double-layer walls where DUROCK cement board is installed over base-layer gypsum boards, apply a water barrier (not a vapor retarder) between the gypsum board and the cement board. If a water barrier was installed, trim any overlap back so that it can be concealed by the application of tile and caulk.

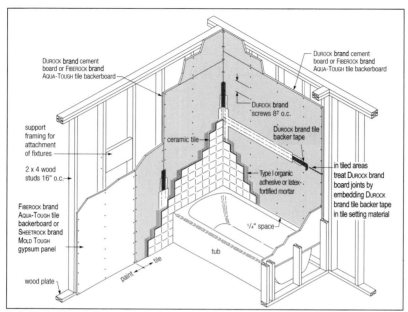

Typical bathtub installation

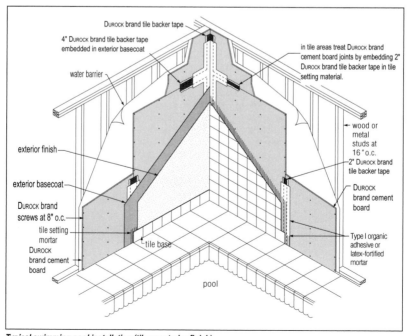

Typical swimming pool installation (tile or exterior finish)

Countertops

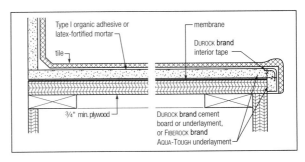

4

For Countertops For DUROCK brand cement board, staple-attach 15-lb. felt or 4-mil polyethylene film to a 3/4" exterior plywood base with galvanized staples. Laminate DUROCK cement board to the membrane using ceramic tile mastic, latex-fortified mortar, or thin-set mortar mixed with acrylic latex additive. Apply thin-set mortar to felt-covered plywood with a 1/4" square-notched trowel and apply mastic with a 5/32" V-notched trowel. Fasten DUROCK brand cement board to plywood with 1-1/4" DUROCK wood screws or 1-1/2" galvanized roofing nails spaced 8" o.c. in both directions and around the edges; or with 1/4" x 7/8" galvanized staples spaced 4" o.c. in both directions and around the edges.

For FIBEROCK Underlayment Install minimum 3/4" exterior grade plywood or OSB base across cabinet supports. Position ends and edges over supports and secure with suitable screws or nails, spaced 12" o.c. max. Position underlayment with joints staggered from base joints. Fit ends and edges closely but do not force together. Fasten panels with corrosion-resistant wood screws, hot-dipped galvanized ring-shank underlayment nails, or roofing nails, spaced 8" o.c. in both directions with perimeter fasteners 1/2" from ends and edges.

For Ceilings Ceiling joists, furring channels or strips must be spaced max. 16" o.c. Framing must be capable of supporting the total ceiling system dead load, including insulation, ceramic tile, bonding materials and cement board, with deflection not exceeding L/360 of the span. When steel framing is used, min. 20 ga. is required.

Apply 1/2" DUROCK brand cement board or FIBEROCK tile backerboard to framing with long dimension across framing. Center end or edge joints on framing and stagger joints in adjacent rows. Fit ends and edges closely, but not forced together, leaving a 1/8" gap. Fasten boards to steel framing with 1-1/4" DUROCK brand steel screws spaced 6" o.c. and to wood framing with 1-5/8" DUROCK brand wood screws spaced 6" o.c. with perimeter fasteners at least 3/8" and less than 5/8" from ends and edges. If necessary, provide additional blocking to permit proper attachment. Edges or ends parallel to framing shall be continuously supported.

Suspended ceiling

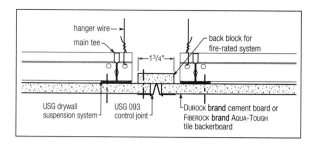

hanger wire —
main tee
back block for
fire-rated system
—1³/4"—

USG drywall
suspension system
USG 093
control joint
DUROCK brand cement board or
FIBEROCK brand AQUA-TOUGH
tile backerboard

Joint Treatment

Fill joints with tile-setting mortar or adhesive and then immediately embed tape and level joints. For small areas where the DUROCK cement board will not be tiled, such as a board extending beyond the tiled area and abutting another surface, treat joints as follows: Seal the DUROCK brand cement board with dilutted Type I ceramic tile adhesive. (Mix four parts adhesive with one part water.) Embed SHEETROCK brand joint tape over the joints and treat fasteners with SHEETROCK brand setting-type joint compound (DURABOND 45 or 90) applied in a conventional manner. Flat-trowel SHEETROCK setting-type joint compound over the board to cover the fasteners and fill any voids to a smooth surface. Finish joints with at least two coats of SHEETROCK brand ready-mixed joint compound. Do not apply ready-mixed or setting-type joint compound over unsealed board.

For areas where FIBEROCK tile backerboard will not be tiled, embed SHEETROCK joint tape in SHEETROCK DURABOND setting-type joint compound and wipe with a joint knife, leaving a thin coating of joint compound over all joints and interior angles. Complete to level of finish specified in project requirements.

Panel Surfacing

Install tile or thin brick and grout in accordance with ANSI A108.4 for Type I organic adhesive or ANSI A108.5 for dry-set or latex-fortified Portland cement mortar and ANSI A108.10 for grouts. Before tile application begins, the moisture content of the DUROCK cement board should be allowed to adjust as closely as possible to the level it will reach in service. Avoid extreme changes in environmental conditions during the curing of the tile-setting material. Provide adequate ventilation to disperse excess moisture.

Resilient Flooring

Fasten FIBEROCK underlayment to subfloor with 1/4"-crown staples. Do not use screws or nails. Fastener length should be approximately equal to combined thickness of underlayment and subfloor. Fasteners should not penetrate through subfloor; long fasteners that penetrate the floor joists may compromise the ability of the subfloor to expand and contract uniformly with natural variations in temperature and humidity. Lay panels flat and press tightly onto subfloor while fastening. Begin fastening where three panels intersect. Affix staples along joints in a zipper pattern at 1" o.c., 1/4" from panel edge. Install staples at 4" o.c. in the field of panels. When using pneumatic tools, apply sufficient pressure on gun to prevent the tool from bouncing. Set pneumatic tool pressure to drive fasteners flush or slightly below underlayment surface. To prevent fastener heads from telegraphing through resilient floor covering, do not countersink more than 1/16" below surface. Fasten one panel at a time. Begin at one end and fan out across the floor. From this point on, refer to FIBEROCK underlayment installation guide and the floor covering manufacturer's installation guide to complete the installation.

4

Finishing Drywall Systems

5

Levels of Gypsum Finishing

The finished appearance of drywall largely depends on the quality of framing and care exercised in applying the drywall panels. The better the framing and cladding, the easier it is to achieve a near-perfect wall. The last remaining challenge is to finish the joints to meet visual appearance expectations. This chapter helps you determine the level of finish quality needed and shows you how to obtain it.

(Note that various organizations provide information about recommended standards or tolerances for finishing of drywall joints. See the Appendix for information about standards and tolerances.)

For instructions on the safe use of joint compounds, texturing materials and related products, see Chapter 13, "Safety Considerations & Material Handling."

Contract documents traditionally use nonspecific terms such as "industry standards" or "workmanlike finish" to describe how finished gypsum board walls and ceilings should look. This practice has often led to confusion about the degree or level of finishing required for a particular job.

Five leading industry trade associations—the Association of the Wall and Ceiling Industries International (AWCI), Ceilings and Interior Systems Construction Association (CISCA), Gypsum Association (GA), Drywall Finishing Council (DWFC) and Painting and Decorating Contractors of America (PDCA)—have combined efforts to collectively adopt a set of industry-wide recommended specifications for levels of gypsum board finish. This specification identifies five levels of finishing, enabling architects to more closely identify the quality of finish required and allowing for better competitive bidding among contractors. American Society for Testing & Materials (ASTM) recognized this specification by including the levels of gypsum board finishing in ASTM C840.

Key factors in determining the quality level required include:

1. The location of the work to be done.
2. The type and angle of surface illumination (both natural and artificial lighting).
3. The orientation of the panels during installation. (See page 106.)
4. The type of paint or wall covering to be used.
5. The method of application.

Critical lighting conditions, gloss paints and thin wall coverings require a high level of finish, while heavily textured surfaces or those that will be decorated with heavy-gauge wall coverings require less attention to final surface quality.

Definitions of the five finishing levels are provided below, together with a matrix that details how each level of finishing should be achieved using SHEETROCK brand joint treatment and finishing products. The matrix also describes the appearance of the finished wall that may be anticipated for each level.

Applications of SHEETROCK brand joint treatment products to joints, beads, trims and corners are described on pages 167–174. Note that the number of layers of compound and the degree of finishing increases at each level.

Finishing-Level Definitions

The following finishing-level definitions are based on GA-214-07, "Recommended Levels of Gypsum Board Finish," and are intended to provide an industry standard for drywall finishing.

Level 0   Used in temporary construction or wherever the final decoration has not been determined. Unfinished. No taping, finishing or corner beads are required. Also could be used where non-predecorated panels will be used in demountable-type partitions that are to be painted as a final finish.

Level 1   Frequently used in plenum areas above ceilings, in attics, in areas where the assembly would generally be concealed or in building service corridors and other areas not normally open to public view. Some degree of sound and smoke control is provided; in some geographic areas, this level is referred to as "fire-taping," although this level of finish does not typically meet fire-resistant assembly requirements. Where a fire resistance rating is required for the gypsum board assembly, details of construction should be in accordance with reports of fire tests of assemblies that have met the requirements of the fire rating imposed.

All joints and interior angles shall have tape embedded in joint compound. Accessories are optional at specifier discretion in corridors and other areas with pedestrian traffic. Tape and fastener heads need not be covered with joint compound. Surface shall be free of excess joint compound. Tool marks and ridges are acceptable.

Level 2   It may be specified for standard gypsum board surfaces in garages, warehouse storage or other similar areas where surface appearance is not of primary importance.

All joints and interior angles shall have tape embedded in joint compound and shall be immediately wiped with a joint knife or trowel, leaving a thin coating of joint compound over all joints and interior angles. Fastener heads and accessories shall be covered with a coat of joint compound. Surface shall be free of excess joint compound. Tool marks and ridges are acceptable.

Level 3   Typically used in areas that are to receive heavy texture (spray or hand applied) finishes before final painting, or where commercial-grade (heavy duty) wall coverings are to be applied as the final decoration. This level of finish should not be used where smooth painted surfaces or where lighter weight wall coverings are specified. The prepared surface shall be coated with a drywall primer prior to the application of final finishes.

All joints and interior angles shall have tape embedded in joint compound and shall be immediately wiped with a joint knife or trowel, leaving a thin coating of joint compound over all joints and interior angles. One additional coat of joint compound shall be applied over all joints and interior angles. Fastener heads and accessories shall be covered with two separate coats of joint compound. All joint compounds shall be smooth and free of tool marks and ridges. The prepared surface shall be covered with a drywall primer prior to the application of the final decoration.

Level 4 This level should be used where residential grade (light duty) wall coverings, flat paints or light textures are to be applied. The prepared surface shall be coated with a drywall primer prior to the application of final finishes. Release agents for wall coverings are specifically formulated to minimize damage if coverings are subsequently removed. The weight, texture and sheen level of the wall covering material selected should be taken into consideration when specifying wall coverings over this level of drywall treatment. Joints and fasteners must be sufficiently concealed if the wall covering material is lightweight, contains limited pattern, has a glossy finish or has any combination of these features. In critical lighting areas, flat paints applied over light textures tend to reduce joint photographing. Gloss, semi-gloss and enamel paints are not recommended over this level of finish.

All joints and interior angles shall have tape embedded in joint compound and shall be immediately wiped with a joint knife or trowel, leaving a thin coating of joint compound over all joints and interior angles. In addition, two separate coats of joint compound shall be applied over all flat joints and one separate coat of joint compound applied over interior angles. Fastener heads and accessories shall be covered with three separate coats of joint compound. All joint compounds shall be smooth and free of tool marks and ridges. The prepared surface shall be covered with a drywall primer like SHEETROCK first coat prior to the application of the final decoration.

Level 5 The highest quality finish is the most effective method to provide a uniform surface and minimize the possibility of joint photographing and of fasteners showing through the final decoration. This level of finish is required where gloss, semi-gloss or enamel is specified, when flat joints are specified over an untextured surface or where critical lighting conditions occur. The prepared surface shall be coated with a drywall primer prior to the application of final decoration.

All joints and interior angles shall have tape embedded in joint compound and be immediately wiped with a joint knife or trowel, leaving a thin coating of joint compound over all joints and interior angles. Two separate coats of joint compound shall be applied over all flat joints and one separate coat of joint compound applied over interior angles. Fastener heads and accessories shall be covered with three separate coats of joint compound.

A thin skim coat of joint compound shall be trowel applied to the entire surface. Excess compound is immediately troweled off, leaving a film or skim coating of compound completely covering the paper. As an alternative to a skim coat, a material manufactured especially for this purpose may be applied such as SHEETROCK TUFF-HIDE primer surfacer. The surface must be smooth and free of tool marks and ridges. The prepared surface shall be covered with a drywall primer prior to the application of the final decoration.

The following matrix helps define the expected appearance of each level and basic requirements for achieving that level. Additional guidelines are offered for meeting the specified finish level using SHEETROCK brand products and application techniques.

Drywall Finishing Levels & Methods

Finishing Level	Final Appearance	How To Achieve Result		
		Joints & Interior Angles	Accessories & Fasteners	Surface
5	No marks or ridges. Entire surface covered with skim coat of compound and ready to prime before decorating with gloss, semi-gloss or enamel, or flat joints or use over an untextured surface.	As in Level 4	As in Level 4	Skim coat plus prime with SHEETROCK Brand First Coat primer before painting or texturing or use SHEETROCK TUFF-HIDE primer Surfacer
4	No marks or ridges. Ready for priming, followed by wall coverings, flat paints or light textures.	Two separate coats of compound over Level 2	Three separate coats of compound	Joints filled and smoothed again. Must be primed with SHEETROCK Brand First Coat before painting or texturing
3	No marks or ridges. Ready for priming, to be followed by heavy texture.	One separate coat of compound over Level 2	Two separate coats of compound	Joints filled and smooth. Must be primed with SHEETROCK Brand First Coat before painting or texturing
2	Tool marks and and ridges okay. Thin coating of compound covers tape; one one coat compound over fastener heads.	Tape embedded in compound and immediately wiped to leave a thin coating of compound over tape	One coat of compound	Free of excess compound
1	Tool marks and ridges acceptable.	Tape embedded in compound	Optional— One coat of compound	Free of excess compound
0	Unfinished	None		

5

Recommended Levels of Paint Finish over Gypsum Board

The recommended level of paint finish over gypsum board wall and ceiling surfaces varies depending on location in the structure, the type of paint applied, the finish achieved on the gypsum board substrate prior to final decoration and the type of illumination striking the surface. The following recommendations from the Drywall Finishing Council Incorporated describe various levels of paint finish as the final decoration over new interior gypsum board surfaces.

Level 0 No painting required. Note that this level is recommended where final decoration is not required.

Level 1
a. When final decoration is undetermined, all appropriately prepared gypsum board surfaces shall have one coat of drywall primer

applied. Drywall primer shall be applied to the mil film thickness and application conditions specified by the primer manufacturer. OR

b. When wall coverings are to be applied, all appropriately prepared gypsum board surfaces shall have one coat of wall covering primer applied. Wall covering primer shall be applied to the mil film thickness and application conditions specified by the primer manufacturer.

Level 2 All appropriately prepared gypsum board surfaces shall have one coat of topcoat material applied to yield a uniform surface. Paint shall be applied to the mil film thickness and application conditions specified by the paint manufacturer. Note that the painted surface may not achieve uniform appearance, color or sheen, but shall be absent of defects caused by the painting contractor's workforce. This level is recommended where economy is of primary concern.

Level 3 All appropriately prepared gypsum board surfaces shall have two separate coats of topcoat material applied to yield a properly painted surface. Paint shall be applied to the mil film thickness and application conditions specified by the paint manufacturer. Note that this is typically recommended for areas having textures (spray or hand applied) over a primed gypsum board surface and the area is not subject to critical lighting. Refer to Drywall Finishing Council document titled, "Recommended Specification for Preparation of Gypsum Board Surfaces Prior to Texture Application." When subjected to critical lighting, a Level 5 gypsum board finish as defined in GA-214-07 ("Recommended Levels of Gypsum Board Finish") is recommended.

Level 4 All appropriately prepared gypsum board surfaces shall have one coat of drywall primer applied to yield a properly painted surface and one separate coat of topcoat material applied to a properly painted surface over the drywall primer. Paint shall be applied to the mil film thickness and application conditions specified by the paint manufacturer. Note that this is typically recommended for smooth surfaces not subject to critical lighting and areas having light to medium texture finishes (spray- or hand-applied over a primed gypsum board surface). Refer to Drywall Finishing Council document titled, "Recommended Specification for Preparation of Gypsum Board Surfaces Prior to Texture Application." When subjected to critical lighting, a Level 5 gypsum board finish as defined in GA-214-07 is recommended.

Level 5 All appropriately prepared gypsum board surfaces shall have one coat of drywall primer applied to yield a properly painted surface. Two separate coats of topcoat material shall be applied over the drywall primer to yield a properly painted surface. Paint shall be applied to the mil film thickness and application conditions specified by the paint manufacturer. Note that this level is recommended where the best paint finish is required, such as under critical lighting conditions or when paints that have a glossy surface are used. Recommended with a Level 5 gypsum board finish as described in the "Recommended Levels of Gypsum Board Finish" (GA-214-07). This system, when combined with the Level 5 gypsum board finish is the most effective method to minimize joint and fastener photographing and provides the most uniform final finish.

Applying Trim Accessories

Trim accessories simplify and enhance the finishing of gypsum board assemblies. The accessories are made with galvanized rust-resistant steel and are easily applied and designed to work together for long-lasting, trouble-free construction. All are suitable for steel-frame and wood-frame construction.

Corner Bead Application

SHEETROCK brand corner reinforcements provide strong, durable protection for outside angle corners, uncased openings, pilasters, beams and soffits. The exposed nose of the bead resists impact and forms a screed for finishing. Corner bead should be installed in one piece unless the length of the corner exceeds stock bead lengths.

5

SHEETROCK **brand paper-faced metal corner bead** is a solid-flange corner bead with a specially formulated paper laminated to its surface. The combination of materials ensures strong corner protection plus an extra bonding mechanism that eliminates edge cracking problems commonly experienced with conventional bare metal bead. USG guarantees against edge cracks when SHEETROCK paper-face bead is used and installed correctly.

The bead is affixed by applying a laminating layer of joint compound between the rough corner and the bead. This is accomplished by:

1. Hand-applying compound to the gypsum board with a 4"–6" drywall knife,
2. Using a mechanical angle applicator to apply compound to the wall surface, or
3. Hopper-applying joint compound to the back of the bead.

Once the joint compound is uniformly applied, the bead is simply pressed into place by hand or with a bead roller, and then finished in a normal fashion.

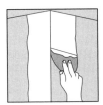 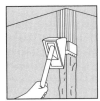 

Hand Application   *Mechanical Application*   *Hopper Application*   *Press in Place*

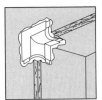 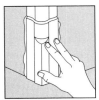

For paper-faced bullnose corner bead, transition corners and caps are available to ensure smooth transitions around corners and from bullnose wall corners to square baseboard corners.

Transition Corner   *Transition Cap*

A variety of SHEETROCK paper-faced trim products are also available. In general, these are installed in the same way as bead. Among them are the following special trim products.

- SHEETROCK and BEADEX brand paper-faced metal inside corner, tape on trim (B2)—forms true, inner 90-degree corner angles.

- SHEETROCK and BEADEX brand paper-faced metal offset inside corner, tape on trim (B2 OS), designed for 135-degree inside corner offset angles.

- SHEETROCK and BEADEX brand paper-faced metal inner cove, tape on trim (SLIC)—creates smooth, rounded inside corners.

- SHEETROCK and BEADEX brand paper-faced metal offset inner cove, tape on trim (SLIC OS)—a softline (bullnose) inside corner for 135-degree offset angles.

- SHEETROCK and BEADEX brand paper-faced metal L-shaped, tape on trim (B4 Series)—a trim used where wallboard abuts suspended ceilings, beams, plaster and concrete walls; also used at untrimmed door and window jambs; available with and without bead.

- SHEETROCK and BEADEX brand paper-faced metal reveal, tape on trim (reveal NB), a modified tape-on "L" trim that can be used to create reveals on soffits, walls and ceilings, around light boxes and other architectural components.

- SHEETROCK and BEADEX brand paper-faced metal J-shaped, tape on trim (B9)—a J-trim that completely surrounds the rough edge of wallboard, providing a strong, clean corner.

- SHEETROCK and BEADEX brand paper-faced metal pre-masked L-shaped, tape on trim (pre-masked L)—provides a serrated paper strip that protects the adjacent surfaces of ceiling or wall intersections. Simply tear away the protective strip after the job is completed, leaving virtually no clean-up of the adjacent surface.

For more information about these and related products, see page 22 in Chapter 1, "Drywall & Veneer Plaster Products," or J1424, *Interior Finishing Products Catalog*. For additional installation information, refer to J1124, SHEETROCK *Brand Paper-Faced Metal Bead and Trim Installation Guide*.

SHEETROCK **Brand Flexible Metal Corner Tape** is a flexible reinforcement that ensures straight, sharp corners on any angle. It provides durable corner protection on cathedral and drop ceilings, arches and around bay windows. The tape is available in two widths: 2-1/16" (with a 1/16" gap between two 7/16"-wide galvanized, rust-resistant steel strips) and 4" (with two 7/8"-wide strips). When folded, the tape forms a strong corner bead. It is applied with standard joint compound, feathered at the edges for a smooth wall surface. It is also useful for joining drywall partitions to plastered walls in remodeling and for repairing chipped and cracked corners. Available in 100' rolls in dispenser box.

To install, cut the tape to the desired length with snips or score with a knife and bend. Notch or angle cut for arches and window returns. Do not overlap at intersections or corners. Apply joint compound to both sides of corner angle, fold tape at its center to form a bead and press the metal strip side into the joint compound. Follow immediately with a thin coat of compound over the tape and let dry. Finish the corner in the conventional manner with additional coats of joint compound.

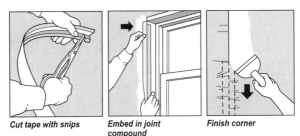

Cut tape with snips   **Embed in joint compound**   **Finish corner**

DUR-A-BEAD **Corner Bead** is a galvanized solid-flange corner bead designed to protect external corners. It may be nailed through the board to wood framing or attached with 9/16" galvanized staples to the board alone—in either wood- or steel-framed construction. A special clinch-on tool also may be used for flange attachment. Bead should be attached at 9" intervals in both flanges with fasteners placed opposite one another. Flange widths available: No. 103, 1-1/4" x 1-1/4"; No. 104, 1-1/8" x 1-1/8".

Clinch-on tool crimps solid-flange beads into place

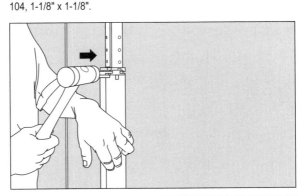

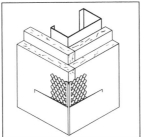

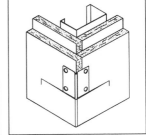

No. 800 Corner Bead   DUR-A-BEAD *Corner Bead*

SHEETROCK **brand No. 800 Corner Bead** is a galvanized fine-mesh, expanded-flange corner bead. It provides exceptional joint compound bond and reinforcement and may be attached with nails or staples directly opposite one another at 9" intervals, just as DUR-A-BEAD is applied. Finishing with three coats of a SHEETROCK brand joint compound is recommended. See 200-A and 200-B on next page. (Only two coats are required with SHEETROCK brand lightweight all-purpose [PLUS 3] ready-mixed joint compound.)

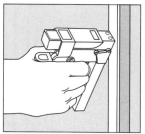
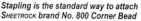

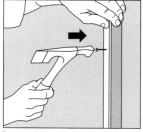

Stapling is the standard way to attach Sheetrock brand No. 800 Corner Bead

For wood studs, nails in both bead flanges are also satisfactory

Metal Trim Application

Sheetrock brand metal trims protect and finish gypsum panels at window framing and door jambs. They can also be used at ceiling-wall intersections and partition perimeters to form a recess for acoustical sealant. Metal trim also serves as a relief joint at the intersection of dissimilar construction materials, such as gypsum board and concrete.

Metal trims provide maximum protection and neat finished edges to gypsum panels at window and door jambs, at internal angles and at intersections where panels abut other materials. The trim pieces are easily installed by nailing or screwing through the proper leg of trim. Various configurations are available depending on the required application.

No. 200-A Sheetrock Brand Metal Trim J-shaped Channel *(1/2" and 5/8" size):* Apply gypsum panels, omitting fasteners at the framing member where trim is to be installed. Leave a space 3/8" to 1/2" wide between edge of panel and face of jamb for installation of hardware. Slip trim over edge of panel with wide knurled flange on room side, and fasten trim and panel to framing. Use the same type of fasteners to attach panels; spacing them 9" o.c., maximum. Finish with three coats of conventional joint compound. (Only two coats are required with Sheetrock brand lightweight all-purpose [Plus 3] ready-mixed joint compound.)

No. 200-B Sheetrock Brand Metal Trim L-shaped Channel *(1/2" and 5/8" size):* Apply gypsum panels the same way as for No. 200-A Trim, omitting fasteners and leaving 3/8" to 1/2" space at jamb. Place trim over edge of panel with knurled flange exposed. Attach trim and panel to framing with fasteners spaced 9" o.c., maximum. Finish with three coats of conventional joint compound. (Only two coats are required with Sheetrock brand lightweight all-purpose [Plus 3] ready-mixed joint compound.)

Nos. 401 and 402 Sʜᴇᴇᴛʀᴏᴄᴋ **Brand Metal Trim J-stop** *(1/2" and 5/8" size)*: Apply the trim to the wall before the gypsum panels go up, by nailing through trim flange into framing. The board is held firmly in place by the short leg of the trim. No additional edge fastening is necessary. Space fasteners 9" o.c. Requires no finishing compound.

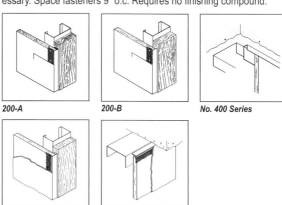

200-A   *200-B*   *No. 400 Series*

801-A   *801-B*

No. 801-A and 801-B Sʜᴇᴇᴛʀᴏᴄᴋ **Brand Metal Trim** *(1/2" and 5/8" size)*: Slip channel-type 801-A trim over the edge of the board, or position L-shaped 801-B trim on the edge of the board with the expanded flange on the room side. Fasten with staples or nails 9" o.c., maximum, for drywall applications. Finish with three coats of conventional joint compound. (Only two coats are required with Sʜᴇᴇᴛʀᴏᴄᴋ brand lightweight [Pʟᴜs 3] all purpose ready-mixed joint compound.)

Control Joint Application

Proper installation of control joints in wall and ceiling membranes should include breaking the gypsum boards behind the control joint. In ceiling construction, the framing should also be broken, and in partitions, separate studs should be used on each side of the control joints. Control joints should be positioned to intersect light fixtures, air diffusers, door openings and other areas of stress concentration.

Gypsum construction should be isolated by control joints where:

a. Partitions or ceilings of dissimilar construction meet and remain in the same plane;

b. Wings of "L," "U" and "T" shaped ceiling areas are joined; and

c. Expansion or control joints occur in the base wall construction and/ or building structure.

Just as important, control joints should be used in the face of gypsum partitions and ceilings when the size of the surface exceeds the following control-joint spacings:

• Partitions, 30' maximum in either direction

• Interior ceilings (with perimeter relief), 50' maximum in either direction

- Interior ceilings (without perimeter relief), 30' maximum in either direction
- Exterior ceilings, 30' maximum in either direction

Ceiling-height door frames may be used as vertical control joints for partitions. However, door frames of lesser height may only be used for this purpose if standard the control joints extend to the ceiling from both corners of the top of the door frame. Ceiling control joints should be located so that they intersect column penetrations, since movement of columns can impose stress on the ceiling membrane.

Control joints, when properly insulated and backed by gypsum panels, have been fire-endurance tested and are certified for use in one- and two-hour-rated walls.

Installation
At control joint locations:

1. Leave a 1/2" continuous opening between gypsum boards for insertion of a surface-mounted joint.

2. Interrupt wood floor and ceiling plates with a 1/2" gap wherever there is a control joint in the structure.

3. Provide separate supports for each control joint flange.

4. Provide an adequate seal or fire-safing insulation behind control joints where sound and/or fire ratings are prime considerations.

Control Joint No. 093: Apply over the face of the gypsum board where specified. Cut to length with a fine-toothed hacksaw (32 teeth per in.). Cut end joints square, butt together and align to provide a neat fit. Attach the control joint to the gypsum board with Bostitch 9/16" type G staples or equivalent, spaced 6" o.c., maximum, along each flange. Remove the plastic tape after finishing with joint compound.

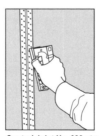

Control Joint No. 093 stapled, finished, tape removed.

Fire-Rated Control Joints

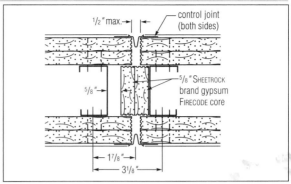

47 STC (SA-860217): 2-hr. Fire Rating

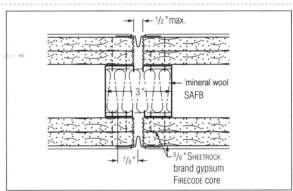

1-hr. Fire Rating

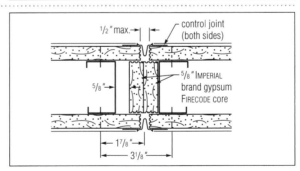

Maximum Spacing—Control Joints

Construction & Location	Max. Single Dimension		Max. Single Area	
	ft.	m	ft.²	m²
Partition-interior	30	9	—	—
Ceiling-interior				
with perimeter relief	50	15	2500	230
without perimeter relief	30	9	900	85
Ceiling-exterior gypsum	30	9	900	85

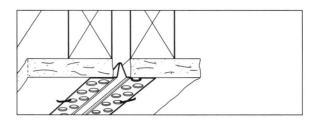

Joint Treatment for Drywall Construction

Application Conditions

Environmental Control Temperature, humidity and airflow should remain constant and as close to occupancy conditions as possible. The potential for finishing and decorating problems is minimal when job environmental conditions match occupancy environmental conditions. Controlling and maintaining environmental conditions is key. Changes and/or fluctuations in temperature, humidity and airflow can have a profound adverse effect on finishing. Temperatures within the building should be maintained within the range of 55°F to 70°F. Adequate ventilation should be provided. Also see "Quality Drywall Finishing in All Kinds of Weather," USG folder J-75.

Check Working Surfaces

Gypsum panels must be tightly fastened to framing members without breaking the surface paper or fracturing the core. Make certain panel joints are aligned. If one panel is higher than another, it becomes difficult to leave sufficient compound under the tape covering the high panel. Blisters, bond failure and cracks can easily develop in these areas.

Open spaces between panels of 1/4" or more should be filled with compound at least 24 hours prior to embedding tape or first-coat work. SHEETROCK brand setting-type (DURABOND) and lightweight setting-type (EASY SAND) joint compounds are recommended for these large fills. When using these setting-type compounds as a fill, joint treatment may begin as soon as the compound has hardened, eliminating the typical 24-hour drying period. Good planning prior to hanging panels can eliminate unnecessary joints.

Care of Equipment

Tools and equipment must be kept clean and in good repair to ensure satisfactory results. With mechanical tools, parts must be replaced when they show signs of wear.

Mixing joint compounds in dirty buckets or failure to wash down the exposed container sides as material is used causes lumps and scratches and usually creates hard working material. With setting-type materials such as SHEETROCK setting-type (DURABOND) and lightweight setting-type (EASY SAND) joint compounds, a residue of dry compounds will shorten the working time of the new batch.

The hardening action of SHEETROCK brand setting-type (DURABOND) and lightweight setting-type (EASY SAND) joint compounds requires that all tools, mixing containers, mud pans, etc., used for application be thoroughly cleaned. Flush and clean these compounds from equipment, and brush before the setting action takes place. Immersion of equipment in water will not prevent hardening of the compound.

Mechanical tool application is not recommended with fast-setting SHEETROCK brand setting-type (DURABOND) and lightweight setting-type (EASY SAND) joint compounds.

Mixing Joint Compounds

1. Mix powder joint compounds in a clean 5-gal. container (preferably plastic). A hand mixer (resembling a commercial potato masher) works well. Power mixing saves considerable time and is recommended particularly in situations where it is convenient to mix in a central location. Power for the mixer may be supplied by a 1/2" heavy-duty electric drill operating at 450 to 650 rpm. Recommend using a USG SHEETROCK mud mixer, designed to prevent the introduction of air. Drills operating at high speeds whip air into the compound, and also accelerate setting of setting-type compounds. (See page 425 for information about mixing paddles.) Small amounts of powder joint compounds may be mixed in a small bowl or mud pan. Keep mixing buckets and tools clean at all times. Containers having any residue of joint compounds may cause premature hardening, scratching and incompatibility problems.

2. Pour the proper amount of clean, drinkable water into a clean container. Use room-temperature water, as very cold or hot water will affect the set time. Ratios of water to product for various applications are shown in the directions on the package. Dirty water (such as that used to clean tools) will contaminate compound and cause erratic setting.

3. Sift powder joint compound into water, allowing complete wetting of the powder.

4. Mix as shown below:

   a. *For powder SHEETROCK brand setting-type (DURABOND) and lightweight setting-type (EASY SAND) joint compounds:* follow mixing directions on the bag. Do not overmix; this may speed up hardening time. Note: Keep compound from being contaminated by any other materials, such as other types of joint compounds, dirty water or previously mixed joint compounds. Contamination will affect the compound's hardening time and other properties. Do not remix if product has started to set. Overmixing or retempering of setting-type joint compounds will affect the set time and reduce strength development.

   Mix only as much compound as can be used within time period shown on the bag (usually about 30 minutes for DURABOND 45 and 1 hour for DURABOND 90, for example).

   The compound will harden chemically after this time period, even under water. Do not attempt to delay hardening by holding wet mix or immersing joint-compound-coated tools in water. Retempering the compound is not recommended.

   An accelerator may be used to alter the set time of the compound. USG gypsum accelerator–high strength was developed for use in conventional basecoat plaster products, but can also be used to reduce the setting time of SHEETROCK brand setting-type (DURABOND or EASY SAND) joint compounds.

The following chart shows the amount of accelerator per unit of joint compound and the resulting set times.

Set Times: USG High Strength Gypsum Accelerator To Setting-Type Joint Compounds

Accelerator Amounts		Approximate Set Time (minutes)*		
Tbls. per Bag	Tbls. per Bread Pan (Approx. 1/4 bag)	EASY SAND/ DURABOND 90 Joint Compound	EASY SAND/ DURABOND 45 Joint Compound	EASY SAND/ DURABOND 20 Joint Compound
1.0	0.22	40	20	10
2.0	0.44	30	10	—
6.0	1.33	20	—	—

* Actual set times may vary due to mixing procedures, temperature, water and other job conditions. When set time is critical, a small test batch should be made to determine required amounts of accelerator.

b. *For* SHEETROCK *brand powder joint compounds (drying type):* Sift powder into water and stir until the powder is uniformly damp, then after approximately 15 minutes, remix vigorously until smooth. Note: Do not add extra water. Use specified amounts of water, as SHEETROCK joint compounds will retain their original mixed consistency over extended periods. On occasion, some slight liquid separation or settlement of compound may take place in the bucket, but a remix will restore the compound to its original consistency.

c. *For* SHEETROCK *brand ready-mixed compounds (drying type):* Mix contents and use at package consistency for fasteners and corner beads. Thin the compound for taping and finishing and for use with mechanical tools. Add water in half-pint increments to avoid over-thinning. Remix and test apply after each water addition. Use either a hand mixer or a drill mixer.

Use cool-to-lukewarm (not hot) water. If compound should accidentally be over-thinned, simply add more compound to thicken, then remix.

To hold the wet mix in a container for use over prolonged periods, wash down the exposed container sides, cover the material with a wet cloth or a thin layer of water and put the lid back on the pail. When needed, pour off water and adjust to a working viscosity.

Ready-mixed compound is sensitive to cold weather and must be protected from freezing. If material freezes in the container, allow it to thaw at room temperature. Do not force the thawing process. Do not pour off any liquid that has separated from the compound. Remix using a power drill mixer until smooth and creamy. Usually thawed compound will again be usable, unless it has been subjected to several freeze-thaw cycles.

Ready-mixed compound can be used in tools and containers previously used for powder compound after normal cleaning.

Hand Tool Application

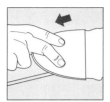

Prefilling "V" joint of SHEETROCK *Brand Gypsum Panels SW*

Prefilling Joints is desirable when there are large gaps between panels. This step is necessary with SW edge board.

Fill the "V" groove between SHEETROCK brand gypsum panels, SW (see diagram), with joint compound such as SHEETROCK brand setting-type (DURABOND 45 or 90) or lightweight setting-type (EASY SAND 45 or 90). Apply the compound directly over the "V" groove with a flexible 5" or 6" joint finishing knife. Wipe off excess compound that is applied beyond the groove. Allow fill compound to harden.

Embedding Tape Make sure no fasteners protrude above the gypsum panel surface. Using a broad steel finishing knife, apply a continuous coat of taping, all-purpose or setting-type joint compound to fill the channel formed by the tapered edges of the panels. Center and lightly press SHEETROCK brand paper joint tape into fresh joint compound. Working within a convenient arm's reach area, embed tape by holding knife at an angle to panel. Draw knife along joint with sufficient pressure to remove excess compound above and below tape and at edges. (See illustration.)

5

Apply a thin coat of taping compound, above; press joint tape into compound; draw knife over tape to remove excess compound, right.

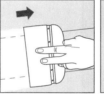

Apply a thin coat of joint compound over tape, above: apply taping compound, all-purpose or setting-type, over fasteners, right.

Leave sufficient compound under the tape for proper bond, but not over 1/32" under edge. While embedding, apply a thin coat of joint compound over the tape (above). This thin coat reduces edge wrinkling or curling and makes the tape easier to conceal with following coats. Allow it to dry completely. (See drying and setting time guides on pages 181 and 184.) Do not use topping compound for embedding tape. Also, do not use fiberglass tape with drying-type joint compound, only with setting-type compound.

Apply all-purpose or setting-type taping compound, at least 6" wide, over all corner beads and trims that are to receive joint compound.

For interior corners, apply compound to each side of the 90° inside corner. Crease the joint tape down the center and embed into joint compound. Use a knife to embed tape into compound, first on one side of the angle, then the other.

Spotting Fastener Heads Use ready-mixed compounds at package consistency or powder compounds mixed per bag directions. Do not add excess water. Apply all-purpose or setting-type joint compound over all fasteners (above, right) immediately before or after embedding tape. Fill only the fastener depression. Apply enough pressure on knife to level compound with panel surface. Allow each coat to dry. Repeat application until fastener depressions are flush with panel surface (normally two or three applications).

Filling Beads Use ready-mixed compounds at package consistency, or powder compounds mixed per bag directions. Apply all-purpose or setting-type compound at least 6" wide over all corner beads (below) and to trims that are to receive compound. Allow each coat to dry. Apply following coats approximately 2" wider than preceding coats. For smoother finishing, the final coat of joint compound may be thinned slightly.

Paper-faced metal drywall bead is applied quickly by applying joint compound to the bead with an installation hopper. Bead is then pressed onto corner.

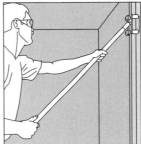

Paper-Faced Metal Beads and Trims Paper-faced metal beads and trims perform the same function as bare metal or vinyl beads and trims, but are applied at the taping stage rather than at the cladding stage of the drywall job. Paper-faced metal bead and trim are preferred because the paper bonds with the joint compound and drywall surface to provide superior resistance to edge cracking and chipping despite the stresses of normal building movement and everyday wear and tear.

Unlike conventional metal or vinyl, which are mechanically attached to the board surface, paper-faced metal beads and trims are adhered using SHEETROCK brand setting-type (DURABOND or EASY SAND) or SHEETROCK brand ready-mixed (taping or all-purpose) joint compounds. Topping compounds are not recommended for embedding bead. The paper facing ensures adhesion of joint compounds, textures and paints for a strong, smooth finish.

Apply the joint compound by hand or mechanically to the wallboard, and then press the bead in place, or apply joint compound by hopper to the inside of the bead. (See illustrations above.) Then mount in position on board corners. Finish the bead in the same manner as other beads.

Applying the Fill Coat After the tape embedding coat is dry, apply a topping or all-purpose compound fill (second) coat approximately 7" to 10" wide over taped joints (shown below), beads and trim. Feather edge of second coat approximately 2" beyond edge of first coat. Spot fasteners with second coat. Allow to dry.

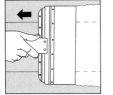

After tape embedding coat is dry, apply topping coat 7" to 10" wide over joints, beads, and trim.

Apply topping compound over joints, fasteners, beads and trim with 2" wider than previous coat.

Bevel edges of butt ends of drywall panels before applying joint compound.

Applying the Finish Coat   After the second coat is dry, smooth tool marks and other protrusions with a finishing knife. Apply a thin finish (third) coat of ready-mixed, topping or all-purpose compound over joints, fasteners, beads and trim. Finish compound should be applied at a slightly thinner consistency. Feather edges of third coats at least 2" wider than second coats (left). SHEETROCK brand lightweight all-purpose (PLUS 3) and dust control joint compounds require only two coats over metal corner beads and fasteners. Joints, fasteners, beads and trim should be finished as smoothly as possible to minimize sanding. Go over the whole job to smooth and touch up with joint compound all scratches, craters, nicks and other imperfections in the dried finish coat.

End Joints   Because ends of gypsum panels are flat and have no taper-like panel edges, end joints are difficult to conceal. Also, exposed paper on ends may cause visible ridging or beading. The following steps are recommended for joint treatment to minimize crowning and/or ridging of end joints:

1. Before attachment, bevel panel ends approximately 1/8" at a 45° angle using a sharp utility knife. This keeps the paper ends apart and reduces expansion problems caused by the raw paper edge. Also, peel back and remove any loose paper from the end.

2. Gypsum panel ends should be loosely butted together. Ends should be separated slightly and not touch.

3. Prefill the recess with compound and allow to set and dry.

4. Apply compound and paper reinforcing tape over the joint in the same manner as for tapered joints. Embed tape tightly to minimize joint thickness, but leave sufficient compound under tape for continuous bond and blister prevention.

5. Finish the end joint to a width at least twice the finish width of a recessed edge joint. This will make the joint less apparent after decoration as the crown will be more gradual.

Finishing Inside Corners   Fold tape along center crease. Apply joint compound to both sides of corner and press folded tape into angle. Tightly embed tape into both sides of angle with finishing knife and let dry. Next, apply a thin coat to one side of angle only. Allow to dry before applying finish coat to other side of angle.

Dry Sanding   Sand joint compounds to prepare gypsum drywall surfaces for decoration. Sand as necessary to remove excess joint compound from tool marks, lap marks and high crowned joints. Fill scratches, craters and nicks with joint compound, then sand. Do not try to remove these depressions by sanding only.

Select sandpaper, a sanding sponge or abrasive-mesh cloth that has the finest grit available. Excessively coarse sandpaper leaves scratches that are visible after decoration. For conventional-weight all-purpose compounds, use #120 grit or finer sandpaper (#200 grit or finer mesh cloth or 100 micron or less polyester film-back abrasive sheets). For lightweight, midweight and topping compounds, use #150

5

grit or finer sandpaper (#220 grit or finer mesh cloth or 80 micron or less polyester film-back abrasive sheets). Only sand surfaces coated with joint compound to avoid scuffing gypsum panel paper. Remove sanding dust before decorating.

Ventilate or use a dust collector to reduce dust in work areas. Use a NIOSH-approved respirator specified for mica and talc when air is dusty. Use of safety glasses is recommended. USG SHEETROCK with dust control can also be used to minimize airborne dust and ease clean up.

Wet Sanding Wet sanding or sponging finished joints, bead, trim and fasteners is suggested rather than dry sanding to avoid creating dust. The best material to use for wet sanding is a high-density, small-celled, polyurethane sponge. When only a touch-up is required, a general-purpose sponge or smooth, soft cloth will work.

Wet sanding avoids creating dust.

To wet sand, saturate the sponge with clean water containing no soap or additives. Water temperature should be cool to lukewarm, not hot. Wring out sponge only enough to eliminate dripping. To remove high spots, moisten the joint compound with the sponge, then pull a joint knife across. Use as few strokes as possible. Excessive rubbing will groove joints. Clean sponge frequently.

Mechanical Tools

Several types of mechanical and semi-mechanical tools are available for applying joint compound. Following are typical tools and steps.

Tools used in the following sequence illustrate typical procedures.

1   Using compound of suitable consistency, mechanically tape all flat joints; wipe down with broad knife. Allow to dry.

2,3   Apply tape and compound to the interior angles. Smooth the tape and compound in the angles with a corner roller and corner finisher. Touch up with a broad knife as necessary.

Apply the first coat to fastener heads and metal accessories. Allow to dry.

4   Apply the fill coat of compound over tape on flat joints using a flat finishing box (above). Using compound of thicker consistency, spot fastener heads and apply a second coat to metal accessories. Allow to dry.

Apply a finish coat of compound to:

– flat joints with a wider finishing box.

– interior corner angles with the corner applicator box.

– metal accessories and fastener heads.

Allow to dry, and smooth lightly as required. Remove all dust before decoration. Do not scuff face paper by over-sanding.

5

Setting-Type Joint Compounds— System Applications

SHEETROCK brand setting-type (DURABOND) and lightweight setting-type (EASY SAND) joint compounds are chemical hardening products with varied working (setting) times for finishing interior gypsum panels and exterior gypsum ceiling boards. These specialized products provide short setting times for fast one-day finishing and extended times (up to 3 hours) to suit individual needs. The following application guide will help you choose the proper product to meet your requirements.

Application Guide—Setting-Type Joint Compounds

Compound Type	Setting Time-Min.	Working Time-Min.	Recommended Application
5	5	75	quick patch
20	20-30	15	application needing very short working time
45	30-80	20	prefill SW panels spot fastener heads embed metal beads
90	85-130	60	all applications
210	180-240	150	embed tape embed metal beads

For One-Day Finishing Use the techniques shown for hand application; mechanical tool application is not recommended for setting-type joint compounds because they may harden in the tools, making them inoperable. If mechanical tool application is required, proceed with caution in selecting a product to ensure enough working time exists for application and thorough cleaning of tools. In the following sequence, steps 1 through 4 should be completed by mid-day. Planning and scheduling according to the setting times of the compounds are essential. For best results, use a compound that will set within 1-1/2 to 2 hours.

(Where SHEETROCK brand gypsum panels, SW edge, are used, the first step is to fill the "V" grooves between panels.)

1. Embed joint tape (fiberglass or paper tape) over all joints and angles.

2. Apply compound over corner reinforcement. For best results, use compound that will set within 1-1/2 to 2 hours.

3. Spot fastener heads.

4. As soon as taping coat has set (hardened even though not dry), apply second (fill) coat over all joints and angles.

5. After the second (fill) coat application has hardened, apply a finishing coat of selected finishing compound to completely cover all joints, angles, corner bead and fasteners.

For SHEETROCK Brand Exterior Ceiling Board Surfaces Use hand application techniques and a SHEETROCK brand setting-type (DURABOND) or lightweight setting-type (EASY SAND) joint compound to treat joints and fasteners in USG exterior ceiling board applications. During periods of near-freezing temperatures, check weather forecast before beginning work. Minimum air, water, mix and surface temperatures of 45°F must be assured until compound is completely dry. Apply joint compound in the following sequence:

1. Prefill joints with compound. After prefill has set, tape all joints and angles in the ceiling with compound and SHEETROCK brand joint tape. When compound sets (hardens), immediately apply a fill coat of compound; allow to harden before finishing.

2. Apply compound over flanges of control joints, metal beads and trim. Spot all fastener heads.

3. After fill coat has set, apply compound finishing coat. Completely cover all joints, angles, beads, control joints and fasteners.

4. After the joint compound has dried, apply one coat of a good-quality latex flat exterior primer to equalize the joint and wallboard surfaces. Then follow with at least one coat of a balanced, good-quality alkyd or latex exterior finishing system as specified by the paint manufacturer.

For Use with SHEETROCK Brand FIBEROCK AQUA-TOUGH Panels In areas to be tiled, for tapered edge joints, embed joint tape with SHEETROCK brand setting-type (DURABOND) 45 or 90. When set, apply a fill coat of the same joint compound. Take precaution not to crown the joint. Wipe excess joint compound from the water-resistant panel surface before it sets. For end joints and interior angles, embed the joint tape with joint compound. A fill coat is not necessary. Take care not to crown the joint. Spot fastener heads at least once with setting-type joint compound. Chapter 4, "Backerboard Installation," provides instructions for tile work and substrates for areas subjected to constant moisture.

Fill and seal all openings around pipes, fittings and fixtures with a thinned-down coat of a good quality tile adhesive. For best results, use tile adhesive both as a sealer and to set the tile. Thin to a paint-like viscosity and apply the thinned compound with a small brush onto the raw gypsum panel core at the cutouts. Allow areas to dry thoroughly prior to application of tile. Before the adhesive dries, wipe excess material from the surface of gypsum panels.

For areas not to be tiled, embed tape with SHEETROCK brand setting-type (DURABOND) or lightweight setting-type (EASY SAND) joint compound 45 or 90 in the conventional manner. Finish with at least two coats of a SHEETROCK brand joint compound to provide joint finishing for painting and wallpapering.

Note: SHEETROCK brand FIBEROCK AQUA-TOUGH panels are not intended for use in areas subject to constant moisture, such as interior swimming pools, gang showers and commercial food processing areas. DUROCK cement board is recommended for these uses.

Drying Time—Joint Compound Under Tape

Standard drying times are based on evaporation of 10 lb. water per 250 ft. reinforcing tape, corresponding to 1/16" to 5/64" wet compound thickness under the tape. The drying times for thicker (or thinner) coats of wet compound between tape and panels will increase (or decrease) in proportion to the wet compound thickness.

These drying times apply when the exposed surface of tape is bare or nearly bare, and when adequate ventilation is provided. A heavy compound coat over tape lengthens drying time.

Drying Time—Joint Compound Under Tape

Temp. °F	60°	70°	80°	90°	100°
Temp. °C	16°	21°	27°	32°	38°
98%	18 D	12 D	9 D	6 D	4-1/2 D
97%	12 D	9 D	6 D	4-1/2 D	3-1/4 D
96%	10 D	7 D	5 D	3-1/2 D	2-1/2 D
95%	8 D	6 D	4 D	2-3/4 D	2 D
94%	7 D	5 D	3-1/4 D	2-1/4 D	41 H
93%	6 D	4 D	2-3/4 D	2 D	36 H
92%	5 D	3-1/2 D	2-1/2 D	44 H	32 H
91%	4-3/4 D	3-1/4 D	2-1/4 D	40 H	29 H
90%	4-1/2 D	3 D	49 H	36 H	26 H
85%	3 D	2 D	34 H	25 H	18 H
80%	2-1/4 D	38 H	27 H	19 H	14 H
70%	38 H	26 H	19 H	14 H	10 H
60%	29 H	20 H	14 H	10 H	8 H
50%	24 H	17 H	12 H	9 H	6 H
40%	20 H	14 H	10 H	7 H	5 H
30%	18 H	12 H	9 H	6 H	4-1/2 H
20%	16 H	11 H	8 H	5-1/2 H	4 H
10%	14 H	10 H	7 H	5 H	3-1/2 H
0	13 H	9 H	6 H	4-1/2 H	3 H
RH	RH = Relative Humidity	D = Days (24 hr.)		H = Hours	

Finishing

Gypsum drywall provides smooth surfaces that readily accept paint, textured finishes and wall coverings. For satisfactory finishing results, care must be taken to prepare surfaces properly to eliminate possible decorating defects commonly referred to as "joint banding" and "photographing." Usually caused by differences between the porosities and surface textures of the gypsum panel face paper and the finished joint compound, joint banding and photographing tend to be magnified by gloss paints. When viewed in direct natural lighting, joints and fasteners in painted walls and ceilings may be visible.

Skim Coating

The best method to prepare any gypsum drywall surface for painting is to apply a skim coat of joint compound. This leaves a film thick enough to fill imperfections in the joint work, smooth the paper texture and provide a uniform surface for decorating. Skim coating is currently recommended when gloss paints are used. It is also the best technique to use when decorating with flat paints.

Skim Coat Application

Finish joints and fasteners in the conventional three-coat manner. After joints are dry, mix joint compound—preferably SHEETROCK brand all-purpose, all-purpose (Midweight) or COVER COAT compound—to a consistency approximating that used for hand taping. Using a trowel, broad knife or long-nap texture roller, apply just enough joint compound to cover the drywall surface. Immediately wipe the compound as tightly as possible over the panel surface using a trowel or broad knife. Note: Do not use setting-type joint compound for thin skim coats. If setting-type compound dries before it sets, bond failure may result. An alternative is spraying SHEETROCK TUFF-HIDE for a level 5 finish.

Finishing and Decorating Tips

1. When sanding joint compound applied over joints, fasteners, trim and corner bead, take care to avoid roughening the panel face paper. Roughing paper during sanding results in raised fibers that can be conspicuous after painting.

2. Make sure all surfaces (including applied joint compound) are thoroughly dry and dust-free before decorating.

3. After conventional finishing of gypsum panel joints and fasteners, apply a skim coat of joint compound over the entire surface. This is the best technique for minimizing surface defects that may otherwise show through after painting if critical lighting conditions exist and/or glossy paints are used. Skim coating fills imperfections in joint work, smoothes the paper texture and provides a uniform surface for decorating. After the skim coat has dried, apply a prime coat of SHEETROCK First Coat for best results. An alternative is spraying SHEETROCK brand TUFF-HIDE.

4. If skim coating or spraying TUFF-HIDE is not done, the next best technique for minimizing decorating problems is to spray-apply a prime coat of First Coat. This paint-like product equalizes joint and wallboard surfaces to help avoid texture or suction variations when the finished paint coats are applied. This procedure minimizes problems with concealment of joints and fasteners.

5. Applying a ceiling or wall texture finish is also considered a suitable method for masking imperfections and diffusing light across wall and ceiling surfaces.

6. Frequent job inspections forestall potential problems and help ensure project specifications are being met. Wall and ceiling surfaces should be inspected after the gypsum panels are installed, when the joints are being treated and after the joints are finished before the surface is decorated. These checks will reveal starved and crowned joints that always show up under critical lighting.

Tip
Use an 8"–10" knife across the joints to inspect for gaps or irregularities.

Priming

Surface Preparation Proper preparation is essential for producing the best possible painted finish. Surfaces must be dry, clean, sound and free of oil, grease and efflorescence. Glossy surfaces must be dulled.

- Metal: Exposed metal should be primed with a good rust-inhibitive primer.

- Concrete: New concrete should age 60 days or more before covering. Fill cracks and level any offsets and voids to the same level as adjacent surfaces with SHEETROCK setting-type (DURABOND) or lightweight setting-type (EASY SAND) joint compound or COVER COAT compound. Apply as many coats as needed to provide a crack-free fill without edge joinings showing through decoration. Be sure to provide a smooth surface free of irregularities in areas exposed to sharply angled lighting.

- Drywall: Treat drywall joints and nailheads with a Sheetrock brand joint treatment system.

Also important for a superior paint job is the equalization of both the porosity and texture of the surface to be painted. The best way to achieve this is to skim coat the entire surface with Sheetrock all-purpose, all-purpose midweight or Cover Coat compound as described above, followed by a prime coat of Sheetrock First Coat. If skim coating is not done, the next best technique for minimizing decorating problems is to spray apply primer surface like Sheetrock Tuff-Hide, or apply a prime coat of Sheetrock First Coat.

Applying Sheetrock Brand First Coat

Specially formulated, fast drying Sheetrock brand First Coat equalizes surface texture and porosity to minimize decorating problems

Sheetrock brand First Coat is a specially formulated flat latex paint product with exceptionally high solids content that provides a superior prime coat over interior gypsum board.

In contrast to sealers or vapor barrier paints, First Coat does not provide a film that seals the substrate surface. Instead, it minimizes porosity differences by providing a base that equalizes the surface absorption and texture of the substrate to minimize "joint banding," "photographing" and other decorating problems. Sheetrock brand First Coat also provides the proper type and amount of pigments and fillers that are lacking in many conventional primers and sealers to equalize the surface textures.

First Coat is designed for fast, low-cost application. It dries to a hard, white finish in less than 30 minutes and can be top-coated within one hour. Not intended as a final coating, it should be painted over when dry. The product comes ready-mixed in 5-gallon and 1-gallon pails.

Mixing Ready-mixed Sheetrock brand First Coat should be stirred gently. Do not thin for brush or roller application. For spray application, if necessary, add water in half-pint increments up to a maximum 1 quart of water per gallon. First Coat may also be tinted.

Applying on Walls and Ceilings Apply a full coverage coat. Material dries to touch in under 30 min. Maintain minimum air, product mix and surface temperature of 55°F during application and until surface is dry. A brush, roller or airless or conventional spray gun may be used.

Brush Use a high-quality, professional paint brush.

Roller Use a high-quality roller with 1/8" to 1/4" nap on smooth and semi-smooth surfaces. Maximum nap length should not exceed 1/2".

Airless Spray Gun Use professional equipment that meets or exceeds the following when spraying through 50' of 1/4" i.d. airless spray hose: output at least 3/4 gallon per minute; pressure at least 2700 psi and accommodates a spray tip of 0.019 to 0.021" and a 30-mesh filter.

Note: Adjust atomizing air pressure and fluid flow rate so that full coverage rate can be achieved by overlapping preceding application with one-quarter to one-half the fan width at a distance of 18" from the surface. Air pressure and flow rates will vary with hose size and length, as well as paint consistency.

SHEETROCK First Coat contains a high level of select pigments and fillers like conventional latex flat paints. When these paints are used in spray equipment previously used to spray PVA sealers (which contain high levels of resin), clogging may occur at the spray gun tip. Use clean or new hoses to avoid this problem.

Coverage First Coat covers approximately 300–500 square feet per gallon of wet-mixed material, depending on factors such as application equipment and technique, condition of the substrate, amount of dilution and thickness and uniformity of coating.

Adding to Wall and Ceiling Textures If you desire slightly better spray properties, wet hide, improved bond, whiteness or surface hardness, First Coat may be added to wet-mixed SHEETROCK brand wall and ceiling textures at a rate of up to 1 gallon of First Coat per 30, 32, 40 or 50-lb. bag of texture. Reduce water quantity to account for the addition of First Coat based on a 1:1 replacement basis. Follow the surface priming recommendations on the bag.

Applying Compound over Concrete

COVER COAT Compound

With ready-mixed COVER COAT, drywall contractors are able to offer ready-to-decorate surfaces on concrete ceilings and columns located above grade. Smooth application and excellent bonding strength make COVER COAT ideal for filling small holes and crevices and for second coats and following covering applications with drywall methods and tools.

COVER COAT compound should not be applied over moist surfaces or areas subject to potential moisture buildup (from condensation or other sources), on ceiling areas below grade, on surfaces that project outside the building, or on other areas that might be subject to moisture, freezing, efflorescence, pitting or popping, movement or other abnormal conditions.

Application

For best results, apply COVER COAT before interior partitions are erected. Mix the compound as directed on the package to the proper consistency to minimize shrinkage. If a thinner consistency is needed for roller application, thin the compound by adding clean water (up to 1 to 1-1/2 gallons per 61.7 lb. carton or pail) and mixing with a hand mixer or low-speed drill-type mixer. If the compound becomes too thin, simply add more additional compound to thicken and remix.

Protect COVER COAT from freezing. During the entire application, maintain temperatures at or above 55°F, and provide heat and ventilation when necessary.

Prepare the concrete surfaces by removing any major protrusions or ridges. New concrete should age 60 days or more before compound is applied. Remove any form or parting oils, grease or efflorescence. All surfaces must be dry, clean and structurally sound. Prime any exposed metal with a good, rust-inhibitive primer. Fill cracks and holes, and level any offsets and voids to the same level as adjacent surfaces with SHEETROCK setting-type (DURABOND) or lightweight setting-type (EASY SAND) joint compound.

Apply as many coats as needed for a crack-free fill without edge joinings that show through decoration. Then apply a skim coat of COVER COAT after the joint compound has hardened (but not necessarily dried). Mix the compound lightly, and test-apply. Add small amounts of water if required. Exercise special care to provide a smooth surface, free of irregularities in areas that will be exposed to sharply angled lighting.

COVER COAT can be applied over joints and ridges left by concrete forms with a flat finisher, broad knife or trowel. Fill in and/or level out small holes and lumps, ridges, lips, etc. with compound. Allow to dry.

For expedient application, two workers are recommended. Apply the first coat of compound to the entire surface area of the ceiling, beam, or column with a flat finisher, long nap roller or broad knife. Keep moving in one direction, making sure that each application overlaps the previous one. Follow this application with a wide rubber squeegee or long-handle drywall blade, 24" or wider, to smooth out each fresh application. Apply SHEETROCK brand paper-faced metal bead on angles and corners as required, embedding and covering both flanges with a smooth fill of COVER COAT compound 3" to 4" wide. Allow to dry (under good drying conditions, 24 hours).

Before applying a second-coat, sand and dust the first coat. Apply second and third coats in the manner described above and perpendicular to the previous coat, or texture at this point if desired. Allow to dry. Sand with fine sandpaper if necessary. For texturing the second coat, simply add water and/or sand. Use a very fluid mix for fine texture, less fluid for coarse effects.

A very rough or uneven concrete surface may require three or more coats applied in the same manner.

COVER COAT compound may be left undecorated, but it is not washable if left unpainted. If decoration is specified, follow directions on the container of the decorating product

(See also USG Technical Data Sheet J-59 for detailed directions, spray application and special-use information.)

Note: Check cracking may occur in excessively deep fills. For this reason, successive coats are recommended for deep fills using joint compound for the first coat.

SHEETROCK Brand Setting-Type Joint Compounds

A SHEETROCK brand setting-type (DURABOND) or lightweight setting-type (EASY SAND) joint compound is equally suitable for filling form offsets and voids left in interior concrete. As with COVER COAT compound, these joint compounds should not be applied over moist surfaces or surfaces subject to moisture or any abnormal conditions.

Application

Grind off high plane differences in concrete level with adjacent area; remove any form oil, efflorescence or greasy deposits.

Prime exposed metal with a good rust-inhibitive primer.

Mix SHEETROCK brand setting-type (DURABOND) or lightweight setting-type (EASY SAND) joint compound according to package directions.

Use compound to fill cracks and holes and level any offsets and voids to the same level as adjacent surfaces. Apply as many coats as needed to provide a crack-free fill without edge joinings that show through decoration. Exercise special care to provide a smooth surface, free of irregularities in areas that will be exposed to sharply angled lighting.

Apply additional coats as required after each has set, but has not necessarily fully dried.

Apply a thick skim coat of joint compound over entire surface. The skim coat must be thick enough to prevent drying out before setting, or bond failure may result. Apply a final skim coat of COVER COAT compound or SHEETROCK brand all-purpose ready-mixed joint compound instead of SHEETROCK setting-type (DURABOND) joint compound.

Before decorating with paint or texture, apply a coat of SHEETROCK First Coat or a good quality, undiluted interior latex flat wall paint over entire surface and allow to dry.

For textured ceiling, apply SHEETROCK ceiling spray texture QT in uniform coat at rate up to 10 SF/lb.

Applying Sealant (Caulking)

For gypsum board assemblies to effectively reduce the transmission of sound, they must be airtight at all points. Perimeters must be sealed with SHEETROCK acoustical sealant, a caulking material that remains resilient. Penetrations for electrical outlets, medicine cabinets, plumbing, heating and air-conditioning ducts, telephone and intercom hookups and television antenna outlets must also be effectively sealed. Sealant is not to be used as a fire-stopping material for through-penetrations and head-of-wall construction joints.

It is crucial that sealing or caulking for sound-control is covered in the specifications, understood by workers of all related trades, supervised by the foremen and inspected carefully during construction.

Applying acoustical sealant has proven to be the least expensive, most cost-effective way to seal assemblies and prevent sound transmission. SHEETROCK acoustical sealant is approved for use in all UL fire-rated assemblies without affecting fire ratings. All references herein to "caulk" or "caulking" indicate use of SHEETROCK brand acoustical sealant.

To be effective, sealant must be properly placed. Placement is as important as the amount used. The technical drawings below indicate correct and incorrect applications of acoustical sealant.

SHEETROCK brand acoustical sealant effectively seals perimeters and openings in walls and ceilings, increasing sound ratings.

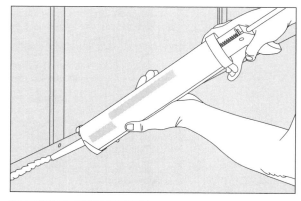

Proper caulking of outlet box (left), and double-layer partition (right).

SHEETROCK brand acoustical sealant applied around pipes and ducts effectively seals the wall to reduce sound transmission. Note: Sealant is not be used as a fire-stopping material for through penetrations and head-of-wall construction joints.

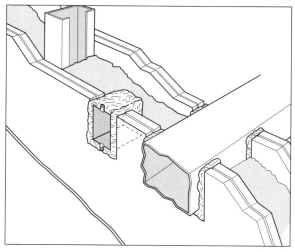

Tests conducted at the USG Research Center demonstrate that reliability of the perimeter seal is increased if perimeter relief does not exceed 1/8". When such a gap around the base-layer perimeter is caulked with a 1/4" bead of sealant, installation of face panels compresses the sealant into firm contact with all adjacent surfaces to form a permanent airtight seal.

The assemblies tested consisted of 2-1/2" steel studs 24 o.c., double-layer Sheetrock brand gypsum panels, SW each side; and 1-1/2" mineral wool SOUND attenuation blankets between studs. Results of sealant conditions are shown below.

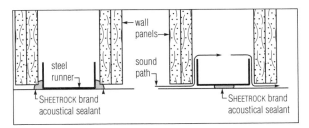

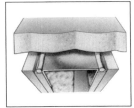

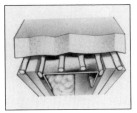

29 STC Unsealed

53 STC Both base layers sealed. No relief on face layers.

53 STC Sealed beneath and on edge of runner track. Base layer not relieved. Face layer relieved and sealed.

Installation

Partition Perimeter Cut gypsum boards for loose fit around partition perimeter. Leave a space no more than 1/8" wide. Apply a 1/4" minimum round bead of sealant to each leg of runners, including those used at partition intersections with dissimilar wall construction. Immediately install boards, squeezing sealant into firm contact with adjacent surfaces. Fasten boards in normal manner. Gypsum panels may have joint treatment applied in normal manner over sealed joints, and gypsum base may be finished normally with veneer plaster. Or, panels may be finished with base or trim as desired.

(See also the "Perimeter Isolation" section on page 131 for caulking application with metal trim over edge of boards where boards intersect dissimilar materials or cracking due to structural movement is anticipated.)

Control Joints Apply sealant beneath control joint to reduce path for sound transmission through joint.

Partition Intersections Seal intersections with sound-isolating partitions that are extended to reduce sound flanking paths.

Openings Apply sealant around all cut outs, such as at electrical boxes, plumbing, medicine cabinets, heating ducts and cold air returns to seal the opening. Caulk sides and backs of electrical boxes to seal them. (Sealant should not be used as a fire-stopping material.)

Door Frames Apply a bead of sealant in the door frame just before inserting face panel.

**Details—use of SHEETROCK
Brand Acoustical Sealant**

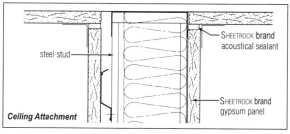

steel stud

SHEETROCK brand
acoustical sealant

SHEETROCK brand
gypsum panel

Ceiling Attachment

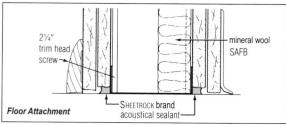

2¼"
trim head
screw

mineral wool
SAFB

SHEETROCK brand
acoustical sealant

Floor Attachment

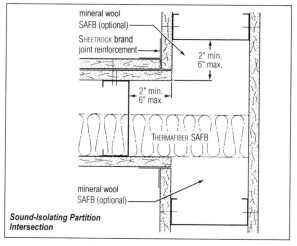

mineral wool
SAFB (optional)

SHEETROCK brand
joint reinforcement

2" min.
6" max.

2" min.
6" max.

THERMAFIBER SAFB

mineral wool
SAFB (optional)

**Sound-Isolating Partition
Intersection**

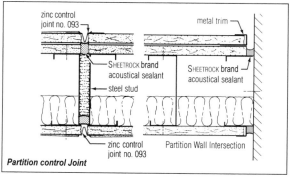

zinc control
joint no. 093

metal trim

SHEETROCK brand
acoustical sealant

SHEETROCK brand
acoustical sealant

steel stud

zinc control
joint no. 093

Partition Wall Intersection

Partition control Joint

Details—use of SHEETROCK brand Acoustical Sealant (continued)

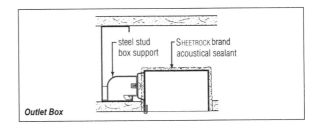

steel stud box support   ⌐SHEETROCK brand acoustical sealant

Outlet Box

Applying Textured Finishes

5

Textured finishes for gypsum board surfaces are often desired for aesthetic reasons, as well as their ability to obscure minor surface imperfections with an economical spray application. USG offers a full line of products to create fine, medium or coarse simulated acoustic texture finishes, as well as sand finishes. A variety of wall patterns can be created by using texture finish products with stipple brushes, pattern devices, rollers, floats, trowels and finishing knives. USG also offers a sound-rated texture finish called acoustical plaster finish. See page 197.

Note: Textured surfaces also can be created with veneer plaster finishes. (See the veneer application section in Chapter 6, "Finishing Veneer Plaster Systems.")

General Limitations

1. Texture finish applications are not recommended below grade or in high-humidity areas.

2. Heavy, water-based texturing materials may cause sag in gypsum panel ceilings under the following adverse conditions: high humidity, improper ventilation, panels applied parallel to framing and panels having insufficient thickness to span the distance between framing. The following table provides the maximum framing spacing for panels that are to be covered with water-based texturing materials.

Frame Spacing—Textured Gypsum Panel Ceilings

| Board Thickness | | Application Method | Max. Framing Spacing o.c. | |
in.	mm	(long edge relative to frame)	in.	mm
3/8	9.5	not recommended	—	—
1/2	12.7	perpendicular only	16	406
1/2*	12.7*	perpendicular only*	24*	610*
5/8	15.9	perpendicular only	24	610

* 1/2" SHEETROCK Brand Interior Gypsum Ceiling Board provides the strength and sag resistance of 5/8" standard board without the added thickness. Note: For adhesively laminated double-layer applications with 3/4" or more total thickness, 24 o.c. max.

3. The following surface preparation directions apply to new drywall and concrete surfaces. When redecorating an old, existing surface with a water-based texture, migrating stains or contaminants from the substrate may leach to the finished surface, resulting in discoloration and staining. (See the preparation directions for "Redecorating Ceilings" on pages 206–208 for more information on the proper surface preparation of existing sur-

faces. See "Ceiling Sag Precautions" on page 345 for more on applying water-based textures and interior finishing materials.)

Preparation

All surfaces must be dry, clean and sound. Glossy surfaces should be dulled. Prime metal with a good rust inhibitive primer. Fill and seal wood surfaces as needed. For new concrete age 60 days or more, before covering; remove form oils, grease and efflorescence. Grind down plane differences, and remove grinding dust and sludge. Fill cracks and holes, and level any offsets and voids to the same level as adjacent surfaces with SHEETROCK brand setting-type (DURABOND), lightweight setting-type (EASY SAND) joint compound or COVER COAT compound. Apply as many coats as needed to provide a crack-free fill without edge joinings that show through decoration. Exercise special care to provide a smooth surface free of irregularities in areas that will be exposed to sharply angled light.

For new drywall, reinforce and conceal drywall joints using SHEETROCK joint tape and joint compound. Fill all fastener depressions with joint compound. Smooth surface scratches and scuffs. Correct plane irregularities, as these are accentuated by sharp, angular lighting.

When prepared surfaces are dry and free of dust, apply a prime coat of First Coat. This product equalizes porosity variations between the gypsum board face paper and the finished joints, minimizing decorating problems such as "joint banding." As a less effective substitute, a good quality, white, interior latex flat wall paint with high solids content may be used. Apply undiluted and allow to dry before decorating.

Note: Application of a prime coat is intended to equalize the surface porosity and provide uniform color. Primers are not intended to reduce sag potential or to prevent migrating stains or contaminants from leaching to the finished surface.

For redecorating old ceilings, see pages 206–208 for proper surface preparation and application of decorating materials.

Powder Texture Finishes

SHEETROCK Brand Ceiling Spray Textures (QT) (Fine), (Medium) (Coarse)

Mixing Use clean vessel equipped with variable-speed power agitator. Sift texture finish into the recommended amount of water, agitating the mix during powder addition. Allow to soak for at least 15 minutes (longer in cold water). Remix until the consistency is creamy, aggregated, and lump-free.

Adjust spray consistency by adding small amounts of powder or water. Do not over-thin, as poor adhesion, lack of hide and texture variation may result.

Equipment Use professional spray equipment, such as a 10-to-1 ratio, double-action piston pump with 7-1/2" stroke, equipped with 4' pole gun having 3/8" to 1/2" round orifice. Use 3/4" to 1" material hose, 3/8" atomizing hose and 1/2" air line from compressor to pump; or rotor-stator pump (L3 or L4) with 5/16" to 3/8" round orifice. Compressor must be adequate for length and size of hose. Keep pressure as low as possible. Plaster mixers or hopper-type applicators also may be used.

Application Apply at rate up to 10 SF per lb. Do not exceed recommended coverage, as subsurface defects, variations in base suction or color differences may show through, or lighter texture may result.

Surfaces with uneven suction may require two coats. Let first coat dry before applying second. Remove splatters immediately from woodwork and trim. Maintain 55°F minimum air, water, product mix and surface temperature of the substrate during application and until surface is dry. Not washable, but can be painted (spray application is recommended) when redecoration is needed.

SHEETROCK **Brand Wall and Ceiling Spray Texture (Unaggregated)**

5

Mixing Use a clean vessel equipped with variable-speed power agitator. In initial mix, stir powder into recommended amount of water according to the package's directions. Agitate during powder addition. Allow to soak for at least 15 minutes (longer in cold water). Remix until the consistency is creamy and lump-free. If additional hardness and bond are desired, add up to 1 gallon of SHEETROCK brand First Coat per bag of SHEETROCK wall and ceiling spray texture. Do not over-thin, as poor adhesion, lack of adequate coverage and texture variation may result.

Equipment Use equipment with #57 fluid nozzle, R-27 air nozzle combination, 1/2" fluid hose, 3/8" air hose, air-powered 4-to-1 ratio materials pump (minimum requirement) with double regulators, 1/2" main line air hose and 7-1/2 to 9-hp gasoline compressor.

Application Apply with suitable spray equipment at rate of 10–25 SF/lb. for spatter and spatter/knockdown patterns, 20–40 SF/lb. for orange peel pattern. Spray using 16" to 20" fan. Hold gun 16" to 18" from surface. Overlap preceding application with 1/2 to 2/3 of fan width. With 75' to 125' of 1/2" hose, use 30 to 40 lb. fluid pressure and 50 to 60 lb. atomizing pressure. Then texture with roller or other tool if required for desired pattern. Flatten raised portions of wet material or sand it when dry to provide further variation. Maintain 55°F minimum air and surface temperature during application and until surface is dry. Avoid drafts while applying, but provide ventilation after application to aid drying. Do not use unvented gas or oil heaters. Spray texture material may be painted after overnight drying. Surface is not washable if left unpainted.

SHEETROCK **Brand Wall and Ceiling Texture (TUF-TEX)**

Mixing Use a clean mixing vessel equipped with a variable speed power agitator. Using drinkable water and clean mixing equipment, slowly add dry powder texture to the recommended amount of water. Mix to a heavy, but lump-free consistency. Allow to soak for at least 15 minutes (longer in cold water). Remix until mixture has a wet, smooth and creamy appearance. Adjust to desired spray consistency by adding small amounts of water to the wet mix. Do not over-thin, as poor adhesion, lack of coverage or texture variation may result. Do not intermix with any materials other than those recommended.

Application Apply by machine or hand to create the desired effect. Application rates will vary depending on the texture pattern. Generally, apply at 10 SF/lb for crow's foot, swirl and stipple patterns; 20–40 SF/lb. for orange peel pattern; and 10–25 SF/lb. for spatter and knock-down patterns. Maintain 55°F minimum air, water, product mix and surface temperature during application and until surface is dry. Avoid drafts while applying product, but provide ventilation after application to aid drying. Do not use unvented gas or oil heaters. Texture material may be painted after overnight drying. Surface is not washable if left unpainted.

SHEETROCK Brand Wall and Ceiling Texture (Multi-Purpose)

Mixing Use a clean mixing vessel equipped with variable-speed power agitator. In initial mix, stir powder into recommended amount of water. Agitate during powder addition. Allow to soak for at least 15 minutes (longer in cold water). Remix until a creamy, lump-free consistency is obtained. Then stir in up to 1 gallon of water. To obtain suitable consistency for texturing as desired, do not use more than the recommended amount of water. Do not over-thin, as poor adhesion, lack of coverage and texture variation may result. Do not intermix with other materials.

Application Apply with brush, roller or suitable spray equipment at rate of 10–20 SF/lb. for crow's foot, swirl and stipple patterns; 10–40 SF/lb. for fine orange peel pattern; then texture with roller or other tool if necessary for desired pattern. For finer textures and designs, use small brush, roller-stippler, whisk broom, comb or other tools. Flatten raised portions of wet material or sand it when dry to provide further variation. Maintain 55°F minimum air, water, product mix and surface temperature during application and until surface is dry. Avoid drafts while applying, but provide ventilation after application to aid drying. Do not use unvented gas or oil heaters. Multi-purpose texture material may be painted after overnight drying. Surface is not washable if left unpainted.

SHEETROCK Brand Texture 12 (Sand Finish) Wall and Ceiling Spray Texture

Mixing Place recommended amount of water in suitable mixing container. Gradually add powder to water. Stir thoroughly with mechanical mixer until completely mixed and lump-free. Soak mix for 15 minutes (longer in cold water). Remix. Gradually add (under agitation) up to 1-3/4 gallons of water to reach desirable spraying consistency. Over-thinning may result in poor adhesion, lack of hiding capability, texture variation and inability to compensate for base suction variations. Do not exceed 3-1/4 gallons total water per bag. Use within 24 hours.

Equipment Spray equipment with #68 stainless-steel fluid nozzle, orifice size .110; air nozzle #101 carbide; atomizing pressure at gun 40–50 psi; air-hose size 3/8" i.d. with 3/8" swivel; fluid hose size 1/2" i.d. with 1/2" swivel; control-hose size 3/16" with 1/4" swivel. Air-driven pump sizes: 4-1/2:1 ratio for hose lengths up to 125'; 7-1/2:1 for lengths up to 200'; 10:1 for lengths over 200'.

Application Apply with spray gun using 24" fan. Hold gun 18" from surface and move parallel to surface. Avoid curved, sweeping strokes. Overlap preceding application with 1/2 to 2/3 of fan width. Apply a full coat in one direction, then immediately cross-spray in opposite direction. Use 1/2" fluid hose with fluid-pressure variable depending on hose length. Air and surface temperatures should be 55°F or higher during application and until surface is dry. Avoid drafts while applying, then provide adequate circulating ventilation to aid drying. Do not use unvented gas or oil heaters. May be painted after overnight drying. Not washable unpainted.

Texture Additives— Optional

a. **Adding latex emulsion to powder texture increasing bond and surface hardness as desired** The more latex additive used, up to 2 pints, the greater the bond and hardness of the dried surface. Surface-priming recommendations still apply.

b. **Adding paint to powder textures** If better wet-and-dry hide, improved surface hardness, wider spray fan and faster spray application are desired, SHEETROCK First Coat or a good-grade, compatible polyvinyl acetate, vinyl-acrylic or acrylic-type paint in white, off-white or pastel colors only may be added to ceiling texture. For First Coat or a compatible paint product, wet-mix at a rate of 1 gallon per 32 or 40 lb. bag of texture by substituting 1 gallon of paint for 1 gallon of water. When adding 1 gallon of paint to a fully diluted mix, the above properties remain appreciably the same, but a somewhat sparser aggregate surface may also result. Also, if aggregate is accidentally brushed off, a lighter colored surface may result. Interior flat, eggshell or semi-gloss paint products can be used. First verify the compatibility of paints to be used with SHEETROCK brand texture products. Surface priming recommendations still apply.

Sound-Rated Texture Finish

USG Acoustical Plaster Finish

Mixing Read mixing and spray application directions completely before proceeding with mixing. Use a 7 cu. ft. or larger paddle-type plaster mixer with rubber-tipped blades (anchor mixer) or a self-contained integral mixing/pumping spray texture tank with horizontal shaft and plaster or texture rig-type paddles mounted on a horizontal shaft. To ensure uniform product performance, mix a minimum of two bags. Add powder to clean, room-temperature water in quantity specified on package. Mix for approximately 5 minutes until lump-free, and a thick, foamy consistency is generated (initial mix will appear dry and heavy).

Note: If material is over-mixed, excessive foam will occur. Add more powder to break down foam and remix until proper foam level is reached. Additional mixing may be necessary during application to maintain foam consistency. Note that this is a chemically setting material; use mixed material within 3–4 hours. (See also Reference P720, USG Acoustical Plaster Finish Submittal Sheet.)

Spray Application All pumps and hoses must be cleaned initially with water, followed by application of approximately one gallon of SHEETROCK brand ready-mixed joint compound prior to spray application to prevent severe aggregate separation or clogging by the clean-out water.

For combined mixing/pumping units: Initially fill mixing hopper with necessary water to flush hoses. Pump all water from hopper, then drop joint compound into material reservoir of pump. Start pumping until compound feeds into hose. Immediately stop pump. Add water and powder in mixing hopper following mixing directions. When USG acoustical plaster finish is properly mixed, pump out and discard joint compound. Turn on atomizing air, material valve and pump (in that order).

5

For pump units only: Add previously mixed finish to material hopper after pumping joint compound into hose. Then follow the start-up procedure as stated for combined mixing/pumping units.

The recommended spray pattern is 1-1/2' to 3' in diameter. The spray gun should be held 2' to 4' from the surface, depending on material density and atomizer pressure. Apply USG acoustical plaster finish evenly, holding pole gun perpendicular to the surface being sprayed and slowly waving it from side to side until area is covered. Then immediately double back, cross-hatching prior coat. Repeat same procedure as necessary until desired thickness is reached.

Elimination of spray lines and section seams is essential in producing an acceptable finish. Do not spray a portion of a ceiling in one day and the final portion on another day, as a noticeable seam will result. If entire ceiling area cannot be sprayed to the final thickness in one day, spray the entire surface with a material coat of uniform thickness (minimum 1/4"). Complete to final thickness the following day using a cross-hatch application. Use natural breaks and boundaries to "frame" pattern edges and conceal seams. To measure average thickness, mark desired thickness on a blunt-tipped object (head of pencil or finishing nail) and insert into finish.

For a different surface color, use a good quality, flat latex paint (white or pastel) and spray apply over dried finish. There will be a minimal loss in NRC value.

Ready-Mixed Texture Finishes

Sheetrock Brand Ready-Mixed Wall and Ceiling Spray Texture

Product Preparation Use a heavy-duty drill fitted with a suitable mixing paddle, and operate it at 400–600 rpm. Excessive or high-speed mixing may produce voids in finished appearance. Mix until consistency is smooth and uniform. Do not mix with other materials in wet or dry form.

Thinning Thinning of texture with water will vary considerably, depending on the finished appearance desired and the method of application to be employed. Applicator should experiment with some of the mixed material prior to use, then adjust water proportions to suit the job. Over-thinning may cause poor bond, pinholes, and cracking.

Coverage Estimated coverage is up to 115 SF/gal. or 400 SF for each 3.5-gal. carton. Actual coverage will vary depending on factors such as the type of texture design, the condition of the substrate surface, the amount of dilution of the product, application technique and the uniformity of the coating.

Application Apply with brush, roller or with suitable professional spray equipment. For spray application, spray using a 16" to 20" fan. Overlap preceding application with 1/2 to 2/3 of fan, applying first in one direction and then in cross direction. Texture must be evenly spread and free from runs, sags and other blemishes. Allow texture to dry before applying paint. Maintain air, texture and surface temperatures of at least 55°F within the working area until texture is completely dry. Texture color may not match color of other texture products. It may be painted after overnight drying, though will not be washable unpainted.

SHEETROCK Brand Ready-Mixed Joint Compound

Mixing and Thinning Although this product is ready to use, slight mixing will increase creaminess of the product. To mix, transfer contents into a suitable vessel. Use a SHEETROCK USG mud mixer on a heavy-duty drill, preferably at 450–600 rpm under load. Higher speeds tend to whip air bubbles into the product. Plunge the mixer paddle up and down in the mix about 10 times before switching on the drill. Mix, adding water as recommended, until smooth and uniform, always keeping the paddle completely immersed.

Experiment with a small amount of mixed material prior to use, adjusting water proportions to match product viscosity to individual requirements. For brush or roller/crow foot pattern, dilute with 1 to 1-1/2 gallon of water per 50 lb.

5

If large areas are being textured, prevent shade differences by sorting out enough boxes bearing identical manufacturing codes to cover entire area. Also, be sure to add exactly the same amount of water to each 50-lb. batch of ready-mixed compound.

Application Material may be brush-, roller- or trowel-applied. Finishes must be evenly spread and free from runs, sags and other blemishes. Some cracking may occur upon drying. Allow each coat to dry before applying following coat. Coverage will depend on the amount of dilution and method of application.

Ready-Mixed Texture Paints

SHEETROCK Brand Wall and Ceiling Texture Paint

Product Preparation Wall and ceiling texture paint is available in two formulas to produce a sand finish (Texture 1) and sanded paste stipple finish (TEXOLITE). These textured products in a paint base may be used directly from the container as supplied. Stir well before applying, but avoid excessive agitation that will entrain air. Thinning with water is not required, and will affect the coating's appearance. If thinning is necessary, add one or two ounces of water per gallon, and stir well. The product can be tinted using universal colorants; incomplete mixing may result in color streaks, however.

Coverage 150–200 SF per gallon, depending on substrate, application method and texture desired.

Application Maintain minimum air, product and surface temperature of 55°F during application and until surface is dry. Can be roller- or spray-applied. Apply a full coverage coat. Provide ventilation after application to encourage drying.

For roller application, cut in corners and trim using a trim brush. Roll surface immediately with a 3/4" nap roller cover. Generously apply in long strokes, keeping the roller cover filled to obtain texture effect. Cross roll area to prevent ridging and framing.

For spray application, use a gun having a #57 fluid nozzle and an A-27 fan cap, or similar equipment. Air hose is typically 3/8" i.d. with 1/2" i.d. material hose. The spray gun should be approximately 18" from the surface. Adjust atomizing air pressure and material flow rate so that a full coverage rate can be achieved by overlapping the preceding application by 1/4 to 1/2 the fan width.

The product dries to the touch in approximately 60 minutes at 72°F/50% RH. Allow to fully dry overnight.

SHEETROCK Brand Ceiling Texture Paint, Coarse Finish Texture

Product Preparation Stir until consistency is smooth and uniform. Up to 1 pint of water per gallon may be added if necessary to adjust consistency. Excessive water will cause cracking and poor bonding. Do not mix with other materials. 2 gallons cover approximately 100 SF on smooth, hard surfaces.

Application Stain blocking sealer may be required on stained or previously decorated surfaces. Maintain surface and air temperature above 55°F. Using a roller, apply texture generously in long strokes. Cross-roll adjoining areas to prevent ridging. Avoid applying in one direction; random spreading will create a more natural appearance. Allow to dry at least overnight before painting.

Creating Texture Patterns

Texture finishes and compounds offer opportunities for a variety of patterns and appearances. The number of patterns that can be created is limitless, but several patterns are particularly popular. Here are some commonly used patterns and information about how to achieve them.

Spatter and Light Orange Peel

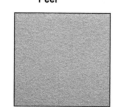

Material for Light Orange Peel and Spatter

- SHEETROCK Brand Wall and Ceiling Spray Texture
- SHEETROCK Brand Wall and Ceiling Texture (TUF-TEX)
- SHEETROCK Brand Wall and Ceiling Spray Texture Ready-Mixed

Application Spray

Equipment Gun equipped with a #57 fluid nozzle and A-27 fan cap.

Procedure Mix products to a thin, latex-paint consistency. For a light orange peel, which is always the first application, atomizing air should be approximately 60 psi, and material feed pressure approximately half the atomizing pressure. When spraying, apply in long, even strokes with no wrist action, holding gun perpendicular to surface and approx. 18" from surface. Apply material as uniformly as possible, avoiding lap marks.

Spatter Coat After fog coat has been applied, allow about 10–15 minutes for surface to partially dry, then apply spattering by removing the A-27 fan cap and reducing atomizing air to approx. 15 psi, and the material feed to approximately 10 psi. While applying spatter coat, move spray gun in a rapid, random fashion, while standing about 6' from the surface. Size of spatters depends on pressures used. Amount (or density) of spatters on surface depends on personal preference.

Orange Peel

Material for Orange Peel

- SHEETROCK Brand Wall and Ceiling Spray Texture
- SHEETROCK Brand Wall and Ceiling Texture (TUF-TEX)
- SHEETROCK Brand Wall and Ceiling Texture (Multi-Purpose)
- SHEETROCK Brand Ready-Mixed Wall and Ceiling Spray Texture

Application Spray

Equipment Same as for light orange peel except atomizing air pressure should be approximately 40 psi, and material feed pressure approximately 20 psi. Degree of orange peel pattern depends on amount of material applied to surface.

5

Knock-Down and Skip-Trowel

Material for Knock-Down and Skip-Trowel

- SHEETROCK Brand Wall and Ceiling Spray Texture
- SHEETROCK Brand Wall and Ceiling Texture (TUF-TEX)
- SHEETROCK Brand Ready-Mixed Wall and Ceiling Texture
- SHEETROCK Brand Ready-Mixed Wall and Ceiling Spray Texture

Application Spray

Equipment Pole gun, hopper, or Binks 7D or Binks 7E2 gun

Knock-Down Procedure Apply as spatter as described previously, using material at a heavy, latex-paint consistency. After spattering surface, wait about 10–15 minutes, then very lightly flatten only tops of spatters with flat blade or flat hand trowel. Again, size of spatters depends on pressures used.

Skip-Trowel Procedure Mix in #30 mesh silica sand (2 cups silica sand/5 gallons of texture). Apply as spatter coat, but at very low pressures to allow for large spatters on surface. Wait approximately 10 to 15 minutes, then use blade as in the knock-down procedure, but applying more pressure.

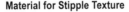

Stipple Texture

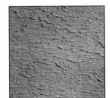

Material for Stipple Texture

- SHEETROCK Brand Wall and Ceiling Texture (Multi-Purpose)
- SHEETROCK Brand Wall and Ceiling Texture (TUF-TEX)
- SHEETROCK Brand Ready-Mixed Wall and Ceiling Texture

Application Hand

Equipment Paint pan or large pail, paint roller 1/4" to 1" nap. Short nap produces lower stipple—fine pattern. Long nap produces higher stipple—coarse pattern.

Procedure for Hand Texturing Mix product to a consistency similar to spatter/knock-down. Completely wet out roller with material, then apply to surface as evenly as possible, covering entire surface. Let partially dry to a "dull wet" appearance, then roll again for desired texture effect.

Crow's Foot

Use same material, equipment and application as for stipple texture, then use texture brush instead of paint roller to texture surface.

Procedure is the same as for roller texture, except that after material has partially dried to dull wet finish, stamp surface with texture brush pre-wetted with texture material for desired stipple finish.

Swirl Finish

Material for Swirl Finish

- SHEETROCK Brand Wall and Ceiling Texture (Multi-Purpose)
- SHEETROCK Brand Wall and Ceiling Texture (TUF-TEX)
- SHEETROCK Brand Ready-Mixed Wall and Ceiling Texture

Application Hand

Equipment Same as for stipple texture, plus wallpaper-type brush.

Procedure Apply as a roller texture. Let surface dry to dull wet finish, then use wallpaper brush to achieve desired swirl texture, rotating brush in circular motion on the wet surface.

Brocade or Travertine

Material for Brocade or Travertine

- SHEETROCK Brand Wall and Ceiling Texture (Multi-Purpose)
- SHEETROCK Brand Wall and Ceiling Texture (TUF-TEX)
- SHEETROCK Brand Ready-Mixed Wall and Ceiling Texture

Application Hand

Equipment Same as for crow's foot texture, plus flat blade.

Procedure Same as for crow's foot. After crow's foot texture has been achieved, wait 10–15 minutes, then knock down tips only by lightly drawing a flat blade across surface.

Other Hand Texture Effects

Textured effects cited above are only a few of the many possibilities. Other effects can be achieved using different texturing tools. A string-wrapped roller, for example, produces an attractive striated stone effect, while cross-rolling gives an interesting squared pattern. For finer designs and textures, use a small brush, roller-stippler, whisk broom, crumpled paper, comb, sponge or similar items. Flattening raised portions of wet material or sanding when dry provides further variations. Material also may be scored to represent block, tile or cut stone outlines. See page 204.

 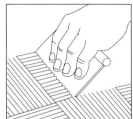 

Interior Patching & Repairing

Finishing of drywall systems often requires patches and repairs of existing walls, or corrections to errors made in erecting new ones. A number of products are available to handle projects ranging from small holes to large breaks and cutouts. Problems in finishes and textures also can be corrected. Following are a few steps for solving several patch and repair problems.

Small Holes

SHEETROCK brand spackling compound, including dust control products, fills small holes and cracks and covers nailheads. Used directly from the container, the compound should be stirred with a putty knife before application. Spread the compound into holes or cracks with a putty knife. Wipe away ridges and let dry approximately 2 hrs. Apply second fill and let dry. Sand lightly to smooth before painting.

SHEETROCK lightweight spackling compound is formulated for low-shrinkage, one-application fills. Stir lightly to ensure uniform consistency, then spread into small holes and cracks with putty knife and smooth. Allow to dry. Sand lightly before painting.

SHEETROCK brand spackling powder is a fast-setting, non-shrinking patching compound. Thoroughly mix 1 lb. of powder into approximately 8 oz. clean, cool water in a clean vessel. Stir until heavy paste is achieved. Press into cracks and holes with putty knife, or use a heavy paint brush to brush into hairline cracks. Use two applications in cracks more than 1/4". Let dry thoroughly and sand lightly before painting.

Larger Holes

SHEETROCK brand plaster of Paris has a working time of about 15 minutes after mixing, then sets hard in 20–30 minutes. Mix 1 lb. of plaster into approximately 6 oz. of clean, cool water in a clean vessel and stir until smooth. Let stand one minute, then remix 1 minute. Wet hole edges with a sponge, then apply compound with putty knife. For holes more than 1" wide and/or more than 1/4" deep, apply first coat to fill opening to within 1/16" to 1/8" of level. Let set, then apply second coat to level.

SHEETROCK brand patching compound, EASY SAND 5 also is a setting-type compound. Mix 2 lb. into approximately 16 oz. of clean, cool water in a clean vessel. Mix until smooth, let soak 1 minute, then remix for 1 minute. Add water in small increments, if desired, to achieve working consistency. Apply with putty knife. For large cracks, fill with compound, cover with SHEETROCK brand paper joint tape, embed tape and let harden. Apply second coat (third if necessary) and let set. Sand and prime when dry. For medium holes up to 2", apply compound around edges and coat perimeter of hole. Crisscross tape over hole and embed. Apply second coat (third if necessary) and let set. Sand and prime when dry.

SHEETROCK brand drywall repair clips enable damaged drywall to be cut away and replaced. After damaged piece has been eliminated, clips are mounted midway on each of the four cut edges. Screw-attach to ensure permanent connection. Measure and cut new panel of the same size and screw-attach to the other end of each repair clip. Remove tabs used for temporary mounting. Finish as with fresh panels.

SHEETROCK drywall repair kit contains drywall clips, fiberglass drywall tape, setting-type joint compound (EASY SAND 90), and plastic spreader. Follow instructions above for drywall clips.

Floor Surfaces   SHEETROCK brand floor patch/leveler repairs and levels substrates before applying new floor covering. May be applied to plywood, hardboard or masonry/concrete surfaces inside and above grade. Surface should be between 40°F and 80°F. Coverage: 0.75 lb. floor patch covers 1 SF at 1/8" thickness; 1.5 lb. covers 1 SF at 1.4"; 2.25 lb. covers 1 SF at 3/8".

Mix 2 parts powder into 1 part water. Stir thoroughly and apply flush with surface using a concrete trowel. Feather into surrounding areas and let dry 4 hours before sanding.

Additive   SHEETROCK brand sand finish paint additive may be added to your favorite paint or varnish to produce a sand-textured finish. Stir in approximately 8 oz. of additive to one gal. of paint. Mix 2–3 hours before painting and let stand. Roller or brush-apply paint in normal fashion.

Resurfacing

Where ceilings or sidewalls are badly disfigured and a fresh surface is desirable, they may be resurfaced using a layer of 1/4" or 3/8" SHEETROCK gypsum panels. Ceilings may also be redecorated with texture finishes. For resurfacing masonry walls, see application of gypsum board to wall furring, described in Chapter 3, "Cladding."

Preparation   Remove all trim (may not be necessary if 1/4" panels are used). To remove trim easily, drive all nails completely through the trim with a pin punch. Remove all loose surfacing material. Fill small holes with joint compound or patching plaster. Patch large holes to the surrounding level with single or multiple layers of gypsum board nailed to framing and shimmed out as required.

Electrical outlet boxes for switches, wall receptacles and fixtures should be extended outward to compensate for the added gypsum panel thickness.

Locate joists and studs by probing or with a magnetic "stud finder." Snap a chalk line to mark their full length and mark their location on the adjacent wall or ceiling. Where great irregularities of surface exist, apply furring strips not over 16" o.c., using wood shingles to shim out to a true, even plane.

Installation Apply SHEETROCK gypsum panels with long dimension placed horizontally or vertically. Fasten with gypsum board nails or drywall screws, spaced 7" o.c. on ceilings, 8" o.c. on walls. Nails or screws must be long enough to penetrate into framing members at least 5/8".

Gypsum panels may be adhesively applied over sound, existing walls (see directions, Chapter 3, page 119) with SHEETROCK setting-type (DURABOND) or lightweight setting-type (EASY SAND) joint compound.

Finish the panels with SHEETROCK paper-faced bead and joint treatment as necessary, and replace all trim.

Redecorating Ceilings

Redecorating cracked, discolored or damaged ceilings with texture can make old ceilings look like new. Spray-applied texture finishes cover minor surface cracks and imperfections and can provide attractive decorative surfaces. Redecorating surfaces previously textured with a large-aggregate (e.g., SHEETROCK brand ceiling spray texture [QT]) is especially effective since these surfaces normally are not easily cleaned, rolled or brush-painted. Yet they are easily spray-painted with texture. These modernized ceilings add value and beauty. Best of all, most jobs can be done in one day without removing rugs, furniture or light fixtures.

Preparation Surface cracks larger than hairline size should be treated with a drywall joint compound and tape, and thoroughly dried, prior to redecorating. Tobacco smoke stains require pre-decorating attention and treatment with special stain-blocking sealer. Remove grease stains using mild detergent. Seal water-stained surfaces with primer specifically recommended by the manufacturer. Remove soot or dirt by air dusting surfaces. Wash mildew-contaminated surfaces with a solution of 1 qt. household bleach such as Clorox® (sodium hypochlorite) to 3 qt. water.

Cover all furniture, rugs, etc. with drop cloths and wear gloves and protective clothing as well as eye protection. For heavy mildew deposits, two applications of the bleach solution may be necessary. On textured ceilings, heavy coats of bleach are not recommended. Mist-coat surface with bleach solution using an aerating device, such as a trigger-type household sprayer. No rinsing of the bleach solution is necessary since this would re-wet the texture and cause serious bond problems. Let bleach dry thoroughly, then respray the surface with SHEETROCK ceiling spray texture.

On previously painted mildew-contaminated surfaces, apply bleach solution with a scrub brush. When dry, rinse the painted surface to remove bleach, dry, and then spray-apply desired texture finish.

Caution: Treatment for mildew will not necessarily prevent its recurrence if humidity, temperature and moisture conditions are favorable for further mildew growth.

Redecorating with Texture

Painted Surfaces Ceilings that have been painted with pastel flat alkyd or latex flat paints can be sprayed with no special pretreatment if free of grease, dirt, smoke stains or other contaminants. Glossy surfaces must be dulled by lightly sanding to develop "tooth" for a good bond. Wash surface with a solution of commercially available wall cleaner. Stained surfaces require application of a stain-blocking sealer. Spot prime bare metal with a good rust-inhibitive primer. After prepared surfaces have thoroughly dried, apply SHEETROCK First Coat.

Previously Textured Surfaces Priming a ceiling previously decorated with a large-aggregate texture (e.g., SHEETROCK ceiling spray texture [QT]) with a paint primer is not necessary if the surface is not stained and is free of grease, dirt, smoke stains or other contaminants. Use only SHEETROCK ceiling spray texture (QT Coarse) to redecorate an aggregated texture surface.

Wallpaper or Vinyl Wall Covering Remove material and prime ceiling surface with appropriate primer prior to texturing.

Plaster Ceilings Surface must be in paintable condition. Prior to texturing, cover with primer-sealer specifically recommended by the paint manufacturer.

Mask surfaces by covering floors and walls with 0.85 to 1-mil-thick polyethylene sheeting, available in 8' to 12' widths, folded and rolled in half for easier handling. Spread polyethylene sheeting on floor, making sure that all areas are completely covered. Next, apply wide masking tape to wall-ceiling intersection, fastening only top of tape to wall and leaving bottom hanging free. Fasten one edge of folded poly sheeting to loose edge of tape, then unfold film to full width. Press tape into firm contact with both wall and sheeting.

Cover Furniture, Cabinets, Light Fixtures and anything that will remain in the room during spraying operation. Lower ceiling light fixtures so they can be quickly and completely covered.

For information on mixing, equipment and application, see pages 194–195.

Equipment Use professional spray equipment such as a hand-held hopper or 10:1 ratio, double-action piston pump with 7-1/2" stroke, equipped with 4' pole gun having 3/8" to 1/2" round orifice. Use 3/4" to 1" material hose, 3/8" atomizing hose and 1/2" air line from compressor to pump. Compressor must be adequate (85 cfm) for length and size of hose. Keep pressure as low as possible. Plaster mixers or hopper-type applicators also may be used.

Application Apply SHEETROCK ceiling spray texture at a rate of up to 10 SF/lb. Do not exceed recommended coverage, as subsurface defects, variations in base suction or color differences may show through, or lighter texture may result. Maintain 55°F minimum air and surface temperature during application and until surface is dry.

Redecorating an Aggregated Textured Surface with Paint

After properly preparing the surface as described on pages 206–207, follow the guidelines below.

Brush application of paint over an aggregated textured ceiling is not recommended. Spray application is preferred. In redecorating by hand, use a long-nap paint roller with 1/2" to 3/4" nap. Any good-quality interior latex or vinyl acrylic paint in flat, eggshell or semi-gloss can be used. Slight dilution of paints with water, particularly high-viscosity types, may be necessary for smoother, easier spreading. Apply paint by rolling in one direction, immediately followed by cross rolling. Use light pressure and avoid over-rolling and saturating the surface to minimize loosening of surface aggregate.

Whether spraying or rolling, avoid drafts while applying, but provide adequate circulation and ventilation to aid drying.

5

Precautions

Ventilate or use a dust collector to avoid creating dust in the workplace. A NIOSH-approved respirator should be used if the air is dusty. Safety glasses are recommended.

Finishing Veneer
Plaster Systems

Advances of Veneer Plaster

Veneer plaster has been growing in popularity in recent years as a wall finishing system. The speed of application for one-coat systems makes it cost-competitive with drywall, and the added smoothness of two-coat veneer provides a rich look that makes decorating easier. Veneer plaster is also durable and resists scuffs, gouges and impact damage.

Note that various organizations provide information about recommended standards or tolerances for finishing veneer plaster systems. See the Appendix for information about standards and tolerances.

For instructions on the safe use of veneer plaster and related products, see Chapter 13, "Safety Considerations & Material Handling."

Veneer Plaster Finishes

Veneer plaster finishes can be used in one- or two-coat applications and can be given smooth or textured surfaces. Each method has its particular advantage.

One-Coat Veneer Finish Provides a hard, monolithic surface at low cost. Complete application—from bare studs to decorated walls and ceilings—takes 48 to 72 hours, provided complete dryness has been reached. Assemblies with one-coat veneer plaster application meet fire and sound requirements, and contribute to shortened construction schedules for added profit.

Two-Coat Veneer Finish Compared to many other finishes, two-coat veneer provides a more durable, abrasion-resistant surface that can be finished to a truer plane than one-coat applications. These finishes can be used with steel or wood framing wherever high quality appearance is desired. They also permit next-day decorating, provided the plaster has fully dried. (See also reference P777.) Assemblies with monolithic gypsum surfaces offer excellent fire and sound ratings.

Job Environment

Maintain building temperature in a comfortable working range, at least 55°F with a relative humidity between 20% and 50%. (See also reference PM10.)

Keep air circulation at a minimum level prior to, during and following application until finish is dry.

If possible, maintain building temperature-humidity combination in the "normal drying" area of the graph on the next page. Where conditions are very dry, relative humidity often can be increased by wetting down the floor periodically. During these periods, make every effort to reduce air movement by closing windows and deflecting a heater blower, if used, and duct output away from the surfaces being plastered.

*Plaster Drying
Conditions*

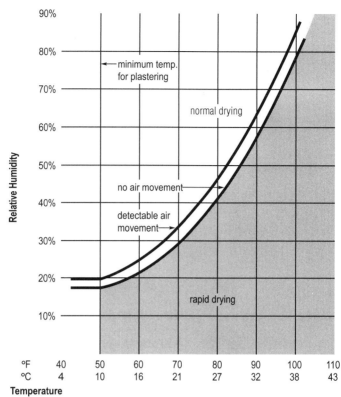

Selection of Joint Treatment System

Under normal working conditions, veneer plaster joints may be treated by applying Imperial brand type P (pressure-sensitive) or type S (staple), and then applying the veneer plaster basecoat or finish to preset the tape. However, there are a number of special situations that require the use of a setting-type joint treatment system:

- If high room temperature, low humidity or excessive evaporation conditions fall in the "rapid drying" area of the graph.
- If metal framing is specified.
- If wood-framing spacing of 24" o.c. and a single-layer gypsum base veneer system are specified (5/8" base with one-coat veneer finish and 1/2" or 5/8" base with two-coat veneer finish).

For any of these conditions, use Sheetrock brand joint tape and setting-type (Durabond) or lightweight setting-type (Easy Sand) joint compound to treat all joints and internal angles. Allow joint treatment to set and dry thoroughly before plaster application.

Grounds

Correct thickness of veneer plaster finish is one of the most important factors in obtaining good results. To ensure proper thickness, all corner beads, trim and expansion joints must be of the recommended type and must be properly set.

Accessories must provide grounds for the following minimum plaster thicknesses:

1. Over IMPERIAL gypsum base, one coat: 1/16 in. (1.6 mm)
2. Over IMPERIAL gypsum base, two coats: 3/32 in. (2.4 mm)

Applying Trim Accessories

Trim accessories simplify and enhance the finishing of veneer plaster assemblies. The accessories are inexpensive, easily applied and designed to work together for long-lasting, trouble-free construction. All are suitable for steel-frame and wood-frame construction.

Corner Bead Application

SHEETROCK brand corner reinforcements provide strong, durable protection for outside angle corners, uncased openings, pilasters, beams and soffits. The exposed nose of the bead resists impact and forms a screed for finishing. Corner bead should be installed in one piece unless the length of the corner exceeds stock bead lengths. Installation notes follow for each product.

SHEETROCK **Brand No. 800 and No. 900 Corner Beads** are galvanized fine-mesh, expanded-flange corner beads specially designed for veneer plaster construction. Apply No. 800 or No. 900 corner bead with nails through the board into wood framing, or to the board alone in wood or steel-framed assemblies with 9/16" galvanized staples spaced 12" o.c. through both flanges. Fasteners should be placed opposite one another in both flanges. Both beads provide superior reinforcement with veneer plaster finishes through approximately 90 keys per linear foot.

Use No. 800 for one-coat applications. It provides the proper 1/16" ground height for one-coat finishing.

Use No. 900 for two-coat applications. It provides the 3/32" ground height needed for two-coat applications.

On masonry corners, hold bead firmly against the corner and grout both flanges with IMPERIAL veneer finish. On monolithic concrete, apply a high-grade bonding agent, such as USG plaster bonder, over the corner before placing the bead and grouting. Preset all beads with a veneer finish.

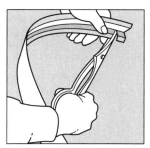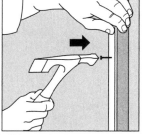

Stapling is the standard way to attach No. 800 corner bead.
For wood studs, nails in both bead flanges are also satisfactory.

Applying Metal Trim

SHEETROCK brand metal trim protects and finishes gypsum base at window framing and door jambs; it can also be used at ceiling-wall intersections and partition perimeters to form a recess for acoustical sealant. It also serves as a relief joint at the intersection of dissimilar construction materials, such as gypsum board and concrete.

No. 800 & 900 Corner Bead

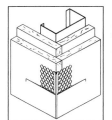

Metal trim provides maximum protection and neat finished edges to gypsum bases at window and door jambs, at internal angles and at intersections where panels abut other materials. It is easily installed by nailing or screwing through the proper leg of the trim. Various configurations are available depending on the required application.

No. 701-A and 701-B SHEETROCK **Brand Metal Trim (1/2" and 5/8" size)** Slip channel-type 701-A trim over the edge of the base or position L-shaped 701-B trim on the edge of the base with the expanded flange on the room side. Fasten with staples or nails 12" o.c. maximum. Both trims are designed to provide proper ground height (3/32") for two-coat veneer finish applications.

No. 801-A and 801-B SHEETROCK **Brand Metal Trim (1/2" and 5/8" size)** Slip channel-type 801-A trim over the edge of the base, or position L-shaped 801-B trim on the edge of the base with the expanded flange on the room side. Fasten with staples or nails 12" o.c. maximum for veneer assemblies. Both trims provide proper ground height for (1/16") for one-coat veneer finish application. Finish with one-coat veneer plaster product of choice.

Nos. 401 and 402 SHEETROCK **Brand Metal Trim (J-stop, 1/2" and 5/8" size)** Apply the trim to the wall before the gypsum base goes up by nailing through the trim flange into the framing; the base is held firmly in place by the short leg of the trim. No additional edge fastening is necessary. Space fasteners 9" o.c. These types do not require finishing compound.

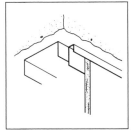

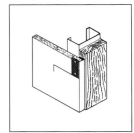

No. 400 Series   *701-A, 801-A*   *701-B, 801-B*

Applying Control Joints

Proper installation of control joints in wall and ceiling membranes should include breaking the gypsum base behind the control joint. In ceiling construction, the framing should also be broken, and in partitions, separate studs should be used on each side of the control joints. Control joints should be positioned to intersect light fixtures, air diffusers, door openings and other areas of stress concentration.

Gypsum construction should be isolated with control joints where:

(a) Partitions or ceilings of dissimilar construction meet and remain in the same plane;

(b) Wings of "L," "U" and "T" shaped ceiling areas are joined; and

(c) Expansion or control joints occur in the base wall construction and/or building structure.

Just as important, control joints should be used in the face of gypsum partitions and ceilings when the size of the surface exceeds the following control-joint spacings:

• Partitions 30' maximum in either direction
• Interior ceilings (with perimeter relief) 50' maximum in either direction
• Interior ceilings (without perimeter relief) 30' maximum in either direction
• Exterior ceilings 30' maximum in either direction

Ceiling-height door frames may be used as vertical control joints for partitions. However, door frames of lesser height may only be used as control joints if standard control joints extend to the ceiling from both corners of the top of the door frame. When planning for control joints in the ceiling, it is recommended that they be located to intersect column penetrations, since movement of columns can impose stresses on the ceiling membrane.

Control joints, when properly insulated and backed by gypsum base panels, have been fire-endurance tested and are certified for use in one- and two-hour-rated walls.

Installation

At control joint locations:

1. Leave a 1/2" continuous opening between gypsum board panels for insertion of surface-mounted joint.

2. Interrupt wood floor and ceiling plates with a 1/2" gap wherever there is a control joint in the structure.

3. Provide separate supports for each control joint flange.

4. Provide an adequate seal or safing insulation behind control joints where sound and/or fire ratings are prime considerations.

Control Joint No. 093 Apply over the face of gypsum base where specified. Cut to length with a fine-toothed hacksaw (32 teeth per in.). Cut end joints square, butt together and align to provide a neat fit. Attach the control joint to the gypsum base with Bostitch 9/16" type G staples, or equivalent, spaced 6" o.c. maximum along each flange. Remove the plastic tape after finishing with veneer plaster.

6

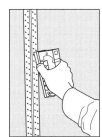 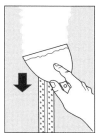 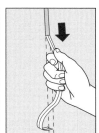

Control Joint No. 093 stapled, finished, tape removed.

**Fire-Rated
Control Joints**

**47 STC
(SA-860217):
2-hr. Fire
Rating**

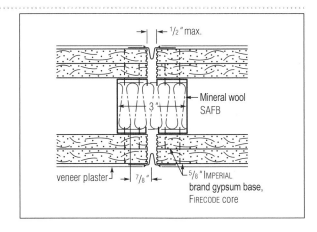

**47 STC
(SA-860302):
2-hr. Fire
Rating**

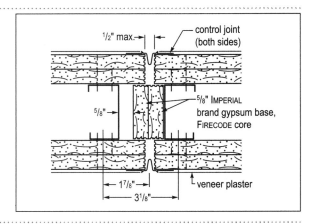

**1-hr. Fire
Rating**

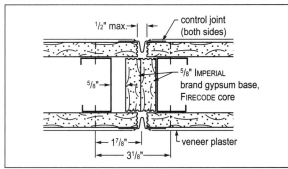

Control Joint No. 093

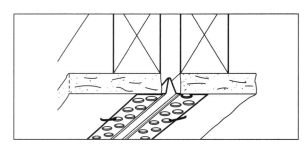

Maximum Spacing—Control Joints

Construction & Location	Max. Single Dimension		Max. Single Area	
	ft	m	ft²	m²
Partition-interior	30	9	–	–
Ceiling-interior				
with perimeter relief	50	15	2500	230
without perimeter relief	30	9	900	85
Ceiling-exterior gypsum	30	9	900	85

Sʜᴇᴇᴛʀᴏᴄᴋ **Brand Control Joint No. 75** Apply to the bottom of the double row of wood joists in radiant-heated ceilings before Iᴍᴘᴇ-ʀɪᴀʟ brand gypsum base is applied. Attach control joint to joists with Bostitch 9/16" type G staples or nails spaced 6" o.c. maximum along each flange. Splice end joints with two pieces 16-gauge galvanized tie wire inserted in the sections. Apply gypsum base over control joint attachment flange and fasten to joist with proper fastener. (See the fastener selector guide in Chapter 1, "Drywall & Veneer Plaster Products.") Space nails 7" o.c., screws 12" o.c. Use control joint as a screed for applying Dɪᴀᴍᴏɴᴅ veneer finish. Remove plastic tape after veneer application.

Joint Treatment & Surface Preparation for Veneer Plaster Construction

For Wood-Framed Assemblies and Normal Drying Conditions Align Iᴍᴘᴇʀɪᴀʟ brand type P (pressure-sensitive) tape over joint and press into place over entire length. Eliminate wrinkles and ensure maximum adhesive bond by pressing entire length of tape with steel finishing knife or trowel. Press tape into corners with corner tool; do not overlap.

Or, attach Iᴍᴘᴇʀɪᴀʟ brand type S tape with spring-driven hand stapler using 3/8" staples. Use two staples at each end of tape; staple remainder at staggered 24" intervals. At wall-ceiling angles, staple every 18" to 24" along ceiling edge only. For wall-to-wall interior angles, staple every 18" to 24" on one edge only, working from top to bottom. Position tape to bridge the joint at all interior corners without overlapping.

Embed tape and fill beads with a coat of veneer plaster and allow to set—but not dry—prior to full veneer plaster application. Slightly underfill in the bead by screeding with edge of trowel after setting the bead. (Best results are obtained by planning the finishing to permit continuous application from angle to angle.)

Simplified, wrinkle-free attachment of self-stick type P Iᴍᴘᴇʀɪᴀʟ brand tape speeds joint reinforcing, boosts production.

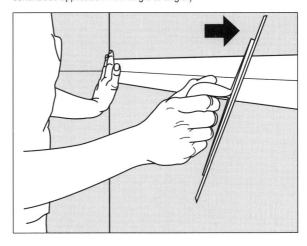

For Steel-Framed Assemblies and Rapid Drying Conditions With steel framing and/or when building temperature-humidity conditions fall in the "rapid drying" area of the graph for steel or wood framing (page 211), SHEETROCK brand joint tape embedded with a SHEETROCK brand setting-type joint compound (DURABOND or EASY SAND) is recommended.

Mix the compound in a clean 5-gal. container (preferably plastic for setting-type compounds). Use a commercial handmixer or a 1/2" heavy-duty 200- to 300-rpm electric drill with a USG mud mixer paddle. Drill speed must not exceed 400 rpm. Use the amount of water shown on the bag, and always sift the powder into the water to ensure complete wetting. Stir according to directions on bag.

Note: Do not contaminate compound with other materials, dirty water or previous batches. Do not retemper batches.

Butter joints with compound using a trowel or steel finishing knife to force compound into the joints. Center SHEETROCK brand joint tape over joint, and press it into the fresh compound with trowel held at a 45° angle. Draw trowel along joint with sufficient pressure to remove excess compound.

After tape is embedded, apply a thin coat of joint compound to reduce possibility of edge wrinkling or curling. Allow thin coat to harden. Then apply a fill coat completely covering the tape and feathering 3" to 4" beyond edges of tape. Allow to harden before finishing. Plaster prefill is not required over SHEETROCK brand setting-type joint compound (DURABOND or EASY SAND).

Note: SHEETROCK brand setting-type joint compound (DURABOND or EASY SAND) and SHEETROCK brand joint tape must be used in the following conditions:

— Where two-coat finish is applied over 1/2" or 5/8" base on 24" o.c. framing

— Where one-coat DIAMOND veneer finish or IMPERIAL veneer finish is applied over 5/8" base on 24" o.c. framing

— Where IMPERIAL gypsum base (blueboard) and veneer plaster is used over steel framing

For Cement Board Substrate Prior to treating DUROCK brand cement board panel joints, apply USG plaster bonder in a continuous film to the joint area according to application directions. Joints should then be treated with SHEETROCK brand joint tape and SHEETROCK brand setting-type joint compound (DURABOND or EASY SAND). Mix and apply following directions on the package. When the joints are completely dry, treat the entire wall surface with USG plaster bonder according to application directions. Then apply DIAMOND veneer basecoat and IMPERIAL veneer finish in a two-coat application.

For Gypsum Fiber Bases This assembly provides added abuse-resistant characteristics when completed. Joints of FIBEROCK brand gypsum panels must be treated with SHEETROCK brand joint tape and setting-type joint compound (DURABOND or EASY SAND) following directions on the package. When the joints are completely dry, treat the entire wall surface with USG plaster bonder according to application directions. Then apply DIAMOND veneer basecoat and IMPERIAL veneer finish in a two-coat application.

For Improved Bond Several products are available to help setting-type joint compounds and veneer plasters work better. USG plaster bonder, used on concrete, cement board, gypsum fiber panels and dry setting-type joint compound surfaces, enhances the plaster's ability to bond to those surfaces. USG plaster accelerator-alum catalyst can also be applied to the substrate surface to help lime-containing veneer plaster adhere to sun-faded plaster base surfaces or setting-type compound at joints. (See page 386.)

To Change Setting Time To reduce the setting time of SHEETROCK brand setting-type joint compounds (DURABOND or EASY SAND), USG high-strength accelerator may be used as a mix additive. USG high-strength retarder can be used to extend the setting and working time.

6

Veneer Plaster Finish Applications

Veneer Plaster Product Compatibility Selector

	Substrate		Finish Plaster										
Basecoat Plaster	CMU	Mono. Concrete	DUROCK® Brand Cement Board	IMPERIAL Brand Veneer Base	RED TOP Finish	STRUCTO Gauge/ Lime	Keenes/ Lime	Gauging/ Lime	Keenes/ Lime/Sand	Gauging/ Lime/Sand	DIAMOND/ IMPERIAL Brand Finish	Deco-rative Interior Finish
IMPERIAL Brand Basecoat	√	√		√	√	√	√	√	√	√	√	√
DIAMOND Brand Veneer Basecoat	√	√	√	√	√	√	√	√	√	√	√	√
IMPERIAL Brand Finish				√								
DIAMOND Brand Veneer Finish		√(2)		√								
DIAMOND Brand Interior Finish (Electric Cable)		√(2)		√								

Notes: (1) FIBEROCK Brand Gypsum Panels may also be used. In both cases, USG™ Plaster Bonder must first be applied. (2) Job sanded. √ = Acceptable.

Mixing and Proportioning

Cage-type mixing paddle is designed to draw material into and through paddle blades to disperse and blend ingredients by shear action rather than folding action of conventional mixers.

All veneer finishes require the addition of water on the job. Water should be clean, fresh, suitable for human consumption and free from mineral and organic substances that affect the plaster set. Water used for rinsing or cleaning is not suitable for mixing because it accelerates the plaster set.

Mechanical mixing is mandatory for veneer finish plasters. Mix no more material than can be applied before set begins. Since veneer finishes set more rapidly than most conventional plasters, always consult package directions for specific setting times.

Veneer plasters will produce mortar of maximum performance when the correct equipment is used and mixing directions are carefully followed. Proper mixing is one of the most important factors in producing mortar of maximum workability.

Use a cage-type mixer paddle or USG mud mixer driven by heavy-duty 1/2" electric drill with a no-load rating of 900 to 1,000 rpm. Do not use a conventional mortar mixer. (For details of the cage-type mixing paddle, mud mixer and available electrical drills, see pages 425–426 and PM9, *Mixing Veneer Plasters and Equipment.*)

For large plaster mixes, use a cage-type paddle in a smooth-sided 16- or 30-gal. container strong enough to withstand impacts that could cause gouging. Do not use brittle containers for mixing.

For smaller plaster mixes, use a mud mixer in a smooth-sided 5- or 15-gal. container strong enough to withstand impacts. (Again, do not use brittle containers for mixing.)

Correct mixing—rapid and with high shear action—is essential for proper dispersion of plaster ingredients. Slow mixing can reduce plasticity of material. Overmixing can shorten working time. Operated at correct speed, the cage-type design paddle mixes thoroughly without introducing excess air into the mix.

Mixing IMPERIAL Brand Plasters

Water requirements for IMPERIAL veneer plasters:
–IMPERIAL veneer basecoat: 5 to 6.25 qt./50 lb. bag.
–IMPERIAL veneer finish: 7 to 8 qt./50 bag.

Place water in a smooth-sided 12- to 16-gal. container. Start mixer, slowly adding plaster and mix at 2-minute intervals to disperse lumps completely. Do not mix more for than 5 minutes. Do not mix more material than can be applied in one hour.

For sand float finish, add up to 12.5 lb. clean silica sand per 50-lb. bag of IMPERIAL veneer plaster to achieve desired texture. The use of more than 12.5 lb. of sand per bag will decrease hardness of surface. (Apply plaster in normal manner, but omit final troweling. After surface has become firm, float to desired texture, using sponge, carpet or other float. Use water sparingly.)

Mixing DIAMOND Brand Plasters

Water requirements for DIAMOND veneer plasters:
–DIAMOND veneer basecoat: 7.5 to 8.75 qt./50-lb. bag
–DIAMOND veneer finish: 12 to 15 qt./50-lb. bag.

Place all but 1 or 2 qt. of water into mixing container. With mixer operating, slowly add one bag of material. If a texture finish is desired, up to 50 lb. clean silica sand may be added per 50-lb. bag of DIAMOND veneer finish. For electric cable heat systems, clean, sharp, fine silica sand must be added as follows: fill coat, 50 lb. but no less than 25 lb. per 50-lb. bag DIAMOND veneer finish; finish coat, at least 12-1/2 lb. per 50-lb. bag plaster. When material is wetted, add more water (1 to 2 qt.) to obtain desired consistency. Mix for minimum of two minutes, but no longer than five minutes.

When DIAMOND veneer finish is job-aggregated, one tablespoon cream of tartar or 1/4 to 1/2 teaspoon of USG retarder for lime-containing plaster products could be added for each bag of plaster to retard set and allow sufficient working time.

Application

Maintain a temperature in all work areas of at least 55°F to 60°F and relative humidity between 20% and 50%. (See also PM10.) Keep air circulation at minimum level during and after application until finish is dry.

IMPERIAL Brand Plasters

Hand Application—Embed IMPERIAL brand tape, type P or S, and fill beads with a tight, thin coat of IMPERIAL brand plaster. Allow to set, and then plaster. (See also "Selection of Joint Treatment System" on page 211.)

Plaster Finishing

IMPERIAL veneer plasters offer a wide range of finish options with two distinct systems:

1. IMPERIAL veneer finish (one-coat)
2. IMPERIAL veneer basecoat with selected hand-applied or spray-applied (two-coat).

6

IMPERIAL Veneer Finish (one-coat) Scratch in a tight, thin coat of IMPERIAL veneer finish over entire area, immediately doubling back with plaster from same batch to full thickness of 1/16" to 3/32". Fill all voids and imperfections. Final trowel after surface has become firm, holding trowel flat and using water sparingly. Do not over-trowel.

For texture finished surfaces, with or without the addition of job-added sand, there is no need to final trowel. The surface is textured naturally as the material firms and water is removed into the base.

Best results are obtained by planning the plastering to permit continuous application from angle to angle. Where joining is unavoidable, use trowel to terminate unset plaster in sharp, clean edge—do not feather out. Bring adjacent plaster up to terminated edge and leave level. Do not overlap. During finish troweling, use excess material to fill and bridge joining.

IMPERIAL Veneer Basecoat (two-coat) Scratch in a tight, thin coat of IMPERIAL veneer basecoat over entire area, immediately doubling back with plaster from same batch to full thickness of 1/16" to 3/32". Fill all voids and imperfections. Leave surface rough and open by cross-raking with a fine-wire rake or broom. Allow basecoat to set to provide proper suction for finish coat.

Finish coat materials are applied by scratching in and doubling back with selected finish—IMPERIAL veneer finish, DIAMOND veneer finish, gauged lime-putty, STRUCTO-GAUGE gauging-lime, RED TOP finish plaster or RED TOP Keenes cement-lime-sand finishes—to achieve a smooth, dense surface for decoration, free of surface blemishes. For textured finishes, floating on textures with additional material is conducted once the surface has become firm, using water sparingly.

For spray-applied finish, mix Keenes cement-lime-sand in proportion of 50 lbs. Keenes cement to 100 lbs. dry double-hydrated lime, and up to 400 lb. but not less than 200 lb. clean, properly graded silica sand with sufficient water to form a smooth consistency for hand application. Apply this mix evenly over a properly prepared IMPERIAL veneer basecoat surface by first applying a well-ground-in scratch coat.

Immediately double back with sufficient material to cover the basecoat to a total thickness of 1/16" to 1/8".

When the surface has become firm by water removal, float it to a uniform blemish-free, flat texture. After floating, and while the application is still wet but totally firm, prepare additional finish material with the consistency adjusted for spray application. With either a hand-held hopper gun or machine-application equipment without catalyst, spray apply the texture to provide a uniform texture appearance. Vary aggregate grading, aggregate proportion, number of passes over the surface, air pressure and nozzle orifice as necessary to achieve the desired appearance.

Spray Texture Finish Mix RED TOP Keenes cement-lime-sand in proportion of 100 lb. Keenes to 50 lb. dry hydrated lime and 400 lb. clean white silica sand, with sufficient water to form a smooth consistency. Alternative finish coat materials for this application may consist of high-strength gauging/lime putty finish, regular gauging/lime putty finish, or various mill-manufactured products. Apply this mix over IMPERIAL veneer basecoat surface that is free of ridges or other imperfections, with either a hand-held hopper gun or machine application equipment without catalyst. Vary aggregate grading, number of passes over the surface, air pressure and nozzle orifice as necessary to achieve desired texture.

Using the selected finish-coat material, mixed for hand-application consistency, apply a tight scratch coat over the properly prepared, set and partially dry basecoat, then double back. When the surface has become firm, float to a uniform, blemish-free, flat texture. Apply selected spray finish material while scratch coat is firm, but not set. Spray texture to a uniform thickness and appearance.

This same procedure can be used with the application of IMPERIAL veneer finish or DIAMOND veneer finish direct to IMPERIAL brand gypsum base.

Limitations: While this method of achieving a textured surface by spraying is expedient, it is not normally recommended because: 1) The properly roughened basecoat may not be uniform in appearance, and any irregularities will photograph through the finish coat, and 2) providing sufficient air pressure and viscosity to achieve proper bond minimizes the degree of texture attainable.

Other IMPERIAL Brand Basecoats

Concrete Block Surface must be porous for proper suction or be roughened/face-scored to provide adequate mechanical bond. Lightly spray walls with water to provide uniform suction. Fill and level all voids, depressions and joints with IMPERIAL veneer basecoat and allow to set. Then apply a subsequent coat, as with gypsum base application, leaving final surface rough and open to provide proper bonding of the finish coat.

Monolithic Concrete Prepare surface with USG plaster bonder applied according to the directions. Fill all voids and depressions with IMPERIAL veneer basecoat and allow to set and partially dry. Then apply basecoat as with gypsum base or concrete block, making sure to rake or broom the applied basecoat surface once the material has become firm for a rough and open surface. This will provide for proper suction for the finish material. Failure to do this may result in delamination of the finish material.

DIAMOND Brand Plasters

DIAMOND Veneer Finish

All adjacent finish materials and finish surfaces must be protected from contact with DIAMOND veneer finish. This includes glass, ceramic materials, metal and wood. Apply wood, plastic or other exposed trim after plaster application.

DIAMOND veneer finish should be applied to IMPERIAL gypsum base that has unfaded blue face paper. Under abnormal conditions where there is no alternative to using gypsum base faded from excessive exposure to sunlight or ultra-violet radiation, precautions should be taken to prevent delamination. Degraded gypsum base is indicated if face paper is not blue or grayish blue. When face paper color has become gray to tan (or if questionable), treat paper with a solution of USG accelerator—alum catalyst or USG plaster bonder.

Degrading may occur when gypsum base has been installed long before the finish is applied.

When used with lime-containing plaster, such as DIAMOND veneer finish, sun-faded IMPERIAL gypsum base face paper should be treated with USG accelerator—alum catalyst or USG plaster bonder. When using USG plaster bonder, a two-coat veneer system (basecoat and finish coat) is required for adequate finish coat smoothness. This precaution is unnecessary when applying products that do not contain lime (IMPERIAL veneer finish, IMPERIAL veneer basecoat and DIAMOND veneer basecoat).

For alum catalyst solution treatment, pour 3 lbs. of alum catalyst slowly into one gal. of water and mix thoroughly. Allow the solution to stand until any undissolved material has settled, then strain the solution into tank-type sprayer (such as a garden sprayer). Spray the solution onto the faded IMPERIAL gypsum base face paper so that it is wet, but not soaked. One gallon of solution should treat 750 SF of IMPERIAL gypsum base. Begin finish plaster application before face paper treated with alum solution is completely dry. **Caution**: Alum treatment shortens the setting time of DIAMOND veneer finish.

Begin application only after joints have been reinforced with glass fiber tape and preset with an application of DIAMOND veneer finish or treated with SHEETROCK brand joint tape and SHEETROCK brand setting-type) joint compound (DURABOND or EASY SAND). Apply a thin, tight scratch coat of this finish over entire working area. Immediately double back with material from same batch to a full 1/16" to 3/32" thickness.

Start the finish troweling as soon as material has become sufficiently firm to achieve a smooth trowel finish, free from trowel marks, voids and other blemishes. Smooth and level the surface with the trowel held flat; use water sparingly to lubricate. Final hard troweling should be accomplished prior to set as indicated by darkening of the surface.

6

A variety of textures ranging from sand float to heavy Spanish can be achieved with DIAMOND veneer finish when job-aggregated with silica sand. Application is the same as for neat DIAMOND veneer finish, except that once the surface has been leveled and sufficient take-up has occurred, begin floating material from the same batch with trowel, float, sponge or other accepted local techniques.

DIAMOND veneer finish plaster also may be textured by skip-troweling. When applying in this manner, eliminate final troweling. When surface has become sufficiently firm, texture with material from same batch prior to set.

Painting or further decoration of DIAMOND veneer finish is recommended and should be specified. However, in many residential applications, DIAMOND veneer finish provides a uniform white color and may satisfy a job's specific acceptance criteria if skip-trowel and float-finish textured finishes are used. DIAMOND veneer finish is formulated to allow quick drying and can be decorated when thoroughly dry using a latex base or breather-type paint. Under ideal conditions, painting can take place in as little as 24 hours, which minimizes costly delays and speeds occupancy. For additional information, see PM15.

Graceful, wavelike swirl texture　　*Unique, skip trowel*　　*Sand-aggregated float finish*　　*Luxurious Spanish texture*

DIAMOND Veneer Basecoat

DIAMOND veneer basecoat provides quality walls and ceilings for residential construction where the superior strength of IMPERIAL veneer basecoat is not essential. DIAMOND veneer basecoat produces a base that aesthetically enhances the finish by providing regulated suction, resulting in exceptional integral bond. Once basecoat is applied and has become firm, the surface is raked or broomed to provide a rough and open surface for the finish coat.

Over Gypsum Base Apply DIAMOND veneer basecoat from 1/16" to 3/32" thickness. When IMPERIAL gypsum base is used, reinforce all joints and interior angles with IMPERIAL brand type P or type S tape. Embed tape and fill beads with DIAMOND veneer basecoat and allow to set, but not dry. After beads and joints have been properly prepared (rough and open), apply a tight, thin coat of DIAMOND veneer basecoat over the entire area, immediately doubling back with plaster from the same batch to full thickness. Fill all voids and imperfections. Leave surface rough and open by cross-raking with a fine wire rake, sponge or fine broom once it has become somewhat firm. Allow basecoat to set to provide proper suction for finish coat.

Over Concrete Block Surface must be porous and develop proper suction to provide adequate mechanical bond. Lightly spray walls with water to provide uniform suction. Fill and level all voids, depressions and joints with Dιaμond veneer basecoat and allow to set. Then apply subsequent coats as with gypsum base application, leaving final surface rough and open to provide proper bonding of the finish coat.

Over Monolithic Concrete Prepare surface with USG plaster bonder applied according to application directions. Fill all voids and depressions with Dιaμond veneer basecoat and allow to set and partially dry. Then apply Dιaμond veneer basecoat as with gypsum base or concrete block. It is essential that the applied basecoat surface be raked or broomed once the material has become firm for a rough and open surface to provide proper suction for the finish coat. Failure to do so may result in delamination of the finish material.

Painting Veneer Plaster

No matter what type of paint or decoration is used, it is essential that the plaster be completely dry. Typically, veneer plasters may be dry in as little as 24 hours. Use a high-quality, undiluted acrylic latex, vinyl or alkali-resistant alkyd paint. Prior to applying a finish, such as epoxy-based finish systems, the veneer plaster must be properly sealed. Quick-drying vinyl acrylic latex or alkali-resistant alkyd primer-sealers are recommended. Polyvinyl acetate (PVA)-based primers should not be used over wet plaster of any kind, including lime-containing plasters. PVA film is subject to rewetting and will almost certainly cause bond loss and subsequent paint delamination. (See also PM15.)

6

Trowel job-sanded Dιaμond brand interior finish plaster over electric cable.

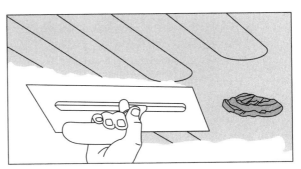

Radiant Heat Plaster System—Dιaμond Veneer Finish

Application-Radiant Heat Cable After Iμperιal gypsum base and joint reinforcement tape have been applied, install electric radiant heating cable in accordance with design requirements and cable manufacturer's specifications. Attach cable to ceiling in such a manner that it is kept taut and does not sag away from the base. All cable connectors and non-heating leads should be embedded (countersunk) into, but not through, the gypsum base so they do not project below the heating wire.

Fill Coat Application Apply job-sanded Dιaμond veneer finish in sufficient thickness to completely cover cable. Trowel plaster parallel to direction of cable but do not use cable as a screed. Level with a trowel, rod or darby to fill any low spots or to remove any high ridges. Use a serrated darby or lightly broom the plaster surface prior to set to provide a key for the finish coat. Average thickness of fill coat should be 3/16".

Finish Coat Application Apply finish coat after fill coat has developed sufficient suction—in good drying weather, about two hours after the fill coat has set; in damp or cold weather usually overnight unless good supplementary heat and ventilation are provided. Use job-sanded DIAMOND veneer finish 1/16" to 3/32" thick, to bring total plaster thickness to 1/4".

Scratch in a tight, thin coat over the entire area, immediately doubling back to full thickness. Fill all voids and imperfections. Scratch and double-back with the same mix of DIAMOND veneer finish. When surface has become firm, hold trowel flat and final-trowel, using water sparingly. Best results are obtained by continuous application of an entire ceiling. Always work to a wet edge to avoid dry joinings.

Texture Finish When finish coat has become sufficiently firm, but not set, float surface to desired texture using a sponge, carpet or other float. Use water sparingly. For heavier texture, additional material from the same batch may be applied to the firm surface to achieve a skip-trowel, Spanish or other texture.

Fissured Finish Spray-apply a maximum 1/8" thickness of SHEETROCK brand ceiling texture finish or similar product over a full, 1/4" thickness of sanded DIAMOND veneer finish. Follow manufacturer's specifications.

At the maximum 1/8" thickness, this product will slightly decrease heating system efficiency, since fissured finishes are formulated with insulating-type aggregates.

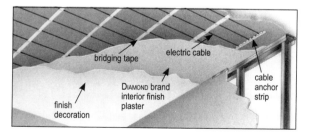

bridging tape — electric cable — cable anchor strip — DIAMOND brand interior finish plaster — finish decoration

Radiant Heat Systems to Monolithic Concrete

Surface Preparation Concrete surface must be structurally sound and clean, free of dirt, dust, grease, wax, oil or other unsound conditions. Treat exposed metal with a rustproof primer. When corrosion due to high humidity and/or saline content of sand is possible, zinc alloy accessories are recommended.

Remove form ridges to make surfaces reasonably uniform and level. Locate uneven ceiling areas and bad gravel pockets, which require filling prior to installing electric cable and filler.

After treating entire surface with USG plaster bonder according to application directions, level it with fill-coat mix of DIAMOND veneer finish. Use a SHEETROCK brand setting-type joint compound (DURABOND or EASY SAND) for minor leveling.

Caution: Temperature of concrete ceiling with bonding agent applied must be above 32°F before filler and finish applications are started, with air temperature above 55°F.

Radiant Heat Cable Application After ceiling surface has been leveled, apply electric radiant heating cable according to design requirements and cable manufacturer's specifications. Attach cable to the ceiling so that it is kept taut and does not sag away from the ceiling. All cable connectors and non-heating leads must be securely attached to concrete ceiling.

Finishing Mix and apply job-sanded fill coat DIAMOND veneer finish according to directions in previous section. Apply 5/16" basecoat parallel to direction of cable, completely covering cable and anchor devices.

Mix and apply finish coat after fill coat has developed sufficient suction. Use job-sanded DIAMOND veneer finish 1/16" to 3/32" thick, to bring total plaster thickness to 3/8". Apply finish coat in same manner described in previous section.

Do not energize heating cable until plaster is thoroughly dry. When either or both the completed radiant heat ceiling and room temperature are below 55°F, the temperature should be increased in 5°F increments for each 24-hr. period until it reaches 55°F.

If completed radiant heat ceiling and room temperature are 55° or higher, thermostat may be set at desired temperature.

(See also PM16, P777 and P838.)

Special Abuse-Resistant Systems

Veneer Plaster over DUROCK Brand Cement Board

For improved impact strength and abrasion-resistance, apply a two-coat veneer plaster system consisting of DIAMOND veneer basecoat and IMPERIAL veneer finish over DUROCK brand cement board, attached to framing. This construction is particularly useful for commercial and institutional applications, such as schools and high-traffic retail locations.

Space wood or steel framing 16" o.c. and install DUROCK brand cement board with long edges either parallel or perpendicular to the framing and with the rough side of panels exposed. Fasteners are spaced a maximum of 8" o.c.

Prior to treatment of panel joints, apply USG plaster bonder in a continuous film to the joint areas according to directions. Joints should then be treated with SHEETROCK joint tape and SHEETROCK setting-type joint compound (DURABOND or EASY SAND). Joint surfaces must be treated with a separate coat of joint compound to fully conceal the paper tape.

When the joint is completely dry, treat the entire wall surface with USG plaster bonder. Then apply DIAMOND veneer basecoat from 1/16" to 3/32" thickness using a scratch and double-back technique. When basecoat plaster is firm, broom the surface to leave it rough and open for a finish application. With basecoat set and partially dry, apply IMPERIAL veneer finish using a scratch and double-back technique. Complete finishing when material is firm. Leave finished surface smooth and dense for decorating.

Veneer Plaster over FIBEROCK Brand Abuse-Resistant Panels

The durability of the already-tough FIBEROCK brand abuse-resistant panels is enhanced by the application of a two-coat veneer plaster system. Apply panels in the same fashion as for cement board above. Then treat joints using SHEETROCK brand joint tape and setting-type joint compound (DURABOND or EASY SAND). When the joints are completely dry, treat the entire wall surface with USG plaster bonder according to the application directions. Then apply DIAMOND veneer basecoat and IMPERIAL veneer finish as described for cement board.

Resurfacing Walls & Ceilings

Veneer plasters may be used to resurface walls that are damaged, or walls that can benefit from a more abuse-resistant surface. However, care must be taken to prepare the wall surface for plaster application.

Make sure old wall coverings and their adhesives have been removed. Wash surface thoroughly. Scrape away any loose paint, and remove and repair any damaged drywall or plaster surface with appropriate patching material. (See "Interior Patch & Repair Products," page 67.) Fill all cracks or holes with SHEETROCK setting-type joint compound (DURABOND or EASY SAND) and joint tape if necessary.

Once joint compound has set and dried, apply USG plaster bonder. Clear over entire wall and ceiling area to be resurfaced.

Mix DIAMOND veneer basecoat and DIAMOND veneer finish as described on page 220, and trowel-apply over surface using a scratch and double-back technique with each coat. Do not over-trowel.

For additional information, see P811.

Decorating with Pigmented Finish Plaster

Decorative Interior Finish System

The USG decorative interior finish system is applied to IMPERIAL gypsum base or other approved substrate. If SHEETROCK brand gypsum panels or other approved substrate are used, the surface must be prepared with SHEETROCK wall covering primer and then with USG plaster bonder to assure a consistent bond.

USG decorative interior finish system utilizes veneer basecoat and finish coat plaster products mixed with pigments that will not affect plaster set. The system must be sealed upon completion.

6

Color is thoroughly mixed into the finish, providing a deep tinted layer that effectively hides mars and prevents chips and scratches from appearing. High-quality colorants are used to ensure color consistency and UV resistance. The system identifies 12 basic colors that can be mixed using a standard tint machine and COLORTREND 888 Universal Machine Colorants. USG recommends using only COLORTREND 888 Universal Machine Colorants. (Colorants from other manufacturers are not recommended, as they may not be compatible with USG materials, may cause color variations and may interfere with the intended product application.) Use the basic USG color formulas and custom colors created using the COLORTREND AMBIANCE™ Fan Deck Selector.

For standard colors using COLORTREND 888 Universal Machine Colorants, the formula selected will produce a 5-gal. batch size. To create a custom color, select a color and formula from the fan deck and color formula book that represents a color somewhat darker than the shade you desire as the finished, dried surface color.

Note that the shade of finished colors depends on many factors. Each color formula yields a slightly different degree of color lightness compared to the color swatch. The texture applied and consistency of the mixed mortar also affect the appearance of the finished surface, and therefore the color. Even the plaster product chosen for the mix (DIAMOND veneer finish, IMPERIAL veneer basecoat, DIAMOND veneer basecoat or IMPERIAL veneer finish) can vary the resulting shade.

Based on these factors, the final dried finish may be up to several shades lighter than the color swatch depicted in the fan deck selector. Note also that wet-mixed mortar appears darker than the selected color swatch, but will lighten in color when set and dry.

Mixing USG decorative interior finish usually consists of DIAMOND veneer finish mixed with colorants and water, but IMPERIAL veneer basecoat, DIAMOND veneer basecoat or IMPERIAL veneer finish also may be used. Mix in 5-gal. pail (14" high, 10-1/4" bottom, 11-1/4" top). Use 6-1/2" of water per batch for DIAMOND veneer finish, 4-1/2" for DIAMOND veneer basecoat, 4" for IMPERIAL veneer basecoat and 5" for IMPERIAL veneer finish. Add the predetermined amount of colorant (COLORTREND Formula) to the water.

The plaster is added to the water in three stages. First, fill the bucket with plaster and stir lightly with an on-and-off action using a 450-rpm, 1/2" drill and blade-type (joint compound) mixing paddle. Add plaster to the top of the bucket and repeat, stirring with on-and-off action. Add plaster a third time and mix completely, ensuring that no colored water splashes out of mixing container.

Using mud mixer, mix approximately 40–45 lbs. of DIAMOND veneer finish with the water, or 60 lbs. of DIAMOND veneer basecoat or IMPERIAL veneer basecoat, or 50 lbs. of IMPERIAL veneer finish. These quantities should fill the container to about 1 to 1-1/2 inches from its top. Finish should be slightly thicker than normal. To ensure color uniformity, each batch must be mixed exactly the same way, by volume and to the same fluidity in a volume-specific container. Note that graded white silica sand may be used for float finishing.

Application Each wall or ceiling must be covered in a continuous application, always continuing joinings of separate mixes prior to either mix setting. Work walls and vaulted ceilings from top to bottom; ceilings from angle to angle. For one-coat semi-smooth texture, apply plaster in random, 1' to 2' strokes at a nominal 1/16" to 1/8" thickness, leaving lap marks as desired. After approximately 20 minutes from initial application, draw a trowel, held almost flat, lightly over the surface with short strokes in various directions. Trowel again as initial set begins (approximately 45 minutes). For two-coat heavy texture, apply first coat to a nominal thickness of approximately 1/8", covering the entire surface. When surface has firmed slightly, apply second coat in short strokes as described above. Two-coat thickness should vary from 1/8" to 1/4". Additional troweling of second coat should be as described above for one-coat finish.

Sealing After finish has set and dried (approximately 24 hours), apply USG decorative finish sealer and maintain a temperature of at least 55°F. Do not shake or box-mix sealer. Apply using brush, roller or sprayer with 0.015" to 0.023" tip. Initially, sealer will appear milky, but will dry clear and colorless. When appearance changes to clear, wipe or roll drips and puddles, then recoat.

For complete information on selecting and applying the appropriate system over drywall, plaster or an existing substrate, see the following USG submittal sheets: P797 (drywall), P808 (existing substrate) or P809 (plaster).

Conventional
Plaster Products

7

A quality plaster job depends on the materials and the application methods at each step of the process, from base to finish coat—as well as the condition of the base materials to which they are applied. USG products are geared to performance—from plaster bases and accessories to finish plaster and lime products—and are designed to work together for a wide range of wall and ceiling applications.

This chapter covers the basic materials for quality plaster wall and ceiling installations.

All USG materials meet the essential requirements of function, economy and speed of installation. To contact a USG sales representative, visit **usg.com**.

Plaster Bases

Proper use of plaster bases with plasters provides a secure bond that is essential to surface strength and resistance to abuse and cracking. While plaster can be installed over many types of substrate and bases, the most common are metal lath and gypsum plaster bases.

Gypsum Plaster Base

ROCKLATH® FIRECODE plaster base is a gypsum lath that provides a rigid, fire-resistant base for the economical application of gypsum plasters. This product requires less basecoat plaster than metal lath. Its specially formulated core is made with mineral materials that enhance the board's resistance to fire exposure. ROCKLATH base is made only in the FIRECODE formulation.

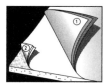

ROCKLATH **multi-ply face paper**

The lath's gypsum core is faced with multi-layer laminated paper engineered to provide proper absorption, check plaster slide and resist lath sag. As illustrated, the three outer layers (1) are highly absorbent, enabling them to draw moisture from the plaster mix uniformly and quickly. This gives the plaster anti-slump strength before it can slide. The inner layers (2) are chemically treated to form a barrier against moisture penetration, which prevents the gypsum core from softening and sagging after the board is in place. The face paper is folded around the long edges, and the ends are square-cut. ROCKLATH base complies with ASTM C37 and C1396.

Key features of ROCKLATH FIRECODE plaster base:

Fire-Resistance When used with gypsum plaster, provides fire ratings of up to 2 hours for partitions, ceilings and column fireproofing.

Strength Adds lateral stability to the structure.

Sound-Resistance Partitions faced with gypsum plaster bases and plaster on both sides have excellent resistance to sound transmission. Resilient attachment further improves ratings, making assemblies suitable for party walls.

Bonding Gypsum plaster bonds to these gypsum plaster bases with a safety factor far higher than required to meet usual construction standards.

Durability Resistant to decay, dry rot, or normal humidity levels; will not attract vermin.

**General
Limitations of
Gypsum Base**

1. ROCKLATH FIRECODE plaster base should be used with gypsum plaster only. (Lime or Portland cement plasters do not bond properly with ROCKLATH base.)

2. Should not be used in areas exposed to excessive moisture for extended periods or as a backing for ceramic tile or similar surfacing materials commonly used in wet areas. (Galvanized metal lath and Portland cement-lime plaster or DUROCK brand cement board systems are recommended for wet areas.)

3. ROCKLATH base is not suitable for veneer plasters and finishes.

Note: Gypsum basecoat plasters have slightly greater dimensional stability than gypsum lath. Therefore, the stability of the lath would govern in design considerations. Refer to the Appendix for coefficients of expansion, data on drying shrinkage and thermal resistance values (R).

Metal Lath

Metal lath mesh material is formed from sheet steel, slit and expanded to form many small openings. It is made in diamond mesh and riblath types and in two different weights to accommodate most applications. Diamond mesh and 3/8" riblath are also available in galvanized steel. (See ASTM C847.)

7

The ends of metal lath bundles are often spray-painted in different colors to indicate various weights to simplify stocking and handling. Check the manufacturer's coding system.

Key Features of Metal Lath:

Strength Provides reinforcement to the plaster embedded within.

Flexibility Can be shaped to ornamental contours to a degree not possible with other plaster bases.

Fire-Resistance When used with gypsum plaster, provides excellent fire-resistance—up to 2 hours for partitions and 4 hours for ceilings and column fireproofing. (See Chapter 10, "System Design Considerations.")

Security Provides excellent protection against penetration or forced entry.

Diamond Mesh Lath

*Self-Furring Diamond
Mesh Lath*

Paper-Back Lath

Flat Riblath

3/8" Riblath

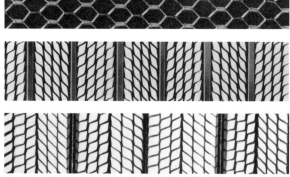

Metal lath is available in following types and styles:

DIAMOND **Mesh Lath** This small-mesh metal plaster base (approximately 11,000 meshes per square yard) is an all-purpose lath suitable for ornamental contour plastering. The small mesh openings conserve plaster and reduce droppings. The product is also available in a self-furring type with 1/4" dimple indentations spaced 1-1/2" o.c. each way, for use as exterior stucco base over sheathing, column fireproofing and replastering over old surfaces.

Paper-Backed Metal Lath Asphalt paper-backed diamond mesh lath is available in regular or self-furring types. This product's asphalt-impregnated paper is factory-bonded to the back of the mesh. The paper is vapor-permeable and complies with Federal Specification UU-B-790a, Type I, Grade D, Style 2.

Paper-backed painted lath is recommended for lath and plaster back-up of interior tile work and other inside work. Paper-backed galvanized lath is a recommended base and reinforcement for some exterior wall construction, including stucco and other machine- or hand-applied exterior surfacing materials.

Flat Riblath A "flat rib" type of lath with smaller mesh openings is more rigid than diamond mesh and is excellent as nail-on lath and for tie-on work on flat ceilings. It is not recommended for contour lathing.

3/8" Riblath A herringbone mesh pattern with 3/8" V-shaped ribs running lengthwise of the sheet at 4-1/2" intervals, with inverted intermediate 3/16" ribs. The heavy ribs provide exceptional rigidity. Used when supports are spaced more than 16" o.c. and not more than 24", and for 2" solid studless metal lath and plaster partitions. Also used as a centering lath for concrete floor and roof slabs. Unsuitable for contour plastering. Minimum ground thickness must be 1".

General Limitations of Metal Lath

1. Should not be used with magnesium oxychloride cement stuccos or stuccos containing calcium chloride additives.

2. In ceiling assemblies, certain precautions concerning construction, insulation and ventilation are necessary for good

performance. A minimum of 1/2 square inch of net free vent area is recommended per square foot of horizontal surface in plenum or other space.

Metal Lath Selector

Type of lath	Recommended Applications					
	Ornamental contour	Over int. substrate	Over ext. substrate[1]	Nail-on/tie-on flat ceiling	Solid partitions	Concrete centering
Diamond Mesh	X			X[3]	X[5]	
Self-Furring		X	X[2]	X[4]		
Flat Riblath				X		
3/8" Riblath					X	X

(1) For example: gypsum sheathing, replastering existing work, column fireproofing. (2) 3.4 lb./yd.^{2} galvanized lath. (3) For tie-on only: supports 16" o.c. max. (4) For nail-on only: supports 16" o.c. max. (5) Supports 16" o.c. max.

Trim Accessories

Corner and Casing Beads

Corner beads should be used on all external plaster corners to provide protection, true and straight corners, and grounds for plastering. Casing beads are used as plaster stops around wall openings and where plaster intersects with other finishes.

Limitation: Galvanized steel accessories are recommended for interior use only. For exterior application and where corrosion due to high humidity and/or saline content of aggregates is possible, zinc alloy accessories are recommended. Galvanized steel should not be used with magnesium oxychloride cement stucco or Portland cement stucco containing calcium chloride additives.

1-A Expanded Corner Bead General-purpose and economical, with wide, expanded, flexible flanges. Preferred for irregular corners. Provides increased reinforcement close to nose of bead.

4-A Flexible Corner Bead Special utility, solid-punch-pattern bead that, by snipping flanges, may be bent to any curved design (for archways, etc.).

Double-X Corner Bead Has full 3-1/4" flanges easily adjusted for plaster depth on columns. Ideal for finishing corners of structural tile and rough masonry. Has perforated stiffening ribs along expanded flange.

Casing Beads Used as a plaster stop. When left exposed, eliminates the need for wood trim around window and door openings. Also recommended at junctions or intersections of plaster with other wall or ceiling finishes, and as a screed. May be used with metal lath, ROCK-LATH FIRECODE plaster base or masonry construction. To ensure proper grounds for plastering, 3/4" casing beads should be used with metal lath, 5/8" beads with all masonry units, 7/8" beads when solid flange is applied under gypsum plaster base, and 1/2" beads when flange is applied over veneer gypsum base. Available in galvanized steel—or zinc alloy for exterior applications.

7

1-A Expanded Corner Bead

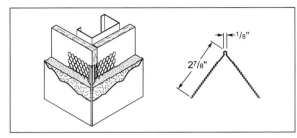

4-A Flexible Corner Bead

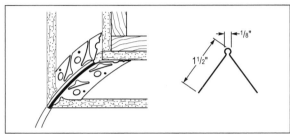

Double-X Corner Bead

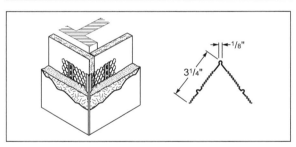

#66 Square Edge Casing Beads (expanded or short flange)

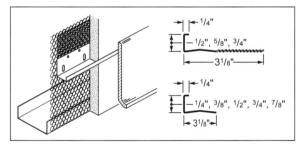

Cornerite and Striplath

Manufactured from strips of galvanized diamond mesh lath; used as reinforcement. Cornerite, bent lengthwise in the center to form a 100° angle, should be used in all internal plaster angles where metal lath is not lapped or carried around; over gypsum lath, anchored to the lath;

and over internal angles of masonry construction. These products are also used as part of the floating angle method of applying gypsum lath to wood framing in order to reduce plaster cracking. Striplath is a similar flat strip used as a plaster reinforcement over joints of gypsum lath and where dissimilar bases join; also used to span pipe chases and as reinforcement of headers over openings.

Cornerite

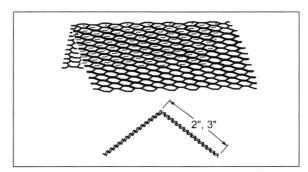

Striplath

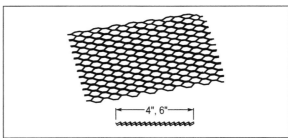

Control Joints

Zinc Control Joints Designed to relieve stresses of both expansion and contraction in large plastered areas. Made from roll-formed zinc alloy, these joints are resistant to corrosion in both interior and exterior uses with gypsum or Portland cement plaster. An open slot, 1/4" wide and 1/2" deep, the joint is protected with plastic tape, which is removed after plastering is completed. (See page 238.) The short flanges are perforated for keying and attachment by wire-tying to metal lath—or by stapling to gypsum lath. Thus the plaster is key-locked to the control joint, which not only provides a plastering ground, but can be used to create decorative panel designs.

Sizes and grounds: No. 50, 1/2"; No. 75, 3/4"; No. 100, 1" (for uses such as exterior stucco).

Maximum Spacing–SHEETROCK Brand Control Joints for Interior Plaster Assemblies

System	Location	Max. single dimension ft.	m	Max. single area ft.²	m²
Metal Lath & Plaster	Partition	30	9	–	–
	Ceiling	50[1]	15	2500	230
		30[2]	9	900	83.6
Gypsum Lath & Plaster	Partition	30	9	–	–
	Ceiling	50[1]	15	2500	230
		30[2]	9	900	83.6

(1) With perimeter relief. (2) Without perimeter relief.

For exterior application where wind pressure exceeds 20 psf, back control joints with 2″ wide butyl tape applied to the sheathing. Install joints with flanges under self-furring lath and attach with Bostitch 9/16″ "G" staples or equal, spaced 6″ apart on each side. Positive attachment of flange to framing through the lath is required using fasteners 12″ o.c. Break supporting members, sheathing and metal lath behind control joints. When vertical and horizontal joints intersect, vertical joint should be continuous; horizontal joint should abut it. Apply sealant at all splices, intersections and terminals.

Control Joint Nos. 50, 75, 100

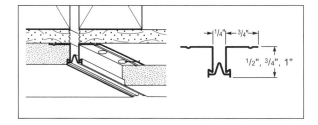

Zinc Control Joint Limitation Where sound and/or fire ratings are prime considerations, adequate protection must be provided behind the control joint. Functions only with transverse stresses. Should not be used with magnesium oxychloride cement stucco or Portland cement stucco containing calcium chloride additives.

Double-V Expansion Joint Provides stress relief to control cracking in large plastered areas. Made with expanded flanges of corrosion-resistant galvanized steel, or zinc for exterior use in 1/2" or 3/4" grounds.

Double-V Expansion Joint

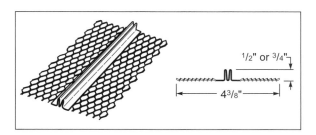

Specifications–Typical Plaster Trim Accessories

Product	Depth or grounds		Flange width		Finish
	in.	mm	in.	mm	
1-A Expanded Corner Bead	–	–	2-7/8	73.0	Galv. or Zinc Alloy
4-A Flexible Corner Bead	–	–	1-1/2	38.1	Galv.
Double-X Corner Bead	–	–	3-1/4	82.6	Galv.
#66 Square Expanded Flange Casing Bead[2]	1/2	12.7	3-1/8	79.4	Galv. or Zinc Alloy
	5/8	15.9	3-1/8	79.4	Galv. or Zinc Alloy
	3/4	19.1	3-1/8	79.4	Galv. or Zinc Alloy
	7/8	22.2	3-1/8	79.4	Galv. or Zinc Alloy
	1	22.2	3-1/8	79.4	Galv. or Zinc Alloy
	1-1/4	22.2	3-1/8	79.4	Galv. or Zinc Alloy
#66 Square Short Flange Casing Bead	1/2	12.7	1-1/4	31.7	Galv. or Zinc Alloy
	3/4	19.1	1-1/4	31.7	Galv. or Zinc Alloy
	7/8	22.2	1-1/4	31.7	Galv. or Zinc Alloy
Cornerite	–	–	2	50.8	Paint or Galv.
	–	–	3	76.2	Paint or Galv.
Striplath	–	–	4	101.6	Paint or Galv.
	–	–	6	152.4	Paint or Galv.
SHEETROCK Brand Zinc Control Joint No. 93	1/2(#50)	12.7	3/4	19.1	Zinc Alloy
	3/4(#75)	19.0	3/4	19.1	Zinc Alloy
	1(#100)	25.4	3/4	19.1	Zinc Alloy
Double-V Expansion Joint	1/2	12.7	2-3/16	76.7	Galv.
	3/4	19.1	2-3/16	76.7	Galv.

(1) Available in zinc, special order only.

Framing Components

Steel framing members offer the advantages of light weight, low material cost, quick erection and superior strength and versatility in meeting job requirements. All are noncombustible.

Steel Studs and Runners Channel-shape and roll-formed from galvanized or corrosion-resistant steel. Used in non-load and load-bearing interior partition and exterior curtain wall systems. Limited chaseways are provided by punch-outs in the web. Assemblies using these studs are low in cost with excellent sound and fire-resistance characteristics. Available in various styles and widths to meet the following functional requirements. (For data on specific framing components, see Chapter 1, "Drywall & Veneer Plaster Products." For installation, see Chapter 2, "Framing.")

Cold-Rolled Channels Formed from 16-ga. steel, black asphaltum, painted or galvanized. Used for furring, suspended ceilings, partitions and ornamental lath. Sizes: 3/4", 1-1/2", 2".

Metal Furring Channels Roll-formed, hat-shaped section of galvanized, 25-ga. steel. May be attached with furring clips or tie wire to the main carrying channels and spaced 16" o.c. for economical screw attachment of ROCKLATH FIRECODE base. This combination provides a base for either adhesively applied acoustical tile or a basecoat plaster. Also available made from 20-ga. galvanized steel for heavier loads and longer spans. Furring channels are noncombustible for exterior walls. They may be spaced up to 24" o.c. Face width 1-1/4", depth 7/8". (See Chapter 1 for Z-furring channels.)

Adjustable Wall Furring Brackets Used to attach 3/4" furring channels to exterior masonry walls. Made of galvanized steel with corrugated edges. Brackets act as supports for horizontal channels 24" o.c. in braced furring systems.

Tie Wire 18-ga. galvanized soft annealed wire for tying metal lath to channels and furring to runner channels.

Hanger Wire 8-ga. for suspended ceiling channel runners when spaced not more than 4'. o.c.

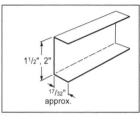

Cold-rolled channel

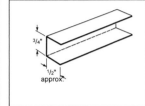

Cold-rolled channel

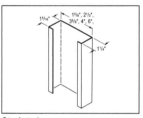

Steel stud

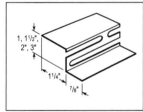

Z-furring channel

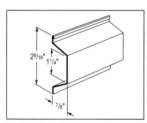

Furring channel

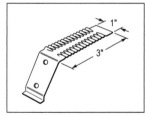

Adjustable wall furring bracket

Tie wire

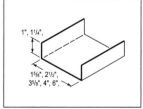

Steel runner

Specifications–Structural Accessories[1]

Product	Size in./ga.	mm
Cold-Rolled Channel[2] [3]	3/4"	19.1
	1-1/2"	38.1
	2"	50.9
Tie Wire/Hanger Wire[3]	8-ga. Coil	4.1
	18-ga Coil	1.2
	8-ga. Bdl.	4.1
	18-ga Hank	1.2
	18-ga.Hank	1.2

Notes: (1) See Chapter 1 for other structural accessories; (2) Painted; (3) Galvanized

Screws A complete line of self-drilling, self-tapping steel screws developed for simple, quick attachment of gypsum boards to steel, wood or gypsum supports. Screws are highly corrosion-resistant and have a Phillips head recess for rapid installation with a special bit and power-driven screw gun. (For complete data and Screw Selector Guide, see Chapter 1.)

Plasters

Plaster Formulation

The main ingredient of all gypsum plasters is gypsum rock—hydrous calcium sulfate—which has a water content of about 20% in chemical combination. During processing, about 3/4 of this chemically combined water is removed from the gypsum rock by means of a controlled heating process called calcination. When water is added at the job, the material crystallizes (sets), reverting to its original chemical composition.

USG plasters are specifically formulated to control setting time and other important characteristics. These depend upon the intended use and method of application, the climatic conditions of the area and job conditions.

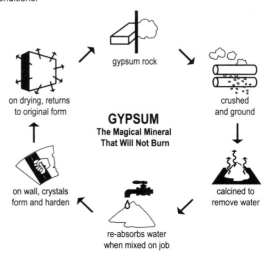

gypsum rock

on drying, returns to original form

crushed and ground

GYPSUM
The Magical Mineral
That Will Not Burn

on wall, crystals form and harden

calcined to remove water

re-absorbs water when mixed on job

Basecoat Plasters

RED TOP Gypsum Plaster

For beauty and durability, the required number of plaster basecoats must be applied as follows:

Three coats, commonly referred to scratch coat, brown coat and finish coat, are required on all metal lath and are desirable on all gypsum lath.

Two coats, scratch/doubleback and finish, are acceptable on gypsum lath and on interior face of rough concrete block, clay tile or porous brick.

Furring is required over the interior surface of exterior masonry wall prior to plastering to prevent damage from seepage and condensation.

Select materials not only for compatibility, but also for the quality of the structure to be plastered. Upgrade plastering specifications when possible.

RED TOP Gypsum Plaster A "neat" gypsum basecoat plaster requiring the addition of aggregate (sand, vermiculite or perlite) and water on the job. It is suitable for hand or machine application. The product can be applied to all standard lath and masonry bases. It provides a plastic working material that will conform to varied designs and help achieve durability in walls and ceilings. Meets ASTM C28. Available in 50-lb. bags. (For additional information, see P752.)

RED TOP Wood Fiber Plaster

RED TOP Wood Fiber Plaster A higher-strength basecoat plaster than RED TOP brand gypsum plaster that can be used without aggregates. Manufactured from selected wood fiber. Only water needs to be added. Wood fiber plaster can be applied to all standard lath and masonry surfaces and is recommended as a scratch coat for metal lath. (Requires aggregate when used in machine applications or when applied to masonry.)

Wood fiber plaster, neat, weighs approx. 1/4 less than a sanded gypsum basecoat. Complies with ASTM C28. Available in 50-lb. bags. (See also P751.)

STRUCTO-BASE Gypsum Plaster

STRUCTO-BASE® Gypsum Plaster USG'S highest-strength basecoat plaster. Designed for use in STRUCTOCORE™ Security Wall Systems, it provides excellent indentation and penetration resistance and is ideally suited for applications requiring the highest levels of abuse-resistance such as: handball courts, hospital corridors and schools. Recommended over metal lath with scratch and brown coats and suitable for hand and machine application. Meets ASTM C28. Available in 50-lb. bags. (See also P753.)

STRUCTO-LITE **Gypsum Plaster** A mill-mixed perlite-aggregate gypsum plaster. It requires only the addition of water. USG's lightest-weight basecoat plaster and the most highly insulated. Provides a plastic working material that will conform to various designs and help achieve durability in walls and ceilings. It can be applied by hand or machine methods on approved plaster bases. Meets ASTM C28. Available in 50-lb. bags. (See also P754.)

STRUCTO-LITE **Pre-Mixed Perlited Gypsum Plaster**

Coverage and Technical Data–Gypsum Basecoat Plasters

Plaster product	Mix	Ratio: aggregate (vol.)/ Basecoat (wt.)		Approx. compressive strength dry[1]		Approx. coverage per ton of gypsum basecoat[2]					
						Gypsum lath		Metal lath		Unit masonry	
		ft.³/100 lb.	m³/ton[3]	lb./in.² (psi)	MPa[4]	yd.²/ton	m²/ton[3]	yd.²/ton	m²/ton[3]	yd.²/ton	m²/ton[3]
RED TOP Gypsum and Two-Purpose Plaster	sand	2.0	1.24	875	6.00	180	165	114	104	140	129
	sand	2.5	1.55	750	5.17	206	190	131	121	160	147
	perlite	2.0	1.24	700	4.82	176	162	112	103	137	126
	perlite	3.0	1.86	525	3.62	224	206	143	132	174	160
	vermiculite	2.0	1.24	465	3.21	171	157	109	100	133	123
	vermiculite	3.0	1.86	290	2.00	215	198	137	126	168	154
STRUCTO-BASE Gypsum Plaster	sand	2.0	1.24	2800 min.[5]	19.30	154	142	99	91	120	110
	sand	2.5	1.55	1900 min.[5]	13.10	185	170	118	109	144	132
	sand	3.0	1.86	1400 min.[5]	9.65	214	197	136	125	167	154
STRUCTO-LITE Gypsum Plaster	regular	–	–	700	4.82	140	129	89[6]	82[6]	109	100
RED TOP Wood Fiber Plaster	neat	–	–	1750	12.06	85	78	54	49	66	60
RED TOP Wood Fiber Plaster	sand	1.0	0.62	1400	9.65	135	124	86	79	105	97

(1) Average laboratory results when tested in accordance with ASTM C472. Figures may vary slightly for products from individual plants. (2) Grounds (including finish coat): gypsum lath (face of lath), metal lath 3/4″ (back of lath), unit masonry 5/8″. (3) Metric ton. (4) Megapascals (MN/m²). (5) Laboratory evaluations for sanded plaster are based on use of graded Ottawa silica sand. (6) Lightweight aggregated plasters are not recommended over metal lath when the finish coat is to be smooth troweled.

Basecoat Plaster Limitations

1. Where sound isolation is prime consideration, use sand aggregate only.

2. Do not use where water or excessive moisture is present. May be applied to exterior soffit equipped with suitable drips and casings and protected from direct exposure to rain and moisture.

3. Not recommended for direct application to substrates coated with bituminous compounds or waterproofing agents.

4. Interior face of exterior walls shall be furred and lathed prior to plastering to prevent seepage and condensation.

5. The only USG plaster recommended for embedding electric heat cables is job-sanded DIAMOND brand veneer finish plaster applied directly to properly prepared monolithic concrete or IMPERIAL brand gypsum base. (See pages 225-227 for more

information.) If IMPERIAL brand gypsum base and job-sanded DIAMOND brand veneer finish are used for a radiant heat system, the cable-sheath operating temperatures must never exceed 125°F. (See also PM16.)

6. Basecoats containing job-mixed lightweight aggregate or STRUCTO-LITE gypsum plaster must be finished with an aggregated finish plaster.

Portland Cement Plaster

This mix is used for interior applications where high-moisture conditions exist, or for exterior stucco applications. Portland cement-based plaster and gypsum plaster are two distinctly different chemical compositions and are not compatible. Gypsum finish plasters should not be directly applied to Portland cement plasters or substrates with out the use of a bonding agent.

Finish Plasters

Conventional plaster walls are finished with gauging plasters and finishing limes or with prepared finishes. USG provides a range of products with a variety of characteristics to meet different performance requirements. From the standpoint of workability, productivity and ease of achieving surface smoothness, the conventional finish plasters described in this section are superior to the veneer finish plasters, which are known best for their surface hardness. (See the Appendix for a comparison of finish plasters.)

Gauging Plasters

RED TOP Gauging Plaster Quick Set

RED TOP Gauging Plaster Slow Set

Lime, when used alone as a finish plaster, does not set, is subject to shrinkage when drying and lacks a hard finish. Gauging plaster is blended into the lime putty in the proper proportions to provide controlled set, early hardness and strength and to prevent shrinkage cracks.

Gauging plasters are carefully ground and screened to proper particle sizes to make the plasters quick-soaking and easily blended with lime putty.

High-strength RED TOP Keenes cement and STRUCTO-GAUGE gauging plaster are to be used only over sanded or wood fiber or veneer basecoat plasters. Over lightweight aggregated basecoats, use gauging plaster that is properly aggregated.

RED TOP **Gauging Plaster** Blends easily with lime putty for durable smooth-trowel or sand-float finishes. Provides high strength, hardness and abrasion resistance superior to many other surfaces. Easily painted or finished. Applied over a gypsum basecoat. Available in Quick Set (30–40 min.) or Slow Set (50–70 min.) and aggregated with perlite fines for lightweight-aggregated basecoats. Meets ASTM C28. Available in 50-lb. bags. (See also P786.)

Structo-Gauge Gauging Plaster Slow Set

Red-Top Keenes Cement

Structo-Gauge **Gauging Plaster** When mixed with lime putty, produces a high-strength, durable, white smooth-trowel finish. Its excellent hardness and abrasion resistance make it ideal for high-traffic areas and other applications requiring durability and abuse resistance. Faster and easier to apply than Keenes cement for smooth-finish surfaces. Should be used over high-strength sanded, veneer plaster or wood fiber gypsum basecoats but not over lightweight-aggregated or Portland cement basecoats or masonry.

Quick Set formulation sets in 30–40 minutes, and is ideal for low-suction veneer basecoats. Slow Set formulation sets in 60–75 minutes and is best suited for use over regular sanded basecoats. Meets ASTM C28. Under equivalent application conditions, Structo-Gauge gauging plaster will provide a harder finish than Red Top gauging plasters. Available in 50-lb. bags. (For more information, see P771.)

Red Top **Keenes Cement** A highly calcined, "dead-burned" white gypsum plaster that produces durable, highly crack-resistant smooth and sand-float finishes when mixed with lime. The only retemperable (reworkable with water) gypsum gauging plaster; it provides the best gauging for lime-sand float finishes and is also suitable for job color. Keenes Cement sets in 3 to 6 hours so it can be floated for an extended time period to provide a densified finish. It can be used as a smooth-trowel finish, offering strong, hard surfaces when densified by extensive troweling through set. This allows installers to mix large batches for job-colored finishes. The product requires a high-strength gypsum basecoat. It must never be used directly over a Portland cement basecoat. Meets ASTM C61. Available in 50-lb. bags. (See also P770.)

7

Finish Limes

The purpose of finish lime is to provide bulk, plasticity and ease of spread for the finish coat. There are two types of finish lime: (1) double hydrate (Type S), and (2) normal or single hydrate (Type N). Each requires different preparation in order to produce a good finish-lime putty.

Ivory **and** Snowdrift **Finish Limes** Autoclaved (double-hydrate) limes that immediately develop high plasticity when mixed with water and do not require overnight soaking. This virtually eliminates the possibility of future expansion within the finish coat due to unhydrated magnesium oxides. These limes are easy to apply and have excellent spreading qualities. Comply with ASTM C206, Type S. Available in 50-lb. bags.

Grand Prize **Finish Lime** Single-hydrate, economical, easy-working, white, uniform plastic. Requires soaking at least 16 hrs. to develop proper plasticity and the degree of hydration for use. Complies with ASTM C206, Type N. Available in 50-lb. bags.

Ivory Finish Lime   *Snowdrift Finish Limes*   *Grand Prize Finish Lime*

Prepared Finishes

Imperial Veneer Finish Plaster

Imperial Veneer Finish Plaster Provides the highest-strength surface hardness and abrasion-resistance. Designed for single-coat application over Imperial gypsum base, or as a high-strength finish over veneer or high-strength sanded basecoats. It is formulated for hand application, providing a smooth-trowel or float or spray-texture finish ready for final surface treatments. Complies with ASTM C5847. Available in 50-lb. bags. (For more information, see P775.)

Diamond Veneer Finish Plaster A white finish formulated for hand application over Imperial gypsum base, or as a finish of a two-coat system over a sanded gypsum basecoat, Imperial veneer basecoat, or Diamond veneer basecoat. Offers a standard strength surface for construction where the extra hardness of Imperial brand finish plaster is not required. This veneer finish is unaggregated for a smooth or skip-trowel finish. When job-aggregated with up to an equal part by weight of clean silica sand, it is extremely adaptable to textured finishes. Complies with ASTM C587. Available in 50-lb. bags. (See also P777.)

Red Top Finish A mill-mixed gauging plaster and lime finish requiring the addition of water only. It has stabilized set, excellent troweling characteristics. The formulation is designed for use over conventional sanded gypsum basecoat, Imperial veneer basecoat and Diamond veneer basecoat. It is not to be used over lightweight aggregate gypsum basecoat. Available in 50-lb. bags. (See also P773.)

Diamond Veneer Finish-Sanded A white sanded finish formulated for hand application over Imperial gypsum base. It can also be used as a finish for a two-coat system over a sanded gypsum basecoat, Imperial veneer basecoat, or Diamond veneer basecoat. It provides a strong, hard surface that resists abrasion and cracking and creates a high-end white finish. This veneer is pre-aggregated for textured or skip-trowel finishes. It can be richly textured to create Spanish, swirl, stippled, float and other types of textures. Complies with ASTM C587. Available in 50-lb. bags. (See also P862.)

Diamond Veneer
Finish Plaster

Red-Top Finish Plaster
Regular Set

Diamond Veneer
Finish Plaster Sanded

Coverage–Finish Plasters(1)

Product	Ratio of Mix (dry wt.)			Approx. Coverage(2)	
	Lime	Gauging	Sand(3)	yd.²/ton	m²/t(4)
IMPERIAL Brand Finish Plaster	–	–	–	360	330
DIAMOND Brand Veneer Finish Plaster	–	–	–	550	510
RED TOP Finish	–	–	–	390	360
RED TOP Gauging Plaster	2	1	8	280	260
RED TOP Keenes Cement	2	1	8	270	250
	2	1	–	430	400
	1	1	–	370	345
STRUCTO-GAUGE Gauging Plaster	1	1	–	380	350
	2	1	–	430	400

(1) Over conventional basecoat plasters; over veneer basecoats, coverage is increased. (2) 1/16″ (1.6mm) thickness.
(3) Natural, uniformly graded, clean silica sand. (4) Metric ton.

Finish Coat Plaster: General Limitations

1. A smooth trowel finish should not be used over lightweight aggregate gypsum basecoat applied over metal lath. Only sand float finishes are recommended over metal lath.

2. Where the gypsum basecoat is STRUCTO-LITE plaster or contains light-weight aggregate (perlite or vermiculite) and a smooth trowel finish is used over any plaster base except metal lath, the finish coat should be RED TOP gauging plaster and lime: a) with addition of 1/2 cu. ft. of perlite fines, or, b) with addition of 50 lb. of No. 1 white silica sand per 100 lb. gauging plaster, or, c) use RED TOP aggregated gauging plaster.

3. Gypsum or lime-based finishes, including Keenes cement, should not be used directly over a Portland cement basecoat or over concrete block or other masonry surfaces.

4. Smooth-trowel high-strength finishes, such as STRUCTO-GAUGE gauging plaster and Keenes cement, must not be used over STRUCTO-LITE plaster or a basecoat with a lightweight aggregate.

5. Gauged-lime putty and RED TOP finish applied over conventional basecoat plasters must age 30 days, be thoroughly dry and properly sealed prior to final surface treatments. Quick-drying vinyl acrylic latex or alkali-resistant alkyd primer-sealers are recommended. (For more information, see PM15.)

6. Primers containing polyvinyl acetate (PVA) are not recommended and should not be specified for use over wet plaster of any kind, or over lime-gauging or lime-containing plasters. The PVA film is subject to rewetting and will almost certainly

7

result in bond loss and subsequent paint delamination. In view of these precautions, strictly follow the paint manufacturers' specific lime-locking product recommendations for painting lime-gauging putty finishes and for lime-containing veneer plaster finishes. (For more information, see PM15.)

Sound-Absorbing Plaster Finish

USG Acoustical Plaster Finish

USG Acoustical Plaster Finish A white, evenly textured plaster finish that is sound-rated and spray-applied. It is used over interior gypsum basecoats and interior monolithic concrete, metal decks and gypsum panel ceilings. As it is chemically setting, it requires only the addition of water. Produces a handsome, natural-white, evenly textured finish. Requires no application of a bonding agent, except over metal decks. Reduces surface preparation time and costs. For use on new or renovation construction. Surface burning characteristics: flame spread 10, smoke developed 25 per ASTM E1042-85. Sound rated: NRC 0.55 for concrete and conventional plaster at 1/2" finish thickness; NRC 0.75 for concrete and conventional plaster at 1" finish thickness, NRC 0.50 for gypsum panels. Use on noncontact surfaces only. (See also P720 and PM15.)

Ornamental Plasters

USG Moulding Plaster Used for specialized work such as ornamental trim or running cornices. The plaster grain is very fine, making it ideal for sharp detail when used neat for cast work. A controlled set provides uniform workability. For running cornice work, add a small amount (maximum 50%) of lime putty to add plasticity and to act as a lubricant for the template. Provides approximately 1.5 cu. ft. per 100 lbs. Complies with ASTM C28. Available in 50- and 100-lb. bags.

HYDROCAL® **White Gypsum Cement** Recommended for ornamental work with thin sections—and for castings made with intricate latex molds. Its high green strength minimizes breakage. Available in 50- and 100-lb. bags.

HYDROCAL **FGR 95 Gypsum Cement** A unique high-strength product used with glass fibers or a glass fiber mat for fabricating lightweight fire-resistant decorated shapes, architectural elements, column covers, cornices and trims. Adapts to most patterns, accepts most coatings. A non-toxic material with zero flame spread, zero smoke developed. In 50- and 100-lb. bags. (For more information, visit **gypsumsolutions.com**.)

USG Moulding Plaster

HYDROCAL *White Gypsum Cement*

HYDROCAL *Gypsum Cement*

Ornamental Plasters–Approximate Yield

Product	Bag size	Approx. volume dry		
	lb.	kg	ft.³/100 lb.	m³/t[1]
USG Moulding Plaster	50 & 100	22.7 & 45.4	1.5	0.94
HYDROCAL White Cement	50 & 100	22.7 & 45.4	1.3	0.81
HYDROCAL FGR 95 Gypsum Cement	100	45.4	1.0	0.62

(1)Metric ton

Special Additives

Plaster Retarders

USG Standard Strength Retarder Recommended for slight to moderate (30 to 45 min.) lengthening of set times of conventional and veneer plasters. Used when required by job or climate conditions. Available in 1-1/2-lb. package. (See also PM7 and P783.)

USG High Strength Retarder Extends setting time of plaster 1 to 3 hours. Especially suitable for conventional plasters where machine application set time alteration is required. Available in 1-1/4-lb. package. (See also PM7 and P783.)

USG Retarder for Lime-Containing Plaster Products Especially formulated for use with lime/finish plasters, such as RED TOP finish, DIAMOND brand veneer finish and gauging/lime plaster finishes. Recommended for slight (20 min.) lengthening of set time. (See also PM7 and P783.)

Retarder Limitations: Using too much retarder can weaken the plaster finish, as excess retarder causes "dry-out,"—a condition where the water required for the chemical set reaction evaporates before adequate setting can take place. USG retarders should never be added directly to the plaster mix. Pre-mixing them with water assures faster and more uniform dispersion for better batch control.

USG Standard Strength Retarder

USG High Strength Retarder

USG Retarder for Lime-Containing Plaster Products

Plaster Accelerators

USG Standard Strength Gypsum Plaster Accelerator Provides slightly quicker setting time (10 to 30 min.) for conventional and veneer plasters when required by job or climate conditions. When used in excess, setting and drying problems can arise. Available in 1-1/2-lb. package. (See also PM8 and P779.)

USG High-Strength Gypsum Accelerator Provides more substantial adjustments to setting times (30 min. to 2 hr.) for conventional plasters. Also may be used to alter set times for setting-type (DURABOND or

Easy Sand) joint compounds. Available in 1-1/2-lb. package. (See also PM8 and P779.)

USG Plaster Accelerator–Alum Catalyst Helps correct plaster performance in dry-out conditions by shortening working times. It is also used to treat sun-faded Imperial brand gypsum base when a lime-containing plaster is to be applied to it. Alum catalyst is used to improve the bond of alkaline veneer plaster to gypsum bases with faded face paper. Available in 1-1/2-lb. package. (See also PM8 and P779.)

Accelerator Limitations: Never add USG standard strength or high strength accelerator directly to the mixing water or mix it with water to form a solution before adding it to the plaster mix. This reduces its ability to accelerate. Instead, sprinkle the accelerator in dry form into the mixer after the plaster has been added. For hand mixing, it can be added either to the dry mix or the plaster slurry.

USG Standard Strength Gypsum Plaster Accelerator *USG High Strength Gypsum Plaster Accelerator* *USG Gypsum Plaster Accelerator Alum Catalyst*

Plaster Bonder

USG Plaster Bonder

USG Plaster Bonder Vinyl acetate homopolymer emulsion is used to enhance adhesion of new plaster to any structurally sound interior surface. Clear or tinted pink to allow visual confirmation of application where desired. May be brush-, roller- or spray-applied. Dries to a film that re-wets when plaster is applied. Compatible with gypsum plaster, concrete, cinder block, stone, gypsum drywall panels and other similar materials. Should not be used around swimming pools or in exceptionally moist areas. Do not apply to underside of concrete roof decks. Required for applications of plaster over Durock brand cement board, Fiberock brand abuse-resistant gypsum fiber panels and monolithic concrete. Available in 1- and 5-gal. containers. (See also P778.)

Acrylic Additive

USG Acrylic Additive

USG Acri-Add™ 100% Acrylic Add-Mix Fortifier Water-based acrylic polymer emulsion admixture designed for interior use with gypsum-based products, and for interior or exterior use with Portland cement-based products. It enhances performance of gypsum plasters, mortars and cement plasters by improving bond strength and water-resistance, minimizing shrinkage cracking, and improving overall durability. It also enhances curing qualities, imparts abrasion resistance and reduces cracking due to tensile and impact stresses. Low odor and color fast. Substitute the fortifier for a portion of the normal amount of mixing water, typically 1:3, but sometimes 1:2 or 1:1 depending on application end product, job site conditions and substrates selected. Available in 1- and 5-gal. containers. (See also P781.)

Conventional Plaster Applications

8

General Planning Procedures

Two ingredients are required for a quality plaster job—quality products and skilled craftspeople using correct lathing and plastering techniques.

USG plaster bases, plasters and plastering accessories are quality, job-proven products designed to work together. But without proper planning and correct installation by the contractor, they cannot be expected to produce the desired results.

This chapter addresses the basic recommendations and installation procedures to produce the best possible job. It describes wood and steel framing, applications of conventional plaster bases in fire- and sound-rated assemblies, and includes frame-spacing and fastener-selector charts.

Various organizations provide information about recommended standards or tolerances for installation of plaster products and systems. See the Appendix for information about standards and tolerances. For instructions on the safe use of plaster and related products, see Chapter 13, "Safety Considerations & Material Handling."

Sound lathing and plastering practices can provide the contractor with (1) greater profit through fewer callbacks, (2) less waste and therefore lower job costs, and (3) high-quality results that produce quicker sales and a favorable business reputation.

Planning the Job

Advance planning by the plastering contractor can mean savings in time and materials cost—and a better-appearing job.

Two areas of planning deserve special attention: hoisting and cleanup. In high-rise work, it is essential to determine the availability of hoisting equipment on the job well in advance of the time when it will be needed. Failure to do so can result in costly delays while the hoist is tied up by other trades.

In all types of jobs, it is wise to plan for cleanup as the work proceeds, not when the job is finished. Contractors who have adopted this practice affirm that it reduces job costs. They have discovered that it is easier, faster and cheaper to spread drop cloths of roofing paper, for example, than to scrape up set plaster. And stuffing electrical boxes with paper before plastering begins is far less costly than digging out set plaster when they are accidentally filled. When machines are shut down, they should be hosed off and thoroughly cleaned—made ready for a fresh start. The benefits from these good working practices add up to faster completions, less down time and equipment maintenance, and more profit.

Estimating Materials

Accurate takeoff and estimating quantities of materials are an essential part of the job planning. Underestimating causes expensive job delays while quantities are refigured and orders placed. Overestimating invariably results in damage or loss of at least part of the surplus materials.

The tables in Chapter 7, "Conventional Plaster Products," contain data needed for accurate estimating: packaging, coverage of various cementitious materials and accessories needed per 100 square yards of finished surface. Similar data on steel studs, runners and screws can be found in Chapter 1, "Drywall & Veneer Plaster Products."

General Job Conditions

Handling and Storage

All successful plaster jobs require adequate equipment: power mixers, mortar boards, scaffolding and tools. Set up enough scaffolding to permit continuous application of both basecoat and finish plasters for a complete section of wall or ceiling. Obtain clean water for washing all mixing tools.

Lath and plaster products should be ordered for delivery to the job just prior to application. Materials stored on the job for longer periods are liable to damage and abuse.

Rather than ship all plaster to the job at one time, fresh plaster should be delivered as needed. Plaster stored for long periods is subject to variable moisture conditions and aging that can produce variations in setting time and performance problems.

Store plastering products inside in a dry location away from heavy-traffic areas. Stack plaster bags on planks or platforms away from damp floors and walls. Store gypsum plaster bases flat on a clean, dry floor; vertical storage may damage edges or deform board. Protect metal corner beads, casing beads and trim from being bent or damaged. All materials used on the job should remain in their packaging or containers until used.

Warehouse stocks of plaster products should be rotated to ensure a supply of fresh materials and to prevent damage to plaster through aging and contact with moisture.

8

Environmental Conditions

1. When outdoor temperatures are less than 55°F, maintain a temperature of 55° to 70°F, with a relative humidity of 20% to 50% both day and night before, during and after plaster application until the plaster is dry. Air should be well distributed, with deflection or protective screens used to prevent concentrated or irregular heat on plaster areas near the air source. It is important to note that temporary open-flame fan heaters give off moisture during use and raise the ambient temperature. Since warmer air holds more water, the relative humidity will decrease while the actual amount of water has increased. (For example, the combustion of 1 gallon of Kerosene gives off over a gallon of water—condensed.) This will delay the dry-out time of your pour, plaster or other wet installations. However, heat may need to be provided to maintain required temperatures (55°F to 70°F).

2. Provide ample ventilation to properly dry plaster during and after application. In glazed buildings, this should be accomplished by keeping windows open sufficiently to provide air circulation. In areas lacking normal ventilation, moisture-laden air must be mechanically removed.

3. To develop proper performance characteristics, carefully control the drying rate of plastering materials during and after application. Plaster should not be allowed to dry too slowly or too fast. If possible, maintain building temperature-humidity combination in the "normal drying" area of the graph on next page. (See also reference PM10.) Excessive ventilation or air movement should be avoided to allow plaster to properly set.

Plaster Drying Conditions

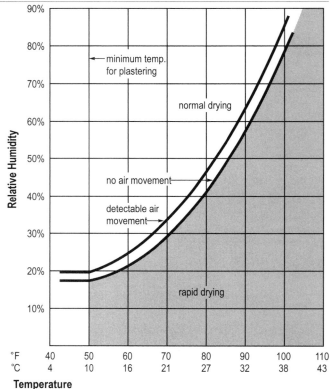

Framing Installation

Requirements for framing with wood and steel studs are the same for plaster and drywall construction and are covered in Chapter 2, "Framing." Maximum frame spacing for plaster base is as follows.

Frame Spacing—Gypsum Base (Ceilings & Sidewalls)

Type Framing	Base Thickness in.	mm	Max. Frame Spacing o.c. in.	mm
Wood	3/8	9.5	16	406
Steel Stud	3/8	9.5	16	406
	3/8	9.5	24[1]	610
3/4 (19.1 mm) Channel Metal Furring	3/8	9.5	16	406
	3/8	9.5	16	406

(1) Three-coat plastering, commonly referred to as scratchcoat, browncoat and finish coat.

Reinforcing

Openings in a gypsum lath-and-plaster system, such as door frames, borrowed lights, etc., cause a concentration of stresses in the plaster, typically at the intersection of heads and jambs. Additional reinforcement (channels, runners, Striplath, self-furring diamond mesh lath) can be used at the weakened areas to distribute concentrated stresses.

Wood or metal inserts used as reinforcing or for attaching cabinets and shelving on nonresilient surfaces should always be applied behind the plaster base to prevent unnecessary damage to the plaster surface. Heavy fixtures, such as water closets and lavatories, should be supported by separate carriers and not by the lath and plaster surface. (See page 284 later in this chapter and "Fixture Attachment" in Appendix p 493.)

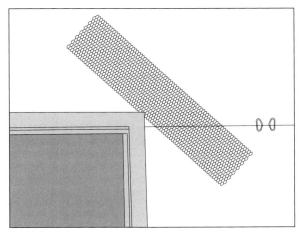

Reinforcing at door

Wall Furring

Exterior wall furring provides a way of spacing the plaster base and plaster away from masonry walls to produce an air space, a chase for services and space for insulation. By furring, uneven walls can be changed to true, even surfaces. Plaster base can be quickly attached, and the uniform plaster base saves plastering material and labor.

Exterior masonry walls should be furred out and a vapor retarder provided if necessary. Several systems are available; each provides structural and cost advantages for special furring conditions.

A professionally designed wall furring system should provide:

1. Protection from moisture seepage.
2. Proper location and need for insulation, air barriers and vapor retarder.
3. Isolation from structural movement. Exterior walls are subject constantly to changing dimensions due to temperature changes and wind loads.

**Wood Strip—
ROCKLATH Base
Furring**

For masonry wall furring, ROCKLATH plaster base and gypsum plaster over wood furring strips is an economical assembly. The wood furring is usually 1 x 2 or 2 x 2 strips spaced 16 o.c. for 3/8" lath, 24" o.c. maximum for 1/2" lath. Apply furring vertically and securely attach to the masonry. If necessary, use small wooden wedges to shim strips to a plumb surface.

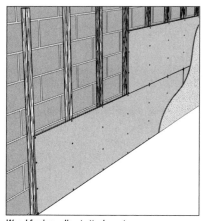

Wood furring—direct attachment

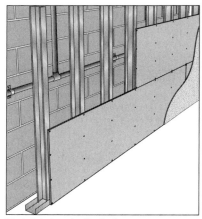

Steel stud—free-standing furring

Installation Apply 2 ft x 8 ft ROCKLATH plaster base at right angles to furring strips with end joints occurring between strips using 1" nails. When ROCKLATH base has been installed, reinforce inside corners with Cornerite.

**Steel Stud—
ROCKLATH Base
Furring**

This free-standing furring assembly consists of ROCKLATH plaster base screw-attached to steel studs and finished with gypsum plaster. The assembly offers a maximum of free space for encasing pipes, ducts or conduits.

Installation Align floor and ceiling runners parallel to wall, positioned to provide required chase space. Attach to concrete slabs with concrete stub nails, power-driven anchors 24" o.c., or appropriate fasteners, to suspended ceilings with toggle bolts, hollow metal fasteners 16" o.c., or appropriate fasteners or to wood framing with 1-1/4" type W screws 16" o.c.

Studs should be selected to limit deflection to L/360 and satisfy applicable stress criteria. Position steel studs vertically in runners, 16" o.c. for 3/8" lath, with all flanges in same direction. The recommended practice for most installations is to anchor only those studs to runners adjacent to door and borrowed light frames. This would also be applicable to partition intersections and corners. In cases where a significant slab live load deflection must be accommodated, the anchoring of these studs may restrict slab movement and cause partition cracking. In these cases, anchoring of these studs may need to be omitted. The services of a design professional are desirable to identify these instances and address them on a case-specific basis. Attach ROCK-LATH base to studs with appropriate screws, and apply 1/2" sanded basecoat plaster, and lime putty finish.

Metal furring

Metal Channel— ROCKLATH Base Furring

For direct attachment with metal furring channels, ROCKLATH plaster base is screwed to furring channels that are attached directly to an exterior masonry wall. The location and type of required air barriers and vapor barrier as specified by the design professional.

Installation Apply channels vertically to masonry not more than 16" o.c. Fasten each channel with hammered or power-driven stud fasteners or appropriate fasteners. If there is a possibility of water penetration, install an asphalt felt protection strip between the furring channel and wall surfaces.

Frame Spacing and Attachment

For Furred Ceilings Fasten 3/4" cold-rolled channel or 3/8" pencil rods directly to bottoms of framing members. On concrete joists, 8-ga. galvanized wire can be put in place before the concrete is poured. Space furring members as shown in the cross-furring member spacing table on next page. For joists spaced about 25" o.c., attachment of 3/4" channels may be on alternate joists; if greater than 25" o.c. but not more than 48" o.c., place attachment at every joist.

On steel joists or beams, place 3/4" cold-rolled channels at right angles to joists; attach with 3 strands 18-ga. galvanized wire.

For Suspended Framing Space 8-ga. wire hangers not more than 4' o.c. in direction of 1-1/2" carrying channels and not over 3' o.c. at right angles to direction of carrying channels. If hanger wires are 3' o.c. in direction of 1-1/2" channels, then channels at right angles may be 4' o.c. Place hangers within 6" of ends of carrying channel runs and of boundary walls, girders or similar interruptions of ceiling continuity. Position and level carrying channel and saddle tie securely with hanger wire.

Position 3/4" cold-rolled channel (cross-furring) across carrying channels, spacing them 12" to 24" depending on type of metal lath to be used, and saddle tie carrying channels with three strands of 18-ga. tie wire.

Apply 3.4-lb. diamond mesh lath, flat riblath or 3/8" riblath as specified with long dimension of sheets across the supports. Details on lathing procedures and control joints follow later in this chapter.

(For Drywall Suspension Systems, see literature 3152/ECM.)

Frame and Fastener Spacing—ROCKLATH Plaster Base

Type Framing	Base Thickness in.	mm	Fastener[1]	Max. Frame Spacing in.	mm	Max. Fastener Spacing in.	mm
Wood stud	3/8	9.5	Nails 13 ga., 1-1/8" long, 19/64" flat head, blued	16	406	5	127
			Staples—16-ga. galv. flattened wire, flat crown 7/16" wide, 1" divergent legs				
Steel stud	3/8"	9.5	1" TYPE S Screws	16	406	12	305
Metal furring	3/8"	9.5	1" TYPE S Screws	16	406	12	305

(1) Metric fastener dimensions: 19/64"=7.5mm; 7/16"=11.1mm; 1"=25.4mm; 1-1/8"=28.6mm.

Maximum Frame Spacing—Metal Lath[1]

Product	Weight lbs./yd.²	kg/m²	Spacing in.	mm
DIAMOND Mesh[2]	2.5	1.4	12[3]	305[3]
	3.4	1.8	24	406
3/8" (9.5mm) Riblath	3.4	1.8	19	610
Flat Riblath	2.75	1.5	16[4]	406
	3.4	1.8	19[5]	483

(1) For spacing on fire-rated constructions, see test reports. (2) 2.5-lb. lath should not be used for ceilings. (3) 16 o.c. permitted with wood framing and 2" solid partition. (4) Spacing of metal ceiling grilles 12" o.c. (5) 24" spacing with solid partition.

Support Area—Hangers

Hanger Size and Type	Max. Ceiling Area per Hanger ft.²	m	Allowable Tensile Load lbs.[3]
9-ga. galvanized wire	12.5	1.2	340
8-ga. galvanized wire	16	1.5	408
3/16" (4.8 mm) mild steel rod [1][2]	20	1.9	546
1/4" (6.4 mm) mild steel rod [1][2]	22.5	2.1	972
3/16" x 1" (4.8mm x 25.4mm) mild steel flat[1][2]	25	2.3	3712

(1) Where severe moisture conditions may occur, rods galvanized or painted with rust-inhibitive paint, or galvanized straps are recommended. (2) Not manufactured by USG. (3) Based on minimum yield 33,000 psi.

8

Maximum Spacing—Main Runner—Carrying Channels

Main Runner C. R. Channel Size in.	mm	Max c. to c. Spacing of Main Runners ft.	mm	Max. Spacing of Hangers Along Runners ft.	mm
3/4	19.1	3	914	2	610
3/4	19.1	2-1/4	686	3[1]	914
1-1/2	38.1	4	1219	3	914
1-1/2	38.1	3-1/2	1067	3-1/2	1067
1-1/2	38.1	3	914	4	1219
2	50.8	4	1219	5	1524
2	50.8	2-1/2	762	6	1829
2	50.8	2	610	7	2134

(1) For concrete joist construction only—where 8-ga. wire may be inserted in joist before concrete is poured.

Maximum Spacing—Cross-Furring Members

Cross-Furring Size	Max. c. to c. Spacing of Cross-Furring in.	mm	Main Runner or Support Spacing ft.	mm
3/4" (19.1 mm) C. R. Channel	24	610	3	914
3/4" (19.1 mm) C. R. Channel	19	483	3-1/2	1067
3/4" (19.1 mm) C. R. Channel	16	406	4	1219

Note: Verify all load values with manufacturer of structural channel.

Applying Plaster Base

Plaster bases may be classified as gypsum base, metal lath base or masonry base. Each of these materials provides a surface for plastering and adds reinforcement to the plaster. As such, they must be rigid enough to accept plaster and produce a secure bond between plaster and base—both necessary to develop strength and resistance to abuse and cracking.

To ensure adequate rigidity of plaster constructions, recommendations for the spacing of supports and fasteners must be strictly followed.

Apply plaster bases to ceilings first and then to partitions, starting at the top and working down to the floor line.

ROCKLATH **Plaster Base** An ideal high-suction rigid base for gypsum plasters. Should be applied face-out with long dimension across supports, and with end joints staggered between courses. Cut lath accurately so it slips easily into place without forcing and fits neatly around electrical outlets, openings, etc. Install any lengthwise raw cut edges at bottom strip or wall-ceiling angle. Apply Cornerite to all interior angles and staple to the lath only.

Metal Lath Should be applied with long dimension across supports and with end joints staggered between courses. Apply Riblath with the rib against supports. Lap ends of metal lath 1" and sides at least 1/2". Lap Riblath by nesting outside ribs. If end laps occur between supports, they should be laced or tied with 18-ga. tie wire. Secure lath to all supports at intervals not exceeding 6". At all interior angles, metal lath should be formed into corners and carried out onto abutting surface.

Clay Tile and Brick Frequently used for plaster bases. Care should be taken to make sure that surfaces are sufficiently porous to provide suction for plaster and are scored for added mechanical bonding. Smooth-surfaced clay tile that is glazed or semi-glazed does not offer sufficient bond for plaster.

Concrete Block A satisfactory base for plaster. The surface should be porous for proper suction, or face-scored for adequate mechanical bond. Units must be properly cured to minimize dimensional changes during and after plastering. Mortar joints should be struck flush.

Monolithic Concrete Ceilings, walls, beams and columns should have a complete and uniform application of USG Plaster Bonder before plastering. This surface treatment produces an adhesive bond suitable for direct application of gypsum plasters.

Plastering Direct to Exterior Masonry Walls Not recommended. Exterior walls are subject to water seepage and moisture condensation that may wet the plaster and damage interior decoration.

Bituminous Waterproofing Compounds Not recommended. These do not provide a good plaster base. Gypsum plasters should not be applied to surfaces treated with these compounds.

Rigid Foam Insulations Not recommended. Such insulations have not proven to be satisfactory bases for direct application of gypsum plaster because of low suction characteristics and low structural strength, which may result in cracking of the plaster.

USG does not recommend direct application of plaster to rigid foam insulation. However, some rigid foam insulation manufacturers have specific directions for application when direct plastering is to be used, as well as detailed specifications for plaster mixes and methods of application to be employed. Confirm local fire code compliance prior to installation.

USG has designed various furring systems (covered earlier in this chapter) that avoid the need to apply plaster to these unsuitable surfaces and do provide high-quality plaster finishes over the inside of exterior walls.

Applying Fasteners

Correct fastener selection and adherence to fastener spacing are extremely important to good plastering performance and absolutely essential in meeting the requirements of specific fire-rated constructions.

8

Gypsum Plaster Bases Attached to framing with screws, nails or staples. Nails, screws and staples should be driven so that the fastener head or crown bears tightly against the base but does not cut the face paper. To prevent core fracturing, they should be driven at least 3/8" away from ends and edges. Staples should be of flattened wire driven so the crown is parallel to wood framing. Screws should be used to attach gypsum plaster bases to steel studs, furring channels or resilient channels.

For screw attachment of single-layer 3/8" ROCKLATH base to steel studs or furring channel, 1" type S bugle head screws are used.

Nail Application Begin from center of base and proceed toward outer ends or edges. When nailing, apply pressure adjacent to nail being driven to ensure base is secured tightly on framing member. Position nails on adjacent ends or edges opposite each other and at least 3/8" from ends and edges. Drive nails with shank perpendicular to plaster base. The nail heads should be driven flush with paper surface but not break paper.

Metal Lath Attach to cold-rolled channel framing with tie wire (minimum 18 ga.) and to wood framing with fasteners engaging two strands or a rib and providing at least 3/4" penetration.

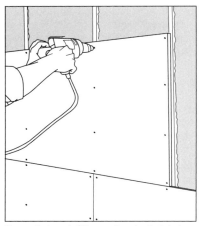

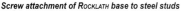

Screw attachment of ROCKLATH base to steel studs

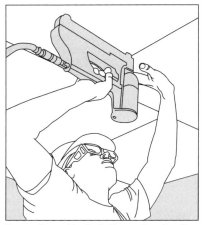

Power nailer used to attache ROCKLATH base to ceiling

Gypsum Lath—Steel Studs

Screw Attachment Fasten to studs spaced 16" o.c. with three 1" type S screws per stud spaced 2" from edge of lath. Type S-12 screws are required for heavier gauges. Drive screws with an electric screw gun.

Gypsum Lath—Wood Framing (Direct)

Nail ROCKLATH plaster base with face out and long dimension across framing members. Stagger end joints in successive courses with ends of lath falling between framing members. Butt all joints together, and cut lath to fit neatly around electrical outlets and other openings.

For ROCKLATH plaster base with 16" o.c. stud spacing, use four fasteners 8" o.c. per 24" width of lath. Place fasteners at least 3/8" from edges and ends of lath. Make sure all interior plaster angles are the floating type, and space first fasteners at least 10" from corner. Reinforce angle with Cornerite stapled to lath surface.

Metal Lath— Wood Framing (Direct)

Apply metal lath with long dimension of sheet across supports. Lap ends of lath at least 1", and if laps occur between supports, lace or tie with 18-ga. tie wire. Attach with fasteners 6" o.c. so that fasteners engage two strands or a rib and provide at least 3/4" penetration.

On walls, place metal lath so that the lower sheets overlap upper sheets and, where possible, stagger ends of lath in adjacent courses.

At all interior angles, form lath into corners and carry out onto abutting surface. Secure lath to joists with 1" galvanized nails or staples to studs, providing minimum 3/4" penetration.

Applying Control Joints

Lath and plaster surfaces will not withstand stresses imposed by structural movement. Additionally, plaster assemblies are subject to dimensional changes caused by fluctuations in temperature and humidity. (See thermal and hygrometric coefficients of expansion in Appendix.) Such surfaces should be isolated from the following structural elements by zinc control joints, casing beads or other means where:

a. A partition or ceiling abuts any structural element other than the floor, a dissimilar wall or partition assembly or other vertical penetration.

b. The construction changes within the plane of a partition, or ceiling and wings of L-, U- and T-shaped ceilings are joined.

In long partition runs, control joints should be provided at maximum 30' o.c. Door frames extending from floor to ceiling may serve as control joints. For less-than-ceiling-height doors, control joints extending from center or both corners of frame to ceiling are effective. If control joints are not used, additional reinforcement is required at corners to distribute concentrated stresses. (Door frame details appear later in this chapter.) In exterior wall furring systems, control joints must be provided at the same locations where control joints in the exterior walls are located, at maximum 30' o.c.

8

Control joints will not accommodate transverse shear displacement on opposing sides of a joint. A joint detail comprising casing beads on each side of the joint opening is typically used to accommodate expansion, contraction and shear. Such joints require special detailing by the designer to control sound and fire ratings, where applicable, as well as dust and air movement. In exterior walls, particular attention is required to resist wind, driving rain, etc., by adequate flashing, backer rod, sealants and gaskets as required.

Large interior ceiling areas with perimeter relief should have control joints spaced at maximum 50' o.c. in either direction; without perimeter relief, 30' o.c. maximum in either direction. The continuity of both lath and plaster must be broken at the control joints. Control joints should be positioned to intersect light fixtures, heating vents, or diffusers, etc., which already break ceiling continuity and are points of stress concentration.

Maximum Spacing—SHEETROCK Brand Control Joints for Interior Plaster Assemblies

System	Location	Max. Single Dimension		Max. Single Area	
		ft.	mm	ft.^{2}	m^2
Metal Lath & Plaster	Partition	30	9144	—	—
	Ceiling	50[1]	15240	2500	230
		30[2]	9144	900	83.6
Gypsum Lath & Plaster	Partition	30	9144	—	—
	Ceiling	50[1]	15240	2500	230
		30[2]	9144	900	83.6

(1) With perimeter relief (2) Without perimeter relief

264

*Sheetrock Brand Control
Joint Nos. 50, 75, 100*

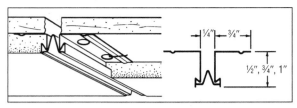

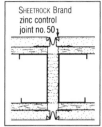

Sheetrock Brand
zinc control
joint no. 50

**Wall control joint
installation**

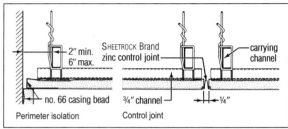

2" min.
6" max.

Sheetrock Brand
zinc control joint

carrying
channel

no. 66 casing bead

¾" channel

¼"

Perimeter isolation

Control joint

Ceiling control joint installation

Installation Provide a break in the lath at location of control joint. Install double framing members—one on each side of the break, and 1/2" to 3/4" apart. Place control joints over all control or relief joints within structural frame of building. Staple or wire tie perforated flanges of control joint to lath. Plaster flush to grounds. Remove factory-applied protective tape after completion of finished surface.

Zinc control joints must be properly insulated or otherwise protected when used in fire-rated assemblies.

Applying Basecoat Plaster

For aesthetically pleasing and durable plaster, certain recommendations should be followed regarding the number of coats applied. Three-coat work is necessary on all metal lath and on edge-supported gypsum lath used in ceilings. Three-coat work is also desirable on all gypsum lath, although two-coat work is acceptable when lath is properly supported and on masonry plaster bases (rough concrete block, clay tile or porous brick).

In preparing for plastering, consider the selection of materials not only for compatibility, but in relation to the quality of the structure to be plastered. It is wise to upgrade plastering specifications when possible.

The "Plaster Product Compatibility Selector" table on page 265 will help you determine which basecoat plaster is appropriate for each possible substrate, and which finish plasters may be used with each basecoat plaster. The table on "Basecoat Plasters for Conventional Plaster Systems" provides a numeric scale comparing the performance of various basecoat plasters over various substrates. The "Basecoat Plaster (Over Metal Lath)" table provides mixing proportions of sand to plaster.

The architect's specifications and the plaster base used will determine the plastering method—either two-coat or three-coat.

Plaster Product Compatibility Selector

Basecoat Plaster	Substrate				Finish Plaster									
	CMU	Mono. Conc.[1]	ML CH-FMG	ML C-Studs	ROCKLATH Plaster Base	RED TOP Finish	STRUCTO-GAUGE/ Lime	Keenes/ Lime	Gauging/ Lime	Keenes/ Lime/ Sand	Gauging/ Lime/ Sand	IMPERIAL Brand Finish	DIAMOND Brand Interior Finish
RED TOP Gypsum Plaster (Lightweight)	√	√	√		√	√	√	√	√	√	√		√
RED TOP Wood Fiber[2] Plaster	√	√	√		√	√	√	√	√	√	√	√	√
STRUCTO-BASE Gypsum Plaster[2]	√	√	√	√	√	√	√	√	√	√	√	√	√
STRUCTO-LITE Gypsum Plaster	√	√	√		√				√[3]	√	√		

Notes: (1) USG Plaster Bonder must first be applied .(2) Job sanded. (3) Red Top Gauging Aggregated/not over metal lath. Monolithic concrete to be treated with USG Plaster Bonder. √= Acceptable

8

Basecoat Plasters for Conventional Plaster Systems

Product	Substrate			Machine Application	Hardness	Productivity
	Metal Lath	Concrete Masonry Unit	Gypsum Lath			
STRUCTO-BASE Gypsum Plaster	1	2	1	yes	1	3
STRUCTO-LITE Gypsum Plaster	4	1	2	yes	4	1
RED TOP Gypsum Plaster	3	3	2	yes	3	3
RED TOP Wood Fiber Plaster	2	2	3	no	2	4

1 = Excellent 2 = Very Good 3 = Good 4 = Acceptable

Basecoat Plaster (Over Metal Lath)

Scratch Coat	Brown Coat
1. STRUCTO-BASE Plaster, sanded 100 lbs. : 2 cu. ft.	STRUCTO-BASE Plaster, sanded 100 lbs. : 3 cu. ft.
2. Wood Fiber, neat, or sanded up to 100 lbs. : 1 cu. ft.	Wood Fiber Plaster, sanded up to 100 lbs. : 1 cu. ft.
3. Wood Fiber, neat, or sanded up to 100 lbs. : 1 cu. ft.	RED TOP Gypsum Plaster, sanded 100 lbs. : 2 cu. ft.
4. RED TOP Gypsum Plaster, sanded 100 lbs. : 2 cu. ft.	RED TOP Gypsum Plaster, sanded 100 lbs. : 3 cu. ft.
5. Wood Fiber, neat, or sanded up to 100 lbs. : 1 cu. ft.	STRUCTO-LITE Plaster (Sand float finish only)
6. Wood Fiber, neat, or sanded 100 lbs. : 1 cu. ft.	RED TOP Gypsum Plaster, perlited 100 lbs. : 2 cu. ft. (sand float finish only)

Two- and Three-Coat Plastering

Two-Coat Plastering with Conventional Plasters Generally accepted for plaster application over gypsum lath and masonry. The basecoat (first) should be applied with sufficient material and pressure to form a good bond to the plaster base and provide full coverage. Then double-back with the same mix to bring plaster out to grounds, straightened to true surface with rod and darby without use of additional water. Leave rough and open to receive the finish coat (second).

Three-Coat Plastering Required over metal lath and edge-supported gypsum lath used in ceilings. It is preferred for other bases because it develops a harder, stronger basecoat. The scratch coat (first) should be applied with sufficient material and pressure to form good full keys on metal lath (and a good bond on other bases), and then cross-raked. The brown coat (second) should be applied after scratch (first) coat has set firm and hard, brought out to grounds and straightened to true surface with rod and darby without use of additional water, and left rough and open to receive the finish coat (third).

To obtain the full hardness, high strength and superior performance available in gypsum basecoat plasters, water, aggregates and setting time must be carefully controlled. In addition, proper mixing and drying of the plaster are required to obtain these superior functional characteristics.

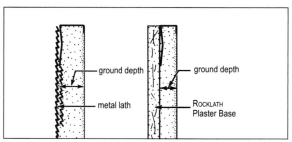

Grounds

Grounds

The thickness of conventional basecoat plaster is one of the most important elements of a good plaster job. To ensure proper thickness, grounds should be properly set and followed.

Grounds may be defined as wooden strips, corner beads (plumbed and aligned) or metal casing beads applied at the perimeter of all openings and other locations.

In addition to these, and especially on walls with no openings and on ceilings, plaster screeds should be installed to ensure plumb and level surfaces. Plaster screeds are continuous strips of plaster, approximately 4" wide, applied either vertically or horizontally and plumb with the finish wall line, allowing for 1/16" finish coat.

Grounds should be set to obtain the following minimum plaster thicknesses:

1.	Over gypsum lath	1/2" (12.7mm)
2.	Over brick, clay tile, or other masonry	5/8" (15.9mm)
3.	Over metal lath, measured from face of lath	5/8" (15.9mm)

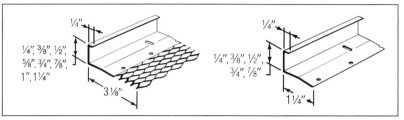

#66 Square Edge Casing Beads
(expanded or short flange)

Mixing

Using the proper type of mechanical mixer will help ensure that the plaster aggregate and water are evenly mixed. Keep the mixer continually clean—an important precaution because partially set material is a powerful accelerator.

Proportioning This refers to weight of gypsum to volume of aggregate. A No. 2 shovel used to add sand to the plaster mix generally carries 15 lb., or approximately one-sixth cubic foot. Thus, a 100:1 mix would use 6 shovels of sand to 100 lb. of gypsum plaster, a 100:2 mix would require 12 to 13 shovels, and a 100:3 mix would use 18 to 19 shovels of sand.

Perlite is generally packaged in bags containing 3 or 4 CF for easy proportioning.

Prepare only one hour's supply of plaster at a time, and do not remix if plaster has started to set. All such plaster should be discarded.

Water All gypsum plasters require adding water. Water should be clean, fresh, suitable for domestic consumption and free from mineral and organic substances, which affect plaster set. Water used earlier for rinsing or cleaning containers and tools should not be used, as this accelerates plaster set.

Only enough water should be added to achieve a workable consistency. Too much water in machine-applied plasters (in excess of 10% more than for hand-applied mixes) or over-aggregated plasters will cause weak, soft walls and ceilings. Excessive water reduces plaster strength and hardness.

Aggregates

Added to conventional gypsum plasters to extend coverage, aggregates reduce shrinkage and help lower cost. Recommended aggregates are: (1) sand, which is denser, stronger and dampens sound transmission better than lightweight aggregates, and (2) perlite, a lightweight aggregate that generally offers better fire resistance, insulation values and reduced weight. For sand-float finishes, the aggregate should be a fine silica sand.

All aggregates should have proper gradation of size as outlined in ASTM C35. Improperly sized aggregates will produce weak walls. Sand should be clean and free of dirt, clay and foreign matter that might affect the setting time of plaster. Perlite-aggregated plasters should not be machine-applied when vertical lift is over 30' or hose length exceeds 150' Maximum recommended proportions for aggregates are shown in following table.

Maximum Aggregate Quantity—Gypsum Plasters

Base	No. Coats[1]	Coat	Under Smooth Trowel Finishes						Under Texture Finishes			
			Sand[2]		Perlite[3]				Sand[2]		Perlite[3]	
			ft.³/ 100 lb.	m³/t		ft.³/ 100 lb.	ft.³/ m³/t		ft.³/ 100 lb.	m³/t	100 lb.	m³/t
Gypsum Lath	3	Scratch	2	1.24		2	1.24		2	1.24	2	1.24
		Brown	3	1.86		2	1.24		3	1.86	3[4]	1.86[4]
	2	Basecoat[5]	2.5	1.55		2	1.24		2.5	1.55	2	1.24
Metal Lath	3	Scratch	2	1.24		—	—		2	1.24	2	1.24
		Brown	3	1.86		—	—		3	1.86	2	1.24
Unit Masonry	3	Scratch	3	1.86		3	1.86		3	1.86	3	1.86
		Brown	3	1.86		3	1.86		3	1.86	3	1.86
	2	Basecoat[5]	3	1.86		3	1.86		3	1.86	3	1.86

(1) Includes finish coat. (2) Approx. 6 No. 2 shovels of sand equal 1 cu. ft. (0.028 m³). (3) In a construction with metal lath as the plaster base, perlite aggregate is not recommended for use in the basecoat plaster, except under a float finish. For a smooth trowel finish over a perlite aggregated basecoat on any plaster base except metal lath, add 1/2 ft.³ of fine silica sand per 100 lb. of gauging plaster, or use aggregated gauging. (4) Only if applied 1″ thick, otherwise 2 ft.³. (5) Basecoat applied scratch and double-back.

Setting Time

The proper setting time for conventional basecoat plasters is generally from 2 to 4 hours after mixing, and this should be checked for close conformity on both the scratch coat and brown coat operations. Normally, plaster shipped to the job will fall in this range. If conditions exist that affect normal setting time, retarders or accelerators may be used.

Retarders The danger of "quick set" plaster is insufficient time to get the plaster from mixer to walls without retempering on mortar board. Retempering will produce a plaster of lower than normal strength. The correction for "quick set" is to add the minimum required amount of retarder in solution with water in the mixer.

Mix a trial batch of formulated product, and determine the set time. Once the set time is known, a measured amount of USG retarder and water mixture can be added to adjust the set. Any available container (wax cup, coffee can, measuring cup, etc.) can be used to measure the retarder/water mixture. Keeping mixing equipment clean between batches helps prevent quick-setting action in subsequent mixes.

Retarder selection will depend on the length of time extension required to handle the job appropriately, and the type of plaster used. USG standard strength retarder is recommended for slight to moderate lengthening of set times and can be used with conventional and veneer plasters. Mix one teaspoon of dry USG standard strength retarder with 5 oz. water to extend the set time of a 100-lb. batch of gypsum plaster by 30–40 minutes or more.

USG high strength retarder is recommended to extend setting times 2 hours or more and is especially suitable for conventional gypsum plasters where machine application set time alteration is required. Mix one teaspoon of dry USG high strength retarder with 5 oz. water to extend the set time of a 100-lb. batch of conventional gypsum plaster by 1–3 hours.

For larger quantities, premix 1 lb. of retarder to 2 gallons of water. Stir to make sure retarder is completely dispersed. Screen out any lumps that may have formed, as they will cause soft discolored spots in the plaster surface. Note that retarder is dispersed in the water, not dissolved. Stir thoroughly before each use.

USG Retarder for Lime Containing Plaster Products is used with such plasters as DIAMOND veneer finish, RED TOP finish and gauging/lime finishes. This retarder may be added directly to the mixing water prior to addition of plaster. As little is 1/4 to 1/2 teaspoon per 50-lb. bag of lime-containing plaster will extend setting time by 20 minutes.

8

Accelerators If plaster does not set for 5 to 6 hours, no harm will be done to the resulting plaster surfaces. However, a "slow set" of plaster (generally taking more than 6 hours) should be avoided by adding accelerator directly to the mixer. Otherwise, the plaster may be subject to a "dry out," particularly in hot, dry weather, and will have a lower than normal strength when finally set. A choice of accelerators is available depending on the degree of acceleration required and the type of plaster being used.

USG standard strength gypsum plaster accelerator is used to slightly modify setting times of veneer and conventional plasters. To maximize the ability of the accelerator, sprinkle 4 oz. of USG standard strength gypsum plaster accelerator in dry form into the mixer for each bag of product after the plaster has been added. This amount of accelerator will reduce set time by 30 minutes.

USG high strength gypsum accelerator is used to reduce setting time of conventional basecoat plaster by 1-1/2 to 2 hours. For best results, sprinkle 2 oz. of USG high strength gypsum accelerator in dry form into the mixer for each bag of product after the plaster has been added.

USG Accelerator—Alum Catalyst is used to correct "dry out" conditions. Accelerating the set of the plaster surface eliminates dry-out shrinkage fissures that occur when the material dries faster than the normal setting time. Another method is fog-spraying the plaster with water from a garden hose to saturate the plaster, and then floating the surface with a wooden float to fill in any already formed fissures.

However, the alum catalyst accelerator can help avert the problem. Mix 1/2 to 1 lb. of USG accelerator—alum catalyst into 3 gallons of water in a garden sprayer. Spray the solution onto the damp plaster surface. Apply it in combination with rewetting to quicken the set time and prevent recurring dry out.

Heating and Ventilation

Plaster must not be applied to surfaces that contain frost. A minimum temperature of 55°F should be maintained for an adequate period to equalize surface temperature prior to, during, and after application of plaster. In cold, damp or rainy weather, properly regulated heat should be provided, but precautions must be taken against rapid drying before set has occurred. This prevents "dry outs."

As soon as set occurs in conventional plasters, free circulation of air should be provided to carry off excess moisture. Heating should be continued to ensure as rapid drying as possible. In hot, dry weather, protect plaster from wind and from drying unevenly or too rapidly before set has taken place. If windows or curtain walls are not in place, exterior openings in the building should be screened.

Applying Finish Plaster

Finish plasters applied to basecoats ready the surface for final wall or ceiling decoration. Finish coats should be applied only to properly prepared basecoats that are rough, open and partially dry.

Trowel Finishes Use this method when a smooth, easily maintained surface is desired, often as a base for paint or wall coverings. The degree of hardness, porosity and polish is determined by the materials and application techniques used. When a smooth-trowel gauged lime putty finish is used over a basecoat containing lightweight aggregate on any plaster base except metal lath, three options are available: 1) add at least 50 lb. of fine silica sand, 2) add 1/2 cu. ft. of perlite fines per 100 lb. of gauging plaster, or 3) use Red Top gauging aggregated.

Trowel finish   *Float finish*   *Spray finish*   *Texture finish*

Finish Plasters for Conventional Plaster Systems

		Easy to Achieve Smooth Surface	Surface Hardness	Productivity	Texture Capability	
					Unsanded	Sanded
Veneer plaster finishes over conventional basecoat	IMPERIAL Veneer Finish*	4	1	4	3	2
	DIAMOND Veneer Finish*	3	3	2	3	2
Lime-gauging finishes over veneer basecoat or conventional basecoat	IVORY/SNOWDRIFT/GRAND PRIZE Finish Lime and STRUCTO-GAUGE Gauging Plaster*	2	3	2	4	2
	RED TOP Finish*	1	4	1	4	2
	Lime–Keenes Cement (Smooth)*	2	3	3	4	N/A
	Lime–Sand-Keenes Cement (Texture)	N/A	3	2	N/A	1
	IVORY/SNOWDRIFT/GRAND PRIZE Lime Finish and RED TOP Gauging Plaster	1	4	3	4	2

*Not recommended for use over lightweight aggregate basecoats.
1 = Excellent 2 = Very Good 3 = Good 4 = Acceptable N/A = Not Applicable

Application To avoid blistering, allow basecoat to dry sufficiently, or use a quick-set gauging plaster. Mix a 50-lb. bag of IVORY or SNOWDRIFT lime with 5-1/2 to 6 gallons of water. Machine-mix for immediate use. For a medium-hard finish, mix 100 lb. STRUCTO-GAUGE plaster or 200 lb. RED TOP gauging plaster to each 200 lb. dry lime (approx. 400 lb. putty). For an extremely hard finish, mix one part STRUCTO-GAUGE Plaster to one part lime.

Scratch in thoroughly, and then immediately double-back to a thickness of not more than 1/16" and trowel to a smooth, dense surface ready for decoration.

Float or Spray Texture Finishes These methods provide attractive, durable finishes where surface textures are desired and are recommended for use over all types of gypsum basecoats. They are the most desirable finishes from the standpoint of crack resistance. The surface texture is easily controlled and can be produced by spray application, or a variety of hand tools.

Application, Sand Float Finish Machine-mix finish in proportion of 100 lb. RED TOP Keenes Cement, 200 lb. lime, approximately 400–800 lb. sand and water to produce a mixture with smooth, plastic consistency.

Scratch in thoroughly over dry basecoat, then immediately double-back to a thickness of not more than 1/8". Hand float to produce a uniform texture free of blemishes. Use water sparingly during floating.

Application, Machine Spray Texture Finish Acceptable finishes can be achieved using either a hand-held hopper gun or other machines specifically designed for spray-applying plaster.

The aggregate size, number of passes over the surface, air pressure and nozzle orifice can be varied to achieve the desired texture. It is best to spray first in one direction and then in another direction, crossing the first path at right angles.

8

Before beginning to spray, test the pattern and make any necessary adjustments to achieve the desired appearance. There are many things that affect the pattern, including the following:

1. **Orifice Size** The smaller the orifice or nozzle tip, the finer the spray.

2. **Air Pressure** If no other changes are made, the higher the air pressure, the finer the spray.

3. **Liquid State** The liquid state of the material should be similar to medium/thick cream, achieved by adding water to the regular mix until it reaches the desired consistency. It is good practice to pass the mix through a screen that will trap all particles larger than the aggregate being sprayed.

The basecoat must be free of ridges or other surface imperfections. Spraying texture finish directly onto it is not normally recommended. The preferred method is to hand-apply a scratch coat before spray-applying finish. Finish materials for this method include gauging plaster (either regular or high-strength), Keenes cement job mixed with lime and silica sand or various single component prepared finishes designated for two-component systems.

With finish coat material mixed for hand application, apply a well ground-in scratch coat over properly set and partially dry brown coat. After scratch coat is applied, double back with sufficient material to cover the basecoat completely. When the surface start to become firm, float it to a uniform, blemish-free flat texture. After scratch and double-back set, and while material is in a wet state, spray material should be prepared using the same proportions as the finish material and mixed to proper fluidity for achieving the final texture finish. Spray texture to a uniform thickness and appearance.

Other Texture Finishes Many pleasing and distinctive textures are possible using various techniques in finishing. Finishes may range from an extremely fine stipple to a rough, heavy or coarse texture. Variety is limited only by the imagination of the designer or the ingenuity of the applicator.

Finish Plaster Limitations Certain precautions must be taken when applying finish coat plasters over various basecoats:

1. A smooth-trowel finish should not be used over lightweight aggregate gypsum basecoat applied over metal lath. A sand-float finish is recommended.

2. Where the gypsum basecoat over any plaster base (except metal lath) is STRUCTO-LITE or contains lightweight aggregate, and a smooth-trowel finish is used, the finish coat should be RED TOP gauging plaster and lime, with the addition of 1/2 cu. ft. of perlite fines or 50 lb. of No. 1 white silica sand per 100 lb. gauging plaster or RED TOP gauging aggregated.

3. Gypsum or lime-base finishes, including Keenes cement, should not be applied directly over a Portland cement basecoat, concrete block or other masonry surfaces.

4. In smooth trowel finishes, gauging plasters that provides an extremely hard surface, such as STRUCTO-GAUGE and Keenes cement, must not be used over STRUCTO-LITE Plaster or a basecoat with a lightweight aggregate.

5. Lime putty cannot be used without the addition of gauging plasters. When used alone as a finish plaster, lime does not set, is subject to shrinkage when drying and lacks hard finish.

Gauging Plasters

RED TOP **Gauging Plasters** Gauging plaster is blended into the lime putty in the proper proportions to provide controlled set, early hardness and strength, and to prevent shrinkage cracks. (See following pages for full description.)

Mixing Add gauging plaster to lime putty in proportion of 1 part dry gauging plaster by weight to 2 parts dry lime by weight, or 1 part dry gauging by volume to 3 parts lime putty by volume. To mix, form a ring of lime putty on mixing board. The volume of putty used depends on wall or ceiling area to be covered. A hod of lime putty weighs approximately 100 lb., and a 12-qt. bucket of lime putty about 35 lb. (50 lb. dry lime equals 100 lb. lime putty). After forming the putty ring, pour clean water into center of ring in correct proportions: 6 qt. water to 100 lb. lime putty; 2 qt. water to each 12-qt. bucket of lime putty. Next, sift slow or quick-set gauging plaster into water; 25 lb. gauging plaster to one hod of lime putty. Thoroughly wet gauging plaster and blend materials thoroughly to prevent gauging "streaks" and provide uniform density.

8

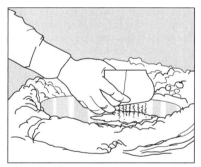
Sift gauging plaster into water

Mix to blend thoroughly

To protect against finish coat check or map-cracking, add 1/2 cu. ft. perlite fines or 50 lb. fine silica sand to every 100 lb. of gauging used. This addition is necessary when applying smooth troweled finishes over lightweight aggregate basecoats. RED TOP gauging aggregated plaster is generally available and eliminates the need for on-the-job measuring.

Application Apply the gauged lime putty over a partially dry basecoat. Scratch in a thin coat, well ground into the basecoat, and double-back with a second coat, filling imperfections. After basecoat has absorbed most of excess water from finish, trowel to densify surface. As final set takes place, water-trowel surface to provide a dense, smooth surface.

STRUCTO-GAUGE Gauging Plaster This high-strength gypsum finishing plaster is used with lime putty to produce an easily applied finish of extreme hardness.

Finish hardness may be altered by adjusting the proportions of lime putty and STRUCTO-GAUGE plaster. Since the material cannot be retempered, using regular Keenes cement is recommended when retempering is a factor. STRUCTO-GAUGE plaster is not recommended where excessive or continued moisture conditions exist. Application must be over high-strength sanded or wood-fibered gypsum basecoats.

Mixing For a hard finish, mix proportions of 100 lb. dry hydrated lime (200 lb. of lime putty) to 100 lb. STRUCTO-GAUGE plaster. For a medium-hard finish, mix proportions of 200 lb. dry hydrated lime (400 lb. of lime putty) to 100 lb. STRUCTO-GAUGE plaster. For best results, machine-mix.

Application Apply like regular finish over partially dried gypsum basecoat. Scratch in thin coat, well ground into base, and immediately double-back with second coat, filling imperfections. Water-trowel to a smooth, hard finish, free of blemishes. Continue to trowel until final set. Clean tools and equipment after each mix.

RED TOP Keenes Cement A high-strength white gypsum plaster used with finish lime putty for extremely hard, dense surfaces. It is the only gypsum plaster that can be retempered. This product has a 3-6 hour set. As with all gypsum plasters, RED TOP Keenes cement is intended for interior use only.

Keenes Cement-Lime Finish is similar in many respects to a lime gauged finish except that Keenes (instead of gauging plaster) is used in varying proportions depending on the hardness required and is generally used as a float finish. If a smooth-trowel hard finish is desired, use STRUCTO-GAUGE gauging plaster. Keenes cement is for interior use over sanded or wood-fibered gypsum basecoats. Do not apply smooth-trowel finish over lightweight aggregate basecoats.

Application, Sand Float Finish A commonly used hard float finish that may be satisfactorily colored. Mix in proportions of 100 lb. Keenes Cement to 200 lb. dry lime and 400–800 lb. sand, with or without lime-proof colors. Apply in same manner as for Keenes Cement-Lime Finish, but instead of final troweling, use a wood, cork, sponge or felt-covered float to bring sand particles to surface to produce a pleasing, durable sand finish.

Application, Keenes Cement-Lime Finish For medium hard finish, mix proportion of 200 lb. lime putty (100 lb. of dry hydrated lime) to 50 lb. Keenes Cement. For a hard finish, use 200 lb. lime putty (100 lb. dry hydrated lime) to 100 lb. Keenes Cement. Apply finish coat over a set high-strength basecoat that has been broomed and is partially dry. Spray with water if surface is too dry, but do not soak. Scratch in thin coat, and then double-back with a second coat to a true surface. Trowel with water to a smooth, glossy finish, free from blemishes, until finish has set.

(See Chapter 7, "Conventional Plaster Products," for lime-gauging ratios and coverage.)

Gauging Plasters—Technical Data

	Set Time with Lime Putty Product (min.)
RED TOP Gauging	slow set 50-75 / quick set 30-40
RED TOP Gauging Aggregated	40-60
RED TOP Keenes Cement	regular 180-360 / quick set 60-120
STRUCTO-GAUGE	slow set 60-75./ quick set 30-40

Finish Limes

The two types of finish lime are: (1) Type S (also called autoclaved, pressure or double hydrate), and (2) Type N (also called normal or single hydrate). Both produce a good finish lime putty, but their preparation differs. The following are important weather precautions.

Cold Weather Where the weather and available water are cold, lime develops better plasticity when soaked overnight. Best conditions are a warm room and water temperature above 50° F.

It is important to note that in cold weather, the lime putty-gauging mixture requires a longer time to set. Therefore, gauging content should be increased or quick-set added to offset the slower setting time.

Proper heat and ventilation are extremely important. Windows should be opened slightly so that moisture-bearing air moves out of the building. Fast drying after setting is essential to a hard finish.

Many cold-weather problems with finish lime are a direct result of improper basecoat conditions. Finish should go over a set, fairly dry basecoat. The basecoat will dry slowly in winter, so heat and ventilation are needed. The water retentivity of lime putty, plus a cold, "green" base, does not provide enough suction to remove excess moisture. Blistering and cracking can occur due to slow set.

Hot Weather Putty should be properly soaked. In direct, hot sunlight, hydrated lime requires 1/2 to 1 gallon more water per 50 lb. Water should be kept cool. Soaking putty in the shade prevents undue water evaporation and helps to prevent curdling and loss of spreading properties. Avoid soaking for periods longer than two or three days.

For application of lime putty-gauging finish plaster, make sure that the basecoat is set and partially dry. If applied over a dried-out basecoat, water will be drawn from the finish coat, resulting in severe check-cracking. Spray the basecoat before applying the finish coat, and trowel coat until final set.

IVORY and SNOWDRIFT Finish Lime Autoclaved (double-hydrate)

Mixing Machine equipment must be clean. Place 5-1/2 to 6 gallons of potable water per 50-lb. bag of lime in mixer. Using a motor-driven, propeller-type mixer, the complete mixing of lime putty takes 2 to 3 minutes and results in a high-quality, easy-working putty. Machine-mixed putty is plastic, and coverage is increased from 10% to 15%. With a paddle-type mixer, the mixing time is about 15 minutes.

8

Hand Mixing—For immediate use, place 5-1/2 to 6 gallons of water per 50 lb. of Ivory or Snowdrift Finish Lime in mixing box. Add finish lime to water, and hoe sufficiently to eliminate lumps. Screen putty through 8-mesh screen before using.

Overnight Soak—Place water hose in bottom of a level soaking box. Sift lime through screen into box. When full, run water slowly, but continuously, until a small amount of excess water is visible over top of lime. If excess water remains on the surface the following morning, absorb it by screening in additional Ivory or Snowdrift Lime. Allow to soak a few minutes, and then blend into putty by hoeing. If necessary, screen through 8-mesh hardware cloth and mix with gauging plaster that meets job requirement.

Application—follows directions for gauging plasters.

Red Top and Grand Prize Finish Limes Single or Normal Hydrate

Machine Mixing Produces a smoother, more plastic putty, easier to use and with better coverage. Use approximately 6 gallons of water to each 50-lb. bag of Red Top or Grand Prize Finish Lime.

Hand Mixing—Slowly sift Red Top or Champion® Lime into water in soaking box. Allow material to take up water for about 20 or 30 minutes, and then hoe briskly to mix thoroughly.

Let mix soak for at least 16 hours to develop full workability and plasticity. For use, screen through 8-mesh hardware cloth and mix with gauging plaster that meets job requirements. Application follows directions for gauging plasters.

Prepared Finishes

USG offers several prepared finishes. Imperial veneer finish, Diamond veneer finish and Red Top finish all shorten construction time and provide hard, abrasion-resistant surfaces. The type of plaster finish used will depend to a large degree on the level of abuse resistance required from the final assembly. (See Appendix for categories of abuse resistance.)

Allow basecoat plaster to set but not completely dry before applying prepared finishes. If basecoat plaster has fully dried, complete misting of the surface is required before applying finish.

Mixing Prepared finishes require the addition of water on the job. Water should be clean, fresh, suitable for human consumption and free from mineral and organic substances that may affect the plaster set. Water used for rinsing or cleaning is not suitable for mixing because it accelerates the plaster set.

Mechanical mixing is mandatory for prepared finishes. Mix no more material than can be applied before set begins. Since prepared finishes set more rapidly than most conventional plasters, always consult package directions for specific setting times. Prepared finishes will produce mortar of maximum performance and workability when the correct equipment is used and mixing directions are carefully followed. Proper mixing is one of the most important factors in producing mortar of maximum workability.

Use a cage-type mixer paddle driven by a heavy-duty 1/2" electric drill with a no-load rating of 900–1,000 rpm. Do not use a propeller-type paddle or conventional mortar mixer. (For details on the cage-type mixing paddle and available electric drills, see pages 425-426 or PM 9, *Mixing Veneer Plasters and Equipment*.)

Mix plaster in 16- or 30-gallon smooth-sided container strong enough to withstand impacts that could cause gouging. Do not use brittle containers for mixing.

Correct Mixing　Rapid mixing with high shear action is essential for proper dispersion of plaster ingredients. Slow mixing can reduce plasticity of the material. Overmixing can shorten working time. Operated at correct speed, the cage-type design paddle mixes thoroughly without introducing excess air into the mix.

IMPERIAL **Veneer Finish**　Scratch in a tight, thin coat of IMPERIAL Veneer Finish over the entire area, immediately doubling back with plaster from the same batch to full thickness of 1/16" to 3/32". Fill all voids and imperfections. Final trowel after surface has become firm, holding trowel flat and using water sparingly. Do not over-trowel.

Best results for IMPERIAL veneer finish are obtained by planning the plastering to permit continuous application from angle to angle. Where joining is unavoidable, use trowel to terminate unset plaster in sharp, clean edge—do not feather out. Bring adjacent plaster up to terminated edge and leave level. Do not overlap. During finish troweling, use excess material to fill and bridge joining.

DIAMOND **Veneer Finish**　Scratch in a tight, thin coat of DIAMOND veneer finish plaster over the entire area, immediately doubling back with plaster from the same batch to full thickness of 1/16" to 3/32". Fill all voids and imperfections. Final trowel after surface has become firm, holding trowel flat and using water sparingly. Do not over-trowel.

A variety of textures ranging from sand float to Spanish can be achieved with DIAMOND veneer finish when job-aggregated with silica sand. (When DIAMOND veneer finish is job-aggregated, one tablespoon of cream of tartar or 1/4 teaspoon of USG Retarder for lime-containing plaster products should be added for each bag of finish to retard plaster and allow sufficient working time.) Application is the same as for neat DIAMOND veneer finish except that once the surface has been leveled and sufficient take-up has occurred, begin floating material from the same batch with trowel, float, sponge or by other accepted local techniques.

DIAMOND veneer finish also may be textured by skip troweling. When applying in this manner, eliminate final troweling. When surface has become sufficiently firm, texture with material from the same batch prior to set.

RED TOP **Finish Plaster**　Scratch in a tight, thin coat of RED TOP finish plaster over entire area, immediately doubling back with plaster from the same batch to full thickness of not more than 1/16". Final trowel to a smooth, dense surface ready for decoration.

8

Ornamental Plasters

Ornamental plasters are used to add decorative treatments such as crown molding, rails, lintels and wall and ceiling details. These features are often screeded in place. More intricate forms are molded, either on the job site or at an off-site location where the forms may be better controlled. In the latter case, the formed pieces are later mounted in place.

Special Additives

USG offers a number of special additives to improve plaster bond or enhance its abuse resistance or performance characteristics. Among those additives are USG Plaster Bonder and USG Acri-Add 100% Acrylic Add-Mix Fortifier.

USG Plaster Bonder is a vinyl acetate homopolymer emulsion that helps bond new plaster to virtually any structurally sound interior surface. Structurally sound surfaces should be clean and free from loose material, dust, dirt, oil, grease, wax, loose paint, mildew, rust or efflorescence. Glossy painted surfaces should be dulled by an abrasive, and adjacent surfaces should be protected using masking tape, soap powder emulsion or other commercially available protective product. Bonder should be hand stirred and applied as is with brush, roller or spray.

USG Acri-Add 100% acrylic add-mix fortifier is an additive that improves bond strength, water resistance, shrink/crack resistance and durability of gypsum or cement-based plaster products. Mix USG Acri-Add with water at a ratio of 1:3, 1:2 or 1:1 and substitute for water in mix of plaster material depending on end use. May be used as an additive for plaster patching, setting-type joint compound patching, mortar and grout fortification, and cement patching. Especially useful in areas subject to vibration and heavy traffic.

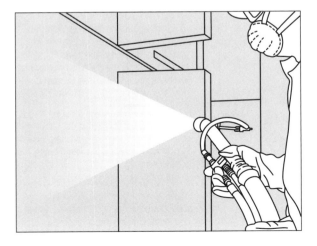

Sound-Absorbing Plaster Finish

**USG Acoustical
Plaster Finish**

Mixing Read mixing and spray application directions completely before proceeding with mixing. Use a 7 cu. ft. or larger paddle-type plaster mixer with rubber-tipped blades (anchor mixer) or a self-contained integral mixing/pumping spray texture tank with horizontal shaft and plaster or texture rig-type paddles mounted on a horizontal shaft. To ensure uniform product performance, mix a minimum of two bags. Add powder to clean, room-temperature water in quantity specified on bag. Mix for approximately 5 minutes until consistency is lump-free, thick and foamy. (Initial mix will appear dry and heavy).

Note: If material is over-mixed, excessive foam will occur. Add more powder to break down foam, and remix until proper foam level is reached. Additional mixing may be necessary during application to maintain foam consistency. Use wet-mixed material within 3–4 hours.

Spray Application All pumps and hoses must be cleaned initially with water followed by approximately one gallon of SHEETROCK brand Ready-Mixed Joint Compound prior to spray application to prevent severe aggregate separation or clogging by the clean-out water.

For combined mixing/pumping units: Initially fill mixing hopper with necessary water to flush hoses. Pump all water from hopper, then drop joint compound into material reservoir of pump. Start pumping until compound feeds into hose. Immediately stop pump. Add water and powder in mixing hopper following mixing directions. When USG Acoustical Plaster Finish is properly mixed, pump out and discard joint compound. Turn on atomizing air, material valve and pump (in that order).

8

For pump units only: Add previously mixed finish to material hopper after pumping joint compound into hose. Then follow the start-up procedure as stated for combined mixing/pumping units.

Recommended spray pattern is 1-1/2' to 3' in diameter. The spray gun should be held 2' to 4' from the surface, depending on material density and atomizer pressure. Apply USG Acoustical Plaster Finish evenly, holding pole gun perpendicular to the surface being sprayed and slowly waving it from side to side until area is covered. Then immediately double back, crosshatching prior coat. Repeat same procedure as necessary until desired thickness is reached.

Elimination of spray lines and section seams is essential in producing an acceptable finish. Do not spray a portion of a ceiling in one day and the final portion on another day as a noticeable seam will result. If entire ceiling area cannot be sprayed to the final thickness in one day, spray the entire surface with a material coat of uniform thickness (minimum 1/4"). Complete to final thickness the following day using a cross-hatch application. Use natural breaks and boundaries to "frame" pattern edges and conceal seams. To measure average thickness, mark desired thickness on a blunt-tipped object (head of pencil or finishing nail) and insert into finish.

USG Acoustical Plaster Finish absorbs sound and gives dramatic appeal to ceilings and other noncontact surfaces.

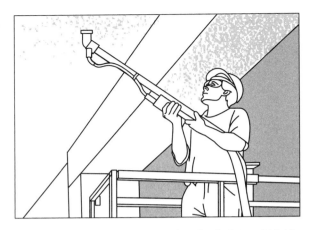

For a different surface color, use a good quality, flat latex paint (white or pastel) and spray apply over dried finish. There will be a minimal loss in NRC value. (For additional information, see Chapter 15, "Building Sciences.")

For additional information, see P720 and PM15.

Replastering Old Plaster Surfaces

In plastering over old plaster surfaces, certain precautions should be exercised to ensure a satisfactory result. Often, the old surface is lime mortar plaster on wood lath, is badly cracked, and usually has been covered with canvas and/or multiple coats of paint.

The following suggestions for lathing and plastering over such old surfaces are listed in order of preference for best results:

1. If the old plaster and lath are removed, 3/8" ROCKLATH plaster base may be applied to the framing and plastered in the same manner as for new work, following all applicable specifications.

2. If the old lath and plaster are left in place, the following methods may be used, after determining that the framing is of adequate size to carry the additional weight of a new plaster finish (average 8 lb./ft.2).

   (a) Apply 1" x 3" furring strips 16" o.c. with 9-ga. nails, 3-1/4" long or of sufficient length to achieve 1-3/4" min. penetration into framing. Then apply 3/8" ROCKLATH base and plaster in same manner as specified for new work.

   (b) Apply 3.4-lb. self-furring Diamond mesh metal lath over old surface by nailing through into framing, using 2" 11-ga. 7/16"-head barbed-shank galvanized roofing nails, 6" o.c. Wire tie side and end laps. Apply plaster in three coats. RED TOP gypsum plaster can be used with max. 2 cu. ft. of sand for scratch coat, max. 3 cu. ft. of sand for brown coat, or with 2-1/2 cu. ft. of sand for scratch and brown coats. Lightweight aggregate should not be used in replastering when using metal lath.

3. If the old plaster is removed and wood lath left in place, all loose laths should be renailed and the lath repeatedly sprayed with water over a period of several hours in order to wet thoroughly. Then replaster as specified in 2(b). Note: If wood lath is not thoroughly nailed and wetted, cracking of the plaster may occur. Finish coat may be smooth trowel or sand float, as desired, mixed and applied per applicable specifications.

(See also reference PM19.)

Door Frames

Hollow metal door frames are shop-fabricated of 16-ga. and 18-ga. primed steel. Floor anchor plates of 16-ga. steel, with two anchor holes to prevent rotation, are welded to trim flanges to dampen door impact vibrations. Jamb anchor clips should be formed of 18-ga. steel, welded in the jamb and head.

Frames used with various plaster systems must be rigidly secured to the floor and partition construction to prevent twisting or other movement. If door frames are free to twist upon impact, cracking of plaster will result and eventually the frames will loosen. In addition to the framing specifications described, door closers are recommended on all oversize doors where the weight, including hardware, is over 50 lb.

8

Grouting of Door Frames   May be required where heavy or oversize doors are used. Check with door manufacturer for their requirements. As a grout, use a 1:2 RED TOP gypsum plaster-sand mix, adding enough water so that the material is stiff but workable. Provide adequate ventilation to allow grout to dry.

Under no condition should the lath and plaster terminate against the trim of the door frame. Grouting of exterior door frames with gypsum plasters is not recommended.

Door frame

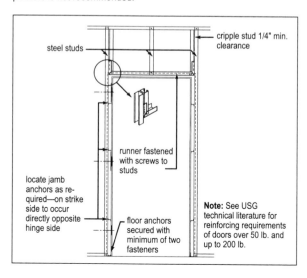

steel studs

cripple stud 1/4" min. clearance

runner fastened with screws to studs

locate jamb anchors as required—on strike side to occur directly opposite hinge side

floor anchors secured with minimum of two fasteners

Note: See USG technical literature for reinforcing requirements of doors over 50 lb. and up to 200 lb.

Elevation cross section

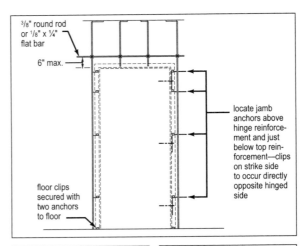

3/8" round rod or 1/8" x 1/4" flat bar

6" max.

floor clips secured with two anchors to floor

locate jamb anchors above hinge reinforcement and just below top reinforcement—clips on strike side to occur directly opposite hinged side

Jamb details

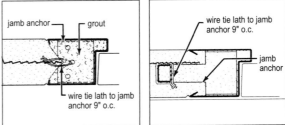

jamb anchor — grout

wire tie lath to jamb anchor 9" o.c.

wire tie lath to jamb anchor 9" o.c.

jamb anchor

Control Joints Also help prevent cracking of plaster at door frames. To break continuity of framing for control joint location, install door frame and place friction-fit cripple studs next to frame uprights. Allow 1/4" clearance for Zinc Control Joints Nos. 50, 75 and 100. Continue with plaster base application using required control joint at break in framing above door frame.

Door Frames with Studless Metal Lath Partitions Follow general directions for fabricating door frames. Use four jamb anchors on each jamb and wire tie to support frame. Use temporary bracing to hold frame until plaster has set.

Door Frames with Stud-Metal Lath Solid Partitions Fabricate as previously described with four jamb anchors welded to trim returns. Anchor frame to floor with power-driven fasteners.

Insert studs into steel door frame. Nest studs in notches of jamb anchor clips and wire tie. Install a 3/8" round rod or a 1/8" x 1-1/4" flat bar across head of door, extending to engage first stud beyond frame. Wire tie bar at each channel intersection.

Grout steel door frames solid with mortar when scratch coat of plaster is applied.

Caulking Procedures

Where a plaster partition is used as a sound barrier, SHEETROCK brand acoustical sealant should be used to seal all cutouts and all intersections with the adjoining structure. Caulking at runners and around the partition perimeter between gypsum lath and/or plaster and the structure is required to achieve sound transmission class (STC) values on the job that approximate those determined by test. Caulking has proven to be the least expensive way to obtain better sound control.

The surfaces to be caulked should be clean, dry and free of all foreign matter. Using an air-pressure-activated or hand caulking gun, apply SHEETROCK brand acoustical sealant in beads about 3/8" round.

Partition Perimeters When gypsum lath is used, leave a space approx. 1/4" wide between lath and floor, ceiling and dissimilar walls. Appropriate metal edge-trim or casing beads applied to the lath may be used to create this space. Fill space with SHEETROCK brand acoustical sealant.

When conventional plaster is applied to metal lath, rake out plaster to form a 3/8" groove at partition perimeter, and fill groove with acoustical sealant. Finish over groove with base or trim as desired.

Openings Apply a 3/8" minimum round bead of acoustical sealant around all cutouts such as at electrical boxes, medicine cabinets, heating ducts and cold air returns to seal the opening.

Electrical Fixtures Apply caulking to the backs of electrical boxes and around all boxes to seal the cutout. Avoid cutting holes back to back and adjacent to each other. Electrical boxes having a plaster ring or device cover for use as a stop for caulking are recommended.

8

Outlet box caulked with SHEETROCK brand acoustical sealant

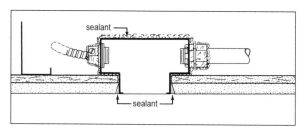

sealant

sealant

Fixture Attachment

Plaster partitions provide suitable anchorage for most types of fixtures normally found in residential and commercial construction. To ensure satisfactory job performance, evaluation of load requirements of unusual or heavy fixtures and preconstruction planning are needed so that attachments will be within the load-carrying capacity of the construction.

The carrying capacity of a given attachment depends upon the strength of the plaster used. Plaster having a compressive strength of at least 900 lb./sq.in. was used to develop the data shown in the Fixture Attachment Load Table on page 493 in the Appendix.

The attachment of fixtures to sound-barrier partitions may impair the sound-control characteristics desired. Refrain from attaching fixtures to party walls so as to avoid a direct path for sound flow. Plastered ceilings are not designed to support light fixtures or troffers, air vents or other equipment. Separate supports should be provided.

In wood-frame construction, fixtures are usually attached directly to the framing or to blocking supports attached to the framing. Blocking or supports should be provided for plumbing fixtures, towel racks, grab bars and similar items. Lath and plaster membranes are not designed to support loads imposed by these items without additional support to carry the main part of the load.

To provide information for proper construction, an investigation of loading capacities of various fasteners and fixture attachments used with plaster partitions was conducted at the USG Research & Technology Center. These fasteners and attachments were tested:

Picture Hooks   A flattened wire hook attached to the wall with a nail driven diagonally downward. Depending on size, the capacity varies from 5 to 50 lbs. per hook. Suitable for hanging pictures, mirrors and other lightweight fixtures from all plaster partitions.

Fiber and Plastic Expansion Plugs   A sheet metal or wood screw driven into a fiber or plastic plug. Annular ribs are provided on outside of plastic plug to assure a positive grip in wall. As screw is inserted, rear end of plug expands and holds assembly in place. Suitable for attaching lightweight fixtures in all partitions (see below).

Fixture attachments

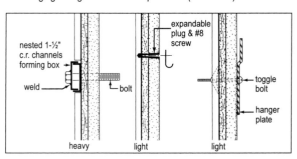

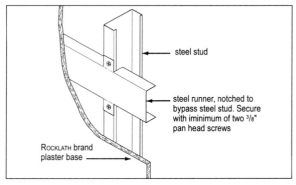

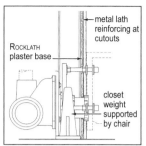

Closet carrier

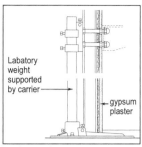

Lavatory carrier

Toggle Bolts Installed in lath and plaster only. Disadvantages of toggle bolt are that when bolt is removed, wing fastener on back will fall down into a hollow wall and a large hole is required to allow wings to pass through wall facings (see page 284 for detail).

Hollow Wall Fasteners Installed in lath and plaster only. One advantage of this type fastener is that threaded section remains in wall when screw is removed. Also, widespread spider support formed by the expanded anchor spreads load against wall material, increasing load capacity.

Bolts and 1-1/2" Channels Two 5/16" bolts welded to 1" channels for use in mounting hanger brackets for heavy fixtures. Two nested channels are securely attached to back of studs in steel-framed partitions (see page 284 for detail).

Angle Brackets Standard 10" x 12" shelving brackets spaced 24" o.c. and fastened to wall with three-hole anchorage. Fastened to steel studs with sheet metal screws or to lath and plaster with toggle bolts or hollow wall fasteners.

Continuous Horizontal Bracing Back-up for fixture attachment is provided with notched runner attached to steel studs with two 3/8" pan head screws (see page 284 for detail).

Slotted Standards With adjustable shelf brackets, are fastened 24" o.c. to steel studs with sheet metal screws or to lath and plaster with toggle bolts or hollow wall fasteners. Normal standard spacing: 24" o.c. for 24" stud spacing, and 32" o.c. for 16" stud spacing. Limited to six shelves per partition height.

Separate Supports Individual carriers or chairs placed in the core wall, recommended where heavy bathroom fixtures such as lavatories and water closets without floor supports are required (see page 284 for detail).

Acoustical Ceiling Design & Application

The development of suspended ceiling systems in the early 1950s produced a shift in thinking about the function of a ceiling in construction. Where conventional ceilings had been regarded simply as a single-plane, fire-protective, finished element, the new suspended ceilings offered access to plumbing, electrical and mechanical components in overhead runs.

Today's suspended ceiling systems provide even more advantages for building construction, including a range of options for acoustical control, fire protection, lighting systems, HVAC, building technology systems and security networks. Vast selections of ceiling designs are available to achieve design considerations such as aesthetic appearance, budget considerations, durability and functional requirements.

Sustainability has also become a major design consideration. Development of today's acoustical ceiling products involves careful selection of building materials, construction methods and design details to create ceilings that consume fewer natural resources to build, maintain and remain viable in the future.

This chapter defines the various types of acoustical ceiling tile and grid products as well as design considerations.

Note that many different organizations provide information and recommended standards or tolerances for installing ceiling suspension systems and acoustical panel and tile products. See the Appendix (Agencies & Organizations, page 488) for more information.

For instructions on the safe use of ceiling suspension systems and acoustical panel and tile products, see Chapter 13, "Safety Considerations & Material Handling."

Suspended Acoustical Ceiling Products

Key components of suspended acoustical ceilings are the suspension grid and acoustical panels. The composition of each can vary depending on the end-use application. The tables within the next few pages describe various grid and tile products available.

Grid Systems

USG offers four primary grid systems. Each performs the same function of suspending panels from the overhead building structure. The systems differ in design, compatibility with certain styles of panels and the resulting appearance of the finished ceiling.

Grid System Types and Profiles

Product Name	Description & Feature/Benefits
DONN™ AX	Non-corrosive aluminum 15/16" exposed grid system ideal for high-humidity or wet-cleaned areas. – Aluminum components can be used in non-magnetic environments and meet USDA/FSIS requirements.
DONN CE	1-1/2" or 15/16" exposed grid systems with factory-applied closed-cell foam gaskets for controlled-environment rooms. – Hot-dipped galvanized body provides unequaled corrosion protection. – Certified for Class 100 clean-room environment per Federal Standard 209(e). – Meets or exceeds all national code requirements, including seismic.
DONN Centricitee DXT/DXLT	9/16" exposed grid offers clean aesthetic. – Patented panel-centering device allows use of standard square-edge panels. – Meets or exceeds all national code requirements, including seismic and fire-rated assemblies up to 2 hours. Design flexibility helps meet life safety codes.
DONN DX/DXL	15/16" exposed tee system. Components for use in general and fire-rated applications. – Maximum economy and design simplicity. – DXL system features more than 80 UL designs with designs up to 3 hours. – Meets or exceeds all national code requirements, including seismic.
DONN DX / DXL Concealed	15/16" concealed tee system. – Supporting grid is completely concealed, providing a monolithic, uninterrupted ceiling plane with up to 50% access to the plenum. – Meets or exceeds all national code requirements, including seismic and fire-rated assemblies up to 3 hours. Design flexibility helps meet life safety codes.
DONN DXLA	15/16" exposed fire rated system. – Maximum economy and design simplicity with UL designs up to 2 hours. – Suitable for use in food processing areas and meets USDA/FSIS requirements.
DONN DXSS	15/16" Type 316 stainless steel grid system. – Resistant to direct and indirect contact with many corrosive agents. – Stainless steel Quick-Release™ clips on cross tees. – Meets USDA/FSIS requirements. – Non-magnetic.

9

Grid System Types and Profiles (continued)

Donn DXW

├── 1¹/₂" ──┤

1-1/2" exposed grid system. Design alternative for high-bay areas and large panel modules.
– Meets or exceeds all national code requirements, including seismic.

Donn Fineline® DXF/DXLF

├─┤/₄"
9/₁₆"

Narrow-profile slotted grid system with 1/4" reveal provides streamlined appearance.
– Reveal accommodates partition attachments and pendant-mounted light fixtures.
– Meets or exceeds all national code requirements, including seismic and fire-rated assemblies up to 1 hour.
– Optional integrated air diffuser.
– Accepts metal ceiling panels for ceiling-area accents without changing grid system.

Donn Fineline® 1/8 DXFF

├─┤/₈"
9/₁₆"

Narrow-profile, slotted grid system with 1/8" reveal provides streamlined appearance.
– Reveal accommodates partition attachments and pendant-mounted light fixtures.
– Meets or exceeds all national code requirements, including seismic and fire-rated assemblies up to 1 hour.
– Optional integrated air diffuser.
– Accepts metal ceiling panels for ceiling-area accents without changing grid system.

Donn ZXLA

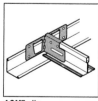

├─15/₁₆"─┤

15/16" exposed, hot-dipped galvanized grid system with aluminum cap, ideal for use in extreme environments.
– Polyester paint finish and stainless steel clip provide unequaled corrosion protection.
– Meets or exceeds all national code requirements, including seismic and fire-rated assemblies up to 2 hours.
– Aluminum-capped grid system, suitable for use in food processing areas, meets USDA/FSIS requirements.

Grid Accessories

A variety of Donn™ grid accessories are available to improve contractor installation efficiency and ensure code compliance. Accessories available include:

- M7 overlapping wall angle
- Seismic accessories
  - ACM7 seismic clip
  - Seismic expansion clip
  - Tee-face sleeves
- Standard and shadow angle moldings, including inside and outside corners and related accessories
- Grid installation and suspension system accessories

ACM7 clip

Note: For up-to-date information for any of the products described in this table, refer to the SC2000 available at **usg.com**.

Ceiling Panels

USG offers a full line of acoustical panels to achieve diverse functional or aesthetic criteria. Selection can be based on varied parameters—texture, budget, acoustical performance, emissions, functional requirements, color, etc. Visit the USG website at **usg.com** or view product selectors at **usgdesignstudio.com**.

Large panels

Logix Linear

The most commonly used panel sizes are 2' x 2' or 2' x 4', typically 5/8" or 3/4" thick. This is the nominal reference; the dimensions actually refer to the module size of the ceiling. Panel sizes are, in fact, 1/4" less than the module dimension in both directions. USG acoustical ceilings are available in a range of formats, from traditional 2' x 2' and 2' x 4' panels to new large-size and plank panels, providing options for enhancing visual interest and maximizing high-NRC areas. (See "Acoustical Requirements" later in this chapter.) A more monolithic look can be achieved with the Logix integrated ceiling system shown above. It can be used to align services (lighting, sprinklers, speakers, etc.) along narrow bands parallel or perpendicular with the main tees. Another option bands perpendicular to main tees, utilizing 6" Halcyon *CLIMAPLUS* or 6" metal Panz utility panels.

9

Ceiling Types, Manufacturing Processes and Applications

USG is the only manufacturer with the capabilities to produce acoustical ceiling panels with five different substrate technologies to achieve the full range of functional and aesthetic needs. Available substrates include cast mineral wool, X-Technology mineral wool, water-felted mineral wool, fiberglass and gypsum panel ceilings.

Ceiling Panel Types and Manufacturing Processes

Process	Construction	Applications	Available Panels
Cast Mineral Wool painted surface ⌐ color-coordinated subtrate ⌐	Formed and baked solid in molds to create a long-lasting, abuse-resistant surface in a range of textures.	Open-plan areas subject to frequent plenum access that require strong sound absorption (NRC) and sound blocking (CAC).	Brio *CLIMAPLUS* "F" Fissured Fresco *CLIMAPLUS* Frost Frost *CLIMAPLUS*
	Through-color masks nicks and scratches.	Enclosed areas requiring speech privacy.	Glacier Summit *CLIMAPLUS* Sandrift *CLIMAPLUS*
	Orients fibers for excellent sound absorption and high noise reduction coefficients (NRC).	Ceilings requiring exceptionally durable, long-lasting panels.	

292

Ceiling Panel Types and Manufacturing Processes (continued)

Process	Construction	Applications	Available Panels
Cast Mineral Wool (continued)	Composition enhances sound blocking (CAC) and resists "breathing" (air passing through panel), so surface stays cleaner, longer. Surface cleans easily with a soft brush or vacuum.	High-visibility areas that require color and/or a range of texture options	
X-Technology Mineral Wool painted surface natural mineral wool	Unique process creates a smooth surface with high noise absorption (NRC) and blocking (CAC). Superior sag resistance and outstanding dimensional stability Surface cleans easily with a soft brush or vacuum.	Open-plan areas that require strong sound absorption (NRC) and sound blocking (CAC) performance. Ceilings that require a level of dimensional stability beyond that of standard water-felted mineral-wool panels. Designs that require a ceiling with a smooth appearance that can be cleaned easily with a soft brush or vacuum.	Astro CLIMAPLUS Eclipse CLIMAPLUS Mars CLIMAPLUS Mars CLIMAPLUS High-NRC Millennia CLIMAPLUS
Water-Felted Mineral Wool painted surface natural mineral wool	Surface perforations aid sound absorption. Creates a variety of surface textures. Surface cleans easily with a soft brush or vacuum. Lowest initial cost. Clean Room panels have a vinyl face and back and sealed edges to meet federal standards for cleanrooms.	General-use areas requiring a balance of acoustical control and economy. High ceilings subject to infrequent plenum access and out of the way of activity below.	Aspen Clean Room CLIMAPLUS Class 100 Clean Room CLIMAPLUS Class 10M-100M Fissured Olympia Micro CLIMAPLUS Pebbled CLIMAPLUS Radar Radar CLIMAPLUS High NRC Radar CLIMAPLUS High CAC Radar CLIMAPLUS High NRC/High CAC Radar Ceramic CLIMAPLUS Rock Face CLIMAPLUS Touchstone CLIMAPLUS
Fiberglass vinyl, fabric or cloth scrim yellow fiberglass	Vinyl- and fabric-surfaced fiberglass offers superior sound absorption (NRC).	Open-plan areas where sound absorption is the highest performance criterion.	Halcyon CLIMAPLUS Halcyon CLIMAPLUS Planks and Large Sizes

Ceiling Panel Types and Manufacturing Processes (continued)

Light weight.	Ceilings that require a very lightweight panel.	Premier Hi-Lite CLIMAPLUS
Washable surface.*		Premier Nubby CLIMAPLUS
	Installations that may benefit from a washable vinyl surface.	

Gypsum Panel

white vinyl surface

white gypsum

Face-laminated gypsum panels Provide dimensional stability and sound blocking (CAC).

SHEETROCK CLEAN ROOM panels have a vinyl face and back and sealed edges to meet USDA/FSIS requirements for food processing areas.

Regulated environments such as cleanrooms and kitchens/ food preparation areas, which require highly cleanable surfaces that resist absorption of chemicals and odors.

Demanding applications subject to moisture exposure, temperature swings and exposure to dirt and grime, such as exterior soffits, marine environments, parking garages and locker rooms.

SHEETROCK Clean Room CLIMAPLUS Lay-in Panel SHEETROCK Vinyl CLIMAPLUS Lay-in Panel

Specialty Ceiling Panel Types & Manufacturing Processes

9

USG offers many innovative specialty ceiling products for use in high-visibility spaces such as lobbies, retail environments, restaurants, entertainment complexes or any space where dramatic focus in important. The company has pioneered affordable and easily installed products utilizing a wide variety of materials and processes to achieve an architect's desired aesthetic.

LIBRETO

GEOMETRIX

CADRE

CURVATURA

Process	Product Pattern	Features/Benefits
Cast Plaster	Cadre	Fiber-reinforced cast gypsum panels offer the look of classic coffered architecture with complete accessibility to above-ceiling utilities. Designs include Contemporary, Historical, Executive and Concepts.
	QUADRA	Four-sided coffer frames give the appearance of molded plaster, with accessibility and sound control.

Roll Forming	CURVATURA	Ceiling system uses curved metal to enable free-flowing, three-dimensional designs.
	GRIDWARE	Open-cell suspension system comprised of main tees and cross tees.
	PARALINE	Decorative and functional linear metal ceiling system.
		COMPÀSSO metal suspension trim allows the creation of free-form ceiling islands or fascias incorporating any standard DONN grid and USG Interiors panel.

	C2 Paired COMPÀSSO	Unique, multi-functional ceiling accents combine form and function. Easily integrate lighting and signage; can also be used as way-finding devices. Available in straight and curved sections in five sizes and custom colors to meet any design need. Easy to install—suspend from ceiling with hanger wire, cable or rods. Applications: Retail spaces, contemporary offices, educational environments, entertainment/gaming.
	CELEBRATION	Metal ceiling panels create a contemporary ceiling surface. Snap into Donn Fineline suspension, concealing the grid. Can also be wall-mounted.

Metal Stamping/Forming	CELEBRATION	Aluminum panels provide durability, accessibility, easy maintenance and sound control. Snap-up installation for shallow plenum areas. Wall-mount options available.

Process	Product Pattern	Features/Benefits
	GEOMETRIX	Three-dimensional metal ceiling panels. Multiple profiles and depths add dimension to ceiling and wall design. Panel depths range from 1-1/4" to 3". 2' x 2' lay-in panels are compatible with 9/16" and 15/16" DONN brand suspension systems. Solid or perforated panels. Available in Flat White, Silver Satin and custom colors.
	GEOMETRIX	Wall-mount solution with using 2' x2' panels installed vertically on walls using a system of mounting tracks, installation clips and perimeter trim. Creates dimensional focal walls that define space and highlight functional areas. Available solid or perforated. Wall-mount also available for CELEBRATION. metal panels. Custom colors available for design versatility.
	PANZ	Aluminum panels provide durability, accessibility, easy maintenance and sound control.
	PANZ Planks and Large Sizes	Range of sizes for large-module ceilings. Available in numerous painted colors and Wood Tones, and a range of perforation patterns. Simple lay-in design provides 100% access. Perforated panels with Acoustibond® sound backer produce .65 NRC without additional acoustical material (enclosed plenum, minimum depth 18"). Available with same edge details as USG acoustical panels.
	LIBRETTO	Gridless metal ceiling system with custom hole patterns. Can be used, with help from USG, to create a custom design tailored to your space. Individually fabricated aluminum panels interconnect to form a continuous, uninterrupted plane. arrier system is concealed and custom-fit, with choice of three perimeter profiles to achieve proper scale. llows for a contoured pattern, a custom graphic, or a standard pattern for a square or rectangular ceiling system.

Welded Assembly

Process	Product Pattern	Features/Benefits
	WIREWORKS	Open-cell ceiling solution of powder-coated wire mesh, compatible with GridWare™ Ceiling System, COMPÁSSO Suspension Trim.

Lexan Polycarbonate

Process	Product Pattern	Features/Benefits
	BILLO	Three-dimensional curved panels punctuate flat ceiling planes with rhythm and depth. 2' x 2' pre-formed, light-weight, lay-in LEXAN® panels create myriad patterns using one simple panel shape. Install into 9/16" narrow profile and standard 15/16" DONN brand suspension systems, allowing full ceiling accessibility. Luminous panels may be backlit with fluorescent strip fixtures or integrated with standard lay-in fixtures.
	TOPO	Pre-formed panels install easily into narrow-profile DONN brand Topo suspension system. Features and Benefits: Two system depths (8" and 12") create varying ceiling topographies. Translucent and opaque opaque LEXAN® infill panels in five colors enhance existing lighting for added visual interest. Optional pre-engineered utility circles accommodate additional lighting and utility access.

9

Process	Product Pattern	Features/Benefits
Lexan Polycarbonate (continued)	Translucents	Fully accessible, flexible, translucent (luminous) infill panels. Can be used with standard DONN brand DX®/DXL™ and Centricitee™ DXT suspension systems or the Curvatura 3-D System and GridWare suspension systems.
	Transparencies	Fully accessible luminous ceiling system provides the aesthetic of sunlit glass block with just a fraction of the weight, cost, and installation time of real glass. Panels consist of nine injection-molded 8" x 8" blocks, fac tory-assembled into a 2' x 2' lay-in panel for fast installation and full accessibility. Special DONN brand Centricitee DXT suspension system is texturized to create "mortar joints." 8" x 89 highlighters, available in five translucent colors. Allows change of color for individual blocks or entire panels.

For more information and quarterly updates, visit **usg.com** and search for the document, SC2000.

Design Considerations for Suspended Acoustical Ceilings

Selecting the right ceiling for a particular application requires careful consideration of a number of factors beginning with the purpose of the space, function, aesthetics, acoustical criteria, sustainability and budget considerations. Features include acoustical performance, sustainability, lighting, structural considerations, environmental conditions and fire performance. Also product features or building needs, such as durability and accessibility to the plenum, require consideration. Aesthetics, on the other hand, address texture, light enhancement, design, configuration and the like. Sustainability addresses environmentally conscious building, which includes both the construction process and ongoing operation and maintenance of the facility. Sustainable design has introduced new criteria such as emissions and recycled content.

USG launched **usgdesignstudio.com** to simplify the ceiling selection and design process. USG DesignStudio helps designers narrow the myriad of design criteria by using online selectors that provide downloadable product details including CAD and REVIT files, specification generators, installation animations and LEED calculators. Designers can use DesignStudio to enter ceiling design criteria, such as NRC, CAC or a fire rating, and it will return results consistent with the search criteria. This dramatically simplifies the ceiling selection, design and specification process.

The type of space will determine the portion of the budget allocated for the ceiling system. If the ceiling simply needs to close off the plenum, without regard to appearance, special functions or acoustical performance, inexpensive grid and tile products are generally selected. "High end" applications, such as hotel lobbies, reception areas or top-quality retail establishments, command more attention and a greater percentage of the interior budget.

Purpose of the Space

Sound control is typically the main objective in ceiling tile selection. However, for situations where appearance criteria outweigh acoustical needs, USG offers several options. For example, a restaurant designer may want to incorporate a sophisticated, high-tech look such as offered by the Curvatura Ceiling System, which includes 3-dimensional vaulted or wavy designs. The system can incorporate metal panels. Compásso trim systems can provide islands of overhead sound absorption, or be left with an open grid.

If acoustical control is a key consideration along with aesthetics, there are several ways to attain it. One is to install a standard acoustical ceiling above the focal point ceilings. An alternative for localized sound control is to use perforated metal panels with floppy poly-bagged fiberglass inserts above the panels. The trade-offs should be carefully evaluated.

Acoustical Requirements

Acoustical sound control performance characteristics are referenced in three different ways: noise reduction coefficient (NRC), ceiling attenuation class (CAC) and articulation class (AC). These are expressed as ratings that can be used to compare products. (See Chapter 15, "Building Sciences," for explanations of these ratings.)

Architects and interior designers use these acoustical rating values to determine which acoustical products will work best to satisfy the requirements of a certain installation. For detailed information about the acoustical performance of particular products refer to the Ceiling Systems catalog (SC2000) available at **usg.com** or the product selector available there or at **usgdesignstudio.com**. The acoustical performance values (CAC, NRC and AC) of USG interior ceiling tile and panel products are independently verified under the Underwriters Laboratories Classification and Follow-Up Services Program.

The key to controlling sound is to design ceiling solutions with products that meet specific sound control performance levels. For areas requiring excellent sound absorption, USG has panels rated as "High NRC" with noise reduction ratings of .70 up to 1.00+. Open or perforated steel specialty products, such as Paraline, Celebration and Curvatura, can also achieve high sound absorption ratings by adding a fiberglass backer to the panels in the plenum area. Using high NRC-rated ceiling systems in combination with wall and floor coverings, furniture, window treatments and other sound-absorbing materials can help to create an ambient acoustic environment free of echoes and reverberations.

"High CAC" panels have CAC values of up to 45. The panels do an excellent job of stopping sound transmission through the plenum. Sound attenuation is even better with the addition of acoustical barriers in the plenum between rooms, as well as acoustical sealant at room perimeters, which stop sound from moving around the ceiling plane.

Reducing speech intelligibility is typically the key objective in open plan facilities. Refer to Chapter 15 for more on acoustics.

Acoustical Ratings

USG offers ceiling panels with enhanced sound-control that absorb sound and reduce sound transmission better than standard panels, significantly improving acoustical comfort, privacy and productivity. Following are some features to consider when selecting a high-performance acoustical ceiling.

High-NRC Panels Absorb More Sound The noise reduction coefficient (NRC) is a measurement of how effectively materials absorb sound. NRC is represented by a number between 0 and 1.00, indicating the amount (percentage) of sound the material will absorb. An NRC of .50 or higher offers significant sound absorption. A panel with an NRC value of .60 will absorb approximately 60% of the sound that strikes it and deflect 40% back into the space. USG panels designed for increased acoustical performance are rated at .70 or above. Halcyon CLIMAPLUS ceiling panels offers the highest rating, 1.00.

High-CAC Panels Reduce Sound Transmission Ceiling attenuation class (CAC) indicates a material's ability to reduce sound transmission. High-CAC panels can improve privacy in enclosed spaces by blocking sound from transmitting up into the plenum and down into adjacent rooms. A CAC of 35 or higher offers significant sound attenuation. A ceiling panel with a CAC of 40 generally reduces transmitted sound by 40 decibels (dB).

Privacy Requirements High acoustical performance is critical for clients that must comply with federal privacy rules. For example, the Health Insurance Portability and Accountability Act (HIPAA) requires that all U.S. physicians' offices, pharmacies and other healthcare facilities in the U.S. protect personal health information. This includes consultation areas, where doctor-patient conversations could be overheard. The Financial Services Modernization Act of 1999, also known as the Gramm-Leach-Bliley Act (GLBA), requires banks, investment companies and other financial institutions to protect customer financial information from inadvertent disclosure. To provide an effective, affordable solution for speech privacy, USG has teamed up with Lencore Acoustics to offer the most comprehensive sound masking ceiling systems available. For more information, see pages 296–297.

USG Ceiling Panels and Acoustical Ratings

| Ceiling Panels | Sound Rating | | Texture | Panel |
	NRC	CAC Min.		Cost
High NRC & CAC Combinations				
Mars CLIMAPLUS High-NRC	.80	35	Fine	$$
Brio CLIMAPLUS	.70	35	Heavy	$$
Eclipse CLIMAPLUS	.70	35	Fine	$$
Eclipse CLIMAPLUS Illusion	.70	35	Fine	$$
"F" Fissured	.70	35	Medium	$$
Fresco CLIMAPLUS	.70	35	Heavy	$$
Frost CLIMAPLUS	.70	35-40[2]	Fine	$$
Mars CLIMAPLUS	.70	35	Fine	$$
Millennia CLIMAPLUS	.70	35	Fine	$$
Millennia CLIMAPLUS Illusion	.70	35	Fine	$$
Radar CLIMAPLUS High-NRC/High CAC	.70	40	Medium	$
Sandrift CLIMAPLUS	.70	38	Medium	$$
Summit CLIMAPLUS	.70	38-40[2]	Fine	$$$
Frost	.70	35-40	Fine	$$
Glacier	.65	35	Heavy	$$
High NRC				
Halcyon CLIMAPLUS	.90-1.00	20-30	Fine	$$
Halcyon CLIMAPLUS Large Sizes	.95	20	Fine	$$$
Halcyon CLIMAPLUS Planks	.90/.95	20	Fine	$$$
Premier Nubby CLIMAPLUS (Foil-Back)	.85/.90	20/25	Fine	$$$

NRC = Noise Reduction Coefficient
CAC = Ceiling Attenuation Class

USG Ceiling Panels and Acoustical Ratings (continued)

Mars *CLIMAPLUS* High-NRC	.80	35	Fine	$$
Millennia *CLIMAPLUS* High-NRC	.75	30	Fine	$$
Premier Hi-Lite *CLIMAPLUS* Perforated	.75	20	Medium	$
Summit *CLIMAPLUS*	.70	38-40²	Fine	$$$
Sandrift *CLIMAPLUS*	.70	38	Medium	$$
Brio *CLIMAPLUS*	.70	35	Heavy	$$
Eclipse *CLIMAPLUS*	.70	35	Fine	$$
Eclipse *CLIMAPLUS* Illusion	.70	35	Fine	$$
"F" Fissured	.70	35	Medium	$$
Fresco *CLIMAPLUS*	.70	35	Heavy	$$
Frost *CLIMAPLUS*	.70	35-40²	Fine	$$
Mars *CLIMAPLUS*	.70	35	Smooth	$$
Millennia *CLIMAPLUS*	.70	35	Fine	$$
Millennia *CLIMAPLUS* Illusion	.70	35	Fine	$$
Radar *CLIMAPLUS* High-NRC	.70	35	Medium	$
Radar *CLIMAPLUS* High-NRC / High-CAC	.70	40	Medium	$
Frost	.70	35-40	Fine	$$
Glacier	.65	35	Heavy	$$
High CAC				
Radar *CLIMAPLUS* High-CAC	.55	40	Medium	$
Radar Ceramic *CLIMAPLUS*	.50	40	Medium	$$
Sheetrock brand Lay-In Ceiling Panel *CLIMAPLUS*	—	35/40	Smooth	$

1. Performance values do not include 129 x 129 or Pedestals products.
2. CAC is 40 when installed in Fineline DXF or Fineline 1/8 DXFF suspension system.
Acoustical Ceiling Systems Selectors Acoustical Ratings 117

9

Sustainability

Sustainable design has become an important criterion in the selection of building products, including suspended ceiling systems. LEED, the most widely accepted national guideline for environmentally conscious building, provides credits for the following categories, for which USG offers ceiling products: energy and atmosphere, materials and resources, and indoor environmental quality.

Sustainability information is available for USG ceiling products. This includes recycled and renewable ingredients and support for healthy environments that addresses VOC content as well has the inhibition of mold, mildew and bacteria. USG ceiling products also include sustainability features for specific uses, such as healthcare or education facilities. Refer to the USG Ceiling Systems Catalog (SC2000) and **usg. com** for additional product information. A LEED calculator is available on **usgdesignstudio.com**.

USG uses responsible manufacturing practices, including clean fuels, waste recycling, and water conservation, which help protect the environment and increase efficiency. In addition, USG takes back approved ceiling panels to recycle into new building products. (For more information, see pages 124 and 298–299.)

See Chapter 16, "Sustainability," for more information on the ways USG products can help achieve sustainability in construction and earn LEED credits.

Lighting & Light Reflectance

Lighting is one of the most important factors to consider in the design of interior spaces. The anticipated use of the space must be clearly understood. Then, the illumination expectations for each space must be well defined. Of course, electrical service capacity must be planned so that it is sufficient to meet current needs as well as future expansion.

Lighting should meet the aesthetic and visual comfort criteria of the occupants given the use of the area. The amount, sources and placement of light will affect the overall mood. Lighting can be dramatic or subdued. Both ambient and task-specific lighting should be provided. Lighting designers and engineers can help determine which artificial light sources work best to complement ambient lighting and meet specific objectives.

Suspended acoustical ceilings play an important role in interior lighting. The suspension system is designed to support the mounting of lighting fixtures and adds flexibility to the placement and future relocation of those fixtures. Further, the panel selection will impact light reflectance and diffusion. See Chapter 16 for more on energy savings through selection of light-reflecting ceiling products. See the Glossary at the end of this book for common lighting terms and definitions.

Lighting Calculations

Interior lighting calculations are generally based on established guidelines for how many luminaires are required in a standard arrangement to provide an average illumination level. A qualified lighting designer or engineer can be a valuable asset to your design team. Using the rated light output at the source and the source-to-surface distance, the engineer can calculate the number, type and placement of the luminaires.

$$\text{Illumination (footcandles)} = \frac{\text{lumens}}{\text{area (sq. ft.)}} \quad \text{or} \quad \text{fc} = \frac{\text{lumens}}{\text{sq. ft.}}$$

Determining the number and placement of luminaires is not as simple as the direct relationship above would suggest. It also is important to take into account absorption of light by wall, ceiling and floor surfaces, the inter-reflection of light, the efficiency or distribution of the luminaires, the shape of the room, etc. Those considerations result in a utilization factor that modifies the light-source-to-useful-light relationship.

$$\text{Illumination (footcandles)} = \frac{\text{lumens} \ \text{X} \ \text{Coefficient of Utilization}}{\text{area (sq. ft.)}}$$

Light Reflectance

Light reflectance, or LR, mentioned earlier in this chapter, is an important factor in determining the amount of source illumination that will be required. Acoustical panels have different degrees of whiteness, surface pattern and texture, all of which affect the amount of light they reflect.

USG tests and measures panel reflectance in accordance with ASTM E1477, Method for Luminous Reflectance Factor of Acoustical Materials by Use of Integrating-Sphere Reflectometers.

High light reflectance (High LR) ceiling panels enable architects and designers to use indirect light effectively. Pendulum, sconce and trim lighting directed at the ceiling produces a wash of light with three specific advantages:

1. Indirect lighting reduces glare against computer terminals, eyeglasses and windows in an office space, creating a more enjoyable and productive work space.

2. Indirect lighting reduces up-front expenses, as fewer fixtures are installed in initial construction.

3. Indirect lighting reduces energy costs.

Applications especially well-suited to High LR panels include open office space, medical facilities, educational settings, libraries and computer rooms. Using light reflectance effectively can bring value to architects and owners by reducing glare, reducing initial construction costs and reducing energy costs. (See Chapter 16 for more on sustainable USG wall and ceiling products.)

USG Ceiling Panels—Light Reflectance Ratings

Note: Cost of panel products is shown in ranges per SF, where $ = < $1.50, $$ = $1.51-$2.50, $$$ = $2.51-$3.50 and $$$$ = > $3.51.

Ceiling Panels	LR1 Cost	Textures Sq. ft.	Panel
Mars *CLIMAPLUS*	.89	Fine	$$
Mars *CLIMAPLUS* High-NRC	.89	Fine	$$
Radar Illusion	.89	Medium	$$
Radar *CLIMAPLUS* Illusion	.89	Medium	$$
Frost *CLIMAPLUS*	.83/.88	Fine	$$
Halcyon *CLIMAPLUS*	.88	Fine	$$
Halcyon *CLIMAPLUS* Large Sizes	.88	Fine	$$$
Halcyon *CLIMAPLUS* Planks	.88	Fine	$$$
Aspen	.87	Medium	$$$
Millennia *CLIMAPLUS*	.87	Fine	$$
Millennia *CLIMAPLUS* High-NRC	.87	Fine	$$
Millennia *CLIMAPLUS* Illusion	.87	Fine	$$
Olympia Micro *CLIMAPLUS*	.87	Fine	$$
Olympia Micro *CLIMAPLUS* Illusion	.87	Fine	$$
Premier Nubby *CLIMAPLUS*	.87	Fine	$$$
Astro *CLIMAPLUS*	.86	Fine	$$
Astro *CLIMAPLUS* Illusion	.86	Fine	$$
Eclipse *CLIMAPLUS*	.86	Fine	$$
Pebbled *CLIMAPLUS*	.86	Medium	$
Rock Face *CLIMAPLUS*	.86	Medium	$$
TouchStone *CLIMAPLUS*	.86	Medium	$$
Aspen Illusion	.85	Medium	$$
Frost	.85	Fine	$$
Radar	.85	Medium	$
Eclipse *CLIMAPLUS* Illusion	.84	Fine	$$
Radar *CLIMAPLUS*	.84	Medium	$
Radar *CLIMAPLUS* High-CAC, High-NRC	.84	Medium	$
Fresco *CLIMAPLUS*	.83	Heavy	$$
Sandrift *CLIMAPLUS*	.83	Medium	$$
Radar Ceramic *CLIMAPLUS*	.82	Medium	$$
Brio *CLIMAPLUS*	.81	Heavy	$$
Fissured	.81	Medium	$
Summit *CLIMAPLUS*	.81	Fine	$$$

9

Dramatic or Theatrical Lighting

Direct, indirect and spot lighting for dramatic effect can be facilitated with the use of curved or undulating ceiling treatments. USG introduced LIBRETTO, COMPÀSSO and CURVATURA ceiling systems to provide just such an avenue for creative expression. These products open up design options well beyond the office environment.

Retail space, entertainment complexes, restaurants and lobbies can be designed with upbeat, upscale lighting. Up-lighting and spotlighting with halogen light sources have become popular design elements. Advancements in LED lighting have created new lighting design options. In specialized spaces, it is even more important to engage the services of a professional lighting designer.

Structural Implications

The grid system becomes a structural component in the ceiling that must safely carry the loads of lighting, air distribution and ceiling panels. These loads are transferred to the building structure through the hanger wires that suspend the ceiling. Performance of the grid system depends on the product's integrity and proper installation. Two standards must be met: ASTM Standard C635, which governs the structural and quality standards of the grid, and ASTM Standard C636, which addresses proper installation to ensure the ceiling's load-carrying capacity and general structural integrity.

Seismic Requirements

Seismic compliance refers to the use of approved systems and designs to provide life safety to building occupants during and after an earthquake. Seismic force levels and design criteria were once considered only in certain earthquake-prone locations, but major revisions to the *International Building Code* (IBC) now require seismic-compliant ceiling systems throughout the U.S.

In addition to geographic location, the current code considers soil type and building function (e.g., hospital, school, etc.). Based on these criteria, more than half of the buildings in the U.S. are now considered to have some level of seismic risk. Design teams, consulting engineers and code officials must work together to analyze these factors and determine the applicable seismic design category (A-F), with F being the most severe. Seismic compliance is now required for every construction project and must be included in the construction documents.

USG DONN brand suspension systems include standard and alternate design solutions for all seismic categories. The alternate designs allow for preferred aesthetic solutions, such as the use of 7/8" wall moulding vs. 2" wall moulding in categories D, E and F. The system performance criteria for a given seismic category are achieved with alternate designs through the use of accessories, including the ACM7 seismic clips and four-way seismic expansion joint clips, shown on the next page.

To find out more about new requirements for seismic ceilings, visit the USG Seismic Ceilings Resource Center (**seismicceilings.com**). The site offers in-depth articles about the governing codes, FAQs and interviews with ceilings experts. The Resource Center also includes a comprehensive library of architectural details, downloadable in PDF

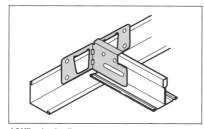

ACM7 seismic clip

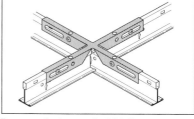

Four-way seismic expansion joint clip

and CAD formats. Refer to Chapter 15 for more on structural movement. USG's seismic suspension system components and alternate designs have been evaluated by ICC Evaluation Services, Inc. Refer to **seismicceilings.com** for the current ICC evaluation report.

Environmental Considerations for Installation

The typical environment for a suspended ceiling system is an enclosed and watertight building with all permanent heating and cooling systems in operation. All residual moisture from plaster, concrete or terrazzo has been dissipated. Temperatures remain in a range from 60°F–80°F, with relative humidity not exceeding 80%. Climatic conditions from outside these boundaries may have adverse effects on the panels and grid.

In some instances, ceiling systems can be specified to be used in certain "non-standard" installations. Standard suspension systems and tiles should be installed in conditions that meet interior environmental requirements as noted above.

9

Higher Humidity Environments

When the ceiling system will be exposed to constant high temperatures and humidity, special panels and grid can be specified. USG Interiors offers panels that will withstand high levels of humidity and temperature without sagging. These panels, categorized as CLIMAPLUS, are standard panels formulated with an added ingredient that remains stable in temperatures up to 104°F, and relative humidity up to 95%.

CLIMAPLUS panels may be used in standard and typical environments as well. The technology allows for flexibility during and after construction, giving the installers the option to install before a building is entirely enclosed. CLIMAPLUS panels, when used with DONN grid systems, carry a lifetime warranty.

In addition to CLIMAPLUS panels, USG offers a number of other special-performance panels that can be used in areas that house swimming pools, kitchens, clean rooms, as well as areas prone to abuse and other non-standard installations.

Grids are also designed for unique situations. DONN AX suspension grid, which is aluminum, stands up especially well in swimming pool areas and other locations with high moisture content. AX is rated as a light-duty system, but its load capacity can be increased to intermediate levels by reducing the hanger wire spacing to 3' o.c.

Steel-bodied grid also is available with aluminum caps (DONN DXLA), as well as an environmental grid with hot-dipped-galvanized bodies and aluminum caps (DONN ZXA and ZXLA). These are offered in heavy- and intermediate-duty ratings.

For extreme environments, DONN DXSS stainless steel grid may be appropriate. A metallurgist should review its use in particularly corrosive environments.

Exterior Suspended Ceiling Applications

Exterior suspended ceilings, subject to environmental extremes, must be horizontally covered and protected. Examples include parking decks, walkways, soffits or protected drive-throughs and building entrances. These applications must address not only temperature and humidity, but also wind. USG offers a variety of products that can perform well in these environments, from standard grid and panel systems to specialty ceilings.

For a standard suspension system in an exterior application, USG recommends using the ZXA/ZXLA environmental grid. The hot-dipped galvanized body, aluminum cap and stainless steel attachment clips make it a non-corrosive system. In conjunction with this grid, USG provides SHEETROCK brand ceiling lay-in tile. These tiles consist of a FIRECODE gypsum core and white stipple vinyl facing. The tiles are durable, cleanable and stain-resistant, making them an ideal choice for exterior applications.

The ZXA grid/gypsum lay-in tile system has been shown to sustain winds up to 120 mph in tests performed by an independent testing lab. The tests used compression posts at each hanger wire location (4' o.c.), and hold-down clips (nails) on each panel. USG recommends this type of installation in exterior conditions, subject to review by a structural engineer for each project on an individual basis. To ensure long-term integrity of the system and the structure, the plenum should be well-ventilated.

Other specialty ceilings also perform well in protected exterior situations. USG manufactures the PARALINE linear pan ceiling system and the CELEBRATION 2'x 2' pan ceiling system. Both may be used in sheltered exterior applications. PARALINE aluminum pans used with the aluminum symmetrical carrier and compression posts have been tested in winds of up to 120 mph (37 psf). CELEBRATION aluminum ceiling panels have also been tested in winds up to 120 mph, snapped into a galvanized FINELINE grid with SHEETROCK brand ceiling lay-in tiles, compression posts and hold-down clips. Both of these systems can be used as a continuous transition from indoors to outdoors. These systems provide architects with multiple options for covered exterior projects.

Fire Safety

Combustibility versus Fire-Rated Assemblies

Fire safety properties of suspended acoustical ceilings are widely misunderstood, largely because there are several fire safety terms that have similar, but different meanings. *Flame Spread, Class A, noncombustible, fire resistance rating*, and *fire-rated assembly* all mean different things.

Non-combustible, defined by ASTM E136, simply means that the material will not burn. The *Class A* designation on products means that the material can be ignited, but will not sustain a flame, and the fire will extinguish itself. *Flame spread* is a measure of the material's self-extinguishing characteristics. *Class A* is defined by the characteristics of both flame spread and smoke, measured in accordance with ASTM E-84. The measurement will determine whether the material can be considered Class A.

None of these terms should be mistaken or substituted for fire-rated assemblies or fire resistance ratings.

Fire Resistance Rating and Fire-Rated Assemblies

Fifteen to twenty percent of all suspended ceilings are sold and installed as fire-rated designs. "Fire resistance rating" is the terminology that has long been used by Underwriters Laboratories (UL) to reference the performance of various types of construction. The ratings relate to fire tests designed to measure the time it takes for a fire to raise the temperature above the ceiling to unacceptable levels.

The term "fire-resistance" leads to the unfortunate misconception that, if Class A materials are used in a grid ceiling, it will stop a fire from spreading, or that it is a "fire-rated" ceiling. That is not necessarily so.

Fire-rated ceilings (or fire-rated assemblies) are tested and certified in their entirety. This includes all the materials used in the construction, from the type of bar joists used to the type and size of acoustical panels. Each ceiling type tested is identified in the *UL Fire Resistance Directory,* which is updated every year.

Because the intense heat of a fire affects different materials in different ways, the materials need to be tested in context, or relative to one another. A fire-rated ceiling assembly duplicates as closely as possible a small portion of the entire building, including, but not limited to concrete, bar joists, light fixtures, grid type, ceiling panel type, floor type, and roof type.

The *Underwriters Laboratories Fire Resistance Directory* lists all of the types of construction that have been tested in an actual fire environment. Although we are concerned primarily with ceilings in this chapter, the tests contained in the book also cover beams, columns, floors, roofs and wall construction. It bears repeating that a fire-rated assembly is the *total construction* as it was built and tested with all of the above. Any deviation from the construction tested leaves serious doubt as to the performance of the rest of the materials in the assembly.

Procedures for a Fire Test

The general method for testing a design for a fire-rated suspended ceiling is to actually build a room that will represent the typical construction and install a suspended ceiling in it. Depending on the type of construction, this room might include an actual concrete slab representing the floor above, bar joists if it is a roof construction, appropriate wall construction, fire-rated Donn brand grid system, and Firecode ceiling board. If the ceiling has light fixtures and air diffusers, these are included too.

All of the UL fire tests are conducted in accordance with ASTM E-119. The assembly passes if no openings occur in the ceiling where flames can get through, or the temperatures in the plenum or of key structural components stay below a prescribed limit for the duration of the test.

Every building material that is used in a fire-rated, tested design is listed in the test report in the UL Directory. Any deviation of the individual materials listed or in the manner it is installed brings the performance of the final construction into question. The ultimate authority on any substitutions or changes rests with the local building official.

Types of Construction Tests

The primary types of fire tests for Donn brand fire-rated grid and USG ceiling panels are based on the type of construction used for the structure. The UL test designation is keyed to those ceiling designs based on the prefix letter of the test:

A - Floor/Ceiling designs comprised of concrete cellular deck with cellular steel floor units and beam support.

D - Floor/Ceiling designs comprised of concrete with steel floor units and beam support.

G - Floor/Ceiling designs comprised of concrete and steel joists.

J or K - Floor/Ceiling designs comprised of pre-cast and field-poured concrete.

L - Floor/Ceiling designs comprised of wood or combination wood and steel joists assemblies.

P - Roof/Ceiling designs.

These letter designations followed by three-digit numbers are the designs called out in the *UL Directory* and written into the specifications. USG offers over 100 tested ceiling designs. Tests that incorporate Donn brand fire-rated grid and Firecode tile and panels are listed on the following pages. For specific information, refer to the latest *UL Fire Resistance Directory.*

Note: The following tests are current as of the writing of this text. Both the tests and the construction specifications shown for them are subject to change from time to time. See the current USG literature and the current UL Fire Resistance Directory to determine the status of a fire-rated design before specifying it.

For more on fire-resistance, see Chapter 15.

Fire Rated Ceilings

Floor/Ceiling Designs	UL Design No.	Assembly Rating (Maximum)	Approved Ceiling Tiles/Panels	Tile/Panel Sizes	Suspension System	Maximum Fix. Size % Ceiling Area	Duct Area per 100 Sq. Ft. of Ceiling Area	Assembly Construction Details
Concrete with Cellular Steel Floor Units and Beam Support Concealed Grid System and Tile	A003	3 hr. R; 3 hr. UR; 3 hr. URB	¾ FR-83	12x12; 12x24	Z-runners	Fluorescent type, 2x4 – 8%	None	2-1/2" concrete; Cellular deck; W10 x 25 beam
Concrete with Steel Floor Units and Beam Support Exposed Grid System and Lay-in Panels	D209	2 hr. R; 1-1/2 hr. UR; 1-1/2 hr. UR; 1-1/2 hr. URB	FR-83; FR-4; M; FR-X1; FC-CB	2x2; 2x4	DXL, DXLA	Fluorescent type, 2x4 – 8%	None	2-1/2" concrete; Cellular or fluted deck W10 x 21 beam
	D215	4 hr. URB; 2 hr. R; 2 hr. UR; 2 hr. URB; 1-1/2 hr. R; 1-1/2 hr UR; 1-1/2 hr URB	¾" FR-83	2x2	DXL, DXLZ, SDXZ	Fluorescent type, 2x4 – 16% Incandescent type, 6-1/2" diam.	113 sq. in.	2-1/2" concrete; Cellular or fluted deck W8 x 15 beam
	D218	3 hr. R; 3 hr. UR; 3 hr. URB; 2 hr. R; 2 hr. UR; 2 hr. URB	FR-83; Metal Pans; M	2x4	DXLP, DXL, DXLZ, SDXL	Fluorescent type, 2x4 – 20%; 5x48 – 10%; 9x48 – 14%; Incandescent type, 6-1/2" diam.	1 air boot per 100 sq. ft.	3-1/4" concrete (3hr.); 2-1/2" concrete (2hr.); Cellular or fluted deck; W8 x 15 beam
	D219	3 hr. R; 3 hr. UR; 3 hr. URB; 2 hr. R; 2 hr. UR; 2 hr. URB; 1-1/2 hr. R; 1-1/2 hr. UR; 1-1/2 hr. URB; 1 hr. R; 1 hr. UR; 1 hr. URB	FR-83; FR-4; FR-X1	2x2; 2x4	DXL, DXLA, DXLT, DXLZ DXLZA, SDXL, SDXLA, ZXLA	Fluorescent type, 12x48 – 16%; 24x24 – 20%; 20x48 – 20%; 20x48 – 24%	144 sq. in.	3-1/2" concrete (3hr.); 2-1/2" concrete (2hr.); Cellular or fluted deck; W8 x 15 beam
Concrete and Steel Joists Exposed Grid System and Lay-in Panels	G201	1 hr. R; 1 hr. UR	FR-X1; FR-83; M	2x2; 2x4	DX, DXLA, DXLZ, SDXL, DXLZA, SDXLA, ZXLA	Fluorescent type, 2x4–8%; Incandescent type, 6-1/2" diam.	None	2" concrete; Metal lath or deck; 10" bar joists 24 to 30" o.c. or Hambro System
	G202	2 hr. R; 2 hr. UR	FR-4; FR-83; FR-X1; Astro-FR; M	2x2; 2x4; 20x60; 24x60	DXL, DXLZ, SDXL	Fluorescent type, 20x48; 20x48/60 – 24%; 2x2 HID – 12%; Incandescent type, 6-1/2" diam.	576 sq. in.	2-1/2" concrete; Metal lath, 10" bar joists 24" or 30" o.c.
	G203	2 hr. R; 2 hr. UR; 2 hr. URB	FR-83; Astro-FR; M	2x2; 2x4; 20x60	DXL, DXLT	Fluorescent type, 2x4 or 20x60 – 16%; Incandescent type, 6-1/2" diam. – 1.4%	254 sq. in. (576 sq. in.)	2-1/2" concrete; Metal lath or deck; 10" bar joists 24" o.c. or Hambro system. W6 x 12 or W8 x 10 beam
	G204	2 hr. R; 2 hr. UR; 2 hr. URB	FR-83; FR-4:m; FR-X1; Astro-FR; (GR-1)	24x24 to 30x60	DXL, DXLA, DXLZ, DSXL, DXLZA, SDXLA	Fluorescent type, 24x24; 24x48; 24x60 – 24%; 2x2 HID; Incandescent type, 6-1/2" diam.	113 sq. in. (576 sq. in.)	2-1/2" concrete; Metal lath or deck; 10" bar joists 30" o.c.; W6 x 12 beam
	G205	3 hr. R; 3 hr. UR; 3 hr. URB	FR-83; FR-X1; FC-CB; FR-4; Astro-FR	2x2; 2x4	DXLT, DXL, DXLZ, DXLA, SDXLA, DXLZA, DXLTZ, DSLTA, DXLTZA	Fluorescent type, 2x4 – 24%; Incandescent type, 6-1/2" diam.	576 sq. in.	3-1/2" concrete (3hr.) or 2-1/2" concrete (2 hr.); 8" bar joists 72" o.c. (2 hr.) 10" bar joists 48" o.c. (3 hr.)
	G211	3 hr. R; 3 hr. UR	FR-83; Fr-R4: FR-X1; FC-CB ; Astro-FR; M	2x2; 2x4	DXL, DXLA DXLZ, ZXLA, SDXL, SDXLA	Fluorescent type, 2x4 – 16%	113 sq. in.	3" concrete; Metal lath; 10" bar joists 24" o.c.
	G213	3 hr. R; 3 hr. UR; 3 hr. URB; 2 hr. R; 2 hr. UR; 2 hr. URB; 1-1/2 hr. R; 1-1/2 hr. UR; 1-1/2 URB; 1 hr. R; 1 hr. 1 hr. URB	FR-4; FR-83; M; FR-X1: FC-CB (1 or 1-1/2 hr.): Astro-FR	2x2; 2x4	DXL, DXLZ, SDXL	Fluorescent type, 2x4 – 24%; Incandescent type, 6-1/2" diam.	154 sq. in.	3-1/2" concrete; metal lath or deck; 10" bar joists 24" o.c.; W6 x 12 beam

9

Fire Rated Ceilings (continued)

Floor/Ceiling Designs	UL Design No.	Assembly Rating (Maximum)	Approved Ceiling Tiles/Panels	Tile/Panel Sizes	Suspension System	Maximum Fix. Size % Ceiling Area	Duct Area per 100 Sq. Ft. of Ceiling Area	Assembly Construction Details
Concrete and Steel Joists Exposed Grid System and Lay-in Panels (continued)	G215	2 hr. R; 2 hr. UR; 2 hr. URB	FR-83: FR-4: FR-X1: Astro-FR; M	2x2; 2x4; 20x60	DXL, DXLZ, SDXL	Fluorescent type, 20x48/60 - 24%; 2x2 HID - 2%; Incandescent type, 6-1/2" diam.	154 sq. in.	3-1/2" concrete; Metal lath; 10" bar joists 24" o.c. or Hambro system; W10 x 21 beam
	G222	2 hr. R; 2 hr. UR; 2 hr. URB	FC-CB	2x2	DXL, DXLA, DXLH, DXLZ, SDXL, SDXLA	Fluorescent type, 2x4 - 12%; Incandescent type, 6-1/2" diam.	57 sq. in.	2-1/2" concrete; Metal lath; 10" bar joists 24 "o.c.p; W8x24 beam 6-1/2" diam.
	G227	2 hr. R; 2 hr. UR; 3 hr. URB	FR-83: Astro-FR; M	2x2; 2x4	DXL, DXLZ, SDXL	Fluorescent type, 2x4 - 16%	57 sq. in.	2-1/2" concrete; Metal lath or deck; 10" bar joists 24" o.c. or Hambro system; W8 x 31 beam
	G228	2 hr. R; 2 hr. UR; 2 hr. URB	AP; AP-3	2x2	DXL, DXLZ, SDXL	Fluorescent type, 2x2 - 12%; Incandescent type, 6-1/2" diam.	57 sq. in.	2-1/2" concrete; Metal lath or deck; 10" bar joists 24" o.c.; W8 x 31 beam
	G230	2 hr. R; 2 hr. UR; 2 hr. URB	FR-83: FR-X1: Astro-FR; M	2x2; 2x4	DXL, DXLA, DXLZ, SDXL, SDXLA, ZXLA, DXLZA	Fluorescent type, 2x4 - 16%	113 sq. in.	2" building units; Floor topping mixture; 10" bar joists 48" o.c.; W8 x 31 beam
	G231	2 hr. R; 2 hr. UR; 3 hr. URB	¾" FR-83	24x24 to 30x60	DXL, DXLA, DXLZ, SDXL, SDXLA, ZXLA	Fluorescent type, 2x4 - 16%	57 sq. in.	2-1/2" concrete Metal lath or deck; 8' bar joists 24" o.c.; W8 x 31 beam
	G259	1-1/2 hr. R; 1-1/2 hr. UR; 1-1/2 hr. URB	FC-CB	2x4	DXL, DXLA, DXLH, DXLZ, SDLX, ZXLA	Fluorescent type, 2x4 - 16%; Incandescent type, 6-1/2" diam.	57 sq. in.	2-1/2" concrete; Metal lath; 10" bar joists 24" o.c.; W8 x 31 beam
	G262	1-1/2 hr. R; 1-1/2 hr. U	AP-1; FR-83: FR-X1: AP-2: (GR-1)	2x2 ILT edge	DXLT, DXLTZ, DXLTA, DXLTZA	Fluorescent type, 2x4 - 24%	113 sq. in.	2-1/2" concrete; Steel deck; 8' bar joists 24" o.c.
	G264	1-1/2 hr. R; 1-1/2 hr. U	AP-1: FR-83: FR-X1: AP-2: Astro-FR	2x2 FL edge	DXLF	Fluorescent type, 2x2 - 24%; Incandescent type, 6-1/2" diam.	113 sq. in.	2-1/2" concrete; Steel deck; 8" bar joists 24" o.c.
	G265	2 hr. R; 2 hr. U; 2 hr. URB	¾" FR-83: FR-X1	2x2; SQ. ILT edge	DXLT, DXLTA, DXLTZ, DXLTZA	Fluorescent type, 2x2 - 24%; Incandescent type, 6-1/2" diam.	113 sq. in	2-1/2" concrete; Metal lath; 10" bar joists 24" o.c.; W8 x 35 beam
Concrete and Steel Joists Concealed Grid System and Tile	G002	2 hr. R; 2 hr. UR	FR-83	12x12; 12x24	Z-runners	Fluorescent type, 2x4 - 24%	576 sq. in.	2-1/2" concrete; Metal lath; 10" bar joists 24" o.c.
	G007	2 hr. R; 2 hr. UR; 2 hr. URB	FR-83	12x12; 12x24; 24x24	Not a USG product	Fluorescent type, 1x4 - 16% or 2x4 - 24%	196 sq. in.	2-1/2" concrete; Metal lath; 10" bar joists 24" o.c.; W10 x 21 beam
	G008	2 hr. R; 2 hr. UR; 2 hr. URB	FR-83	12x12 to12x24	DXL, DXLZ, SDXL (DE, DT, DEN, PAT, BPA/PAT, E, BPC)	Fluorescent type, 1x4 - 12% or 2x4 - 16%	288 sq. in.	2-1/2" concrete; Metal lath or deck; 10" bar joists 24" o.c.; W8x31 beam
	G040	2 hr. R; 2 hr. UR	FR-83	12x12; 12x24	DXL, DXLA, ZXLA, (DE, DT), DXLZ, SDXL	Fluorescent type, 2x4 - 16%	113 sq. in.	2-1/2" concrete; Metal lath; 10" bar joists 24" o.c.; W10x19 beam
	G267	1-1/2 hr. R; 1-1/2 hr. UR	FR-83: AP; AP-3; FR-X1: M	2x2	DXL, DXLZ, SDXL	Fluorescent type, 2x4 - 24%; Incandescent type, 6-1/2" diam.	113 sq. in.	2-1/2" concrete; Steel deck; 8" bar joists 24" o.c.

Fire Rated Ceilings (continued)

Floor/Ceiling Designs	UL Design No.	Assembly Rating (Maximum)	Approved Ceiling Tiles/Panels	Tile/Panel Sizes	Suspension System	Maximum Fix. Size % Ceiling Area	Duct Area per 100 Sq. Ft. of Ceiling Area	Assembly Construction Details
Concrete and Steel Joists Concealed Grid System and Tile (continued)	G268	3 hr. R; 3 hr. UR; 3 hr. URB	¾" AP-3	2x2	DXL, DXLZ, SDXL	Fluorescent type, 2x4 – 12%; Incandescent type, 6-1/2" diam.	57 sq. in.	2-5/8" concrete; Metal lath; 10" bar joists 28" o.c.; W8x31 beam
Pre-cast and Field Poured Concrete Exposed Grid System and Lay-in Panels	J201	2 hr. R; 2 hr. UR	FR-83; FR-4; M; FR-X1; AP; AP-1; AP-3	2x2; 2x4; 20x60	DXL, DXLT, DXLZ, SDXL, DXLA, SDXLA, ZXLA, DXLTA, DXLTZA	Fluorescent type, 2x4 – 24%; Incandescent type, 6-1/2" diam.	576 sq. in.	2-1/2" concrete floor with 6" concrete stems
	J202	2 hr. R; 2 hr. UR	FR-83; FR-X1; AP; AP-1; AP-2; AP-3	2x2; 2x4	DXL, DXLT, DXLZ, SDXL, DXLTZ, DXL DXLZ, SDXL	Fluorescent type, 2x4 – 14%; Incandescent type, 6-1/2" diam.	57 sq. in.	Precast concrete; 2" desk; Stems 4' o.c.
Wood or Combination Wood and Steel Joists Assemblies Exposed Grid System and Lay-in Panels	L202	1 hr. UR; Finish Rating: 15 min.	FR-83; FR-4; M; FR-X1; Astro-FR	2x2; 2x4; 20x60; 24x60	DXL, DXLZ, SDXL, Acoustical tent, DXLT, DXLTA, DXLTZ	Fluorescent type, 20 x 48/60 or 2x4 – 16%; Incandescent type, 6-1/2" diam.	110 sq. in.	Wood floor; 2x10 wood joists 16" o.c.
	L206	1 hr. UR; Finish Rating: 17 min.	FR-83; FR-X1; M; FC-CB	2x2x3/4; 2x4	DXL, DXLA, DXLT, DXLTA, DXLTZ, DXLZ, DXLZA, SDXL, SDXLA	Fluorescent type, 2x4 – 8%; Incandescent type, 6-1/2" diam. – 0.5%	110 sq. in.	Wood floor; 2x10 wood joists 16" o.c.
	L211 (P237)	2 hr. UR; Finish Rating: 75 min.	FR-4; FR-83; FRxX1; M	2x4	DW (For drywall), DXL, DXLA, SDXL, DXLZ, SDXLA, ZXLA (for panels)	Fluorescent type 1x4 – 16%; 2x2 – 20%; 2x4 – 24%; Incandescent type, 6-1/2" diam.	576 sq. in.	Wood floor; 2x10 wood joists 16" o.c.; ½" Firecode C Gypsum Panel Ceiling w/6" fiberglass insulation
	L212 (P238)	FR-41 hr. UR; Finish Rating: 17 min.	FR-4	2x2; 2x4	DXL, DXLZ, SDXL	Fluorescent type, 1x4 – 12%; 2x2 – 16%; 2x4 – 24%; Incandescent type, 6-1/2" diam.	576 sq. in., Linear air returns.	Wood floor; 2xs10 wood joists 16" o.c.; Panels back-loaded with 6" fiberglass
Wood or Combination Wood and Steel Joist Assemblies Concealed Grid System and Tile	L006	1 hr. UR; Finish Rating: 12 min.	FR-83	12x12; 12x24	Not a USG product	Fluorescent type, 12x48; 20x48; 20x60 –14%	81 sq. in, Linear air returns	Wood floor; 2x10 wood joists 16" o.c.

Roof/Ceiling Designs	UL Design No.	Assembly Rating (Maximum)	Approved Ceiling Tiles/Panels	Tile/Panel Sizes	Suspension System	Maximum Fix. Size% Ceiling Area	Duct Area per 100 Sq. Ft. of Ceiling Area	Assembly Construction Details
Exposed Grid and Lay-in Panels	P230	1-1/2 hr. R; 1-1/2 hr. UR; 1-1/2 hr. URB	FR-4; fr-83: FR-X1; M; AP (1 hr. only); AP-3; Astro-FR; Metal Pans	2x2; 2x4; 20x60	DXL, DXLA, DXLP, DXLT, DXLTA, DXLTZ, DXLZ, DXLZA, SDXL, SDXLA, ZXLA	Fluorescent type, 2x4 – 24%; Incandescent type, 6-1/2" diam.; 2x2 HID	255 sq. in. (576 sq. in. for 1 hr.)	Unlimited insulation; Gypsum panels or Durrock ® on steel deck; 10" bar joists 72" o.c.; W6 x 12 beam
	P237	2 hr. R; 2 hr. UR; 2 hr. URB	FR-4; FR-83; FR-X1; M	2x4	DGL *for drywall) DXL, DXLA, DXLZ, DXLZA, SDXL, SDXLA (for panels), ZXLA	Fluorescent type, 1x4 – 16%; 2x2 – 20%; 2x4 – 24%; Incandescent type, 6-1/2" diam.	144 sq. in. Linear air returns	Unlimited insulation; Steel deck; 8" bar joists 72" o.c.; ½" Firecode C Gypsum Panel Ceiling w/ 6" fiberglass insulation
	P254	1 hr. R; ¾ hr. UR; ¾ hr. URB	3/4" FR-83	2x2 FL edge	DXLF	Fluorescent type, 2x2 or 2x4 – 24%; Incandescent type, 6-1/2" diam.	113 sq. in.	Unlimited insulation; Gypsum wallboard; Steel roof deck, 10" bar joists 48" to 72" o.c.

9

Fire Rated Ceilings (continued)

Roof/Ceiling Designs	UL Design No.	Assembly Rating (Maximum)	Approved Ceiling Tiles/Panels	Tile/Panel Sizes	Suspension System	Maximum Fix. Size % Ceiling Area	Duct Area per 100 Sq. Ft. of Ceiling Area	Assembly Construction Details
	P254	1 hr. R; ¾ hr. UR; ¾ hr. URB	¾" FR-83	2x2 FL edge	DXLF	Fluorescent type, 2x2 or 2x4 – 24%; Incandescent type, 6-1/2" diam.	113 sq. in.	Unlimited insulation; Gypsum wallboard; Steel roof deck, 10" bar joists 48" to 72" o.c.
	P268	1-1/2 hr. R; 1-1/2 hr. UR; 1-1/2 hr. URB	¾" FR-83; 5/8" FR-4	2x2	DXL, DXLA, ZXLA, DXLZ, SDXL, DXLZA, SDXLA	Fluorescent type, 2x4 – 24%	576 sq. in.	Metal roof deck panels; glass fiber insulation; steel roof purlins 60" o.c.; ceiling panels back-loaded with 6" fiberglass

Additional UL design are: P201, P202, P203, P213, P214, P235, P238, P241, P245, P246, P255, P257, P267, P269

Standards for Suspended Acoustical Ceilings

The most common source of voluntary standards is the American Society for Testing and Materials (ASTM). ASTM standards are widely referenced in all major building codes. ASTM is a not-for-profit organization that provides a forum for industry, consumer and regulatory body representatives, as well as other interested parties, to meet on a common ground and develop standards for products, installations and product testing methods. See the Appendix (ASTM Standards, page 499).

Building Codes Applicable to Suspended Acoustical Ceilings

The International Building Code (IBC) was first published by the International Code Council (ICC) in 2000 upon consolidation of the three major codes. The three major codes consolidated were the *Uniform Building Code* (UBC), *Standard Building Code* (SBC), and *BOCA National Building Code* (BOCA).

Regional building code authorities generally have adopted a form of the IBC. Several city and/or state code authorities, such as the State of New York, City of New York, City of Los Angeles, State Architects Office for State of California and the California State Fire Marshal, have added requirements for acoustical ceilings and their suspension systems, based on specific local needs.

In addition, there are several other codes that may have some influence over suspended ceiling construction, depending on the application. They include the *National Electric Code* (NEC) and the *Life Safety Code—NFPA 101*, both written by a committee of the National Fire Protection Association, Inc., and the *International Mechanical Code* (IMC), produced by the International Code Council.

Product Specifications

Project specifications have become coordinated almost entirely with the use of standardized, organized systems developed or adopted by the American Institute of Architects (AIA) and the Construction Specifications Institute (CSI). AIA adopted MASTERSPEC as a primary specification system. CSI developed MASTERFORMAT as the guideline in its Manual of Practice for a complete system of construction documentation. Online tools such as e-Specs developed by InterSpec also facilitate specification standards and leverage BIM technology. The website **usgdesignstudio.com** includes BIM content with e-specs integration.

Standard construction documents, particularly project and product specifications, streamline the bidding process while defining product and project quality. The project manual includes bid forms, contract conditions, drawings and specifications, and addenda and modifications.

Heating, Ventilation and Air Conditioning

Air distribution is an integral part of many suspended ceiling systems, and the delivery of heated and cooled air to the spaces below the ceiling is a major factor in the design of any ceiling system. The architect or designer must consider the amount of air flow and the distribution of the air from the HVAC equipment which is required to service a particular area. Typically, the air is delivered through diffusers in the ceiling system and is controlled by the amount of pressure produced by the HVAC equipment.

The movement and discharge of air into a conditioned space has a direct effect on the quality of the acoustical environment within the space. The acceptability of the sound caused by air movement depends on its loudness, its sound spectrum and its relationship to other sounds existing within the space.

Loudness of the air supply being delivered through an air diffuser is measured in decibels. The air diffusers are rated based on noise criteria (NC) for a given air flow in cubic feet per minute (CFM). In most cases, the sound caused by air movement must be kept to a low level so as to not interfere with communication within the space. Sometimes, however, a relatively higher noise level can be used to mask or cover other undesirable sounds and/or to provide for conversational privacy.

Acoustical design should be based on a thorough analysis of the practical requirements of the conditioned space. The design generally incorporates a balance between sounds: those caused by air movement and other existing sounds, communication, noise penetrating through the building exterior and sounds from adjacent spaces. The typical benchmark for noise produced by an air diffuser is a maximum of 35 NC in an office environment.

USG offers standard 2' x 2' air diffusers for 9/16" grid ceilings, as well as linear air boots for the PARALINE linear metal ceiling system. The air diffuser interface with the ceiling surface must maintain visual appeal and provide a clean, discreet slot for air flow. These diffuser units offer four-way air flow capability for optimum directional control and are available in one-, two-, three- or four-slot versions for maximum flexibility in air delivery requirements.

The chart on the following page lists design ranges for noise criteria (NC) for various indoor spaces.

Sound Control Guidelines for Air Handling Systems

Type of Area		Noise Criteria Range
Residences	Apartment houses, 2 and 3 family units	30-40
Hotels	Ballrooms, Banquet rooms	30-40
	Halls and corridors, Lobbies	35-45
	Garages	40-50
Hospitals and Clinics	Operating rooms, Wards	30-40
	Laboratories, Halls and corridors, Lobbies and waiting rooms	35-45
Offices	Conference rooms	25-35
	Reception rooms	30-40
	General open office, Drafting rooms	35-50
	Halls and corridors	35-55
Auditoriums	Multi-purpose halls	25-30
	Semi-outdoor amphitheaters, Lecture halls, Planetarium	30-35
	Lobbies	35-45
Schools	Libraries	30-40
	Classrooms	30-40
	Laboratories	35-45
	Recreation halls	35-50
	Corridors and halls	35-50
Public Buildings	Public libraries, Museums, Court rooms	30-40
	Post offices. General banking areas, Lobbies	35-45
	Washrooms and toilets	40-50
Restaurants, Cafeterias	Restaurants	35-45
	Cafeterias	40-50
Stores, Retail	Clothing stores	35-45
	Department stores, Small retail stores	40-50
	Supermarkets	40-50
Sports Activities, Indoor	Coliseums	30-40
	Bowling alleys, Gymnasiums	35-45
	Swimming pools	40-55
Transportation	Ticket sales office	30-40
	Lounges and waiting rooms	35-50

Source: American Society of Heating, Refrigerating and Air-Conditioning Engineers, Inc.
Noise Criteria (NC) is important to the design of the HVAC system and selection of the proper air diffuser.

Installation of Suspended Acoustical Ceilings

The appearance of a suspended acoustical ceiling depends on both the materials used and the quality of the installation. USG manufactures components to meet ASTM C635 to ensure material, structural and other quality standards. Installation must meet ASTM 636 to ensure the ceiling is level and securely attached as prescribed.

Measuring and planning are key first steps in the installation process. Measurement and placement of the tees will be on center (o.c.), meaning from the center of one to the center of the next. Several components are involved:

Wall Angle: L- shaped metal strips that provide a continuous finished edge around the perimeter of the ceiling, where it meets the wall.

Main Tees: Metal framing members that run the full length or width of the room (preferably perpendicular to joists) between the wall angles and perform as the primary support for the ceiling's weight. They are hung by hanger wire from joists or other supports above.

Cross Tees: Secondary support members for individual ceiling panels that snap into main tees at right angles. They generally come in two lengths: 4', used for both 2' x 4' and 2' x 2' grid patterns; and 2' for

2' x 2' only. Some suspension systems offer 3', 5' and 8' cross tees for off-module applications.

Ceiling Panels: Supported by the grid along all four edges, these lay in the open areas once the grid is assembled.

Hanger Wire: Typically 12 gauge, specified by most local building codes to support the main runners, every 4' o.c., along the entire length of each main runner.

Planning

Start with a drawing of the room that shows all walls, including bays, alcoves, beams and stairwells. Note which direction the joists are running, then determine the center line of the room's long dimension. (If the center line is perpendicular to the joists, installation of the tees will be easier.)

Locate the main tees by starting at the center line and marking 4' intervals to each side wall. If more than 2' remain between the last mark and the side wall, place the main tees at these locations. If less than 2' remain, locate the first two main tees 2' to either side of the center line and place all other main tees at 4' intervals. This procedure ensures symmetrical border panels of the largest possible cut size.

Locate cross tees at 2' intervals perpendicular to the main tees. Follow the same procedure as above to be sure border panels are the same size. For a 2' x 2' grid pattern, indicate additional 2' cross tees by bisecting each 2' x 4' module.

9

Tools

See Chapter 14, "Tools & Equipment," for information about applicable tools.

Step-By-Step Installation

Refer to the Ceilings & Interior Systems Construction Association's *Ceiling Systems Handbook* for detailed installation recommendations as well as environmental conditions (temperature and relative humidity) recommendations for proper installation.

1. Choose the desired ceiling height, maintaining at least 3" clearance below the lowest duct, pipe or beam. Measure and mark the walls at corners 7/8" above the desired ceiling height.

2. Snap a chalk line and test for level. Measuring down from joists, or up from floor, is not recommended, since either might not be level.

3. Install the wall angle with its top edge at the chalk line, spacing nails 2' o.c. or closer.

4. Cut inside angles at 90° and miter outside angles at 45°, fitting them snugly together.

5. Stretch a string taut along the positions the main tees will occupy to ensure level. A nail inserted between the wall and the wall angle at marked locations serves as a good anchor for this purpose.

6. Stretch another string across the room where the first row of cross tees will be located. This identifies where the first pre-punched slots need to fall. Check to be sure the cross-tee string is at 90° to the main tee string via the 3-4-5 method.

7. Install lag screws or screw eyes tightly into joists or suitable substrate at 4' intervals, then attach the hanger wire (18-ga. for residential, 12-ga. for commercial). The wires should extend 6" below the string line.

8. Bend wires 3/4" above the string line with pliers.

9. In each row, trim the main tee so that the cross-tee slot will line up with the cross-tee string.

10. Mount main tees, resting their cut ends on the wall angle and attaching wires by pulling them through the round hanger holes in the main tees. After checking the string line to be sure the tee is level, bend the wire up and around, twisting the wire tightly at least 3-1/2 turns to secure it. If the nearest hanger hole is not directly below the screw eye, adjust the hanger length accordingly or punch new holes at those locations.

11. Install cross tees, making sure they are adequately connected to main tees. (They "click" in place when properly seated.) Where two cross tees intersect in the same slot, insert the second cross-tee's end to the left of the first cross-tee. Where a cross-tee is installed without an opposing cross-tee, a nail must be slipped into the opening of the cross-tee clip to maintain the pull-out value for the cross-tee. This is known as an ashlar condition.

12. Lay in panels, beginning at one corner and completing row by row. Tilt each panel up through the opening and lower it to rest squarely on all four tees.

Other tips: Install light fixtures and wiring before installing the ceiling system. Cut tees with aviation snips, first the stem and then the flanges. Cut panels with a utility knife and straight edge, cutting the face first. Cut panels should be 3/4" larger than the opening. To install panels around obstructions, draw the exact locations on the panels and cut them out; cut the panel from the hole to side to enable fitting. To trim for Shadowline edge, use a utility knife to cut the panel, first at the face, then from the edge, to the same depth as Shadowline. If windows, stairwells, etc., extend above the ceiling plane, build suitable valances and attach the wall angle.

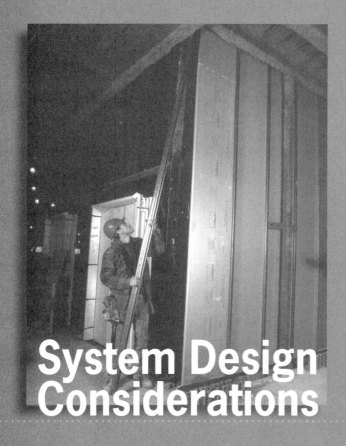

System Design Considerations

10

System Technical Data

USG leads the industry in developing high-performance systems to meet specialized requirements for modern building design and in documenting their performance at recognized testing laboratories. These systems provide fire resistance, sound control, structural capacity and aesthetics. All are constructed of quality products and released only after thorough testing and field trial.

In most instances, fire resistance and often sound-attenuation performance applies equally to systems constructed with gypsum panels and gypsum bases. Gypsum base with veneer plaster finish provides an acceptable alternative to gypsum panels. Therefore, the term "gypsum board" is used throughout this chapter to refer to both types of products. Only where performance differs greatly are the products treated separately.

Structural Criteria

Design of any structure must take into account the kinds of conditions that will exist and the resulting stresses and movements. Load-bearing walls include the exterior walls of a building, as well as some interior walls. These structures must be designed to carry the weight of the structure, its components, and other loads that occur once the building is occupied.

The amount of axial load that structural members can bear will vary with the amount of lateral load (pressure from wind or other horizontal stresses) that the final assembly may incur.

Manufacturers of structural components, particularly of steel framing (studs, runners and joists), provide maximum allowable loads for various components under specific conditions. These typically start at 5 psf lateral loads and increase in 5 or 10 psf increments to about 40 psf. Interior partitions are typically designed for 5 psf lateral loads. Gypsum board is used to clad both load-bearing and non-load-bearing walls.

Interior non-bearing partitions are not designed to carry axial loads. Limiting heights are based on stress or deflection limits for given lateral loads. Height limitations depend on the gauge of the steel used, dimensions of the stud, stud spacing, and the allowable deflection limit.

Curtain walls are not regarded as load-bearing walls and are not designed to carry axial loads. However, finished curtain wall assemblies do need to withstand wind loads within certain stress or deflection limits. Limiting height tables from the framing manufacturer should be consulted.

Load-span as it relates to the allowable height of the wall capacity of steel studs is based on the following factors (as applicable):

1. AISI *Specification for the Design of Cold-Formed Steel Structural Members*
2. Yield strength of the steel
3. Structural and physical properties of members
4. Bending stress of the steel stud
5. Axial load on the stud

6. Shear stress of the stud

7. Allowable deflection of the stud

8. Web crippling of stud at supports

9. Lateral bracing

Stud Selection

Selection of a stud gauge and size must take into account a number of factors. The key consideration is whether the assembly is for a load-bearing (having the ability to support the structural loads of the intended building), non-load-bearing or curtain wall application. Other variables include anticipated wall height, weight and dimensions of mounted fixtures, fire rating desired, sound attenuation needed, anticipated wind loads, insulation requirements, deflection allowance and desired impact resistance.

In general, stronger or heavier studs are needed to accommodate taller walls. Stronger studs also reduce deflection and vibration from impacts such as slamming doors. Wider studs may be needed to accommodate insulation requirements. Fire-resistant systems are usually designed, tested and classified based on using the lightest gauge, shallowest stud depth and maximum stud spacing as indicated in the assembly description. Stud gauge and depth may be increased without affecting the fire-resistance rating of the assembly.

Strength and performance characteristics can be achieved in a variety of ways. Wall strength can be increased by using heavier gauge material, stronger stud designs, narrower stud spacing or larger web dimensions. Studs typically are selected to maintain cost control and design integrity. Increased strength requirements generally are met by first increasing steel gauge or stud style before increasing stud dimensions.

10

Steel studs are typically manufactured in two different styles:

– Studs designed for non-load-bearing interior drywall partition applications have a minimum 1-1/4" flange width on both sides. The web design incorporates a cutout for bracing and for electrical, communication and plumbing lines.

– Studs designed for load-bearing drywall partition applications have varying flange widths ranging from 1-3/8" to 2". Cutouts in the web accommodate bracing, utility service and mechanical attachments.

Fire & Sound Tests

Fire and sound test data aid in comparing and selecting materials and constructions. In addition, these data frequently are essential for securing acceptance by the building code or authority having jurisdiction. The USG *Fire-Resistant Assemblies* SA100 provides tested fire resistance for various systems. Acoustical performance can be found in SA200 *Acoustical Assemblies*. Both fire and sound performance selectors may be found at **usgdesignstudio.com**.

Fire resistance refers to the ability of an assembly to serve as a barrier to fire and to confine its spread to the area of origin. Spread of fire from one area to another occurs because (a) the barrier collapses, (b) openings in the barrier allow passage of flame or hot gases or (c) sufficient heat is conducted through an assembly to exceed specified temperature limitations. These characteristics form the basis for judging when an assembly no longer serves as a barrier in a test.

A fire-resistance rating denotes the length of time a given assembly can meet the criteria above under precisely controlled laboratory conditions. All tests are conducted in accordance with ASTM E119 "Standard Test Methods for Fire Tests of Building Construction and Materials." The standard is also known as ANSI/UL 263 and NFPA 251. The ratings are expressed in hours and apply to walls, floor- and roof-ceiling assemblies, beams and columns. Refer to page 450 for a full discussion of the significance of laboratory fire resistance testing.

For assemblies tested at Underwriters Laboratories Inc. (UL), or any fire test facility, ratings are specific to the designs tested. Unless described in the design, insulation may not be added to floor- or roof-ceiling assemblies under the assumption that the rating either will remain the same or improve. Addition of insulation in the concealed space between the ceiling membrane and the floor or roof structure may reduce the hourly rating of an assembly by causing premature disruption of the ceiling membrane and/or higher temperatures on structural components under fire exposure conditions.

Sound control refers to the ability to attenuate sound passing through a partition.

The Sound Transmission Class (STC) is a widely used rating of sound attenuation performance. It is tested per ASTM E90 and rated per ASTM E413.

The Impact Insulation Class (IIC) is a numerical evaluation of a floor-ceiling assembly's effectiveness in retarding the transmission of impact sound, also determined from laboratory testing. IIC is tested per ASTM E492 and rated per ASTM E989.

The Noise Reduction Coefficient (NRC) is a measure of sound absorption. This is an important consideration for controlling acoustics within a confined area.

The Ceiling Attenuation Class (CAC) applies to acoustical ceilings and is tested per ASTM E1414 for horizontally adjacent spaces.

Fire and sound tests are conducted on USG products assembled in a specific manner to meet requirements of established test procedures. Substitution of materials other than those tested or deviation from the specified construction may adversely affect performance and result in failure. For complete information on test components and construction, refer to the test report.

Typical Fire Systems

A large number of systems have been designed and tested for fire resistance. The systems vary greatly in both design and performance. Nevertheless, certain basic system designs are commonly used. As a frame of reference, several typical designs and their accompanying fire ratings are shown below for both wood- and steel-framed assemblies.

Below are a series of notes that apply to many of the fire tests:

1. Two recent tests, UL Design U419 for non-load-bearing partitions and UL Design U423 for load-bearing partitions, permit

SHEETROCK brand gypsum panel products and IMPERIAL brand gypsum base products to be applied horizontally or vertically in partitions without compromising the fire rating. When either of these tests is listed with a USG system, the system can then be built with the panels oriented in either direction.

2. The two fire tests indicated above also demonstrated that when FIRECODE or FIRECODE C Core products are used, the horizontal joints on opposite sides of the studs need not be staggered (as was previously required).

3. In partition systems indicating the use of 5/8" SHEETROCK brand gypsum panels, FIRECODE Core, or 1/2" SHEETROCK brand gypsum panels, FIRECODE C Core, it is permissible to substitute 5/8" FIBEROCK brand panels without compromising the fire rating.

4. Where insulation is shown in assembly drawings, a specific product may be required to achieve the stated fire rating. Glass fiber insulation cannot be substituted in all cases for mineral wool insulation.

5. In fire-rated non-load-bearing partitions, steel studs should not be attached to floor and ceiling runners.

Wood Frame Partitions

1-hr. Rating
UL Design U305
Drywall System

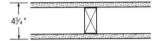

Studs:	Wood 2 x 4
Stud spacing:	16" o.c.
Gypsum panel:	5/8" SHEETROCK brand FIRECODE Core gypsum panel, or 5/8" SHEETROCK brand FIRECODE Core MOLD TOUGH gypsum panel, each side.
Panel orientation:	Vertical or horizontal.
Attachment:	1-7/8" cement-coated nails spaced 7" o.c.
Joints:	Exposed or taped and treated according to edge configuration.
Insulation:	Optional.
Perimeter:	Should be caulked With SHEETROCK brand acoustical sealant.

Veneer Plaster System

Studs:	Wood 2 x 4
Stud spacing:	16" o.c.
Gypsum panel:	5/8" IMPERIAL brand gypsum base FIRECODE Core, each side.
Panel orientation:	Vertical or horizontal.
Attachment:	1-7/8" cement-coated nails spaced 7" o.c.
Joints:	Taped.

Finish:	3/32" Dɪᴀᴍᴏɴᴅ or Iᴍᴘᴇʀɪᴀʟ veneer finish both sides.
Insulation:	Optional.
Perimeter:	Should be caulked with Sʜᴇᴇᴛʀᴏᴄᴋ brand acoustical sealant.

**2-hr. Rating
UL Design U301
Drywall System**

6″

Studs:	Wood 2 x 4
Stud spacing:	16" o.c.
Gypsum panel:	Two layers of 5/8" Sʜᴇᴇᴛʀᴏᴄᴋ brand Fɪʀᴇᴄᴏᴅᴇ Core gypsum panel, or 5/8" Sʜᴇᴇᴛʀᴏᴄᴋ brand Fɪʀᴇᴄᴏᴅᴇ Core Mᴏʟᴅ Tᴏᴜɢʜ gypsum panel each side.
Panel orientation:	Horizontal or vertical—joints of face layer staggered over joints of base layer.
Attachment:	Base layer—1-7/8" cement-coated nails spaced 6" o.c. Face layer—2-3/8" nails 8" o.c.
Joints:	Exposed or taped and treated.
Perimeter:	Should be caulked with Sʜᴇᴇᴛʀᴏᴄᴋ brand acoustical sealant

Veneer Plaster System

Studs:	Wood 2 x 4
Stud spacing:	16" o.c.
Gypsum panel:	Two layers of 5/8" Iᴍᴘᴇʀɪᴀʟ brand gypsum base Fɪʀᴇᴄᴏᴅᴇ Core.
Panel orientation:	Horizontal or vertical—joints of face layer staggered over joints of base layer.
Attachment:	Base layer—1-7/8" cement-coated nails spaced 6" o.c. Face layer—2-3/8" nails 8" o.c.
Joints:	Taped.
Finish:	3/32" Dɪᴀᴍᴏɴᴅ or Iᴍᴘᴇʀɪᴀʟ veneer finish both sides.
Perimeter:	Should be caulked with Sʜᴇᴇᴛʀᴏᴄᴋ brand acoustical sealant.

**Steel Frame
Partitions**

**1-hr. Rating
UL Design U419
Drywall System**

4⅞″

Studs:	Steel 362S125-18 (minimum).
Stud spacing:	24" o.c.
Gypsum panel:	5/8" SHEETROCK brand FIRECODE Core gypsum panel or 5/8" SHEETROCK brand Mold-Tough FIRECODE Core gypsum panel each side.
Panel orientation:	Vertical or horizontal.
Attachment:	Type S screws 8" o.c.
Joints:	Taped and treated.
Insulation:	Optional.
Perimeter:	Should be caulked with SHEETROCK brand acoustical sealant.

Veneer Plaster System

Studs:	Steel 362S125-18 (minimum).
Stud spacing:	24" o.c.
Gypsum panel:	5/8" IMPERIAL brand gypsum Base FIRECODE Core, each side.
Panel orientation:	Vertical or horizontal.
Attachment:	Type S screws 8" o.c.
Joints:	Taped (paper) and treated.
Finish:	3/32" DIAMOND or IMPERIAL veneer finish both sides.
Insulation:	Optional.
Perimeter:	Should be caulked with SHEETROCK brand acoustical sealant.

10

2-hr. Rating
UL Design U411, U412 or U419
Drywall System

wall thickness
varies with
actual design

Studs:	Steel 250S125-18.
Stud spacing:	24" o.c.
Gypsum panel:	Two layers of 5/8" SHEETROCK brand FIRECODE Core gypsum panel, or 1/2" SHEETROCK brand FIRECODE C gypsum panel, Core, each side.
Panel orientation:	Vertical or horizontal—joints of face layer staggered over joints of base layer.
Attachment:	Base layer—1" Type S screws 8" o.c. Face layer—laminated with joint compound or attached with 1-5/8" Type S screws 12" o.c.

Joints:	U411, exposed or taped and treated; U412, outer layer taped and treated.
Perimeter:	Should be caulked with SHEETROCK brand acoustical sealant.

Veneer Plaster System

Studs:	Steel 250S125-18.
Stud spacing:	24" o.c.
Gypsum panel:	Two layers of 5/8" IMPERIAL brand gypsum base, FIRECODE Core, or 1/2" IMPERIAL gypsum base, FIRECODE C Core.
Panel orientation:	Vertical or horizontal—joints of face layer staggered over joints of base layer.
Attachment:	Base layer—1" Type S screws 8" o.c. Face layer—laminated with joint compound or attached with 1-5/8" Type S screws 12" o.c. Face layer—2-3/8" nails 8" o.c.
Joints:	Taped (paper) and treated.
Finish:	3/32" DIAMOND or IMPERIAL veneer finish both sides.
Perimeter:	Should be caulked with SHEETROCK brand acoustical sealant.

Wood Floor/ Ceilings

1-hr. Rating
UL Design L501 or L512
Drywall System

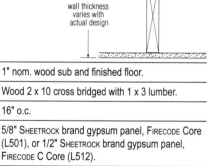

wall thickness
varies with
actual design

Floor:	1" nom. wood sub and finished floor.
Joists:	Wood 2 x 10 cross bridged with 1 x 3 lumber.
Joist spacing:	16" o.c.
Gypsum panel:	5/8" SHEETROCK brand gypsum panel, FIRECODE Core (L501), or 1/2" SHEETROCK brand gypsum panel, FIRECODE C Core (L512).
Panel orientation:	Perpendicular to joists.
Attachment:	1-7/8" cement-coated nails spaced 6" o.c.
Joints:	Taped and treated.

Veneer Plaster System

Floor:	1" nom. wood sub and finished floor.

Joists:	Wood 2 x 10 cross bridged with 1 x 3 lumber.
Joist spacing:	16" o.c.
Gypsum panel:	5/8" IMPERIAL brand gypsum base, FIRECODE Core (L501), or 1/2" IMPERIAL brand gypsum base, FIRE CODE C Core (L512).
Panel orientation:	Perpendicular to joists.
Attachment:	1-7/8" cement-coated nails spaced 6" o.c.
Joints:	Taped.
Finish:	3/32" DIAMOND or IMPERIAL veneer finish both sides.

Steel Floor/ Ceilings

3-hr. Rating
UL Design G512
Drywall System

16"

Floor:	2-1/2" concrete on corrugated steel deck or riblath over bar joist—includes 3-hr. unrestrained beam.
Joists:	Type 12J2 min. size, spaced 24" o.c. (riblath); Type 16J2 min. size, spaced 24" o.c. (corrugated steel deck).
Furring channel:	25-ga. spaced 24" o.c. perpendicular to joists; 3" on each side of wallboard end joints—double-strand saddle tied.
Gypsum panel:	5/8" SHEETROCK Brand Gypsum Panel, FIRECODE C Core.
Panel orientation:	Perpendicular to furring.
Attachment:	1" Type S screws 12 " o.c.
Joints:	End joints backed with wallboard strips and at tached to double channels.

10

Veneer Plaster System

Floor:	2-1/2" concrete on corrugated steel deck or riblath over bar joist—includes 3-hr. unrestrained beam.
Joists:	Type 12J2 min. size, spaced 24" o.c. (riblath); Type 16J2 min. size, spaced 24" o.c. (corrugated steel deck).
Furring channel:	25-ga. spaced 24" o.c. perpendicular to joists; 3" on each side of wallboard end joints—double-strand saddle tied.
Gypsum panel:	5/8" IMPERIAL brand gypsum base, FIRECODE C Core.
Panel orientation:	Perpendicular to furring.
Attachment:	1" Type S screws 12 " o.c.

| Joints: | End joints backed with wallboard strips and attached to double channels. |
| Finish: | 3/32" DIAMOND or IMPERIAL veneer finish both sides. |

Wood Stud Partitions

Suitable for residential and light-commercial construction where combustible framing is permitted, wood stud partition design includes single and double-layer gypsum board facings, single- and double-row studs, those with insulating blankets, and those with resilient attachment. Performance values of up to 2-hr. fire resistance and 59 STC can be obtained.

Wood Stud Partitions

Steel Stud Partitions

Suitable for all types of construction, these designs include single- and multi-layer gypsum board facings, with and without sound attenuation blankets. Performance values of up to 4-hr. fire resistance and 62 STC can be obtained.

Steel Stud Partitions

Sound Control Systems

USG fire-rated partition systems offer a range of assemblies that are highly effective in isolating all types of sound. Resilient channel systems offer improved sound attenuation to direct attachment systems.

In steel-framed construction, USG systems provide economical sound isolating systems without the excess weight or space required of masonry construction. Systems are designed to control not only mid and high frequencies, but also low frequencies prevalent in music and mechanical equipment environments. Partition systems include both load-bearing and non-load-bearing designs.

For assistance with specific project requirements, visit **usgdesignstudio.com**.

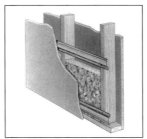 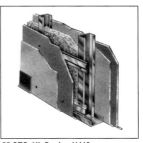

50 STC, UL Design U311,
BBN-760903

55 STC, UL Design U412 or
U419, SA800421

Area Separation Fire-Wall/Party-Wall Systems

USG area separation fire walls/party walls are recommended for constructing common walls with fire-resistive protection for adjacent properties. These lightweight, non-load-bearing gypsum drywall assemblies are designed as vertical fire barriers for fire walls and party walls separating occupancies in wood-frame apartments and townhouses.

Large-size gypsum panels used in conjunction with steel studs and runners quickly become thin, space-saving walls offering excellent privacy. Their engineered performance and low labor and material costs make these systems superior to the usual masonry construction.

Solid Type area separation fire/party walls feature independently framed interior gypsum panel surfaces on both sides of the fire wall or party wall. This system may be used in buildings up to four stories high (44') and with all common floor-ceiling heights found in multi-family housing. It is suitable for exterior walls with appropriate weather-resistant cladding when building offsets are desired.

10

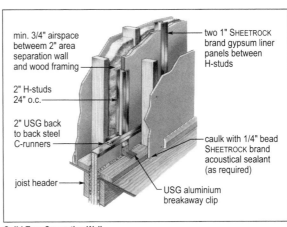

min. 3/4" airspace
betweem 2" area
separation wall
and wood framing

2" H-studs
24" o.c.

2" USG back
to back steel
C-runners

joist header

two 1" SHEETROCK
brand gypsum liner
panels between
H-studs

caulk with 1/4" bead
SHEETROCK brand
acoustical sealant
(as required)

USG aluminium
breakaway clip

Solid-Type Separation Wall

Fire Resistance: Separation walls offer 2-hr. and 3-hr. fire ratings.

Sound Isolation: STC ratings up to 60 are available.

Lightweight: These drywall assemblies weigh at least 50% less than masonry walls, a characteristic that speeds up installation.

Weather Resistance: Moisture-resistant components permit installation in any weather, and can help eliminate costly winter construction delays.

Solid-Type Separation Wall

Solid-type separation walls consist of two 1" thick SHEETROCK brand gypsum liner panels installed vertically between 2" steel C-runners. Panel edges are inserted in 2" steel H-studs spaced 24" o.c.

C-runners should be installed at the top and bottom of the wall, as well as back-to-back between vertical panels at a convenient height above each intermediate floor. H-studs are attached on both sides to adjacent wood framing at intermediate floors, the bottom chords of attic trusses, and at the roof line with 0.063" aluminum angle clips designed to break away when exposed to fire, thus permitting a fire-damaged structure to fail while the fire barrier remains intact. Refer to the architectural specifications in SA925, *USG Area Separation Wall Systems,* for exact clip placement.

With 2" mineral wool sound attenuation blankets (SAB) stapled to each side of liner panels, the assembly obtains a 3-hr. fire-resistance rating, allowing separate selection and construction of tenant walls.

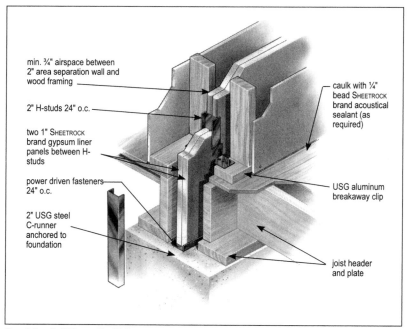

min. ¾" airspace between 2" area separation wall and wood framing

2" H-studs 24" o.c.

two 1" SHEETROCK brand gypsum liner panels between H-studs

power driven fasteners 24" o.c.

2" USG steel C-runner anchored to foundation

caulk with ¼" bead SHEETROCK brand acoustical sealant (as required)

USG aluminum breakaway clip

joist header and plate

Foundation–Solid Separation Wall

Foundation—
solid separation wall

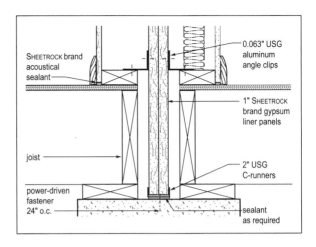

SHEETROCK brand
acoustical
sealant

0.063" USG
aluminum
angle clips

1" SHEETROCK
brand gypsum
liner panels

joist

2" USG
C-runners

power-driven
fastener
24" o.c.

sealant
as required

Installation

Layout A minimum of 3/4" clearance must be maintained between an area separation wall and wood framing. A 3" space is required to accommodate insulation thickness (for the 3-hr. wall). Mineral wool insulation fire blocking at intermediate platforms is required in all cases.

Foundation Position 2" C-runners at floor and securely attach to foundation with power-driven fasteners at both ends, spaced 24" o.c. Space adjacent runner sections 1/4" apart. When specified, caulk under runner at foundation with min. 1/4" bead of acoustical sealant.

First Floor Install H-studs and liner panels to a convenient height (max. 2') above the floor line. Install two thicknesses of 1" liner panels vertically in C-runner with long edges in H-stud. Erect H-studs and liner panels alternately until wall is completed. Cap top of panels with horizontal C-runner. Fasten C-runner flanges at all corners both sides with two 3/8" type S screws.

Intermediate Floors and Bottom of Trusses Cap top of liner panels and H-studs with C-runner. Attach C-runner for next row of panels to the C-runner below with end joints staggered at least 12".

Fasten the C-runners together with double 3/8" screws at ends and 24" o.c. Attach all H-studs to adjacent framing with an aluminum breakaway clip. Clips securing H-studs and vertical C-runners to adjacent wood framing on both sides should be attached with one 3/8" type S screw. Clips securing H-studs and vertical C-runners to adjacent wood framing on only one side and with exterior exposure on the other side should be attached with two 3/8" type S screws. Attachment to the wood framing should be done with one 1-1/4" type W or S screw.

Locate the horizontal C-runner joint within 2' of the intermediate floor. Install fire blocking between the solid wall system and adjacent framing at floor lines, bottom of truss line, and any other locations required by the applicable code. Note that for walls with exterior exposure on opposite side, clips should be spaced maximum 4' o.c. vertically.

10

330

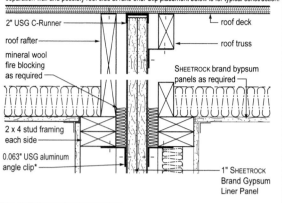

Details - UL Design U336

Note: As required by code, 5/8" SHEETROCK brand gypsum panels, FIRECODE Core, may be used as underlayment to untreated roof sheathing with panels extending 4' on both sides of area separation wall and possibly roof side at rake end. Clip placement below is for typical construction.

2" USG C-Runner

roof rafter

mineral wool fire blocking as required

2 x 4 stud framing each side

0.063" USG aluminum angle clip*

roof deck

roof truss

SHEETROCK brand bypsum panels as required

1" SHEETROCK Brand Gypsum Liner Panel

Intersection at roof

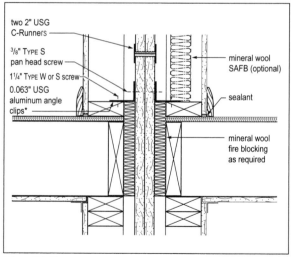

two 2" USG C-Runners

3/8" TYPE S pan head screw

1¼" TYPE W or S screw

0.063" USG aluminum angle clips*

mineral wool SAFB (optional)

sealant

mineral wool fire blocking as required

Intermediate floor

*Note: When installing the solid-type wall and its height is over 23 feet, up to a maximum height of 44 feet, the aluminum clips shall be vertically spaced a maximum of 10 feet on center for the upper 23 feet of the wall and 5 feet on center for the remaining portion of the wall below the 23 foot increment.

Roof Continue erecting H-studs and liner panels for succeeding stories as described. Cut the liner panels and H-studs to roof pitch and length as necessary. At roof, cap liner panels and H-studs with C-runner. Attach all H-studs to adjacent framing with an aluminum breakaway clip. Again, clips used to secure H-studs and vertical C-runners to adjacent wood framing on only one side and with exterior exposure on the other side require attachment to each vertical framing member with two 3/8" type S screws.

Sound Attenuation Fire Blankets For direct attachment to 1" liner panels, install blankets with joints staggered and attach them with seven staples driven through each blanket. Blanket installation within cavities is friction fit between stud framing.

Interior Finish Apply specified gypsum panels to wood studs and joists with screws or nails in conventional manner.

Good Design Practices

Clip Attachment Solid systems with adjacent wood framing on both sides require an aluminum breakaway clip to the wood framing on either side of the H-stud. Clips should be attached to the H-studs and vertical C-runners with one 3/8" type S screw, and to the wood framing with one 1-1/4" type W or S screw (3-hole leg of clip).

Solid systems with exterior exposure and with adjacent wood framing on only one side require an aluminum breakaway clip on the side of the H-stud toward the wood framing. Clips are attached to each vertical framing member with two 3/8" type S screws, and to the wood framing with one 1-1/4" type W or S screw (3-hole leg of clip). Exterior exposure is limited to 15 psf wind load, and requires vertical clip spacing of 4' o.c. maximum. For use with the solid system, these clips may be attached to adjacent wood framing.

10

Sound Control Construction For maximum sound control seal the entire perimeter and between the horizontal, back-to-back C-runners at the intermediate levels with a minimum 1/4" bead of SHEETROCK brand acoustical sealant. Carefully seal around all gaps and cutouts for lights, cabinets, pipes, ducts, electrical boxes, etc. to minimize sound leakage. Back-to-back penetrations of the gypsum panel diaphragm and flanking paths should be eliminated.

USG Shaft Walls

Cavity Shaft Walls

USG cavity shaft walls are non-load-bearing, fire-resistant gypsum board partition systems for enclosing shafts, air ducts and stairwells. Designed for erection from one side, USG shaft walls offer superior performance and greater economy than other designs.

The engineered design of the C-H stud system provides a simpler, thinner, lighter-weight assembly. It offers faster installation and lower material costs, which reduce total in-place costs. It also saves on structural framing costs. For example, masonry shaft enclosures in high-rise buildings can weigh up to 45 psf, whereas lightweight USG shaft walls range from 9 psf (2-hour assembly) to 16 psf (3-hr. assembly).

USG shaft walls provide up to 4-hr. fire resistance and sound ratings to 51 STC. Designs are available for intermittent lateral loads up to 15 psf. For sustained pressure in air returns, design uniform pressure loads should not exceed 10 psf.

Maximum partition heights depend on expected pressures. For elevator shafts, the applied pressure load is selected by the designer based on elevator cab speed and the number of elevators per shaft. Instead of using only deflection criteria, USG design data considers several additional factors in determining limiting partition heights. These include:

Bending Stress The unit force that exceeds the stud strength.

End Reaction Shear Determined by the amount of force applied to the stud (at the supports) that will bend or shear the J-runner or cripple the stud.

Deflection The actual deflection under a load. Allowable deflection is based on the amount of bowing under load that a particular wall can accommodate without adversely affecting the wall finish.

A wide range of product and installation combinations is available to meet performance requirements: Intermittent air pressure loading of 5, 7-1/2, 10, 15 psf; vertical heights in three stud sizes and four steel thicknesses to accommodate lobbies and mechanical rooms. Assemblies can be constructed with fire-resistance ratings from 2-hr. to 4-hr. For more information, consult USG Technical Folder SA926, *USG Cavity Shaft Wall Systems.*

Single-layer both sides
(UL Designs U415 and U467)

Double-layer one side
(UL Designs U415 and U438)

Horizontal Shaft Walls

Cavity shaft walls installed horizontally provide economical construction for fire-resistive duct protection, corridor and other ceilings and stairway soffits. They are also ideal for ceilings over office areas in pitched-roof buildings and in modular buildings where ceiling framing is independent of the floor above. With 1" liner panels inserted into USG C-H studs 24" o.c. and triple-layer 1/2" Sʜᴇᴇᴛʀᴏᴄᴋ brand gypsum panels, Fɪʀᴇᴄᴏᴅᴇ C Core, screw attached to studs, the system provides greater spans and 2-hr. protection from fire either inside or outside the duct.

With double-layer 1/2" Sʜᴇᴇᴛʀᴏᴄᴋ brand gypsum panels, Fɪʀᴇᴄᴏᴅᴇ C Core, screw attached to studs, the assembly provides suitable 2-hr. fire-resistive ceiling construction for corridors and stairs. One-hour fire-rated construction is offered with single-layer 1/2" Sheetrock brand gypsum panels, Firecode C Core.

No other drywall shaft assembly provides such an economical horizontal application.

Installation of Vertical Shaft Walls

Studs and Liner Panels Position USG J-runners at the floor and ceiling with the short leg toward the finish side of the wall. Securely attach the runners to the structural supports with power-driven fasteners at both ends and max. 24" o.c. With steel-frame construction, install floor and ceiling runners and J-runners, or E-studs on columns and beams before they are fireproofed. Remove spray fireproofing from runners and E-studs before installing the gypsum line panels. For other structural steel fireproofing requirements, use Z-shaped stand-off clips secured to the structural steel before the fireproofing application. The above is only applicable in areas where it is code mandated.

Cut the liner panels 1" less than floor-to-ceiling height, and erect vertically between J-runners. Where the shaft walls exceed the maximum available panel height, position the liner panel end joints within the upper and lower third points of the wall. Stagger joints top and bottom in adjacent panels. Screw studs to runners on walls over 16'.

Use steel C-H studs 3/8" to not more than 1/2" less than floor-to-ceiling height, and install them between liner panels with the liner inserted in the groove. Install full-length steel E-studs or J-runners vertically at T-intersections, corners, door jambs and columns. Install full-length E-studs over gypsum liner panels on both sides of closure panels. Frame openings with vertical E-studs or J-runners at edges, horizontal J-runners at head and sill, and reinforcing as specified. Suitably frame all openings to maintain structural support for the wall.

Install floor-to-ceiling steel E-studs on each side of steel door frames designed for hinged doors and jamb struts on each side of elevator door frames to act as strut studs. Attach strut studs to floor and ceiling runners with two 3/8" type S-12 pan-head screws. Attach strut studs to jamb anchors with 1/2" type S-12 screws. Over steel door frames, install a cut-to-length section of J-runner and attach it to the strut stud with 3/8" type S-12 pan-head screws.

10

Gypsum Panel Attachment

For a single-layer, one-side, one-hour wall, apply 5/8" SHEETROCK brand gypsum panels, FIRECODE Core, to the "C" side of the C-H studs. Position the gypsum panels vertically and fasten them to the studs and runners with 1" type S screws 12" o.c. (UL Design U415 or U469).

For a double-layer, one side, two-hour wall, apply the base layer of 1/2" SHEETROCK brand gypsum panels, FIRECODE C Core, or 5/8" gypsum panels, FIRECODE Core, vertically or horizontally to the studs with 1" type S screws 24" o.c. along the edges and in the field of the panels. For vertical application, apply the face layer of 1/2" panels, FIRECODE C Core, vertically and fasten it to the studs and J-runners with 1-5/8" type S screws 12" o.c. along the edges and in the field of the panels, staggered from the screws of the base layer. Joints between the base and face layers should be staggered. For horizontal applications, apply the face layer horizontally and attach it over the base layer with 1-5/8" type S screws 12" o.c. in the field, along the vertical edges and to the floor and ceiling runners. Attach the face layer to the base layer with 1-1/2" long type G screws midway between the studs and 1" from the horizontal joint (UL Design U415 or U438).

For a single-layer both sides, two-hour wall, apply 1/2" SHEETROCK brand gypsum panels, FIRECODE C Core, or 5/8" panels, FIRECODE Core, vertically or horizontally to both sides of the studs. Fasten the gypsum panels with 1" type S Screws 12" o.c. along the vertical edges and in the field (UL Design U415 or U467).

For a single 3/4" layer one side, two-hour wall, apply 1" liner panels on one side, between 4" steel C-H studs, 24" o.c., install 3" Mineral wool insulation in the cavity, and 3/4" gypsum panels, ULTRACODE Core, on the other side. Position the panels vertically or horizontally, and fasten them to the studs and runners with 1-1/4" type S screws 8" o.c. (UL Design U415 or U492).

For a double-layer, two-hour wall, with DUROCK brand cement board, install 1-1/2" mineral wool insulation in the stud cavity. Apply a base layer of 5/8" SHEETROCK brand gypsum panels, FIRECODE Core, vertically or horizontally, and attach with 1" type S screws 24" o.c. along the vertical edges and in the field of the panels. Install the face layer of 1/2" DUROCK brand cement board by lamination to the gypsum panels with 4" wide strips of organic adhesive applied with a 3/4" notched trowel midway between the studs and fasten to the studs with 1-5/8" DUROCK brand screws 6" o.c. (UL Design U415 or U459).

For a double-layer, two-hour resilient wall, apply a base layer of 1/2" SHEETROCK brand gypsum panels, FIRECODE C Core, to resilient channels with end joints staggered; fasten with 1" type S screws 12" o.c. Apply face layer of 1/2" gypsum panels, FIRECODE C Core, vertically with joints staggered; fasten to channels with 1-5/8" type S screws 12" o.c. (UL Design U415).

For triple-layer, three-hour wall, install three layers of 5/8" gypsum panels, FIRECODE C Core, vertically or horizontally on corridor side of studs. Use 1" type S self-drilling, self-tapping bugle-head screws, spaced 24"/16" o.c. (vertical/horizontal orientation) for the first layer; mid-layer 1-5/8" TYPE S screws, spaced 24"/16" o.c. (vertical/horizontal orientation). Apply the third layer using 2-1/4" TYPE S screws, spaced 16" (vertical board application) or 12" o.c. (horizontal board application). Finish joints with paper tape and joint compound (UL Design U415).

For horizontal shaft wall installation, two-hour membrane, install three layers of 1/2" gypsum panels, FIRECODE C Core, to horizontally installed C-H and/or E-studs. Install the base layer with the edges parallel to the studs and attached with 1" type S screws 24" o.c. Apply the middle layer in the same manner with joints offset 2' and attached with 1-5/8" type S screws 24" o.c.; and apply the face layer perpendicular to the studs and attached with 2-1/4" type S screws 12" o.c. Place the face-layer end joints between the studs and secure them with 1-1/2" type G screws 8" o.c.

Vent Shaft

USG Vent Shaft System provides a 2-hr. fire-rated enclosure (UL Design U505 or U529) for vertical shafts in apartments and other types of multi-story buildings. The assembly is particularly suited for relatively small and widely separated mechanical, service and ventilator shafts. USG Shaft Walls are preferred where service and mechanical lines and equipment are consolidated within the building core.

Installation

Support Member Attachment Install 1" x 2" x 25-ga. galvanized steel angles as runners on floor and sidewalls by fastening through their short legs. Steel angles may be used as ceiling runners. Install side angle runners 30" long and centered for attachment of horizontal bracing angles.

Bracing Angle Attachment (UL Design U505) Install 1" x 2" x 25-ga. galvanized steel bracing angles horizontally at quarter-points between the floor and ceiling and spaced max. 5' o.c. Position the long leg vertically for board attachment and fasten to sidewall angles with 1" type S screws.

Gypsum Panel and Liner Application Install 5/8" gypsum panels, FIRECODE Core, or 1/2" FIRECODE C Core panels, vertically on the shaft side and fasten to angles and runners with 1" type S screws 16 o.c. Apply setting-type or lightweight setting-type joint compound or ready-mixed joint compound (all-purpose or taping) on the back side of the liner panels and strip or sheet-laminate to the shaft-side board. Install a second set of floor and sidewall angle runners (and ceiling angles, if required) with the long legs against the liner panels. Attach the liner to the runners and angles with 2-1/4" type S screws 12" o.c. and at least 6" away from the liner edges.

Laminate the floor-side face board to liner panels with joint compound and install vertically. Joints should be offset 12" from one layer to the next, and moderate pressure should be applied to ensure good adhesive bond. Fasten to the liner panels with 1-1/2" type G screws. Drive the screws approximately 24" from the ends of the board and 36" o.c. along lines from vertical edges. Temporary bracing may be used instead of screws to maintain bond until adhesive is hard and dry. Caulk the perimeter with acoustical sealant to prevent air infiltration. Complete the assembly with the appropriate drywall or veneer finish application.

10

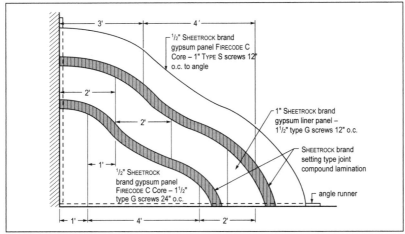

Vent Shaft Enclosure

Floor/Ceiling Assemblies

Wood Frame Floor/Ceilings

These designs, which are suitable for all types of wood-framed residential and commercial buildings, include those with single- and double-layer gypsum board facings, and other assemblies with mineral wool insulation sound attenuation blankets and resilient attachment.

Performance values of up to 2-hr. fire resistance, STC 60 and IIC 69 can be obtained, as well as a non-fire-rated assembly with STC 57 and IIC 53.

Wood-frame—direct attachment.

Wood-frame—with resilient attachment and mineral wool SAFB.

USG publishes data for more than 20 tests conducted on resilient wood-frame ceiling assemblies including the only 1-hr. residential gypsum board system for 48" joist spacing. For complete listings, refer to Technical Folder SA924, *Drywall/Wood Framed Systems,* and the *Fire-Resistant Assemblies* SA100.

Sound Control Floor/Ceilings

Several floor/ceiling systems have been developed to provide exceptional sound control as well as fire resistance in wood-framed assemblies.

The systems require two layers of 5/8" gypsum panels, FIRECODE Core, applied over resilient channels and 3" batts of mineral wool sound attenuation fire blankets (SAFB) installed within the cavity. More detailed information is provided in Technical Folder SA924, *Drywall/Wood Framed Systems.*

Noncombustible Floor/Ceilings

Noncombustible ceilings with steel furring channels conceal and protect structural and mechanical elements above a lightweight fire-resistant layer of gypsum board. The furring channels, to which gypsum board is screw-attached, are wire-tied to bar joists, or wire-tied to suspended 1-1/2" main runner channel grillage. Panels are also screw-attached below a direct suspension system.

Furred Ceiling

Suspended Ceiling

For long-span suspension beneath large ducts or pipes, steel studs are substituted for furring channels. With foil-back gypsum board, the ceiling is effective as a vapor retarder. Also, the board provides a firm base for adhesively applied acoustical tile.

Performance values of up to 3-hr. fire resistance (3-hr. beam) and STC 43 and IIC 60 have been obtained on certain specified systems.

Beam & Column Fire Protection 10

Beam Fire Protection

Beam fire protection consists of double or triple layers of 5/8" gypsum board (FIRECODE Core and FIRECODE C Core) screw-attached to framework of steel runners and metal angles. These lightweight assemblies are easily and economically installed and provide 2-hr. and 3-hr. beam protection.

Installation

Framing System Install ceiling runners parallel to and at least 1/2" away from the beam. Position metal angles with 1-3/8" leg vertical. Fasten ceiling runners to steel floor units with 1/2" type S-12 pan head screws spaced 12" o.c.

Fabricate channel brackets from 1-5/8" steel runners; space brackets to provide the clearance shown in the specific design selected. (See illustrations on pages 338–339.) When steel runners are used for corner runners, cope or cut away legs of the runner used for brackets to allow insertion of the corner runner. When metal angles are used for corner runners, slit the channel bracket runner legs and bend the runner to a right angle. Install channel brackets 24" o.c. along the length of the beam, and fasten them to ceiling runner with 1/2" type S-12 pan head screws.

Install lower corner runners parallel to the beam. Set steel runner corner runners in coped channel brackets. Apply metal angles to the outside of the channel brackets with the 7/8" leg vertical, and fasten with 1/2" type S-12 pan head screws.

Gypsum Board For 2-hr. assemblies, apply the vertical base-layer board and attach it to the ceiling and corner runners with 1-1/4" type S screws spaced 16" o.c. Install the base layer to the beam soffit overlapping vertical side panels and fasten with 1-1/4" Type S screws 16" o.c. Apply face-layer boards so the soffit board supports the vertical side boards. Fasten the face layer to runners with 1-7/8" type S screws spaced 8" o.c.

For 3-hr. assemblies, apply base-layer boards and attach them to ceiling and corner runners with 1" type S screws spaced 16" o.c. Apply the middle layer over the base layer, and attach it to the brackets and runners with 1-5/8" type S screws spaced 16" o.c. Install hexagonal mesh over the middle layer at the beam soffit. Extend the mesh 1-1/2" up the sides of the beam, and hold it in place with the 1-5/8" screws used to attach middle layer. Apply the face layer over the middle layer and wire mesh, and fasten it to brackets and runners with 2-1/4" type S Screws spaced 8" o.c. Apply all layers so soffit panels support vertical side boards.

Finishing Construction Apply corner bead to bottom outside corners of face layers, and finish with joint treatment as directed in Chapter 5, "Finishing Drywall Systems," or with veneer plaster finish described in Chapter 6, "Finishing Veneer Plaster Systems."

UL Design N501
(beam only)

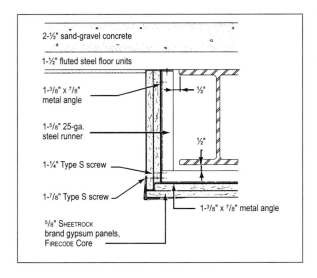

2-½" sand-gravel concrete

1-½" fluted steel floor units

1-³/8" x ⁷/8" metal angle — ½"

1-⁵/8" 25-ga. steel runner — ½"

1-¼" Type S screw

1-⁷/8" Type S screw

1-³/8" x ⁷/8" metal angle

⁵/8" Sheetrock brand gypsum panels, Firecode Core

UL Design N505
(beam only)

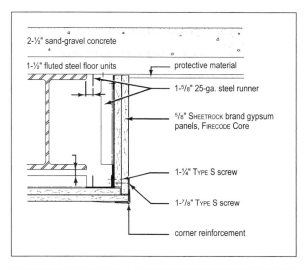

2-½" sand-gravel concrete

1-½" fluted steel floor units

protective material

1-⁵/₈" 25-ga. steel runner

⁵/₈" SHEETROCK brand gypsum panels, FIRECODE Core

1-¼" TYPE S screw

1-⁷/₈" TYPE S screw

corner reinforcement

UL Design N502
(beam only)

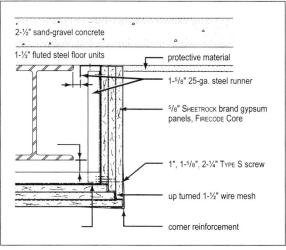

2-½" sand-gravel concrete

1-½" fluted steel floor units

protective material

1-⁵/₈" 25-ga. steel runner

⁵/₈" SHEETROCK brand gypsum panels, FIRECODE Core

1", 1-⁵/₈", 2-¼" TYPE S screw

up turned 1-½" wire mesh

corner reinforcement

10

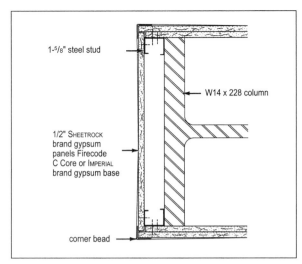

1-⁵/₈" steel stud

W14 x 228 column

1/2" SHEETROCK
brand gypsum
panels Firecode
C Core or IMPERIAL
brand gypsum base

corner bead

**Column Fire
Protection**

Steel column fire protection with lightweight and compact gypsum board enclosures offers fire ratings of 2, 3 or 4 hours depending on the type of construction. The board is held in place by a combination of wire, screws and steel studs. All attachments are mechanical; there's no waiting for adhesives to dry. (See USG Technical Folder SA920, *Plaster Systems* for more detailed information.)

Penetration Fire-Stop Systems

**Penetration Fire
Stops**

**USG Fire-Stop
Systems for
Floor and Wall
Penetrations**

Fire can pass from floor to floor or into adjacent spaces through oversized floor or wall penetrations, including poke-through openings required for plumbing, telecommunication lines or other utility service.

USG fire-stop systems for floor and wall penetrations employ FIRECODE compound to block smoke and flame from passing through openings in concrete floors and gypsum panel walls. Several different UL-classified through-penetration systems are available. Description of these systems may be found in Technical Folder SA727, *USG Fire-Stop Systems.* These systems are classified in accordance with the standards ASTM E814 and UL 1479.

Water-Managed EIFS

Masonry Exterior

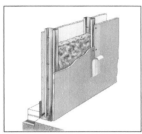

Gypsum Drywall Interior

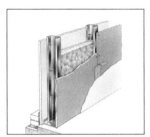

Veneer Plaster Interior

Installation When its use is called for, cut safing insulation with a serrated knife to a width slightly wider than the opening. Compress and tightly fit insulation with nominal density of 4.0 pcf completely around the penetrant. Note that the insulation thickness varies from system to system. Mix FIRECODE compound according to the directions on the container. Using a trowel, putty knife or spatula, scoop the compound from its container and work it into the penetration opening. Apply compound to the thickness called for in fire-rated assembly on top of the safing insulation.

10

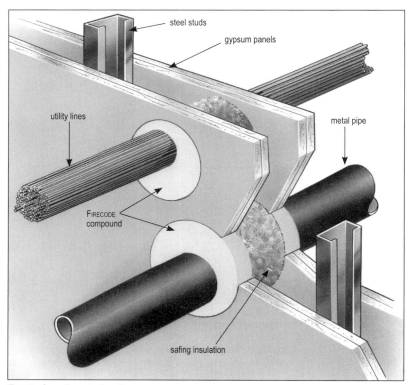

Fire stop for wall penetration, UL System No. W-L-1027 (metal pipe) and W-L-3023 (utility lines)

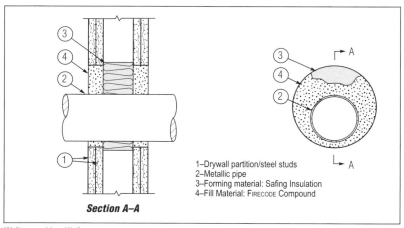

1–Drywall partition/steel studs
2–Metallic pipe
3–Forming material: Safing Insulation
4–Fill Material: FIRECODE Compound

Section A–A

Wall assembly—UL System No. W-L-1027 (metal pipe); F Rating—2 hr., T Rating—0 hr.

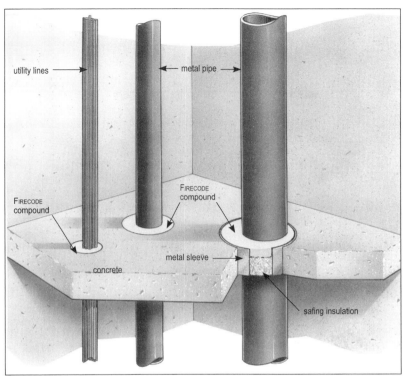

*Fire stop for floor
penetration, UL System Nos.
C-AJ-1081 and C-AJ-3045*

Head-of-Wall Construction Joints

Construction joints—where two fire-rated assemblies intersect—are evaluated under ASTM E1966 for their ability to resist flame and temperature transmission, as well as hose stream, where required. Head-of-wall construction joints are intersections of wall to floor/ceiling or roof/ceiling. Other construction joints include wall to wall (expansion joint application), floor to floor (building joint application) and floor to wall.

Test parameters for head-of-wall assemblies are similar to those established for through-penetration fire stops, discussed earlier. Systems may be tested and prescribed for either static (no floor or roof movement) or dynamic (to accommodate live-load deflection) conditions.

Head-of-wall construction joints have common features, including:

a) Fire-rated assemblies for both the wall and floor/ceiling or roof/ceiling,

b) A joint treatment system consisting of a forming material, such as mineral wool safing insulation, to pack into openings, and a fill material, such as FIRECODE compound, to seal all openings and passages.

Restraining angles also may be required to achieve the necessary flame and temperature barriers.

USG has had several head-of-wall assemblies tested under standard ASTM E1966. The illustration shows a head-of-wall assembly for a dynamic construction joint.

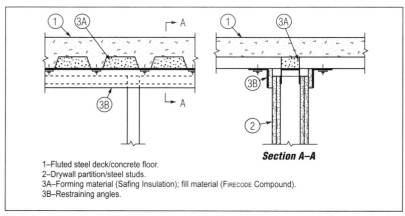

Section A–A

1–Fluted steel deck/concrete floor.
2–Drywall partition/steel studs.
3A–Forming material (Safing Insulation); fill material (FIRECODE Compound).
3B–Restraining angles.

Head-of-wall joint treatment system for fluted steel deck/concrete floor or roof/ceiling and gypsum wallboard wall assembly—UL System HW-D-0002.

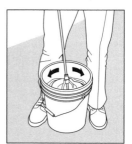

FIRECODE Compound mixes easily with water (or activator) at the job site. There's less waste than with caulking tube products.

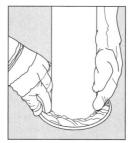

When required by the specific system, Safing Insulation, the forming material, is fit snugly into the penetration.

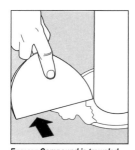

FIRECODE Compound is troweled into the penetration to block particulate, fire, sound, smoke and air movement through the floor or wall.

Air, Water & Vapor Control

Air and Water Filtration

Flashing and sealants, as shown in construction documents and as selected by the architect and/or structural engineer, should be provided to resist air and water infiltration. They should be installed in appropriate locations to maintain continuity of air/water barriers, particularly at windows, doors and other penetrations of exterior wall.

All gypsum sheathing must be covered with No. 15 asphalt felt or an approved water and infiltration barrier to ensure water-tight construction. Asphalt felt should be applied horizontally with 2" overlap and attached to sheathing. Sheet barriers should be stapled to the sheathing according to manufacturer's directions. Accessories for stucco finishes should be made of zinc alloy with weep holes 12" o.c.

Vapor Retarders and Air Barriers

Proper use and placement of vapor retarders are critical factors in modern, energy-efficient construction. Improper placement of a vapor retarder could produce condensation in exterior wall stud cavities and cause deterioration of the structure.

In cold climates, a vapor retarder is required on the warm interior side of the wall to restrict moisture from the warmer, humid air inside the building from penetrating through wall surfaces and causing condensation on colder surfaces within the cavity.

In climates where high temperature and humidity conditions are sustained, placement of a vapor retarder may be recommended on the exterior side. In any case, location and placement of vapor retarders should be determined by a qualified design professional.

Two vapor retarders in a single wall will trap water vapor between them and create moisture-related problems in core materials.

When a polyethylene vapor retarder film is installed on ceilings behind gypsum panels under cold conditions, it is recommended that ceiling insulation (batts or blankets) be installed before the board. If loose fill insulation is to be used above the ceiling, it must be installed immediately after the ceiling board is installed during periods of cold weather. Also the plenum or attic space should be properly vented. Failure to follow these guidelines can result in moisture condensation behind the gypsum panels, causing board sag.

Note: Although nearly all vapor retarders are also air barriers, not all air barriers are vapor retarders. Standard SHEETROCK brand gypsum panels, DUROCK cement board, SHEETROCK gypsum sheathing, No. 15 felt and industry building wrap and other common construction materials serve as air barriers, but not as vapor retarders.

Ceiling Sag Precautions

Water-based textures, interior finishing materials and high ambient humidity conditions can produce sag in gypsum ceiling panels if adequate vapor and moisture control is not provided. The following precautions must be observed to minimize sagging of ceiling panels:

1. Where vapor retarder is required in cold weather conditions, the temperature of the gypsum ceiling panels and vapor retarder must remain above the interior air dew-point temperature during and after the installation of panels and finishing materials.

2. The interior space must be adequately ventilated and air circulation must be provided to remove water vapor from the structure.

Most sag problems are caused by condensation of water within the gypsum panel. The placement of vapor retarders, climate, insulation levels and ventilation requirements will vary by location and climate, and should be reviewed by a qualified design professional if in question.

Good Design Practices

A common error in buildings with suspended ceilings is to neglect treatment of drywall surfaces within the ceiling plenum on exterior walls. Since the plenum is not visible, care should be taken to make sure that this area is not overlooked. The drywall application and joint treatment should be carried all the way to the spandrel beam or floor structure above. Exterior ceilings and soffits are other areas that may be forgotten. Ceilings, soffits and cutouts for pipe, conduit, knee braces and vent penetrations should be carefully treated to avoid compromising the effectiveness of the vapor retarder and/or air barrier.

Penetrations in the exterior wall for windows, doors, outlets, HVAC and other fixtures or devices must be closed tight with sealant or tape.

Control joints should be carefully flashed and/or sealed to prevent water infiltration. Also, particular care should be taken to ensure the integrity of the envelope for airtightness, vapor diffusion and thermal resistance, particularly at intersections and hidden penetrations. Details for floor/wall and roof/wall connections are the most difficult and important design challenges.

Planning, Execution & Inspection

Factors Affecting Results

Today's proven-quality products and high-performance systems permit installation of attractive, durable, trouble-free interiors that meet designers' specifications and owners' needs. By using correct installation procedures and equipment, contractors can combine these products into systems with high-quality results, thus reducing customer dissatisfaction, poor productivity, callbacks and decreased profitability.

This chapter identifies products and equipment, environmental factors, handling and storage, installation, workmanship and inspection that can affect the end results of a project.

Selection of Materials

In recent years, technological advances in building construction have resulted in new products and systems. Each requires systematic evaluation of performance and appearance characteristics in relation to cost, before selection and use. Evaluation may be done through benefit-cost analysis or life-cycle cost analysis, which considers the total cost of an assembly throughout its useful life. Building materials selection should always be based on total performance, including maintenance, not simply on initial construction cost or a budgeted cost figure. The following items merit consideration in systematically selecting products and systems for gypsum construction.

Satisfying User Needs

To satisfy the owner's functional requirements, it is a basic requirement to match products and systems to the end performance desired. For instance, high-traffic areas such as corridors may require hard-wearing, abuse-resistant surfaces made of specially designed products. Where quiet surroundings or isolation from noise is needed, systems with high resistance to sound transmission and surfaces that provide sound absorption are essential. In common walls between apartments, where greater cavity widths are needed to enclose plumbing lines, a system with adequate space in the cavity is called for. The objective is always to select products and systems that will improve the total performance of the building components.

Meeting Regulatory Requirements

The performance of gypsum construction products and systems must comply with regulatory requirements established by local, state and federal agencies. Local and state building codes and insurance and lending agency requirements should be considered in material selection.

Identifying Critical Performance

Any selection of appropriate materials should reflect product or system limitations. Structural factors, such as limiting height and span, required number of screws, metal thickness, bracing spacing or maximum frame and fastener spacing, should be carefully considered since they affect the flexural properties and strength of an assembly. Yield strength of all steel is not the same. Substitution by size alone is not recommended. System performance following any substitution of material or compromise in assembly design cannot be certified and may result in failure under critical conditions. It is important to note that extreme and continuous high humidity or temperatures may result in sag, joint deformation, poor appearance and possible deterioration of gypsum surface materials. Sealing and painting recommendations are important for proper performance of paints and other finishes.

Performance Requirements

Fire Resistance Select ASTM E119 fire-tested assemblies to comply with regulatory requirements, and construct the assembly according to specifications. If an assembly does not comply, work may be halted by the building inspector or installation may be rejected after completion.

Sound Control Owners' needs and regulatory requirements dictate the sound control needed. Many assemblies are available to meet various requirements. Sound test data is obtained under ideal laboratory conditions per ASTM procedures, except as noted. For assemblies to approach testing performance, strict attention must be given to construction details, such as acoustical sealant and installation. The isolation expected from an assembly can be negated by penetrations, perimeter leaks, accidental coupling of decoupled elements, incompatible surrounding structures and other faulty installation practices. The isolation may also be compromised by flanking sound, e.g., structure-borne sound carried via continuous concrete floors and other building elements, bypassing the sound-rated assembly.

Structural Strength and Stability Select systems that provide adequate strength and acceptable deflection under live and dead loads as described in published USG performance tables. Shear or torque loads caused by shelving, sanitary basins, light fixtures and other accessories should also be considered. Shear forces from wind or earthquake may also require consideration. Cracking probably will occur in assemblies of sufficient strength or stiffness if adequate reinforcing is not provided.

Water and Moisture Choose products and systems that offer adequate resistance to water and high-moisture conditions. Gypsum wallboard products are not suitable under conditions of extreme and sustained moisture. Durock cement board is recommended as a substrate for ceramic tile under these conditions. Products manufactured from steel or other materials subject to corrosion must have a protective coating equal to the service conditions envisioned.

11

Humidity and Temperature Determine the environmental conditions to be expected during construction and use. Control the job environment or select products that offer high performance under these conditions. Plaster products should be installed at uniform temperatures that will remain above 55°F for 48 hours prior to and until 48 hours after application. Products may gradually deteriorate under sustained temperatures over 125°F. High humidity and temperatures may cause problems with veneer plaster, finishes, gypsum plasters and gypsum board products.

Durability High-strength gypsum plaster, veneer plaster products and abuse-resistant drywall and gypsum fiber products offer high compressive strength and surface hardness to resist damage from impact and abrasion. For long-lasting, problem-free interiors, select products to meet functional needs.

Appearance Color, texture and surface gloss affect the final appearance of interior surfaces. Texture finishes offer a wide variety of effects for distinctive appearances. Glossy finishes highlight surface defects; textures hide minor imperfections.

Cleanability and Maintenance Select products according to functional requirements for washability and resistance to fading, staining and scuffing. While aggregated ceiling texture finishes cannot be washed, they can be painted if redecoration is needed.

Light Reflection Select colors and finishes to meet appearance standards, illumination levels and other functional requirements. Strong side-lighting from windows or surface-mounted light fixtures may reveal even minor surface imperfections. Light striking the surface at an angle exaggerates surface irregularities. These conditions, which demand precise installation, increase chances for callbacks and should be avoided. If critical lighting cannot be changed, the effects can be minimized by any of the following procedures: skim coating the gypsum panels, applying SHEETROCK brand Tuff-Hide Primer Surfacer, applying SHEETROCK First Coat primer, finishing the surface with texture finish, or installing draperies and blinds, which soften shadows. As a preventive measure, use strong parallel-to-the-surface job lights to ensure a flat, acceptable joint-compound finish prior to priming, texturing and/or painting.

Interface and Compatibility Materials that come into contact with each other must be compatible. Differences in thermal or hygrometric expansion, strength of substrates or basecoats in relation to finish coats, strength of drywall or plaster finishes in relation to certain types of paint coatings, thermal conductivity and galvanic action can cause problems. (Tables of thermal and hygrometric coefficients for selected products can be found in the Appendix. Contact specific manufacturers for recommendations should questions arise.) Following are some precautions associated with gypsum construction:

1. Gypsum surfaces should be isolated with control joints or other means where necessary to abut other materials, isolate structural movements and remain within gross area limits of the drywall surface.

2. Certain types of plaster may be applied directly to concrete block. However, with plaster over poured-in-place concrete, a bonding agent such as USG plaster bonder must be used.

3. Due to expansion differences, the application of high-pressure plastic laminates to gypsum panels or plaster generally is not satisfactory.

4. IMPERIAL brand gypsum base and regular SHEETROCK brand gypsum panels do not provide sufficient moisture resistance as a base for adhesive application of ceramic tile in wet areas. Use FIBEROCK interior AQUA-TOUGH panels, FIBEROCK AQUA-TOUGH tile backerboard or DUROCK cement board.

5. Install resilient thermal gaskets around metal window frames to keep condensation from damaging wall surface materials. The gasket may also reduce galvanic action and resultant corrosion, which occurs when two dissimilar metals contact in the presence of moisture.

Vapor Control Proper placement of vapor retarders is critical in modern construction, with its increased use of thermal insulation to facilitate energy conservation.

Incorrect placement or omission of a vapor retarder may result in condensation in the exterior wall stud cavities. Cold climates typically call for a vapor retarder on the warm interior side of the wall. For warmer, humid climates with sustained high temperatures, one may be required on the outside of the exterior wall of air conditioned buildings. A qualified mechanical engineer should determine the proper location. Refer to local building codes for requirements in your project area.

Two vapor retarders on opposite sides of a single wall can trap water vapor between them and create moisture-related problems in the cavity materials.

When polyethylene vapor retarder film is installed on ceilings behind gypsum panels under cold conditions, it is recommended that ceiling insulation be installed before the board is installed or immediately after (if the insulation is blown in). Also, the plenum or attic space should be properly vented. Failure to follow these procedures can result in moisture condensation on the back side of the gypsum panels, causing board sag. See Chapter 15, "Building Sciences," for more information.

Handling & Storage

Even quality products can contribute to application problems and job failures if not protected from damage and improper handling. Generally, gypsum products should be stored inside at temperatures above freezing, protected from moisture and external damage and used promptly after delivery.

11

Inspection

Products should be inspected for damage and proper quantity upon receipt at distributor locations and when delivered on the job. Incorrect quantities may result in job delays due to shortages or extra cost for overages that are wasted. Check products for such physical damage as broken corners or scuffed edges on gypsum board, wet board and bent or corroded steel studs and runners. Inspect containers for evidence of damage that may affect the contents. Look for damaged or torn bags, which could result in waste or preset plaster finishes. Report any damaged material or shortages immediately.

Storage

Enclosed protection from the weather is required for the storage of all gypsum products. Though not recommended, outdoor storage for up to one month is permissible if products are stored above ground and completely covered. Plastic covers used to protect gypsum board during shipment via rail are intended to provide temporary protection from moisture exposure and should be removed upon receipt at the distributor's location. Do not store gypsum products on gypsum risers. Use wood risers to prevent moisture from wicking up and wetting material. Various problems can result when these products get wet or are exposed to direct sunlight for extended periods.

If no job site moisture is anticipated, store gypsum boards flat on a clean, dry floor to prevent permanent sag, damage or deformity, such as wavy edges. Do not store board vertically. If board is stored on risers, they should be evenly spaced no more than 28" apart and within 2" of the ends of the board. The risers should also be placed directly under each other vertically.

Stack bagged goods and metal components off of damp floors and walls. Corrosion on corner bead, trim and fasteners may bleed through finishing materials. Ready-mixed joint compounds that have been frozen and thawed repeatedly lose strength, which may weaken the bond.

Locate stored stocks of gypsum products away from heavy-traffic areas to prevent damage from other trades. Keep materials in their packages or containers until ready for use to protect them from dirt, corrosion and distortion. Damaged board edges are more susceptible to ridging after joint treatment. Boards with rough ends will require remedial action before installation. Otherwise, deformation or blistering may occur at end joints.

Using Fresh Material

If possible, gypsum construction products should be scheduled for delivery to the job just prior to application. Materials risk damage if stored for long periods. To minimize performance problems caused by variable moisture conditions and aging, fresh plaster and veneer plaster finishes should be received on the job frequently.

Job Conditions

Many product failures can be directly traced to unfavorable job conditions. These problems may occur during product application, or they may not appear until long after job completion.

Recommendations for proper job conditions, given in the appropriate product application chapters here, should be closely followed. If job conditions are unfavorable, correct them before product installation. The following environmental factors can present problems in gypsum construction.

Temperature

Temperature can have a dramatic effect on the performance of gypsum products. Install gypsum products, joint compounds and textures at comfortable working temperatures continuously above 50°F. In cold weather, provide controlled, well-distributed heat to keep the temperature above minimum levels. For example, if gypsum board is installed at a temperature of 28°F, it expands at the rate of 1/2" for every 100 linear feet when the temperature rises to 72°F. At low temperatures, the working properties and performance of plasters, veneer plaster finishes, joint compounds and textures are seriously affected. They suffer loss of strength and bond if frozen after application and may have to be replaced. Ready-mixed compounds deteriorate from repeated freeze-thaw cycles, lose their workability and may not be usable. Avoid sudden changes in temperature, which may cause cracking from thermal shock.

Humidity

High humidity—either from atmospheric conditions or on-the-job use of wet materials like concrete, stucco, plaster and spray fireproofing—often creates the potential for problems. In certain kinds of gypsum board, water vapor is absorbed, which softens the gypsum core and expands the paper. As a result, the board may sag between ceiling supports. Sustained high humidity increases chances for galvanized steel components to rust, especially in marine areas where salt air is present. High humidity can cause insufficient drying between coats of joint compounds, which can lead to delayed shrinkage and/or bond failure. Jobs may be delayed because extra time for drying is required between coats of joint compound.

Low humidity speeds drying, especially when combined with high temperatures and air circulation. These conditions may lead to dryouts in veneer plaster finishes and conventional plaster. While working time may be reduced under such conditions, they can also lead to edge cracking of the joint treatment, crusting and possible contamination of fresh compound, and check and edge cracking. Handle gypsum board carefully to prevent cracking or core damage during erection.

Moisture

Wind-blown rain and standing water on floors increase the humidity in a structure and may cause the problems previously described under high humidity conditions. Water-soaked gypsum board and plasters have less structural strength and may sag and deform. Their surfaces when damp are extremely vulnerable to scuffing, damage and mildew. Note that conventional drywall products should not be used in areas that have high humidity or the presence of moisture. SHEETROCK brand MOLD TOUGH gypsum panels or FIBEROCK AQUA-TOUGH interior panels may be used in areas where occasional moisture or humidity are present. These panels are not intended for use in areas subject to constant moisture, however, such as interior swimming pools, gang showers and steam rooms. DUROCK brand cement board is recommended for these applications.

Ventilation

Ventilation should be provided to remove excess moisture, permit proper drying of conventional gypsum plasters and joint compounds, and prevent problems associated with high-humidity conditions. For veneer plaster finishes, to prevent rapid drying and possible shrinkage, poor bond, chalky surfaces, and cracking, air circulation should be kept at a minimum level until the finish is set. Rapid drying also creates problems with setting-type joint compounds, gypsum plasters, and finishes when they dry out before setting fully and, as a result, don't develop full strength.

Sunlight

Strong sunlight for extended periods will discolor gypsum panel face paper and make final surface treatment difficult. The blue face paper on veneer gypsum base will fade to gray or tan from excessive exposure to sunlight or ultraviolet radiation. Applying finishes containing alkali (lime) to this degraded base may result in bond failure unless the base is treated with an alum solution or bonding agent. (For more information, see page 386 and PM4, *Sun-Faded IMPERIAL brand gypsum base,* from USG.)

Movement in Structures

Modern structural design uses lighter but stronger materials capable of spanning greater distances and extending buildings higher than ever before. While meeting current standards of building design, these frames are more flexible and offer less resistance to structural movement. This flexibility and resulting structural movement can produce stresses within the usually non-load-bearing gypsum assemblies. Unless perimeter relief joints are provided to isolate movement, when accumulated stresses exceed the strength of the materials in the assembly, they will seek relief by cracking, buckling or crushing the finished surface.

Structural movement and most cracking problems are caused by deflection under load, physical change in materials due to temperature and humidity changes, seismic forces or a combination of these factors.

Concrete Floor Slab Deflection

Dead and live loads cause deflection in the floor slab. If this deflection is excessive, cracks can occur in partitions at the midpoint between supports. If partition installation is delayed for about two months after slabs are completed, perhaps two-thirds of the ultimate creep deflection will have taken place, reducing chances of partition cracking. This is usually a one-time non-cyclical movement.

Wind and Seismic Forces

Wind and seismic forces cause a cyclical shearing action on the building framework, which distorts the rectangular shape to an angled parallelogram. This distortion, called racking, can result in cracking and crushing of partitions adjacent to columns, floors and structural ceilings.

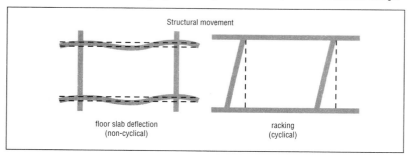

Structural movement

floor slab deflection
(non-cyclical)

racking
(cyclical)

To resist this racking, building frames must be stiffened with shear walls and/or cross-bracing. Light steel-frame buildings are diagonally braced with steel strapping. Wood-frame structures are strengthened with let-in cross-bracing and/or shear diaphragms of structural sheathing. On larger buildings, racking is resisted by shear walls and windbracing without considering the strength added by finishing materials. Moreover, the partitions must be isolated from the structure to prevent cracking caused by racking movement and distortion.

Thermal Expansion

All materials expand with an increase in temperature and contract with a decrease. In tall concrete or steel-frame buildings, thermal expansion and contraction may cause cracking problems resulting from racking when exterior columns and beams are exposed or partially exposed to exterior temperatures. Since interior columns remain at a uniform temperature, they do not change in length.

Exposed exterior columns can be subjected to temperatures ranging from over 100°F to -30°F, and therefore will elongate or contract in length. The amount of expansion or contraction of the exposed columns depends on the temperature difference and several other factors. (Structural movement caused by thermal differentials accumulates to the upper floors.) However, the stiffness of the structure resists the movement and usually full unrestrained expansion is not reached. A gypsum board wall 100' long will expand 0.54" when the temperature rises 50°F.

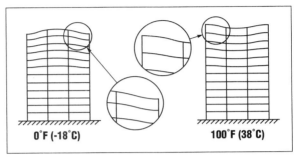

0°F (-18°C)   **100°F (38°C)**

Racking, resulting from thermal movement, is greatest in the outside bays of upper floors in winter when temperature differentials are largest. To prevent major changes as described above, apply proper insulation to exterior structural members. The design should call for control joints to relieve stress and minimize cracking of surfaces.

Hygrometric Expansion

Many building materials absorb moisture from the surrounding air during periods of high humidity and expand; they contract during periods of low humidity. Gypsum, wood and paper products are more readily affected by hygrometric changes than are steel and reinforced concrete. Gypsum board will expand about 1/2" per 100' with a relative humidity change from 13% RH to 90% RH. (See Appendix for coefficients.) Unless control joints are provided, hygrometric changes create stresses within the assembly, which result in bowed or wavy walls, sag between supports in ceilings, cracking and other problems.

11

Relief Joints

Select gypsum assemblies to provide the best structural characteristics to resist stresses imposed on them. As described previously, these systems must resist internal stresses created by expansion and contraction of the components and external stresses caused by movement of the structure. The alternative solution is to provide control and relief joints to eliminate stress buildup and still maintain structural integrity of the assembly.

To control external stresses, partitions and other gypsum construction must be relieved from the structural framework, particularly at columns, ceilings and intersections with dissimilar materials. In long partition runs and large ceiling areas, control joints are recommended to relieve internal stress buildup. Methods for providing relief and control joints are shown in Chapters 3, 4, 5, 6 and 8. These recommendations, for normal situations, provide for 1/4" relief. Relief joints for individual structures should be checked for adequacy by the design engineer to prevent cracking and other deformations.

Cracking in High-Rise Structures

Contractors who install commercial partitions and ceilings should be aware of cracking problems caused by structural movement, deflection, expansion and contraction. These problems, described previously, are not due to faulty materials. Anticipated structural movement in the frame and floor system should be taken into account in the design of the building. It is prudent to solve potential problems with preventive measures before installation rather than attempting repairs afterward.

Some types of construction can be expected to cause cracking in gypsum assemblies if not handled properly. Following are indications of potential problems:

Flat Plate Design Particularly with column bay sizes exceeding 20'.

Exposed Exterior Columns and Shear Walls On buildings over 12 floors high and located in a cold climate.

Reinforced Concrete Structures Erected in cold weather, with partitions installed too soon thereafter. Creep deflection in the floor slab, a cause of partition cracking, is retarded in cold weather and accelerated in warm weather.

Structures Without Shear Walls or Proper Bracing Particularly if the plan is long and narrow, presenting a large wall area to withstand wind load.

Gypsum Systems Without Expansion Joints Long partition runs and large ceiling areas must have control joints to compensate for hygrometric and thermal expansion and contraction. Placement of control joints must be noted in the architectural or design plans.

When one or more of these conditions exists, it is wise to notify the owner, architect and general contractor of the possible problems and recommend corrective measures. If corrective measures are effective, all involved will be rewarded with a satisfactory performance, and costly complaints will be avoided.

Structurally Generated Noise

Loads of varying intensity can cause structural movement, which generates noise when two materials rub or work against each other. In high-rise buildings, variable wind pressure can cause the structure to drift or sway, causing structural deformation. Such deformation imparts racking stresses to the non-load-bearing partition and can create noise.

As another annoyance, lumber shrinkage often results in subfloors and stair treads squeaking under foot traffic. This can be avoided by using adhesive to provide a tight bond between components and prevent adjacent surfaces from rubbing together.

Acoustical performance values (STC, NRC, CAC, IIC) are based on laboratory conditions. Field conditions such as lack of sealants, outlet boxes, back-to-back boxes, medicine cabinets, flanking paths, doors, windows and structure-borne sound can diminish acoustical performance values. These individual conditions usually require the assessment of an acoustical engineer.

USG assumes no responsibility for the prevention, cause or repair of these job-related noises.

Lumber Shrinkage

In wood-frame construction a common problem encountered is fastener pops, often caused by lumber shrinkage in drywall framing. Shrinkage occurs as lumber dries. Even kiln-dried lumber can shrink, warp, bow and twist, causing boards to loosen and fasteners to fail. Gypsum surfaces can also crack, buckle, or develop joint deformations when attached across the wide dimension of large wood framing members such as joists. Typically, this installation occurs in stairwells and high wall surfaces where the gypsum finish passes over mid-height floor framing, as in split-level houses.

Framing lumber, as commonly used, has a moisture content of 15% to 19%. After installation, the lumber dries to approximately 10% moisture content and consequently shrinks, particularly during the first heating season.

Wood shrinks most in the direction of the growth rings (flat grain), somewhat less across the growth rings (edge grain) and very little along the grain (longitudinally). Shrinkage tends to be most pronounced away from outside edges and toward the center of the member. When nails are driven toward the central axis, shrinkage leaves a space between the board and the nailing surface, as shown in the drawings on the next page.

Based on experiments conducted by the Forest Products Laboratory and Purdue University, the use of shorter nails results in less space left between the board and nailing surface after shrinkage than with longer nails having more penetration. Using the shortest nail possible with adequate holding power will result in less popping due to shrinkage. Longer nails, however, usually are required for fire-rated construction, as specified by design requirements. Choose the proper nail length from the "Selector Guide for Gypsum Board Nails" on page 44.

Specifically, the annular drywall nail, with an overall length of 1-1/4", has equivalent holding power to a 1-5/8" coated cooler-type nail, but the shorter length of the nail lessens the chances for nail popping due to lumber shrinkage.

The floating interior angle system effectively reduces angle cracking and nail pops resulting from stresses at intersections of walls and ceilings. (See intersection detail on page 134 of Chapter 3, "Cladding.") Gypsum boards should be floated over the side face of joists and headers and not attached. To minimize buckling and cracking in wall expanses exceeding one floor in height, either float the board over second-floor joists using resilient channels or install a horizontal control joint at this point. See Chapter 2, "Framing," for partition corner detail.

11

Using 2-1/2˝ nails

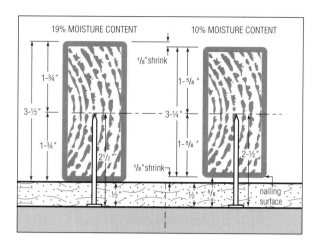

Using 1-1/2˝ nails

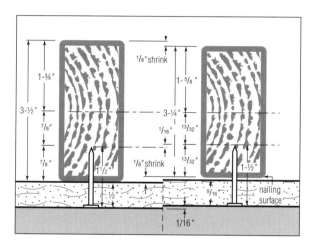

Workmanship

USG products are quality-tested and job-proven for fast, economical installation and problem-free results. Unfortunately, sometimes these products fail to achieve optimum performance after installation due to improper or unspecified application.

**Following
Directions**

The major cause of job problems and poor product performance after application is failure to follow manufacturer's directions and architect's specifications.

Application procedures should be checked regularly to conform to current manufacturer's recommendations. Product modifications to upgrade in-place performance may require slight changes in mixing or application methods. New products may require the adoption of entire new procedures and techniques.

**Meeting
Specifications**

Construction specifications are designed to provide a given result, but unless specified construction materials and methods are used and the proper details followed, the actual job performance will probably fall short of requirements. Excessive water usage, oversanding, improper surface preparation, substitution of materials, skimping and shortcuts should not be tolerated, because they lead, inevitably, to problems.

**Drywall
and Plaster
Tolerances**

Standards of acceptability for installation of framing, drywall panels and joint treatment vary in different parts of the United States. Nevertheless, several organizations, including the Association of the Wall and Ceiling Industries International, Metal Lath/Steel Framing Association, Gypsum Association and ASTM International have published recommendations, standards and/or tolerances that may be required for a specific project. Similarly, references for tolerances and quality in plaster work have been published by AIA MasterSpec and Diehl's *Manual of Lathing and Plastering*. Contractors and their customers should reach agreement before starting the project regarding which tolerance standards will be used to judge acceptability of the work. See the Appendix for further information on tolerances.

Equipment Selection

11

A large selection of equipment is available for gypsum construction and particularly for mechanical application of veneer plaster and texture finishes, conventional plasters and joint treatments. (See Chapter 14, "Tools & Equipment.") The mechanical spray equipment chosen should be based on the type of material and the situations presented on each job. The size of the job, delivery volume required, portability and access through doorways also deserve consideration. Low maintenance and accessibility of parts for cleanup are important factors.

Using the wrong equipment for the job can cause serious problems. Improper equipment affects production as well as strength, workability, setting time and finished appearance.

Mixing

Equipment should provide the correct mixing action and mixing speed. Equally important are proportioning and mixing procedures, as shown in Chapters 5, 6 and 8. Poor mixing practices adversely affect material performance and can cause various problems.

Pumping

Equipment should have capacity sufficient for the job, hose size and pumping distance, and should be kept in good repair. To minimize abrasive wear in the pump mechanism, the pump type should be suitable for the aggregate and mixes being used. High plaster/sand ratios, small-diameter hoses and leakage increase the possibility of aggregate packing in the pump and hose. Use large-diameter hoses and no more hose length than needed. Small-diameter, long hoses cause pumps to wear faster and may lead to quick-set and low-strength problems in fluid materials.

Spraying

Nozzle or orifice size of the spray gun and air pressure used must be suitable for the material being applied. Improper nozzles and incorrect air pressure affect the spray pattern and may cause stoppage and aggregate fallout. With most veneer plaster finishing, a catalyst tank with metering device is required to adjust setting time.

Product Quality

Gypsum construction products from USG provide economical, problem-free installation and high performance in fire- and sound-rated systems. During manufacture, products are carefully controlled to meet specific performance standards when applied according to directions and under proper job conditions.

Complaint Procedure

Should a probable product deficiency appear, stop using the suspected defective material immediately and ask your supplier to notify USG at once so that a representative can investigate the complaint and take remedial action. Do not continue to use improperly performing materials, because the labor cost of replacement or reworking far exceeds the material cost.

Sampling

Obtain samples of the material that fully represent the complaint condition for analysis. Save bags, wrappers and packages (or write down the production codes). These labels will identify place and time of manufacture. For some complaints, samples of related materials, such as aggregates, are also necessary. Weather conditions, mixing times and proportions of ingredients should be fully reported.

Substitution and Certification

USG will provide test certification for published fire, sound and structural data covering systems designed and constructed according to its specifications. Tests on USG products are conducted to meet the exact performance requirements of established test procedures specified by various building code agencies. Any substitution of materials or compromise in assembly design cannot be certified and may result in failure of a system in service, especially under critical conditions of load or fire exposure. Substitution of materials usually will nullify acceptability of applicable fire tests, as well.

How to Inspect a Job

Proper job inspection by the construction trades during installation may reveal potential problem areas or procedures that may produce unsatisfactory results. Corrective action taken immediately is usually less costly than callbacks to repair—and perhaps rebuild—walls and ceilings after the job is completed.

A thorough understanding of job details, schedules and specifications is necessary to conduct proper inspection. If the assembly is to meet fire- and sound-rating requirements, then construction details must also be known.

All walls and ceilings must be judged by these criteria and the contract conditions. Thus, it is important that drawings and specifications be complete, accurate and easily understood.

The job inspection phase of supervision is most important, and in many cases, will determine the success of the job. An accurate check should be made of the following major categories so that best results can be obtained.

Schedule of Inspection

Conduct inspections at the following stages:

– When the job is almost ready for materials delivery, to check environmental conditions and plan for delivery.

– When materials are delivered to the job.

– When framing is erected but before board or lath application.

– When gypsum board base layer and/or face layer are applied.

– When joints are treated; when veneer plaster finish or conventional plaster is applied.

– When the job is substantially completed.

Delivery and Storage

As materials are delivered, check the following:

– First, check for shipping damage.

– Materials meet specifications and are in good condition.

– Materials are stored properly: gypsum boards flat on the floor and bagged goods flat on a raised platform. Protect from moisture and damage by abuse.

– Framing materials are protected from damage and moisture.

Framing Inspection

Framing members, either wood or metal, must meet architect's specifications and be free of defects. During and after framing construction, make the following inspections:

– See that wood and steel framing materials meet specifications as required by local building codes, regulations and standards. Also verify that sizes and gauges are appropriate based on limiting height tables.

11

- Check accuracy of alignment and position of framing, including bracing if required, according to plans and details. Make sure load-bearing steel studs are directly underneath the members they support.

- See that partitions are acceptably straight and true and ceilings are acceptably level.

- Spacing of studs and joists does not exceed maximum allowable for the system.

- Look for protrusions of blocking, bridging or piping, and twisted studs and joists that would create an uneven surface. Correct before board attachment.

- Make sure there is appropriate blocking and support for fixtures and board.

- See that window and door frames and electrical and plumbing fixtures are set for the board thickness used.

- Check for proper position and attachment of resilient and furring channels.

- Review all wood and steel framing for compliance with minimum framing requirements outlined in Chapter 2.

- Examine steel studs at corners, intersections, terminals, shelfwalls and door and borrowed light frames for positive attachment to floor and ceiling runners. All load-bearing and curtain wall studs are attached to runner each side, top, and bottom. All load-bearing studs sit tight against web of runner. Verify that appropriate gauge is used.

- See that steel stud flanges in field all face the same direction.

- See that preset door frames are independently fastened to floor slab and that borrowed light frames are securely attached to stud and runner rough framing at all jamb anchors.

Suspending Grillage

- Measure spacing of hangers, channels and studs to see that they are within allowable limits.

- Check ends of main runner and furring channels to ensure that they are not let into, supported by, or in contact with abutting walls. Main runners should extend to within 6" of the wall to support a furring channel.

- Make sure furring channel clips are alternated and that furring channel splices are properly made.

- Ensure that mechanical equipment is independently supported and does not depend on grillage for support.

- Inspect construction surrounding light fixtures and openings to see that recommended reinforced channel support is provided.

Inspecting Drywall & Veneer Plaster Installations

Base Layer
- Verify that material being used complies with specifications and requirements of fire or sound rating.
- Make sure that proper perpendicular or parallel application of board is being used and that end joints are staggered.
- See that the recommended fasteners are being used, spaced and set properly.
- Check for proper use of acoustical sealant.
- Inspect installation to make sure thermal insulating or sound attenuation fire blankets are properly attached and fitted.
- Be certain vapor retarder is installed, if required, and sealed properly.
- Review appropriate system construction and application, and inspect for compliance with laminating recommendations and other construction procedures.
- See that required control joints are properly located and installed per architect's drawings.

Face Layer
- Verify material compliance.
- Look for high-quality workmanship. Cracked or damaged-edge boards should not be used. Board surfaces should be free of defects; joints should be correctly butted and staggered.
- Check for proper application method—perpendicular or parallel.
- Ensure that all drywall panels are in the same, even plane after installation, to prevent joint-finishing issues.
- Examine fasteners for compliance with specifications, proper spacing and application.
- Review adhesive application method and see that recommendations and specifications are being followed. Consult the setting time table on page 181 and the drying time table on page 184 for guidance.
- Inspect trim, corner beads and related components for alignment, grounds, secure attachment and proper installation.
- Make sure that acoustical sealant is applied around electrical outlets and other penetrations and that it completely seals the void.

11

Fasteners
- Make sure recommended or specified fasteners are used. Use of a specific fastener may be required by fire tests.
- See that fasteners are applied in such a manner that the board is flat against the framing.
- Observe whether board is held tightly against framing during application. Test for loose board by pushing adjacent to the fastener. See that face paper is not broken when fastener is

driven. If necessary, a second fastener should be driven within 1-1/2" of the faulty one.

- Examine fastener positions. Fasteners should be at least 3/8" in from edges and ends. Screws should not be set too deep; the screw head should be just below the surface of the wall-board.

- Make sure that fastener heads in veneer plaster assemblies are flush with the gypsum base surface, not dimpled.

Adhesives

- Ensure that adhesive is applied to clean, dry surfaces only.

- Make sure that board is erected within allowable time limit after adhesive is applied, so proper bond can be obtained.

- Measure size of bead and spacing, and see that a sufficient quantity is applied.

- Make sure temporary fastening and shoring holds panel tightly in place.

- Review appropriate adhesive application methods and inspect for compliance. (See Chapter 3, "Cladding.")

Inspecting Drywall Joint Treatment

- Make sure panel surface is ready for joint treatment, and fastener heads are properly seated below panel surface. Anything protruding above the plane of the drywall surface must be removed or sanded below the plane. Gaps between adjacent panels should be prefilled with joint compound before taping begins. When a gap wider than 1/8" is prefilled, the compound must be allowed to set or completely dry before taping.

- See that recommended mixing directions are followed. (See Chapter 5, "Finishing Drywall Systems.") Only clean water and mixing equipment should be used. SHEETROCK brand Setting-type (DURABOND) and Lightweight Setting-type (EASY SAND) joint compounds cannot be held over or retempered.

- Inspect joints and corners to see that tape is properly embedded and covered promptly with a thin coat of joint compound. Only compounds suitable for embedding should be used. Avoid heavy fills.

- Make sure compound is used at its heaviest workable consistency and not over-thinned with water.

- Make sure joint compound is allowed to dry thoroughly between coats. Exception: SHEETROCK brand setting-type (DURABOND) and lightweight setting-type (EASY SAND) joint compounds need only be set prior to a subsequent application.

- Inspect second and third coats over joints for smoothness and proper edge feathering.

- Ensure that fastener heads and metal trim are completely covered.

- Check that the paper surface of the gypsum board has not been damaged by sanding.

- Make sure that all finished joints are smooth, dry, dust free and sealed before decoration.

**Inspecting
Veneer
Plaster Joint
Treatment**

– Ensure that corner bead is properly attached and aligned at all outside corners.

– Verify that control joints are properly installed where required.

– Check for proper joint reinforcement. Under normal working conditions, joints of veneer plaster systems may be treated by applying IMPERIAL brand Type P (pressure-sensitive) or Type S (staple) to the joints and then applying the veneer plaster basecoat or finish to preset the tape. However, there are a number of special situations that require the use of a setting-type joint treatment system:

- With high building temperature, low humidity or excessive evaporation conditions that fall in the "rapid drying" area of the graph. (See page 211.)

- When metal framing is specified.

- When wood-framing spacing of 24" o.c. and a single-layer gypsum base veneer system is specified (5/8" base with one-coat veneer finish and 1/2" or 5/8" base with two-coat veneer finish).

Under any of these conditions, use SHEETROCK brand joint tape and Setting Type (DURABOND) or Lightweight Setting-Type (EASY SAND) joint compound to treat all joints and internal angles. Allow joint treatment to set and dry thoroughly before plaster application.

– Make sure that IMPERIAL brand tape is not overlapped at intersections.

– Verify that all taped, preset IMPERIAL brand base joints are set before plaster application begins.

– If gypsum base paper is faded, ensure proper treatment. (See page 386.)

11

Inspecting Conventional Plaster Installations

Plaster Base

– Verify that material being used complies with specifications and fire- or sound-tested construction.

– Review appropriate system construction and application, and inspect for proper installation practices.

– Check for proper application of base perpendicular to framing members, and see that end joints are staggered.

– Check for cracked and damaged edges of plaster base. These should not be used.

– Be sure recommended fasteners or clips are used and spaced properly.

– Check for proper use of acoustical sealant.

– Inspect installation to make sure that insulating blankets are properly attached and fitted.

– Be sure adequate supports are in place for fixture and cabinet applications.

Grounds for Plastering

The thickness of basecoat plaster is one of the most important elements of a good plaster job. To ensure proper thickness of plaster, grounds should be properly set and followed. Check the following points:

- All openings have specified plaster grounds applied as directed.
- If plaster screeds are used, the dots and continuous strips of plaster forming the screed have been applied to the ground thickness to permit proper plumbing and leveling.
- Grounds have been set for recommended minimum thickness for particular plaster base being used. (See Chapter 8, "Conventional Plaster Applications.")
- Control joints should be installed as required for materials and construction with lath separated behind joint.

Job Conditions for Plastering

This phase of inspection is also important. Periodically make an accurate check of the following points:

- At no time should plastering be permitted without proper heating and ventilation.
- A minimum temperature of 55°F has been maintained for an adequate period before plastering, during plaster application and until the plaster is dry. Circulation of air is necessary to carry off excess moisture in the plaster, and a uniform temperature in a comfortable working range helps to avoid structural movement due to temperature differential.
- Check that precautions have been taken against rapid drying before plaster set has occurred to prevent "dryouts."
- Check temperature during damp, cold weather where artificial heat is provided.
- Check that window and door openings have been covered during hot, dry weather to prevent rapid drying due to uneven air circulation.

Plaster Application

After determining what materials are to be used on the job, refer to correct mixing and application procedures described in Chapter 8.

The visible success of the job is at stake with the finish plaster coat, and required measures should be taken to finish correctly:

- Check plaster type and mixing operation.
- See that proper plaster thickness is maintained.
- Inspect plaster surfaces during drying. Setting of basecoat plaster is indicated by hardening of plaster and darkening of surface as set takes place. Plaster that has set but not yet thoroughly dried will be darker in color than the unset portion. This accounts for the mottled effect as the plaster sets.
- Consult architect's specifications to see that proper surface finish is being used.
- Check temperature of building for proper finish plaster drying conditions.

Cleanup

For a complete job, cleanup is the final stage. All scaffolding, empty containers and excess materials should be removed from the job site. Floors should be swept and the building and site left in good condition for decoration and finishing.

11

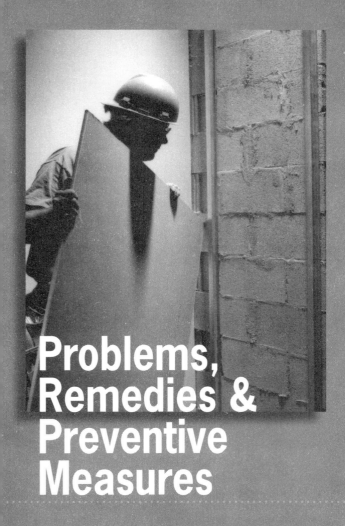

Problems,
Remedies &
Preventive
Measures

Chapter 11 discussed problems associated with gypsum construction, some of which are beyond the control of contractors working from construction documents. However, many issues result from improper job conditions and application practices, which are the responsibility of the contractor, and thus controllable. These problems are outlined in this chapter, as well as corrective remedies and preventive measures.

Drywall Construction

Unsatisfactory results usually show up first in the areas over joints or fastener heads. Improper application of either the board or joint treatment may be at fault, but other conditions existing on the job can be equally responsible for reducing the quality of the finished gypsum board surface. This section will address the possible causes.

To help determine the root cause of a problem, what follows is a physical description of each defect, along with a discussion of the factors causing unsatisfactory results. Also provided is a checklist, as well as an index to the numerically listed problems, causes, remedies and preventions. By checking each numerical item listed for the defect, the precise underlying cause can be determined and corrected.

Note that, because proper installation procedures for FIBEROCK brand products sometimes vary from the procedures used to install conventional drywall panels and gypsum base, associated problems and remedies will vary as well. See the most current literature on FIBEROCK brand panels for recommendations to avoid installation problems.

Description of Defect

Fastener imperfections A common defect, which takes on many forms, including darkening, localized cracking, depressions over fastener heads and/or pops or protrusions of fasteners or the surface area immediately surrounding them. Usually caused by improper framing or fastener application.

Joint defects Generally occur in a straight-line pattern and appear as ridges, depressions or blisters at the joints or darkening over the joints or in adjacent panel areas. Imperfections may result from incorrect framing or joint treatment application, or climatic conditions if remedial action has not been taken.

Loose panels Result of improper contact with framing, and leads to rattling when impacted or shifting when pressure is applied to the surface. Caused by improper application of panels, framing out of alignment or improper fastening.

Joint cracking Appears either directly over the long edge or butt ends of boards, or may appear along the edge of taped joints. Often caused by structural movement and/or hygrometric and thermal expansion and contraction, or by excessively fast drying of joint compounds.

Field cracking Usually appears as diagonal crack originating from a corner of a partition or intersection with structural elements. Also may be seen directly over a structural element in center of a partition. May originate from corners of doors, light fixtures and other weak areas in the surface created by penetration. Caused by movement described previously. (See also "Door and Window Openings" on page 94 for use of control joints to minimize cracking.)

Angle cracking Appears directly in the apex of wall-ceiling or interior angles where partitions intersect. Also can appear as cracking at edge of paper reinforcing tape near surface intersections. Can be caused by structural movement, improper application of joint compound in corner angles or excessive build-up of paint.

Bead cracking Shows up along edge of flange of a metal corner bead. Caused by improper bead attachment or faulty bead or joint compound application.

Wavy surfaces Boards are not flat but have a bowed or undulating surface. Caused by improper board fit, misaligned framing or hygrometric or thermal expansion. (See also "Handling and Storage" on page 104 and Chapter 13, "Safety Considerations & Material Handling," for proper procedure to keep boards flat before installation.)

Board sag Occurs in ceilings, usually under high-humidity conditions. Caused by insufficient framing support for board, board too thin for span, improperly installed or mislocated vapor retarder, unsupported insulation directly on ceiling panels or improperly fitted panels. Refer to appropriate chapters for proper job ventilation, storage and frame spacing, particularly with water-based texture finishes.

Surface defects Fractured, damaged or crushed boards after application may be caused by abuse or lumber shrinkage. (See also discoloration, below.)

Discoloration Board surface has slight difference in color over joints, supports or fasteners. Caused by improper paint finishing or uneven soiling and darkening from aging or ultraviolet light.

Water damage Stains, paper bond failure, softness in board core or mold growth. Caused by sustained high humidity, standing water or improper protection from water leakage during transit and storage. (See page 104 and Chapter 13 for proper handling, storage and environmental conditions.)

Checklist for Drywall Problems

12

To find the specific cause for a problem described above, check all numerical references listed in the particular category on the following pages.

Fastener imperfections	5, 8, 9, 10, 11, 12, 13, 14, 15, 16, 17, 18
Joint defects	1, 5, 6, 7, 11, 19, 20, 21, 22, 23, 24, 25, 26, 27, 28, 29, 30, 31
Loose panels	5, 8, 9, 10, 12, 13, 14, 15, 16, 17, 18
Joint cracking	5, 9, 20, 21, 22, 26
Field cracking	6
Angle cracking	20, 22
Bead cracking	20
Wavy surfaces	5, 8, 22
Board sag	5, 7, 14
Surface defects	2, 6, 28, 29, 30, 31
Discoloration	27, 28, 29, 30
Water damage	2, 4

Dyrwall Panel Problems

The following pages outline common defect allegations of drywall panels and their probable causes, as well as recommended remedies and prevention techniques.

1. Panels—Damaged Edges

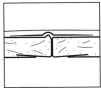

Fig. 1

Cause: Paper-bound edges have been damaged or abused. May result in ply separation along edge or loosening of paper from gypsum core, or may fracture or powder the core itself. Damaged edges are more susceptible to ridging after joint treatment (Fig. 1).

Remedy: Cut back any severely damaged edges to sound board before application.

Prevention: Avoid using board with damaged edges that may easily be compressed or can swell during contact with moisture. Handle gypsum panels with reasonable care.

2. Panels—Water-Damaged

Cause: During transit or storage, water has damaged panels from heavy rain, floods, broken pipes, etc. Water-damaged panels may be subject to scuffing and may develop paper bond failure or paper delamination from the gypsum core after application. They also may easily warp and deform. Dissolved glue from bundling tapes may damage board faces and cause them to stick together. If stored wet, they may be subject to mold. Prolonged soaking or exposure to water can soften gypsum core and destroy bond of the paper to the core.

Remedy: The amount and duration of water exposure are both critical factors in preventing excessive losses. As soon as possible, dry wet board completely before using. Moisture induced delamination should not be present after thorough drying. Paper that is not completely bonded when the panel is moist often will reestablish its bond when the panel is thoroughly dry. If delamination exists after thorough drying, remove loose paper and patch area with SHEETROCK brand setting-type (DURABOND or EASY SAND) joint compound. Replace board if there is extensive loose paper. Handle board cautiously, and re-pile with bundles separated by spacer strips of gypsum board.

Prevention: Protect panels from any and all high moisture conditions. Check incoming board for water stains or dampness. Protect panels during shipment and storage. Do not erect damp panels; this may result in paper bond failure. Replace boards that have soft cores.

3. Panels—Paper Delamination

Cause: Manufacturing conditions, water damage.

Remedy: Manufacturing conditions or water damage causing delamination often can be treated as above under #2. If board is received on the job with paper delaminating, inspect delivery to determine extent of damage. Do not install or finish prior to contacting a USG representative. If delamination is minor, peel back paper to where it soundly bonds to board and treat with joint compound (ready-mix or setting-type).

Prevention: Protect panels from water exposure.

4. Panels—Mold

Cause: Mold can occur on almost any surface depending on heat and humidity conditions. Gypsum panels that have become wet for any reason are susceptible to mold growth.

Remedy: Ordinary soap and water may be used to clean moderately affected surfaces. Proper ventilation and/or heat should be used to thoroughly dry the affected area. Mold growth may occur again if proper conditions are not maintained. Where mold growth is extensive, a qualified construction professional should assess the situation.

Prevention: Keep gypsum panels and the job site area as dry as possible to prevent mold spores from blooming.

5. **Panels—
   Improperly
   Fitted**

Cause: Forcibly wedging an oversized panel into place bows the panel and builds in stresses, preventing it from contacting the framing (Fig. 14, page 378). Following fastening, a high percentage of fasteners on the central studs will most likely puncture the paper. This may also cause joint deformation.

Remedy: Remove panel, cut to fit properly and replace.

Prevention: Always fasten panels so that the board hangs flat against framing without binding against previously installed panels. Apply pressure to hold panel tightly against framing while driving fasteners.

6. **Panels—
   Surface
   Fractured
   after
   Application**

a. **Cause:** Heavy blows or other abuse has fractured finished wall surface. Break is too large to repair with joint compound.

Remedy 1: Cut a square-shaped section around damaged area with a utility knife or keyhole saw (Fig. 2). Then cut a plug of the same dimensions from a sound gypsum panel. Slip SHEETROCK brand drywall repair clips onto all four edges of the prepared hole and screw attach (Fig. 3). Mount replacement section and screw attach to clips (Fig. 4). Remove repair clip tabs (Fig. 5) and finish all four sides with joint tape and compound. Apply and feather out second and third coats, sand and prime. This remedy meets requirements of ASTM E119 testing for repairing one-hour fire-rated wall. All patching components—except drywall—available in SHEETROCK brand drywall repair kit.

12

Fig. 2

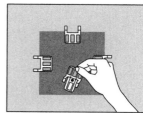

Fig. 3

Fig. 4

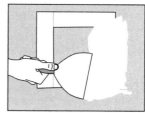

Fig. 5

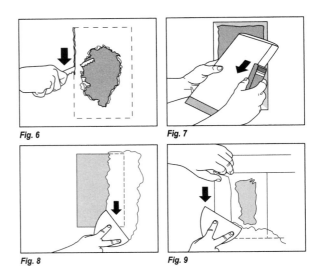

Fig. 6

Fig. 7

Fig. 8

Fig. 9

Remedy 2: Cut a square-shaped or triangular section around damaged area with a utility knife or keyhole saw (Fig. 6); use a rasp or sanding block to slope edges inward at 45°. Cut corresponding plug from sound gypsum panel, sand edges to exact fit (Fig. 7). Butter edges (Fig. 8), and finish as a butt joint with joint compound (Fig. 9).

Remedy 3: An alternate repair technique (sometimes referred to as "California patch," "butterfly patch" or "hot patch") involves cutting a corresponding plug approximately 1-1/2" wider and longer that the cutout in the wall. Next, score through the back paper and core, snap the core and then peel the core away from the face paper so that an overlapping section remains around the perimeter of the plug. Edge the plug with joint compound, and insert it into the damaged area. The overlapping face paper is used in lieu of tape for finishing with joint compound. Although this may be an acceptable method for certain applications, note that the resulting repair is weaker and more difficult to finish than the methods noted above, because the patch will remain above the existing plane of the wall or ceiling. This technique should not be used to repair fire-rated walls.

b. **Cause:** Attaching panel directly to flat grain of wide-dimensional wood framing members, such as floor joists or headers. Shrinkage of wood causes fracture of board.

Remedy: As noted above, where appropriate, or repair as for joint ridging.

Prevention: To provide a flexible base to allow for movement of framing, attach resilient channels to framing members and apply panels. Allow 1/2" of space at bottom edges of board for movement. Or, attach board directly to studs but allow 1/4" separation between panels, and install zinc control joint No. 093. (See single-layer application on page 115.)

c. **Cause:** Knife scoring beyond corner of cutout for electrical boxes, light fixtures or door and window openings produces cracks in panel surface.

Remedy: Repair cuts with joint compound and tape before finishing.

Prevention: Stop score marks at corners, and cut openings accurately.

d. **Cause:** Abnormal stress buildup resulting from structural deflection or racking discussed previously (in section 6A above).

Remedy: Relieve stress, provide adequate isolation and retape, feathering joint compound over board area to disguise buildup.

Prevention: Provide proper isolation from structure to prevent stress buildup.

e. **Cause:** Excessive stresses resulting from hygrometric and/or thermal expansion and contraction.

Remedy: Correct unsatisfactory environmental conditions; provide sufficient relief. Retape, feathering joint compound over board area.

Prevention: Correct improper job conditions, and install control joints for relief in long partition runs and large ceiling areas. (See pages 171–173.)

7. **Panels— Ceiling Sag after Installation**

a. **Cause:** Too much weight from overlaid insulation, exposure to sustained high humidity, vapor retarder improperly installed or wetting causes ceiling panels to sag after installation. Board that is too thin for framing space also results in sag.

Remedy: Remove sagged board or fur ceiling using resilient channels. Apply another layer of board. (Note that leveling of surface with joint compound will not correct problems resulting from improper framing, unusual weight loads or recurring high moisture conditions.)

Prevention: Follow recommended frame spacing and attachment procedures, and use only recommended products. SHEETROCK brand interior gypsum ceiling board is recommended, where available. (See "Ceiling Sag Precautions" on page 345.)

b. **Cause:** Water-based textures tend to wet face paper and weaken gypsum core, causing ceiling panels to sag after installation.

Remedy: Same as 7a above.

Prevention: See Chapter 3, "Cladding," for proper frame spacing and application procedures. See also "Ceiling Sag Precautions" on page 345.

12

Framing Problems

8. **Framing— Members out of Alignment**

Cause: Due to misaligned top plate and stud, hammering at points "X" (Fig. 10) as panels are applied on both sides of partition will most likely result in nail heads puncturing paper or cracking board. Framing members more than 1/4" out of alignment with adjacent members make it difficult to bring panels into firm contact with all nailing surfaces.

Remedy: Remove or drive in problem fasteners, and only drive new fasteners into members in solid contact with board.

Prevention: Check alignment of studs, joists, headers, blocking and plates before applying panels, and correct before proceeding. Straighten badly bowed or crowned members. Shim out flush with adjoining surfaces. Use adhesive attachment.

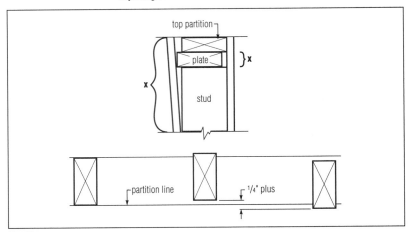

Fig. 10

9. Framing—Members Twisted

Cause: Framing members have not been properly squared with plates, presenting angular nailing surface (Fig. 11). When panels are applied, there is danger of puncturing paper with fastener heads or of reverse twisting of member as it dries out, with consequent loosening of board and probable fastener pops. Warped or wet dimension lumber may contribute to deformity.

Remedy: When moisture content in framing has stabilized after one heating season, remove problem fasteners and re-fasten with carefully driven type W screws.

Prevention: Align all twisted framing members before board application. (See also wood framing requirements on page 71.)

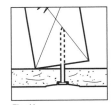

Fig. 11

10. Framing—Protrusions

Cause: Bridging, headers, fire stops or mechanical lines have been installed improperly so as to project beyond face of framing, preventing panels from contacting nail surface (Fig. 12). Result is loose boards. Fasteners driven in area of protrusion will most likely puncture face paper.

Remedy and Prevention: Align all twisted framing members before board application. (See also wood framing requirements on page 71.)

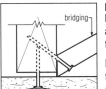

Fig. 12

11. Framing (Steel)—Panel Edges out of Alignment

Cause: Improper placement of steel studs or advancing in the wrong direction when installing panels can cause misalignment of panel edges and give the appearance of ridging when finished.

Remedy: Fill and feather out joint with joint treatment.

Prevention: Install steel studs with all flanges pointed in the same direction. Then install panels by advancing in the direction opposite the flange direction (Fig. 13).

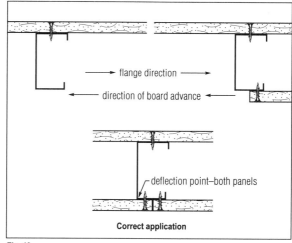

flange direction

direction of board advance

deflection point—both panels

Correct application

Fig. 13

Fastener Problems

12. Fasteners— Puncturing of Face Paper

Cause: Poorly formed nail heads, careless nailing, excessively dry face paper or soft core or lack of pressure during fastening (Fig. 14). Nail heads that puncture paper and shatter core of panel (Fig. 15) have little grip on board.

Remedy: Remove improperly driven fastener, hold panel tightly and properly drive new fastener.

Prevention: Correct faulty framing, and properly drive nails to produce tight attachment with slight uniform dimple (Fig. 16). (See previous Framing Problems.) Nail head should bear on paper and hold panel securely against framing member. Use proper fastener or adhesive application. Screws with specially contoured heads are recommended to eliminate cutting and fracturing. If face paper becomes dry and brittle, its low moisture content may aggravate nail cutting. Raise moisture content of board and humidity in work area.

12

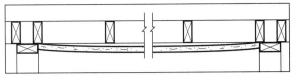

Fig. 14

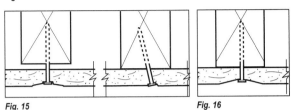

Fig. 15　　　　　　　　　　　　　*Fig. 16*

13. Fasteners— Nails Loosened by Pounding

Cause: Applying panels to the second side of a partition can loosen nails on the opposite side. This is particularly true when lightweight, soft lumber, undersized studs or furring are used.

Remedy: Check panels for tightness on the partition side where panels were first applied. If looseness is detected, strike each nail head an additional hammer blow, being careful to not overdrive.

Prevention: Use proper framing methods. Use type W screws or adhesive application. Apply hand pressure to hold panel tight against framing while driving fasteners.

14. Fasteners— Unseated Nails

Cause: Flexible or extremely hard framing or furring does not permit nails to be properly driven. May result from undersized framing members, type of wood used, supports that exceed maximum allowable frame spacing or lack of hand pressure during fastening.

Remedy: Replace nails with 1-1/4" type W screws.

Prevention: Use proper framing methods. (See Chapter 2, "Framing.") Use type W screws or adhesive application. Apply pressure to hold panel tight against framing while driving fasteners.

15. Fasteners— Loose Screws

Cause: Using the wrong type screw for the application or an improperly adjusted screw gun results in a screw stripping or not seating properly.

Remedy: Remove faulty fastener and replace with a properly driven screw.

Prevention: Use screws with combination high/low threads for greater resistance to stripping and pullout; set screw gun clutch to proper depth.

16. Nail Pops From Lumber Shrinkage

Cause: Improper application, lumber shrinkage or a combination of both. With panels held reasonably tight against framing member and proper-length nails, only severe shrinkage will generally cause nail pops. But if nailed loosely, any inward pressure on panel will push nail head through its thin covering pad of compound. Pops resulting from "nail creep" (movement of nail resulting from lumber shrinkage) occur

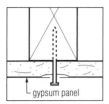

gypsum panel

Fig. 17

when shrinkage of the wood framing exposes nail shank and consequently loosens the panel. (See "Lumber Shrinkage" page 357.)

Remedy: Repairs usually are necessary only for pops that protrude 0.005" or more from face of board (Fig. 17). Smaller protrusions may require repair if they occur in a smooth gloss surface or flat-painted surface under extreme lighting conditions. Those that appear before or during decoration should be repaired immediately. Pops that occur after one month's heating or more are usually caused by wood shrinkage and should not be repaired until near end of heating season. An often effective procedure for resetting a popped nail is to place a 4" broad knife over the nail and hit with hammer to seat flush with surface. A more permanent method is to drive proper nail or type W screw about 1-1/2" from popped nail while applying sufficient pressure adjacent to nail head to bring panel in firm contact with framing. Strike popped nail lightly to seat it below surface of board. Remove loose compound, apply finish coats of compound and paint.

Prevention: Proper nail application; use of lumber meeting framing requirements (page 71); attachment with type W screws or by adhesive application (Chapter 3).

17. Fasteners— Panels Loosely Fastened

Cause: Framing members are uneven because of misalignment or warping; lack of hand pressure on panel during fastening. Head of fastener alone cannot pull panel into firm contact with uneven members. (See No. 5.)

pressure

Fig. 18

Remedy: With nail attachment, during final blows of hammer, apply additional pressure with hand to panel adjacent to nail (Fig. 18) to bring panel into contact with framing.

Prevention: Correct framing imperfections before applying panels; for a more solid attachment, use 1-1/4" type W screws or adhesive method. (See Chapter 3.) Apply pressure to hold panel tightly against framing while driving fasteners.

12

18. Fasteners— Bulge Around Fastener

Cause: Overdriving fasteners, driving them with the wrong tool or failing to hold board firmly against framing while driving can puncture and bulge face paper and damage core of board. Application of joint compound or texture finish that wets the board paper can also result in board bulging or swelling around fastener.

Remedy: Drive screw fastener close to damaged area, clean out damaged paper core, repair with SHEETROCK brand setting-type (DU-RABOND) or SHEETROCK brand lightweight setting-type (EASY SAND) joint compound, and refinish.

Prevention: Use correct tool and drive fasteners properly. Also, see No. 17.

Joint Problems

19. Joints— Blisters in Tape

Cause: Insufficient or overly thin compound used under the tape, tape not initially pressed into good contact with the compound, overly thick (dry) compound used, or too much compound forced from under tape by application of excessive tool pressure when embedding.

Remedy: Open up blistered area by slitting tape. Fill cut with joint compound and press tape back in place with knife blade. When dry, smooth to level finish.

Prevention: Provide sufficient compound under entire length of tape.

20. Joints— Edge Cracking

a. **Cause:** After joint treatment, straight narrow cracks along edges of tape may result from too rapid drying because of high temperature accompanied by low humidity or excessive drafts; improper application such as over-dilution of joint compound; use of wrong compound (topping instead of taping); excessive joint compound under tape; failure to follow embedding with a thin coat over tape; or cold, wet application conditions, which also may cause poor bond.

This problem, difficult to see when it first occurs, may not be discovered until decoration begins. However, the cause can be attributed to some aspect of the taping operation.

Remedy: Especially in hot, dry and/or drafty conditions, carefully examine all joints after taping applications have dried; repairs are more economical at this stage. Cut away any weakly bonded tape edges. Fill hairline cracks with cut shellac (2- to 3-lb.). Then groove out larger cracks with a sharp tool, coat with shellac and allow to dry. Finally, refill with joint compound or cover cracks with complete joint treatment, including reinforcing tape. Feather to surface level with plane of board.

Prevention: Use either SHEETROCK brand setting-type (DURABOND) or lightweight setting-type (EASY SAND) joint compound, which have the best built-in resistance to cracks. Place shielding devices over room openings to prevent drafts. Do not apply joint treatment over hot surfaces. Dampen floors if extra low room humidity condition is suspected. During cold weather, control heat at minimum of 55°F and supply good ventilation.

b. **Cause:** After joint treatment, cracks along edges of corner bead or trim can result from the same unsatisfactory conditions listed above for tape. Also can be caused by impact on the bead.

Remedy: Remove applied joint compound. Securely fasten corner bead or trim to framing beneath panels. Refinish bead with joint compound.

Prevention: Use SHEETROCK brand paper-faced metal tape on bead and trim, which eliminates edge cracking.

21. Joints— Center Cracking

a. **Cause:** Abnormal stress buildup resulting from structural deflection or racking as discussed in Chapter 15, "Building Sciences."

Remedy: Relieve stress. Provide adequate isolation, and retape, feathering joint compound over broad area to disguise buildup.

Prevention: Provide proper isolation from structure to prevent stress buildup.

b. **Cause:** Excessive stresses resulting from hygrometric and/or thermal expansion and contraction. (See also Chapter 15.)

Remedy: Correct unsatisfactory environmental conditions. Provide sufficient relief, and retape, feathering joint compound over broad area.

Prevention: Correct improper job conditions, and install control joints for relief in long partition runs and large ceiling areas. (See pages 171–173.)

22. Joints— Angle Cracking

a. **Cause:** Too much compound applied over tape at apex of angle.

Remedy: After compound is completely dry, smooth out excess compound at apex. Fill only hairline cracks with compound. Do not apply additional compound, which will build up.

Prevention: Keep excess compound from corner, leaving only a small amount or no compound in apex.

b. **Cause:** Slitting or scoring reinforcing tape during application. May result from incorrect tool use

Remedy: If crack extends through the tape, retape and finish.

Prevention: Use proper tools for corner treatment.

c. **Cause:** Structural movement from two separate supports or framing members, which react independently to applied loads. Often occurs in wall-ceiling angles where wall is attached to top plate and ceiling is attached to floor or ceiling joists running parallel to top plate.

Remedy: Remove fasteners closer than 6" from angle, and then retape and finish.

Prevention: Use "Floating Interior Angle" application described on page 134.

d. **Cause:** Structural or thermal movement resulting from two dissimilar materials or constructions.

Remedy: Remove tape, provide relief, finish with appropriate trim and caulk as required.

Prevention: Use channel-type or angle-edge trim over gypsum board where two dissimilar surfaces interface.

e. **Cause:** Excessive paint thickness; application of paint under poor conditions.

Remedy: Correct unsatisfactory job conditions. Scrape away cracked paint. Fill and feather with joint compound. Prime and paint.

Prevention: Provide proper job conditions. Apply recommended thickness of prime and finish coats of paint.

23. Joints—High Crowns

Cause: Excessive buildup of compound over joint; compound not feathered out beyond shoulders; improper bedding of tape; framing out of alignment or panel edges not tight against framing; improperly adjusted or worn tools; misuse of tools.

Remedy: Sand joints to flush surface. Take care to avoid scuffing paper by oversanding.

12

Prevention: Embed tape properly, using only enough compound to cover it and fill taper depression or tape itself at butt joints. Feather compound wide enough to conceal.

24. Joints— Excessive and/or Delayed Shrinkage

Cause: (1) Atmospheric conditions—slow drying and high humidity; (2) Insufficient drying time between coats of compound; (3) Excessive water added in mixing compound; (4) Heavy fills. When a second coat of joint compound is applied over compound that has not yet dried, the first coat will dry more slowly, and shrinkage will occur later than is typical. This slow shrinkage is termed "delayed shrinkage."

Remedy: See "Starved Joints," below.

Prevention: Allow each coat of joint compound to dry thoroughly before applying succeeding coat, or use a low-shrinkage joint compound.

25. Joints— Starved Joints

Cause: This is a form of delayed shrinkage caused chiefly by insufficient drying time between coats of compound. May also be caused by insufficient compound applied over tape to fill taper, over-thinning or over-smoothing of compound. Shrinkage usually progresses until drying is complete.

Remedy: Use fast-setting joint compound (such as DURABOND or EASY SAND) or reapply a full cover coat of heavy-mixed compound over tape. Since this is heaviest application, most shrinkage will take place in this coat, making it easier to fill taper properly.

Prevention: Allow each coat of joint compound to dry thoroughly before applying succeeding coat, or use a low-shrinkage joint compound.

26. Joints— Ridging

Cause: All building materials grow or shrink in response to changes in temperature and humidity. When they are confined to a specific space, such as gypsum panels in a partition or ceiling, they are put under stress, either compression or tension, depending on the temperature or humidity conditions. These stresses are relieved when the panel bends outward in the region of the joint. Once this bending takes place, the system sets and never returns to normal. It becomes progressively worse with each change of temperature or humidity. This progressive deformation appears as a continuous ridge along the length of joint, with a uniform, fine, ridge-like pattern at the center.

Remedy: (1) Let ridge develop fully before undertaking repairs; usually a period of six months is sufficient. Make repairs under average room environmental conditions. (2) Smooth ridge down to reinforcing tape without cutting through it. Fill concave areas on either side of ridge with light fill of compound. After this is dry, float a very thin film of compound over entire area. (3) Examine area with strong side lighting to make certain that ridge has been concealed. If not, use additional feathering coats of compound. Redecorate. Ridging may recur, but is usually less severe. Continuous wetting will aggravate condition.

Prevention: Where available, use SHEETROCK brand gypsum panels, SW edge, which feature a rounded edge designed to prevent ridging. Follow general recommendations for joint treatment (Chapter 1) and approved application procedures, which include back-blocking and laminated double-layer application to minimize potential ridging problems (Chapter 3, "Cladding"). Pay particular attention to temperature, ventilation, consistency of compound, prompt covering coat over tape, minimum width of fill, finish coats and required drying time between coats.

Finishing Problems

27. Finish— Discoloration

a. **Cause:** Differences in suction of panel paper and joint compound may lighten paint color or change gloss or sheen in higher-suction areas. This is most common when conventional oil-based paints are used, and may also be caused by texture differences between the face paper and finished joint compound or by over-thinning of paint. May also occur over fasteners in ceilings subjected to severe artificial or natural side lighting. Suction differences may cause greater amounts of texturing material to be deposited over high-suction areas, resulting in color differences when viewed from an angle. Before painting, face panel paper may be darkened from exposure to sunlight.

Remedy: Redecorate.

Prevention: Before painting or texturing, apply a prime coat of Sheet-rock brand First Coat or undiluted interior flat latex paint with high solids content. Avoid roughening surface paper when sanding joint compound. Use strong job lights parallel to the surface to ensure a flat, acceptable joint compound finish prior to priming, texturing and/or painting.

b. **Cause:** The use of preservatives in paint formulation. As the scientific community learns more about health hazards, additives to many products are changed or eliminated. Mercury, for example, was banned for use in paints in 1990. Some additives may cause a reaction resulting in an off-color appearance.

Remedy: A high-quality finish coat will generally produce an acceptable finish.

Prevention: A good quality primer or Sheetrock brand First Coat and finish paint coat properly applied according to the paint manufacturer's recommendations will prevent most discoloration problems.

28. Finish—Gloss Variation With High-Gloss Paints

Cause: Differences in suction of panel paper and joint compound, or texture differences between the face paper and finished joint compound (as stated in 27a above). The problem is accentuated by strong side lighting with slight angle of incidence to ceiling or wall surface.

Remedy: Redecorate.

Prevention: Before painting with a high-gloss paint, apply a skim coat of joint compound over the entire wall surface or use a veneer plaster system. If skim coating is not done, the next best preventative measure is to apply a prime coat of Sheetrock brand First Coat.

29. Finish—Joint Darkening

Cause: This condition occurs most commonly with color-tinted paint rather than white. It is most severe when applied in humid weather when joints have not fully dried.

12

Remedy: Apply a prime coat of SHEETROCK First Coat and repaint. (Repaint only after all surfaces are thoroughly dry.)

Prevention: Be sure joints are thoroughly dry before painting. (See "Drying Time" on pages 183–184).

**30. Finish—
Shadowing**

Cause: Temperature differentials in outside walls or top-floor ceilings cause collection of airborne dust on colder spots of interior surface. Results in photographing or shadowing over fasteners, furring or framing. Most severe with great indoor-outdoor temperature variation.

Remedy: Wash painted surfaces, remove spots with wallpaper cleaner or redecorate surfaces. Change air filters regularly.

Prevention: Use double-layer application with adhesively applied face layer. Use separately framed free-standing interior wall surface and insulate in void to reduce temperature difference between steel or wood components and panels.

**31. Finish—
Decorating
Wallboard
Damaged by
Over-Sanding**

Cause: Paper fibers of the exposed gypsum panel surface are scuffed and raised by over-sanding of the joints or use of sandpaper that is too coarse.

Remedy: Correct severe paper fiber raise with a light skim coat of a drying-type joint compound. Minor fiber raise may be treated by light sanding with very fine sandpaper or wiped down with a damp sponge or cloth.

Prevention: Good finish work with compound, feathered edges, etc. reduces the need for sanding, in general, limiting exposure to this kind of problem.

Veneer Finish Construction

Many problems associated with veneer plaster construction have the same cause, remedy and prevention as with drywall systems. Similarity of problems appears in application of the base, framing irregularities, cracking due to structural movement, hygrometric and thermal expansion and fastener imperfections. The additional problems that follow specifically relate to veneer finish construction. If a solution to your specific problem with veneer finish construction is not described, check similar problems for drywall construction found earlier in this chapter.

**Application
Problems**

**1. Mixing—
Foaming
Action in Mixer**

Cause: Use of USG plaster accelerator—alum catalyst as an accelerator when limestone aggregate is used.

Remedy: None. Dispose of batch.

Prevention: Use molding plaster or quick-set gauging plaster as an accelerator when limestone aggregate is used, or use sand aggregate. Also, avoid entraining air from mixing with high-speed mixing paddle or wrong kind of paddle.

2. **Setting Time—Variable Set Time Within Batch**

Cause: Insufficient or excessive mixing.

Remedy: None. Dispose of batch.

Prevention: Use proper drill speed; follow recommended mixing times. (See pages 219–221.)

3. **Slow Set— IMPERIAL and DIAMOND Interior Finish Plaster/ Basecoat**

a. **Cause:** High air and mixing water temperature, in excess of 100°F.

Remedy: Proper use of accelerator.

Prevention: Avoid extremes of air and water temperatures.

b. **Cause:** Contaminated mixing water or contaminated sand.

Remedy: None.

Prevention: Use drinkable water only.

c. **Cause:** Excessive use of retarder.

Remedy: None. Dispose of batch.

Prevention: Follow recommendations for mix proportions and use of additives.

4. **Quick Set— IMPERIAL and DIAMOND Interior Finish Plaster/ Basecoat**

a. **Cause:** Low air and water temperature below 40°F.

Remedy: None. Dispose of batch.

Prevention: Avoid extremes of air and water temperatures.

b. **Cause:** Contaminated mixing water; dirty mixing equipment.

Remedy: None. Dispose of batch.

Prevention: Use drinkable water only. Clean set plaster residue from equipment after each batch. Always use clean mix equipment.

c. **Cause:** Excessive use of accelerator.

Remedy: None. Dispose of batch.

Prevention: Follow recommendations for mix proportions and use of additives.

5. **Quick Set— IMPERIAL Finish Plaster and DIAMOND Interior Finish Plaster Only/Basecoat**

Cause: Contamination; excessive use of aggregate and/or accelerator.

Remedy: None. Dispose of batch.

Prevention: Use drinkable water. Clean set plaster residue from equipment after each batch. Always use clean mix equipment. Follow recommendations for mix proportions and use of additives.

6. **Workability— Still Working**

Cause: Mixing action has improper or insufficient shear.

Remedy: None. Use remainder of batch, if at all workable.

Prevention: Follow recommendations for mixing time, drill speed and type of mixing paddle. (See pages 219–221.)

12

In-Place Problems

7. Bond Failure— Delamination of Finish Coat

Cause: Basecoat not left rough and open (rough for mechanical key and open as in porous); finish coat not properly scratched into basecoat to have necessary keying.

Remedy: Remove loose material, brush basecoat thoroughly, apply bonding agent and refinish.

Prevention: Follow application recommendations. (See Chapter 6, "Finishing Veneer Plaster Systems.")

8. Bond Failure— DIAMOND Interior Finish Plaster

Cause: Application over faded (not normal blue color) gypsum base.

Remedy: Remove loose material, brush base clean, apply bonding agent and refinish.

Prevention: Do not store or apply base where it will be exposed to sunlight for an extended time. Where exposed, spray faded base with USG accelerator–alum catalyst or USG plaster bonder before finish is applied. (See No. 9 below.)

9. Sun-Faded Gypsum Base

Cause: Exposure of gypsum base to sunlight for an extended period of time.

Remedy: When used with lime-containing plaster, such as DIAMOND interior finish, sun-faded IMPERIAL brand gypsum base face paper should be treated with USG accelerator-alum catalyst or USG plaster bonder. This precaution is unnecessary when applying products that do not contain lime (IMPERIAL finish and basecoat plaster, and DIAMOND veneer basecoat plaster). For alum catalyst solution treatment, pour three pounds of USG accelerator-alum catalyst slowly into one gallon of water and mix thoroughly. Allow the solution to stand until all undissolved material has settled. Then strain solution into tank-type sprayer (such as garden sprayer). Spray solution onto faded face paper so that it is wet but not soaked. One gallon of solution should treat 750 SF of IMPERIAL gypsum base. Begin finish plaster application before face paper treated with alum solution is completely dry. Caution: Alum treatment shortens setting time of DIAMOND brand interior finish.

Prevention: See Problem No. 8.

10. Cracks— Joint Cracking

a. **Cause:** IMPERIAL Tape overlapped at joint intersections.

Remedy: On large cracks, apply SHEETROCK brand joint tape and ready-mixed joint compound (all-purpose or taping). For minor cracks, flush out area with SHEETROCK ready-mixed joint compound (all-purpose or taping).

Prevention: Avoid overlapping tape at all joint intersections, including those at angles.

b. **Cause:** Improper steel stud placement. Gypsum base application advanced in wrong direction relative to flange direction.

Remedy: Repair with joint tape and ready-mixed joint compound (all-purpose or taping).

Prevention: Install steel studs with all flanges pointing in same direction. Arrange gypsum base application so lead edge of base is attached to open edge of flange first. (See Framing [Steel]—Panel Edges out of Alignment on page 377.)

c. **Cause:** Overly rapid drying conditions.

Remedy: Repair with joint tape and ready-mixed compound (all-purpose or taping).

Prevention: Liberally sprinkle floor with water to raise humidity. Use joint tape and joint compound (such as DURABOND or EASY SAND) on all joints. Allow compound to dry thoroughly before applying finish. Where steel stud framing is used, apply SHEETROCK brand joint tape and setting-type joint compound (DURABOND or EASY SAND).

d. **Cause:** IMPERIAL tape with steel framing.

Remedy: Repair with SHEETROCK brand joint tape and ready-mixed compound (all-purpose or taping).

Prevention: Because of its increased strength and hardness use only SHEETROCK brand joint tape and setting-type joint compound (DURABOND or EASY SAND).

11. Cracks—Field Cracking

Cause: Gypsum base installed with vertical joints extending from corners of door and window openings.

Remedy: Apply SHEETROCK brand joint tape and setting-type (DURABOND) joint compound. Then finish with ready-mixed joint compound (all-purpose or taping). Prime and seal. As this treatment is cosmetic, it is not guaranteed that cracks will not reopen.

Prevention: Install zinc control joint No. 093 or cut base to fit around openings with joints centered above openings, not at corners.

12. Cracks— Craze and Map Cracking

Cause: Veneer plaster application too thin. Also can be caused by too rapid drying.

Remedy: Apply spackling putty. Prime and seal.

Prevention: Apply recommended thicknesses for both one- and two-coat work. Avoid excessive ventilation, which may cause rapid drying. When weather is hot and dry, sprinkle floor with water to raise humidity.

12

13. Blemishes —Blistering

a. **Cause:** Loose paper on gypsum base as a result of improper cutting or from "peelers" caused by careless handling.

Remedy: Cut and remove unbonded paper, apply bonding agent if gypsum core is exposed, and refinish.

Prevention: Follow proper handling and cutting procedures.

b. **Cause:** Troweling too early and lack of absorption; excessive material buildup.

Remedy: Minimize troweling and allow finish to become firm. Finish trowel over freshly set surface to eliminate blisters.

Prevention: Apply material in uniform thickness with minimum amount of troweling to produce smooth surface.

14. **Blemishes— Joint Ridging and Beading**

Cause: Joints not preset; excessive ventilation and poor heat control. Most likely to occur with one-coat applications.

Remedy: Repair with SHEETROCK brand ready-mixed compound (all-purpose or taping).

Prevention: Preset all joints before veneer finish application; keep ventilation to minimum and control heat. In extremely hot, dry weather use SHEETROCK brand joint tape and setting-type (DURABOND or EASY SAND) joint compound as alternative joint reinforcement.

15. **Blemishes— Spalling at Exterior Corners**

Cause: Use of solid-flange drywall corner bead.

Remedy: Remove all loose material and corner bead. Install expanded-flange corner bead and refinish.

Prevention: Use expanded-flange corner bead.

16. **Stains— Staining and Rusting**

Cause: Use of improper fasteners, or exposed, improperly prepared metal trim.

Remedy: Apply rust-locking primer over stains.

Prevention: Use recommended coated fasteners. (See Chapter 1, "Drywall & Veneer Plaster Products.") Apply rust-locking primer to all exposed metal.

17. **Soft, Weak Surface— Dryouts**

Cause: Too rapid drying conditions.

Remedy: Fog-spray surface with water or alum solution to provide setting action. When set, apply ready-mixed joint compound (all-purpose or taping) for acceptably smooth surface.

Prevention: Avoid extending set and/or temperature and humidity conditions, which cause rapid drying.

18. **Soft, Weak Surface— Crumbly Areas**

Cause: Use of excessive amount of sand aggregate and/or retarder.

Remedy: Treat soft areas with penetrating sealer.

Prevention: Allow minimum ventilation; use only recommended amounts of aggregate or retarder. Avoid prolonged set.

Cement Board Construction

DUROCK brand cement board systems require careful adherence to published installation procedures and high standards of workmanship. The following pages outline common defect allegations and their probable causes, as well as recommended remedies and prevention techniques.

1. **Interior Tile System— Surface Fractured**

Cause: Heavy impact punctures from moving equipment or vandalism. Holes resulting from previous fixture attachment.

Remedy: If tile can be removed without damaging the cement board, remove damaged tile by cutting and chipping tile. Scrape or grind bond coat down to skim coat. Tape any cracks with DUROCK brand tape. Re-set tile and grout.

If tile cannot be removed without causing excessive damage to the board, remove the damaged section by cutting through the tile and board. Install additional framing by screw attaching to existing framing at the same plane behind edge of existing surface so that the perimeter of existing and new panels will be supported. Cut a patch of cement board that closely fits the opening. Apply a generous amount of organic adhesive to the edges of existing and new panel. Install panel and attach to framing with appropriate fasteners. Smooth and level adhesive at panel joints. Let adhesive cure for 24 hours before setting and grouting new tile.

2. Delamination— Basecoat or Mortar

Cause: Improper mixing procedures or improper base coating techniques.

Remedy: Remove all material that is not properly bonded to the panel surface. Apply a bonding agent, such as Larsen's WELD-CRETE; then reapply basecoat to the area.

Prevention: Always use the proper amount of clean, potable water when mixing the material. Too much water will significantly reduce the bond strength of the material. Apply the material using a scratch-and-double-back method. The tight scratch coat keys the material into the panel surface.

2. Delamination— Tile and Thin Brick

Cause: Allowing the mortar to skin over before setting the tile or brick. Not back-buttering or not applying sufficient mortar to the back of the tile.

Remedy: Scrape the mortar from the panel surface. Apply a bonding agent and allow to dry. Apply fresh mortar to the panel, and back-butter the tile and push into place.

Prevention: Do not allow the mortar to skin over. Back-butter the tile, slide into place, and beat in to ensure 100% coverage.

12

Texture Finishes

USG texturing materials offer a wide range of decorative yet practical finishes. Properly used, they can provide interest and variety in decoration while covering minor defects in the base surface. However, certain working conditions, application techniques or equipment problems can cause unsatisfactory results. The following list describes potential problems, probable causes, remedies and prevention techniques for various situations.

Mixing Problems

1. Mixing— Lumping of Wet Mix

Cause: Too much water added to initial mix, making lumps difficult to break up.

Remedy and Prevention: Initial amount of water added to mix should be slightly less than recommended. After lumps are broken up, add remaining water.

2. Mixing—Slow Solution Time

Cause: Insufficient soaking and/or use of very cold water.

Remedy and Prevention: Allow materials to soak for up to two hours, as necessary, if using cold water. Minimum recommended temperature for air, water, mix and wall surface is 55°F.

3. Mixing—Wet Mix Too thin

Cause: Addition of excessive water during initial mix. Also, insufficient soaking time in cold water.

Remedy and Prevention: Use recommended amount of water to proper consistency. Allow materials to soak up to two hours, if necessary, when using cold water.

Application Problems

4. Application— Excessive Aggregate Fallout in Spraying

Cause: Excessive air pressure at nozzle; holding gun too close to surface being sprayed.

Remedy and Prevention: Use proper air pressure for type of material to be sprayed. (Consult appropriate USG data sheet for recommended air pressure.) Hold spray gun at proper distance from surface to prevent excessive bounce or fallout of aggregate.

5. Application— Flotation of Aggregate

Cause: Over-dilution of job mix and/or lack of adequate mixing after water is added to control consistency.

Remedy and Prevention: Add correct amount of water as directed on package to ensure proper suspension of materials in mix. Make certain that water is blended into mix.

6. Application— Poor Coverage with Spray Finishes

Cause: Not enough water to bring texture material to proper spray viscosity and/or improper application, such as moving spray gun too slowly, overloading spray surface and using incorrect spray pressure.

Remedy and Prevention: Add proper amount of water as directed on package. Use correct spray gun pressure and application technique to ensure uniform texture with maximum coverage.

7. Application— Poor Hide

Cause: Over-dilution of mix causing reduction in hiding power. Insufficient water in spray finishes causes poor material atomization, resulting in surface show-through. Also caused by over-extending material or choosing incorrect spray pressure package.

Remedy and Prevention: Add proper amount of water as directed on package. Use correct spray gun pressure and application technique to ensure uniform texture with maximum coverage.

8. Application— Poor Bond or Hardness

Cause: Over-dilution of job-mix results in thinning out of binder in texture. Contamination or intermixing with other than recommended materials can destroy bonding power.

Remedy and Prevention: Add proper amount of water as stated in bag directions. Always use clean mixing vessel and water. Never intermix with other products (except materials as recommended).

9. **Application— Stoppage of Spray Equipment**

Cause: Contamination of material or oversized particles can cause clogging of spray nozzle orifices. Also caused by using incorrect nozzle size.

Remedy and Prevention: Prevent contamination during mixing. Use correct nozzle for aggregate size of texture material.

10. **Application— Unsatisfactory Texture Pattern**

Cause: Improper spray pressure and/or worn spray equipment, either fluid or air nozzle. Also improper spraying consistency of mix and/or spraying technique.

Remedy and Prevention: Use recommended amount of water to ensure proper spraying consistency. Handle spray equipment correctly to achieve best results. Make certain that spray accessories are in good working condition; replace when necessary.

11. **Application— Unsatisfactory Pumping Properties**

Cause: Mix too heavy. Pump equipment worn or of insufficient size and power to handle particular type of texture.

Remedy and Prevention: Use recommended amount of water to ensure proper spraying consistency. Make sure that equipment is in good repair and capable of pumping heavy materials.

12. **Application— Texture Buildup**

Cause: Texturing over a high-suction drywall joint (surface not properly primed) and/or allowing too much time between roller or brush application and texturing operation. Over-dilution of texture material will produce texture buildup over joint.

Remedy and Prevention: Before texturing, apply a prime coat of SHEETROCK brand First Coat or an undiluted, interior flat latex paint with high solids content. Use correct amount of water when mixing texture material. Allow safe time interval between application and final texturing.

Finish Surface Problems

12

13. **Finish Surface— Poor Touchup**

Cause: Touchup of a textured surface to completely blend with the surrounding texture is extremely difficult. A conspicuous touchup is caused either by texture or color variance.

Remedy: Perform touchup operation with extreme care; otherwise, re-texture entire wall or ceiling area.

14. **Finish Surface— Joint Show- Through**

Cause: Over-thinned or over-extended texturing material does not adequately hide the normal contrast between joint and gypsum panel paper. Also caused by improperly primed surface.

Remedy: Use correct amount of water when mixing texture material and apply at recommended rate of coverage until joint is concealed.

Prevention: Before texturing, apply a prime coat of SHEETROCK brand First Coat or undiluted, interior flat latex paint with high solids content.

15. Finish Surface— White Band or Flashing Over Gypsum Panels

Cause: High-suction gypsum panel joint causes a texture variation, which often appears as a color contrast.

Remedy: Allow texture to dry, and paint entire surface.

Prevention: Before texturing, apply a prime coat of SHEETROCK brand First Coat or undiluted, interior flat latex paint with high solids content.

16. Finish Surface— White Band or Flashing Over Concrete

Cause: Damp concrete surface on which leveling compound has dried completely can produce results similar to those of high-suction joint.

Remedy: Allow texture to dry, and paint entire surface.

Prevention: Allow concrete to age for at least 60 days for complete dryout. Before texturing, apply a prime coat of SHEETROCK brand First Coat or undiluted, interior flat latex paint with high solids content.

17. Finish Surface— Joint Darkening

Cause: Application over damp joint compound, especially in cold and/or humid conditions.

Remedy: Allow texture to dry completely, and paint entire surface.

Prevention: Allow joint compound to dry completely before priming and texturing. Before texturing, apply a prime coat of SHEETROCK brand First Coat or an undiluted, interior flat latex paint with high solids content.

Conventional Plaster Construction

All USG basecoat and finish plasters are carefully manufactured and thoroughly tested before shipment. Along with the functional characteristics offered, USG plasters are carefully formulated for use under normal, prevailing weather conditions and with aggregates commonly used in the market.

Plasters are adversely affected by aging and abnormal storage conditions, use of the wrong aggregate and improper proportioning, all of which may affect the set, hardness and working properties of the material. Most plaster problems result from the following situations:

1. Adverse atmospheric and job conditions.
2. Set conditions that are too fast or slow.
3. Poor quality and incorrect proportioning of aggregate.
4. Improper mixing, application or thickness of basecoat or finish.
5. Incorrect lathing practices.
6. Dirty or worn mixing or pumping equipment.

Basecoat and finish coat plasters are so closely interrelated that problems pertaining to their use are treated together. No attempt is made here to discuss problems that might occur due to structural deficiencies. These were covered previously in this chapter. Plaster problems are classified under the specific existing condition. These are discussed in order, in the following groups:

1. Plaster cracks.
2. Blemishes.
3. Color variations and surface stains.
4. Weak, soft walls.
5. Bond failure.
6. Other problems.

Cracking Problems

Problem: Connecting vertical or horizontal cracks at somewhat regular intervals, often in a stepped pattern. Also may be diagonal in appearance.

Material: Plaster over metal or gypsum lath.

   a. **Cause:** Plaster too thin, insufficient plaster grounds.

   Remedy: Patch affected area.

   Prevention: Apply plaster to proper thickness.

   b. **Cause:** Weak plaster (through dryout or slow set).

   Remedy: Spray with alum solution to accelerate set.

   Prevention: Add accelerator to plaster mix to bring setting time to normal range.

   c. **Cause:** Excessive use of aggregate.

   Remedy: Patch affected area.

   Prevention: Use proper proportions of aggregate and plaster.

   d. **Cause:** Failure to use Striplath reinforcement at potential weak points.

   Remedy: Cut out, reinforce and repair.

   Prevention: Install proper reinforcing.

   e. **Cause:** Expansion of rough wood frames.

   Remedy: Remove plaster and lath as necessary. Seal frames and patch.

   Prevention: Seal frames. Cut basecoat along grounds prior to set. Install control joints over frames.

Material: Plaster over unit masonry.

   a. **Cause:** Structural movement of masonry units.

   Remedy and Prevention: Correct masonry construction, provide movement relief, patch.

Material: Plaster over brick, clay tile or concrete block at door openings.

   a. **Cause:** Poor lintel construction, improper frame construction.

   Remedy: Patch affected area.

   Prevention: Use proper frame and lintel construction with self-furring metal lath reinforcement.

12

Problem: Fine cracks, random pattern, generally 1" to 3" apart. Includes shrinkage cracks, crazing, alligatoring and chip cracks.

Material: Gauged lime-putty finish over gypsum basecoat, used with any plaster base.

  a. **Cause:** Insufficient gauging plaster-shrinkage of lime. Insufficient troweling during setting. Applied finish too thick. Basecoat too wet or too dry and too little or too much suction.

   Remedy: Apply spackling putty and primer-sealer.

   Prevention: Use sufficient gauging plaster, trowel sufficiently or properly condition basecoat before applying finish.

Problem: Fine cracks, irregular pattern, generally 6" to 14" apart; map cracking.

Material: Trowel finishes over gypsum basecoat—unit masonry plaster base.

  a. **Cause:** Finish coat applied too thick.

   Remedy: Patch affected area.

   Prevention: Apply finish coat to 1/16" thickness but not more than 1/8".

  b. **Cause:** Improper timing of final troweling.

   Remedy: Patch affected area.

   Prevention: Water-trowel as final set takes place (not before) to provide dense, smooth surface.

  c. **Cause:** Retempering gauged lime putty.

   Remedy: Discard batch; make up new gauge.

   Prevention: Gauged lime putty should not be retempered once it has started final set.

Problem: Random pattern, usually less than 12" apart, called map, shrinkage or fissure cracking.

Material: Basecoat over masonry.

  a. **Cause:** High suction of masonry base.

   Remedy: If bond to base is sound and cracks are open 1/16" or more, fill by troweling across cracks with properly aggregated plasters. If bond is sound, finish over fine cracks with highly gauged trowel finish or float finish. If curled at edges and bond is not sound, remove and reapply using proper plaster method.

   Prevention: Wet masonry with water to reduce suction before basecoat application.

  b. **Cause:** Under-aggregating of basecoat; slow set.

   Remedy: Same as above in "a."

   Prevention: Use 3 CF of aggregate per 100 lb. gypsum plaster. (See Chapter 8, "Conventional Plaster Applications," for proper proportion of aggregates.) Discontinue use of job-added retarder and accelerator, if necessary, to obtain proper set.

  c. **Cause:** Dryout condition.

Remedy: Spray basecoat either with water or alum solution to thoroughly wet plaster. Proceed same as above.

Prevention: In hot, dry weather, protect plaster from drying too rapidly before set. Spray plaster during set time if necessary.

Problem: Cracking at wall or ceiling angles.

Material: Plaster over gypsum lath.

a. **Cause:** Thin plaster.

Remedy: Cut out and patch.

Prevention: Follow correct application procedure.

b. **Cause:** Failure to use Cornerite reinforcement.

Remedy and Prevention: Same as above in part "a."

Blemishes

Problem: Water-soluble, powdery crystals on surface, generally white but may be colored. Can be brushed off.

Material: Basecoat and finish plaster over concrete block or clay tile.

a. **Cause:** Efflorescence. As masonry units dry, water-soluble salts from units or mortar joints leach out and are deposited on the plaster surface.

Remedy: After plaster surfaces are thoroughly dry, brush off efflorescence, apply oil-based sealer and paint.

Prevention: On interior walls, eliminate source of moisture, remove efflorescence before plastering; decorate with oil-based sealer and paint. On exterior walls, eliminate moisture source, fur out, lath and plaster.

Problem: Pops or peak-like projections which fall out and create little craters or pits; often with final radial cracks.

12

Material: Gauged lime-putty finish.

a. **Cause:** Unslaked lime in mortar which slakes and swells after it is applied.

Remedy: Remove core of "pops" and patch after popping has ceased.

Prevention: Allow sufficient soaking time for normal hydrated lime or use double-hydrated lime or a prepared finish such as RED TOP finish plaster.

b. **Cause:** Contamination from foreign matter.

Remedy: Same as above in part "a."

Prevention: Eliminate source of impurity.

Material: Gypsum basecoat and finish.

a. **Cause:** Lumpy or undissolved retarder added on job. Retarder lumps swell or "pop" when wet.

Remedy: Cut out spots and patch affected area.

Prevention: Completely disperse retarder before adding to mix water; mix well to distribute retarder throughout plaster.

Problem: Blisters in finish coat occur during or immediately after application.

Material: Gauged lime-putty finish.

   a. **Cause:** Base too green (wet); insufficient suction; too much water used in troweling.

   Remedy: After finish has set, trowel with very little water.

   Prevention: Do not apply finish over green basecoat.

   b. **Cause:** Finish too plastic.

   Remedy: Same as above in part "a."

   Prevention: Add small amount of very fine white sand to putty or increase amount of gauging plaster.

Problem: Excess material (slobbers) on finish surface.

Material: Gauged lime-putty finish.

   a. **Cause:** Improper joining technique, excessive or improper troweling leaves excess material on finished surface.

   Remedy: Scrape off excess material before decoration. Seal surface when plaster is dry.

   Prevention: Previously applied finish should be cut square for completion of finish. Avoid excessive troweling at joining.

Problem: Peeling paint.

Material: Gauged lime-putty finish.

   a. **Cause:** Paint applied over wet plaster.

   Remedy: Scrape off peeled paint, allow plaster to dry, and re-decorate.

   Prevention: Be sure plaster is dry before decorating, and use a breather-type paint.

   b. **Cause:** Weak finish. Plaster worked through set.

   Remedy: Scrape off peeled paint, patch and decorate.

   Prevention: Do not retemper or trowel finish after set.

Color Variations and Surface Stains

Problem: Streaks and discoloration.

Material: Lime finishes, gauged with gauging plaster or Keenes Cement.

   a. **Cause:** Lime and gauging plaster not thoroughly mixed.

   Remedy: Seal and decorate.

   Prevention: Follow recommended mixing procedures.

   b. **Cause:** Too much water used in troweling.

   Remedy: Same as above in "a."

   Prevention: Apply as little water as possible in troweling.

c. **Cause:** Dirty tools or water.

Remedy: Same as above in "a."

Prevention: Wash tools and use clean water.

Problem: Light and dark spots.

....

Material: Float finish.

a. **Cause:** Improper technique or too much water used in floating.

Remedy: Seal and paint to get uniform color.

Prevention: Follow recommended application procedures.

b. **Cause:** Spotty suction on basecoat that was dampened unevenly by throwing water on with a brush rather than by spraying with a fine nozzle.

Remedy: Same as above.

Prevention: Dampen basecoat uniformly using a fine spray.

Problem: Light or flat spots in light-color paint.

....

Material: Oil-based paint over gauged lime-putty finish.

a. **Cause:** Surface painted too soon after plastering (alkali in lime saponifies paint); paint pigments not limeproof.

Remedy and Prevention: Apply primer-sealer and repaint.

....

Material: Any colored paint over any plaster finish.

b. **Cause:** Non-uniform absorption results in uneven surface gloss and coloration.

Remedy and Prevention: Apply primer-sealer and repaint.

Problem: Yellow, brown or pink staining—yellowing.

....

Material: Any lime-putty finish over any basecoat and plaster base; generally occurs while surface is damp.

a. **Cause:** Contaminated aggregate.

Remedy: Apply primer-sealer and repaint.

Prevention: Use clean aggregate.

b. **Cause:** By-product of combustion from unvented fossil fuel space heaters.

Remedy: Same as above in "a."

Prevention: Vent heaters to outside.

c. **Cause:** Tarpaper behind plaster base; creosote-treated framing lumber; tar or tar derivatives used around job; sulfur or chemical fumes.

Remedy: Same as above in "a."

Prevention: Use asphalted paper. Remove source of air contamination.

12

Problem: Rust.

Material: Plaster over any plaster base.

a. Cause: Rusty accessories; or any protruding metal.

Remedy: Apply rust-locking primer-sealer and decorate.

Prevention: Use accessories made of zinc alloy or with hot-dip galvanizing. Do not use accessories that show rust prior to installation.

Soft, Weak Walls

Problem: Soft, white, chalky surfaces, occurring during hot, dry weather, usually near an opening.

Material: Gypsum basecoat over any plaster base.

a. **Cause:** Dryout. Too much water has been removed before plaster can set.

Remedy: Spray with alum solution or plain water to set up dryout areas.

Prevention: Screen openings in hot, dry weather; spray plaster during set; raise humidity by sprinkling floor with water.

Problem: Soft, dark, damp surfaces occurring during damp weather.

Material: Gypsum basecoat over any plaster base.

a. **Cause:** Sweat-out. Too little ventilation allows water to remain in wall for an extended period after plaster set. Some plaster has redissolved.

Remedy: Dry walls with heat and ventilation. If sweat-out condition continues, there is no remedy; remove and replaster.

Prevention: Properly heat and ventilate during plastering.

Problem: Soft, dark, damp surfaces, occurring in freezing weather.

Material: Gypsum basecoat over any plaster base.

a. **Cause:** Frozen plaster.

Remedy: If plaster freezes before set, no remedy except to remove and replaster.

Prevention: Close building, supply heat.

Problem: General condition; soft, weak walls; not spotty or due to slow set.

Material: Gypsum basecoat over any plaster base.

a. **Cause:** Too much aggregate or fine, poorly graded aggregate.

Remedy: No remedy; remove and replaster.

Prevention: Use properly graded aggregate and correct proportioning.

Problem: Weak plaster.

Material: Gypsum basecoat.

a. **Cause:** Extremely slow set.

Remedy: Spray with alum solution to accelerate set.

Prevention: Add accelerator to plaster mix to bring setting time within normal range.

Material: Gauged lime-putty finish over any basecoat.

a. **Cause:** Too little gauging with insufficient troweling; retempering; basecoat too wet.

Remedy: No remedy; remove and replaster.

Prevention: Use proper ratio of gauging to lime putty. Do not retemper plaster. Trowel adequately to ensure desired hardness.

Bond Failure

Problem: Basecoat separation.

Material: Gypsum basecoat over gypsum or metal lath.

a. **Cause:** Too much aggregate, plaster application over frost on lath, freezing of plaster before set, addition of lime or Portland cement, excessive delay in plaster application after mixing, extremely slow set, or retempering.

Remedy: No remedy except to replaster.

Prevention: Provide proper job conditions during plastering. Follow correct mixing and application procedures.

Problem: Brown coat separation from scratch coat.

Material: Gypsum basecoat plasters.

a. **Cause:** Weak scratch coat.

Remedy: None; remove and replaster.

Prevention: Use proper aggregate amount. Avoid retempering.

b. **Cause:** Failure to provide mechanical key in scratch coat.

Remedy: Roughen scratch coat and replaster.

Prevention: Cross-rake scratch coat to provide rough surface for brown coat.

c. **Cause:** Dryout of scratch coat.

Remedy: Water-spray scratch coat for thorough set before brown coat application.

Prevention: Provide proper job conditions during plastering; screen openings in hot, dry weather. Water-spray plaster during set. Raise humidity by sprinkling floor with water.

12

Problem: Finish coat separation.

Material: Gauged lime-putty finish applied over gypsum brown coat.

a. **Cause:** Brown coat too smooth, too dry, wet or weak; finish improperly applied.

   Remedy and Prevention: Strip off finish, correct condition of brown coat and replaster.

b. **Cause:** Frozen finish coat.

   Remedy and Prevention: Remove finish, provide sufficient heat during plastering, reapply finish.

c. **Cause:** Incomplete hydration of finish lime.

   Remedy and Prevention: Remove finish; using properly proportioned double-hydrated lime or a prepared finish, reapply finish.

Other Problems

Problem: Slow Set. See "Soft, Weak Walls."

Problem: Quick Set. Plaster sets before it can be properly applied and worked.

Material: Gypsum basecoat over any plaster base.

a. **Cause:** Dirty water, tools or mixing equipment; excessive use of accelerator.

   Remedy: Discard material as soon as it begins to stiffen; do not retemper.

   Prevention: Use clean water, tools and equipment.

b. **Cause:** Mixing too long.

   Remedy: See above in "a."

   Prevention: Reduce mixing time.

c. **Cause:** Poor aggregate.

   Remedy: See above in "a."

   Prevention: Use clean, properly graded aggregate or add retarder.

d. **Cause:** Error in manufacture.

   Remedy: See above in "a." Send samples to manufacturer's representative.

   Prevention: Add retarder.

e. **Cause:** Machine-pumping and application that exceed limits of time and distance pumped for plaster being used.

   Remedy: See above in "a."

   Prevention: Add retarder. Use plaster designed for machine application.

Problem: Erratic Set—lack of uniformity in set.

Material: Gauged lime putty over gypsum basecoat.

a. **Cause:** Variable temperature.

Remedy and Prevention: Maintain uniform job temperature. In cold weather, heat building to min. 55°F.

Problem: Works hard or short, loses plasticity and spreadability. Does not carry proper amount of aggregate.

Material: Gypsum basecoat over any plaster base.

a. **Cause:** Aged or badly stored plaster.

Remedy: Obtain fresh plaster and mix equal parts with aged plaster or use less aggregate.

Prevention: Use fresh plaster.

b. **Cause:** Over-aggregating.

Remedy: None.

Prevention: Use proper proportioning.

Material: Gauged lime putty over gypsum basecoat.

a. **Cause:** Aged lime, partially carbonated; warehoused too long or improperly.

Remedy: None.

Prevention: Use fresh material.

b. **Cause:** Improper soaking, slaking. Low temperature during putty preparation.

Remedy: None.

Prevention: Use proper lime-putty preparation procedure. Do not soak at temperatures below 40°F.

Problem: Soupy Lime—too fluid for proper gauging and application.

Material: Lime putty.

a. **Cause:** Incorrect soaking.

Remedy: None.

Prevention: Follow directions for type of lime being used.

b. **Cause:** Cold weather, cold mixing water.

Remedy: None.

Prevention: The gelling action of lime is retarded when material is soaked in temperatures less than 40°F with cold water. Use warm water to quicken gelling.

Problem: Lime material too lumpy for proper blending with gauging plaster.

Material: Lime putty.

a. **Cause:** Old lime.

Remedy: None.

Prevention: Use fresh lime.

12

b. **Cause:** Damp lime.

   Remedy: None.

   Prevention: Protect lime from moisture on job and in storage.

c. **Cause:** Incorrect soaking.

   Remedy: None.

   Prevention: Follow soaking directions for type of lime used.

d. **Cause:** Excessive evaporation.

   Remedy: Add proper quantity of water and allow to soak.

   Prevention: Cover lime box with tarpaulin to reduce evaporation.

Safety Considerations & Material Handling

This chapter is an overview of the health and safety concerns that should be addressed when USG's products and systems are used—both at home in do-it-yourself projects or at professional construction sites. The chapter is not intended to be a comprehensive review, but instead outlines some major issues and refers to other reputable sources for information and assistance. We recommend that contractors seek the assistance of safety professionals, especially at the professional construction site, as there are many factors to be considered that are not included here.

Introduction

Construction can be a dangerous activity. This is intuitive to many people, but it is also borne out by government statistics that show construction to be one of the occupations most likely to result in severe injury or death.

The key to safety is training. Training leads to familiarity with the hazards and how to avoid them, and is the foundation of any safety program. For construction professionals, guidance is provided by federal OSHA regulations and comparable state laws and regulations. These resources are invaluable.

For home owners taking on gypsum-related projects themselves, the best approach is to be familiar with Material Safety Data Sheets (MSDS) and product warnings, literature produced by the Gypsum Association and guides issued by state and federal agencies, as well as manuals or instructions on any tools that are used.

Safety risks can be caused by both physical dangers and health hazards. Physical hazards include falling objects, panels breaking and electrical hazards, for example. Health hazards are often less obvious and include potential long-term harm to the lungs and other organs caused by exposure to crystalline silica, mold, fungus or mildew that can grow on building materials after they get wet or dust that can be created when sanding or finishing joints. Some of these hazards may pose immediate symptoms or medical conditions, while others may have a delayed effect. In addition, hazardous health effects can occur from a single exposure or as a result of long-term exposure. Thus, this part of safety awareness depends heavily on education. Warning labels and MSDSs are the primary initial sources of health hazard information.

Handling Wallboard & Other Panel Products

SHEETROCK brand gypsum panels, IMPERIAL brand gypsum base, DU-ROCK brand cement board, SECUROCK glass-mat sheathing, and FI-BEROCK brand gypsum panels are all heavy panels whose handling by machine or by hand poses the risk of serious injury.

Forklift Safety

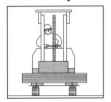

Board products and ceiling tile will initially be moved by a forklift or similar device. It is absolutely essential that the equipment be rated capable of handling the loads. The forks should always be long enough to extend completely through the width of the load. Forks should also extend far enough apart to support the load so that it will not break or fall. Gypsum panels are brittle compared to other building products, such as lumber. If not properly supported, individual panels or a whole lift can break.

SHEETROCK gypsum panels and IMPERIAL gypsum base:

- Fork spacing between supports should be one-half the length of the panels or base being handled so that a maximum of 4' extends beyond the supports on either end.

FIBEROCK gypsum panels:

- Fork spacing should be similar to the above except that a maximum of only 3' should extend beyond the supports on either end. Fork carriage spread in the range of 46" to 84" is suitable for handling most common lengths of board and panels. Sometimes gypsum board manufacturers offer to band lifts of board at each end. This will aid in preventing deflection of the board when it is picked up with a forklift but it is not a substitute for proper fork spacing. Banding will not prevent board from breaking if the forks are not spaced far enough apart.

Other key items of forklift safety include:

- Always follow the forklift manufacturer's operating and maintenance instructions, especially concerning load limits.
- Always wear a safety belt when operating a forklift.
- Never move the forklift with the load elevated more than a few inches above the floor or ground surface.
- Never stand below or near a raised load.
- Observe all traffic rules in the loading or warehouse area.
- Never disable equipment back-up alarms or other safety devices.
- In heavy traffic areas, use a spotter to regulate forklift, pedestrian and other traffic.

13

– When parking a lift truck, set the parking break and lower the forks to the floor. Turn truck off.

For more information on forklift safety, see:

OSHA CFR, (800) 321-OSHA (6742)

National Safety Council, (800) 621-7619; **nsc.org**

Stacking Board

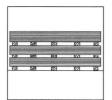

Generally, it is safer to stack board flat.

Gypsum Association literature states unequivocally that board should be stacked flat because stacking boards vertically against a wall poses a safety hazard. According to the *Handling and Storage of Gypsum Panel Products: A Guide for Distributors, Retailers, and Contractors*, Gypsum Association publication GA-801-07:

"Stacks of gypsum board are very heavy and can become unstable if proper stacking and handling procedures are not followed. Workers must always be extremely careful when stacking or working in an area where gypsum panel products are stacked. For example, a 4' wide by 12' long by 1/2" thick gypsum board can weigh over 80 pounds; this means a stack of only 25 boards weighs over a ton" (page 2). The capacity of the floor to support the load whenever wallboard is stacked must be examined and considered when stacking panel products.

"The safest way to store gypsum panel products on a job site is to stack them flat on risers that are placed on a solid surface. Storing gypsum panel products on edge leaning against wall framing can pose a serious hazard. Panels stacked on edge can easily become unstable, and the entire stack can accidentally topple or slip, which in turn can result in serious injury or even death" (page 9).

While the vertical stacking of paneled material should be minimized, there are some situations where stacking the board flat creates different safety hazards. For example, in residential construction where rooms are small and hallways narrow, vertically stacking against the wall allows installers to move around the room.

Also in residential construction, floor load limits often are not sufficiently high to be able to accommodate a concentrated point load of gypsum panels, cement board or gypsum fiber panels in the center of the floor; instead, the safer procedure in this situation is to distribute the board in vertical stacks around the sides of the room. Sometimes, when different sizes or widths of board are required (for example, 5/8" for the ceiling and 1/2" for the walls) vertical stacking makes it easier for the wallboard hangers to find the board they need.

While vertical stacking of panel material can be appropriate and helpful it can also pose a falling hazard. When vertical stacking is used, be sure to leave at least 4" to 6" of space between the bottom of the first board in the stack and the wall. Leaving less than 4" creates a risk that the stack could be pulled over; leaving more than 6" applies too much weight laterally against the wall. Warning tape or signage should be used to alert people of the potential for leaning wallboard to fall if disturbed.

Vertical stacking

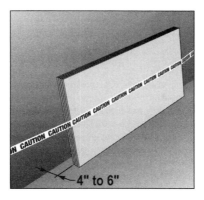

4" to 6"

Storage Conditions

Protecting wallboard and other products from rain, snow, sunlight and wind is important. Not only can the weather damage the board by soaking it, but exposure to weather can do other harm not immediately obvious. For example, moisture could affect the bond of the face paper to the gypsum core in a way that later creates problems in application and finishing. Also, ultraviolet (UV) exposure from sunlight will ruin the ability of plaster base panels (blue board) to act as a substrate for some veneer plasters.

If wallboard is left unprotected and then installed, moisture in the wallboard can provide conditions favorable for mold, mildew and fungus growth, which, as discussed below, poses not only aesthetic problems, but also serious health consequences.

Although board products are very heavy, high winds across their flat surfaces can provide "lift" just as with an airplane wing, and thus wind can send heavy pieces of gypsum wallboard flying through the air, causing damage and serious injuries.

(For more information on proper storage, see the Gypsum Association publication *Handling and Storage of Gypsum Panel Products: A Guide for Distributors, Retailers, and Contractors*, GA-801-07, available through **gypsum.org**.)

13

Lifting

SHEETROCK brand gypsum panels, SECUROCK glass-mat sheathing, IMPERIAL brand gypsum base, DUROCK brand cement board, FIBEROCK brand gypsum panels, joint compound packages (buckets or boxes), and bags of plaster and ceiling tile packages are all very heavy, awkward loads that pose the risk of severe back injury. Proper lifting techniques should always be observed. Keep the load close to your body and use your legs, not your arms, to lift. Use mechanical assistance, such as pallet lifters or hand dollies, wherever possible. Manual lifting and carrying should be confined to the shortest distance possible.

(For more information, consult the National Safety Council, (800) 621-7619; **nsc.org**.)

Other Physical Hazards

Pallets

Almost all pallets used to transport joint compound, plaster, plaster bags, ceiling tile, cement board and other construction materials are made of wood. Pallets that are defective or incomplete (missing pieces) should be carefully unloaded and discarded from service. Not only will a broken pallet cause a spill and loss of the product, but it could also lead to serious injuries or death if heavy materials fall. Pallets are usually designed for specific applications; using pallets for different applications than they were originally designed for can create a hazardous condition.

(For more information, consult the National Wooden Pallet and Container Association, (703) 519-6104; **nwpca.com**.)

Eye Protection

Safety glasses or goggles protect eyes from a variety of hazards.

Eye protection should be worn at all times, not just when using power equipment. Some products, such as plasters containing lime, pose the risk of a chemical burn, which could result in the loss of eyesight. Eye protection (safety glasses or goggles) also protects the eyes from dust. (For more information, consult the National Safety Council, (800) 621-7619; **nsc.org**.)

Five-Gallon Bucket Child Drowning Warning

In the mid-1980s health officials noticed a pattern in some drowning deaths of very young children (less than three years of age). Several hundred deaths were reported of children drowning after falling into five-gallon buckets that were being used for household purposes (cleaning, storage, etc.). Some children drowned in as little as a few inches of liquid. Investigation showed that while children this age were developed enough to stand up and lean over into the bucket, their muscles were not strong enough to pull them out. USG led the industry in putting a warning of this hazard on its five-gallon pails. It is a good example of a simple physical hazard that is not obvious. Many parents who would not dream of leaving their small children alone in a bathtub or by a pool might not recognize that a five-gallon bucket with a few inches of water also poses a drowning hazard.

Plaster Burn Warning

Occasionally people will use gypsum plaster in an art class or at home for projects. Sometimes, instead of an imprint of a hand, for instance, they will try to make a cast of the whole hand or other body part, completely enclosing it. This can lead to a serious injury because, as the plaster sets, it traps the hand or other body part, and enough heat

Directions
Protect from moisture during storage and on the job.

In cold weather, heat the interior of the building to a minimum of 55F (13C) for an adequate period before the application of plaster, while basecoat and nish is being applied and until the nish is dry. Air circulation should be kept at a minimum level during this period.

Mixing
Use a cage-type paddle mixer (see PM19, "Mixing Equipment for Veneer Plasters") driven by a heavy-duty drill capable of producing 900-1000 rpm minimum under no load. Place approximately 9 to 11 qts. (8.5-15.1 L) of clean water in a 12- to 15-gallon, smooth-sided container, and with mixer operating, slowly add one bag of plaster. Mix for a minimum of two minutes, but not longer than ve minutes, to disperse all lumps completely. Keep mixing equipment and all tools clean.

This nish will set in about one hour. Do not mix more material than can be used in 30 minutes. Do not retemper.

Use and Application
Where Norfolk Special Veneer Plaster is applied directly to veneer plaster base, rst reinforce all joints and interior angles (see P517, "Imperial" Brand Tape, and PM5, "Veneer Plaster Joint Reinforcement Systems"). Particular joint reinforcement procedures vary with framing methods and drying conditions.

Fill all voids and imperfections. Final trowel after surface has become rm, holding trowel at and using water sparingly. Do not overtrowel.

Best results are obtained by applying the plastering to permit continuous application from angle to angle. Where joining is unavoidable, use the trowel to terminate unset plaster in sharp clean edge—do not feather out. Bring adjacent plaster up to terminated edge and leave level. Do not overlap. During nish troweling, use excess material to ll and bridge joining.

This material also can be used for the popular skip-trowel texture nish. Once the nish has become suf ciently rm, but before setting, texture with material from the same batch, but do not nal trowel. Other types of texture surfaces can be achieved, but may require using additional aggregate. For sand oat nish, add up to 10-15 lbs. (4.5-6.8 kg) of clean silica sand per 50-lb. bag of Norfolk Special Veneer Plaster to achieve the desired texture. The use of more than 15 lb. of sand per bag will decrease the hardness of the surface. Apply plaster in the normal manner but omit nal troweling.

Start initial oat nishing as soon as the material has become rm enough to permit removal of trowel marks, voids and other blemishes. Final oat nishing must be accomplished prior to set, using water sparingly to avoid shading problems.

For heavier textures, apply suf cient material from the same batch using a trowel, sponge or other accepted method.

Norfolk Special Veneer Plaster provides a white, smooth trowel, oat or texture nish ready for decoration. The nish may be left undecorated if skip-trowel, oated or other textured nishes are utilized and the nish is acceptable.

Ingredients
Plaster of paris CAS 26499-65-0; crystalline silica (sand) CAS 14808-60-7; calcium sulfate CAS 777 18-9; and hydrated lime CAS 39455-23-3.

⚠ WARNING
When mixed with water, this material hardens a then slowly becomes hot – sometimes quickly. D NOT attempt to make a cast enclosing any part body using this material. Failure to follow these instructions can cause severe burns that may re surgical removal of affected tissue or amputatio limb. This material is strongly alkaline and conta with dust or when wetted can cause burns or irritation to the skin, eyes, nose, throat or upper respiratory system. Avoid eye and skin contact c inhalation of dust. If dusty, wear an NIOSH/MSH approved dust respirator. Prolonged and repeat exposure to respirable crystalline silica may cau lung cancer. Use proper ventilation to reduce dl exposure. Wear eye and skin protection. If eye contact occurs, immediately ush thoroughly wi water for 15 minutes. Get medical attention. If si contact occurs, wash thoroughly with water. Do ingest. If ingested, call physician immediately. Product safety information: (800) 507-8899.
KEEP OUT OF REACH OF CHILDREN.

Notice
We shall not be liable for incidental and conseq damages, directly or indirectly sustained, nor fo loss caused by application of these goods not in accordance with current printed instructions or other than the intended use. Our liability is expr limited to replacement of defective goods. All cl shall be deemed waived unless made in writing within thirty (30) days from date it was or reasor should have been discovered.

United States Gypsum Company
125 South Franklin Street
Chicago, Illinois 60606-4678
A Subsidiary of USG Corporation

P654-50BAG/4-00
Printed and Produced in U.S.A.
© 2000, United States Gypsum Company

is given off in the setting of the plaster to cause serious burns. For many years USG has placed the following warning on plaster products to alert users to this danger.

△ WARNING!

When mixed with water, this material hardens and becomes very hot—sometimes quickly. DO NOT attempt to make a cast enclosing any part of the body using this material. Failure to follow these instructions can cause severe burns that may require surgical removal of affected tissue or amputation of limb. Dust can cause eye, skin, nose, throat or respiratory irritation. Avoid eye contact and inhalation of dust. Wear eye protection. If eye contact occurs, flush thoroughly with water. If dusty, wear a NIOSH/MSHA-approved respirator. Prolonged and repeated exposure to respirable crystalline silica can cause lung disease and/or lung cancer. Use proper ventilation to reduce dust exposure. Do not ingest. If ingested call physician. Product safety information: (800) 507-8899.

KEEP OUT OF REACH OF CHILDREN.

Inappropriate Use of Plasters, Joint Compounds or Other Products

People sometimes use construction materials in situations for which they are not designed, which can cause serious risks of injury or death.

For example, gypsum plaster should not be used to anchor porch, stadium or balcony railings where the plaster will be exposed to the weather. This is a dangerous misuse of gypsum plaster. Rain and snow weakens and dissolves exposed gypsum plaster. The resulting railing failure can cause death or at the very least, serious injury, e.g., to people falling from the balcony or to people on the ground below. In another example of misuse, a person using gypsum plaster as a substitute for the dietary calcium supplement prescribed by a physician can bring about serious medical problems. No gypsum-based construction product is designed for human consumption.

13

Health Hazards

Perhaps the greatest change in safety programs for the construction industry in the past several decades is the still-growing appreciation of the hazards posed by various chemicals or substances once used or still used in construction materials. These include, for example, asbestos, lead and silica. Note that no USG products currently contain any asbestos or lead.

Silica

Crystalline silica quartz is respirable and can pose a long-term health risk, including cancer and other severe and debilitating diseases if inhaled. All dust should be avoided, not just silica-containing dust. Excessive dust strains the lungs and overcomes the body's defense systems. Every step should be taken to avoid generating dust. All of the following strategies should be pursued to minimize dust exposure:

- Avoid dust generation with power tools. Wherever a product can be scored and snapped—as is the case with all of USG's gypsum panel products—this method should be used rather than power tools to trim the board.

- Where power tools are used, dust-control mechanisms should be employed. Even consumer power tools come with dust control kits, some of which hook up to shop vacs.

- Similarly, when mixing plaster or joint compound in powder form, care should be taken to create as little dust as possible when emptying the bags into the mixer. Ventilation or, better yet, a local exhaust should always be provided for the dust.

- Final finishing of joint compound may create excessive dust if the worker is not properly trained to apply joint compound. For years USG and other manufacturers in the industry have recommended wet sanding to reduce or eliminate dust levels. More recently, several equipment manufacturers have offered sanding equipment that uses a combination of wetting and/or local exhaust to remove the dust as it is being created.

Mold, Mildew and Fungus

Mold, mildew and fungus are all microorganisms that can, under the right conditions, find a suitable environment in which to grow and survive on building materials. Most often this growth is caused by moisture leaking into the building, although condensation, temperature, pH, lack of exposure to sunlight and several other factors also are involved.

In the past, mold and mildew were considered primarily as an aesthetic problem that spoiled the appearance of the walls or ceilings and only secondarily as a mild health hazard affecting people with allergies or asthma. Today, the picture has dramatically changed as medical science recognizes that not only can these microorganisms cause potentially severe health problems in people with asthma or allergies, but they also can sometimes pose serious health threats even to people who do not have these conditions.

The best way to address mold, mildew and fungus is to make sure that building materials do not get wet before installation and are not exposed to moisture inside the finished building. Traditional building practices, such as management of water away from the interior of the structure, not only constitutes the foundation of good construction practice, but also is the best way to avoid the growth of mold, mildew and fungus. Remove any building products from the job site that are wet or have mold on them.

Fungicides and Mildewcides

Joint compounds are treated at the factory with fungicides to prevent mold growth in the bucket before the product is used, and to retard the growth of mold and mildew after the product is applied on walls and ceilings. The kinds and formulations of fungicides and mildewcides have changed over the years. For example, decades ago joint compounds contained mercury-based biocides. These were discontinued by most manufacturers as the health hazards of mercury became better known. The quantity of mildewcide or fungicide used in USG joint compounds is minute—less than 0.1 weight-percent. This quantity is less than the reporting requirements of OSHA's Hazard Communication Standard.

For more information, see the websites for EPA's Indoor Air Quality Home Page, the American Lung Association and Canada's Indoor Environmental Program; they are listed at the end of this chapter.

Safety Tips for Installing Ceilings

Safety helmets, safety goggles/glasses and gloves are just three examples of safety equipment for use when installing acoustical ceilings.

– Always wear a safety helmet on the job site.

– Wear eye goggles whenever there is the possibility of eye injury, e.g., when using power-actuated tools, when doing overhead drilling or when hammering or drilling into concrete.

– Wear rubber-soled shoes for good traction.

– Do not wear baggy or torn clothing, as they may catch on objects or moving equipment parts and cause injuries or falls.

– Use a kit or tool belt to carry tools.

– Be very careful when using sharp tools or materials. If you are cut by a tool, obtain proper first aid immediately to avoid infection. If the injury is serious, seek professional help immediately.

– Practice good housekeeping: keep work areas free of debris and neatly stack construction materials and panels. Secure these if necessary to prevent falling or sliding.

– Use personal protective equipment to guard against the hazards of falling, flying or splashing objects, or exposure to harmful dusts, mists, fumes, vapors or gases. If respiratory protection is required, be sure respirator users are in good health, medically certified and properly fitted with the equipment.

13

Electrical Tools and Cables

Know how to properly use and maintain the power tools used for ceiling installations. Power-operated hand tools should be double insulated or grounded. Defective tools must be successfully repaired before use. Do not use electrical tools in wet conditions (e.g., wet floors). Do not hoist or lower a power tool by its electrical cord.

The owner's manual is an excellent source of safety and operational information. Always review the specific equipment's manual prior to operation. If you do not have an owner's manual you can usually obtain one from the equipment manufacturer either by phone or through the Internet.

All cable in the work area must be covered or elevated to prevent damage. Frayed or worn electric cable must never be used. Extension cords must be protected against damage from traffic, sharp corners and projections. Flexible cord must be in continuous lengths without splices. When properly made, molded or vulcanized splices may be used.

When tools are equipped with guards, these must never be removed. Belts, gears, shafts or other moving parts must be guarded if there is any possibility of exposure to moving parts.

Powder-Actuated Tools (e.g., Powder Fastening Tool)

These tools should be used only by workers who are properly trained and certified. Powder-actuated tools must be oiled, cleaned and tested each day to make certain that safety devices are working properly. Always review the specific equipment's owner's manual prior to operation. Other tips are as follows:

- Loaded tools must not be left unattended.
- Leave tools unloaded until ready to use.
- Never point powder-actuated tools at anyone.
- Always wear protective eyewear (goggles) when using these tools.
- Never use tools in an explosive atmosphere.
- Use only cartridges and fasteners that are supplied by the manufacturer.
- Inspect for any constriction each time before use.
- Use equipment only with the material it was designed for, as specified in the owner's manual. Using these tools on other surfaces can create a hazard.

Saber and Band Saws

Ensure proper training on how to use these tools before operating them. Always wear safety goggles when operating saws. Always review the specific equipment owner's manual prior to operation. Do not wear loose clothing that could get caught in the moving blade.

Scaffolding

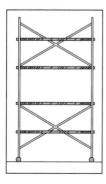

- The height of a scaffold must not exceed four times the minimum base dimension.
- Footings must be rigid and capable of supporting the maximum intended load without settling.
- Do not use barrels, boxes, bricks, concrete blocks or other unstable objects to support scaffolds.
- Casters on wheels must be locked to prevent movement.
- Use cross or diagonal bracing (or both) to properly brace scaffolds. Scaffolding must be upright, rigid and square. Make certain that poles, legs or uprights are plumb and securely braced to prevent displacement or swaying.
- Scaffolds with platforms 10' or more above the ground must have guardrails and toeboards installed on all open sides and ends.

- Scaffolds 4' to 10' high ("Baker" scaffolds) and with a minimum horizontal dimension of less than 45" must have guardrails installed on all open sides and ends of their platforms.
- When scaffolding is used as a passageway or work is to be performed underneath, a screen (No. 18 gauge U.S. Standard wire 1/2" mesh or equivalent) must be provided between the toeboard and guardrail and must extend the entire length of the opening.
- Scaffold planking must overlap a minimum of 12" or be secured from movement.
- Planks must extend over end supports not less than 6" and not more than 12".
- An access ladder or equivalent safe access must be provided.
- Weak or damaged scaffolding parts or components (braces, brackets, ladders, etc.) must be immediately fixed or replaced. Refer to the specific equipment owner's manual prior to operation.

Portable Scaffolds

Portable scaffolds must be leveled and checked for safety each time they are moved. Do not adjust leg screws more than 12". Move scaffolds only when the floor is level and free of obstructions.

Ladders

- Do not use ladders with broken or missing rungs or steps, broken side rails or other defects.
- Do not use ladders as horizontal platforms, runways or scaffolds.
- Keep ladders out of doorways, driveways and passageways.
- Do not use metal ladders for electrical work or in areas where they may contact electrical conductors.
- Set a ladder so that its base stands 1' of horizontal distance from the wall for every 4' of ladder height. The base of the ladder must be level and stable.
- The top of the ladder side rails must extend at least 36" above a landing.
- The area around the top and bottom of a ladder must be kept clear.
- When climbing up or down a ladder hold the side rails with both hands, and carry tools in a kit or on a tool belt.
- The feet of portable ladders must be placed on a substantial base (e.g., floor) before being used. Portable ladders must be secured at the top to prevent movement.

13

Additional Sources of Safety Information

Safety information is easier to find than ever before. OSHA and state agencies have done a tremendous amount of work in creating and making available materials that describe job site hazards—and how to prevent them—in clear, simple ways. Most of this material is available on the Internet. Trade associations such as the Gypsum Association also make their materials available to the people who use Association members' products.

Organizations referenced throughout this chapter as sources for safety information are below. To contact any of these organizations, see "Agencies & Organizations" on pages 488–492 of the Appendix.

- Occupational Safety & Health Administration (see OSHA), US Department of Labor
- National Safety Council (see NSC)
- National Wooden Pallet and Container Association (see NWPCA)
- American Society of Safety Engineers (see ASSE)
- American Industrial Hygiene Association (see AIHA)
- Gypsum Association (see GA)
- Ceiling and Interior Systems Construction Association (see CISCA); for further information about safety practices in installing ceilings, see the latest edition of (CISCA) *Ceiling Systems Handbook.*

Government agencies and non-profit organizations that may provide useful safety and health information are as follows:

EPA's Indoor Air Quality Home Page   Contains information for homeowners, schools, commercial buildings and environmental professionals on indoor air quality. It has extensive links to sites (**epa. gov/iaq**).

American Lung Association A national education program designed to help you make informed choices to improve indoor your environment (**lungusa.org** and **healthhouse.org**).

Canada's Indoor Environmental Program   The Indoor Environmental Program integrates experimental, analytical and modeling competencies in the areas of lighting, acoustics, ventilation, indoor air quality, thermal comfort, energy efficiency and environmental psychology (**nrc.ca/irc/ie**).

Also listed below are several sources that you may want to consult further. Again, for professional construction, the advice and assistance of a safety professional is highly recommended.

- OSHA/National Association of Home Builders. *Jobsite Safety Handbook.* **nahb.org**
- Gypsum Association. *Handling and Storage of Gypsum Panel Products: A Guide for Distributors, Retailers, and Contractors* Publication GA-801-07. **gypsum.org**
- Ceilings & Interior Systems Contractors Association (CISCA) **cisca.org**
- U.S. Department of Labor, OSHA/OICA publications. **osha.gov**

   Ground Fault Protection on Construction Sites—OSHA 3007

   Personal Protective Equipment—OSHA 3077

Fall Protection in Construction—OSHA 3146

Stairways and Ladders—OSHA 3124

– The following publications are available from the Superintendent of Documents, U.S. Government Printing Office, Washington, DC. **gpo.gov**

Controlling Electrical Hazards—OSHA 3075

Hand and Power Tools-OSHA 3080

– Information available for purchase from the American National Standards Institute (ANSI):

ANSI A10.2-44 Safety Code for Building Construction

ANSI A10.3-70 Safety Requirements for Explosive-Actuated Fastening Tools

ANSI A12.1-67 Safety Requirements for Floor and Wall Openings, Railings, and Toe Boards

ANSI A14.1 1-68 Safety Code for Portable Wood Ladders. Supplemented by ANSI A14.1a-77

ANSI A14.2-56 Safety Code for Portable Metal Ladders, Supplemented by ANSI A14.2a-77

ANSI A14.3-56 Safety Code for Fixed Ladders

ANSI Z87.1-68 Practice of Occupational and Educational Eye and Face Protection

ANSI Z89.2-69 Practices for Respiratory Protection

ANSI Z89.1-69 Safety Requirements for Industrial Head Protection

13

Tools & Equipment

The Tool for the Task

Suitably designed tools are essential for high-quality workmanship. Using the right tools for specific jobs can improve efficiency and reduce labor costs. This chapter contains an extensive sampling of tools designed to meet the needs of acoustical, drywall and plaster contractors. Some of the more commonly used hand tools can be found at building material dealers, hardware stores and home centers.

Framing & Acoustical Ceiling Installation Tools

Magnetic Spirit Level	Ensures that steel framing members are level and plumb. Typical length is 4'; available in 2'–7' lengths.	
Chalk Line	A device that holds retractable chalk line and chalk. Also used as plumb bob.	
String Line	Strong nylon string that is stretched taut between two distant points, such as midpoints on ceiling grid wall	angles, so that additional components can be aligned to the same level plane.
Water Level	Useful for ceiling grid installation. Water in transparent hose will be level at two distant points.	
Laser Alignment Tool	Utilizes a visible laser beam for all construction alignment jobs. Provides maximum accuracy and speed for laying out partitions and leveling suspended ceiling grids.	

Circular Saw

Cuts wood and steel studs, runners and joists of various gauges with appropriate abrasive metal-cutting blade. Hand-held and portable, it ensures easy on-site cutting and trimming. Use a carbide-tipped blade for cutting DUROCK cement board and FIBEROCK gypsum panels.

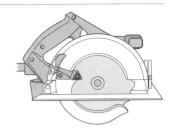

Chop Saw

Cuts wood and steel framing members with an abrasive metal blade. Its steel base can be placed on a bench, saw horse or floor for fast and efficient gang-cutting of members.

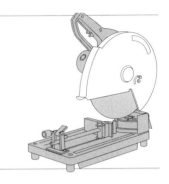

Band Saw

Use in cutting wood and steel framing members; a variety of models are available.

Cut-off Saw

Uses an abrasive blade and provides more power than a circular saw. Gas-powered models available.

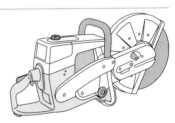

Power Fastener Driver

Drives fasteners into concrete or steel for attachment of framing members. Powder-driven model shown. Also available in air-driven models.

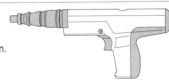

14

Lather's Nippers — Used in wire-tie attachment of metal lath, ceiling grid and framing components.

Metal Snips — Used to cut steel framing components and trims. Several sizes and styles available, including those that make curved cuts.

Lineman's Pliers — Square-nosed pliers with flat jaws and integral wire cutter. Flat jaws are used for joining wires, such as suspension ceiling tie wires, together by twisting; cutter is used for quickly removing excess.

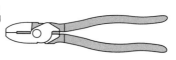

Locking Pliers/ Clamps — Holds steel framing and acoustical grid members in place during screw attachment. Adjustable lock mechanism in the grip ensures that clamps hold securely.

Spring Clamps — Faster and easier to use than locking clamps, and excellent for light-duty applications.

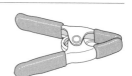

Acoustical Punch Pliers — Used for punching holes in acoustical ceiling grid main tees for hanger wire attachment, or in wall angle to be secured by pop rivets.

Pop Rivet Tool

Used to flare and secure pop rivets through prepared holes. Useful for securing wall angle to acoustical ceiling grid.

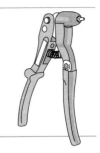

Serrated Knife

Makes cutting insulation easy.

Board & Lath Application Tools

Steel Tape Rule

Retractable steel tape measure is essential for accurate measurements in preparation for cutting and attaching board.

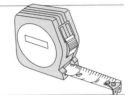

T-Square

4' square is indispensable for making accurate cuts across the narrow dimension of board products. Also available in 54" length.

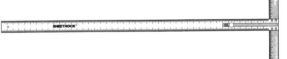

Utility Knife

The standard knife for cutting board products. Uses replaceable blade; extra blades store in handle.

14

Hook-Bill Knife

Useful for trimming gypsum boards and for odd-shaped cuts. (Also known as linoleum knife.) Carbide-tipped version useful for scoring DUROCK brand cement board.

Drywall Saw

Used for cutting gypsum boards quickly and easily. Has short blade and coarse teeth.

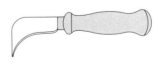

Keyhole-Type Utility Saw

Used for cutting small openings and making odd-shaped cuts. Sharp point and stiff blade can be punched through board for starting cut.

Circle Cutter

Used to cut arcs and circles in gypsum board. Calibrated steel shaft allows accurate cuts up to 16" diameter.

Electric Router

Used for cutting openings in gypsum panels for electrical boxes, heating ducts and other passageways. Specialty bits are used for cutting cement board or fiber-reinforced gypsum panels.

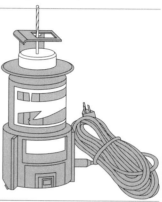

Tack Claw

A screw driver with claw head attached that can be used to remove misapplied fasteners.

Rasp

Smooths rough-cut edges of gypsum boards quickly and efficiently. Manufactured model features replaceable blade and clean-cut slot to prevent clogging. Job-made model at right consists of metal lath stapled to a wood block.

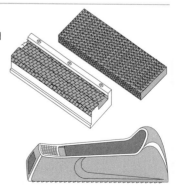

Kick Lifter

Panels are lifted off the ground into place by stepping on this device.

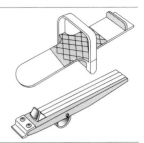

Panel Lift

Lifts and holds drywall onto ceilings and sidewalls with rollers for easy movement.

Lather's Hatchet

The standard nailing and cutting tool for gypsum lath.

Drywall Hammer

Waffle-patterned convex face designed to compress gypsum panel face and leave desired dimple.

Electric Screw Gun

Drives drywall screws in gypsum board attachment. Special chuck and tip control screw depth to ensure that screw is set at desired depth. Also used for steel-stud framing and acoustical ceilings.

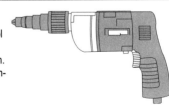

14

Cordless Drill	Operates with power from battery pack that can be readily recharged.	
Pistol-Type Stapler	Used for staple attachment of corner beads, Striplath, Cornerite and fiberglass mesh tape.	
Electric or Pneumatic Stapler	Used for faster staple attachment applications.	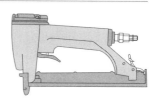

Caulking Equipment

Cartridge-Type Caulking Gun	Aids uniform application of adhesive. Hand-operated apparatus uses 29-oz. cartridges. Size of caulk bead determined by	cut of cartridge nozzle. Smaller version uses 10-oz. cartridges.
Bead Bulk-Type Caulking Gun	Used for high-volume applications. Cylinder is reloaded from bulk container of adhesive. Trigger mechanism withstands rough usage and	offers minimum resistance to large bulk load of adhesive. Gun has 1-qt. capacity.

| **Loader Pump** | Pump clamps on 5-gal. container to mechanically load bulk-type adhesive hand guns. |  |

| **Pail Extruder** | Used for high-volume extrusion of adhesives from pails. |  |

Mixing Equipment

| **Hand Mixer** | Used for hand-mixing joint compounds. Available in several styles. Model with rounded edge is especially effective for scraping material from sides of mixing bucket. |  |

| **Heavy-Duty Drill** | Use a 1/2" heavy-duty electric drill operating at a speed of 450–650 rpm for joint compound, 300–600 rpm for textures. Use a 1/2" electric drill with a no-load rating of 900–1,000 rpm for mixing veneer plasters. |  |

14

| **Joint Compound and Texture Mixing Paddle** | Designed for joint compounds and textures. |  |

Veneer Plaster Mixer

Recommended as the mixer for USG veneer plaster finishes, this cage-type paddle provides high shear action necessary for proper dispersion of plaster ingredients in mixing water and to develop high plasticity in the mix.

Plaster and Stucco Mixer

Used for stucco and conventional plasters (not suitable for veneer plaster finishes). Standard paddle-type mixer is available with capacities from 5 to 7 cu. ft. in either electric or gasoline-powered models.

Lime Mixer

Used for mixing lime. A vertical drum mixer that consists of an electric motor (which drives shaft-mounted paddles) mounted atop an open-end drum. Typically made in 16- and 30-gal. sizes to accommodate one- and three-bag mixing assignments.

Drywall Finishing Tools

Taping Knives

4", 5" and 6" knives designed for taping, fastener spotting, angle taping and finishing.

Finishing Knives

8" or wider knives designed for finish coating. Drywall finishing knives are available with blade widths from 1" up to 24". Offset-handle and long-handle models also available.

Mud Pan	Used to carry joint compound. Shaped like a bread pan. Edge of the pan is used for blade-cleaning. Available in a wide range of sizes and material composition.	
Tape Holder	Holds tape rolls up to 500' and attaches to belt.	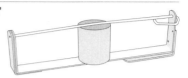
Banjo	Draws paper tape through a compartment filled with joint compound so that both materials are simultaneously applied to joints.	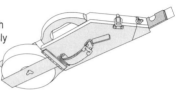
Convertible Hopper	Holds and dispenses joint compound evenly onto paper-faced corner bead. Will accommodate both 90° and bullnose bead configurations.	
Outside Roller Tool	Used to press paper-faced corner beads into place for precise trim alignment.	
Hand Sander	Sandpaper attached with end clamps to the base plate. Models include those with wood or aluminum handles.	

14

Pole Sander — Enables working large areas with longer strokes and reach.

Vacuum Power Sander — Used for fast and easy sanding of large areas. Vacuum dramatically reduces the amount of airborne particles.

Mechanical Taping Tools

This line of specialized equipment is designed to speed and facilitate high-volume taping and joint finishing operations.

Hand Pump — Fills mechanical tools from 5-gal. pail.

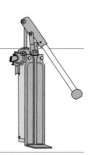

Automatic Taper — Applies a metered amount of compound onto the tape, places the tape on the wall and cuts the tape to length. Works for flat joints and corners. The original taper is sold under the Bazooka® trade name.

Corner Roller — Used to embed tape in corner and force excess compound from under tape prior to using the corner applicator head.

| **Corner Applicator Head** | Attaches to pole to wipe down and feather taping compound on both sides of a corner in one pass. This head is also used as an attachment with corner finishing box for application of topping. |  |

| **Corner Finishing Box** | Used to apply joint compounds to corners with an appropriate attach- | ment, such as the corner applicator head or paper-faced bead applicator head. |

| **Paper-Faced Bead Applicator Head** | Used to apply taping compound to corners prior to application of paper-faced bead. Attaches to corner finishing box. | |

| **Flat Finisher Box** | Places a defined layer of compound 7"–12" wide on flat surfaces. Various handle | lengths available to reach different height ceilings. |

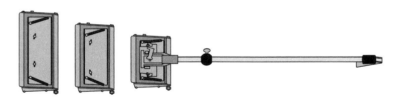

Plaster Tools

14

| **Trowel** | Available in several styles and in lengths from 10" to 16". Trowels are the standard tools for veneer plaster and conventional plaster work. Also used by drywall finishers. | 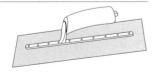 |

| **Hawk** | Suitable for carrying any cementitious material by a hand applicator—joint compound, plaster, veneer finishes and stucco. Available in sizes from 8" x 8" to 14" x 14". |  |

Margin Trowel   A narrow trowel used to touch-up small areas, and for cleaning tools and equipment.

Pointer Trowel   Pointed trowel enabling finishing of sharp angles.

Angle Trowel   For interior corner finishing of veneer plaster and drywall jobs.

Browning Rod   Used for leveling base coats of plaster, across grounds or screeds. Also known as a straight edge. Available in lengths from 4' to 8'.

Feather Edge   Enables feathering of plaster, generally from corners, intersections or terminations, out onto the plaster plane and into the field of already-applied plaster. Similar to straight edge with precision tapered edge.

Slicker   A tool with a beveled edge often used in place of a darby to level and smooth plaster coats.

Darby   Used for leveling, smoothing or floating plaster base coat. Made of wood, metal-edged wood or all metal. Notched darby is for scratching basecoats.

Float

Used for leveling and straightening finish coat or to correct surface irregularities. Also used to produce a sand-finish effect on plaster surfaces. Floats typically are faced with hard rubber (shown), but may also be made of sponge rubber, cork, felt or carpet.

Angle Float

Used for inside corner work with conventional plasters. Can be used for either brown or finish coat.

Blister Brush

Used to keep the plaster finish wet while finish troweling. This felt-pad brush can also be used for wet-sanding joint compound.

Water Sprayers

Used to spray water or alum solutions on plaster surfaces. Also used to soak and clean surfaces for removal of wallpaper or other undesired finishes. Compressed air tank is available in different models.

Scarifier

A wire-barbed tool used to rake the wet surface of the scratch coat, so that the brown coat can key and bond correctly.

14

Scrub Brush

Used for cleanup. Residue on tools or containers will affect performance of material.

Hand Texture Equipment

Stucco Brush

Used to create a variety of textures from stipple to swirl to splash dash.

Texture Brush

Tandem-mounted brushes cover large area to speed texturing job. The texture brush may be attached to a pole for greater reach. Available in many sizes and styles.

Roller

Standard paint roller is adapted to particular type of finish required. Roller sleeves available include short-nap, long-nap and carpet type in standard 9" and 18" widths.

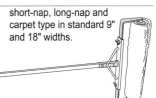

Roller Pan

Used with roller. Some models can hold up to 25-lb. supply of mixed texture.

Wipedown Blade

Used for cleaning of walls after application of ceiling texture. Straight wipedown blade is also used to knock down splatters to produce splatter-knockdown surface texture.

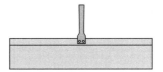

Glitter Gun

For spraying glitter on wet texture ceilings. Hand-crank model (shown) is most economical but is not as efficient as air-powered type (not shown).

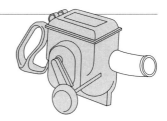

Coating Spray Equipment

Airless Spray Equipment

Specifically designed airless spray pumps deliver paint, joint compound, and specialty caulks fast and efficiently. The material is pumped at high pressure with a single piston pump through a high pressure hose. The high pressure atomizes the material as it leaves the spray tip without the aid of additional air pressure.

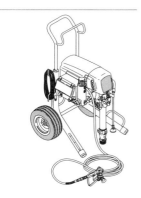

Spray Texture Equipment

Hand-Held Hopper Gun

This machine, with a spray gun and material hopper mounted together to form an integral unit, handles most types of drywall texture and fine-aggregate finish plaster materials. Material is gravity-fed through the hand-held hopper. Compressed air is introduced at the spray-nozzle orifice where texture material is atomized and applied to substrate.

Universal Spray Machines

When machine speed, air pressure and/or nozzle are adapted to the material used, equipment in this group can handle drywall textures, veneer plaster finishes and conventional plasters, stucco and fireproofing materials. Several factors must be considered in the selection of new equipment of this type, including: the type of material to be sprayed, type of finish desired, output volume required, the distance (horizontally and vertically) that the material is to be pumped, and portability of the machine through the halls and doorways in a building. The following information is general in nature, offered to aid in the selection of new spray equipment.

Equipment is discussed in terms of the commonly used types of pumping devices. Prospective equipment buyers should discuss their individual needs with manufacturers and users of the equipment.

Four pump types are available: rotor-stator (Moyno), peristaltic (squeeze-type), piston (single- and multi-piston), and diaphragm. While the delivery of material is sufficient with each of these pump types, the mechanical differences may result in operational preferences of one type over the rest. Each operator must determine which will work best for his or her application. Depending on the size, much of this equipment is trailer or truck mounted.

14

**Rotor-Stator
(Moyno) Pump**

This pump uses a screw mechanism to pump material forward through a cylinder. The auger-type rotor is powered by an electrical or gas motor. It rotates in place within a stationary metal sleeve that is lined with a pliable material such as rubber or neoprene (the stator) to assure rotor-to-stator contact and stop back flow. The auger (rotor) moves material from the hopper into the cylinder (stator) and drives it through the hose.

Rotor-stator pumps have a relatively high wear

incidence with abrasive aggregates such as sand or perlite. However, they are particularly suited for pumping textures with polystyrene aggregates, since they are not abrasive and reduce pumping resistance. In addition, the smooth, constant delivery action makes rotor-stator pumps a good choice for very fine textures. The trailer-mounted rig shown is equipped with two separate self-contained mixing tanks and two rotor-stator pumps.

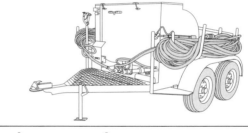

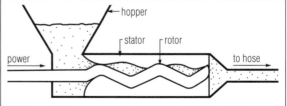

Moyno roto-stator

Peristaltic Pump

The action of this type of pump is like that of a wheel running lengthwise over a hose, squeezing material in the hose forward (the pump is sometimes called a "squeeze-type" pump). Multiple rollers pass over the pumping line and ensure smooth, constant material delivery. Offers the same benefits as the rotor-stator

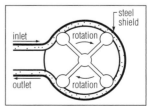

Peristaltic (squeeze-type) pump

pump. Designed for long wear. Excellent for relatively low-volume installations. The peristaltic pump set-up shown includes a hopper to hold material and is mounted on wheels for easy movement on the job site.

Piston Pumps

Piston pumps operate by drawing material into a cylinder through one port and out through another. The material is drawn into a large main cylinder and then into a smaller surge cylinder. The two-stage process ensures continuous material flow and equalizes pressures within the chambers to keep pulsations at an acceptable level. Actual material flow into the hose is dictated by the action in the surge cylinder.

The piston ram only displaces about half of the material in the cylinder and into the hose. As that action takes place at one end of the piston, a check valve opens at the other end, drawing more material into the main cylinder to renew the process.

These are high-volume pumps that can be metered for moderately fine textures.

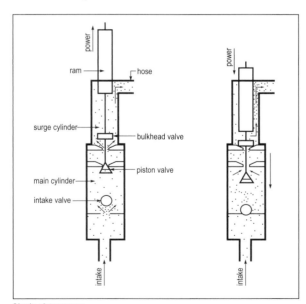

Single-piston pump

14

Diaphragm Pump

A diaphragm pump's operation is similar to a piston pump's in that it draws material into a chamber with one action and discharges it with another. The difference is that the diaphragm itself enables the chamber size to expand and contract. As the diaphragm moves in one direction, material is drawn from the hopper into the chamber through a check valve. When the diaphragm moves in the other direction, that check valve closes and another opens, allowing material to move into the hose.

The special advantage of a diaphragm pump is that the diaphragm separates the mechanical action of the pump from the material flow, making cleanup and maintenance easier. The set-up shown here has a material hopper placed above the pump, and the wheeled cart also has a self-contained compressor.

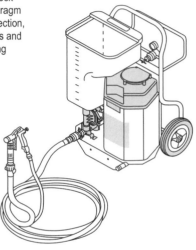

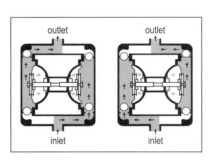

Hoses, Guns & Nozzles

Hoses

Used to carry material from pump to nozzle. Hoses vary in type and generally have a diameter of 3/4" to 1".

Pole Guns

Used with any universal spray machine as well as largest of drywall texture machines described earlier in this section. Their length allows any operator to spray moderately high ceilings without scaffolding or stilts. Model shown has electric start-stop control. Also available with air start-stop control.

Texture Guns

Professional-type equipment for specific texture applications is manufactured by Binks, Graco and others. Each gun is designed for specific product applications. For instance the Binks Model 7E2 type texturing gun is used for high volume or heavy texture designs, while the Binks Model 7D type is for lighter textures. Follow the manufacturer's guidelines for selection to meet particular applications.

Nozzles

Provide for a variety of spray textures, and vary in orifice openings from 1/4" to 5/8".

Those used for conventional texturing are never larger than 1/2".

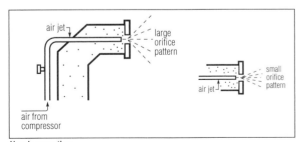

Nozzle operation

14

Spray Shield

Wide aluminum or plastic shield protects abutting wall or ceiling against overspray during spraying operation. Various widths available.

Miscellaneous Equipment

Joint Compound & Adhesive Spreaders

Used for applying joint compound in laminated gypsum panel assemblies. A notched trowel is commercially available. Depending on the notch configuration, these are often sufficient for job applications.

The spreader shown (below left) is easily assembled on the job. Stainless or galvanized sheet steel make the best spreaders. A good spreader blade has about the same stiffness as a plasterer's trowel.

Notches should be an inverted "V" shape, 1/2" deep, 3/8" wide at the base and spaced 1-1/2" to 2" o.c. A piece of wood dowel or window stop attached near top edge of blade provides a grip.

The laminating spreader shown (below right) applies properly sized beads of adhesive at correct spacings.

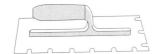

Gypsum Board Dolly

Used for efficient transport of gypsum boards around the floors of a building. The load, centered over large side wheels, is easily steered and moved by one worker.

Folding Trestle Horse

Top surface provides work surface or stand-on work platform. Legs adjust in increments.

Scaffold

Portable and easy to set up. Wheels lock for safety and security. Wide variety of sizes and types of scaffold are available to meet job requirements.

Stilts

Convenient way to reach high areas on drywall, veneer plaster and plaster jobs. Strapped to legs and feet to give applicator full mobility plus height needed for ceiling work. Stilts have articulated joints to flex with ankle movement. Available in fixed-height and adjustable-height types (adjustable, articulated model shown).

Floor Scrapers

Scrapers have hardened steel blades and long handles to speed cleaning of floors after application of joint compound, plaster or texture materials. Blades are often replaceable.

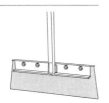

Canvas Drop Cloths

Used to protect floors and furniture from dropped material and overspray while working in finished and/or occupied areas. They are available in a variety of different sizes and materials.

14

Manufacturers

The following tool manufacturers provided illustrations or information for the creation of this chapter.

Ames Taping Tools and Systems, Duluth, GA

Bjorklund Manufacturing, Kirkland, WA

Dewalt Industrial Tool Company, Hampstead, MD

Empire Level Manufacturing Corporation, Mukwonago, WI

Force-Flo Inc., Cleveland, OH

Graco Inc., Minneapolis, MN

Hilti, Inc., Tulsa, OK

Hyde Manufacturing Company, Southbridge, MA

ITW, Glendale Heights, IL

IRWIN Industrial Tools, Huntersville, NC

Malco Products, Inc., Annandale, MN

Marshalltown Trowel Company, Marshalltown, IA

Milwaukee Electric Tool Company, Brookfield, WI

Pla-Cor Inc., Santee, CA

PLS – Pacific Laser Systems, San Rafael, CA

Porter-Cable Corporation, Jackson, TN

Quikspray, Inc., Port Clinton, OH

Roto-Zip Corporation, Cross Plains, WI

Bosch Power Tools, Mount Prospect, IL

Spectra-Precision Inc., Dayton, OH

Spray Force Manufacturing, Fresno, CA

Stanley Tools, New Britan, CT

Wallboard Tool Company, Long Beach, CA

Wind-Lock Corp., Leesport, PA

Titan Tool Inc., Plymouth, MN

USG Sheetrock Tools, Chicago, IL

Building Sciences 15

This chapter reviews building science principles that relate to design, selection and installation of gypsum panel products. The topics include building movement, fire resistance, heat transfer, sound transmission and vapor control.

USG Design Studio, **usgdesignstudio.com**, is an excellent source for identifying USG products and systems that fulfill a project's required design performance. This online tool was developed for construction professionals including architects, interior designers, specification writers and contractors who should find the site intuitive and easy to navigate. USG Design Studio provides specific information related to fire, acoustics, sustainability and moisture resistance and allows for ease of product comparison, selection and specification, specification fulfillment and identification of LEED credit information for USG products.

Structures

Structural Movement

This section will analyze how buildings move, and how that movement relates to partition construction techniques.

From calm breezes to violent winds, movement impacts the structural integrity of buildings and other structures to varying degrees. When forces are severe enough, such as with extreme hurricane or tornado activity with the possibility of total destruction, evacuation becomes necessary, and life safety is the primary concern. Proper design will help to prevent damange, and, in extreme conditions, may prevent personal injury during evacuation. In some geographical areas, movement from seismic conditions affects the structure. In either case, the forces of movement influence the basic structure and eventually transfer to the sub-elements of the building—including partitions and ceilings. If not properly addressed, there may be distress to these sub-elements, perhaps to the point of failure.

The type of distress most often associated with plaster and drywall membranes is cracking, which is a break or fissure originating on the surface of or within the membrane. Cracking is due to one primary cause: a concentration of stresses that, at a sufficient level, exceeds the maximum strain capacity of the material, at which point the stress is relieved in the form of a break.

Movement stresses are always present and may be transferred to the membrane from the structure, set up in the membrane by dimensional changes due to varying temperature and moisture conditions, or may result from other types of external force, such as impact or vibration directly on the membrane. Stress build-up may be controlled by reducing the transfer of stress from the structure (perimeter relief, slip connections, etc.) and provision of integral stress relief mechanisms (control/expansion joints).

Flat plate concrete construction is used in a large portion of residential high-rise buildings. It experiences two types of movement. In one case, the frame (particularly on upper floors and usually if exterior columns are exposed to major changes in temperature), is subjected to racking. Partitions are distressed by racking of structural elements

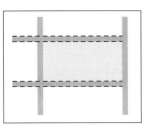

Frame Movements Cause Racking Cracks

that surround and support them. In that case, cracks typically occur in the partition's corners as the outside columns move up and down. Crushing occurs in opposite corners, and diagonal cracks are possible in the partition face. In effect, the partition is forced to become a shear wall with insufficient strength to resist much force. Cracking due to racking will be seasonally affected by thermal expansion and contraction, since the stress reverses with prolonged changes in outside temperature.

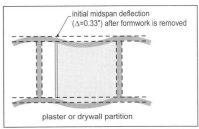
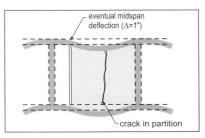

Cracking caused by slab deflection

The other type of movement relates to deflection of the slab, which in flat plate construction increases for some time after the structure is built due to plastic creep of the concrete. Cracks occurring in partitions due to this type of movement result from flexural tension as the wall panel tries to follow the deflection of the structural floor. Distress and the potential for cracks due to flexural tension will decrease with time, as the deflection process diminishes and eventually becomes stable.

The design professional can calculate the amount of movement anticipated as a result of racking stresses. Expected slab deflection is calculated based on the initial dead load, with compensating partition and ceiling details providing for an amount ranging from two to five times the initial dead load deflection. Following are some general considerations for the design of partition and ceiling assemblies and the use of perimeter relief or control joints:

- Distress problems are usually most serious when partitions are tightly connected to the structural frame or partition membranes abutted to the structure, rather than supported by some kind of suspension system.

- In high-rise buildings (more than eight stories) a relief joint must be incorporated at the periphery of the partition, which allows sufficient vertical movement for the anticipated conditions.

15

- Initial and creep deflection can be reduced with a stiffer floor system, or with a pan-joist structure and a suspended ceiling. With flat plate construction, perimeter relief and/or control joints should be used to compensate for deflection of the floor and ceiling.

Control joints of varying types are time-proven means to accommodate stress relief. The design professional should analyze the structure and determine when, where and which type is required. The following section explains the use of different types of control joints.

Expansion joints (also referred to as building control joints) prevent structural cracks due to the movement of a building based on structural materials (concrete, steel), length of structure, area temperature variations, foundation conditions, occupancy, etc. Expansion joints extend entirely through the footing, foundation and superstructure of a building. They consist of a complete frame (separated with spaces between structural members), and filled, or bridged, with a compressible and resilient material with a suitable joint closure on the outer face.

Expansion joints are needed:

- Where a long, narrow structure abuts a rigid mass.
- At ends of a low structure between two heavy masses, and at appropriate intervals of approximately 150'.
- When a new building adjoins an existing building.
- In freestanding buildings at intervals of approximately 200'.
- When interior and exterior temperature differentials are extreme (e.g., a cold storage building connected to a warm building).

Construction joints are horizontal or vertical features introduced into the building design to conform to material limitations, such as the amount of concrete that can be poured in a day's operation, the size of components or panels selected, aesthetic considerations, etc. Generally these joints are located at ledges or other architectural features including window jambs, heads or sills.

Control joints are used to limit cracking in partitions and ceilings. Within the face of a partition or ceiling, it is a control joint; at the perimeter, it is a perimeter relief joint or a slip joint. A control joint is effective in limiting cracking due to tensile or compressive movement in a membrane resulting from thermal, hygrometric and structural effects. In the case of shear movement as discussed relative to flat plate construction, perimeter relief or slip joints are necessary at the perimeter interfacings.

Proper installation of control joints in wall and ceiling membranes requires breaking the lath or gypsum panels behind the control joint. In ceiling construction, the framing should also be broken, and in partitions, separate studs should be used on each side of the joint, with the runner track separated at that location.

The following illustrations show some suggested locations for perimeter relief and control joints.

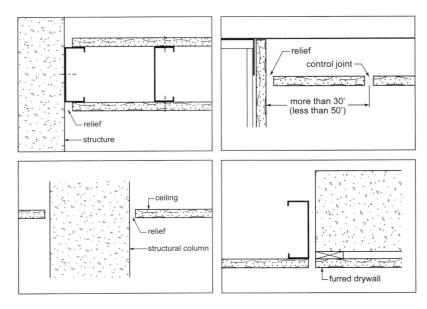

Building materials are affected by variations in temperature and humidity, identified as thermal and hygrometric expansion characteristics and seen in the chart below.

Material	Thermal Expansion Characteristics	Hygrometric Expansion Characteristics
Gypsum panels and bases	9.0×10^{-6} in./(in. °F)	7.2×10^{-6} inches/inch/% R.H.
Gypsum plaster (sanded 100:2, 100:3)	7.0×10^{-6} in./(in. °F)	1.5×10^{-6} inches/inch/% R.H
Gypsum wood fiber plaster (sanded 100:1)	8.0×10^{-6} in./(in. °F)	2.8×10^{-6} inches/inch/% R.H
Gypsum FiberPanels (AR)	7.0×10^{-6} in./(in. °F)	3.5×10^{-6} inches/inch/% R.H

Control joints should be used to accommodate potential movement due to hygrometric and thermal variations. Sudden changes in temperature may cause cracking from thermal shock. The use and location of control joints is the responsibility of the design professional. Following are conditions requiring placement of control joints or other means to provide isolation from movement:

- Partition, furring or column fireproofing abutting a structural element (except floor) or dissimilar wall or ceiling.

- Ceiling or soffit abutting a structural element, dissimilar wall or partition or other vertical penetration.

- Construction changes within the plane of the partition or ceiling.

- Partition or furring run exceeding 30'.

- Ceiling dimensions exceeding 50' in either direction with perimeter relief; 30' without relief.

- Exterior soffits and ceilings exceeding 30' in either direction.

- At joints of wings of "L"-, "U"- and "T"-shaped ceiling areas.

15

The following illustrations depict typical perimeter relief and control joint details:

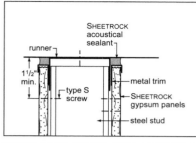
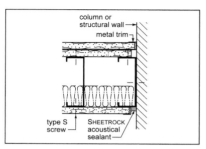
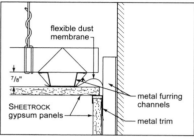
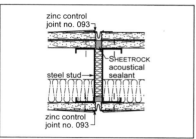

Ceiling-height door frames may be used as **vertical control joints** in partitions. Door frames of lesser height will require control joints extending to the ceiling (structure) from both corners of the top of the frame. Control joints in ceilings should be located to intersect column penetrations, light fixtures and air diffusers that can impose stresses on the ceiling membrane. Experience has shown that to relieve stresses in Portland cement-stucco surfaces, control joints should be spaced no more than 10' apart. When a gypsum-based system abuts a different material, or construction changes within the plane of the assembly, a relief mechanism should be provided. A control joint in a partition should extend through a bulkhead/soffit condition with the same consideration for separation of the membrane and framing. The ratio of length to width in ceiling membranes should be in the range of 1:1. A Portland cement plaster ceiling formed of 10' x 10' panels (100 SF) is considerably less prone to cracking than a soffit that is 2' x 50' (100 SF).

Introducing a control joint into a partition or ceiling membrane that is part of a fire-rated assembly necessarily creates an opening for flame and temperature transmission. For gypsum drywall ceilings, Underwriters Laboratories provides "generic" details for maximum one-hour floor/ceiling assemblies in the G500 and L500 series. Since typical fire tests of floor/ceiling assemblies incorporate an end joint backed with a continuous gypsum strip, the detailing for control joints in ceiling membranes for higher ratings should be acceptable to a code jurisdiction. For partitions, details were tested at an independent fire test facility on a two-hour partition using gypsum panel strips as back-up members in one case, and mineral wool insulation in another. The details are considered pertinent to one-hour assemblies as well. Development of special details to satisfy head-of-wall conditions are a new twist that must be considered by the design professional as required by code.

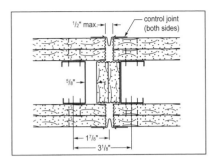
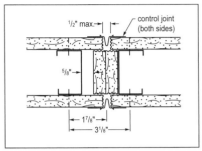

Gypsum surfaces may buckle or crack when firmly anchored across the flat grain of wide dimensional lumber. The gypsum does not react like wood in response to moisture changes. Therefore, the gypsum surface should either "float" over the wood or be provided with a control joint mechanism.

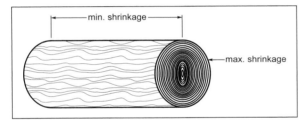

With platform framing, the condition can be addressed by using resilient channels on the wood frame studs and spanning the gypsum panels across the wood member. Another option is to use a control joint at the bottom edge of the top and first floor studs. This places the joint where the greatest amount of shrinkage and dimensional change needs to be absorbed. The gypsum panels are applied horizontally with a 1/4" separation between panels at the control joint location. The bottom gypsum panel is applied with its top edge aligned with the bottom of the top plates. One-quarter inch shims placed on the top edge provide the proper spacing. The upper gypsum panel is not nailed below the level of the toe plate, thus allowing the edge to float over the header joist. The control joint can be finished with a Control Joint No. 093 or with wood molding applied so as not to restrict movement of the gypsum panel above the joint.

15

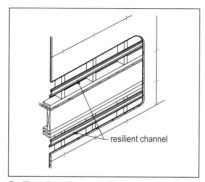

Resilient channels on wood frame studs; gypsum panels spanning wood member

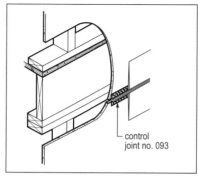

Control joint at bottom edge of top- and first-floor studs

In areas of earthquake activity, structures are designed and constructed to resist the lateral forces induced by seismic disturbances. Per the *International Building Code*, gypsum drywall and plaster membrane ceilings do not require lateral bracing when walls or partitions brace them, and the walls are no more than 50' apart. Where walls do not brace the ceiling, independent bracing designed by a structural engineer is required. Light fixtures are to be supported independently of the ceiling runners.

Direct-hung suspended acoustical ceilings, while not subjected to the same stresses as continuous membranes, are affected by seismic forces. Damage is often exhibited by the battering and collapsing of the edges of the ceilings at walls and partitions, and dropping of light fixtures. The common type of lateral bracing for suspended ceilings consists of diagonal (45°) wires connected between the ceiling runners and/or tees and the floor or roof structure above. The spacing of the diagonal braces is a function of the lateral force produced by the ceiling, lights, partitions, etc., and the load capacity of the wires and their connection to the ceiling system members and the structure above. The load brought into the brace points is a horizontal force, and the wire braces are tension diagonals. This results in a vertical uplift component that is usually addressed with a vertical compression strut.

Seismic requirements must be determined by the building code in effect. The Gypsum Association addresses this through its "Seismic Bracing of Steel Stud/Gypsum Board Partitions – Design Tables (GA-350)." The Drywall Information Trust Fund (CA) has an Evaluation Report, ER-4071, addressing seismic connections. CISCA has information available relative to seismic criteria with acoustical ceiling systems.

It is important to realize that several different movement factors influence the performance of interior finish systems. These must be considered by the design professional for proper detailing, and the detailing must be properly installed by the contractor. Improper design or installation leads to undesirable results.

Abuse-Resistance

Abuse-resistance has become a key wall system selection factor. Designers and their clients have realized that it is often less expensive from a life-cycle perspective to invest in abuse-resistant materials in critical areas as a first cost than to pay high ongoing costs to maintain and repair regular drywall partitions.

Abuse-resistance may be defined as the ability to resist three levels of damage: (1) Surface damage from abrasion and/or indentation; (2) Penetration through to the wall cavity from sharp or blunt impact; (3) Security breach through the entire assembly from ballistics or forced entry. (For more detailed information on abuse resistance, see USG Abuse-Resistant Systems, publication SA929.

Surface Damage: Abrasion and Indentation Resistance

Interior partitions in high-traffic areas are subject to surface damage caused by ordinary contact with people and furniture, as well as from impacts with objects like mail carts, hospital gurneys and cleaning equipment. Surface damage can consist of abrasion (scratching) or indentation (denting). The surface durability, or abuse resistance, of partitions is improved by increasing the surface and core strength of the partition facing, by applying a coating or wall covering over the surface, or by increasing the thickness of the partition facing.

Penetration: Hard- and Soft-Body Impact Resistance

In more demanding environments, interior partitions can be exposed to impacts that penetrate through the partition into the wall cavity, causing damage that is both costly to repair and potentially dangerous. Impacts of this nature are of two types: hard body impact results from direct concentrated contact with a tool or hard object; soft body impact results from bodily contact with the building's human occupants. Penetration resistance is improved by increasing the core strength of the partition facing, or by incorporating impact-resistant material into the back of the partition facing.

Testing

Testing for abuse resistance is defined by ASTM C1629, "Standard Classification for Abuse-Resistant Non-Decorated Interior Gypsum Panel Products and Fiber-Reinforced Cement Panels." This specification covers surface abrasion, indentation and impact tests. Impact tests take two forms: hard and soft body. They also establish three levels of performance (referred to as classification levels; see table on page 451), which help design professionals make informed decisions.

Abrasion Testing Abrasion resistance is evaluated by a test known as ASTM D4977. The test has been modified by using a total load of 25 pounds to better abrade the samples. The depth of the abrasion after 50 cycles is used to determine a level of performance.

15

Surface Abrasion Test Apparatus

Indentation Testing Indentation resistance is measured using ASTM D5420 and Gardner Impact Test Apparatus. This test method drops a 2 lb weight from a height of 36" onto a 5/8" hemispherical die, then measures the depth of the resulting indentation.

Indentation Test Apparatus

Impact Testing The standard accepted test to determine soft body impact performance is ASTM E695, which uses a leather bag filled with steel pellets to a weight of 60 pounds. The bag is dropped a known distance and in a prescribed arc impacting the test wall. The distance of the drop (which affects the energy of the impact) is increased until the bag breaches the panel being tested, or the permanent set of the panel, after the impact, is greater than the thickness of the tested panel.

Leather Bag Used for Soft Body Impact Test

Hard Body Testing Apparatus The hard body impact test measures resistance to penetration of a wall panel when impacted by a rigid body. Failure in the hard body is reached when the impacting head completely penetrates through the test panel—or when the permanent set after impact is greater than the thickness of the panel being tested.

A nominal 2' x 2' (610 mm x 610 mm) panel specimen is mounted to the apparatus frame. A ramming arm impactor strikes the wall specimen while swinging in an arc. The impactor is dropped from a fixed height to impart specific design energy to the wall specimen. Weights are progressively added to the impactor to increase the design impact energy until specimen failure occurs. For each impact, a new test specimen is used.

Hard Body Text Apparatus

Performance Classification Table
Surface Abrasion Performance, ASTM D4977

Classification Level	Abraded Depth Maximum, Inches (mm)
1	0.0126 (3.2)
2	0.059 (1.5)
3	0.010 (0.3)

Indentation Performance, ASTM D 5420

Classification Level	Indentation Maximum, Inches (mm)
1	0.150 (3.8)
2	0.100 (2.5)
3	0.050 (1.3)

Soft Body Impact, ASTM E 695

Classification Level	Soft Body Minimum ft-lbf (J)
1	90 (122)
2	195 (265)
3	300 (408)

Hard Body Impact

Classification Level	Hard Body Minimum ft-lbf (J)
1	50 (68)
2	100 (136)
3	150 (204)

15

Fire Resistance

This section presents the fundamentals of fire resistance. Testing and product performance are the main focal points.

Building Codes

Today's buildings are constructed to conform to one or more building codes designed to protect human health and safety, and property. One of the prime considerations of all building codes is fire protection. Elaborate requirements, based on laboratory tests, must be adhered to. Most USG products offer fire-resistance advantages.

The National Board of Fire Underwriters (NBFU) founded Underwriters' Laboratories (UL) in 1894, partially as a result of the extensive use of electricity needed to light the 1893 Columbian Exposition (the Chicago World's Fair). In 1895, NBFU pioneered the first electrical code. The Underwriters published the first building code in 1905 and the first model code in 1930. These codes have been refined through the years.

One of the results of these refinements was the development of uniform standard fire tests. The performance of building materials and construction types under standard test procedures has become the accepted criterion of fire resistance. Fire protection requirements are based on the building's occupancy and characteristics. Requirements are met by using materials and construction that has performed up to the specified degree in laboratory tests. Most local building codes are modeled after one model code—the *International Building Code* (IBC). This model code classifies buildings according to their occupancy and construction type, which in turn determine the degree of fire resistance required. Fire resistance of a material or type of construction is established by the hours of the fire resistance rating of the various elements. Once the types of construction have been classified, the permissible heights and areas are established.

Fire Endurance Tests

Structural—(ASTM E119, UL263 and NFPA 251)

This is the standard test for rating the fire resistance of columns, girders and beams, as well as wall-partition, floor/ceiling and roof/ceiling assemblies. The standard is published by three organizations, ASTM, UL and NFPA, and is essentially the same for all three. The structural elements subjected to the test must support the maximum design loads applied throughout the test period. Columns, beams, girders and structural decks should remain stable in the sense of carrying the load without failure. This test does not imply that the test specimen will be suitable for use after the exposure. Some specimens are so damaged after one hour of exposure that they would require replacement, even though they meet all of the requirements for a 4-hr. rating.

Fire resistance classifications are based on results of tests conducted on assemblies (systems) created with specific materials and built in a specified manner; therefore, variations from the test conditions or the construction specifications (including, but not limited to, the type and size of materials and the method of construction) will affect the results of fire tests. Because fire exposure conditions vary with changes in a wide variety of factors, including the amount, nature and distribution of available fuel; ventilation; and the size, configuration and other characteristics of the compartment, the test method contained in the ASTM E119 standard should not be considered to be representative of all fire conditions. Fire resistance ratings created through use of the ASTM E119 test method reflect a relative measure of comparative assembly's performance under specific fire test conditions. ASTM E119 test results should not be construed as having determined performance of an assembly under different conditions.

The test procedure consists of the fire endurance test for all assemblies and, in addition, a hose stream test for partition and wall assemblies. The test specimen must meet the following requirements to pass the test.

An assembly must resist heat transmission so that temperatures on the side opposite the fire may be maintained below designated values. The temperature of the unexposed surface is measured by thermocouples attached directly to the surface. In the case of walls and partitions, one thermocouple is located at the center of the assembly, one in the center of each quarter section, and the other four at the discretion of the testing authority.

The hose stream test consists of subjecting a duplicate sample to one-half of the indicated fire exposure (but not more than one hour), then immediately to a jet stream of water from a fire nozzle at a prescribed pressure and distance. (See table on page 457 for conditions of hose stream test.)

The time-temperature curve used for the furnace is shown below. The temperature is obtained from the average readings of 9 thermocouples symmetrically located near all parts of the assembly, and placed 6" from the exposed surface of the walls and partitions or 12" from the exposed surface of floors, ceilings and columns.

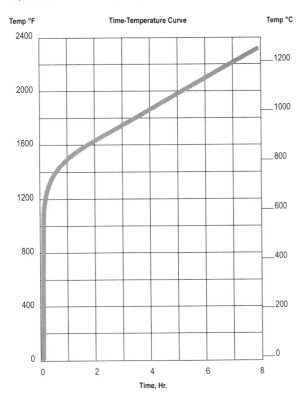

15

Walls and Partitions—Load-Bearing

The area exposed to the fire is at least 100 SF, with neither dimension less than 9'. The vertical edges are unrestrained. A superimposed load is applied to the assembly throughout the fire endurance and hose tests to develop, theoretically, the maximum working stresses contemplated by the design. The test is considered successful if the assembly has:

- Sustained the applied load during the fire endurance test without permitting the passage of flame or gases hot enough to ignite cotton waste placed on the unexposed side.
- Withstood the hose stream test.
- After cooling, sustained the dead load of the test assembly, plus twice the superimposed load.
- Maintained a heat rise of not more than 250°F on average or more than 325°F at any thermocouple, on the unexposed side during the fire endurance test.

Walls and Partitions—Non-Load-Bearing

The area exposed to the fire is at least 100 SF, with neither dimension less than 9'. The vertical edges are unrestrained. The test is considered successful if the assembly has:

- Sustained the fire endurance test without permitting the passage of flame or gases hot enough to ignite cotton waste placed on the unexposed side.
- Withstood the hose stream test. (See page 457 for conditions of hose stream test.) Maintained a heat rise of not more than 250°F, average or more than 325°F, at any thermocouple, on the unexposed side during the fire endurance test.

Columns—Non-Loaded

There is a loaded version of this test, but it is seldom used. The size of the column is representative of the design, materials and workmanship for which classification is desired (and in no case less than 8' in length). The protection is applied in accordance with the methods of acceptable field practice, with the column in a vertical position. The applied protection is restrained from longitudinal thermal expansion by steel plates or concrete attached to the ends of the steel column. The temperature of the steel column is taken from four groups of at least three thermocouples. Two groups, one at each end, are located 2' from each end of the column. The other two groups are equally spaced between those two points.

The thermocouples at each level are arranged to measure the temperature of the various elements of the steel section (such as web and flanges). The test is considered successful if the heat transmitted through the protection does not raise the average temperature at any of the levels above 1,000°F and does not raise the temperature more than 1,200°F at any thermocouple.

Floor/Ceiling and Roof/Ceiling Assemblies

Floor and roof tests are conducted in much the same manner as wall tests, but with the assembly horizontal and the fire applied from the underside. Thermocouples are used both inside the furnace to measure its temperature and on the unexposed side of the assembly structural members and at other points of interest. In these tests, it is assumed that the members supporting the assembly are not damaged by the fire. If light fixtures, air ducts, etc. are to be part of the contemplated design, they are included in the specimen.

The area of the specimen to be exposed to the fire is as least 180 SF, with neither dimension less than 12'. Beams and girders included in the test are at least 8" from the walls of the furnace. They are mounted in the same manner that they would be in the actual construction.

A load is applied to the assembly, which is calculated to develop (theoretically) the maximum working stresses in each member, as contemplated by the design.

The test is considered successful if the assembly:

- Sustains the applied load for the length of the test without permitting the passage of flame or gases hot enough to ignite cotton waste placed on the unexposed side.
- Maintains a temperature increase of not more than 250°F average on the unexposed side during the test.

For "restrained" assemblies with beams spaced more than 4' o. c., the beam rating will be 1/2 of the rating of the assembly or 1 hour, whichever is greater.

Fire Resistance and Gypsum Panels

A common misconception is that there are just two basic types of drywall—regular and type X—and beyond this difference, drywall products from various manufacturers are about the same. However, laboratory fire tests by United States Gypsum Company and various independent testing organizations provide strong evidence that there are significant fire-performance differences between drywall products from various manufacturers.

It is well known in the construction industry that the single most important characteristic of gypsum drywall is its fire resistance. This is provided by the principal raw material used in its manufacture, $CaSO_4$-$2H_2O$ (gypsum). As the chemical formula shows, gypsum contains chemically combined water (about 50% by volume). When gypsum drywall panels are exposed to fire, the heat converts a portion of the combined water to steam. The heat energy that converts water to steam is thus used up, keeping the opposite side of the gypsum panel cool as long as there is water left in the gypsum, or until the gypsum panel is breached.

In the case of regular gypsum panels, as the water is driven off by heat, the reduction in volume within the gypsum causes large cracks to form, eventually causing the panel to fail. In a special fire test designed to demonstrate the relative performance of different types of gypsum cores (described later in this section), it was shown that in a fire with a temperature of 1,850°F, a 5/8" thickness of regular-core gypsum panels would fail in this manner in 10 to 15 minutes. Type X gypsum panels, such as SHEETROCK brand FIRECODE gypsum panels, have glass fibers mixed with the gypsum to reinforce the core of the panels. These fibers have the effect of reducing the extent of and size of the cracks that form as the water is driven off, thereby extending the length of time the gypsum panel can resist the heat without failure.

15

Fire test results indicate that the same thickness of the type X gypsum drywall exposed to the same temperature (1,850°F) will last 45 to 60 minutes.

USG has developed a third-generation gypsum drywall product called SHEETROCK brand FIRECODE C gypsum panels that provides even greater resistance to the heat of fire. The core of FIRECODE C contains more glass fibers than type X—but also a shrinkage-compensating additive, a form of vermiculite that expands in the presence of heat at about the same rate as the gypsum in the core shrinks (from loss of water). Thus the core becomes highly stable in the presence of fire and remains intact even after the combined water is driven off. Tests have shown that this third-generation product resisted the fire for more than two hours, as compared to 45 to 60 minutes for the type X, and 10 to 15 minutes for the regular panel under the same test conditions.

Figures 1, 2 and 3 show the actual test that was conducted at USG's research facility in which the regular-core SHEETROCK brand gypsum panels, type X-core SHEETROCK brand FIRECODE gypsum panels and special C-core SHEETROCK brand FIRECODE C gypsum panels were compared. All three samples of drywall were 5/8" thick and were exposed to gas-fired burners producing a temperature of 1,850°F. Each sample was 13" by 13" in size and had a 12 lb-9 oz weight on top to dramatize the point at which the sample failed.

Figure 1 *Figure 2* *Figure 3*

In Fig. 1 the test has been in progress for about 12 minutes, and the regular-core SHEETROCK brand gypsum panel has just failed. The heat from the fire has caused enough water loss to make the gypsum panel crack severely and lose its ability to support the live load. In Figure 2, the test has been in progress for 57 minutes, and the type X SHEETROCK brand FIRECODE board has developed a large crack and is starting to fail. The glass fibers in the type X gypsum core have given it the strength to last nearly five times as long as the regular panel under applied load. In Figure 3, the test has just been terminated at 2 hours, 2 minutes with still no sign of failure of the type C core SHEETROCK brand FIRECODE C gypsum panel. The type C panel has resisted failure for twice as long as the type X panel and 10 times as long as the regular panel. This test proves that the dimensional stability achieved by the vermiculite additive and the strength provided by the glass fibers produce panels that are highly superior to even the type X fire-rated products.

Fire Doors (UL 10b and NFPA 252)

The tests of fire doors and windows are concerned only with their ability to stay in position during a fire in order to close the opening against flame penetration—and to withstand the effects of a hose stream.

Conditions for Hose Stream Test

Resistance Period	Water Pressure at Base of Nozzle (psi)	kPa	Duration of Application, Min. per 100 ft.² (9.3m²) Exposed Area
8 hr. and over	45	310	6
4 hr. and over if less than 8 hrs.	45	310	5
2 hr. and over if less than 4 hrs.	30	207	2-1/2
1-1/2 hr. and over if less than 2 hr.	30	207	1-1/2
1 hr. and over if less than 1-1/2 hr.	30	207	1
Less than 1 hr., if desired	30	207	1

Building codes often call for a door with a lower rating than what is required of the wall in which it is mounted. This is because heat transfer through the door is not a factor (considering the door composition and the details involved in its installation) and because the door must withstand the hose stream after the full exposure of the test.

Surface Burning Characteristics (ASTM E84, ANSI 2.5, NFPA 225 and UL 723)

The characteristics of interior finish materials that are related to fire protection are:

- Tendency for fire to spread over the surface of the material when exposed to flame.
- Quantity of smoke developed when burning.

Materials that have high flame spread and produce large quantities of smoke are considered undesirable, especially when used in areas where people assemble or are confined. The flame spread test (surface burning characteristics of building materials) is often referred to as the Steiner Tunnel Test in honor of its originator.

In the test, a 20" x 25' sample, which is installed as the "roof" of a rectangular furnace, is subjected to a fire of controlled severity. The fire is 12" from one end of the sample. From ignition the distance and time of flaming of the sample material, along with the smoke it produces, are compared with similar figures for red oak and inorganic reinforced board, which are arbitrarily assigned values of 100 and 0, respectively, for these characteristics. (The indices developed in the tunnel test are relative, but enough is known about the surface burning characteristics of materials to make these indices reliable for building code specifications.)

Smoke is measured by means of a photoelectric cell connected to an ammeter, which indicates changes in smoke density. This density influences occupants' ability to visually locate exit markers and egress paths in a fire.

Most building codes divide materials into four classes, based on the flame spread indices. The numbering and range of each class vary with the different codes, but they generally follow this pattern based on flame spread index:

Class I (Class A): 0–25   Class III (Class C): 76–200

Class II (Class B): 26–75   Class IV (Class D): over 200

The smoke developed index is 450 or less for each class.

15

Surface Burning Characteristics (per ASTM E84)

Product	Flame Spread	Smoke Developed
SHEETROCK Brand Gypsum Panels	15	0
SHEETROCK Brand Interior Gypsum Ceiling Board	15	0
SHEETROCK Brand Lay-In Ceiling Tile	15	0
SHEETROCK Brand Exterior Gypsum Ceiling Board	20	0
SHEETROCK Brand Gypsum Panels, Water-Resistant	20	0
DUROCK Cement Board, Underlayment	5	0
FIBEROCK Brand Panels	5	0
SECUROCK Roof Board	5	0

Through-Penetration Fire Stops (ASTM E814)

ASTM E119 is the guide for assessing the fire performance of most building assemblies and materials. However, ASTM E814, "Standard Test Method for Fire Tests of Penetration Firestop Systems," has been developed in recognition of the special role fire stops play in fire protection when a fire-resistant assembly is penetrated by a pipe, duct or other building component. This standard test is applicable to through-penetration fire stops of various materials and types of construction.

Fire stops are intended for use in openings in fire-resistive walls and floors. They consist of materials that fill the opening around penetrating items such as cables, cable trays, conduits, ducts and pipes—and their means of support. (See Chapter 10, "System Design Considerations," for more on through-penetration fire stops.)

The test method considers the resistance of fire stops to an external force simulated by a hose stream. Two ratings are established for each fire stop. An F rating is based on flame occurrence on the unexposed surface, while the T rating is based on the temperature rise and flame occurrence on the unexposed side of the fire stop.

A fire stop shall be considered as meeting the requirements for an F rating when it remains in the opening during the fire test and hose stream test and meets these requirements:

- Withstands the fire test for the rating period without permitting flame to pass through openings, or no flaming occurs on any element of the unexposed side of the fire stop.

- Does not develop any opening, during the hose stream test that would permit water from the stream to project beyond the unexposed side.

A fire stop shall be considered as meeting the requirements for a T rating when it remains in the opening during the fire and hose stream tests within the above limitations for F rating—and the transmission of heat through the fire stop (during the rating period) does not raise the temperature of any thermocouple on its unexposed surface—or on any penetrating item—more than 325°F above its initial temperature.

Head-of-Wall Construction Joints

Construction joints, where two fire-rated assemblies intersect, are evaluated under UL Standard 2079 for their ability to resist flame and temperature transmission, as well as the hose stream, where required. Head-of-wall construction joints occur at the intersections of wall to floor/ceiling or roof/ceiling. Other construction joints include wall to wall (expansion joint application), floor to floor (building joint application) or floor to wall. (See Chapter 10 for more on head-of-wall construction joints.)

Test parameters for head-of-wall assemblies are similar to those established for through-penetration fire stops, above. Systems may be tested and prescribed for either static (no floor or roof movement) or dynamic (to accommodate live load deflection) conditions.

Head-of-wall construction joints have common features including (a) fire-rated assemblies for both the wall and floor/ceiling or roof/ceiling, (b) a joint treatment system consisting of a forming material such as mineral wool safing insulation to pack into openings and (c) a fill material such as FIRECODE compound to seal all openings and passages. Restraining angles also may be required to achieve the necessary flame and temperature barriers.

USG has had several head-of-wall assemblies tested under standard UL-2079.

Heat Transfer

This section reviews the science of heat transfer as it relates to the built environment—including factors that influence selection of insulation.

Heat is defined as the result of vibration of molecules in any substance. The more rapidly the molecules vibrate, the higher the temperature. Therefore, heat can be defined as a form of energy. Temperature is the intensity, not quantity of heat.

Heat will flow only from a warm surface to a colder surface. For instance, a building heated to 75°F will lose heat to the outside atmosphere if the outside temperature is lower than 75°F. During such movement, heat will travel by a combination of these methods: conduction, convection and radiation. All materials resist heat transfer to a certain degree.

Insulation is any material that retards heat transfer. Structural insulation provides both insulating and structural properties to the building. Fill insulation's only function is to provide insulation. Reflective insulation reflects, and thus retards, the flow of radiant heat energy

The degree of insulation efficiency of any material is determined mainly by the number of air cells it contains. In almost all cases, the thermal resistance of an insulating material is in direct proportion to the number of its air cells. (Exceptions to this are materials, such as aluminum foil, that insulate by reflecting radiant heat.) The individual, minute air cells, because of their size, do not permit transfer of heat through convection since the air space is too small to allow air movement. Air cells resist transfer of heat by radiation since some of the radiated heat striking dead air space is not transmitted to the surface on the other side. Little heat is transmitted by conduction because the continuity of the material is broken by air cells.

In any discussion of heat loss or insulation values, the Btu (British thermal unit) is the unit of measure for a quantity of heat. To make the heat

15

unit applicable for determining the relative insulation values of various materials, a coefficient of transmission, commonly known as the "U" factor, is used. U factor is the amount of heat expressed in Btus that will pass through a combination of materials and air spaces, such as the construction of a builc ing's roof, ceiling, floor or sidewall in a given time period. The heat loss U is computed on the basis of each degree difference in opposing temperatures per SF per hr. It must be noted that the coefficient is taken from air-to-air and not surface-to-surface. U factors can be used to determine fuel savings resulting from use of insulating materials.

To obtain the U factor for part of a building, it is necessary to know the conductivity coefficient of each individual building material included in the construction. There are two measures of heat flow through building materials. Conductivity, k refers to the amount of heat that will pass through one SF of homogeneous material one inch thick in one hour for each degree Fahrenheit of temperature difference between two surfaces. Conductance, the C factor, refers to the transfer of heat through varying thicknesses of one material or any combination of materials.

Such materials as hollow tile, building paper, roofing or concrete block are examples of materials that are difficult to appraise on the basis of a one-inch thickness. Basically the difference between the C factor and the k factor is that the C factor refers to the actual thickness of the material, however variable, and the k factor always refers to a one-inch thickness. Both factors represent the rate of heat transfer between two surfaces. Either C or k factors (or both) may be combined (with due consideration) for whatever air spaces may be present to make up the U factor for the total coefficient of a wall section or for any section of the building. Installed resistance factor R of a specific insulation product is the sum of the mass resistance (1/C) and the resistance of any adjacent air spaces and air surfaces.

Sound Transmission

This section includes basic sound transmission principles, plus information USG has accumulated from experience, research and close association with acoustical consultants. (See Chapter 9, "Acoustical Ceiling Design & Application," for information on USG acoustical ceiling products.)

Sound is transmitted in a wave motion as an elastic medium produced by a vibrating object. The vibrations move the particles of the medium (such as air) adjacent to it, back and forth, creating an alternate compression and rarefaction of the medium. These disturbances move away from the source in a wave motion, much as a ripple moves along the surface of water when a stone is dropped in.

The speed of sound, or velocity, depends only on the density and elasticity of the medium through which it is traveling. The velocity in air at room temperature is 1,130 feet per second; in steel it is 16,500 feet per second; in hardwood, it is 13,000 feet per second.

Sound control breaks down into three distinct areas:

- *Airborne sound transmission:* Sound traveling through the air and subsequently through partitions and openings.
- *Impact sound transmission:* Originates by contact with the structure and travels through the structure. Thus, it is governed by a completely different set of values than airborne sound.
- *Architectural acoustics:* Refers to the handling of sound within a single area (reflection, reverberation, absorption, etc.). It does not address sound transmission through elements of the structure.

Airborne Transmission

The control of airborne sound in any building is determined by the applicable building codes. Among the most important factors used for sound control are:

- *Mass:* Sound waves must overcome the mass (weight) of a medium before the particles of the medium can be set into motion to transmit sound. Mass may be a factor in the reduction of impact sound transmission. It is most effective—though unpredictable—in the lower frequencies.
- *Isolation:* The retardation of the flow of airborne and structure-borne sound through an assembly or use of special materials, methods of construction and designs. Decoupling is one isolation method, in which the elements of a partition are separated to retard transmission of structure-borne sound.
- *Damping:* When the full capabilities of mass and isolation have been utilized, the next logical step is damping. Damping is the process of introducing fibrous sound-absorbing material into the partition to increase the transmission loss. (Damping in floor/ceiling construction has a wider application for impact sound than for airborne sound.) There are several ways to introduce damping beyond just insulation in the plenum.
- *Leaks:* Any leak in a partition that will allow air to pass will also leak sound. Small holes in a wall, openings for electrical boxes and plumbing, cracks around doors are all leaks that will allow sound to pass, destroying the noise reduction effectiveness of the wall.
- *Limpness:* A limp member (such as a lead sheet) does not vibrate easily. As a result, sound is dampened.
- *Flanking Paths:* Sound waves have sufficient energy to set any construction (assembly) in motion. That means that sound can bypass a sound partition by activating the floor that the partition rests on. Flanking paths are as important to impact sound as to airborne sound.

- *Masking Level:* Background noise (such as from air conditioning or human activities), also known as masking level, plays an important part in the apparent acoustical performance of a partition. A partition for an apartment located in an area that has considerable amount of outside or "street" noise may prove quite satisfactory, while the same partition in a quiet neighborhood would be unsatisfactory. The difference is the background noise, which "masks" the sound being transmitted through the partition.

• *Impact Sound Isolation*: Impact sound is also transmitted by vibration, but the energy setting the floor, ceiling or wall into vibration is supplied by a physical act, such as footsteps, dropping a toy or a frying pan, moving furniture or slamming a door.

Noise Reduction Coefficient (NRC)

Noise reduction coefficient (NRC) is a measure of the sound absorption characteristics of an acoustical product. The standard ASTM test method for determining the sound absorption (NRC) of acoustical materials is ASTM C423. A specimen of material approximately 8 SF is placed in the center of the room on an elevated platform 16" high. Prior to placing the acoustical material in the room, the reverberation time is determined, then measured after the acoustical material has been placed. The difference in the two measured times is used to calculate the effectiveness of the acoustical material in absorbing sound.

The actual NRC value is determined by averaging the sound absorption values in the four main frequency bands of 250, 500, 1,000 and 2,000 Hz. These values represent most of the range of the human voice. The greater the NRC, the better the overall sound absorption of the acoustical material, providing a room that will have less reverberation and echo.

Ceiling Attenuation Class (CAC)

Ceiling attenuation class (CAC) is a numerical rating used to characterize sound traveling between two horizontally adjacent spaces sharing a common ceiling plenum. CAC is measured using test standard ASTM E1414. Sound is introduced into a room and measured in that room. Then the same sound is measured in the adjacent room (the other side of the partition from where sound was introduced). The CAC value is calculated using sound measurements in both rooms. Any sound that could pass directly through the partition is already calculated and factored out. The goal is to measure only the sound that is passing from the first room to the second room *through* the ceiling. That means that the wall's contribution to sound transmission must be accounted for (mathematically) and eliminated. Higher CAC values indicate greater attenuation of sound into and through the plenum.

Articulation Class (AC)

Articulation class (AC) refers to a single numerical rating used to identify the degree of transmitted speech intelligibility between office spaces. This rating is particularly useful for open plan offices. AC provides an indication of the degree to which occupants will be able to understand and/or be disturbed by conversation occurring elsewhere in the office space. AC is determined by following the test procedure outlined in standard ASTM E1111, which measures sound levels in a source space and then at varying distances beyond a barrier screen. The derived value is a combination of the sound reflection characteristics and sound absorption characteristics of the acoustical product being tested in a prescribed assembly.

Vapor Control

Basic Principles

Air holds water in the form of water vapor (a gas). The amount of water retained depends on the air temperature; warm air holds more moisture than cool air. Moisture problems in buildings stem from excess water vapor in the air.

Condensation occurs when warm, moist air is cooled and is no longer able to hold all the water vapor present. Moisture is released in the form of dew, fog, rain or snow. The dew point is the temperature at which condensation begins to occur. Air at the dew point is saturated or at 100% relative humidity (RH, the percentage of air's saturation at a particular temperature).

The weight of water vapor is usually measured in grains per pound of dry air. A pint of water weighs about 7,000 grains (one pound).

The psychrometric chart below provides the values for vapor conditions that are typically encountered in structures. Refer to the chart and figures a–e as they relate to the following examples.

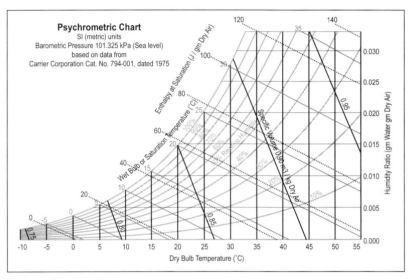

At a temperature of 70°F and 80% RH, the air is holding 88 grains of water vapor per pound of dry air (Figure a below) and is capable of holding up to 110 grains/lb when saturated (Figure b below). If the temperature is lowered to 60°F, the air is capable of holding only 78 grains of water vapor (Figure c below) and condensation of the excess water (88-78=10 grains) will occur.

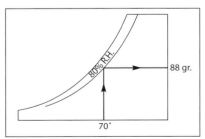

a

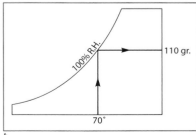

b

15

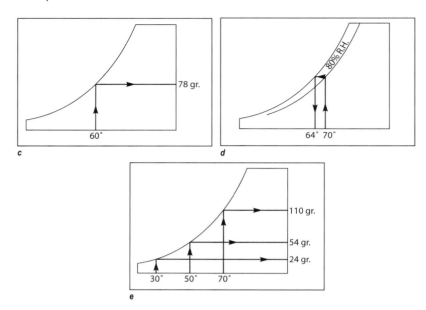

c

d

e

The dew point is found along the 100% RH line, thus the dew point of 70°F air at 80% RH is 64°F (Figure d above).

As illustrated in these examples, temperature directly affects the air's ability to retain water vapor. Referring to Figure e above, a pound of air at 70°F can hold 110 grains of water vapor, but if the temperature is lowered to 50°F, it retains only 54 grains—and at 30°F just 24 grains, having given up 3/4 of its water vapor to condensation.

An example of condensation is when warm air comes in contact with a cold object such as a window pane or an iced drinking glass. The film of air next to the glass is cooled, causing it to give off its water vapor in the form of droplets that cling to the glass.

Surface condensation (similar to the type that forms on window panes) will occur on interior building walls in certain cases, such as shower walls where humidity is high, kitchens during cooking and on single-pane windows. Surface condensation takes place when the surface's temperature is below the dew point of the surrounding air.

Condensation can also take place within a wall, even though enough insulation is provided to prevent surface condensation. Generally in cold weather, a temperature equal to the dew point exists somewhere in the wall if the inside air is moist. If the moist inside air can reach this part of the wall, internal condensation will occur.

Water vapor travels from points of higher vapor pressure to points of lower pressure. Thus, the inside air with a high moisture content (due to cooking, washing, showers, perspiration, humidifiers) has a high vapor pressure, which results in the water vapor migrating towards the outside of the walls.

Internal condensation can be controlled by one or a combination of the following methods:

- Insulation can be used to move the dew point to a less harmful location in the construction; the condensation will still occur.
- Ventilation of the moist air before it reaches the area of the dew point temperature within the wall. This method is highly effective.
- Vapor barrier installation will restrict the flow of water vapor to the area of dew point temperatures.

Ventilation replaces the vapor-laden air with dry, outside air with a lower RH, and thus a lower dew point. This approach minimizes moisture problems and is most effective in attics, crawl spaces, bathrooms, kitchens and other areas of high humidity.

A barrier to keep vapor from entering the construction cavities is the most practical answer to internal condensation. To be effective, a barrier, called a vapor retarder, must be located in a portion of the wall that never reaches the dew point.

Vapor retarders are classified in terms of the amount of water vapor they allow to pass through a material, in a measurement called "perms." A perm is a vapor transmission rate of 1 grain of water vapor per square foot, per hour, per inch of mercury vapor pressure difference. Materials having a perm rate of 1 or less are considered good vapor retarders.

No part of the exterior construction beyond (towards the outside) the actual, intended retarder should be less permeable than the retarder itself. It is usually impossible to achieve a perfect barrier, since there are nearly always penetrations (such as for water, ventilation, electrical, cable, etc.) that allow moisture into the cavity. Consequently, some vapor will pass into the construction, and unless the construction is open enough to allow the vapor to pass, it will condense.

The location of the vapor retarder varies by geography and climate. In cold climates, it is generally installed on the "warm" side of the exterior wall—the inside face. In hot, dry or humid climates, it may be determined that no vapor retarder is needed. In any case, it is recommended that a mechanical engineer be consulted regarding both the location and the type of vapor retarder.

Condensation problems can be prevented at much less expense than what it will cost to correct them. The chart on the next page shows that it is very difficult to correct many of these situations after the construction is completed, while precautions taken during construction are so inexpensive that to omit them is a false economy.

15

Condensation in Interior Spaces

Causes	Remedies
Attics	
Condensation is caused by vapor entering an attic through ceilings, attic doors and from the basement through stud walls.	Ventilate attic well, install vapor retarders and seal attic doors and stud-wall tops. Paint ceilings below.
Basements	
Most often encountered in the summer, condensation takes place when warm, humid air contacts cool basement walls and floors. Water leakage through walls is another source of moisture problems in basements, but this is not caused by condensation.	Ventilation may help, although heavy foliage and shade near a structure often reduce its effectiveness. If the dew point of outside air is higher than the temperature of basement walls, ventilation will increase condensation. Mechanical dehumidifiers are probably the most effective solution, although calcium chloride and other moisture-absorbing materials will help. Insulating the walls may prevent surface condensation, but any moisture coming through the walls will collect behind the insulation.
Floors	
Usually occurs when concrete slabs are poured on soil.	Concrete floors should be installed over gravel, cinders or other insulating material and should be provided with good drainage and perimeter insulation at the edges of the slab.
Bathrooms	
This is an intermittent problem caused by hot water baths and showers.	Install exhaust fan of ventilator to remove moisture-laden air to the outside, and decorate with vapor-resisting materials such as tile, plastic wall covering or oil paint.
Kitchens and Laundries	
This is also an intermittent problem caused by cooking and washing.	Same as bathrooms.
Windows	
Single-pane windows, coupled with high inside humidity, bring about condensation, which damages window frames and paint. Double-pane windows do not allow condensation up to about 33% RH at 70°F, whereas single panes will become moist at 14% RH.	Install double-pane windows or storm windows.
Exterior Walls	
Surface condensation often occurs on the exterior walls and ceilings of uninsulated structures. In these cases, unobserved condensation is also likely within the walls and ceilings.	Insulate walls with vapor retarder/wall insulation or with a separate vapor retarder. If this is impractical, paint the inside walls with non-breathing paint. (Consult with paint manufacturer for thickness required.)
Closet Walls	
Since closets are not heated, the outside walls become colder, causing condensation	Same as exterior walls.

Sustainability

A Construction Priority

In a world ever more challenged by global environmental issues, sustainability has become a major focus across the building design and construction industry, placing a growing demand on material producers, architects and contractors to demonstrate environmental awareness and to implement "green" approaches. The development of new building materials and the production and application of current components are increasingly driven by concerns for their effects on our climate, the earth's existing and potential natural resources, rising energy and operational costs, and the quality of our lives.

Sustainability as a key factor in the production and use of building materials is a relatively new concept. In the past, most manufacturers were unprepared to make substantial investments in environmentally friendly production processes or in the development of quality materials that minimized consumption of natural resources. The sophisticated technologies needed to measure and monitor sustainability criteria in production processes were not available. Furthermore, the industry did not have the guidance of environmental testing standards, sustainability related building codes, and the government regulations needed to set universal production and application benchmarks, as we have today.

During the last decade, the industry's intensifying focus around environmental impact has significantly boosted its ability to manage critical sustainability factors. With the involvement and support of professional associations like United States Green Building Council (USGBC) and the National Association of Home Builders (NAHB), along with product ratings, assessment tools and production standards, practical guidelines have been identified to ensure that sustainability is consistently achieved. Many governments throughout the world, as well as cities and states within the U.S., have established specific green building requirements and have enacted regulations demanding compliance. These requirements are aimed at promoting sustainability beginning with building construction through the development's life cycle.

Almost 30 years ago, USG developed progressive product designs, manufacturing methods and resource uses that actively incorporated the principles of environmental responsibility. These measures included treatment of waste water, closed loop manufacturing processes and use of recovery, and recycled products such as paper and metal slag.

What Is Sustainability?

There are probably as many ways to define "sustainability" as there are industry sectors and sciences. USG has adopted a working definition that applies to building sciences and the building materials industry—acknowledging that our actions have a positive or negative impact on the environment and future generations. These actions must be analyzed throughout raw material selection, manufacturing, distribution, use and end-of-life disposal, including recycling and/or reuse of our products to minimize our overall environmental impact. USG defines sustainability as the knowledge and management of these impacts. The company continually looks for ways to minimize its use of natural resources and substitute them with repurposed materials.

USG's approach to sustainability promotes functional, as well as corporate responsibility and accountability. Sustainability goals are applied equally to product design and manufacture, distribution capabilities, business operations, customer support functions and vendor relations. USG evaluates and adjusts its production processes and operating efficiencies in order to achieve the best possible ratio of resource consumption to manufacturing and distribution productivity. USG incorporates the basic design requirements of long-term product sustainability into its existing and new product solutions.

Each decision made in the selection and use of USG products is based on careful consideration of their environmental effects over time. The aim is to minimize—or eliminate altogether—the possibility of a negative impact on our present and future environment. This decision-making process requires a comprehensive evaluation of every aspect of a given product's positive and negative characteristics. The process is laborious and continuous, but it results in the design and production of building components that meet our sustainability criteria: durability, life and product safety and reducing long-term environmental impact.

USG's EcoBlueprint™ commitment underscores the company's dedication to environmental sustainability through manufacturing and providing the most innovative products and services to customers for creating sustainable spaces.

EcoBlueprint™
USG's Environmental Sustainability Commitment

Minimize Our Footprint Wherever Possible	Support Our Customer's Needs	Consciousness in All We Do
• Utilize water, energy and other resources more efficiently • Find innovative ways to reduce and reuse waste • Transform manufacturing by-products into valuable new resources	• Base innovative products on solid building science • Extend our high performance and environmentally friendly product and service offerings	• Embedded in our core values • Continue our industry leadership position • Visit **usg.com/ecoblueprint** for more information

Achieving Sustainability

Research and long-term assessment, in combination with on-the-job experience, shows that building sustainability is best achieved through a holistic or whole building design approach. This includes consideration of all aspects of the design solution, e.g., site selection and preservation, building orientation and landscaping; material selection and operational energies; natural resource impact; and occupant and community impact.

The principles of sustainable design take into account every aspect of a product's life cycle: from the resources required for its manufacture, inventory and distribution—to known and possible interactions with its intended environment. This full-scale analysis takes place at the front end of the design and development process and involves all design disciplines working together. This process allows sustainability to be accurately gauged based on a comprehensive understanding of the product's actual and potential environmental impact characteristics. And it results in lasting, quality materials that support the facility's flexibility and functionality.

16

Sustainable Product Design & Production

Designing sustainable building products involves integration of factors such as conservation of natural resources, avoidance of harmful emissions, materials recycling capabilities, and manufacturing efficiencies—plus life health and safety. Expertise in terms of construction technologies, building and material science, and product applications and systems is an essential ingredient in successful sustainable product design.

Product Evaluation

Throughout the development stage, products are tested for performance characteristics and environmental impacts. Assessment procedures are conducted throughout this stage to measure a product's sustainability in the context of both manufacturing and practical use.

Sustainability standards are considered at each step of the evaluation process. These include benchmarks such as the whole-building Green Building Rating System® established by LEED® (USGBC's Leadership in Energy and Environmental Design) and NAHB's Green Building Standards protocols, along with product guidelines and standards, and federal and state environmental regulations and codes. Product design is thoroughly assessed, both in USG's research and manufacturing facilities and at independent field test sites. The aim of this rigorous evaluation process is to identify the results of a material's environmental interactions across a broad spectrum, including its reactions to climate, air quality, interior furnishings and other key built environment variables.

Environmental Management in Production

For more than a century, USG has been a leader of responsible environmental management among major U.S. corporations. Innovative processes pioneered by the company, such as the use of synthetic gypsum (also known as FGD gypsum), slag mineral wool, and recycled paper and metal in many of our wallboard and ceiling products, enable the company to manufacture high-quality goods while managing consumption of energy and other natural resources. Many of USG's manufacturing processes, material designs and product systems are patented, reflecting the industry-wide reputation for continuous innovation, expertise and leadership that the company has earned and maintained over the years.

Water Use

USG has been in the forefront of developing processes that reduce fresh water resource usage. Through water management, treatments and recycling practices, USG has greatly reduced effluents and placed significantly less demand on their plant's local water treatment facilities.

Energy Conservation and Emissions

USG manufacturing processes are designed and operated to minimize energy use, emissions and pollution through long-standing evaluation and conservation programs. In addition, the company recaptures and recycles energy wherever possible by incorporating energy management processes within its manufacturing systems.

The Economics of Sustainability

Clearly, sustainable product development and use has proven to be not only environmentally responsible, but also a sound business approach. From that standpoint alone, commitment to sustainability is a global imperative and a mandate for materials producers, architects, designers and builders. Sustainable products are an important component in building and resource economics including life cycle costs, as well as from a purely "green," ecological perspective.

Today, many architects, developers and owners demand building materials and construction technologies that consistently deliver energy efficiency, preserve the integrity of the surrounding land, and ensure a clean, healthy indoor environment. Our customers can be confident that USG products take the lead in fulfilling the most stringent Indoor Environmental Quality requirements.

At USG, we understand that a whole design solution approach applies to sustainable product design and manufacture and represents a powerful, practical competitive advantage for builders and contractors. The use of sustainable materials in the course of a building project helps

16

to eliminate sources of negative environmental impact and therefore satisfy environmentally conscious customers. This, in turn, promotes better, more lasting business relationships and stronger builder-contractor reputations.

From the owner's or developer's perspective, the use of sustainable building components results in cost-effective structures that perform at higher levels of efficiency, comfort and occupant safety throughout their life cycles. As a result, their investment in sustainable construction is more likely to deliver a favorable return and to maintain long-term economic value.

Clearly, sustainability is no longer optional or limited to the custom-built marketplace, but is requested across the construction industry. USG responds with products and services that meet or exceed today's environmental standards and leads development of future product offerings.

Essential Elements of a Sustainable Building

Any structure that meets the criteria necessary for true sustainability must be physically and ecologically suitable for long-term human occupancy. In general, it must:

- Be structurally and environmentally safe and healthy throughout its entire life cycle.
- Support and facilitate the building's basic functions—shelter, security and accessibility—during the life of the structure, despite changes in intended use (e.g., healthcare or educational facility).
- Incorporate design, materials, construction and continuous-use characteristics that actively minimize or eliminate negative environmental impacts.
- Integrate positively with its surrounding ecosystem—the physical, geographic and organic components of its environment.

Architects, builders, and contractors face real challenges in the development and construction of a sustainably designed building. Fortunately, the demands of green building can be successfully met with an understanding of the components of sustainability and of the standards and practices that combine to achieve it.

Basic Measures of Sustainability

The broad spectrum of products and systems used in the course of a building project has a major bearing on the finished structure's sustainability. Each product—ceilings, walls, flooring and so on—contributes to or detracts from the total building's sustainability. To develop an accurate understanding of the building's overall sustainability, it is important to determine the environmental impact of its individual components and systems.

Measuring Building Energy

All manufactured building materials require various forms of energy to produce and distribute. The total amount of energy used to manufacture a given material and then to transport it to its point-of-use stage is called **embodied energy**. This is a critical measure of a product's sustainability.

A calculation of embodied energy combines the energy needed to extract and transport raw materials used as product ingredients; to manufacture the item ready for installation or use; and then to transport the finished product to the distributor. This chain of events is often referred to as "cradle to market." Other terms describing the product's life stage evaluation for energy and other life cycle assessment criteria is "cradle to grave," which also includes installation, life and maintenance, demolition and transportation to disposal and land filling: "Cradle to cradle" is the cradle-to-grave process, except that disposal and landfill are replaced with reuse or recycling.

The aggregate embodied energy of all materials used to construct the finished building including the construction process itself is known as **building embodied energy**. This measure provides an accurate calculation of the structure's initial environmental impact. The building's designer must carefully analyze a given product's performance characteristics for intended application in the built environment.

Operational energy is the energy consumed to maintain required levels of occupant comfort, temperature and relative humidity, lighting and acoustical integrity, equipment use and other factors of continuous use. Conventional buildings typically have an operational energy nine times greater than their embodied energy over a fifty-year life cycle. Selection of high-performance building materials can reduce a building's operational energy requirements. These relative advantages must be weighed in building materials selection and again, may help with whole building sustainability ratings.

Interior Environmental Factors

The ways that individual products relate strongly influence operational energy and occupant health and can cumulatively react in an indoor environment. Materials that emit harmful vapors may require additional air-exchange capacity that, in turn, increases operational energy.

Many of these vapors fall into the category of **volatile organic compounds** (VOCs). Commonly found in the built environment (including building materials, paints, carpeting, cleaning supplies and furnishings), VOCs are organic chemicals such as formaldehyde, that are given off as gases. VOCs may be present during any or all stages of a building's life cycle—materials manufacturing, construction and occupancy—and may pose real health and comfort issues. Architects must be especially alert to the risk of VOCs when they develop product and design specifications. Builders and contractors must recognize the potential dangers of VOCs relative to the products they install and may adjust their construction methods in accordance with best practices.

Additional information concerning specific wall, ceiling and flooring product characteristics and recommended applications, installation techniques and sustainability ratings can be obtained on the USG

16

website at **usg.com** by navigating to specific product pages or **usgdesignstudio.com**.

Sustainability Through Performance

Indoor Environmental Quality Moisture & Mold Resistance	Acoustics	Durability	Life Safety	Indoor Air Quality
SHEETROCK Mold-Tough Gypsum Panels	USG Acoustical Ceiling Systems	USG Abuse-Resistant Panels	USG Fire-Related Gypsum Systems	USG Zero and Low Emitting Ceiling Panels and USG Zero Emitting SHEETROCK gypsum panels
DUROCK Cement Board	USG Acoustical Gypsum Systems	DUROCK Cement Board	USG Seismic Solutions	SHEETROCK Mold Tough Gypsum Panels
FIBEROCK AQUA-TOUGH Underlayment and Tile Backerboard	SHEETROCK Acoustical Sealant	SHEETROCK Paper Faced Beads		FIBEROCK AQUA-TOUGH Underlayment and Tile Backerboard
CLIMAPLUS Ceilings	LEVELROCK Floor Underlayment	USG Plaster Systems USG Cast Ceilings		SHEETROCK Dust Control Joint Compound
SECUROCK Roof Board				DUROCK Cement Board

Indoor environmental quality, or IEQ, encompasses all interior environmental factors and is a major component of overall building sustainability. IEQ considers all of a structure's interior environmental factors that affect the safety, health and well-being of its occupants. Characteristics such as relative occupant comfort, humidity, ventilation and air circulation, and acoustics and lighting are used to form a comprehensive assessment of IEQ. Another key determinant of IEQ is **indoor air quality** (IAQ), which evaluates the level of interior building pollutants, including mold and mildew, ventilation and air circulation, cleaning solvents and VOCs. Additionally, mold and moisture resistance, acoustics, durability and life safety can be components of IEQ.

Considerable research into the effects of indoor environmental quality shows that the impact of IEQ on building inhabitants is substantial. In commercial office buildings, for example, high IEQ promotes stronger occupant productivity, reduced absenteeism and lower levels of employee turnover. General measures of workforce health are also more positive. In contrast, low workplace IEQ is reflected in reduced productivity, higher absenteeism and turnover, and more frequent health-related issues among employees.

As discussed earlier in this chapter, sustainability relies in large part on environmentally responsible approaches to process management and optimal use of raw materials. Sustainable product design and continuous assessment must be incorporated into every aspect of materials development, production and distribution in order to minimize the environmental impact of manufacturing. Producers should follow procedures in accordance with the EPA's **Three Rs of Sustainability**: reduce, reuse, recycle.

- **Reduce:** Products and packaging designed to minimize the amount of raw materials and energy consumed during the manufacturing process greatly contribute to overall sustainability. Light-weight materials typically require less energy to transport. Production waste can also be minimized through the use of high-efficiency design and manufacturing processes. USG uses raw materials very efficiently, for example, within drywall production, using all but 3% of the raw material input to make up the finished panels, and a portion of that remaining 3% utilized as transportation spacers (also known as "dunnage").

• **Reuse:** Responsible deconstuction of construction projects allows for reuse of the building components. For example, products like wall partitions, ceilings and lumber, if carefully removed, can be reused in the construction of a new project. Brick is an example of a commonly reused material. By reusing material, the environmental footprint of producing new products is dramatically decreased.

• **Recycle:** Materials that are discarded or damaged in the course of manufacturing can be efficiently reprocessed into the same product. This waste can also be reused to manufacture differ-

ent products with shared ingredients or it can be repurposed for altogether new applications. The extensive use of recycling processes at every stage of manufacturing is a major element of USG's environmental management strategy. Effective recycling during manufacturing substantially reduces raw material consumption, energy demands and landfill waste.

For alternatives to landfill disposal of gypsum panel waste, contact your local USG sales representative or visit **usg.com**.

Best Sustainability Practice at USG

USG has, over the course of its century-plus history, led the building sector's effort to develop and supply environmentally friendly, fully sustainable construction materials. Today, sustainability is integrated into the manufacture of every USG wall, ceiling and flooring product.

For example, USG's SHEETROCK and FIBEROCK AQUA-TOUGH lines of gypsum panels meet nearly every criterion of sustainable design. The panels have extremely low embodied energy, high recycled content, and are free of VOC and formaldehyde emissions.

USG makes extensive use of synthetic gypsum (also known as "recaptured" or FGD gypsum), a by-product of flue gas desulfurization (FGD)—the scrubbing technology utilized by many coal-fired power plants to reduce undesirable sulfur dioxide emissions. Synthetic gypsum is chemically refined and purified in processes that USG helped to pioneer and used as an alternative to naturally occurring gypsum. In terms of sustainability, synthetic gypsum provides the same attributes as natural gypsum. In addition, landfilling is avoided by utilizing this waste by-product.

USG ceiling systems are another example of its leadership in developing best sustainable manufacturing practices. As a case in point, in late 2006, USG became the first manufacturer to provide zero-VOC and formaldehyde-emitting ceiling panels, while meeting the highest standards of antimicrobial protection. Ingredients used in many USG ceiling products include environmentally friendly mineral wool made from steel slag, as well as recycled paper and renewable corn- and wheat-starch binders. In addition, several of USG's metal specialty ceilings and ceiling and drywall suspension systems utilize recycled steel and aluminum.

16

USG leads the building industry in the development of high-performance components designed to meet specifications and construction requirements, including sustainability, to enhance building performance, and to streamline the building process. For detailed design and installation information, specifications and additional sustainability suggestions, access the USG website at **usg.com** and navigate to specific product web pages. Or, consult our online Design Studio at **usgdesignstudio.com**.

Sustainable building design must be supported with construction methods and technologies that comply with relevant building codes and that adhere to the specific product's recommended installation procedures. Sealants, joint compounds, adhesives and paint, for example, should be applied according to the manufacturer's specifications. This will help to ensure the integrity of the project's sustainable design and will support its durability and value over time. Professionals may obtain detailed, up-to-date installation information by navigating to relevant USG product descriptions on our website.

Best Practices

Manufacturing Conservation

100% recycled face and back paper since the 1960s	Waste water reused in the manufacturing process
One of the nation's top users of waste paper helping avoid landfill	Reduced product packaging to minimize construction to waste
Pioneered the use of synthetic gypsum from flue gas desulfurization of U.S. coal-fired power plants	New plants are among the most energy efficient in the world
Excellent recovery rates at gypsum and ceilings plants	Wallboard manufacturing contributes less than 0.01% to the world's greenhouse gas emissions
Regional wallboard recycling options available	Nationwide ceiling recycling program

Sustainability Assessment Tools

Numerous tools exist to help guide construction professionals in the evaluation of sustainability characteristics of manufacturers and their products. Generally, these tools can be categorized as codes, standards and guidelines. They provide accurate, useful decision-making support when determining preferred project materials; gathering application, installation and building life cycle information; or comparing an individual product's performance properties.

Of these guidelines, one of the most reliable and comprehensive assessment standards was created by the American Society for Testing and Materials (ASTM). Designated ASTM E2129, "Standard Practice for Data Collection for Sustainability Assessment of Building Products," the tool analyzes a manufacturer's commitment to sustainable product development across five relevant criteria, including:

1. Materials (product feedstock)
2. Manufacturing
3. Operational performance of installed product
4. Indoor environmental quality
5. Corporate environmental policy

Each of these criteria is further broken into sub-categories designed to obtain specific descriptive and quantitative data regarding the producer's demonstrated sustainability performance and manufacturing environment. Companies that supply building materials advertised as sustainable should be able and willing to provide information on their responses to ASTM E2129 protocols upon request. See **usg.com/ecoblueprint**.

A number of trade associations across the United States provide environmentally focused building guidelines and standards. Among the most influential is the U.S. Green Building Council (USGBC), a nonprofit coalition of leaders drawn from across the building industry and formed to promote sustainable building. USG is proud to be a founding and charter member of the Council.

Today, the LEED ("Leadership in Energy and Environmental Design") Green Building Rating System developed by USGBC is the most widely accepted national guideline for environmentally responsible building. LEED provides technical guidance and third-party certification measures that evaluate project sustainability by analyzing critical aspects of building design and construction. A project may receive one of four levels of LEED certification by earning points in six categories of assessment.

For more information on the LEED rating system, visit the USGBC website at **usgbc.org/leed**. Projects that seek LEED certification can review the assessment tool at **usgdesignstudio.com** and can consult the USG Sustainability Tables containing pertinent product and plant information at **usg.com/ecoblueprint**.

USG also works in close partnership with trade and professional organizations, such as the National Association of Home Builders (NAHB), a leading voice in residential construction. NAHB's National Green Building Program has resources and tools to help builders, remodelers, home building associations and homeowners learn how to build green. More information about the NAHB home certification program can be accessed on the association's website at **nahbgreen.org**.

In addition, USG has worked with NAHB and other associations to present demonstrations and professional training workshops on recommended construction recycling procedures and related sustainability and environmental management topics.

Product Testing & Standards

Vigorous product testing and the development of new materials and installation technologies have helped to promote building and product sustainability, increase manufacturing efficiency and apply upgraded performance standards to the built environment. Today, a variety of independent, nonprofit organizations work to support continuous improvement across the building industry.

Organizations such as the Collaborative for High Performance Schools (CHPS) promote research, testing and the development of effective environmental management strategies for schools and other special-

16

ized building projects, such as healthcare facilities. More information on CHPS is available via its website at **chps.net**.

Environmentally focused organizations like CHPS make significant contributions to public health and safety and to our understanding of best environmental management practices. They also help the building industry to better manage its ongoing development of sustainable products and processes.

USG is proud of its leadership in the environmental sustainability arena, and takes great pride in its many partner associations, including:

USGBC

NAHB

Responsible Solutions to Mold Coalition

Alliance for the Sustainable Built Environment

AIA Cornerstone Partners

California Climate Action Registry

Wildlife Habitat Council

'USGBC' and related logo is a trademark owned by the U.S. Green Building Council and is used by permission.

USG Sustainability Design Tools

USG also serves as a knowledge center in support of our customers and other building professionals throughout the industry. The company delivers expert advice, reliable information and comprehensive consulting support to builders, contractors, architects and engineers—both through our central offices and on-site. USG customers and others can also find sustainable solutions on our website at **usg.com**. Users can quickly to access relevant, up-to-date information on product applications, specifications, installation techniques, design ideas and tools and current regulations. (For example, the Suspended Ceilings publication, SC2000, contains a sustainable ceilings selection chart, catalog and more helpful information.) Please visit our websites at:

usg.com

usg.com/ecoblueprint

usgdesignstudio.com

getmoldfacts.com

sustainableceilings.com

seismicceilings.com

The USG LEED Report Tool

All the LEED information you need for the USG products you select

A Fast and easy way to dynamically generate a custom Microsoft Word document with LEED credit information for USG products

- Complete information package in just 3 steps
- Calculates recycled content of products based on MR 4.1 & 4.2 formulas
- Includes list of test protocols and definitions
- Includes summary of LEED credits applicable to USG products

16

USG: America's Building Industry Leader

About USG Corporation

Chicago-based USG has a long history of leadership in producing innovative building construction products. Since its founding in 1902, USG's focus has been on quality and innovation in the development of gypsum plasters and cements for the construction industry. The company revolutionized the industry in the early 1930s with the introduction of ROCKLATH gypsum lath, a paperbound gypsum board that replaced wood and metal lath as a base material for conventional plaster. As USG perfected systems to join panels together, it introduced the SHEETROCK® brand drywall systems that have gone on to become an authority in the worldwide building industry.

Innovation at USG continues to this day. In the past 30 years, the company has pioneered major advances in DUROCK brand cement board construction, lightweight SHEETROCK brand joint compounds, high-performance sound-control assemblies, fire-rated systems, high-strength veneer plasters and drywall surface preparations.

Recent innovations have been in the area of FIBEROCK brand abuse-resistant and SHEETROCK brand MOLD TOUGH gypsum panels, SECUROCK Glass-Mat exterior sheathings and plaster products. Additionally, in 2006, USG became the first manufacturer to offer formaldehyde-free ceiling panels with the highest-level of antimicrobial protection. These new ceiling products are also characterized by high mold and mildew resistance and low VOC (volatile organic compounds) emissions.

USG products are used across the full range of construction projects, from major commercial developments, to residential housing projects, to simple home improvements. USG's flagship brands, including SHEETROCK brand gypsum panels and finishing products, CLIMAPLUS ceiling panels, and DUROCK brand cement board, are recognized worldwide for their quality, performance and cost-effectiveness.

With facilities in more than 30 countries, USG, a multi-billion-dollar Fortune 500 company, is one of the world's leading producers of gypsum wallboard, joint compound and related products, and acoustical ceiling panels, suspension systems, and specialty ceiling systems. USG distributes its products across North America, Europe, the Middle East, Africa, Latin America, the Caribbean and the Pacific Rim—through local, regional and national wholesalers and building-materials suppliers.

The USG family of products is focused on creative building solutions that set new standards for productivity and efficiency, helping contractors and architects deliver quality building projects and innovative designs. USG's core values include:

Safety We adhere to the highest standards for effective accident prevention and safe operating practices to prevent injuries.

Integrity We maintain the highest standards of behavior by being honest and ethical in our conduct.

Service We anticipate customer needs and are the most responsive, dependable and easiest company to do business with.

Innovation We strive to develop creative customer-desired products and services.

Diversity We are committed to promoting diversity of thought, ideas, perspectives and people.

Efficiency We streamline end-to-end processes across business lines, customers and suppliers.

Quality We maintain the highest operational standards in the industry.

USG is also fully committed to responsible environmental management. In fact, it has been corporate policy for over 100 years to manage natural resources effectively. The company continuously seeks ways to minimize use of natural materials and substitute them with repurposed materials. (See Chapter 16, "Sustainability," for specific information on sustainability at USG.)

USG Building Materials

USG offers a wide variety of quality products and integrated, performance-engineered systems. Our building systems are designed to consider all major factors: cost, sound control, moisture resistance, abuse resistance, fire resistance, structural capacity, aesthetics, sustainability, and overall utility and function.

Current USG Building Systems and Component Products

System Applications	Product Examples
Tile and Flooring	• Cement Board • Fiber Board • Tile Membrane • Floor Patch • Floor Primer/Sealer • Mortars and Mastics • Poured Self-leveling Floor Underlayment
Interior Panels and Finishes	**Gypsum-Based** • Gypsum Board • Mold-Resistant Gypsum Board • MH Gypsum Board • Abuse-Resistant Fiber Board • Joint Compound • Drywall Tape • Corner Bead • Tools • Primers

17

(continued on next page)

Current USG Building Systems and Component Products (cont.)	
	Plasters
	• Plaster Base Board
	• Veneer Plaster
	• Tools
Exteriors	• Exterior Wall Panels
	• Roofing Panels
Structural	• Structural Panels
Ceilings	• Tile
	• Grid
	• Specialty
	• Drywall Suspension

New USG Products

Since the *USG Handbook Centennial Edition* was published in 2001, the company has introduced new products:

- Sheetrock brand gypsum panels, Mold Tough—A non-combustible, moisture- and mold-resistant paper-faced gypsum core (drywall) panel that addressed the rising concerns regarding mold and indoor air quality.

- Securock brand glass-mat sheathing—A non-combustible, moisture- and mold-resistant panel designed for use under exterior claddings where conventional gypsum sheathing products had been used.

The Manufacture of Gypsum Products

All gypsum products are manufactured from a mineral rock (gypsum) that is gray to white in color and is found in abundant deposits around the world. Basic gypsum consists of calcium sulfate chemically combined with water of crystallization ($CaSO_4 + 2H_2O$). The combined water makes up about 20% of gypsum rock's weight (50% by volume) and gives the material its characteristic fire-resistive qualities and high adaptability to varied construction use.

After gypsum rock is mined or quarried, it is crushed, dried, and ground to a flour-like consistency. It is then calcined (heated) to remove most of its chemically combined water. The resulting material, commonly known as "plaster of Paris," is mixed with water and other ingredients and sandwiched between two sheets of specially manufactured paper to form various types of gypsum board. The powdery, calcined material may also be formulated and packaged for use as gypsum plaster or cement.

Gypsum manufacturers began incorporating recycled paper facings into gypsum board more than 50 years ago, while synthetic gypsum was first integrated into the core of gypsum board almost a quarter of a century ago. It is this constant desire to improve the basic gypsum product line that has driven the gypsum manufacturing industry to be a leader in the production of environmentally conscious building materials. Mined gypsum has been the traditional raw material used for drywall and plaster products. In the past few decades, however, more and more "synthetic" or "recaptured" gypsum has been used in the manufacturing process. Advanced processes, many developed by USG, enable the conversion of certain industrial waste products to form this synthetic gypsum.

For example, many of our nation's power plants burn coal, which emits sulfur dioxide and other pollutants. The technology used to capture and treat these harmful emissions—called "flue gas desulfurization" (FGD)—creates a residual product that can be purified and processed to form high-performance synthetic gypsum. This material delivers all the durability, fire resistance, low cost and ease of installation of naturally occurring gypsum rock.

Gypsum boards are produced using a highly automated, continuous process. After the paper-sandwiched gypsum core has set, the boards are cut to length, dried, prefinished as required, and packaged for shipment. Rigorous quality-control measures are applied throughout the manufacturing process.

Cement board products have some of the same characteristics as gypsum board, with the added advantage of moisture resistance. At USG, they are formed in a continuous process using aggregated Portland cement slurry, with polymer-coated, glass-fiber mesh completely wrapping the edges and front and back surfaces. Cement board is most typically used as a substrate beneath ceramic tile on walls and floors. A wide variety of board sizes are available for floor, wall, ceiling and countertop installations.

The ongoing advancement of gypsum construction products depends on maintaining quality, while reducing construction time and cost. This is the focus of specialists at the USG Research and Technology Innovation Center.

Products for Manufactured Housing and Industrialized Construction

USG provides a wide assortment of products specifically designed for use in manufactured housing and industrialized applications. Examples include gypsum board, joint treatments, metal beads and trims, special sealants, primers, cement board and texture products, all distributed under the SHEETROCK MH brand.

Industrial Products

LEVELROCK **Brand Floor Underlayment** Poured gypsum floor underlayment systems provide an economical way to achieve lightweight, fire-resistant, sound-rated, self-leveling floors in residential and light-commercial construction. Gypsum floor underlayment can be applied to a variety of substrates for both new construction and rehab flooring. Typical applications are less labor-intensive than many other types of construction and provide the additional advantages of high fire ratings and sound isolation that characterize gypsum systems. Other benefits of gypsum floor underlayments (unmatched by other commonly specified underlayment):

- Compressive strengths up to 5,000 psi. They can be applied over plywood at thicknesses of only 0.75 inches.

- Crack-free surfaces. In addition, their slight expansive nature seals openings around pipes and other penetrations to enhance sound control.

- Quick installation. Up to 30,000 SF can be installed in a day, and fast setting permits the return of light construction traffic within hours.

17

To learn how gypsum floor underlayments can save money and provide project solutions, visit **usg.com**.

Plaster Casting and Glass-Fiber Reinforced Gypsum Products USG Moulding Plaster and HYDROCAL Brand White Gypsum Cement are ornamental plasters for specialized cast work, such as ornamental trim, running cornices, and castings. HYDROCAL Brand FGR-95 Gypsum Cement is designed for use with chopped glass fibers or glass fiber mat to fabricate lightweight, fire-resistant decorated shapes, architectural elements, column covers, cornices and trims.

Agricultural and Landscaping Products USG's Industrial Gypsum Division has many other specialty products for diverse applications such as: agricultural soil supplements, landscaping erosion control, plastic and pharmaceutical fillers, bridge deck repair and more.

Online Tools & Contact Information

USG provides a variety of online tools to help building professionals gather product information and specifications, compare products against relevant codes and regulations, and review design and application ideas and effective installation procedures. The website is continuously updated to ensure that it contains the most current and accurate data. Information is presented in ways that are easy to access and apply.

Visitors may access our corporate homepage at **usg.com** and then easily navigate across the site to topics of particular interest. Or, they may go directly to selected topics by opening the following application- and product-specific pages:

downwithdust.com

getmoldfacts.com

gypsumsolutions.com

levelrock.com

usgdesignstudio.com

seismicceilings.com

sheetrocktools.com

sustainableceilings.com

Appendix

Agencies & Organizations

ACI	ACI International (American Concrete Institute) P.O. Box 9094 Zip code 48333 38800 Country Club Drive Farmington Hills, MI 48331	Phone: 248-848-3700 Fax: 248-848-3701 Website: www.concrete.org E-mail: BKStore@concrete.org
AGC	Associated General Contractors of America 2300 Wilson Boulevard, Suite 400 Arlington, VA 22201	Phone: 703-548-3118 Fax: 703-548-3119 Website: www.agc.org E-mail: info@agc.org
AFPA	American Forest & Paper Association 1111 19th Street NW, Suite 800 Washington, DC 20036	Phone: 202-463-2700 Fax: 202-463-2785 Website: www.afandpa.org E-mail: info@afandpa.org
AIA	American Institute of Architects 1735 New York Avenue NW Washington, DC 20006	Phone: 202-626-7300 Fax: none Website: www.aia.org E-mail: aiaonline@aiamail.aia.org
A Ins. A	American Insurance Association 1130 Connecticut Avenue NW, Suite 1000 Washington, DC 20036	Phone: 202-828-7100 Fax: 202-293-1219 Website: www.aiadc.org E-mail: info@aiadc.org
AIHA	American Industrial Hygiene Association 2700 Prosperity Avenue, Suite 250 Fairfax, VA 22031	Phone: 703-849-8888 FAX: 703-207-3561 Website: www.aiha.org Email: infonet@aiha.org
AISI	American Iron and Steel Institute 1140 Connecticut Avenue NW, Suite 705 Washington, DC 20036	Phone: 202-452-7100 Fax: 202-463-6573 Website: www.steel.org E-mail: none
ANSI	American National Standards Institute 25 West 43rd Street, 4th Floor New York, NY 10036	Phone: 212-642-4900 Fax: 212-398-0023 Website: www.ansi.org E-mail: info@ansi.org
APA	APA, The Engineered Wood Association (formerly: American Plywood Association) 7011 South 19th Street Tacoma, WA 98466-5333	Phone: 253-565-6600 Fax: 253-565-7265 Website: www.apawood.org E-mail: help@apawood.org
ASA	Acoustical Society of America 2 Huntington Quadrangle, Suite INO1 Melville, NY 11747-4502	Phone: 516-576-2360 Fax: 516-576-2377 Website: http://asa.aip.org E-mail: asa@aip.org
ASC	Adhesive and Sealant Council, Inc. 7101 Wisconsin Avenue Suite 990 Bethesda, MD 20814	Phone: 301-986-9700 Fax: 301-986-9795 Website: www.ascouncil.org E-mail: info@ascouncil.org

ASHRAE	American Society of Heating, Refrigerating and Air Conditioning Engineers 1791 Tullie Circle NE Atlanta, GA 30329	Phone: 800-527-4723 or 404-636-8400 Fax: 404-321-5478 Website: www.ashrae.org E-mail: ashrae@ashrae.org
ASSE	American Society of Safety Engineers 1800 E. Oakton Street Des Plaines, IL 60018	Phone: 847-699-2929 Fax: 847-768-3434 Website: www.asse.org E-mail: customerservice@asse.org
ASTM	American Society for Testing and Materials 100 Barr Harbor Drive West Conshohocken, PA 19428-2959	Phone: 610-832-9585 Fax: 610-832-9555 Website: www.astm.org E-mail: service@astm.org
AWCI	Association of the Wall & Ceiling Industries International 513 West Broad Street, Suite 210 Falls Church, VA 22046	Phone: 703-538-1600 Fax: 703-534-8307 Website: www.awci.org E-mail: info@awci.org
BIA	Brick Industry Association (formerly: Brick Institute of America) 1850 Centennial Park Drive, Suite 301 Reston, VA 20191	Phone: 703-620-0010 Fax: 703-620-3928 Website: www.gobrick.com E-mail: brickinfo@bia.org
CISCA	Ceiling and Interior Systems Construction Association 405 Illinois Avenue, Unit 2B St. Charles, IL 60174	Phone: 630-584-1919 Fax: 630-584-2003 Website: www.cisca.org E-mail: cisca@cisca.org
CSI	Construction Specification Institute 99 Canal Center Plaza, Suite 300 Alexandria, VA 22314	Phone: 703-684-0300 or 800-689-2900 Fax: 703-684-0465 Website: www.csinet.org Email: csi@csinet.org
DWFC	Drywall Finishing Council, Inc. 11392 Park Lane Garden Grove, CA 92840	Phone: 909-595-2208 Fax: none Website: www.dwfc.org E-mail: none
EIMA	EIFS Industry Members Association 3000 Corporate Center Drive, Suite 270 Morrow, GA 30260	Phone: 800-294-3462 or 770-968-7945 Fax: 770-968-5818 Website: www.eima.com E-mail: lwidzowski@eima.com
GA	Gypsum Association 810 First Street NE, Suite 510 Washington, DC 20002	Phone: 202-289-5440 Fax: 202-289-3707 Website: www.gypsum.org E-mail: info@gypsum.org

GSA	U.S. General Services Administration 1800 F Street NW Washington, DC 20405	Phone: 202-501-0800 Fax: 202-219-1243 Website: www.gsa.gov E-mail: none
HUD	U.S. Department of Housing & Urban Development 451 Seventh Street SW Washington, DC 20410	Phone: 202-708-1112 Fax: 202-619-8129 Website: www.hud.gov E-mail: none
ICC	International Code Council 500 New Jersey Avenue NW, 6th Floor Washington DC 20001-2070	Phone: 888-422-7233 Fax: 202-783-2348 Website: www.iccsafe.org E-mail: webmaster@iccsafe.org
ML/SFA	Metal Lath/Steel Framing Association; now a division of National Association of Architectural Metal Manufacturers (see NAAMM)	
NAAMM	National Association of Architectural Metal Manufacturers 800 Roosevelt Road Building C, Suite 312 Glen Ellyn, IL 60137	Phone: 630-942-6591 Fax: 630-790-3095 Website: www.naamm.org E-mail: info@naamm.org
NAHB	National Association of Home Builders 1201 15th Street NW Washington, DC 20005	Phone: 800-368-5242 or 202-266-8200 Fax: 202-266-8400 Website: www.nahb.com E-mail: info@nahb.com
NCMA	National Concrete Masonry Association 13750 Sunrise Valley Drive Herndon, VA 20171-4662	Phone: 703-713-1900 Fax: 703-713-1910 Website: www.ncma.org E-mail: ncma@ncma.org
NCSBCS	National Conference of States on Building Codes and Standards 505 Huntmar Park Drive, Suite 210 Herndon, VA 20170	Phone: 703-437-0100 Fax: 703-481-3596 Website: www.ncsbcs.org E-mail: none
NEMA	National Electrical Manufacturers Association 1300 North 17th Street, Suite 1752 Rosslyn, VA 22209	Phone: 703-841-3200 Fax: 703-841-5900 Website: www.nema.org E-mail: none
NFPA	National Fire Protection Association 1 Batterymarch Park Quincy, MA 02169-7471	Phone: 617-770-3000 Fax: 617-770-0700 Website: www.nfpa.org E-mail: custserv@nfpa.org
NFoPA	National Forest Products Association This organization is now American Forest & Paper Association (see AFPA)	

NIBS	National Institute of Building Sciences 1090 Vermont Avenue NW, Suite 700 Washington, DC 20005-4905	Phone: 202-289-7800 Fax: 202-289-1092 Website: www.nibs.org E-mail: nibs@nibs.org
NLS	National Lime Association 200 North Glebe Road, Suite 800 Arlington, VA 22203	Phone: 703-243-5463 Fax: 703-243-5489 Website: www.lime.org E-mail: natlime@lime.org
NSC	National Safety Council 1121 Spring Drive Itasca, IL 60143-3201	Phone: 630-285-1121 Fax: 630-285-1315 Website: www.nsc.org E-mail: info@nsc.org
NTIS	National Technical Information Service U.S. Department of Commerce 5285 Port Royal Road Springfield, VA 22161	Phone: 703-605-6000 Fax: 703-605-6900 Website: www.ntis.gov E-mail: info@ntis.gov
NWPCA	National Wooden Pallet & Container Association 1421 Prince Street, Suite 340 Alexandria, VA 22314-2805	Phone: 703-519-6104 Fax: 703-519-4720 Website: www.nwpca.com E-mail: none
OSHA	Occupational Safety & Health Administration U.S. Department of Labor 200 Constitution Avenue Washington, DC 20210	Phone: 800-321-6742 Fax: none Website: www.osha.gov E-mail: none
PCA	Portland Cement Association 5420 Old Orchard Road Skokie, IL 60077	Phone: 847-966-6200 Fax: 847-966-8389 Website: www.cement.org E-mail: info@cement.org
PDCA	Painting and Decorating Contractors Of America 1801 Park 270 Drive, Suite 220 St. Louis, MO 63146	Phone: 800-332-7322 or 314-514-7322 Fax: 314-514-9417 Website: www.pdca.org E-mail: memberservices@pdca.org
RAL	Riverbank Acoustical Laboratories 1512 S. Batavia Avenue Geneva, IL 60134	Phone: 630-232-0104 Fax: 630-232-0138 Website: http://riverbank.alion-science.com E-mail: riverbankinquiries@alionscience.com
SIPA	Structural Insulated Panel Association P.O. Box 1699 Gig Harbor, WA 98335	Phone: 253-858-7472 Fax: 253-858-0272 Website: www.sips.org E-mail: help@sips.org

TCNA	Tile Council of North America, Inc. 100 Clemson Research Boulevard Anderson, SC 29625	Phone: 864-646-8453 Fax: 864-646-2821 Website: www.tileusa.com E-mail:info@tileusa.com
TPI	Truss Plate Institute 218 N. Lee Street, Suite 312 Alexandria, VA 22314	Phone: 703-683-1010 Fax: 866-501-4012 Website: www.tpinst.org E-mail: info@tpinst.org
UL	Underwriters' Laboratories, Inc. 333 Pfingsten Road Northbrook, IL 60062-2096	Phone: 847-272-8800 Fax: 847-272-8129 Website: www.ul.com E-mail: cec@us.ul.com
ULC	Underwriters' Laboratories of Canada 7 Underwriters Road Toronto, ON M1R 3B4 Canada	Phone: 866-937-3852 or 416-757-3611 Fax: 416-757-8727 Website: www.ulc.ca E-mail: customerservice@ulc.ca
WHI	Intertek Testing Services 3933 U.S. Route 11 Cortland, NY 13045	Phone: 607-753-6711 Fax: 607-756-9891 Website: www.intertek-etlsemko. com E-mail: icenter@intertek.com

Fixture Attachment—Drywall & Plaster Systems

Fixture Attachment Load Table[3]

Fastener Type	Size in.	mm	Base Assembly	Allowable Withdrawal Resistance lbf.	N[1]	Allowable Shear Resistance lbf.	N[1]
toggle bolt or hollow	1/8	3.2	1/2" gypsum base or panels	20	89	40	178
wall fastener	3/16	4.8		30	134	50	223
	1/4	6.4		40	178	60	267
	1/8	3.2	1/2" gypsum base or panels	70	312	100	445
	3/16	4.8	& 25 ga. steel studs	80	356	125	556
	1/4	6.4		155	690	175	779
no. 8 sheet metal screw	—	—	1/2" gypsum base or panels	50	223	80	356
type S bugle head screw	—	—	& 25 ga. steel base	60	267	100	445
type S-12 bugle head screw	—	—	1/2" gypsum base or panels & 20 ga. steel insert	85	378	135	601
type S pan head screw	—	—	25 ga. steel to 25 ga. steel	70	312	120	534
two bolts welded to	3/16	4.8	grab bar attachment	175	779	200	890
steel insert	1/4	6.4		200	890	250	1113
bolt welded to 1-1/2"	1/4	6.4	plumber's bracket	200	890	250	1113
channel	5/16	7.9	see drawing on page 140	200	890	300	1334
plug and screw	#6	—	metal or gypsum	10	45	40	178
	#8	—	lath and plaster(2)	20	89	50	222
	#12	—		30	133	60	267
toggle bolt or	1/8	3.2	Metal or gypsum	75	334	50	222
hollow wall fastener	3/16	4.8	lath and plaster(2)	125	556	140	623
	1/4	6.4		175	778	150	667

(1)lbf and Newton for force measurements in American standard and SI units respectively. (2) Plaster having compressive strength of at least 900 psi was used to develop this data. (3) Values for steel system connections are based on standard gage thicknesses of 0.0179 inches for 25 ga., and 0.0329 inches for 20 ga. material. Consult the manufactured of the framing for different thicknesses of materials

Drywall, Plaster & Acoustical Ceiling Installation Tolerances

Standards of acceptability for installation of framing, drywall panels and joint treatment vary in different parts of the United States. Nevertheless, several organizations, including the Metal Lath/Steel Framing Association, Gypsum Association and American Society for Testing and Materials (ASTM), have published recommendations, standards and/or tolerances that may be required for a specific project.

Similarly, references for tolerances and quality in plasterwork and acoustical ceilings are available. References for tolerances and quality in plasterwork have been published by AIA MasterSpec and Diehl's "Manual of Lathing and Plastering." For acoustical ceilings construction, see the appropriate ASTM standards (page 474) or "Code of Practices for Acoustical Ceiling System Installation" in the Ceilings and Interior Systems Construction Association (CISCA) *Ceiling Systems Handbook.*

Contractors and their customers should reach agreement before starting the project regarding which tolerance standards will be used to judge acceptability of the work.

Gypsum Board Screw Usage

The number of fasteners used to install gypsum board varies with framing spacing, screw spacing, panel orientation and panel size. The charts below show estimated screw usage per thousand square feet of gypsum board for both horizontal and vertical board attachment. Allowance should be made for loss.

Horizontal Board Attachment (Screws/1000 ft.^{2})

Framing Spacing

4' x 8' Board	Screw Spacing (Inches)			
	8	12	16	24
8″	2844	2031	1625	1219
12″	1969	1406	1125	844
16″	1531	1094	875	656
24″	1094	781	625	469
4' x 10' Board				
8″	2800	2000	1600	1200
12″	1925	1375	1100	825
16″	1488	1063	850	638
24″	1050	750	600	450
4' x 12' Board				
8″	2780	1980	1590	1190
12″	1900	1360	1090	820
16″	1460	1050	840	630
24″	1030	730	590	440

Vertical Board Attachment (Screws/1000 ft.^{2})

Framing Spacing

4' x 8' Board	Screw Spacing (Inches)			
	8	12	16	24
8″	2844	1969	1531	1094
12″	2031	1406	1094	781
16″	1625	1125	875	625
24″	1219	844	656	469
4' x 10' Board				
8″	2800	1925	1488	1050
12″	2000	1375	1063	750
16″	1600	1100	850	600
24″	1200	825	638	450
4' x 12' Board				
8″	2771	1896	1458	1021
12″	1979	1354	1042	729
16″	1583	1083	833	583
24″	1188	813	625	438

Metric Terms & Equivalents

Basic Units

Quantity	Metric (SI) Unit	Symbol	U.S.A. equivalent (nom.)[1]
Length	millimeter	mm	0.039 in.
	meter	m	3.281 ft.
			1.094 yd.
Area	meter	m²	10.763 ft.²
			1.195 yd.²
Volume	meter	m³	35.314 ft.³
			1.307 yd.³
Volume (Fluid)	liter	L	33.815 oz.
			0.264 gal.
Mass (Weight)	gram	g	0.035 oz.
	kilogram	kg	2.205 lb.
	ton	t	2,204 lb.
			1.102 tons
Force	newton	N	0.225 lbf.
Temperature (Interval)	kelvin	K	1.8°F
	degree celsius	°C	1.8°F
Temperature	celsius	°C	(°F-32)5/9
Thermal Resistance	K•m²		5.679 ft.²•hr•°F
	W		Btu
Heat Transfer	watt	W	3.412 Btu/hr.
Pressure	kilopascal	kPa	0.145 lb./in.² (psi)
	pascal	Pa	20.890 lb./ft.² (psf)

(1) To convert U.S.A. units to SI units, divide by U.S.A. equivalent

Prefixes (Order of Magnitude)

Prefix	Symbol	Factor
mega	M	$1000000 = 10^{+6}$
kilo	k	$1000 = 10^{+3}$
centi[1]	c	$0.01 = 10^{-2}$
milli	m	$0.001 = 10^{-3}$
micro	μ(mu)	$0.000001 = 10^{-6}$

(1) Limited use only.

Metric Conversion

The table on the following page provides metric equivalents for the dimensions of USG products. "Soft" conversions merely apply a conversion factor that translates feet and inches (according to which the products were manufactured) into metric units; "hard" metric measurements are given for products actually manufactured in metric sizes.

Metric Equivalents

Dimension	Conversion Type[1]	in. or ft.	mm[2]
SHEETROCK Brand Gypsum Panels			
Thickness	Soft	1/4"	6
		3/8"	10
		1/2"	13
		5/8"	16
		3/4"	19
		1"	25
Width	Hard	24"	600
		48"	1200
Length	Hard	8'	2400
		10'	3000
		12'	3600
USG Ceilings Ceiling Tiles			
Thickness	Soft	3/4"	19
		5/8"	16
Width	Hard	24"	600
		48"	1200
Length	Hard	24"	600
		48"	1200
Steel Stud Framing			
Thickness (gauge)[3]	Soft	0.0209 (25)	0.53
		0.0270 (22)	0.69
		0.0329 (20)	0.84
Depth	Soft	1-5/8"	41
		2-1/2"	64
		3-1/2"	89
		3-5/8"	92
		4"	102
Length	Hard	8'	2400
		10'	3000
		12'	3600
Mineral Wool Insulation			
Thickness	Soft	1"	25
		1-1/2"	38
		2"	51
		3"	76
		4"	102
		6"	152
Width	Hard	16"	400
		24"	600
Length	Hard	48"	1200

(1) Conversion Type: "Soft" is metric relabeling with no physical change of dimension; "hard" is a physical change to the metric dimension shown.
(2) Conversion factors: Inches X 25.4 = mm; Feet X 304.8 = mm.
(3) Thickness shown is for standard steel gauge. Consult SSMA documents for information regarding current steel framing designations and base steel thickness. Some drywall steel is thinner than the standard gauge specified.
Notes: Availability: Items above are not stocked in metric lengths or widths. Minimum quantity orders may be required. Lead time should be determined; upcharges may apply. Geographic availability may vary and should be verified for the project location.
Lengths: Shown on SHEETROCK Brand Gypsum Panels and steel stud framing for illustration purposes only.
Framing Spacing: 16" o.c. converts to 400 mm o.c.; 24" converts to 600 mm o.c.

Specification Standards

The following listings contain existing standard specifications that apply to USG materials described in this handbook. Where ASTM, local codes, etc., require product variance, consult your USG representative.

Specification Standards

Product	ASTM Designation
Plaster	
RED TOP gypsum plaster	C28
RED TOP wood fiber plaster	C28
STRUCTO-LITE plaster	C28
RED TOP gauging plaster	C28
RED TOP keenes cement	
regular	C61
quick trowel	C61
STRUCTO-GAUGE plaster	C28
STRUCTO-BASE plaster	C28
IMPERIAL plaster	C587
DIAMOND plaster	C587
Gypsum Lathing	
ROCKLATH plaster base 3/8″ & 1/2″	C37
IMPERIAL gypsum base 1/2″ & 5/8″	C588
Lime	
RED TOP and GRAND PRIZE finish limes	C206 type N
IVORY finish lime	C206 type S
Gypsum Panels[1]	
SHEETROCK Brand (plain) (foil-back)	C1396
SHEETROCK Brand sq. edge	C1396
SHEETROCK Brand tap. edge	C1396
SHEETROCK Brand bev. edge	C1396
5/8″ SHEETROCK Brand FIRECODE Core	C1396
SHEETROCK Brand FIRECODE C core	C1396
SHEETROCK Brand ULTRACODE panels	C1396
SHEETROCK Brand gypsum coreboard panels	C1396
SHEETROCK Brand shaft wall liner panels	C1396
SHEETROCK Brand exterior gypsum ceiling board	C1396
SHEETROCK Brand interior gypsum ceiling board	C1396
FIBEROCK Brand Abuse-Resistant panels	C1278
FIBEROCK Brand Abuse-Resistant VHI panels	C1278
FIBEROCK Brand Aqua-Tough Interior panels	C1278
FIBEROCK Brand Tile Backerboard panels	C1278
FIBEROCK Brand Underlayment panels	C1278
Cement Panels	
DUROCK Brand cement board	C1325, C1186 (ANSI A 118.9)
Roof Boards	
SECUROCK Roof board	C1278
Sheathing	
SHEETROCK Brand gypsum sheathing	C1396
FIBEROCK Brand Aqua-Tough Exterior sheathing	C1396
Joint Treatment	
SHEETROCK Brand joint compounds	C475

Specification Standards (continued)

Product	ASTM Designation
Accessories	
Structural steel joists, runners	C645, C955, A568, A653, A792 (alum.-zinc coating), A591 (galv. coating)
25, 22 ga. studs, 25, 22 ga. runners	C645, A568 (steel), A653, A463 (alum. coating), A792 (alum.-zinc coating) A591 (galv. coating)
20 ga. studs, 20 ga. runners	C645, A568 (steel), A653 (galv. coating), A792 (alum.-zinc coating) A591 (galv. coating)
Resilient channels	A568 (steel), A525 (galv. coating), A792 (alum.-zinc coating)
Zinc Control Joints	C841
Dur-A-Bead corner bead	C1047
Sheetrock Brand metal trims	C1047
Shaft wall/area separation wall studs	A653 A792 (alum.-zinc coating) A591 (galv. coating)
Drywall screws	C1002, C954
Sheetrock Brand acoustical sealant	C834
Acoustical Units—Prefabricated	
Cast ceiling panels	E1264
Water-felted ceiling panels	E1264
Ceiling Suspension System	
Donn	C635

(1) ASTMC1396 is the consolidated product standard for gypsum board products. It replaces separate standards C36, C79, C442, C630, C931, and C960. The obsolete standards may stil be used in the building code of some jurisdictions.

ASTM Application Standards

There are also standards for application of many of the products in this Handbook. See the specification standards listed below for more information.

Application Standards

Product	Application Standard
Standard Practice for Installation of Metal Ceiling Suspension Systems for Acoustical Tile and Lay-In Panels	C636
Specification for Installation of Steel Framing Members to Receive Screw-Attached Gypsum Panel Products	C754
Specification for Application and Finishing of Gypsum Board	C840
Specification for Installation of Interior Lathing and Furring	C841
Specification for Application of Interior Gypsum Plaster	C842
Specification for Application of Gypsum Veneer Plaster	C843
Specification for Application of Gypsum Base to Receive Gypsum Veneer Plaster	C844
Specification for Installation of Load-Bearing Steel Studs and Related Accessories	C1007
Specification for Application of Gypsum Sheathing	C1280
Standard Practice for Application of Ceiling Suspension Systems for Acoustical Tile and Lay-In Panels in Areas Requiring Moderate Seismic Restraint	E580

ASTM Standards for Performance Specifications & Test Methods

Performance Specifications and Test Methods

ASTM E84, Standard Test Method for Surface Burning Characteristics of Building Materials, describes the method of establishing Flame Spread and Smoke Developed values.

ASTM E119, Standard Test Methods for Fire Tests of Building Construction and Materials, describes the method of establishing fire-resistant hourly ratings for floor/ceiling and/or roof/ceiling construction assemblies. Underwriters Laboratories, Inc. Fire Resistance Designs are established under this test method.

ASTM E136, Standard Test Method for Behavior of Materials in a Vertical Tube Furnace at 750 °C, describes the method for determining the acceptability of a material for use in noncombustible construction.

Fed. Standard 209(E), Clean Room and Work Station Requirements for Controlled Environments, describes the method of establishing Clean Room Classification values. See also ISO 14644-1.

ASTM C367, Standard Test Methods for Strength Properties of Prefabricated Architectural Acoustical Tile or Lay-in Ceiling Panels, describes the method of establishing strength properties of acoustical ceiling tiles and panels.

ASTM E413, Standard Classification for Rating Sound Insulation, provides criteria to establish Ceiling Attenuation Class (CAC) of an acoustical ceiling, similar to STC ratings for walls.

ASTM C423, Standard Test Method for Sound Absorption and Sound Absorption Coefficients by the Reverberation Room Method, describes the method of establishing Noise Reduction Coefficient (NRC) values.

ASTM C473, Standard Test Methods for Physical Testing of Gypsum Panel Products, describes the test methods used to establish the physical cahacteristics of gypsum board and panel products.

ASTM C627, Standard Test method for Evaluating Ceramic Floor Tile installation Systems Using the Robinson Floor Type Tester, provides a standardized procedure for evaluating performance of ceramic floor tile installations under conditions similar to actual specific usages.

ASTM C635, Standard Specification for the Manufacture, Performance and Testing of Metal Suspension Systems for Acoustical Tile and Lay-in Panel Ceilings, provides classification criteria by load capacity, along with manufacturing tolerance, coating, and inspection criteria for suspension systems.

ASTM C636, Standard Practice for Installation of Metal Ceiling Suspension Systems for Acoustical Tile and Lay-In Panels, provides for the installation of individual components, such as hangers, carrying channels, main runners, cross runners, splines, assembly devices and ceiling fixtures.

ASTM C645, Standard Specification for Nonstructural Steel Framing Members, covers nonstructural steel framing members in interior construction assemblies

ASTM C754, Standard Specification for Installation of Steel Framing Members to Receive Screw-Attached Gypsum Panel Products, describes installation of drywall grid systems.

ASTM C840, Standard Specification for Application and Finishing of Gypsum Board, provides standard methods for hangin and finishing various type of gypsum board products.

ASTM C841, Standard Specification for Installation of Interior Lathing and Furring, is the installation standard for plaster and lath. It applies to plaster and lath ceilings.

ASTM 1177, Standard Specifications for Glass Mat Gypsum Substrate, covers the requirements for glass mat gypsum substrate designed to be used as exterior substrate or sheathing for weather barriers.

ASTM C1396, Standard Specifications for Gypsum Board, is a consolidated standard covering required properties for gypsum board. This standard consolidates and replaces ASTM Standards C36, C79, C442, C630, C931 and C960.

ASTM C1629 / C1629M – 06, Standard Classification for Abuse-Resistant Nondecorated Interior Gypsum Panel Products and Fiber-Reinforced Cement Panels, establishes classifications of abuse resistance based on minimum abuse-resistance performance of nondecorated interior gypsum panel products and fiber-reinforced cement panels (abuse-resistant wall panels).

ASTM E1110, Standard Classification for Determination of Articulation Class, provides criteria to establish ceiling Articulation Class (AC) of an acoustical ceiling, generally applies to open plan ceilings in lieu of a NRC rating.

ASTM E1111, Standard Test Method for Measuring the Interzone Attenuation of Ceiling Systems, describes the method of establishing Articulation Class (AC) values.

ASTM E1264, Standard Classification for Acoustical Ceiling Products (replaced Federal Spec. SS-S-118 "Sound Controlling Acoustical Tiles and Panels"), provides general classification by type and form, acoustical rating qualification, light reflectance coefficient qualification, and surface burning fire classification of acoustical ceiling tiles and panels for use in specifying a ceiling panel or tile.

ASTM E1414, Standard Test Method for Airborne Sound Attenuation Between Rooms Sharing a Common Ceiling Plenum (Adaptation of the AMA-I-II-1967 "Test Method for Ceiling Sound Transmission Test by Two-Room Method"), describes the method of establishing Ceiling Attenuation Class (CAC) values.

ASTM E1433, Standard Guide for Selection of Standards on Environmental Acoustics, is intended to assist acoustical consultants, architects, specifiers and others in understanding ASTM standards in environmental acoustics, as referenced in E413, E1110, E1264, etc.

ASTM E1477, Standard Test Method for Luminous Reflection Factor of Acoustical Materials by Use of Integrating-Sphere Reflectometers, describes the method of establishing Light Reflectance (LR) values.

ASTM E492, Standard Test Method for Laboratory Measurement of Impact, covers the laboratory measurement of impact sound transmission of floor-ceiling assemblies using a standardized tapping machine.

Products/UL Designations

The USG products listed below are identified in the UL Fire Resistance Directory by the designations shown.

Products/UL Designations

UL Type Designation	Drywall, Cement Board and Plaster Board Products
R	SHEETROCK Brand Gypsum Panels
SCX	SHEETROCK Brand Gypsum Panels, FIRECODE Core
C	SHEETROCK Brand Gypsum Panels, FIRECODE C Core
SCX	SHEETROCK Brand Gypsum Panels, FIRECODE Core, MOLD TOUGH
C	SHEETROCK Brand Gypsum Panels, FIRECODE C Core, MOLD TOUGH
AR	SHEETROCK Brand Abuse-Resistant Gypsum Panels
SLX	SHEETROCK Brand Gypsum Liner Panels
ULTRACODE	SHEETROCK Brand Gypsum Panels, ULTRACODE Core
SHX	SHEETROCK Brand Gypsum Sheathing, FIRECODE Core
USGX	SECUROCK Brand Glass-Mat Sheathing
IPR	IMPERIAL Brand Plaster Base
IP-X1	IMPERIAL Brand Plaster Base (Type X)
IP-X2	IMPERIAL Brand Plaster Base (Type C)
IP-X3	IMPERIAL Brand Plaster Base, ULTRACODE Core
FRX-G	FIBEROCK Brand Panels
FRX-G	Securock Roof Board
DCB	DUROCK Brand Cement Board
UL Type Designation	**Acoustical Tile and Panel Products**
FC-CB	Gypsum Lay-In Ceiling Panel
AP, AP-1	CAST FIRECODE Ceiling Product (SANDRIFT, CLIMAPLUS, FROST, GLACIER, "F" FISSURED Ceiling Panels) WET FELTED FIRECODE Ceiling Product (Fissured, Radar, Radar CLIMAPLUS Ceiling Panels)
FR-83	WET FELTED FIRECODE Ceiling Product (Illusion, Aspen, Fissured, Pebbled, Radar CLIMAPLUS, Radar CLIMAPLUS High NRC/CAC, Touchstone Ceiling Panels)
FR-83	WET FELTED FIRECODE Ceiling Product (Rock Face CLIMAPLUS)
FR-4	Radar Ceramic CLIMAPLUS
FR-2	WET FELTED FIRECODE Ceiling Product
M	Clean Room CLIMAPLUS
FR-X1	X Technology FIRECODE Ceiling Product (ECLIPSE CLIMAPLUS)
ASTRO-FR	X Technology FIRECODE Ceiling Product (ASTRO CLIMAPLUS)

Permeance—USG Products

Permeance—USG Products

Moisture Vapor Permeance

Product[1]	Finish	Perms[2,3]
Gypsum Panels		
3/8" SHEETROCK Brand Regular		35
1/2" SHEETROCK Brand Regular		35
1/2" SHEETROCK Brand Regular	1-coat flat latex paint	30
1/2" SHEETROCK Brand Regular	2-coats flat latex paint	30
1/2" SHEETROCK Brand Regular	2-coats gloss enamel (oil)	1
5/8" SHEETROCK Brand Regular		30
5/8" SHEETROCK Brand FIRECODE Core		25
1/2" SHEETROCK Brand FIRECODE C Core		30
5/8" SHEETROCK Brand FIRECODE C Core		25
1/2" SHEETROCK Brand MOLD TOUGH		30
5/8" SHEETROCK Brand MOLD TOUGH FIRECODE C Core		30
5/8" SHEETROCK Brand MOLD TOUGH FIRECODE Core		25
1" SHEETROCK Brand Gypsum Liner Panel		25
Gypsum Base		
1/2" IMPERIAL Brand		30
1/2" IMPERIAL Brand	DIAMOND Brand Veneer Finish	25
1/2" IMPERIAL Brand	1 Coat IMPERIAL Veneer Finish	5
1/2" IMPERIAL Brand	IMPERIAL Brand Veneer Basecoat/ IMPERIAL Brand Veneer Finish	8
5/8" IMPERIAL Brand		25
1/2" IMPERIAL Brand FIRECODE C		30
5/8" IMPERIAL Brand FIRECODE C		25
3/8" gypsum base and 1/2" gypsum plaster, metal lath and 3/4" gypsum plaster		20
Gypsum Sheathing		
1/2" SHEETROCK Brand Gypsum Sheathing, Regular		25
1/2" SECUROCK Glass-Mat Sheating		33
5/8" SECUROCK Glass-Mat Sheathing FIRECODE Core		26
1/2" FIBEROCK AQUA-TOUGH Exterior Sheathing		20
5/8" FIBEROCK AQUA-TOUGH Exterior Sheathing		25

(1) All foil-back products, less than 0.06 perms.
(2) All tests comply with ASTM E96 (desiccant method).
(3) Grain per sq. ft. per in. of water vapor pressure difference (grain/ft.^{2}-h.-in.-Hg) (grams/m^2/24 hours).
(4) Comply with Federal Specification CCC-2-408C, Type I
(5) Data based on physical testing. Values greater than 10 were rounded to the nearest 5 perms. Values less than 10 were rounded to the nearest integer.

Thermal Coefficients of Linear Expansion of Common Building Materials

Unrestrained 40°–100°F. (4°–38°C)

Material	Coefficient x10⁻⁶in./ (in.°F)	x10⁻⁶ mm/ (mm.°C)
Gypsum Panels and Bases	9.0	16.2
Gypsum Plaster (sanded 100:2, 100:3)	7.0	12.6
Wood Fiber Plaster (sanded 100:1)	8.0	14.4
STRUCTO-LITE Plaster	7.3	13.1
Aluminum, Wrought	12.8	23.0
Steel, Medium	6.7	12.1
Brick, Masonry	3.1	5.6
Cement, Portland	5.9	10.6
Concrete	7.9	14.2
Fir (parallel to fiber)	2.1	3.8
Fir (perpendicular to fiber)	3.2	5.8

Hygrometric Coefficients of Expansion (Unrestrained)

	Inches/Inch/% R.H. (5%–90% R.H.)
Gypsum Panels and Bases	7.2×10^{-6}
Gypsum Plaster (sanded 100:2, 100:3)	1.5×10^{-6}
Wood Fiber Plaster (sanded 100:1)	2.8×10^{-6}
STRUCTO-LITE Plaster	4.8×10^{-6}
Vermiculite Gypsum Plaster (sanded 100:2)	3.8×10^{-6}

Thermal Resistance Coefficients of Building & Insulating Materials[1]

Thickness			Density		Resistance (R-Value)	
in	mm	Product	lb/ft³	kg/m³	hr.ft.²°F/Btu	K.m²/W
2, 2-1/2	50.8-63.5	Mineral Wool Insulation	2.5	48.1	7.7-9.3	1.23
3, 3-1/2	76.2-88.9	Mineral Wool Insulation	2.5	48.1	11.1-13.0	1.94
5-1/4, 6	133.4-152.4	Mineral Wool Insulation	2.5	48.1	19.4-22.2	3.35
1	25.4	Extruded Polystyrene Insulation	2.2	35.2	5.00	0.88
1/2	12.7	SHEETROCK Brand Gypsum Panels	43	690.2	0.45	0.08
5/8	15.9	SHEETROCK Brand Gypsum Panels	43	690.2	0.56	0.10
1/2	12.7	SHEETROCK Brand Gypsum Panels, FIRECODE C Core	50	800.9	0.45	0.08
5/8	15.9	SHEETROCK Brand Gypsum Panels, FIRECODE and FIRECODE C Core	50	800.9	0.56	0.10
1/2	12.7	IMPERIAL Brand Gypsum Base	43	690.2	0.45	0.08
5/8	15.9	IMPERIAL Brand Gypsum Base	43	690.2	0.56	0.10
1/2	12.7	IMPERIAL Brand Gypsum Base, FIRECODE C Core	50	800.9	0.45	0.08
5/8	15.9	IMPERIAL Brand Gypsum Base, FIRECODE and FIRECODE C Core	50	800.9	0.56	0.10
3/8	9.5	ROCKLATH Plaster Base	50	800.9	0.32	0.06
1/2	12.7	SHEETROCK Brand Gypsum Sheathing	50	800.9	0.45	0.08
1/2	12.7	SECUROCK Glass-Mat Sheathing	48	769	0.5	0.09
5/8	15.9	SECUROCK Glass-Mat Sheathing FIRECODE Core	52	833	0.5	0.09
1/2	12.7	Sanded Plaster	105	1681.9	0.09	0.02
1/2	12.7	Plaster with Lightweight Aggregate	45	720.8	0.32	0.06
4	101.6	Common Brick	120	1922.2	0.80	0.14
1/2	12.7	DUROCK Brand Cement Board	72	1153.3	0.26	0.05
1/2	12.7	DUROCK Brand Exterior Cement Board	72	1153.3	0.26	0.05
4	101.6	Face Brick	130	2082.4	0.44	0.08
1	25.4	Portland Cement Stucco with Sand Aggregate	116	1858.1	0.20	0.04
4	101.6	Concrete Block, 3-oval Core, Cinder Aggregate			1.11	0.20
8	203.2	Concrete Block, 3-oval Core, Cinder Aggregate			1.72	0.30
12	304.8	Concrete Block, 3-oval Core, Cinder Aggregate			1.89	0.33
—	—	Vapor-Permeable Felt			0.06	0.01
—	—	Vapor-Retarder Plastic Film		Negl.	—	
1	25.4	Stone			0.08	0.01
1 x 8	25.4-203.2	Wood Drop Siding			0.79	0.14
3/4 x 10	19.1-254.0	Beveled Wood Siding			1.05	0.18
3/4, 3-1/2	19.1-88.9	Plain Air Space, non-reflective[2]			0.92	0.17
		Wet Felted Ceiling Tiles				
		Cast Ceilings Tiles				
		X Tech Mineral Wool Ceiling Tiles				
		Fiberglass Ceiling Tiles				

(1) All factors based on data from 1981 ASHRAE Handbook of Fundamentals, Factors at 75°, mean temperature. (2) Conditions: heat, flow horizontal; mean temperature 50°F; temperature differential 30°F; E (emissivity) 0 82.

USG Plant Locations

USG Plant Locations

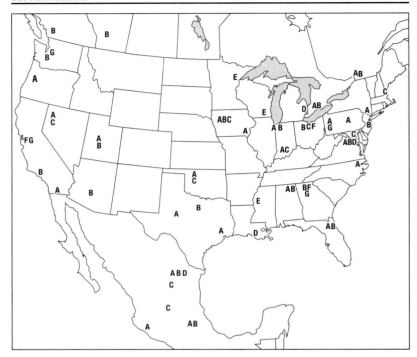

Legend	
A	Gypsum Board
B	Joint Treatment and Textures
C	Gypsum Plasters
D	Cement Board Products
E	Acoustical Ceilings
F	Acoustical Suspension Systems and Specialty Products
G	Trim

A Gypsum Board

Aliquippa, PA
Baltimore, MD
Bridgeport, AL
East Chicago, IN
Empire, NV
Fort Dodge, IA
Galena Park, TX
Hagersville, Ontario, Canada
Jacksonville, FL
Monterrey, Mexico
Montreal, Quebec, Canada
Norfolk, VA

Plaster City, CA
Puebla, Mexico
Ranier, OR
Shoals, IN
Sigurd, UT
Southard, OK
Sperry, IA
Stony Point, NY
Sweetwater, TX
Tecoman, Mexico
Washingtonville, PA

B Joint Treatment and Textures

Auburn, WA
Baltimore, MD
Bridgeport, AL
Calgary, Alberta, Canada
Chamblee, GA
Dallas, TX
East Chicago, IN
Fort Dodge, IA
Gypsum, OH
Hagerville, Ontario, Canada

Jacksonville, FL
Monterrey, Mexico
Montreal, Quebec, Canada
Phoenix, AZ
Port Reading, NJ
Puebla, Mexico
Sigurd, UT
Surrey, British Columbia, Canada
Torrance, CA

C Gypsum Plasters

Baltimore, MD
Boston, MA
Fort Dodge, IA
Gypsum, OH
Puebla, Mexico

San Luis Potosi, Mexico
Shoals, IN
Saltillo, Mexico
Southard, OK
Empire, NV

D Cement Board

Baltimore, MD
Detroit, MI
Monterrey, Mexico

New Orleans, LA

E Acoustical Ceilings

Cloquet, MN
Greenville, MS

Walworth, WI

F Acoustical Suspension Systems and Specialty Products

Cartersville, GA
Oakville, Ontario, Canada

Stockton, CA
Westlake, OH

G Trim

Auburn, WA
Stockton, CA

Wierton, WV
Cartersville, GA

Glossary

abrasion resistance Durability that enables interior partitions in high-traffic areas to resist surface damage from contact with people, furniture, etc. Achieved by increasing the surface and core strength of the partition facing, by applying a coating or wall covering over the surface, or by increasing the thickness of the partition facing.

absorption The taking up and holding (or sometimes dissipating) of matter or energy, as a sponge takes up water. Absorption is the opposite of reflection. *See also* **porosity**.

abuse resistance A property that helps protect a material such as gypsum board from surface damage (abrasion and indentation).

accelerator An additive that shortens the setting time for gypsum plasters or setting-type joint compounds.

acoustical ceiling A system with highly effective sound-absorbing and/or sound attenuating qualities.

acoustical ceiling board (lay-in panel) Acoustical material used in conjunction with a lay-in grid system, usually in 24" x 24" or larger panels.

acoustical consultant (acoustical engineer, acoustician) A trained professional qualified to recommend solutions to sound problems and to design facilities to meet specific sound criteria.

acoustical panels Normally a 24" x 24" or larger piece of pre-finished material (with various surface finishes) installed in a suspension system to provide improved sound absorption.

acoustical sealant Special caulking material designed to seal gaps and cracks to reduce sound flanking in an assembly. For example, SHEETROCK acoustical sealant from USG.

acoustical tile Normally a 12" x 12" or 12" x 24" piece of pre-finished material (with various surface finishes) installed in a concealed suspension system or adhered to a ceiling or upper wall surface to provide sound absorption.

acoustic privacy Prevention of the passage of airborne sound—and dampening of impact sound. Achieved by installing assemblies between two spaces.

acoustics A science dealing with the production, control, transmission, reception and effects of sound, and the process of hearing.

admixture Any substance added to a plaster component or plaster for the purpose of modifying its properties.

aggregate Sand, gravel, crushed stone or other material that is a main constituent of Portland cement concrete and aggregated gypsum plaster. Also, polystyrene, perlite and vermiculite particles used in texture finishes.

AIA American Insurance Association, successor to the National Board of Fire Underwriters and Nonprofit Organization of Insurance Companies. Also *American Institute of Architects*.

airborne sound   Sound traveling through air and subsequently through partitions and openings.

all-purpose joint compound   A material formulated and manufactured for use in taping and/or finishing gypsum panel products.

ambient light   The generally available surrounding or pervading light in an interior space, including outside light entering through windows.

amplitude (sound)   The maximum pressure displacement from the at-rest position of the particles of the transmitting medium. The amplitude of a sound wave is determined by the energy of the sound source.

anchor   A metal securing device embedded or driven into masonry, concrete, steel or wood.

anchor bolt   A heavy, threaded bolt embedded in a building's foundation to secure the sill to the foundation wall, or the bottom plate of the exterior wall to the concrete floor slab.

annular ring nail   A deformed shank nail with improved holding qualities specially designed for use with gypsum board.

ANSI   American National Standards Institute, a nonprofit national technical association that publishes standards covering definitions, test methods, recommended practices and materials specifications. Formerly the American Standards Association (ASA) and the United States of America Standards Institute (USASI).

architectural acoustics   The handling of sound within a single area (reflection, reverberation, absorption, etc.). It does not address sound transmission through elements of the structure.

Architecture 2030   A U.S. nonprofit environmental advocacy group that addresses climate change and the global greenhouse gas (GHG) emissions produced by the building sector.

area separation wall   A residential fire wall, usually with a two- to four-hour rating, designed to prevent the spread of fire from an adjoining occupancy. An area separation wall extends from the foundation to or through the roof. Identified by codes as a *fire wall, party wall* or *townhouse separation wall.*

articulation class   A classification that rates the degree of speech recognition that can be transmitted through ceilings or partitions.

ASA   American Standards Association. Now referred to as American National Standards Institute (ANSI).

ASTM International   Formerly American Society for Testing and Materials. A nonprofit technical society that publishes definitions, standards, test methods, recommended installation practices and materials specifications.

attenuate   To resist the passage of sound energy.

attenuation   In acoustics, the diluting or holding back of the energy of sound waves as they pass through a material. Materials are rated for their ability to prevent sounds from traveling through them. *See also* **ceiling attenuation class, CAC.**

back blocking A short piece of gypsum board adhesively laminated behind the joints between each framing member to reinforce the joint. Also, a method of attaching additional framing to support gypsum board where no framing is present.

backup strips Pieces of wood nailed at the ceiling-sidewall corner to provide fastening for ends of plaster base or gypsum panels.

balloon frame A method of framing exterior walls in which studs extend the full length or height of the wall, running past/not stopping at each floor line.

bar joist An open-web, flat-truss structural member used to support a floor or roof structure. The web section is made from bar or rod stock, and chords are usually fabricated from "T" or angle sections.

basecoat The first layer or layers of plaster applied over a lath or other substrate. The first application is normally called a "scratch coat." The second application is a "brown coat."

basecoat floating The finishing action of spreading, compacting and smoothing basecoat plaster to a reasonably true plane.

batten A narrow strip of wood, plastic, metal or gypsum board used to conceal an open joint.

beam A load-bearing member spanning a distance between supports.

bearing A support area on which a construction assembly rests, such as the point on bearing walls where the weight of the floor joist or roof rafter is borne.

bed To set firmly and permanently in place.

bending Bowing of a member that results when a load is applied laterally between supports.

board foot (Bd. Ft.) A segment of wood with nominal dimensions of 1" thick x 12" wide x 1' long. Lumber is sold by the board-foot measure.

bonding agent A material applied to a surface to improve the quality of the bond between it and the succeeding plaster application. For instance, monolithic concrete and cement board require the addition of a bonding agent before plaster is applied.

brick veneer Non-load-bearing brick facing applied to a wall to present the appearance of solid-brick construction. Bricks are fastened to a backup structure with metal ties embedded in mortar joints.

bridging Framing members attached between floor joists to distribute concentrated loads over more than one joist and to prevent joist rotation. Solid bridging consists of joist-depth lumber installed perpendicular to and between the joists. Cross-bridging consists of pairs of braces set in an "X" form between joists.

brown coat The second coat in three-coat gypsum plaster application.

building codes Legal requirements concerning construction and occupancy—intended to safeguard public health and safety. Sustainable building design must be supported with construction methods and technologies that comply with relevant building codes and that adhere to the specific product's recommended installation procedures.

building construction joint *See* **construction joint**.

CAC *See* **ceiling attenuation class**.

calcine To change the chemical composition of a mineral by heating it, ranging from the removal of chemically combined water through the reduction of the mineral to its oxide state.

calcined gypsum A dry powder, primarily calcium sulfate hemihydrate, resulting from calcination of gypsum; a cementitious base used in the production of most gypsum plasters. Also called *plaster of Paris*; sometimes called *stucco*.

calcium sulfate The chemical compound $CaSO_4$.

calculations Determinations by mechanical engineers of the total loss (or gain) for a building resulting from heat transfer through the ceilings, walls, floors, windows, doors and any other surface exposed to the elements.

camber Curvature built into a beam or truss to compensate for loads that will be encountered when it is in place, and the load is applied. The crown is placed upward. Insufficient camber results in unwanted deflection when the member is loaded.

cant beam A beam with edges chamfered or beveled.

cant strip A triangular section laid at the intersection of two surfaces to ease or eliminate the effect of a sharp angle or projection.

carbon-neutral A building that produces net zero carbon emissions. This is achieved by calculating emissions, reducing them through design and conservation, substituting fossil energies with renewable energies, and offsetting remaining emissions through actions such as purchasing carbon offsets or planting trees that absorb carbon.

carrying channel The main supporting member of a suspended ceiling system to which furring members or channels attach.

casement A glazed sash or frame hung to open like a door.

casing Trim around windows, doors, columns or piers.

ceiling attenuation class (CAC) A sound rating developed especially for acoustical ceilings. Ratings are determined by AMA1-II ceiling sound transmission tests. Results were previously called *CSTC value*.

Ceiling STC (CSTC) Now obsolete. *See* **ceiling attenuation class (CAC)**.

cement board A factory-manufactured panel, 5/16" to 5/8" thick, 32" to 48" wide, and 3' to 10' long, made from aggregated and reinforced Portland cement.

certification, LEED A nationally recognized benchmarking system for sustainable construction. LEED® provides technical guidance and third-party certification measures that evaluate project sustainability by analyzing critical aspects of building design and construction. A project may receive one of four levels of LEED certification by earning points in six categories of assessment.

chalk line A straight working line made by snapping a chalked cord stretched between two points, transferring chalk to a surface.

CHPS Collaborative for High Performance Schools (CHPS), an organization that promotes research, testing and development of effective environmental management strategies for schools and other specialized building projects, such as healthcare facilities.

cladding Gypsum panels, gypsum bases, gypsum sheathing, cement board, etc. applied to framing; can refer to both sides of the framing.

Class A A fire classification for a product with a flame spread rating of no more than 25 and a smoke-developed rating not exceeding 50, when tested in accordance with ASTM E84.

Coefficient of Thermal Conductance (c) The amount of heat (in Btu) that passes through a specific thickness of a material (either homogeneous or heterogeneous) per hr., per SF, per °F. Measured as the temperature difference between the material's two surfaces.

The "c" value of a homogeneous material equals the "k" value divided by the material thickness:

$c = k/t$ where t = thickness of material in inches.

It is impractical to determine a "k" value for some materials, such as building paper or materials formed as a thin membrane; only "c" values are given for these.

Coefficient of Thermal Conductivity (k) A convenient factor that represents the amount of heat (in Btu) that passes by conduction through a 1" thickness of homogeneous material, per hr., per SF, per °F. Measured as temperature difference between the material's two surfaces.

Coefficient of Heat Transmission (U) Total amount of heat that passes through an assembly of materials, including air spaces and surface air films. Expressed in Btu per hr., per SF, per °F temperature difference between inside and outside air (beyond the surface air films). "U" values are often used to measure heat transmission through wall and ceiling assemblies, floors and windows.

Note: "k" and "c" values cannot simply be added to obtain "U" values. "U" can be obtained only by adding the thermal resistance (reciprocal of "c") of individual items and dividing the total into 1.

Coefficient of Hygrometric Expansion *See* **hygrometric expansion**.

Coefficient of Thermal Expansion *See* **thermal expansion**.

column A vertical load-bearing member.

combustible Capable of burning. *See also* **noncombustible**.

comfort, occupant Characteristics including humidity, ventilation, air circulation, acoustics and lighting, used to form a comprehensive assessment of IEQ.

compression Force that presses particles of a body closer together.

compression strength The measure of a material's maximum unit resistance to a crushing load. Expressed as force per unit of cross-sectional area, e.g., pounds per square inch (psi).

concrete footing Generally, the wide, lower part of a foundation wall that spreads the weight of a building over a larger area. Its width and thickness vary according to the weight of the building and the type of soil on which the structure is erected.

condensation The water produced when warm, moist air is cooled.

conduction, thermal The transfer of heat from one part of a body to another part of that body, or to another body in contact, without any movement of bodies involved. The hot handle of a skillet is an example. The heat travels from the bottom of the skillet to the handle by conduction.

construction joint A designed separation of materials within construction that allows movement of all component parts of the building in any plane. (Movement may be caused by thermal, seismic, wind loading or any other force.) The separation is accomplished by one of the following methods: (1) manufactured devices suitable for this application, (2) field fabrication of suitable materials. Construction joints are sometimes confused with *control joints*.

construction practices Methods used by a contractor and crew throughout the work performed on site to build or remodel a structure—from demolition/initial site work through all phases of construction. Proper construction practices include aspects such as appropriate material delivery times and storage and drying times to avoid later indoor air quality problems with moisture and mold.

construction waste Materials to be disposed of—from the manufacturing process, construction or demolition. For information on alternatives to the use of landfills for gypsum product waste disposal, contact your local USG Sales Representative or visit USG's website (**usg.com**).

control joint A division within the face of a partition or ceiling, the purpose of which is to limit cracking due to tensile or compressive movement in a membrane resulting from thermal, hygrometric or structural effects.

convection Transmission of heat from one point to another by movement of a liquid or a gas (e.g., water or air). Natural convection is caused by expansion of a liquid or gas when it is heated. Expansion reduces the density of the medium, causing it to rise above the cooler, denser portions of the medium. Gravity heating systems are examples of the profitable use of natural convection. The air, when heated by the furnace, becomes less dense (consequently lighter) and rises, distributing heat to the various areas of the building without any type of blower. When a blower is used, the heat transfer method is called *forced convection*.

core (of gypsum board) The hardened material filling the space between the face and back papers. It consists substantially of rehydrated gypsum with additives.

corner brace A structural framing member used to resist diagonal loads that cause racking of walls and panels due to wind and seismic forces. May consist of a panel or diaphragm, or a diagonal flat strap or rod. Bracing must function in both tension and compression. If the brace performs only in tension, two diagonal tension members must be employed in opposing directions as "X" bracing.

corner post Timber or other member forming the corner of a frame. May be solid or built-up as a multi-piece member.

cradle to cradle A calculation of environmental impacts (both negative and positive) across a material's life cycle. Product cradle to cradle may evaluate the embodied energy of the product and would include energy needed to extract and transport raw materials used as product ingredients; to manufacture the item ready for installation or use; to transport the finished product to the distributor; to install, use and maintain it; to deconstruct it at the end of its useful life; and then to reuse or recycle it. Other terms describing the product's life stages for energy use and other life cycle assessment criteria include "cradle to market," which includes all the same processes as cradle to cradle, except the product is disposed in a landfill, versus being recycled or reused at the end of its use.

cradle to gate A portion of a product's life cycle covering manufacture ("cradle") and handling up until it leaves the factory ("gate"). This does not include transportation or use of the product, nor its disposal at the end of its use. Environmental product declarations (EPD) are used to assess sustainability for this phase.

creep Plastic flow or deformation of a material or a composite resulting from the sustained application of a force or load. Creep is typically greater at higher temperatures.

creep deflection Permanent deflection in a building system caused by deformation under a sustained force or load. An example is the sag in a new building's concrete floor slab caused by sustained dead and live loads on the floor. This deformation or sag often causes partition cracking when the center of a partition span occurs near the area of greatest creep deflection. Creep deflection is a structural problem that decreases after a building stabilizes, one or two years after construction. Another cause of partition cracking, sometimes confused with that from creep deflection, is racking of structural components. Partition cracking caused by racking (as a result of thermal expansion and contraction or wind loads on the building) must be treated, for example by the proper placement and installation of control or expansion joints.

cripple A short stud such as that used between a door or window header and the top plate.

critical light Strong, angular or harsh light that can show imperfections in reflecting surfaces. Most common sources are skylights, wall sconces and directed track lights such as those used in art galleries.

crowned joint Over-filling (with compound) the location where two boards or panels meet.

curtain wall Exterior wall of a building that is supported by the structure and carries no part of the vertical load except its own. Curtain walls must be designed to withstand wind loads and transfer them to the structure.

cycle (acoustic) One full repetition of a motion sequence during periodic vibration. Movement from zero to +1, then back to zero to -1, then back to zero. Frequency of vibration is expressed in Hertz (cycles per second; *see also* **frequency**).

daylighting Admitting natural light into a space with consideration of distributing light at uniform levels, controlling glare and reflections and reducing the need for artificial light.

darby A hand float or trowel used by plasterers and concrete finishers in preliminary floating and leveling operations.

dead load Load on a building element contributed by the weight of the building materials.

decibel (dB) A measure adopted for convenience to represent vastly different sound pressures. The sound pressure level (SPL) in decibels is 10 times the logarithm to the base 10 of the squared ratio of the sound pressure to a reference pressure of 20 micropascals. This reference pressure is considered the lowest value at 100 Hz that the ear can detect. For every 10 dB increase or decrease in SPL, a sound is generally judged to be about twice or half as loud as before the change.

decoupling Separation of elements to reduce or eliminate the transfer of sound, heat or physical loads from one element to the other.

deflection Displacement that occurs when a load is applied to a member or assembly. The dead load of the member or assembly itself causes some deflection—as may occur in roofs or floors at mid-span. Under applied wind loads maximum deflection occurs at mid-height in partitions and walls.

deflection limitation Maximum allowable deflection is dictated by the bending limit of the finish material under the required design load (usually 5 psf for interior partitions). Often expressed as ratio of span (L) divided by a criterion factor (120, 180, 240, 360). For example, in a 10' (or 120") high wall, the allowable deflection under L/240 criterion equals 120"/240 or 1/2" maximum. Selection of limiting heights and spans is frequently based on minimum code requirements and accepted industry practice. However, USG recommendations are as follows: (a) L/240 for gypsum panel surfaces and veneer plaster finish surfaces, (b) L/360 for conventional lath and plaster surfaces and any brittle material finishes. Horizontal applications such as floors require special consideration for the increased deflection due to the dead load. The contribution to deflection from these dead loads requires stiffer floor systems, especially for large format heavy stone, marble or tile floors.

deformation Change in the shape of a body brought about by the application of a force—either internal or external. Internal forces may result from temperature, humidity or chemical changes. External forces from applied loads can also cause deformation.

degree day A unit representing daily mean temperature of one degree below 65°F. An indication of heat load required over a given period of time.

density The quantity per unit volume of a material; the mass of a substance per unit volume.

design load Combination of weight (dead load) and other applied forces (live loads) for which a building or part of a building is designed.

desulfo gypsum Calcium sulfate dehydrate (gypsum) produced as a byproduct of scrubbing industrial smoke stacks to meet environmental clean air standards. Also known as *synthetic gypsum.*

dew point The temperature at which air becomes saturated with moisture and below which condensation occurs.

direct lighting Lighting aimed at objects or surfaces. Direct lighting mounted in ceilings de-emphasizes the ceiling surface and highlights horizontal surfaces below, such as work surfaces and the floor.

door buck Structural element of a door opening; may be the frame, as in the case of heavy steel frames.

dot A small lump of plaster placed on a surface (usually scarified basecoat) between grounds to assist the plasterer in obtaining the proper plaster thickness and to aid in aligning the surface.

double-hung window Window sash that slides vertically and is offset in a double track.

double-up Successive plaster coat applications with no setting or drying time allowed between coats; usually associated with veneer plastering. The double-up coat is applied (from the same mix) to a scratch coat over a gypsum base.

drip Interruption or offset in an exterior horizontal surface, such as a soffit, immediately adjacent to the fascia. Designed to prevent the migration of water back along the surface.

drywall Generic term for interior surfacing material, such as gypsum panels, applied to framing using dry construction methods, e.g., mechanical fasteners or adhesive. *See also* SHEETROCK **brand gypsum panels**.

Dyne (acoustics) A unit of force required to accelerate one gram of mass at a rate of 1 cm per second.

echo Sound reflected back to the source from a reflective surface, received with enough interval and loudness to be distinguished from the original sound.

ecological footprint The impact that an entity such as an operating facility, individual, city or nation has on the local, regional or global ecosystem. Factors include direct and indirect consumption of natural resources and waste production.

edge (of gypsum board) The paper-bound edges of a manufactured panel.

efflorescence A deposit of white, powdery, water-soluble salts on the surface of masonry or plaster. It is caused by the migration of the dissolved salts to the surface. Also called *whiskering* or *saltpetering*.

embodied energy The total amount of energy used across a product's life. Usually cradle to gate or cradle to market embodied energies are used to compare construction products and are a critical measure of a product's sustainability. Generally, the lower the product's measure of embodied energy, the higher its sustainability rating.

emissions Vapors that may be off-gassed by building components. Some are harmless in themselves, but may react with moisture or vapors from other products, including carpeting, paint and adhesives, and even furnishings, to form potentially hazardous airborne compounds.

emissivity The relative ability of a surface to emit radiant heat.

end (of gypsum board) The ends perpendicular to the paper-bound edges, as manufactured. The gypsum core is always exposed on the ends.

energy conservation Reducing energy use and waste by various means, including equipment efficiencies, insulation and business practices.

EPA The U.S. Environmental Protection Agency.

EPD Environmental product declarations. A standardized tool based on life cycle analysis used to rate the environmental performance of a product.

expansion joint *See* **building construction joint** *and* **construction joint**.

exterior insulation and finish systems (EIFS) Exterior cladding assembly consisting of a polymer finish over a reinforcement adhered to foam plastic insulation that is fastened to masonry, concrete, building sheathing or directly to the structural framing. The sheathing may be cement board, gypsum sheathing or another acceptable substrate.

extrapolate To project tested values, assuming a continuity of an established pattern, to obtain values beyond the limit of the test results. Not necessarily reliable.

F & T ratings Flame-resistance and temperature ratings usually associated with "through-penetration" testing. F rating (flame-resistance rating) is the time period a firestop system remains in place during an ASTM E814 fire test. T rating is the time period it takes for the temperature on the unexposed surface, the firestop and the penetrating item to rise 325 °F above the initial temperature.

factor of safety Ratio of the ultimate unit stress to the working or allowable stress.

fascia board Board fastened to the ends of the rafters or joists forming part of a cornice.

fast track A building method that telescopes or overlaps phases of the traditional design-construction process.

fatigue Condition of a building material under stress. Involves some degree of loss of the material's power of resistance as a result of repeated application of stress, particularly if stress reversals occur as with positive and negative cyclical loading.

feather Gradual thinning of joint compound from the thickness over the joint to the outer edge of a coat.

finish coat Final layer of plaster applied over a basecoat or other substrate.

finish coat floating Spreading, compacting and smoothing the finish coat plaster or stucco to a specified surface texture.

finishing compound *See* **topping compound**.

fire blocking A construction element used as an obstruction in a cavity for the purpose of resisting the passage of flame.

fire endurance Measure of elapsed time during which an assembly continues to exhibit fire resistance under specified conditions of test and performance. As applied to elements of buildings, fire endurance is measured by the methods and to the criteria defined in ASTM E119, Standard Test Methods for Fire Tests of Building Construction and Materials and ASTM Methods E814, Fire Tests of Penetration Firestop Systems.

fire hazard classification Rating of interior and surface materials based on testing according to ASTM Standard E84.

fireproof Able to withstand damage from fire. Use of this term in reference to buildings is discouraged because few, if any, building materials can withstand extreme heat for an extended time without some effect. The term *fire-resistive* or *resistant* is more descriptive for this purpose.

fire resistance A relative term, used with a numerical rating or modifying adjective to indicate the extent to which a material or structure resists the effects of fire.

fire-resistive Refers to properties or designs that resist effects of any fire to which a material or structure may be expected to be subjected.

fire-retardant Denotes a substantially lower degree of fire resistance than "fire-resistive." Often used to describe materials that are combustible, but have been treated to retard ignition or spread of fire under conditions for which they were designed.

firestop system A system for protecting against the spread of fire through a penetration in a wall or floor where a pipe or other penetrant passes through a fire-rated system. A firestop is the specific construction using materials designed to fill the annular space around the penetrant for the purpose of preventing the passage of fire through the fire-resistive partition or floor/ceiling assembly.

fire wall A fire-resistant partition extending to or through the roof of a building to retard the spread of fire. *See also* **area separation wall**.

flame-proof Able to resist ignition and flame propagation under test conditions.

flame spread An index of the capacity of a material to spread fire under test conditions, as defined by ASTM Standard E84. Materials are rated by comparison with the flame-spread index of red oak flooring (assigned a value of 100) and inorganic reinforced cement board (assigned a value of 0).

flammable A combustible material's capability to ignite easily, burn intensely or have rapid rate of flame spread.

flanking paths Paths by which sound travels around an element intended to impede it, usually a structural component that is continuous between rooms and rigid enough to transmit the sound. For example, a partition separating two rooms can be "flanked" by the floor, ceiling or walls surrounding the partition if they run uninterrupted from one room to the other. Ducts, conduits, openings, structural elements, rigid ties, etc., can be sound flanking paths. The acoustic effect of sound flanking paths is dependent on many factors.

flashing Strips of metal or waterproof material used to make joints waterproof, as in the joining of curtain wall panels.

flexural strength The maximum load sustained by a standard specimen of a sheet material when subjected to a bending force.

footcandle Measurement of light emitted over distance. One footcandle is the amount of direct light thrown by one candela onto a surface one foot away and equal to one lumen per square foot.

footing The lower extremity of a foundation or load-bearing member that transmits and distributes the load to the substrate or soil.

force Amount of applied energy to cause motion, deformation or displacement and stress to a body.

form oil Oil applied to the interior surface of formwork to promote easy release from the concrete when forms are removed.

foundation Component that transfers the weight of the building and its occupants to the earth.

framing member A stud, plate, track, joist, furring or other support to which a gypsum panel product or metal plaster base is attached.

frequency (sound) The number of complete vibrations or cycles or periodic motion per unit of time.

furring Means of supporting a finished surfacing material away from the structural wall or framing. An element for mechanical or adhesive attachment of paneling. Also used to level uneven or damaged surfaces or to provide space between substrates.

gable Uppermost portion of the end wall of a building that comes to a triangular point under a sloping roof.

gauging plaster Used in combination with lime putty, this material provides setting properties to increase dimensional stability during drying, and provides initial surface hardness in lime finish coats.

girder A beam, especially a long, heavy one; the main beam supporting floor joists or other smaller beams.

global warming Increase in global temperatures resulting from many natural and man-made causes including the emission of gases that trap the sun's heat within Earth's atmosphere.

grain The weight of water vapor in air is usually measured in grains per pound of dry air. A pint of water weighs about 7,000 grains (one pound).

green A term to describe freshly applied plaster that has set, but has not dried.

green building Design, construction and product selection that minimizes a structure's impact on the natural environment.

Green Cross International An organization whose mission is to "help ensure a just, sustainable and secure future for all by fostering a value shift and cultivating a new sense of global interdependence and shared responsibility in humanity's relationship with nature."

Green Globes An international organization that provides a rating system for building owners and managers to assess the environmental performance of existing buildings.

GreenGuard Environmental Institute (GEI) An industry-independent, ANSI-authorized, nonprofit developer of standards for indoor products, environments and buildings.

Green Guide A database of green building materials and products for schools, healthcare and other facilities.

Green Home Building Standards (Model Green Home Building Standards) A whole-building rating system developed by the National Association of Home Builders.

greenhouse effect The effect when light transfers through a medium (e.g., the atmosphere or glass) and is refracted and reflected, giving off heat upon impact. The more the light bounces around and is trapped, the more the light transfers into heat.

greenwash The overstating of benefits of the sustainable properties of a product, process or structure. To market a product as sustainable even though its green characteristics may be minimal or offset by other unsustainable factors.

ground (1) A piece of wood or metal attached to the framing or plaster base so that its exposed surface acts as a gauge to define the thickness of plaster to be applied. (2) Plaster thickness. *See also* **screed.**

grout Gypsum or Portland cement plaster used to fill crevices or hollow metal frames. More commonly a mixture of cement, water and sand used to fill spaces between ceramic tile.

gusset A wood or metal plate riveted, bolted, glued or pressed (wood trusses) over joints to transfer stresses between connected members.

gypsum The mineral consisting primarily of fully hydrated calcium sulfate, $CaSO_4 \cdot 2H_2O$ or calcium sulfate dihydrate.

gypsum fiber panels Gypsum panels with fiber reinforcement concentrated on each face of the panel. They are part of a new-technology series of panel products called FIBEROCK brand panels, which produce stronger, more abuse-resistant, water-resistant walls and ceilings than those produced with conventional drywall. There are variations for interior drywall applications in dry and wet areas, sheathing applications and flooring applications. Very-high impact (VHI) products are further reinforced on the backside by a fiberglass mesh.

gypsum lath A gypsum board used as the base for application of gypsum plaster.

gypsum moulding plaster A calcined gypsum plaster used primarily for plaster casts or molds, sometimes used as a gauging plaster.

gypsum neat plaster A calcined gypsum plaster without aggregate; common usage is for gypsum plaster as a basecoat.

gypsum plaster The generic name for a family of powdered cementitious products consisting primarily of calcined gypsum with additives to modify physical characteristics, and having the ability, when mixed with water, to produce a plastic mortar or slurry that can be formed to the desired shape by various methods and will subsequently set to a hard, rigid mass.

gypsum sheathing Gypsum board used as a backing for exterior surface materials, manufactured with water-repellent paper and a water-resistant core. Newer versions of gypsum sheathing have a glass mat facing.

gypsum, synthetic A chemical form of gypsum—often a byproduct of a manufacturing process. The production process may be included as a descriptor of the material, e.g., *Flue-gas desulfurization (FGD) synthetic gypsum.* Synthetic gypsum comes from substances recovered or recaptured as a byproduct of removing polluting gases from the stacks of burning coal. (Sulfur dioxide, chemically combined with limestone, produces gypsum and carbon dioxide. The more sulfur in the coal, the more gypsum is produced.) Because this process captures harmful materials that would otherwise be released into the atmosphere, these materials are referred to as *recaptured gypsum.*

harmonic (acoustics) A secondary tone of a frequency that is a whole-number multiple of the frequency of a fundamental tone.

high-performance building A building that is energy- and water-efficient, healthy and comfortable for its occupants.

header A horizontal framing member across the ends of the joists. Also the member over a door or window opening in a wall.

head of wall A type of construction joint where two fire-rated assemblies intersect. Head-of-wall assemblies occur where a wall intersects a floor/ceiling or roof/ceiling. In these construction intersections, a fire-protective assembly is needed to protect against the spread of fire. An example is where a partition intersects a fluted steel deck. Head-of-wall and other construction joints are evaluated under UL Standard 2079 for their ability to resist flame and temperature transmission, as well as the force and expansion from a hose stream.

heat A form of energy thought to be characterized by the rate of vibration of the molecules of a substance. The hotter the substance, the faster the molecules vibrate. On the other hand, when there is no heat present, it is thought the molecules will be at rest, which theoretically occurs at absolute zero, -459.7 °F (-273.2 °C or 0.0 K).

heat quantity (Btu) A common unit of measure of the quantity of heat—British thermal unit (Btu). One Btu is the amount of heat required to raise one pound of water from 63°F to 64°F (1 Btu = 1055.06 J). This is about the amount of heat given off by one wooden match. A pound of coal can produce 13,000 Btu.

heat transfer Heat always flows toward a substance of lower temperature until the temperatures of the two substances equalize. Heat travels by one or more of three methods: conduction, convection or radiation.

heel of rafter The seat cut in a rafter that rests on the wall plate.

hemihydrate The dry powder, calcium sulfate hemihydrate, resulting from calcination of $CaSO_4 \cdot 2H_2O$, calcium sulfate dihydrate. *See also* **calcined gypsum**.

Hertz Unit of measure of sound frequency, named for Heinrich H. Hertz. One Hertz (Hz) equals one cycle per second.

holistic design Integration of all building's systems to maximize sustainable and/or economic functioning by considering many factors including use of energy and other resources, building materials, site preservation and indoor air quality. The goal is a structure that can operate at its maximum efficiency, enhance user health, comfort and productivity and have the least environmental impact.

honeycomb Any substance or material having multiple cells such as those built by the honeybee. Some hollow-core doors use the honeycomb principle in their construction.

HUD U.S. Department of Housing and Urban Development, a federal agency.

HUD Manufactured Home Standards Officially, the Manufactured Home Construction and Safety Standards, a national, pre-emptive building code covering manufactured homes. Includes the following agencies: DAPIA—Design Approval Primary Inspection Agency, and IPIA—Production Inspection Primary Inspection Agency.

HVAC Heating, ventilating and air conditioning. (The American Society of Heating, Refrigerating & Air Conditioning Engineers, Inc. *ASHRAE Guide* is a leading technical reference source.)

hydrate To chemically combine with water, as in the hydration of calcined gypsum or slaking of quicklime. Also, the product resulting from this combination.

hygrometric expansion All materials, particularly those of organic origin, expand and contract in relation to their moisture content, which varies with environment. The Hygrometric Coefficient of Expansion is expressed in *inches per inch per percent of relative humidity.* Example: gypsum board has a coefficient of 7.2 x 10^{-6} in. per in per % R.H. This means that with an increase in relative humidity of from 10% to 50%, a gypsum board wall 300' long will have an unrestrained linear expansion of 1.0368" or 1-1/32".

IEQ Indoor environmental quality and occupant comfort. An important criterion for green, or sustainable, building design. Includes humidity, ventilation and air circulation, acoustics and lighting.

impact isolation class (IIC) A single number rating used to compare and evaluate the performance of floor-ceiling constructions in isolating impact noise.

impact noise rating (INR) Obsolete rating system for floor-ceiling construction in isolating impact noise. INR ratings can be converted to approximate IIC ratings by adding 51 points (with a variation of 1 or 2 points).

impact sound pressure level (ISPL) The sound (in decibels), measured in a receiving room, resulting from the transmission of impact sound through floor construction, produced by a standard "tapping" machine.

impact sound transmission Sound that originates by contact with the structure and travels through the structure.

incident sound Noise that is directly received from the source, as distinguished from sound that is reflected from a surface.

incombustible *See* **noncombustible**.

indirect lighting Reflected light. For ceilings, this is typically light from luminaires, distributed upward. This type of lighting is used to reduce glare and hot spots, providing a more uniform source of light.

industrial construction Construction of residential or commercial structures (in a factory environment) that will later be assembled on the building site. Includes HUD-Code manufactured homes as well as residential and commercial modular construction.

insulation (thermal) Any material that measurably retards heat transfer. There is wide variation in the insulating value of different materials. A material having a low density (weight/volume) will usually be a good thermal insulator.

integrated design Also referred to as **holistic** or **whole building design.** A design method that integrates, early in the process, the whole building team, including all disciplines. For a sustainable building, resource efficiencies, indoor air quality and other goals can be achieved most effectively with this approach.

intensity A measure of acoustic energy per unit area of a sound wave. Measured in watts per square meter or micro-watts per square centimeter. The intensity is proportional to the square of the amplitude.

interpolate To estimate untested values that fall between tested values.

ISO International Standards Organization, an organization similar in nature to ASTM.

jamb One of the finished upright sides of a door or window frame.

jamb stud A wood or metal stud adjacent to the door jamb.

joint banding The visible striping of each panel joint—usually a result of over-sanding or uneven absorption of the primer due to differences in surface texture. More noticeable under critical lighting.

joint tape A type of paper, fabric or glass mesh commonly used with joint compounds to reinforce the joints between adjacent gypsum boards.

joist A small beam that supports part of the floor, ceiling or roof of a building.

joist hanger A metal shape formed to hang on the main beam—to provide support for the end of a joist.

Keene's cement (RED TOP Keenes Cement) An anhydrous gypsum plaster characterized by a low mixing water requirement and special setting properties. Primarily used with lime to produce a hard, dense finish coat.

key Grip or mechanical bond of one coat of plaster to another coat, or to a plaster base. A key may be accomplished by the penetration of wet mortar or crystals into paper fibers, perforations or scoring irregularities, or by the embedment of the lath.

kiln-dried lumber Lumber that has been dried and seasoned with carefully controlled heat in a kiln.

Label Service (UL) A program allowing a manufacturer to place Underwriters Laboratories Inc. labels on its products that have met UL requirements. A UL representative visits the manufacturing location to obtain samples of the products for testing. In some cases, UL also purchases samples on the open market for testing. The public is thereby assured that products bearing the UL label continually meet its specifications.

lamination Placing a layer of gypsum board over either another gypsum board or another type of substrate using an adhesive product for attachment.

landfill avoidance Practices that minimize the amount of debris that goes into landfills. Approaches include deconstruction, in which materials from an existing building are methodically removed, separated and either reused in the new structure or recycled.

laser level A mechanical device whose primary function is to establish level or plumb lines on a construction site with an very high degree of precision. In acoustical ceiling installations, a laser level uses a high-intensity light beam that rotates in a level plane. See Chapter 14, "Tools & Equipment," for more information.

lath A metal or gypsum (or wood in the past) material applied to interior wall or ceiling structures to serve as a base for plaster.

lay-in panel Any panel designed to be supported by an accessible suspension system.

leaks (sound) Small openings at electrical boxes and plumbing, cracks around doors, loose-fitting trim and closures that allow sound to pass through, reducing the acoustical isolation of a wall, floor or ceiling system.

ledger strip Strip fastened to the bottom edge of a flush girder to help support the floor joists.

LEED® (Leadership in Energy and Environmental Design) A whole building rating system developed by the U.S. Green Building Council (USGBC) to evaluate project sustainability by analyzing critical aspects of building design and construction. A project may receive one of four levels of LEED certification by earning points in six categories of assessment. LEED is the most widely accepted national guideline for environmentally responsible building. It also provides technical guidance and third-party certification measures.

life cycle assessment (LCA) An approach used to measure a product's or building's environmental performance, from raw materials through manufacture, transportation, installation, use, recycling and waste management. USG defines sustainability in terms of building and resource economics as well, including life cycle costs.

life cycle cost (LCC) The cost of a building system over its useful life, including installation, use (e.g., related energy costs), anticipated repairs and maintenance.

life-cycle costing Selection of the most economical material and systems based on initial costs, maintenance costs and operating costs for the life of the building.

life cycle inventory (LCI) A collection of data to facilitate life cycle assessment and environmental impact studies. NREL (the National Renewable Energy Laboratory) and its partners have created the U.S. LCI Database to provide "a cradle-to-grave accounting of the energy and material flows into and out of the environment that are associated with producing a material, component or assembly."

limiting height The maximum height for design and construction of a partition or wall without exceeding the structural capacity or allowable deflection under given design loads.

limpness Characteristic of a member that reduces vibration, thereby dampening sound.

lintel A horizontal member spanning an opening such as a window or door. Also referred to as a *header*.

live load Part of the total load on structural members that is not a permanent part of the structure. May be variable, as in the case of loads contributed by occupancy, and wind and snow loads.

load The force provided by weight, external or environmental sources such as wind, water and temperature, or other sources of energy.

load-bearing partition A partition designed to support a portion of the building structure.

locally sourced material Construction materials that are extracted and processed near the location where these materials are used (in the manufacturing and installation into a finished building). Use of local materials minimizes energy consumption for transportation.

loudness A subjective response to sound pressure. The loudness of sound is not directly proportional to the amount of sound pressure or energy. Moreover, the apparent loudness—the way the sound is heard by a human—varies from person to person. *See also* **decibel**.

louver An opening with slanted fins (to keep out rain and snow) used to ventilate attics, crawl spaces and wall openings.

lumen A standard unit for measuring light emission. Generally speaking, one lumen is the amount of light emitted by one candle. More specifically, a lumen is the unit of measure for the flow of light through a unit solid angle from a uniform point source equal to one candela. One candela roughly approximates the intensity of light emitted by a single burning candle.

luminaire A complete lighting unit, consisting of a lamp or lamps, together with parts designed to distribute the light, to position and protect the lamps and to connect to the power source.

masking sound Background noise used to cover unwanted sounds, provide privacy or avoid a "quiet" area that otherwise may be acoustically "dead."

mass Property of a body that resists acceleration and produces the effect of inertia. The weight of a body is the result of the pull of gravity on the body's mass.

mechanical bond The attachment created when plaster penetrates into or through the substrate or envelops irregularities in the substrate's surface.

member A general term for a structural component of a building, such as a beam or column.

metric terms Metric units shown as equivalents in this Handbook are from the International System of Units in use worldwide, as established by the General Conference of Weights and Measures in 1960. Metric terms in the Handbook comply with the Metric Conversion Act of 1975, which committed the United States to a coordinated voluntary conversion to the metric system of measurement. For more on metric conversion, see the Appendix.

miter A joint formed by two pieces of material cut to meet at an angle.

model code Building code written and published by a building-official association, available to states, counties and municipalities for adoption (for a fee) in lieu of their own, e.g., the *International Building Code* (IBC).

modular building A structure intended for residential or commercial use that is at least partially completed in a factory complying with state or local code requirements.

module (1) In architecture, a selected unit of measure used as a basis for building layout; (2) In industrialized housing, a three-dimensional section of a building, factory-built, shipped as a unit and interconnected with other modules to form the complete building. Single-family units factory-built in two halves are usually referred to as "sectionals."

modulus of elasticity (E) Ratio between stress and unit deformation, a measure of the stiffness of a material.

moisture management Construction and maintenance methods that protect a building from the structural and indoor air quality problems that can result from condensation or water intrusion.

moment of inertia (I) Calculated numerical relationship (expressed in inches to the 4th power) of a member's resistance to bending. Moment of inertia is a function of the member's cross-sectional shape and size. A measure of the stiffness of a member based on its shape. Larger moments of inertia indicate greater resistance to bending for a given material.

mortar A mixture of gypsum plaster or Portland cement with aggregate or hydrate lime (or both) and water to produce a trowelable fluidity.

moulding (also molding) Narrow decorative strip applied to a surface.

MTS The Institute for Market Transformation to Sustainability. An organization that promotes sustainable product standards.

mud Slang term for **joint compound**.

mud pan Rectangular, angle-sided pan, shaped like bread pan, used by joint finisher to handle portions of joint compound. Straight-cut lip of pan ensures that taping knife can be regularly cleaned.

mullion Vertical bar or division in a window frame separating two or more panes.

muntin Horizontal bar or division in a window frame separating multiple panes or lites.

nail pop The protrusion of a nail from a wall or ceiling, usually attributed to the shrinkage of or use of improperly cured wood framing.

NBFU National Board of Fire Underwriters, now merged into the American Insurance Association.

NBS National Bureau of Standards, a federal agency.

neutral axis The plane through a member (at the geometric center of the section in symmetrical members) where the fibers are neither under tensile nor compressive stress.

NFPA National Fire Protection Association. An international technical society that disseminates fire prevention, fire fighting and fire protection information. NFPA technical standards include the *National Electrical Code*, which is widely adopted.

noise reduction coefficient (NRC) Arithmetic average of sound absorption coefficients at 250, 500, 1,000 and 2,000 Hz.

nominal Term indicating that the full measurement is not used. Usually slightly less than the full net measurement, as with 2" x 4" studs that have an actual size when dry of 1-1/2" x 3-1/2".

noncombustible Definition paraphrased from the ICC 2009 *International Building Code*:

1. Material of which no part will ignite and burn when subjected to fire.
2. Material having a structural base of noncombustible materials as defined, with a surface not over 1/8" thick that has a flame spread rating of 50 or less.

The term does not apply to surface finish materials.

octave Interval between two sounds having a basic frequency ratio of two. The formula is 2n times the frequency, where n is the desired octave interval. The octave band frequency given in sound test results is usually the band center frequency. Thus the 1,000 Hz octave band encompasses frequencies from 707 Hz to 1,414 Hz (n=± 1/2). The 1,000 Hz one-third octave band encompasses frequencies from 891 Hz to 1,122 Hz (n = ± 1/6).

OSU Ohio State University, an independent fire-testing laboratory, currently not active.

parapet wall An extension of an exterior wall above and/or through the roof surface.

parting oil Material used to prevent bonding of concrete to a surface, such as to forms. Parting oil on concrete surfaces must be removed, along with grease and efflorescence, before gypsum products are applied.

passive solar Design strategies that contribute to a building's needed supply of heat (water and air) without an energy input (pumps or fans). For example, windows and building mass collect heat without the need for power. Passive solar designs are categorized as direct gain, sunspaces or Trombe walls.

penny (d) A suffix designating the size of nails, such as 6d (penny) nail, originally indicating the price, in English pence, per 100 nails. Does not designate a constant length or size, and will vary by type (e.g., common and box nails).

performance specification A statement of how a building element must perform—as opposed to describing equipment, products or systems by name.

perimeter relief A gap left around the perimeter of a wall, floor or ceiling membrane, such that it will not be in direct contact with the membrane of adjoining assemblies. This gap is normally caulked with acoustical sealant.

perm A unit of measurement of Water Vapor Permenance (ASTM E96). *See also* **permeance**.

permeability The property of a porous material that permits a fluid (or gas) to pass through it. In construction, commonly refers to water vapor permeability of a sheet material or assembly and is defined as water vapor permeance per unit thickness, using a metric unit of measure (metric perms per centimeter of thickness). *See also* **permeance**.

permeance (water vapor) The ratio of the rate of water vapor transmission (WVT) through a material or assembly (between its two parallel surfaces) to the vapor pressure differential between the surfaces. The metric unit for measuring permeance is the metric perm, 1 g/24 h. x m^2 x mm Hg; U.S. unit, 1 grain/h x ft.^{2} x in. Hg.

photographing *See* **shadowing**.

photovoltaics (PVs) Devices that convert sunlight directly into electricity. PVs generate power without noise, pollution or fuel consumption.

pilaster Projecting, square column or stiffener forming part of a wall.

pillar Column supporting a structure.

pitch of roof Slope of the surface, generally expressed in inches of vertical rise per 12" horizontal distance, such as "4-in-12 pitch."

plaster base Gypsum panel with specially treated face paper to serve as a stable backing for plaster applications. Two types of plaster base are available; one type is usually 3/8" thick, 16" wide and 4' long and is used for conventional (thick) coat plastering. The other is typically 1/2" or 5/8" thick and 4' wide (lengths vary) and is used for veneer plaster system applications.

plaster bonder *See* **bonding agent**.

plate "Top" plate is the horizontal member fastened to the top of the studs or wall on which the rafters, joists or trusses rest. The "sole" plate is positioned at bottom of the studs or wall.

platform Floor surface raised above the ground or floor level.

platform framing Technique of framing where walls can be built and tilted up on a platform floor, and in multi-story construction are erected sequentially from one platform to another. Also known as *Western framing*.

plenum (1) Chamber in which the air pressure is higher (as in a forced-air furnace system) than that of the surrounding air. (2) The space above a suspended ceiling.

plenum barrier Vertical surface framed from the structure above to the finished ceiling and sealed to prevent the passage of air.

porosity The propensity of certain materials, such as wallboard paper, to absorb water.

Portland cement Hydraulic cement produced by pulverizing clinker consisting essentially of hydraulic calcium silicates, usually containing one or more forms of calcium.

post-consumer waste Recycled materials that have been used and discarded by households or commercial uses.

pre-consumer waste Materials and by-products of manufacturing. Also known as **post-industrial waste**. Includes waste generated by manufacturers, such as trimmings and overruns that are used to manufacture additional products.

prescription specification Traditional procedure used on building projects to describe by name products, equipment or systems to be used.

purlin Horizontal member in a roof supporting common rafters, such as at the break in a gambrel roof. Also, a horizontal structural member perpendicular to main beams in a flat roof.

3 Rs of sustainability (reduce, recycle, renew) USG seeks to maximize all three, as follows:

> **Reduce** Products and packaging designed to minimize the amount of raw materials and energy consumed during the manufacturing process greatly contribute to overall sustainability. Lightweight materials typically require less energy to transport. Production waste can also be minimized through the use of high-efficiency design and manufacturing processes. In drywall production, USG uses 97% of the raw material in its finished panels. A portion of the remaining 3% is utilized for transportation spaces (also known as "spacers" or "dunnage").

> **Recycle** Effective recycling during manufacturing reduces raw material consumption, energy demands, and landfill waste. Materials that are discarded or damaged in the course of manufacturing are reprocessed into the same product. This waste is also reused to manufacture different products with shared ingredients, or repurposed for altogether new applications. The extensive use of recycling processes at every stage of manufacturing is a major element of USG's environmental management strategy.

> **Renew** Responsible manufacturing minimizes the environmental impact of resource consumption by utilizing renewable materials that are regenerated in a shorter time frame than conventional resources. Key ingredients of grain-based fuels used as sources of production energy, for example, are renewable in less than two years.

racking Forcing out of plumb of structural components, usually by wind, seismic stress or thermal expansion or contraction.

radiation Transfer of heat energy through space by wave motion. Although the radiant energy of heat is transmitted through space, no heat is present until this energy strikes and is absorbed by an object. Not all of the radiant heat energy is absorbed; some is reflected to travel in a new direction until it strikes another object. The amount reflected depends on the nature of the surface the energy strikes. This fact explains the principle of insulating foil and other similar products that depend on reflection of radiant heat for their insulating value.

rafter Framing member forming the slanting frame of a roof or top chord of a truss. Also known as *hip, jack* or *valley rafter* depending on its location and use.

rafter tail The part of a rafter that extends beyond the wall plate—the overhang.

rapidly renewable materials (RRM) Raw materials such as cork, bamboo and straw, that can be re-grown quickly and are therefore considered sustainable.

ready-mixed plaster A calcined gypsum plaster with aggregate added during manufacture. A powder product that requires the addition of water.

recycled content The percent of the total material content (by the combination of post-consumer waste, pre-consumer material and post-industrial material) versus the percent of content that is virgin material.

reflected heat *See* **radiation.**

reflected sound Sound that has struck a surface and "bounced off." Sound reflects at the same angle as light reflects in a mirror; the angle of incidence equals the angle of reflection. Large curved surfaces tend to focus (concave) or diffuse (convex) the sound when reflected. However, when the radius of the reflecting surface is less than the wavelength of the sound, this does not hold true. Thus, a rough-textured surface has little effect on diffusion of sound.

reflective insulation Material that reflects and thus retards the flow of radiant heat. The most common type is aluminum foil. The effectiveness of reflective barriers is diminished by the accumulation of dirt and by surface oxidation.

relative humidity The ratio of actual water vapor pressure to the saturation water vapor pressure at the same temperature, expressed as a percentage.

renewable energy Energy from natural resources that replenish themselves, such as the sun, wind, rain, tides and geothermal sources.

resonance The production of relatively intense sound vibrations by exposure to a small sound stimulus. Every medium and object has a resonant frequency at which it will, under favorable conditions, re-radiate a received sound of the same frequency.

retarder An admixture used to delay the setting action of plasters or other cementitious materials.

reverberation The perpetuation of sound within a space after the source has ceased, such as an echo.

reverberation time The number of seconds it takes for the sound pressure to die down to one-thousandth of its original value after the source has ceased.

ridge Peak of a roof where the roof surfaces meet at an angle. Also may refer to the framing member that runs along the ridge and supports the rafters.

rise Measurement in height of an object. The converse is "fall."

riser Vertical face of a step supporting the tread in a staircase.

rough framing Structural elements of a building or the process of assembling elements to form a supporting structure where finish appearance is not critical.

sabin Measure of sound absorption of a surface, equivalent to 1 SF of a perfectly absorptive surface.

safing Firestop material in the space between a floor slab and a curtain wall in multi-story construction.

safing off Installation of fire safety insulation around floor perimeters, between floor slab and spandrel panels. Insulation helps retain integrity of fire-resistance ratings.

scab Small piece or block of wood that bridges several members or provides a connection or fastening between them.

screed To level or straighten a plaster coat application with a rod, darby or other similar tool.

screed (noun) *See* **ground.** Screeds are made from basecoat plaster; they are created between plaster dots or grounds.

section modulus (S) Numerical relationship, expressed in inches to the third power, of the resistance to the stress of a member. Section modulus is equal to the moment of inertia divided by the perpendicular distance from the neutral axis to the extremity of the member.

set The hardening and hydration of a gypsum plaster or setting-type joint compound. *See also* **setting time.**

setting time The elapsed time required for a gypsum plaster or setting-type joint compound to attain a specified hardness and strength after mixing with water.

shadowing An undesirable condition where the joint finish shows through the surface decoration.

shaft wall Fire-resistant wall that isolates the elevator, stairwell and vertical mechanical chase in high-rise construction. This wall must withstand the fluctuating (positive and negative) air-pressure loads created by elevators or air distribution systems.

shear Force that tends to slide or rupture one part of a body from another part of the body or from attached objects.

sheathing Plywood, gypsum, wood fiber, expanded plastic or composition boards encasing walls, ceilings, floors and roofs of framed buildings. May be structural or non-structural, thermal-insulating or non-insulating, fire-resistant or combustible.

SHEETROCK Leading brand of gypsum panel for interior wall and ceiling surfaces, developed and improved by United States Gypsum Company.

shoring Temporary member placed to support part of a building during construction, repair or alteration. Also may support the walls of an excavation.

sill Horizontal member at the bottom of a door or window frame. Provides support and closure.

sill plate Horizontal member laid directly on a foundation on which the framework of a building is erected.

slab Flat (although sometimes ribbed on the underside) reinforced concrete element of a building that provides the base for the floor or roofing materials.

SMaRT© A multiple sustainability attribute product rating system/standard.

soffit Undersurface of a projection or opening; bottom of a cornice between the fascia board and the outside of the building; underside of a stair, floor or lintel.

sole plate *See* **plate**.

sound A wave motion in an elastic medium caused by a vibrating object.

sound absorption The dissipation of sound by conversion of the acoustical energy into heat or another form of energy. Friction produces heat as the energy passes over and agitates the fibers of a sound-absorbing material.

sound attenuation Reduction of sound energy as it passes through a conductor (which resists the transmission).

sound barrier A material installed in a plenum or partition to prevent the passage of sound from one area to another. Sound-deadening board and lead sheet or special insulations make good sound barriers.

sound control Measures taken to control three types of sound: airborne sound transmission, impact sound transmission and architectural acoustics.

sound damping The use of fibrous sound-absorbing material in a partition to reduce sound transmission. Damping in floor/ceiling construction has a wider application for impact sound than for airborne sound.

sound insulation, isolation Use of building materials or constructions that reduce or resist the transmission of sound. Decoupling is one isolation method, in which the elements of a partition are separated to retard transmission of structure-borne sound.

sound leak Opening in a partition that allows air (and sound) to pass through. Examples include small holes in a wall, openings for electrical boxes and plumbing, and cracks around doors.

sound pressure The change in pressure resulting from vibration in the audible frequency range. Conversational speech at close range produces a sound pressure of about one dyne per sq. cm.

sound pressure level (SPL) Expressed in decibels, the SPL is 20 times the logarithm to the base 10 of the ratio of the sound pressure to a reference pressure of 20 micropascals. *See also* **decibel**.

sound transmission The transfer of sound energy from one space to another, through air, structure or other conductor. Unwanted sound in a room may be the result of sound transmission from sources outside the room. The degree to which sound transmission is acceptable depends on the quantity and source of the sound and the use of the adjacent space. Sound transmitted at a level below the receiving room ambient level would be acceptable.

sound transmission class (STC) A single-number rating for evaluating the effectiveness of a construction system in isolating audible airborne sound transmission across 16 frequencies. Higher numbers indicate more effectiveness. Tested per ASTM E90.

span Distance between supports, usually beams or joists.

spandrel beam Horizontal member that spans exterior columns or other vertical structural elements and supports a floor or roof.

spandrel wall Exterior wall panel, usually between columns, that extends from the window opening on one floor to one on the next floor.

speed of sound In air varies with atmospheric pressure and temperature, but is the same at all frequencies. For most architectural work, the speed of sound should be taken as 1,130' per second.

splayed hangers Hangers installed at an angle rather than perpendicular to the support grid or channel.

spot To treat fastener heads with joint compound material. As the fastener sets below the surface of the board, an indentation is formed, allowing a recess, which is filled by spotting.

square edge In context of acoustical tile, a square-edge is not beveled and creates a hairline joint when installed. Drywall panels also may have square edges, although they are typically tapered.

starved joint A poorly bonded joint, resulting from inadequate adhesive.

stile Vertical outside member in a piece of millwork, such as a door or sash.

stirrup Hanger to support the end of the joist at the beam.

stop Strip of wood fastened to the jambs and head of a door or window frame against which the door or window closes.

strain Unit deformation in a body as a result of stress.

stress Unit resistance of a body to an outside force that tends to deform the body by tension, compression or shear.

stringer Heavy horizontal timber that supports other members of the frame in a wood or brick structure. Also a support for steps.

structure-borne sound Sound energy imparted directly to and transmitted by the elements of a structure. Plumbing noises traveling through pipes are a good example.

strut Slender structural element that resists compressive forces acting lengthwise.

stucco (1) A mixture of Portland cement and aggregate designed for use on exterior or interior surfaces exposed to high levels of moisture. May also contain hydrated lime to improve working characteristics. (2) A gypsum plaster mix including aggregate for use on interior surfaces. (3) Calcined gypsum used to produce plaster, gypsum wallboard and related products. This terminology is specific to the gypsum processing industry.

stud Vertical load-bearing or non-load-bearing framing member.

subfloor Rough or structural floor placed directly on the floor joists or beams to which the finished floor is applied. As with resilient flooring, an underlayment may be required between subfloor and finished floor.

substrate Underlying material to which a finish is applied, or by which it is supported.

surface burning characteristic Rating of interior and surface finish material providing indexes for flame spread and smoke developed, based on testing conducted according to ASTM Standard E84.

suspended ceiling A ceiling that is hung from the structure typically with wire hangers.

sustainable design Design that considers all environmental and human health and well-being aspects, as well as resource efficiency. USG's SHEETROCK and FIBEROCK AQUA-TOUGH lines of gypsum panels meet nearly every criterion of sustainable design: low embodied energy, high recycled content and free of VOC and formaldehyde emissions.

synthetic gypsum A chemical product consisting primarily of calcium sulfate dehydrate ($CaSO_4 \cdot 2H_2O$) derived primarily from an industrial process. *See also* **Desulfo gypsum**.

take-up The loss of water from plaster into the absorptive substrate during application, as evidenced by a moderate stiffening of the plaster coat.

tapered edge An edge formation of gypsum board that provides a shallow depression at the paper-bound edge to receive joint reinforcement. Typical edge on drywall panels; edges may also be square.

taping compound (embedding compound) A compound specifically formulated and manufactured for use in embedding of joint reinforcing tape at gypsum board joints.

task lighting Lighting directed to a specific work surface or area.

temper To bring plaster to the proper consistency by moistening and mixing.

temperature Measurement of the intensity (not quantity) of heat. The Fahrenheit (°F) scale places the freezing point of water at 32° and the boiling point at 212°. The Centigrade or Celsius (°C) scale, used by most countries and in scientific work, places the freezing point of water at 0° and the boiling point at 100°. On the Kelvin (K) scale, the unit of measurement equals the Celsius degree and measurement begins at absolute zero 0° (-273°C).

tensile strength Maximum tensile stress that can be developed in a given material under axial tensile loading. Also the measure of a material's ability to withstand stretching.

tension Force that tends to pull the particles of a body apart.

thermal expansion All materials expand and contract to some extent with changes in temperature. The thermal coefficient of linear expansion is expressed *inches per inch per degree Fahrenheit*. Example: gypsum board has a coefficient of 9.0 x 10^{-6} in. per in. per °F. This means that with an increase in temperature of 50°, a gypsum board wall 100' in length will have a linear expansion of 0.54" or an excess of 1/2". The expansion characteristics of some other building materials are more pronounced. For example, a 50° temperature increase would produce expansion in a 100' length of approx. 3/4" in aluminum, 3/8" in steel and 1/2" in concrete.

thermal resistance (R) Resistance of a material or assembly to the flow of heat. It is the reciprocal of the heat transfer coefficient: (1/C, or 1/U)

For insulating purposes, low "c" and "U" values and high "R" values are the most desirable.

thermocouple A thermoelectric junction of two dissimilar metals used to measure temperature differences.

threshold Raised member at the floor within the door jamb. Its purpose is to provide a divider between dissimilar flooring materials and/or serve as a thermal, sound or water barrier.

through-penetration An opening through a fire-resistive partition or floor/ceiling assembly to provide for an item (such as piping) to pass through it. Through-penetrations usually require the use of a firestop system to protect against the spread of fire through the opening.

through-penetration firestop A system for sealing through-penetrations in fire-resistant floors, walls and ceilings.

time-temperature curve Rate at which the temperature increases in a fire-testing furnace. Developed by ASTM, NFPA and UL, this curve is adhered to in all fire-resistive testing.

toenail Method of fastening two boards or studs together as in a "T" by driving nails into the board that forms the stem of the "T" at an angle so they enter the other board and cross each other.

tone A sound that produces a definite sensation of pitch, loudness and timbre.

tongue-and-groove joint A joint where the projection or "tongue" of one member engages the mating groove of the adjacent member to minimize relative deflection and air infiltration. A method widely used in sheathing, flooring and paneling. Tongues may be in "V," round or square shapes.

topping compound A compound specifically formulated and manufactured for use over taping or all-purpose compounds to provide a smooth, level surface for applying decoration.

transmission loss (TL) The decrease in energy during transmission from one surface of a medium to another, such as, through a panel or wall.

tread The horizontal plane or surface of a stair step.

trimmer Double joists or rafters framing the opening of a stairwell, dormer opening, etc.

truss Open, lightweight framework of members, usually designed to replace a large beam where spans are great.

TSP (trisodium phosphate) A cleaning agent used to remove grease, soot and paint dust from a surface, usually in preparation for painting.

U of C University of California, an independent fire-testing laboratory.

"U" factor The coefficient of heat transfer, "U" equals 1 divided by (hence, the reciprocal of) the total of the resistances of the various materials, air spaces and surface air films in an assembly. *See also* **thermal resistance**.

Underwriters Laboratories, Inc. (UL) A not-for-profit laboratory operated for the purpose of testing devices, systems and materials as they relate to life, fire and casualty hazards, in the interest of public safety.

USASI United States of America Standards Institute, now referred to as American National Standards Institute.

U.S. Green Building Council (USGBC) A nonprofit coalition of leaders drawn from across the building industry whose purpose is to promote sustainable building. USG is proud to be a founder and charter member of the Council. The LEED (Leadership in Energy and Environmental Design) Green Building Rating System developed by USGBC is the most widely accepted national guideline for environmentally responsible building.

vapor retarder A material used to retard the flow of water vapor through walls and other spaces where it may condense at a lower temperature.

velocity The speed of sound in air at room temperature is 1,130' per second; in steel, 16,500' per second; in hardwood, 13,000' per second. The speed sound travels depends only on the density and elasticity of the medium through which it passes. Its speed is unaffected by loudness and frequency.

veneer plaster Calcined gypsum plaster specially formulated to provide specific workability, strength, hardness and abrasion resistance characteristics when applied in thin coats (1/16" to 3/32" nom.) over veneer gypsum base or other approved base. The term *thin-coat plaster* is sometimes used in reference to veneer plaster.

volatile organic compounds (VOCs) Chemicals, such as formaldehyde, that are harmful when released (off-gassed) from building products after installation. VOCs are also found in cleaning supplies and furnishings and are also emitted by some plants, trees, microorganisms, and even by humans. VOCs may be present during all stages of a building's life cycle—materials manufacturing, construction/installation and occupancy—and may pose real health and comfort issues.

water-absorption The amount of water absorbed by a material under specified test conditions. Commonly expressed as a weight percent of the test specimen.

water-repellent paper Gypsum board paper surfacing that has been formulated or treated to resist water penetration.

water vapor transmission The rate of water vapor flow, under steady specified conditions, through a unit area of a material, between its two parallel surfaces. Metric unit of measurement is 1 g/24 h. x m² x mm Hg. *See also* **permeance**.

watt A basic unit of power equal to 10,000,000 dyne-cm.

wave front The surface of the wave sphere created when sound waves radiate from the source in all directions, forming a spherical shape.

wavelength (sound) A wave is one complete cycle of sound vibration passing through a medium (such as air) from compression through rarefaction and back to compression again. The physical length of this cycle is termed the wavelength. Wavelengths in air vary from about 11/16" for a 20,000-cycle per second (*see* **frequency**) sound, to approximately 56'-6" for a 20-cycle per second sound (the two approximate extremes of human hearing sensitivity). There are waves outside of this range, but generally, they cannot be heard by humans.

weep hole A small aperture at the base of an exterior wall cavity intended to drain trapped moisture.

wet sand To smooth a finished joint with a small-celled wet sponge. This method produces less dust than is created by the dry sanding method.

WHI Warnock Hershey International, an independent fire-testing laboratory.

whole design solution A design approach that considers and integrates all building systems, starting with the early design stages—for optimum efficiency and sustainability in the structure. Also **holistic, integrated** or **whole building design.**

wind power Energy from wind, usually collected by wind turbines.

wood-fibered plaster A calcined gypsum plaster containing shredded or ground wood fiber added during manufacture.

zero-net energy building (ZEB) or **net zero energy building** A building that has a net energy consumption of zero over a year.

Key Word Index

Alphabetical Index to Tables

Contact Information

To contact your local USG sales representative, visit **usg.com** and select "Contact USG." For product information, visit **usg.com** and select "Products."

Additional Copies

For additional copies of *The Gypsum Construction Handbook*, Sixth Edition, visit **rsmeans.com** or call (800) 334-3509.

Notes

Notes

Notes

Notes

Notes

Notes